U0450168

本书为
国家社会科学基金青年项目
两河流域乌尔第三王朝赋税制度研究
（批准号：17CSS007）
结项成果（鉴定等级：优秀）

A STUDY OF TAXATION DURING
THE THIRD DYNASTY OF UR

古代两河流域
乌尔第三王朝赋税制度研究

刘昌玉 著

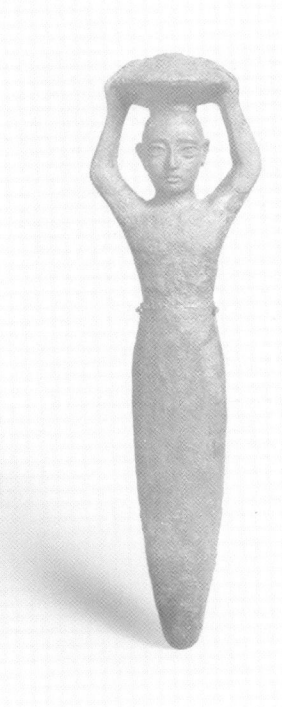

中国社会科学出版社

图书在版编目(CIP)数据

古代两河流域乌尔第三王朝赋税制度研究/刘昌玉著. —北京：中国社会科学出版社，2021.6
ISBN 978 - 7 - 5203 - 8353 - 0

Ⅰ.①古… Ⅱ.①刘… Ⅲ.①赋税制度—研究—乌尔 Ⅳ.①F813.09

中国版本图书馆 CIP 数据核字(2021)第 072915 号

出 版 人	赵剑英
责任编辑	耿晓明
责任校对	李　军
责任印制	李寡寡

出　　版	中国社会科学出版社
社　　址	北京鼓楼西大街甲 158 号
邮　　编	100720
网　　址	http://www.csspw.cn
发 行 部	010 - 84083685
门 市 部	010 - 84029450
经　　销	新华书店及其他书店

印　　刷	北京明恒达印务有限公司
装　　订	廊坊市广阳区广增装订厂
版　　次	2021 年 6 月第 1 版
印　　次	2021 年 6 月第 1 次印刷

开　　本	710×1000　1/16
印　　张	24.5
字　　数	402 千字
定　　价	98.00 元

凡购买中国社会科学出版社图书,如有质量问题请与本社营销中心联系调换
电话:010 - 84083683
版权所有　侵权必究

目 录

引 言 ·· (1)

第一章 乌尔第三王朝概况 ·· (19)
第一节 地理概况 ··· (19)
第二节 历史概况 ··· (22)
第三节 文献概况 ··· (26)

第二章 核心区 bala 税 ·· (31)
第一节 核心区概况 ··· (32)
第二节 税收管理 ··· (52)
第三节 温马行省的 bala 税 ·································· (69)
第四节 拉伽什—吉尔苏行省的 bala 税 ··················· (86)
第五节 其他行省的 bala 税 ································· (109)

第三章 外围区 gun$_2$ ma-da 税 ·································· (117)
第一节 外围区概况 ·· (117)
第二节 文献与术语 ·· (124)
第三节 外围区 gun$_2$ ma-da 税的征收 ··················· (141)

第四章 附属国 gun$_2$ 税 ·· (149)
第一节 附属国概况 ·· (149)
第二节 术语与文献概况 ······································ (152)
第三节 附属国 gun$_2$ 税解析 ······························· (156)

第五章　王室 maš-da-ri-a 税 ……………………………… （173）
　　第一节　乌尔第三王朝王室概况 ……………………… （174）
　　第二节　术语与文献概况 ……………………………… （181）
　　第三节　王室税的征收 ………………………………… （184）
　　第四节　王室税的变革 ………………………………… （198）

第六章　神庙 zag-u 税 …………………………………… （203）
　　第一节　神庙体系概况 ………………………………… （203）
　　第二节　术语与文献 …………………………………… （207）
　　第三节　神庙 zag-u 税的征收 ………………………… （210）

第七章　赋税制度与国家治理 …………………………… （216）
　　第一节　舒尔吉时期的赋税制度 ……………………… （216）
　　第二节　阿马尔辛时期的赋税制度 …………………… （220）
　　第三节　舒辛时期的赋税制度 ………………………… （225）

结　语 ……………………………………………………… （229）

附　录
　　附录一　古代两河流域历史框架 ……………………… （236）
　　附录二　乌尔第三王朝年名 …………………………… （238）
　　附录三　乌尔第三王朝月名 …………………………… （245）
　　附录四　度量衡单位对照 ……………………………… （253）
　　附录五　动物（牲畜）的种类与级别 ………………… （255）
　　附录六　缩写词 ………………………………………… （260）
　　附录七　原始档案目录 ………………………………… （272）

参考文献 …………………………………………………… （321）

中外文专有名词对照表 …………………………………… （372）

后　记 ……………………………………………………… （383）

图 目 录

图 1-1 古代两河流域版图 ……………………………………（21）
图 1-2 乌尔第三王朝版图 ……………………………………（23）
图 2-1 bala 税对应的楔形文字 ………………………………（32）
图 2-2 乌尔第三王朝核心区版图 ……………………………（35）
图 2-3 温马行省版图 …………………………………………（36）
图 2-4 拉伽什—吉尔苏行省版图 ……………………………（43）
图 2-5 bala 税流转过程示意图 ………………………………（110）
图 3-1 乌尔第三王朝外围区版图 ……………………………（119）
图 6-1 zag-u 税对应的楔形文字 ……………………………（207）

表 目 录

表1-1　乌尔第三王朝统治者 …………………………………（24）
表1-2　乌尔第三王朝主要遗址出土文献数量统计 ……………（28）
表1-3　乌尔第三王朝各位统治者时期文献数量统计 …………（29）
表2-1　乌尔第三王朝内行省统计表 ……………………………（33）
表2-2　尼普尔行省总督任期 ……………………………………（40）
表2-3　拉伽什—吉尔苏行省总督任期 …………………………（44）
表2-4　温马行省总督任期 ………………………………………（46）
表2-5　伊利萨格里格行省总督任期 ……………………………（47）
表2-6　行省总督任期一览表 ……………………………………（48）
表2-7　bala税文献数量及比例统计表 …………………………（67）
表2-8　温马行省bala税形式统计表 ……………………………（70）
表2-9　温马行省bala税纳税月份统计表 ………………………（84）
表2-10　拉伽什—吉尔苏行省bala税形式统计表 ………………（87）
表2-11　拉伽什—吉尔苏行省bala税的征收对象统计表 ………（90）
表2-12　拉伽什—吉尔苏行省的粮仓种类一览表 ………………（91）
表2-13　拉伽什—吉尔苏行省的储藏室种类一览表 ……………（93）
表2-14　拉伽什—吉尔苏行省的船文献统计表 …………………（98）
表2-15　拉伽什—吉尔苏行省的食用大麦术语统计表 …………（104）
表2-16　拉伽什—吉尔苏行省bala税纳税月份统计表 …………（108）
表2-17　乌尔第三王朝内行省bala税纳税月份统计表 …………（114）
表3-1　乌尔第三王朝外围区统计表 ……………………………（121）
表3-2　gun$_2$ ma-da文献统计分析表 …………………………（143）
表3-3　普图里乌姆gun$_2$ ma-da税缴纳情况 …………………（146）

1

表 3-4	提兰、阿尔曼和扎克图姆拖欠 gun$_2$ ma-da 税情况	(147)
表 3-5	gun$_2$ ma-da 税缴纳额度一览表	(148)
表 4-1	乌尔第三王朝附属国统计表	(151)
表 4-2	乌尔第三王朝附属国税术语不同写法	(153)
表 4-3	包含术语 gun$_2$ 的文献统计表	(154)
表 4-4	附属国 gun$_2$ 税文献统计分析表	(155)
表 4-5	附属国阿丹顿纳税统计分析表	(160)
表 4-6	附属国乌鲁阿纳税统计分析表	(165)
表 4-7	附属国孜姆达尔纳税统计分析表	(172)
表 5-1	乌尔第三王朝王妻统计表	(176)
表 5-2	乌尔第三王朝国王儿女统计表	(177)
表 5-3	王室税术语形式	(182)
表 5-4	王室税术语不同时期文献分布统计表	(183)
表 5-5	乌尔第三王朝王室税术语不同遗址出土文献分布统计表	(183)
表 5-6	乌尔第三王朝王室税文献统计分析表	(184)
表 5-7	王室税加乌尔三大节日统计表	(198)
表 5-8	王室税加各个节日文献统计分析表	(200)
表 6-1	乌尔第三王朝 zag-u 文献统计表	(208)
表 6-2	乌尔第三王朝神庙 zag-u 税统计分析表	(208)
表 6-3	神庙 zag-u 税贡献的主要神	(211)

引　言

^dŠul-gi nita-kala-ga lugal Uri₅^{ki}-ma lugal-an-ub-da-limmu₂-ba
舒尔吉，强大之人，乌尔之王，天下四方之王

  赋税是国家财政的重要支柱，古代两河流域文明国家机器的运转同样也离不开赋税。赋税指为了维持国家机器的运转而无偿地、强制地向民众征收的货币和实物的总称。① 赋税的一大特征是其强制性，"赋税是政府机器的经济的基础，而不是其他任何东西的经济的基础"②。英国古典经济学家亚当·斯密指出："人们必须拿出自己的一部分收入，给君主或国家，作为一笔公共收入。"③ 日本财政学者小川乡太郎在《租税总论》中认为，赋税为国家支付一般经费之目的，依其财政向一般人民强制征收之财。④ 赋税是国家用以取得财政收入的重要手段，列宁说："所谓赋税，就是国家不付任何报酬而向居民取得东西。"⑤ 马克思将赋税概括为："赋税是官僚、军队、教士和宫廷的生活来源，一句话，它是行政权的整个机构的生活来源。"⑥ 国家的治理与赋税的征收密不可分，国家是赋税产生和存在的

---

① 何盛明主编：《财经大辞典》下卷，中国财政经济出版社1990年版，第2022页。
② 《马克思恩格斯选集》第3卷，人民出版社2009年版，第376页。
③ ［英］亚当·斯密：《国民财富性质和原因的研究》下册，郭大力、王亚南译，商务印书馆1974年版，第383页。
④ ［日］小川乡太郎：《租税总论》，萨孟武译，商务印书馆1935年版，第11页。
⑤ 《列宁全集》第32卷，人民出版社1958年版，第275页。
⑥ 《马克思恩格斯选集》第1卷，人民出版社2012年版，第766页。

必要条件，"国家存在的经济体现就是捐税"①。

　　古代两河流域文明（约公元前3200—前330年）②是人类历史上最早的文明之一，其在绵延三千年的历史发展历程中，经历了若干个时期和王朝，出现过以城市为主体的城邦、囊括两河流域局部地区的区域性国家，以及跨地区的帝国这三种国家形态，③在古波斯帝国灭亡之后逐渐被世人遗忘。直到19世纪，欧洲探险家在中东地区的游历探险、考古发掘以及楔形文字的破译，这一文明才重见天日。④1857年，亚述学这一门新兴学科的诞生，标志着古代两河流域文明和楔形文字的研究走上了正轨，世界上为数不多的亚述学研究者一代代地传承，一层层地揭开这一古老文明的神秘面纱。

　　在公元前3千纪的两河流域，国家经济（财政收入）并不依靠人头税的征收，而是依靠徭役与实物税。从早王朝时期到阿卡德王国时期，捷姆迭特纳色、乌卡伊尔（Uqair）和乌鲁克的城邦联盟向乌鲁克的伊南娜神庙提供食物，作为供品和神庙人员的日常开销，这可以看作是乌尔第三王朝核心行省bala税的前身。⑤在早王朝时期的恩美台纳铭文、⑥阿卡德王国的萨尔贡铭文⑦与拉伽什第二王朝的古地亚铭文⑧中，有关于劳动力（劳役）征用的相关记载。此外，乌鲁卡基那的改革铭文规定，废除神庙管理者的

---

① 《马克思恩格斯全集》第1卷，人民出版社1972年版，第181页。
② 又名美索不达米亚文明。两河流域（Mesopotamia），音译为"美索不达米亚"，源自古希腊语 Μεσοποταμία，意为"河流之间的土地"。这里的"两河"指幼发拉底河和底格里斯河。关于古代两河流域历史的时段划分，主要参考：A. L. Oppenheim, *Ancient Mesopotamia*, Chicago-London：University of Chicago Press, 1964; M. Van de Mieroop, *A History of the Ancient Near East*, ca. 3000 – 323 BC, Malden-Oxford-Carlton：Blackwell Publishing, 2007; 刘文鹏主编《古代西亚北非文明》，中国社会科学出版社1999年版；于殿利《巴比伦与亚述文明》，北京师范大学出版社2013年版。
③ 关于古代两河流域文明发展过程中的三种国家形态，参见 M. Van de Mieroop, *A History of the Ancient Near East*, ca. 3000 – 323 BC, Malden-Oxford-Carlton：Blackwell Publishing, 2007.
④ 关于古代两河流域的考古发掘历史，参见拱玉书《西亚考古史（1842—1939）》，文物出版社2002年版。
⑤ 本书中的苏美尔语单词和语义符一律用正体，阿卡德语单词一律用斜体。由于乌尔第三王朝的赋税名称很难准确译成汉语，加之其含义在不同学者中存在争议，本书不按中国学术界的惯例译成汉语，而是按国际亚述学惯例只给其拉丁化形式。
⑥ D. R. Frayne, *Presargonic Period (2700 – 2350 BC)*, The Royal Inscriptions of Mesopotamia Early Periods, Volume 1, Toronto-Buffalo-London：University of Toronto Press, 1998, pp. 193 – 236.
⑦ D. Frayne, *Sargonic and Gutian Periods (2334 – 2113 BC)*, The Royal Inscriptions of Mesopotamia Early Periods, Volume 2, Toronto-Buffalo-London：University of Toronto Press, 1993, pp. 7 – 39.
⑧ D. O. Edzard, *Gudea and His Dynasty*, The Royal Inscriptions of Mesopotamia Early Periods, Volume 3/1（RIME 3/1），Toronto-Buffalo-London：University of Toronto Press, 1997, pp. 68 – 100.

dubsig 税以及其他税目，渔民、园丁、牧民从免除赋役改革政策中获得好处。① 在早王朝时期，就已经有了王室税、土地灌溉税等税目。这些税目的起源与演变，为乌尔第三王朝赋税制度的建立和发展奠定了基础。

乌尔第三王朝（又称乌尔帝国，公元前 2112—前 2004 年）② 作为苏美尔人建立的典型区域性国家，是苏美尔文明发展的最高峰，也是公元前 3 千纪世界文明中建立中央集权制国家的典范。虽然它只存在了短短一百余年的时间，但是却在古代世界历史长河中占据非常重要的地位，并且留下了数以万计的楔形文字泥板文献，其中许多文献涉及赋税内容，包含与赋税相关的术语。乌尔第三王朝的赋税制度研究，对于我们了解和认识古代两河流域的政治制度、经济制度、军事与外交制度，乃至上古西亚文明的历史发展都具有重要的理论意义，并且对于今天我国进行的税制改革也具有一定的借鉴与参考价值。

一　选题意义

赋税是维系国家机器正常运转的经济基础和物质条件，研究赋税制度是打开乌尔第三王朝国家之谜的一把钥匙。赋税是国家财政收入的主要来源，研究乌尔第三王朝的赋税制度有助于深入了解其经济结构。赋税的征收不仅关系国家财政收入的多寡，而且关系到民众负担的轻重，进而影响经济的发展。赋税制度是国家财政经济制度的重要内容，研究乌尔第三王朝的赋税制度有利于进一步全面了解其经济制度。

---

① D. R. Frayne, *Presargonic Period (2700 – 2350 BC)*, *The Royal Inscriptions of Mesopotamia Early Periods*, Volume 1, Toronto-Buffalo-London: University of Toronto Press, 1998, pp. 259 – 265.

② 在古代两河流域年代学研究中，共存在三种不同的年代学："高年代学"（High Chronology）、"中年代学"（Middle Chronology）和"低年代学"（Low Chronology）。本书采用的是传统上被普遍接受的"中年代学"，即认为乌尔第三王朝的时间范围是公元前 2112—前 2004 年，参见 A. L. Oppenheim, *Ancient Mesopotamia: Portrait of a Dead Civilization*, Chicago: University of Chicago Press, 1964。除此之外，还有学者认为"高年代学"可能更加准确，参见 P. J. Huber, "Astronomical Dating of Babylon I and Ur III", *Monographic Journals of the Near East*, Vol. 1/4 (1982), pp. 1 – 19; P. J. Huber, "Astronomical Evidence for the Long and against the Middle and Short Chronologies", in P. Åström (ed.), *High, Middle or Low? Acts of an International Colloquium on Absolute Chronology held at the University of Gothenburg 20th-22nd August 1987*, Göteborg: Paul Åströms Förlag, 1987/89, pp. 5 – 17.

赋税是以国家为主体的一种分配形式，即只存在于文明国家阶段。恩格斯说："捐税是以前的氏族社会完全没有的。"① 赋税是国家凭借政治权力对民众进行的强制的和无偿的索取，赋税的这种强制性是与国家权力分不开的，国家权力是赋税产生的前提，研究乌尔第三王朝的赋税制度有助于认识其政治结构。赋税的征收不仅影响和制约国家机构的运转效率，而且关乎民众的生活和社会的稳定，进而影响国家的盛衰。赋税制度是联结经济基础和上层建筑的纽带，运用辩证唯物主义与历史唯物主义的观点和方法，从历史学的角度考察古代两河流域乌尔第三王朝赋税制度的历史地位和作用，从解读原始楔形文字文献——尤其是从大量未发表的新泥板文献——入手，以古代两河流域乌尔第三王朝贡赋税性质为抓手，深入地剖析乌尔第三王朝的政治组织、经济制度和社会结构的演进状况，这对于我们正确理解古代西亚两河流域的社会经济形态有着重要的意义。

乌尔第三王朝赋税制度研究属于早期文明史的研究内容，但是，如果从"一切历史都是当代史"的现代史学观念来看，乌尔第三王朝赋税制度的研究对于我们深入了解现代文明也具有重要意义。通过系统整理古代两河流域乌尔第三王朝的楔形文字赋税泥板文献，考察乌尔第三王朝赋税的本质与特征，对乌尔第三王朝的赋税制度进行专题研究，深入剖析其对世界古代文明起源与发展的重要性。从问题史学的理念入手，研究古代文明，比如乌尔第三王朝的赋税制度，对于我们理解现代文明，理解现代文明的产生、发展和成熟具有重要的借鉴意义。乌尔第三王朝的赋税制度作为古代世界赋税制度的典范，对我国目前供给侧改革背景下的税制改革具有重要的借鉴意义。乌尔第三王朝赋税制度的研究属于国际人文学科合作的成果，对国际亚述学的发展具有重要的推动作用，对国人研究亚述学等人文学科在国际上增强话语权具有重要的现实意义。

二　研究综述

赋税制度是亚述学研究的重要课题之一，长期以来，与两河流域后期

---

① 《马克思恩格斯选集》第4卷，人民出版社1972年版，第167页。

形成完善的赋税制度相比,[①] 乌尔第三王朝的赋税制度研究始终是亚述学界的一个悬而未决的课题,这是因为用以构建乌尔第三王朝赋税制度的原始文献资料不仅零散而且缺失,许多经济文献只是简单记载了与赋税相关的术语,而对于这些零散术语的解释在学术界也存在不小的争议。由于赋税是国家经济有效运转的前提,虽然迄今为止并没有发现专门的乌尔第三王朝的赋税档案资料,不过对乌尔第三王朝赋税制度进行构建是我们研究乌尔第三王朝乃至古代两河流域经济制度史无法规避的论题。有关乌尔第三王朝赋税制度的研究始于20世纪初,相关的论著极少涉及多种赋税的综合性研究,主要集中于对单一税种的研究,可以细分为涉及核心区 bala 税、外围区 gun_2 ma-da 税、王室 $maš_2$-da-ri-a 税、神庙 zag-u 税等税种的研究。根据乌尔第三王朝专题的研究特点,赋税制度研究的前提依据是乌尔第三王朝的数十万块刻在泥板上的经济文献或者经济档案,这些文献主要出土于伊拉克南部的几个遗址,包括普兹瑞什达干、温马、吉尔苏、尼普尔、乌尔、伽尔沙纳和伊利萨格里格等。

(一) 涉及赋税的经济档案整理

由于历史的原因,古代两河流域出土的楔形文字泥板文献主要被一些欧美发达国家的博物馆、图书馆和私人藏家保存收藏,亚述学者们对这些文献档案进行了整理和翻译,其中一部分成果与乌尔第三王朝的赋税内容相关。自1911年,英国亚述学家兰登出版了英国阿什摩利博物馆所藏的68件涉及赋税的乌尔第三王朝经济泥板文献以来,[②] 国外学者又陆续出版发表了大量涉及赋税的乌尔第三王朝经济文献档案,每次出版的数量少至只有一篇,[③] 多则数千篇文献不等,比如法国亚述学家西格里斯特和日本亚述学家尾崎亨共同整理出版了美国耶鲁大学博物馆所藏的3024件乌尔第三王朝经济泥板,[④] 其中大多涉及赋税领域。由于乌尔第三王朝的经济文献被分散收藏于

---

① 参见国洪更《亚述赋役制度考略》,中国社会科学出版社2015年版。
② S. Langdon, *Tablets from the Archives of Drehem*, Paris: Librairie Paul Geuthner, 1911.
③ 比如: C. Liu, "An Ur III Tablet from Southwestern University", *Aula Orientalis*, Vol. 32, No. 1 (2014), pp. 175 – 176.
④ M. Sigrist, T. Ozaki, *Neo-Sumerian Administrative Tablets from the Yale Babylonian Collection*, Part 1 – 2, Madrid: Consejo Superior de Investigaciones Científicas, 2009.

世界各地，并被发表于不同的期刊或著作，这就为专题研究工作造成不便。为了解决这种弊端，亚述学者们不遗余力地搜集、整理已经发表的经济文献，更重要的是建立专门的楔形文字文献档案数据库。1991 年，西格里斯特和五味亨（即后来的尾崎亨）合著的《乌尔第三王朝综合出版目录》一书，[①] 共搜集到了 28021 篇当时已经发表的乌尔第三王朝经济文献，其中大多数档案文献涉及赋税。2015 年，意大利罗马大学的博士加西亚—文图拉整理出版了自 1997 年至 2014 年间国际亚述学界有关乌尔第三王朝研究的成果目录，其中包括赋税文献的发表情况。[②] 此外，需要强调的是，目前由美国加州大学洛杉矶分校亚述学家英格伦（R. K. Englund）主持的"楔形文字数字图书馆"（Cuneiform Digital Library Initiative，简称 CDLI）项目[③]和西班牙马德里高等科学研究院亚述学家莫利纳（M. Molina）主持的"新苏美尔语文献数据库"（西班牙语：Base de Datos de Textos Neo-Sumerios，简称 BDTNS，英语：Database of Neo-Sumerian Texts）项目，[④] 汇集了世界上最丰富的乌尔第三王朝经济文献资料，其中绝大多数为已经出版发表的文献，也包括少数未发表的文献，这些文献是我们研究乌尔第三王朝赋税制度的第一手资料，也为研究乌尔第三王朝赋税制度提供了最基本以及最重要的前提条件。当然，仍然还有相当数量的乌尔第三王朝经济管理文献尚未发表和编目，它们被收藏在某博物馆、大学图书馆或者私人手中，甚至仍然在伊拉克或叙利亚的地下尚未发掘出土，这些不知数目的潜在文献资料很可能也涉及赋税，甚至可能还会有意想不到的系统赋税档案。对此，我们只能寄希望于将来相关文献资料的不断出现。这么说的话，本书的研究成果也只是暂时的、而绝非最终的结论。

（二）多项赋税制度的综合性研究

关于乌尔第三王朝赋税制度的综合性研究成果目前还没有出现，较为

---

① M. Sigrist, T. Gomi, *The Comprehensive Catalogue of Published Ur III Tablets*, Bethesda：CDL Press，1991.

② A. Garcia-Ventura, "Ur III Studies：Bibliography 1997 – 2014", *Studia Orientalia*, Vol. 3 (2015), pp. 22 – 47.

③ https：//cdli. ucla. edu/.

④ http：//bdtns. filol. csic. es/.

系统的是施拉坎普和保莱蒂合写的德语词条"税收"（Steuer A），其中的第三部分专门讲的是乌尔第三王朝的赋税，但也只是简略地列举了这一时期可能存在的赋税种类，包括 bala 税、gun₂ ma-da 税、maš/maš₂-a-ša₃-ga 税、maš₂-da-ri-a 税、zag-u 税等。① 其余对于乌尔第三王朝赋税的研究基本都是个案研究，即只关注于某一个税种进行研究，主要涉及 bala 和 gun₂ ma-da 这两种税。造成这种研究格局和特点的原因，主要是乌尔第三王朝属于早期文明的范畴，作为构建早期国家经济形态要素的赋税制度尚处于萌芽或初级阶段，还没有发展到完善和系统的程度，在古代文献中也没有发现这一时期有系统的赋税档案。现代学者们只能依靠经济文献档案中提到的一些可能与赋税相关的术语，来间接求证乌尔第三王朝的赋税制度，这也就造成了学者们倾向于研究某一种赋税的个案研究特点。

（三）单项赋税制度的个案研究

1. 涉及 bala 税的研究

最早研究乌尔第三王朝 bala 税的学者是耶鲁大学亚述学教授哈罗。② 他利用在当时数量有限的普兹瑞什达干（即今伊拉克的德莱海姆）文献，区分了 bala 这个术语的不同含义，认为 bala 是地方（行省总督和神庙主管）向中央（尼普尔祭祀中心）缴纳牲畜的一种贡赋，每个行省中按月轮流缴纳，并且指出尼普尔行省不需要缴纳 bala 税。他借用了古希腊的术语"近邻同盟"（Amphictyonies）③ 的概念，进一步认为 bala 税是将分散的苏美尔—阿卡德城邦相结盟，其职责是向国家的宗教中心尼普尔贡献祭祀所用的牺牲。虽然由于文献数量的局限性，但是他的这一研究成果基本上肯定了 bala 作为一种赋税的结论，为后来的 bala 税研究指明了方向。1987年，哈佛大学亚述学教授斯坦因凯勒（P. Steinkeller）发表了跨时代的论

---

① I. Schrakamp, P. Paoletti, "Steuer", *Reallexikonder Assyriologie und Vorderasiatischen Archäologie*, Vol. 13 (2011–2013), pp. 163–164. 最新关于乌尔第三王朝赋税的概述，参见：S. Alivernini, "Management of Resources and Taxation in an Early Mesopotamian Empire: the Case of the Third Dynasty of Ur", in Mynarova, J., Alivernini, S. (eds.), *Economic Complexity in the Ancient Near East, Management of Resources and Taxation (Third-Second Millennium BC)*, Prague: Charles University, 2020, pp. 69–86.

② W. W. Hallo, "A Sumerian Amphictyony", *Journal of Cuneiform Studies*, Vol. 14 (1960), pp. 88–114.

③ 关于古希腊术语"近邻同盟"，参见 H. Chambers, "Ancient Amphictyonies, Sic et Non", in W. W. Hallo (ed.), *Scripture in Context III*, Winona Lake: Eisenbrauns, 1983, pp. 39–59.

文《乌尔第三王朝行政与经济组织：核心区与外围区》一文，[①] 正式提出乌尔第三王朝地方行政区划的三分法原理，即核心区（或核心行省）、外围区（或外围行省）和附属国的概念，并且对应于经济方面指出，核心行省缴纳 bala 税，边远行省缴纳 gun₂ ma-da 税，为乌尔第三王朝赋税制度的研究奠定了基础。他关于乌尔第三王朝的行政区分三分法，直到今天也是学者们普遍遵循的原理，并且成为研究乌尔第三王朝政治制度和经济制度的基础。斯坦因凯勒的研究不仅依赖普兹瑞什达干文献，还增加了温马和吉尔苏的文献，他并不反对哈罗关于 bala 税是地方向中央以牲畜形式缴纳的一种赋税的观点，但是却认为这只是 bala 税的"冰山一角"，还应该有更多的原则和规定。对此，他提出了关于 bala 税的三个基本原则：[②] 第一，bala 税的形式以每个行省所产的物品为主（并不仅仅是牲畜），包括农产品和自然资源（粮食、芦苇、木材）；第二，bala 税是双向的，当行省完成既定的 bala 税义务后，可以从中央或再分配中心获取其他所需产品作为回报；第三，bala 税被发送到邻近该行省的再分配中心，相当一部分 bala 税由中央机构在该行省范围内进行再分配或者直接消费，或者直接拨付给王室成员。总之，斯坦因凯勒认为，bala 税是一种具有再分配性质的赋税，各行省主要以农副产品形式向中央缴纳，而中央作为回报，将其从外围区征收的牲畜再分配给行省，完成产品的再分配。在斯坦因凯勒之后，关于 bala 税的研究朝着越来越清晰的方向发展。日本早稻田大学亚述学教授前田彻连续发表了两篇论文，[③] 总结了乌尔第三王朝每个行省 bala 税的具体缴纳月份，指出每个行省的 bala 税缴纳月份并不是固定不变的，并且总结了 bala 税文献的格式记录特点。还有一位研究 bala 税的学者是美国俄克拉荷马大学的沙拉赫博士，她依据温马、吉尔苏和普兹瑞什达干出土的文献，撰写出了研究 bala 税的专著《行省税与乌尔第三王朝》，[④] 通过充

[①] P. Steinkeller, "The Administrative and Economic Organization of the Ur III State: The Core and the Periphery", in M. Gibson, R. D. Biggs (eds.), *The Organization of Power: Aspects of Bureaucracy in the Ancient Near East*, Chicago: The Oriental Institute of the University of Chicago, 1987, pp. 15 – 34.

[②] P. Steinkeller, "The Administrative and Economic Organization of the Ur III State: The Core and the Periphery", in M. Gibson, R. D. Biggs (eds.), *The Organization of Power: Aspects of Bureaucracy in the Ancient Near East*, Chicago: The Oriental Institute of the University of Chicago, 1987, pp. 28 – 29.

[③] T. Maeda, "Bal-ensí in the Drehem Texts", *Acta Sumerologica*, Vol. 16 (1994), pp. 115 – 164; T. Maeda, "Šà-bal-a in Umma Tablets: Bal duty of the Ensí of Umma", *Acta Sumerologica*, Vol. 17 (1995), pp. 145 – 174.

[④] T. Sharlach, *Provincial Taxation and the Ur III State*, Cuneiform Monographs 26, Leiden: Brill, 2004.

分的证据证明 bala 是一种行省税,并且论述了温马和吉尔苏行省 bala 税的运转状况,认为乌尔第三王朝的财政基础根植于各行省所缴纳的赋税。需要指出的是,沙拉赫关于 bala 税的研究只是集中于温马和吉尔苏两个行省,对于乌尔第三王朝的其他行省并没有涉及。

2. 涉及 gun_2 ma-da 税的研究

关于外围行省缴纳的 gun_2 ma-da 税,最早对其进行专门研究的是密歇根大学亚述学教授米哈洛夫斯基,他在《乌尔第三王朝的外邦贡赋》一文[①]中,依据自己收集到的 20 件文献,将 gun_2 ma-da 解释为一种朝贡体系,是乌尔第三王朝边防区(或军事缓冲区)向中央缴纳的一种贡赋,主要的贡赋形式是牲畜。美国康奈尔大学亚述学教授欧文在其《城市长老的赋税》一文中,[②] 主要考证了乌尔第三王朝东北部的一些小城市的赋税情况。斯坦因凯勒的《乌尔第三王朝行政与经济组织:核心区与外围区》一文的后半部分是专门研究 gun_2 ma-da 税的,他利用所收集的近 100 件文献,认为 gun_2 ma-da 是乌尔第三王朝外围区向中央缴纳的一种赋税,并且最早发现了关于这种赋税征收的一个规律,即作为赋税形式的牛和羊大致是按照 1∶10 的比例进行征收,同时他还对 gun_2 ma-da 税的税率、负责官员、征收、运输以及管理进行了初步的研究。斯坦因凯勒对 gun_2 ma-da 税的研究虽然看似近乎完美,但也还是引起了学者们的质疑。1992 年,日本学者前田彻在《乌尔第三王朝的防御区》一文[③]中,列举了 89 个外围区(或军事防御区),并且详细考证了这些地区缴纳的 gun_2 税(或贡)或 gun_2 ma-da 税(或贡)情况,他不同意斯坦因凯勒将 gun_2 税作为 gun_2 ma-da 税简写形式的观点,而是认为两者指的是两种不同的贡税,同时前田彻将 gun_2 ma-da 税的建立同舒辛 3 年的税制改革相联系,尤其是与王朝的再分配中心——普兹瑞什达干的 mu-DU 体系改革相关。前田彻对 gun_2 ma-da 税的研究从个案的角度初步解决了乌尔第三王朝外围区的贡税制度,但是就这一特殊地区的实际作用以及具体的行政管理制度等方面,尚留有进一步研究的广阔空间。

---

① P. Michalowski, "Foreign Tribute to Sumer in Ur III Times", *Zeitschrift für Assyriologie und Vorderasiatische Archäologie*, Vol. 68 (1978), pp. 34–49.

② D. I. Owen, "Tax Payments from Some City Elders in the Northeast", *Acta Sumerologica*, Vol. 3 (1981), pp. 63–76.

③ T. Maeda, "The Defense Zone during the Rule of the Ur III Dynasty", *Acta Sumerologica*, Vol. 14 (1992), pp. 135–172.

3. 涉及 maš₂-da-ri-a 税的研究

关于 maš₂-da-ri-a 术语的界定在亚述学界存在争议，早期的学者从这个术语的本义出发，倾向于将其定义为一种"山羊的献祭"或者是一种祭祀供品。① 在 20 世纪 80 年代末、90 年代初，学者们对 maš₂-da-ri-a 的研究掀起了一个小高潮，基本上不是专门的研究，而是在研究乌尔第三王朝专题史中涉及 maš₂-da-ri-a 术语，并且对这一术语的认识也在不断演进。前田彻在著名的关于普兹瑞什达干 mu-DU 文献的研究成果中，② 探讨了 maš₂-da-ri-a 加乌尔第三王朝三大节日（ezem-mah，a₂-ki-ti，šu-numun）的用法以及含义，认为这是属于舒辛 3 年经济改革的一部分，但是他认为 maš₂-da-ri-a 是一种礼品，而不是一种税。前田彻关于 maš₂-da-ri-a 加节日术语的研究，后来被德国慕尼黑大学的亚述学教授扎拉伯格和法国亚述学者西格里斯特所承袭。扎拉伯格在其名著《乌尔第三王朝的祭祀历书》中，③ 详细研究了用 maš₂-da-ri-a 修饰节日时的用法以及文献特征，认为 maš₂-da-ri-a 指一种与王室有关的赋税，由地方行省和神庙向中央缴纳，主要是用于国家的重大节日祭祀和王室成员的日常消费。西格里斯特在其专著《德莱海姆》中，④ 系统研究了普兹瑞什达干出土文献及其机构的运转管理情况，他也认为 maš₂-da-ri-a 术语指的是一种礼品，由乌尔中央向地方行省、外围区以及神庙所征收，用于国家的祭祀活动。最后一位研究 maš₂-da-ri-a 的是奥地利维也纳大学的亚述学教授泽尔茨，他从语言学（尤其词源学）角度探讨了 maš₂-da-ri-a 的词源为"被牵到一边的山羊"，根据早王朝时期文献，他认为，这个术语的意思和使用方式在乌尔第三王朝并没有发生改变，指的是一种与山羊有关的供品或者赋税。⑤

---

① A. L. Oppenheim, *Catalogue of the Cuneiform Tablets of the Wilberforce Eames Babylonian Collection in the New York Public Library*: *Tablets of the Time of the Third Dynasty of Ur*, New Haven: American Oriental Society, 1948, p. 30.

② T. Maeda, "Bringing (mu-túm) Livestock and the Puzrish-Dagan Organization in the Ur III Dynasty", *Acta Sumerologica*, Vol. 11 (1989), pp. 98 – 99.

③ W. Sallaberger, *Der kultische Kalender der Ur III-Zeit*, Berlin and New York: Walter de Gruyter, 1993, pp. 160 – 170.

④ M. Sigrist, *Drehem*, Bethesda: CDL Press, 1992, pp. 190 – 192.

⑤ G. J. Selz, "Maš-da-ri-a und Verwandtes. Ein Versuch über da-ri'an der Seite führen': ein zusammengesetztes Verbum und einige nominale Ableitungen", *Acta Sumerologica*, Vol. 17 (1995), pp. 251-274.

引 言

4. 涉及神庙税的研究

神庙在乌尔第三王朝，乃至整个古代两河流域历史上都占有重要的地位。关于两河流域神庙赋税的研究成果却并不是很多，这主要是学者们对古代术语的认识上存在争议，容易将宗教献祭品、供品和礼品同赋税的概念相混淆，它们之间的界线并不是很清晰。[1] 目前可以肯定的一种神庙税是什一税（zag-u），它是乌尔第三王朝所建立的一种赋税，后来影响了两河流域的神庙体系，甚至成为犹太什一税的起源，影响到了欧洲中世纪的什一税。[2]

5. 涉及其他可能的税种研究

除了 bala 税和 gun$_2$ ma-da 税之外，学界对乌尔第三王朝其他赋税种类的研究十分零散和匮乏。由于能够得到的研究资料非常零散与缺失，以及对相关的术语含义的探讨尚存在诸多争议，从而导致迄今学界对这一时期赋税的研究尚未形成完整的体系。诸如，有的学者认为 šu-gid$_2$（向牧羊人征收的一种牲畜税）[3] 和 maš-a-ša$_3$-ga（土地灌溉税）[4] 也分别指一种赋税。此外，诸如神庙供品（a-ru-a, sa$_2$-du$_{11}$, nidba, šu-a-gi-na, kaš-de$_2$-a,

---

[1] 关于乌尔第三王朝的宗教神庙祭祀与供品的研究，参见 R. L. Zettler, *The Ur III Temple of Inanna at Nippur: The Operation and Organization of Urban Religious Institutions in Mesopotamia in the Late Third Millennium B. C.*, Berlin: Dietrich Reimer Verlag, 1992; W. Sallaberger, *Der kultische Kalender der Ur III-Zeit*, Berlin and New York: Walter de Gruyter, 1993; M. Such-Gutiérrez, *Beiträge zum Pantheon von Nippur im 3. Jahrtausend*, Rome: Herder Libreria editrice, 2003.

[2] E. Salonen, *Über den Zehnten im alten Mesopotamien: Ein Beitrag zur Geschichte der Besteuerung*, Helsinki: Suomalaisen Kirjallisuuden Kirjapaino Oy, 1972, 亦可参见刘昌玉、应俊《欧洲什一税源于古代两河流域》，《中国社会科学报》2018 年 10 月 29 日。

[3] D. C. Snell, "The Ur III Tablets in the Emory University Museum", *Acta Sumerologica*, Vol. 9 (1987), p. 228; A. L. Oppenheim, *Catalogue of the Cuneiform Tablets of the Wilberforce Eames Babylonian Collection in the New York Public Library: Tablets of the Time of the Third Dynasty of Ur*, New Haven: American Oriental Society, 1948, p. 5.

[4] P. Steinkeller, "The Renting of Fields in Early Mesopotamia and the Development of the Concept of 'Interest' in Sumerian", *Journal of the Economic and Social History of the Orient*, Vol. 24 (1981), pp. 113 – 145; K. Maekawa, "Agricultural Texts of Ur III Lagash of the British Museum (IV)", *Zinbun*, Vol. 21 (1986), pp. 122 – 125; H. Neumann, "Grundpfandbestellung und Feldabgabe unter rechts-und sozialvergleichendem Aspekt (mit Bemerkungen zur Lesung und Interpretation von CST 60, 11 und MVN III 336, 11)", in H. Klengel and J. Renger (eds.), *Landwirtschaft im alten Orient: Ausgewählte Vorträge der XLI. Rencontre Assyriologique Internationale Berlin*, 4. – 8. 7. 1994, Berliner Beiträge zum Vorderen Orient 18, Berlin: Dietrich Reimer Verlag, 1999, pp. 137 – 148.

siskur₂，nig₂-diri)、礼品（nig₂-ba）、结婚礼（nig₂-mussa）① 这些术语是否也是指一种税，目前学界也存在较大的争议，而且它们到底是否适合借用今天的税收概念，也是一个尚未解决的问题。鉴于此，本书并未将上述不确定具体含义的术语纳入赋税的考察范围。作者寄希望于随着更多研究资料的发现与解读，以及我们对于古代赋税和现代赋税含义以及之间关系的更深入认识，届时我们可能会对这些术语有新的理解，甚至是更新的研究成果。

由于古代语言文字的障碍以及原始材料的缺乏，国内学者对于乌尔第三王朝的赋税制度研究尚处于空白，对于古代两河流域各时期赋税制度的研究成果也寥寥无几。目前仅有国洪更《亚述赋役制度考略》一书②系统研究了亚述时期的赋税制度，以及国内学者对于古埃及③、古罗马④和中世纪⑤赋税制度的研究，对于乌尔第三王朝的赋税制度研究具有一定的参考与借鉴价值。

综上所述，无论是涉及多项赋税制度的综合性研究，还是集中于单项赋税的个案研究，都从不同的角度揭示了乌尔第三王朝赋税的不同方面，有关学者的前期研究成果奠定了进一步深入研究这一主题的基础。然而，尽管涉及乌尔第三王朝赋税的论著数量不少，但是基本上都是针对于单项赋税的个案研究。除了萨拉赫、前田彻等人的少数研究成果之外，大多数研究成果属于探讨其他问题时顺便提及赋税内容，或者只是针对某个涉及赋税术语的词源学解释，而非系统的专门研究，更没有涉及赋税制度的专题性研究。总体而言，上述研究尚有一些需要完善之处：第一，以往的研

---

① W. Sallaberger, *Der kultische Kalender der Ur III-Zeit*, Berlin and New York: Walter de Gruyter, 1993.
② 国洪更：《亚述赋役制度考略》，中国社会科学出版社2015年版。
③ 郭丹彤：《论古代埃及的赋税体系》，《东北师大学报》（哲学社会科学版）2016年第3期。
④ 王三义：《古罗马"赋税名目"考略》，《史学月刊》2002年第6期；王三义：《罗马税制的积弊与戴克里先税制改革》，《世界历史》2007年第1期；徐国栋：《罗马人的税赋——从起源到戴克里先登基》，《现代法学》2010年第5期；崔国强：《罗马帝国税收钱币化探析》，《外国问题研究》2018年第3期。
⑤ 顾銮斋：《英国中古前期的税收习惯》，《世界历史》2014年第6期；顾銮斋：《赋税制度与欧洲政治制度的演进》，《史学理论研究》2014年第2期；熊芳芳：《从"领地国家"到"税收国家"：中世纪晚期法国君主征税权的确立》，《世界历史》2015年第4期；顾銮斋：《赋税变迁与欧洲文明》，《光明日报》2018年8月13日。

究基本都关注单项赋税,我们需要从整体上来考察乌尔第三王朝的赋税制度,及其对乌尔第三王朝国家治理与国家兴衰的影响;第二,以前的研究更多的是关注乌尔第三王朝的 bala 税和 gun_2 ma-da 税,而对于 $maš_2$-da-ri-a 税和 zag-u 税的研究略显单薄,并且对于这些术语的具体含义的考察尚存在争议;第三,过去的研究更多的是局限于当时的社会背景,造成了税、贡、供和礼的术语混淆,甚至一概称为"费用"(fee)来研究,在与现代税收概念的联系方面尚需要进一步斟酌与考究。因此,我们要从总体上全面地评估与考察乌尔第三王朝的赋税制度,及其对早期文明国家形态的发展演变所起的经济作用。

三 研究方法

文献研究的方法。乌尔第三王朝赋税制度属于亚述学研究的范畴,亚述学(Assyriology)是一门通过释读相关楔形文字文献来研究古代两河流域历史文化的综合性人文学科。故此,解读相关的楔形文字文献是乌尔第三王朝赋税制度研究的前提和基础。迄今为止,考古学家在西亚两河流域发掘的乌尔第三王朝楔形文字泥板数量多达十余万块。[①] 其中绝大多数是经济管理文献,从中筛选出与乌尔第三王朝赋税制度相关的文献,是本研究最为基础的工作。由于乌尔第三王朝的经济文献被分散在世界各国的博物馆、图书馆和私人藏家所收藏,借助于世界两大楔形文字文献数据库"楔形文字数字图书馆"(CDLI)和"新苏美尔语文献数据库"(BDTNS),我们可以收集到绝大多数相关文献,但是仍然有数量颇丰的文献分散在世界各地且尚没有发表。通过释读、翻译未发表的与赋税相关的原始楔形文字泥板文献,包括泥板临摹、拉丁字母音译、中英文翻译和术语注解,收集相关的文献资料和甄别史料成为乌尔第三王朝赋税制度研究的重要任

---

① 据莫利纳在2008年时的统计,乌尔第三王朝经济文献共计87241件,其中已发表的有74225件,尚未发布的有13016件,参见 M. Molina, "The Corpus of Neo-Sumerian Tablets: An Overview", in S. J. Garfinkle and J. C. Johnson (eds.), *The Growth of an Early State in Mesopotamia: Studies in Ur III Administration*, Madrid: Consejo Superior de Investigaciones Científicas, 2008, p. 20. 目前乌尔第三王朝的泥板文献的具体数目无从考证,随着新文献的不断被发现、释读,这个数目会持续保持增长态势。

务。乌尔第三王朝没有留下关于赋税征收的成文法律条文和档案资料，梳理各类涉及赋税制度的文献是乌尔第三王朝赋税制度研究的主要目标。需要指出的一点是，在乌尔第三王朝的文献中，已经明确记载有征税人的相关术语（enku 或者 en-ku$_3$），① 这些"征收人"包括库南那（Ku-Nanna）、② 卢伽尔奈萨吉（Lugal-nesage）、③ 塞塞什（Sheshesh）、④ 乌尔巴巴（Ur-Baba）、⑤ 乌尔吉吉尔（Ur-gigir）、⑥ 乌尔玛米（Ur-mami）、⑦ 乌尔宁伽尔（Ur-Ningal）、⑧ 乌尔乌图（Ur-Utu）、⑨ 乌尔辛（Ur-Suen）、⑩ 乌玛米（Umami）⑪ 等。因此，乌尔第三王朝赋税制度研究的基础是对文献的考证，即对文献史料进行内证和外证及其相互印证来选取可信、合适的材料。

定量分析与定性分析相结合的方法。乌尔第三王朝赋税制度属于经济学研究范畴，文献来源是数以万计的经济文献，对这些文献中的数据进行统计与计算是本书的基础技术工作。通过大量的图表、数据来准确描述乌尔第三王朝赋税制度的各个方面，利用 Filemaker 软件建立专业的数据库，

---

① M. W. Green, "Early Sumerian Tax Collectors", *Journal of Cuneiform Studies*, Vol. 36 (1984), pp. 93 – 95.

② 文献 UET 3 1310（IS 6，Ur）. 注意：根据国际亚述学惯例，文献的表示方式为"原始文献出处（文献日期，文献地点）"。本书引用的楔形文字原始文献出处的字母缩写，参见牛津大学"亚述学缩写"规范，网址为 http://cdli.ox.ac.uk/wiki/abbreviations_for_assyriology，最近浏览日期：2021 年 1 月 1 日。"原始文献出处"后面的"（文献日期，文献地点）"（IS 6，Ur）表示"伊比辛 6 年，地点为乌尔"。其中，S 代表舒尔吉、AS 代表阿马尔辛、SS 代表舒辛、IS 代表伊比辛、- - 代表统治者名字不详，undated 代表统治者及统治年份均不详，后面的数字表示统治年份，罗马数字 i—xii 代表月份，d 代表闰月，比如 IS 6 表示"伊比辛统治第 6 年"，SS 6 viii 5 表示"舒辛统治第 6 年，第 8 月，第 5 日"，S 48 xid 表示"舒尔吉统治第 48 年，闰 11 月"；关于"文献地点"，Drehem 代表德莱海姆（普兹瑞什达干）、Girsu 代表吉尔苏、Irisagrig 代表伊利萨格里格、Nippur 代表尼普尔、Umma 代表温马、Ur 代表乌尔。

③ 文献 BPOA 1 1086（undated，Umma）.

④ 文献 AfO 24 pl. 17 Truro 1（S 36，Girsu），RSO 83 343 5（S 45 x，Drehem）.

⑤ 文献 STA 11（AS 1，Umma），YOS 4 3（SS 6 viii 5，Umma）.

⑥ 文献 BPOA 6 1053（--xi，Umma），YOS 15 204（undated，Umma）.

⑦ 文献 SNAT 345（AS 4，Umma），SNAT 347（AS 4，Umma），TCL 5 6046（AS 4，Umma）.

⑧ 文献 UET 3 48（undated，Ur）.

⑨ 文献 BPOA 6 1004（S 45，Umma），BPOA 1 1206（AS 8 xii，Umma），AAICAB 1/3 pl. 249 Bod S 306（SS 2，Umma），TCBI 2/2 1（SS 6 – 9，Umma），UTI 5 3186 + 3415（SS，Umma），ZA 95 191（SS 7 – IS 1，Umma），Nisaba 23 65（undated，Umma），SNAT 537（undated，Umma）.

⑩ 文献 UTI 4 2577（S 46 xi，Umma），AUCT 3 479（AS 6）.

⑪ 文献 BPOA 2 2345（S 36 vii，Umma）.

涉及赋税种类、赋税形式、税源、税率、征税目的和用途、税务官员、赋税时限、来源文献及时间等数据的整理与统计工作。经济史的研究建立在对大量统计数据的分析与利用的基础上，乌尔第三王朝赋税制度的研究也不例外，由于缺乏专门的赋税档案文献和法律，这就需要我们对数量众多的零散文献证据进行甄别、统计、整理与分析，从而窥探乌尔第三王朝赋税制度的本质与特征。

鉴古知今与以今律古的历史研究方法。乌尔第三王朝赋税制度的研究虽然属于世界古代史亚述学的范畴，似乎距离我们今天的中国当代史很遥远，但是如果从"一切历史都是当代史"、探索一切历史问题都是从提出问题开始，对于乌尔第三王朝赋税制度的研究，自然也需要具有问题意识，从而体现历史研究所具有的重要借鉴作用。作为早期文明的代表，古代两河流域历史上的乌尔第三王朝是最早关于国家治理的典范，利用赋税的杠杆作用调控国家的经济与政治，从而引导早期国家形态演变的历史走向。这些宝贵的历史经验即使过去了数千年，对于今天我国的税收体制改革也具有一定的借鉴作用。正如刘家和先生所言："要深入认识今天的中国，就不能不深入认识今天的世界；要深入认识今天的世界，就不能不深入认识近代及中古之世界；要深入认识近代及中古之世界，就不能不深入认识古代之世界。这仍然是从当代的中国人出发，但又是一条思路，一条今日中国人必不可少的思路。所以，如果只看事情的一面，那么世界古代文明史就是遥远而无足轻重的；如果追寻事情的总体，那么世界古代文明史就是虽远犹近而不能不深研的了。"[①]

四　难点问题

赋税的征收一般是固定的，由国家的法律或国王敕令来颁布确定，但是乌尔第三王朝缺乏规定赋税征收的法令以及系统记录赋税征收的档案文献资料，以至于我们只能依据间接资料来窥探乌尔第三王朝的赋税制度，

[①] 刘家和、廖学盛主编：《世界古代文明史研究导论》，北京师范大学出版社2010年版，第19页。

不同于后来时期（如古罗马、① 西欧中世纪②）的赋税有详细的法律条文或者明文规定，乌尔第三王朝的这些间接资料比较零散，其中涉及的赋税术语又往往还有其他不同的含义，需要从数以万计的经济文献中进行甄别与筛选，并且把各种资料进行互证。加之乌尔第三王朝的赋税体系尚未创建，零散的赋税种类之间存在着何种关系，也是我们需要重点考证的方面。研究乌尔第三王朝赋税制度需要花费很大精力去搜集、整理材料，直接材料的缺乏增加了本研究的难度。

赋税制度随着早期文明国家的诞生，经历一个曲折复杂的过程，即由简单的、原始的直接税制演变为间接税制，再进一步发展为发达的直接税制。税制的发展要受到社会经济条件的制约，在早期社会，由于社会生产力水平比较低，自给自足的自然经济占主导地位。在这种以土地为中心的农业经济中，国家财政收入的主要部分，只能来自按土地面积征收的土地税和按人口征收的人头税以及灶税、窗户税等，这些赋税是早期的、原始的直接税。马克思说："直接税，作为一种最简单的征税形式，同时也是一种最原始最古老的形式，是以土地私有制为基础的那个社会制度的时代产物。"③ 长期以来，学界对早期文明和国家形态的研究重点在于政治和文化领域，而对早期国家的经济状况的认识一直比较模糊，这就严重制约了我们对构建早期文明国家形态的深入了解。由于基本上缺乏直接的证据材料，导致乌尔第三王朝赋税制度研究的基础更为薄弱，这大大增加了本研究的难度。

乌尔第三王朝的赋税制度研究属于专业性很强的亚述学范畴，不仅需要基本的楔形文字（主要是苏美尔语楔形文字）知识功底以及古代两河流域历史和考古的基础知识，还需要在释读楔形文字泥板过程中，对所涉及的一些晦涩难懂的苏美尔语和阿卡德语术语的词源进行严谨的推敲和判断，准确地把握相关术语的内涵与外延，这需要研究者具有丰富的亚述学专业知识。此外，乌尔第三王朝赋税制度属于经济学领域的问题，研究者

---

① 王三义：《古罗马"赋税名目"考略》，《史学月刊》2002年第6期；王三义：《罗马税制的积弊与戴克里先税制改革》，《世界历史》2007年第1期；徐国栋：《罗马人的税赋——从起源到戴克里先登基》，《现代法学》2010年第5期。

② 顾銮斋：《赋税制度与欧洲政治制度的演进》，《史学理论研究》2014年第2期；熊芳芳：《从"领地国家"到"税收国家"：中世纪晚期法国君主征税权的确立》，《世界历史》2015年第4期。

③ 《马克思恩格斯全集》第8卷，人民出版社1961年版，第543页。

需要把握和评断古代的税、贡、礼、供、费等术语之间的界限，以及深入考究它们与今天税收概念之间的关系。综合运用历史学、考古学、经济学、亚述学等多学科知识也增加了本研究的难点。

五 基本思路

乌尔第三王朝的赋税制度与乌尔国家的政治、经济和社会生活等方面密切相关，所以要研究赋税制度，我们首先要对乌尔第三王朝的具体情况有一个总体上的了解和认识。因此，本书专门用一章来宏观介绍乌尔第三王朝的概况，作为探讨各项赋税制度的历史背景。乌尔第三王朝的历史虽然只有短短百余年时间，但是却留下了数以十万计的楔形文字泥板文献资料，成为我们还原这段历史的最直接证据，也是研究其赋税制度的第一手资料来源。本书注重实证研究，坚持论从史出，在分析前人关于古代两河流域赋税制度研究成果的基础上，通过梳理乌尔第三王朝的核心行省税、外围行省税、附属国税、王室税、神庙税，研究税制改革与乌尔第三王朝国家治理之间的关系，从赋税制度对乌尔第三王朝政治和经济等诸方面的作用来认识乌尔第三王朝的兴衰演进，进而总结早期文明国家的历史发展规律。

第一章介绍乌尔第三王朝的概况。首先介绍乌尔第三王朝的地理概况，包括地理条件与位置、自然环境特征以及行政区划，接着介绍乌尔第三王朝的历史概况，分析乌尔第三王朝由建立到扩张、由盛而衰的历史发展过程，进而分析乌尔第三王朝的灭亡原因。最后，介绍乌尔第三王朝的各种文本文献，包括经济管理文献、王室铭文、书信、信使外交文献、文学文献、法律文献等，分析普兹瑞什达干、温马、吉尔苏、尼普尔、乌尔、伊利萨格里格的经济管理文献特征及其对研究乌尔第三王朝赋税制度的重要性。

第二章探讨核心行省的 bala 税。首先介绍了乌尔第三王朝行省制度的发展演变和组织结构等基本情况，具体介绍核心行省（核心区）的构成以及每个行省的具体情况。然后，重点分析核心行省的 bala 税，包括其术语和词源含义、赋税形式、赋税来源（纳税人）、赋税运送、赋税目的地（收税人）及其用途、税率、税务官员等基本情况。最后具体探讨温马行省和拉伽什—吉尔苏行省的 bala 税具体情况。

第三章分析外围行省的 gun$_2$ ma-da 税。概述乌尔第三王朝的外围行省（或称外围区、军事缓冲区）概况及组成，乌尔中央对外围行省的管理和控制以及外围区对乌尔第三王朝的意义和作用等基本情况。介绍了 gun$_2$ ma-da 税的赋税形式、赋税来源（纳税人）、赋税运送、赋税目的地（收税人）及其用途、税率、税务官员等内容。

第四章研究附属国的 gun$_2$ 税。通过区分 gun$_2$ 税和 gun$_2$ ma-da 税的术语含义，介绍了 gun$_2$ 税的赋税形式、赋税来源（纳税人）、赋税运送、赋税目的地（收税人）及其用途、税率、税务官员等内容。

第五章研究王室 maš$_2$-da-ri-a 税。首先考证 maš$_2$-da-ri-a 术语的词源及使用范畴，接着介绍 maš$_2$-da-ri-a 税的征收方式、课税形式、赋税用途等基本情况，进而分析 maš$_2$-da-ri-a 税同乌尔王室之间的关系。

第六章讨论神庙 zag-u 税。首先介绍乌尔第三王朝的神庙体系以及发展演变，分析神庙经济和神庙势力在古代两河流域历史上的地位和作用，然后分析什一税的起源与发展演变、征收的物品、征收的渠道和方式、征收什一税的目的等内容。

第七章探讨赋税制度与乌尔第三王朝国家治理之间的密切关系，通过舒尔吉、阿马尔辛和舒辛三位国王统治时期进行的税制措施，分析乌尔第三王朝政治、经济与文明的发展与兴衰。

在结论部分，我们归纳和总结了乌尔第三王朝赋税制度的特点和历史意义，以及赋税制度与乌尔第三王朝的政治、经济与文化发展之间的关系。

第一章　乌尔第三王朝概况

乌尔第三王朝（公元前2112—前2004年）是古代两河流域文明历史发展过程中的一个短暂的却又重要的王朝，上承苏美尔城邦时期和阿卡德王国，下启古巴比伦王国，是两河流域苏美尔人所建立的一个中央集权制国家，又称新苏美尔帝国（Neo-Sumerian Empire）或者复兴的苏美尔（Sumerian Renaissance）。[①] 据《苏美尔王表》记载，[②] 这是乌尔城（今伊拉克穆凯吉尔遗址）第三次作为王朝的首都，所以被称为乌尔第三王朝。苏美尔人、阿卡德人和阿摩利人是乌尔第三王朝的主要民族成分，苏美尔语是主要的用语，不过阿卡德语在王朝的北部地区也得到了普遍使用。由于首都乌尔是月神南那（阿卡德语称为辛）的主要祭祀地，所以月神在乌尔第三王朝占据十分重要的地位。

第一节　地理概况

古代两河流域，又称美索不达米亚（Mesopotamia），这个词源于古希腊语，意为"河流之间的土地"。古代两河流域人们对这个地区并没有一个统一的名称，而是以他们所居住的城市名或者王国名来命名。例如，苏美尔人称"苏美尔（地区）"为 ki-en-gi，称"阿卡德（地区）"为 ki-uri，此外表示"地区"的苏美尔术语 kalam 也特指苏美尔地区。

从今天的世界版图来看，古代两河流域的大部分地区位于今天伊拉克

[①] A. Becker, "Neusumerische Renaissance? Wissenschaftliche Untersuchungen zur Philologie und Archäologie", *Baghdader Mitteilungen*, Vol. 16 (1985), pp. 229–316.

[②] T. Jacobsen, *The Sumerian King List*, Assyriological Studies 11, Chicago: University of Chicago Press, 1939；[美] 雅各布森编：《苏美尔王表》，郑殿华译，生活·读书·新知三联书店1989年版。其中乌尔第一王朝和乌尔第二王朝处于早王朝时期，属于苏美尔城邦。

境内，少部分位于今天的叙利亚东部、土耳其南部和伊朗西南部地区。这里的"两河"指幼发拉底河（Euphrates，全长约2600千米）和底格里斯河（Tigris，全长约1850千米），其名称也是源于古希腊语，它们的苏美尔语名称分别是buranun和idigna。① 这两条河流均发源于土耳其境内亚美尼亚高原，向东南流向波斯湾。西边的幼发拉底河流经土耳其、叙利亚和伊拉克境内，东边的底格里斯河流经土耳其和伊拉克境内，这两条大河分别有若干支流，形成了一个庞大的河流网，被称为新月形地带，其中幼发拉底河的支流自北向南主要是巴里赫河和喀布尔河，底格里斯河的支流自北向南主要是大扎布河、小扎布河和迪亚拉河。今天我们知道，这两条大河在今伊拉克南部巴士拉附近汇合成为一条河——沙特—阿尔阿拉伯河，然后才注入波斯湾，可是在古代，这两条大河是分别流向波斯湾的。在乌尔第三王朝时期，波斯湾的海岸线要比今天向内缩进240多千米，结果是今天版图上处于内陆的乌尔和埃利都两城在古代其实都是沿海城市。譬如，文献中就有乌尔港口停泊船只的记载。②

在地理区划上，两河流域以今伊拉克首都巴格达为界，以北称为亚述（Assyria），以南称为巴比伦尼亚（Babylonia），其中巴比伦尼亚又以尼普尔（今伊拉克的努法尔）为界，以南称为苏美尔（Sumer），以北称为阿卡德（Akkad）（见图1-1）。③

乌尔第三王朝大致处于两河流域南部地区，也即苏美尔—阿卡德地区：东抵伊朗高原的西部及扎格罗斯山脉，西达幼发拉底河中游，北临底格里斯河上游的亚述地区，南至波斯湾沿岸。

两河流域南部是平坦的冲积平原，平缓的河水携带大量泥沙沉淀，抬升河床，河水漫过河堤甚至改变河道。由于两河流域南部的气候干燥而炎热，大多数地区年降雨量在250毫米以下，土壤干而坚硬，在每年的4—6月间，安纳托利亚以及库尔德斯坦的高山积雪融化后，两河开始泛滥，这里的农业依赖两河的河水进行人工灌溉，发展灌溉农业。如果像希罗多德所说的"埃及是尼罗河的赠礼"的话，那么美索不达米亚就是底格里斯河

---

① 在《圣经》中，源自希伯来语，底格里斯河被称为Hiddekel，幼发拉底河被称为Prat。

② J. J. van Dijk, "Une insurrection générale au pays de Larša avant l'avènement de Nūradad", Journal of Cuneiform Studies, Vol. 19 (1965), pp. 21–22.

③ 刘文鹏主编：《古代西亚北非文明》，中国社会科学出版社1999年版，第203—204页。

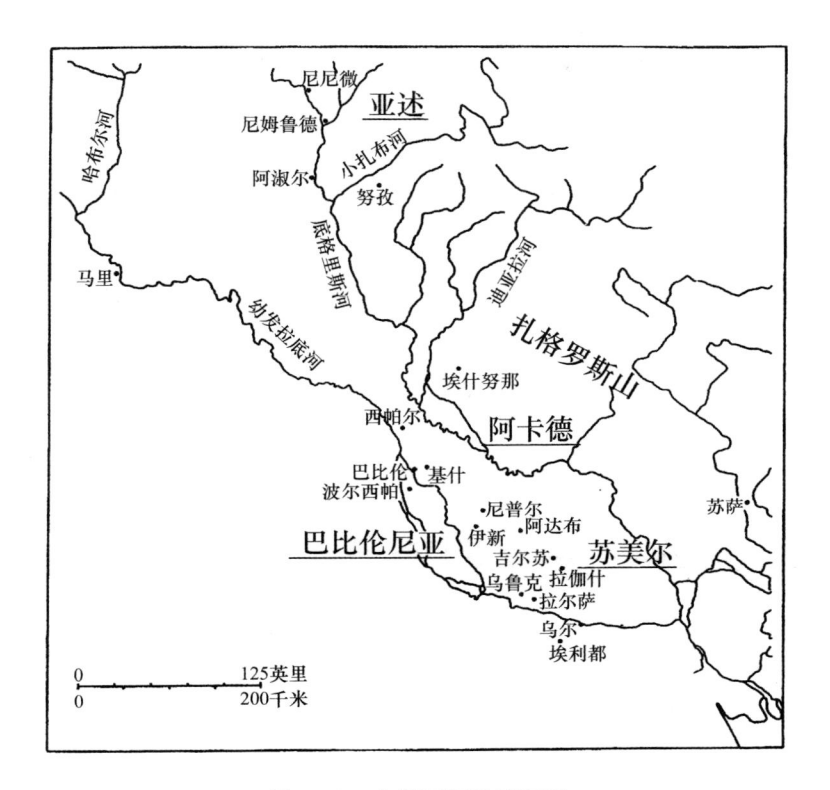

图 1-1 古代两河流域版图

资料来源：引自 M. T. Roth, *Law Collections from Mesopotamia and Asia Minor*, Atlanta: Scholars Press, 1997, p. xi。

和幼发拉底河的赠礼。① 两河流域南部的主要自然资源是水源和肥沃的土地，这里孕育世界上最早的农业，主要的农产品有大麦、小麦、芝麻、蔬菜和椰枣，② 牲畜主要有牛、绵羊和山羊。③ 古代两河流域人们利用冲积平

---

① S. Bertman, *Handbook to Life in Ancient Mesopotamia*, New York: Facts On File, 2003, p. 4.
② 关于乌尔第三王朝的农业和食物，参见 K. Maekawa, "Agricultural Production in Ancient Sumer", *Zinbun*, Vol. 13 (1974), pp. 1-60; H. Brunke, *Essen in Sumer: Metrologie, Herstellung und Terminologie nach Zeugnis der Ur III-zeitlichen Wirtschaftsurkunden*, München: Herbert Utz Verlag, 2011; H. Brunke, "On the Role of Fruit and Vegetables as Food in the Ur III Period", in L. Milano (ed.), *Paleonutrition and Food Practices in the Ancient Near East towards a Multidisciplinary Approach*, History of the Ancient Near East, Monographs 14, Padova: S. A. R. G. O. N. Editrice e Libreria, 2014, pp. 339-352.
③ 关于乌尔第三王朝的牲畜，参见 M. Stepien, *Animal Husbandry in the Ancient Near East*, Bethesda: CDL Press, 1996.

原区的黏土制作成泥板,用河边生长的芦苇制成笔,在泥板上"压"出形同"楔子"的文字——楔形文字。① 河流和沼泽提供了芦苇和渔业资源,② 芦苇被用来编席、篮和箱,以及造船和建房。与今天中东盛产石油类似的是,古代两河流域人们已经学会了利用沥青,他们在幼发拉底河的希特(Hit)地区开采沥青,将其涂在船身上防漏,涂在墙壁和屋顶上防水,以及用来黏合泥砖等。③ 不过,两河流域南部缺乏石料、大型木材、金属和矿产资源,而这些资源基本都是靠从两河流域附近地区进口,这也催生了最早的跨区域贸易。④ 大致上,普通木材来自扎格罗斯山脉和麦鲁哈(西南亚印度河流域或东非埃塞俄比亚),⑤ 建筑庙宇和宫殿的高大杉木、柏木和雪松来自地中海沿岸的黎巴嫩山脉和阿玛努斯山,硬石料(如闪长岩)来自伊朗和马干(阿曼),铜来自安纳托利亚、高加索、阿曼、塞浦路斯和伊朗,锡来自伊朗、高加索和阿富汗,白银来自陶鲁斯山脉,黄金来自埃及和印度,青金石来自阿富汗。

乌尔第三王朝的行政区分为中央行政区和地方行政区。中央行政区上至国王,下至各级官吏,有着严格的等级划分和职业分工。地方行政区采取三分法的划分,分为核心区、外围区和附属国三种类型(见图1-2)。

第二节 历史概况

大约公元前2154年,库提人灭亡了阿卡德王国。库提人对两河流域的统治主要维持在两河流域北部地区,⑥ 而南部地区的许多苏美尔城邦趁

---

① C. B. F. Walker, *Reading the Past*: *Cuneiform*, Berkeley and Los Angeles: University of California Press, 1987; I. Finkel, J. Taylor, *Cuneiform*, London: British Museum, 2015.

② 关于乌尔第三王朝的渔业资源,参见 R. K. Englund, *Organisation und Verwaltung der Ur III-Fischerei*, Berliner Beiträge zum Vorderen Orient 10, Berlin: Dietrich Reimer Verlag, 1990.

③ R. Moorey, *Ancient Mesopotamian Materials and Industries*: *The Archaeological Evidence*, Winona Lake: Eisenbrauns, 1999, pp. 332 - 334.

④ 参见刘昌玉《从"上海"到下海:早期两河流域商路初探》,中国社会科学出版社2019年版。

⑤ 国洪更、吴宇虹:《古代两河流域和巴林的海上国际贸易——楔形文字文献和考古发现中的狄勒蒙》,《东北师大学报》2004年第5期;刘昌玉:《麦鲁哈与上古印度洋——波斯湾海上贸易》,《浙江师范大学学报》(社会科学版)2016年第5期。

⑥ D. Frayne, *Sargonic and Gutian Periods (2334 - 2113 BC)*, The Royal Inscriptions of Mesopotamia Eary Periods, Volume 2, Toronto-Buffalo-London: University of Toronto Press, 1993.

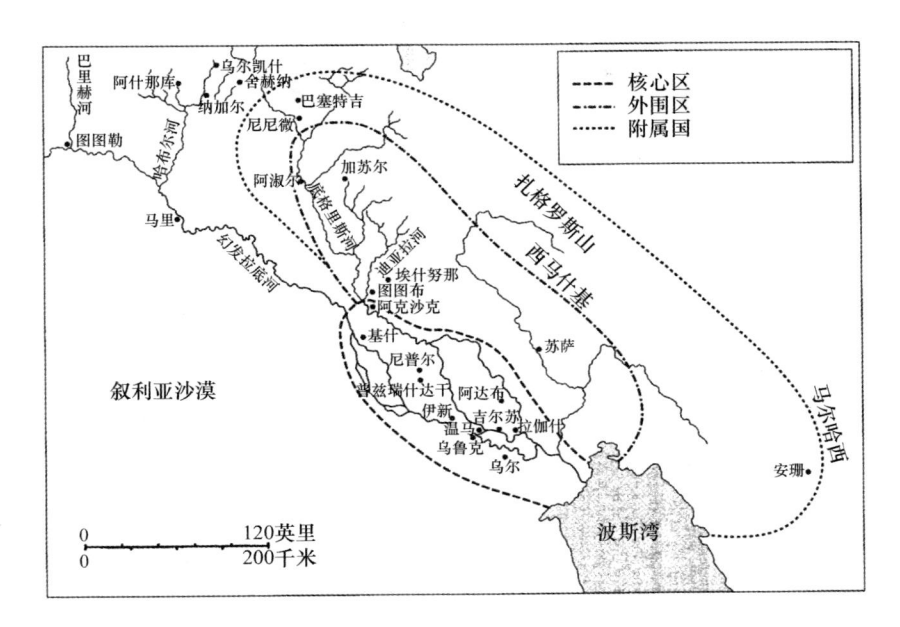

图1-2 乌尔第三王朝版图

资料来源：引自 M. Van de Mieroop, *A History of the Ancient Near East (ca. 3000–323 BC)*, Second Edition, Oxford: Blackwell Publishing, 2007, p.75.

机独立，恢复了早王朝时期的城邦分立状态，以拉伽什城邦作为代表。其中最著名统治者叫古地亚，他发展国内经济，为自己建造了大量的雕像，留下了丰富的修建神庙的记录。这一时期苏美尔文化的复苏为接下来的乌尔第三王朝的繁荣奠定了文化基础。① 与此同时，在政治上，库提人对两河流域的统治也激起了两河流域人们的激烈反抗，乌鲁克的乌图赫伽尔（Utu-hegal）打败库提末王提里干（Tirigan），把库提人赶出了两河流域。乌图赫伽尔以乌鲁克为都，建立了乌鲁克第五王朝（因乌鲁克城第五次作为王朝首都，故名）。他任命乌尔纳姆（可能是乌图赫伽尔的兄弟）为乌尔城的总督。但是乌图赫伽尔的统治只有短短7年，王位就被乌尔纳姆取得。② 乌尔纳姆将首都从乌鲁克迁到乌尔，

---

① D. O. Edzard, *Gudea and His Dynasty*, The Royal Inscriptions of Mesopotamia Eary Periods Volume 3/1, Toronto-Buffalo-London: University of Toronto Press, 1997; W. H. Ph. Römer, *Die Zylinderinschriften von Gudea*, Alter Orient und Altes Testament 376, Münster: Ugarit-Verlag, 2010.

② N. De Zorzi, "The Death of Utu-hegal and Other Historical Omens", *Journal of Cuneiform Studies*, Vol. 68 (2016), pp. 129–151.

建立了乌尔第三王朝。

乌尔第三王朝历时108年（公元前2112—前2004年），共有五位国王（lugal）组成，他们分别是（见表1-1）：

表1-1　　　　　　　　乌尔第三王朝统治者

国王	统治时间	在位时长
乌尔纳姆（Ur-Nammu）	公元前2112—前2095年	共18年
舒尔吉（Shulgi）	公元前2094—前2047年	共48年
阿马尔辛（Amar-Suen）	公元前2046—前2038年	共9年
舒辛（Shu-Suen）	公元前2037—前2029年	共9年
伊比辛（Ibbi-Suen）	公元前2028—前2004年	共24年

根据《苏美尔王表》的记载，五位国王父子相继。《苏美尔王表》记录如下：[①]

Unug$^{ki\,giš}$tukul ba-an-sag$_3$	乌鲁克被武力打败，
nam-lugal-bi uri$_2$^{ki}-še$_3$ ba-DU	其王权被带到乌尔。
Uri$_2$^{ki}-ma Ur-^{d}Nammu lugal	（在）乌尔，乌尔纳姆为王，
mu 18 i$_3$-ak	（他）统治了18年。
^{d}Šul-gi dumu^{d}Ur-Nammu-ke$_4$	乌尔纳姆之子舒尔吉（继任为王），
mu 48 i$_3$-ak	（他）统治了48年。
^{d}Amar-^{d}EN.ZU dumu^{d}Šul-gi-ke$_4$	舒尔吉之子阿马尔辛（继任为王），
mu 9 i$_3$-ak	（他）统治了9年。
Šu-^{d}EN.ZU dumu^{d}Amar-^{d}EN.ZU	阿马尔辛之子舒辛（继任为王），
mu 9 i$_3$-ak	（他）统治了9年。
I-bi$_2$-^{d}EN.ZU dumu Šu-^{d}EN.ZU-ke$_4$	舒辛之子伊比辛（继任为王），
mu 24 i$_3$-ak	（他）统治了24年。
5 lugal	五位国王

[①] T. Jacobsen, *The Sumerian King List*, Assyriological Studies 11, Chicago: University of Chicago Press, 1939, pp. 123-125；[美]雅各布森编：《苏美尔王表》，郑殿华译，生活·读书·新知三联书店1989年版，第39—42页。

第一章 乌尔第三王朝概况

mu-bi 108 ib$_2$-ak	共统治了 108 年。
Uri$_2^{ki}$-ma ^{giš}tukul ba-an-sag$_3$	乌尔被武力打败，
nam-lugal-bi I$_3$-si-in^{ki}-še$_3$ ba-DU	其王权被带到伊新，
I$_3$-si-in^{ki}-na Iš-bi-Er$_3$-ra lugal	（在）伊新，伊什比埃拉为王。

关于乌尔第三王朝的五位国王之间的谱系关系，一直以来是学术界争议比较大的问题。显然，从诸多文献证据中，学者们否认了《苏美尔王表》有关乌尔国王们之间"父子相继"的论述。从文献的蛛丝马迹证据，我们大致可以推断，舒尔吉是乌尔纳姆之子，而王朝最后三位国王阿马尔辛、舒辛和伊比辛很可能都是舒尔吉的儿子，即三人之间是兄弟关系。[①]但是有学者认为，乌尔纳姆是舒尔吉的亲生父亲，舒辛和伊比辛是舒尔吉的亲生儿子，而阿马尔辛则是舒尔吉的侄子。具体来言，乌尔纳姆与瓦塔尔图姆生了舒尔吉，舒尔吉与舒尔吉西姆提生了舒辛，舒尔吉与阿比西姆提生了伊比辛，而乌尔第三王朝第三位国王阿马尔辛则是乌尔纳姆与瓦塔尔图姆所生的另一个儿子（名字不详）与塔兰乌兰（Taram-Uram，她是阿皮尔金与一不知名女子所生）所生。[②] 这一结论虽然看似新颖，但是并没有得到学术界太多关注和认同，笔者对此持保留意见。

乌尔第三王朝的历史经历了四个阶段：统一、扩张、巩固和衰亡。在统一阶段，即乌尔纳姆统治时期以及舒尔吉统治前半期，乌尔第三王朝的统治者致力于统一苏美尔地区的城邦以及征服阿卡德地区。在扩张阶段，即舒尔吉统治后半期，乌尔统治者通过政治结盟与军事相结合的方式，来征服东部和东北部的邻近地区。在阿马尔辛统治时期，乌尔第三王朝国力强盛，大量的国家管理信息被记录，国家达到鼎盛时期。在衰亡阶段，即舒辛和伊比辛统治时期，王朝在达到极盛之后不久，就迅速地衰落瓦解，由于王朝统治下的行省陆续脱离中央而独立，王朝面临严重的经济危机，随着外来势力的入侵等原因，乌尔第三王朝最终于公元前 2004 年被其之

[①] J. L. Dahl, *The Ruling Family of Ur III Umma*: *A Prosopographical Analysis of an Elite Family in Southern Iraq 4000 Years Ago*, Publications de l'Institut historique-archéologique néerlandais de Stamboul 108, Leiden: Nederlands Instituut voor het Nabije Oosten, 2007, p. 2.

[②] P. Michalowski, "Of Bears and Men: Thoughts on the End of Šulgi's Reign and on the Ensuing Succession", in D. S. Vanderhooft and A. Winitzer (eds.), *Literature as Politics, Politics as Literature*: *Essays on the Ancient Near East in Honor of Peter Machinist*, Winona Lake: Eisenbrauns, 2013, pp. 285–320.

前的附属国埃兰所灭亡。①

第三节　文献概况

　　乌尔第三王朝虽然只有短短的百余年时间,但是留下了数以十万计的文献资料,是公认的世界古代史上留传文献资料最丰富的一个时期。② 乌尔第三王朝的文献种类繁多,包括苏美尔王表、③ 王室铭文、④ 文学作品、⑤ 书信、⑥ 法

---

① J. L. Dahl, *The Ruling Family of Ur III Umma*: *A Prosopographical Analysis of an Elite Family in Southern Iraq 4000 Years Ago*, Publications de l'Institut historique-archéologique néerlandais de Stamboul 108, Leiden: Nederlands Instituut voor het Nabije Oosten, 2007, p. 1.

② M. Molina, "The corpus of Neo-Sumerian tablets: an overview", in S. J. Garfinkle and J. C. Johnson (eds.), *The Growth of an Early State in Mesopotamia*: *Studies in Ur III Administration. Proceedings of the First and Second Ur III Workshops at the 49th and 51st Rencontre Assyriologique Internationale*, London July 10, 2003 and Chicago July 19, 2005, Biblioteca del Proximo Oriente Antiguo 5, Madrid: Consejo Superior de Investigaciones Científicas, 2008, pp. 19 – 53; C. Liu, *Organization, Administrative Practices and Written Documentation in Mesopotamia during the Ur III Period (c. 2112 – 2004 BC)*: *A Case Study of Puzriš-Dagan in the Reign of Amar-Suen*, Kārum-Emporion-Forum: Beiträge zur Wirtschafts-, Rechts-, und Sozialgeschichte des östlihen Mettelmeerraums und Altvorderasiens 3, Münster: Ugarit-Verlag, 2017, p. 3.

③ T. Jacobsen, *The Sumerian King List*, Assyriological Studies 11, Chicago: University of Chicago Press, 1939;［美］雅各布森编:《苏美尔王表》,郑殿华译,生活·读书·新知三联书店1989年版,第39—42页。

④ D. Frayne, *Ur III Period (2112 – 2004 BC)*, The Royal Inscriptions of Mesopotamia Early Periods Volume 3/2 (RIME 3/2), Toronto: University of Toronto Press, 1997.

⑤ S. N. Kramer, *Sumerian Mythology*: *A Study of Spiritual and Literary Achievement in the Third Millennium B. C.*, Philadelphia: University of Pennsylvania Press, 1972; T. Jacobsen, *The Harps That Once …*: *Sumerian Poetry in Translation*, New Haven and London: Yale University Press, 1987; B. R. Foster, *From Distant Days*: *Myths, Tales, and Poetry of Ancient Mesopotamia*, Bethesda: CDL Press, 1995; B. Alster, *Proverbs of Ancient Sumer*: *The World's Earliest Proverb Collections*, Volume I-II, Bethesda: CDL Press, 1997; B. Alster, *Wisdom of Ancient Sumer*, Bethesda: CDL Press, 2005; J. Black, et al., *The Literature of Ancient Sumer*, Oxford: Oxford University Press, 2004; G. Rubio, "Sumerian Literature", in C. S. Ehrlich (ed.), *From an Antique Land*: *An Introduction To Ancient Near Eastern Literature*, Lanham: Rowman & Littlefield Publishers, 2009, pp. 11 – 75; N. Samet, *The Lamentation over the Destruction of Ur*, Mesopotamian Civilizations 18, Winona Lake: Eisenbrauns, 2014.

⑥ P. Michalowski, *The Royal Correspondence of Ur*, PhD dissertation, Yale University, 1976; P. Michalowski, *Letters from Early Mesopotamia*, Atlanta: Scholars Press, 1993; P. Michalowski, *The Correspondence of the Kings of Ur*: *An Epistolary History of an Ancient Mesopotamian Kingdom*, Mesopotamian Civilizations 15, Winona Lake: Eisenbrauns, 2011.

第一章 乌尔第三王朝概况

律文献①以及经济管理文献,其中以经济管理文献的数量最为丰富,截至目前已有大约十余万计的经济管理文献被发表,这些文献大约被世界上 40 个国家的至少 758 个博物馆、图书馆和私人所收藏,② 另外还有数量不确定的文献在世界各地的拍卖机构进行交易,甚至依然被埋藏于伊拉克的土堆之下,尚未被发掘出土,或者已经出土尚未被发表面世,不为学者们所知。乌尔第三王朝的楔形文字文献,除了王室铭文是刻写在砖块上,其他绝大多数文献的书写材料都是泥板(clay tablet)。③ 由于这些泥板文献分布极为分散,给学者们系统研究乌尔第三王朝的社会经济史造成了不小的困难,学者们通过不懈努力,搜集、整理已经发表的文献信息,④ 并且统一汇编入数据库中保存,为乌尔第三王朝的研究提供了方便。目前,有两个关于乌尔第三王朝经济泥板文献最重要的网上在线数据库,一个是西班牙马德里高等科学研究院资助的"新苏美尔语文献数据库"(Database of Neo-Sumerian Texts,简称 BDTNS),⑤ 包含乌尔第三王朝经济文献共计 101944 件(截至 2021 年 1 月 1 日);另一个是美国加利福尼亚大学洛杉矶分校、英国牛津大学和德国马克斯·普朗克历史科学研究所共同资助的"楔形文字数字图书馆计划"(Cuneiform Digital Library Initiative,简称 CDLI),⑥ 该数据库包含目前世界上最齐全的楔形文字文献资料,乌尔第三王朝文献是其中十分重要的组成部分,共有文献 104419 件(截至 2021 年 1 月 1 日)。以后者的数据为例,

---

① A. Falkenstein, *Die neusumerischen Gerichtsurkunden*, Munich: Verlag der Bayerischen Akademie der Wissenschaften, 1956 – 1957; P. Steinkeller, J. N. Postgate, *Third-Millennium Legal and Administrative Texts in the Iraq Museum, Baghdad*, Mesopotamian Civilizations 4, Winona Lake: Eisenbrauns, 1992; M. Molina, "New Ur III Court Records Concerning Slavery", in P. Michalowski (ed.), *On the Third Dynasty of Ur: Studies in Honor of Marcel Sigrist*, Boston: American Schools of Oriental Research, 2008, pp. 125 – 143. 亦可参见刘昌玉、吴宇虹《乌尔第三王朝温马地区法庭判案文件译注与简析》,《古代文明》2011 年第 2 期。

② M. Molina, "Archives and Bookkeeping in Southern Mesopotamia during the Ur III period", *Comptabilités*, Vol. 8 (2016), p. 2.

③ 泥板也是古代两河流域楔形文字的主要书写材料,它是就地取材,利用两河流域南部的黏土,其粘性十分强,黏土加水后制成泥板,写上文字后自然晒干,十分坚硬,或者经火烧制成为更硬的砖。参见 M. P. Streck, "Tafel (tablet)", *Reallexikon der Assyriologie und Vorderasiatischen Archäologie*, Vol. 13 (2011 – 2013), pp. 400 – 401.

④ 参见 M. Sigrist, T. Gomi, *The Comprehensive Catalogue of Published Ur III Tablets*, Bethesda: CDL Press, 1991, 该书搜集整理了 1991 年以前已经发表的乌尔第三王朝经济文献情况。

⑤ http://bdtns.filol.csic.es/.

⑥ https://cdli.ucla.edu/.

乌尔第三王朝的经济文献主要来自以下七个遗址：温马、吉尔苏、普兹瑞什达干、尼普尔、乌尔、伽尔沙纳①和伊利萨格里格②，其中又以前三个遗址（温马、吉尔苏、普兹瑞什达干）的文献数量为最多，具体的统计数字如表1-2（截至2021年1月1日）：③

表1-2　　　　乌尔第三王朝主要遗址出土文献数量统计

遗址名称	文献数量	所占比例
温马	32176	31.56%
吉尔苏	27892	27.36%
普兹瑞什达干	16137	15.83%
乌尔	4491	4.41%
尼普尔	3531	3.46%
伊利萨格里格	2665	2.61%
伽尔沙纳	1648	1.62%
其他	13404*	13.15%
共计	101944	100%

数据来源：BDTNS。

*包括不清楚来源地的文献和其他来源地的文献。其他来源地文献包括西阿雅档案（SI.A-a）、图兰伊里档案（Turam-ili）和乌尔努斯卡档案（Ur-Nuska），参见 S. Garfinkle, *Entrepreneurs and Enterprise in Early Mesopotamia: A Study of three Archives from the Third Dynasty of Ur*, Cornell University Studies in Assyriology and Sumerology 22, Bethesda: CDL Press, 2012.

乌尔第三王朝的经济文献按照档案性质，可以分为私人档案（尼普尔私人档案、图兰伊里档案、西阿雅档案），乡村不动产档案（阿拉德姆档案、舒埃什塔尔档案、伽尔沙纳档案），神庙档案（尼普尔），行省

---

① 主要参见 D. I. Owen, R. Mayr, *The Garšana Archives*, Cornell University Studies in Assyriology and Sumerology 3, Bethesda: CDL Press, 2007; A. Kleinerman, D. I. Owen, *Analytical Concordance to the Garšana Archives*, Cornell University Studies in Assyriology and Sumerology 4, Bethesda: CDL Press, 2009; D. I. Owen, *Garšana Studies*, Cornell University Studies in Assyriology and Sumerology 6, Bethesda: CDL Press, 2011.

② 主要参见 D. I. Owen, *Cuneiform Texts Primarily from Iri-Saĝrig/Āl-Šarrākī and the History of the Ur III Period*, Nisaba 15/1-2, Bethesda: CDL Press, 2013.

③ 注意：这里统计的文献包括已经出版的文献和未出版的文献，对于文献的来源地存在一些争议和错误之处。

档案（温马、吉尔苏、伊利萨格里格），以及王家机构档案（乌尔、普兹瑞什达干）。

乌尔第三王朝历时 108 年，其文献的时间分布是不均匀的，首王乌尔纳姆时期和末王伊比辛中后期的文献数量极少，绝大多数文献主要集中于舒尔吉后半期、阿马尔辛时期和舒辛时期，以及伊比辛统治初期。根据 BDTNS 数据库的统计，其具体文献数量分布如下（截至 2021 年 1 月 1 日）：①

表 1-3　　　　　　乌尔第三王朝各位统治者时期文献数量统计

时期	文献数量	所占比例
乌尔纳姆	23	0.02%
舒尔吉	17975	17.63%
阿马尔辛	22929	22.49%
舒辛	20390	20.00%
伊比辛	7516	7.38%
不清楚	33111	32.48%
共计	101944	100%

数据来源：BDTNS。

本书所论及的乌尔第三王朝赋税制度研究，主要的文献资料来源是普兹瑞什达干文献（或称德莱海姆文献）、温马文献和吉尔苏文献，其中尤以普兹瑞什达干文献为最重要。这些档案文献有其不同的记录特征、记录内容和记录格式，由于这些文献大都没有经过系统的考古发掘，而是由非法盗挖经文物市场获得，所以需要对其来源地进行重新认定。我们判定一件乌尔第三王朝经济文献一般依据其记录内容、记录格式、文献中所含月名格式、专有名词（人名、地名等）等信息来认定。② 这些泥板文献的大

---

① 亦可参见 M. Molina, "The Corpus of Neo-Sumerian Tablets: An Overview", in S. J. Garfinkle and J. C. Johnson (eds.), *The Growth of an Early State in Mesopotamia: Studies in Ur III Administration*, Biblioteca del Proximo Oriente Antiguo 5, Madrid: Consejo Superior de Investigaciones Científicas, 2008, pp. 19-53; M. Molina, "Archives and Bookkeeping in Southern Mesopotamia during the Ur III period", *Comptabilités*, Vol. 8 (2016), pp. 1-19.

② W. Sallaberger, "Ur III-Zeit", in W. Sallaberger and A. Westenholz (eds.), *Mesopotamien: Akkade-Zeit und Ur III-Zeit*, Orbis Biblicus et Orientalis 160/3, Freiburg: Universitätsverlag, 1999, pp. 207-210.

小规格不一，目前已知的最大的一块泥板文献达 1663 行，① 而大部分泥板文献的长度在 5—15 行之间，长、宽尺寸大约 4—5 厘米。大约有 1/3 的泥板文献加盖印章，使用滚筒印章在泥板上滚压印纹，印纹有图有文，印文内容大都是印章持有者的信息。②

在内容上，乌尔第三王朝经济文献记录的是资本（如劳动力、动物、物品、工时、商品等）的情况，记录的是资本从一个机构（地区）到另一个机构（地区）的进出情况，或者在一个机构内部的运转情况，或者在特殊地点和时间里的存在状况。③ 从记录内容和记录格式上划分，乌尔第三王朝的经济文献（又称为账目、档案）可以分为年账、月账和日账文献。年账一般都是总结性的账目，或者平衡账目（结算），包括数个年名，行文上包含十余行至数十行之多，有的还分为多栏。月账是一个月的账目统计情况，不一定逐日记录，从几天到 30 天不等，最后以月名结束。日账最为常见，出现的也最多，多简洁明了，大多由 5—8 行组成，往往包含详细的日期、月名和年名。

普兹瑞什达干、温马和吉尔苏三个遗址出土的乌尔第三王朝楔形文字经济文献是本书研究最重要的资料来源和依据，此外还有其他遗址文献（如尼普尔、乌尔、伽尔沙纳和伊利萨格里格等）中涉及赋税的内容（或含有赋税术语），因此如何从数量庞大的文献资料库中选取有用的资料，则成为本研究的前提和基础。通过创建数据库，选取、收集包含赋税术语和信息的有用文献资料，并且对其时间、地点、人物、格式等信息进行列表分类，成为本研究需要完成的又一项准备工作。从数据库资料所包含的诸多不同种类的赋税术语信息内容中，bala 这一赋税术语的信息最为丰富，也是我们最先要研究的一个税种。

---

① 文献 MVN 15390（S 37 iii – vii）.
② 刘昌玉：《乌尔第三王朝滚印研究》，《西泠艺丛》2016 年第 12 期。
③ P. Steinkeller, "Archival Practices at Babylonia in the Third Millennium", in M. Brosius (ed.), *Ancient Archives and Archival Traditions: Concepts of Record-Keeping in the Ancient World*, Oxford: Oxford University Press, 2003, pp. 37 – 58.

第二章 核心区 bala 税

乌尔第三王朝核心区（核心行省或内省）位于两河流域的南部地区，是乌尔第三王朝地方政府中最重要的一环，表示核心区"赋税"的术语为 bala（又可读作 bal），这是一个苏美尔语单词。bala 是一个多义词，有如下的含义：（1）"循环、翻转、交叉"，其对应的阿卡德语为 *nabalkutu*，（2）"倾倒、祭酒（仪式）"，其对应的阿卡德语为 *naqû* 或者 *tabāku*，（3）"统治时期、任职期、轮转、翻转"，其对应的阿卡德语为 *palû*，[①] 此外还有"反叛、升起、引水、转移、携带、煮沸、改变、违反、换算"[②]等诸多意思。在乌尔第三王朝的经济文献中，bala 这一术语指的是劳动者的服务期，即劳动者为行省各部门服劳役的时期。[③] 这个词并没有"赋税"的含义，它被认定为一种赋税也经历了学者们长时期的争论，最终才被绝大多数学者所认同。加芬克尔（Steven Garfinkle）认为，bala 是一种从乌尔第三王朝行省提取资源的系统，并且将资源指向乌尔，资源被运送到苏美尔世界的宗教中心——尼普尔，这是 bala 系统的基本组成部分之一。[④] 当 bala 这一术语指一种赋税时，它可以指行省向中央缴费的一种轮转（或循环）体系，即每个行省按照既定时间段依据固定的额度向中央缴纳实物

[①] J. -J. Glassner, "Les Temps de l'Histoire en Mésopotamie", in A. de Pury (ed.), *Israël Construit son Histoire*, Paris: Monde de la Bible, 1996, p. 171.

[②] S. Tinney (ed.), *Pennsylvania Sumerian Dictionary B*, Philadelphia: University Museum, 1984, pp. 64 – 75; J. A. Halloran (ed.), *Sumerian Lexicon: A Dictionary Guide to the Ancient Sumerian Language*, Los Angeles: Logogram Publishing, 2006, p. 28.

[③] T. Sharlach, *Provincial Taxation and the Ur III State*, Cuneiform Monographs 26, Leiden: Brill, 2004, p. 16.

[④] S. Garfinkle, "SI. A-a and His Family: the Archive of a 21st Century (BC) Entrepreneur", *Zeitschrift für Assyriologie und Vorderasiatische Archäologie*, Vol. 93, No. 2, 2003, pp. 180 – 181.

的一种赋税体系。

由于 bala（如图 2-1）这个苏美尔语单词具有多种含义，在乌尔第三王朝的经济文献中所记载的术语 bala 也自然有其不同的意思，所以在本书所依据和引用的文献资料中，我们需要谨慎辨析每处 bala 的具体指代意思，排除与赋税无关的含义，并且对其中有歧义的术语进行比较分析，以确定其真正的含义。bala 体系是连接乌尔第三王朝中央政府（王室家族）和地方政府（行省）之间最重要的经济桥梁，[①] 也是乌尔第三王朝中央政府对地方行省进行直接统治的体现，以及乌尔第三王朝加强中央集权统治的内在表现。

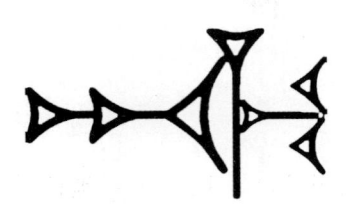

图 2-1　bala 税对应的楔形文字

第一节　核心区概况

乌尔第三王朝是中央集权的统一国家。在中央，国王是国家最高权力的代表，位于最高层；王室成员次之，位居第二层；丞相（sukkal-mah，又译"大维齐尔"或"苏卡尔马赫"）是主管行政事务的最高长官，他和主管宗教事务的最高长官大祭司（zabar-dab$_5$，"扎巴尔达卜"）一同位居第三层，直接听命于国王[②]。在地方，乌尔第三王朝依据"三重区域"政策进行管理，将地方区划为：核心区（core）、外围区（periphery）、附属国（vassal state）。其中，核心区和外围区一同构成了乌尔第三王朝的行省单位，分别称为内行省和外行省，即行省的"二元制"结构。

[①] 其他连接乌尔第三王朝中央与地方之间的赋税种类可能还要 mašdaria 税、恩利尔神庙的 nesag 税（"初熟的果子"仪式），以及 šu-gid$_2$ 税，参见 T. Sharlach, *Provincial Taxation and the Ur III State*, Cuneiform Monographs 26, Leiden: Brill, 2004, p. 17.

[②] W. Sallaberger, "Ur III-Zeit", in W. Sallaberger and A. Westenholz (eds.), *Mesopotamien: Akkade-Zeit und Ur III-Zeit*, Freiburg: Universitätsverlag, 1999, pp. 121 – 392; S. J. Garfinkle, "Was the Ur III State Bureaucratic? Patrimonialism and Bureaucracy in the Ur III Period", in S. J. Garfinkle and J. C. Johnson (eds.), *The Growth of an Early State in Mesopotamia: Studies in Ur III Administration. Proceedings of the First and Second Ur III Workshops at the 49th and 51st Rencontre Assyriologique Internationale*, London July 10, 2003 and Chicago July 19, 2005, BPOA 5, Madrid: Consejo Superior de Investigaciones Científicas, 2008, pp. 55 – 61.

第二章 核心区 bala 税

核心区的确定需要同时满足两个标准，一是行省的最高长官是恩西（ensi₂），二是行省必须向中央缴纳 bala 税。如果只满足一个条件，则不能称其为核心行省。① 根据文献中的证据，我们收集了以下可能满足这两个条件的地区，通过对其统计分析，以确定乌尔第三王朝的核心行省（内行省）数量（见表 2-1）。

表 2-1　　　　　　　乌尔第三王朝内行省统计表

地名	是否有恩西	是否缴纳 bala 税	出土文献数量②
阿达布	是	是	174
阿哈	是	是	—
阿皮亚克	是	是	—
巴比伦	是	是	—
达卜鲁姆	是	否	—
埃莱什	是	否	—
埃什努那	是	是（也缴纳 gun₂ ma-da 税）	155
吉尔塔卜	是	否	—
拉伽什—吉尔苏	是	是	27892
卡扎鲁	是	是	—
基什	是	是	6
库特哈	是	是	—
马腊德	是	是	—
尼普尔	是	否	3531
普什	是	是	—
西帕尔	是	是	3
苏萨	是	是（也缴纳 gun₂ ma-da 税）	76
舒鲁帕克	是	是	3
温马	是	是	32176

① 唯一的一个例外是尼普尔，它是乌尔第三王朝的宗教中心，虽然有恩西，但是不需履行 bala 税的义务，可以看作一个特殊的行省。
② 数据来源：BDTNS 数据库统计（截至 2021 年 1 月 1 日）。

续表

地名	是否有恩西	是否缴纳 bala 税	出土文献数量
乌尔	王室领地	是（由神庙主管负责）	4491
乌鲁克	王室领地	是（由神庙主管负责）	23
乌鲁姆	是	是	—
伊利萨格里格	是	是	2665
伊新	是	是	4
伊西姆舒尔吉	是	是（也缴纳 gun_2 ma-da 税）	—
伊舒	是	否	—

基于上述统计结果，我们得知，乌尔第三王朝共设立有 19 个核心区，由北到南排列分布如下（见图 2-2）：西帕尔、阿哈（提威）、乌鲁姆、普什、库特哈、巴比伦、基什、卡扎鲁、阿皮亚克、马腊德、尼普尔、伊利萨格里格、伊新、阿达布、舒鲁帕克、温马、拉伽什—吉尔苏、乌鲁克、乌尔。

在空间地理位置上，核心区北起西帕尔（今伊拉克的阿布哈巴赫，Abu Habbah），南至乌尔，东、西范围差不多是在底格里斯河和幼发拉底河之间的区域，大致位于今天伊拉克首都巴格达以南的区域。迪亚拉河流域的两个行省埃什努那和伊西姆舒尔吉，均位于今伊拉克巴格达稍北部区域，以及位于埃兰的苏萨（今伊朗东南部）也有可能属于内行省。这三个行省一方面缴纳 bala 税，另一方面也缴纳 gun_2 ma-da 税，比如埃什努那直到舒辛统治时期才向中央缴纳 bala 税，之前都是缴纳 gun_2 ma-da 税，[1] 这体现了这三个行省的不稳定性，它们位于乌尔第三王朝的边疆地区，很可能会随着其与中央的关系远近而调整自己的政策。

这 19 个内行省以尼普尔为界，以北的阿卡德地区包括 10 个，以南的苏美尔地区包括 9 个，虽然北部的行省数量要多于南部，但是南部的苏美尔地区依然是乌尔第三王朝的核心地带，南部的行省向中央缴纳的赋税要远远多于北部行省，比如拉伽什—吉尔苏行省每年有三至四个月都要向中

---

[1] C. Reichel, *Political Changes and Cultural Continuity in the Palace of the Rulers of Eshnunna (Tell Asmar) from the Ur III Period to the Isin-Larsa Period*, PhD diss, University of Chicago, 2001.

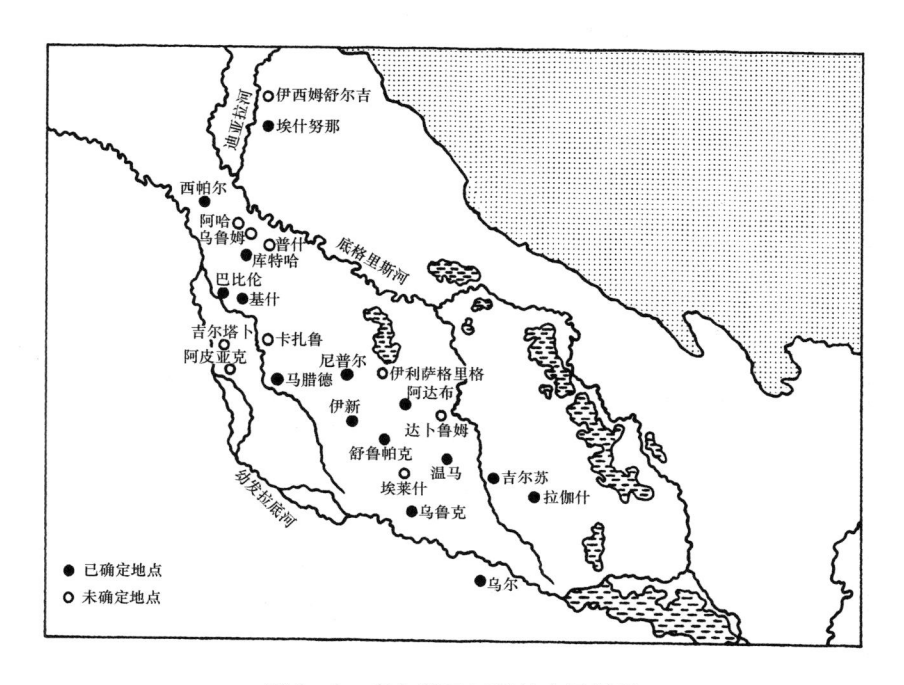

图 2-2　乌尔第三王朝核心区版图

资料来源：引自 P. Steinkeller, "The Administrative and Economic Organization of the Ur III State: the Core and the Periphery", in McG. Gibson, R. Biggs (eds.), *The Organization of Power Aspects of Bureaucracy in the Ancient Near East*, Chicago: The Oriental Institute of the University of Chicago, 1987, p. 18.

央缴纳 bala 税，多于平均水准的 3—4 倍，而北部的许多行省（如巴比伦、普什、阿哈）只需缴纳平均水准赋税的 1/3。

在行政组织上，核心区是"一点一环"的建构模式。其中，"一点"是指主要以一个城市为中心，即中心城市，作为该行省的政治、经济和文化中心。"一环"是指在中心城市的周围分布大小不一、数量不等的城镇和村庄，每个村镇又下设若干个"组"或者"区块"（a-ša₃），作为最基本的行政单位。例如温马行省内包括大约 50 个城镇和村庄，其中比较重要的有：阿姆利马、阿皮沙尔、阿萨如姆达基、丁提尔、伽尔沙纳、伽尔库如达、伊杜拉、卡马里、卡尔达希、卡尔卡尔、马什坎、纳格苏、沙尔

35

巴特、扎巴兰等。①（见图2-3）

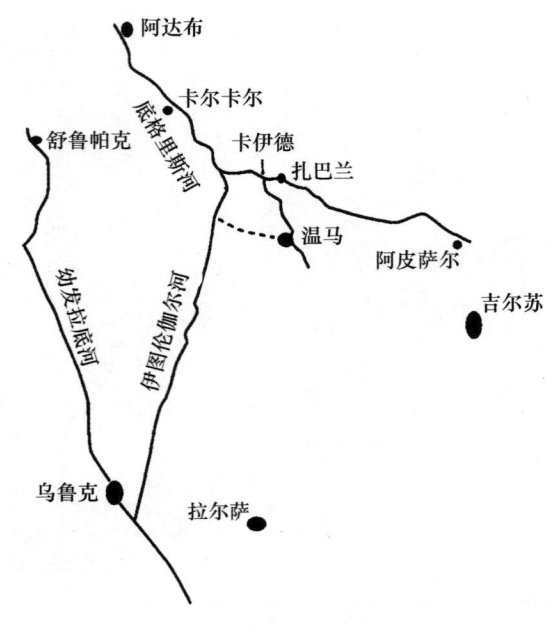

图2-3 温马行省版图

资料来源：引自J. L. Dahl, *The Ruling Family of Ur III Umma: A Prosopographical Analysis of an Elite Family in Southern Iraq 4000 Years ago*, PIHANS 108, Leiden：Nederlands Instituutvoor het Nabije Oosten, 2007, p. 34.

一 中央行省

在总共19个内行省中，乌尔、乌鲁克和尼普尔这三个行省属于"中央行省"，它们都具有首都的性质，类似于中国历史上元朝中书省的直辖地区——腹里②。这三个行省在行政和组织管理方面都与中央政府有着密切的联系，而与其他内行省有明显的区别。三个行省区域内都有王室成员的官邸（类似于行宫），作为王室成员的长期或者短期的居住场所，比如

---

① M. Stepien, *From the History of State System in Mesopotamia-The Kingdom of the Third Dynasty of Ur*, Warsaw: Uniwersytetu Warszawskiego i Dyrekcje Instytutu Historycznego, 2009, pp. 56–57.

② 参见李治安《元代行省制度》，中华书局2011年版；张金铣《元代地方行政制度研究》，安徽大学出版社2001年版。

伊比辛还是王子的时候，于舒辛 9 年第 10 月分别在尼普尔、乌尔和乌鲁克居住过。① 此外，在这三个行省中的宗教活动（神庙的祭祀活动）也多属于中央政府的任务，属于国家级的宗教活动。我们知道，乌尔第三王朝的宗教活动分为两类：一类是国家级宗教活动，由国王亲自或者由其代表代理主持进行，主要包括王宫中的神庙活动，以及国家的主神祭祀活动，比如尼普尔的恩利尔和宁利尔神庙、乌尔的南那神庙、乌鲁克的伊南娜神庙等；另一类是行省级别的宗教活动，由行省长官（恩西）或其他高官主持进行。国家级的宗教活动所需的动物祭品主要来自普兹瑞什达干动物管理机构，而那里的动物最初则来源于地方向中央缴纳的各种形式的赋税。

（一）乌尔

乌尔位于两河流域最南端，它既作为一个行省单位，又是乌尔第三王朝的首都，是乌尔国家的政治、经济和文化中心，乌尔第三王朝的国王在其铭文中自称为"乌尔的国王"（lugal Urim$_5^{ki}$-ma）。乌尔遗址的考古发掘开始于 1918 年，一直持续到 1934 年，主要由英国考古学家伦纳德·伍利主持。② 虽然大多数考古发掘成果在年代上属于早王朝时期，但是也不乏乌尔第三王朝时期的发掘成果，比如乌尔纳姆的塔庙遗址，神庙女祭司的驻地，以及舒尔吉和阿马尔辛的陵墓等。

与其他内行省不同，乌尔行省没有总督（恩西）一职，而是由首席神庙主管"沙卜拉"（šabra）负责乌尔行省的行政事务，并且和其他核心地省一样支付和接收 bala 税。

乌尔文献档案属于乌尔第三王朝的中央王室档案，③ 最早的文献起于舒尔吉 13 年，④ 最晚的文献终于伊比辛 23 年。⑤ 需要强调的是，由于乌尔第三王朝伊比辛统治时期其他地区的文献都在其统治前期中止，所以乌尔

---

① M. Sigrist, "Le deuil pour Šu-Sin", in H. Behrens, D. Loding, M. T. Roth (eds.), *Dumu-é-dub-ba: Studies in Honor of Åke W. Sjöberg*, Occasional Publications of the Samuel Noah Kramer Fund 11, Philadelphia: The University Museum, 1989, pp. 499 – 505.

② L. Woolley, *Ur Excavations at Ur*, London: Ernest Benn Ltd, 1954, pp. 12 – 13, 122 – 162；拱玉书《西亚考古史（1842—1939）》，文物出版社 2002 年版，第 142—149 页。

③ M. Widell, *The Administrative and Economic Ur III texts from the City of Ur*, Piscataway: Gorgias Press, 2003.

④ 见文献 RA 30 118 2 (S 13 vi).

⑤ 见文献 UET 3 711 (IS 23 xii 22).

文献成为伊比辛统治中后期唯一的文献来源，对于我们研究伊比辛时期的统治、乌尔第三王朝晚期的政治经济史，以及乌尔第三王朝的灭亡都具有十分关键的作用。

（二）乌鲁克

乌鲁克（今伊拉克瓦尔卡）位于乌尔的西北部，靠近幼发拉底河东岸，是乌尔第三王朝王室成员的所在地，相当于行宫。乌鲁克遗址主要是由德国考古学家发掘，但是处于乌尔第三王朝时期的发掘成果比较少，比如乌尔纳姆在埃安那神庙区的塔庙遗址。① 所以我们对于乌鲁克的认识主要来源于文献资料。

乌尔第三王朝的建立者乌尔纳姆很可能与乌鲁克第五王朝的唯一国王乌图赫伽尔是兄弟关系。② 后来，乌尔纳姆取代乌图赫伽尔成为国王，将首都从乌鲁克迁到乌尔，建立乌尔第三王朝。虽然乌尔最终取代了乌鲁克，但是在乌尔第三王朝，乌鲁克似乎依然保留着特殊的地位，这也说明了乌尔第三王朝的前身与乌鲁克有着密切的联系。此外，乌尔第三王朝的国王们还自称和早王朝时期乌鲁克的国王吉尔伽美什是"兄弟"关系，和乌鲁克保护神伊南娜是"姐弟"关系，③ 他们试图以此来加强同乌鲁克历史上的英雄人物之间建立亲属关系。

乌鲁克是王室成员的驻地，王子担任乌鲁克行省的总督或者将军。和其他行省不同，文献中极少有乌鲁克总督"恩西"和将军"沙基那"的记载，可能乌鲁克行省由国王或中央政府直接管辖，具体行政事务由代表国王的伊南娜神庙最高女祭司所任命的官员（如"沙卜拉"和"萨加"）负

---

① 拱玉书：《西亚考古史（1842—1939）》，文物出版社 2002 年版，第 124—128 页；R. W. Roehmer, "Uruk-Warka", in E. M. Meyers（ed.）, *The Oxford Encyclopedia of Archaeology in the Near East*, Volume 5, New York and Oxford: Oxford University Press, 1997, p. 296.

② B. Hrouda, *Isin-Išan Bahriyat III: Die Ergebnisse der Ausgrabungen 1983 – 1984*, Bayerische Akademie der Wissenschaften 94, Munich: C. H. Beck Verlag, 1987, pp. 108 – 111.

③ G. Castellino, *Two Shulgi Hymns（B，C）*, Studi semitici 42, Rome: Istituto di studi del Vicino Oriente, Universita, 1972, pp. 256 – 257; J. Klein, "Šulgi and Gilgameš: Two Brother-Peers（Šulgi O）", in B. L. Eichler（ed.）, *Kramer Anniversary Volume: Cuneiform Studies in Honor of Samuel Noah Kramer*, Alter Orient und Altes Testament 25, Kevelaer: Verlag Butzon & Bercker and Neukirchen-Vluyn: Neukirchener Verlag, 1976, pp. 271 – 292; P. Michalowski, "Charisma and Control: On Continuity and Change in Early Mesopotamian Bureaucratic Systems", in McG. Gibson and R. D. Biggs（eds.）, *The Organization of Power: Aspects of Bureaucracy in the Ancient Near East*, Studies in Ancient Oriental Civilization 46, Chicago: The Oriental Institute of the University of Chicago, 1987, pp. 58 – 66.

责，比如支付和接收 bala 税。所以实际上，乌鲁克行省的最高行政长官不是"恩西"或"沙基那"，而是神庙主管"沙卜拉"和"萨加"①。不过需要说明的是，乌鲁克缴纳和接收 bala 税的记录在文献中很少出现，可能这不是乌鲁克行省的主要义务。

（三）尼普尔

尼普尔（今伊拉克努法尔）处于乌尔第三王朝核心行省的中间位置，是古代两河流域的主神恩利尔与其妻宁利尔的居住地。尼普尔不仅是乌尔第三王朝的宗教首都，也是整个古代两河流域文明的祭祀中心和宗教圣地，享有十分重要的地位。恩利尔的神庙"埃库尔"位于尼普尔城内，而宁利尔的神庙位于尼普尔城南部的一个小城吐玛尔。② 由于其宗教中心的地位，尼普尔也作为乌尔第三王朝的三个首都之一。

尼普尔遗址的考古发掘工作，主要在 1888—1900 年由美国宾夕法尼亚大学考古队完成，出土的乌尔第三王朝经济文献大多数都是私人档案。1948 年，美国芝加哥大学考古队再次对尼普尔进行了考古发掘，发掘出了乌尔第三王朝时期的伊南娜神庙和恩利尔的"埃库尔"神庙遗址。③ 尼普尔文献最早起于舒尔吉 21 年，④ 终止于伊比辛 8 年。⑤

同其他许多核心行省一样，尼普尔行省也是由总督"恩西"负责行政事务，尼普尔总督的位子由一个叫乌尔美兰的家族世袭。⑥ 他们负责管理伊南娜的神庙区，并且居住于其内。乌尔的一些王室成员也很可能居住在尼普尔。与其他核心行省不同的是，尼普尔行省不需要向中央缴纳 bala 税，它是乌尔第三王朝所有核心行省中唯一一个不需要缴纳 bala

---

① P. Steinkeller, "On Rulers, Priest and Sacred Marriage: Tracing the Evolution of Early Sumerian Kingship", in K. Watanabe (ed.), *Priests and Officials in the Ancient Near East*, Heidelberg: Winter, 1999, pp. 103 – 136.

② M. Yoshikawa, "Looking for Tummal", *Acta Sumerologica*, Vol. 11 (1989), pp. 285 – 291.

③ R. L. Zettler, *The Ur III Temple of Inanna at Nippur: The Operation and Organization of Urban Religious Institutions in Mesopotamia in the Late Third Millennium B. C.*, Berliner Beiträge zum Vorderen Orient 11, Berlin: Dietrich Reimer Verlag, 1992, pp. 8 – 10.

④ 见文献 Iraq 22 pl. 18 5 NT 490 (S 20 ii).

⑤ 见文献 NATN 533 (IS 8 iii).

⑥ W. W. Hallo, "The House of Ur-Meme", *Journal of Near Eastern Studies*, Vol. 31, No. 2 (1972), pp. 87 – 95; R. L. Zettler, "The Geneaology of the House of Ur-Me-me: a Second Look", *Archiv für Orientforschung*, Vol. 31 (1984), pp. 1 – 9.

税的行省，其原因与它特殊的宗教地位密切相关。不过，尼普尔行省虽然不需缴纳 bala 税，但是它却可以接收 bala 税。尼普尔行省的总督有义务将接收的 bala 税物品（主要是牲畜）用于各种祭祀活动，献给尼普尔的众神。① 虽然被赦免了 bala 税义务，但是尼普尔还是要向中央政府提供其他赋役义务。② 根据文献记载，我们可以暂时复原尼普尔总督的任职期限。

表2-2　　　　　　　　　　尼普尔行省总督任期

总督名字	任期时间
乌尔纳尼卜伽尔（Ur-Nanibgal）	舒尔吉 44 年—45 年
古地亚（Gudea）	舒尔吉 48 年
阿胡玛（Ahuma）	阿马尔辛 1 年
卢伽尔美兰（Lugal-melam）③	阿马尔辛 1 年—9 年
达达（Dada）	舒辛 4 年—伊比辛 3 年

需要特别指出的是，在尼普尔行省内，距离尼普尔城东南大约 8 千米处，是乌尔第三王朝的国有贡牲中心——普兹瑞什达干，它虽然在地里上位于尼普尔行省内，但是不归尼普尔行省管辖，而是直属于中央政权的特殊机构。1962 年至 1966 年间，意大利学者布切拉蒂（Giorgio Buccellati）在实地考察了德莱海姆之后，写道："这个遗址从未被系统发掘，所有的泥板都来自（20）世纪初的非法挖掘。然而，盗挖者留下的大大小小的盗

---

① C. Liu, *Organization, Administrative Practices and Written Documentation at Puzriš-Dagan during the Reign of Amar-Suen*, PhD dissertation, Ruprecht-Karls-Universität Heidelberg, 2015; C. Liu, *Organization, Administrative Practices and Written Documentation in Mesopotamia during the Ur III Period (c. 2112 – 2004 BC): A Case Study of Puzriš-Dagan in the Reign of Amar-Suen*, Kārum-Emporion-Forum: Beiträge zur Wirtschafts-, Rechts-, und Sozialgeschichte des östlihen Mettelmeerraums und Altvorderasiens 3, Münster: Ugarit-Verlag, 2017; 以及王光胜、吴宇虹《乌尔帝国阿马尔辛王的贡牲中心结构和总管研究》，《历史教学》2013 年第 18 期。

② 见文献 NYPL 47（S 43 or AS 4 v 15），SACT 1 1（S 44 i 12），TCND 18（IS 2 vii 18）。

③ 这个人名 Lugal-me-lam$_2$ 也可以拼写为 Lugal-me-me（卢伽尔麦麦）。参见 W. W. Hallo, "The House of Ur-Meme", *Journal of Near Eastern Studies*, Vol. 31, No. 2 (1972), pp. 87 – 95.

洞清晰可见，无疑这些泥板都来自同一个地区。这个地区位于整个遗址的北部，在中心高地以北约 175 米处。在中心高地似乎没有盗洞痕迹。"① 多年后，英国学者亚当斯（Robert M. Adams）也对德莱海姆进行了实地考察，他写道："德莱海姆土丘，即古代的普兹瑞什达干，在遗址西北部的体积为 560×275×8.5 米，东南部有一个小的塔庙遗址。这一地区的海拔大多位于 2 米之下。表面多含盐分且柔软疏松，没有多少土壤堆积，在之前的盗洞地带有一些土壤遗存。整个地层信息仅限于乌尔第三王朝至拉尔萨王朝时期。"②

普兹瑞什达干是一个针对牲畜和其他产品的再分配中心。它是由乌尔第三王朝的第二位国王舒尔吉在其统治的第 39 年所设立，一直持续运营到末王伊比辛统治的第 2 年结束，一共存在了约 30 年。我们对普兹瑞什达干机构的早期历史不是很清楚。很可能，普兹瑞什达干机构的雏形是埃萨格达纳机构。在 2007 年之前，③ 普兹瑞什达干出土的泥板文书都没有经过系统科学的考古发掘，全部都是非法盗挖所得，目前这些泥板被世界各地的博物馆、图书馆和私人藏家所收藏。绝大多数的普兹瑞什达干泥板文书记录的是动物的运转与交易，当然也有少数文书涉及其他产品，比如"鞋档案"涉及各类鞋被运到乌尔，"财宝档案"记录了银饰及其他贵金属产品被送到乌尔王室。第三类档案是"舒尔吉西姆提档案"，也叫"早期德莱海姆档案"。普兹瑞什达干文献起于舒尔吉 26 年，④ 结束于伊比辛 3 年。⑤

二 地方行省

除了上述的三个首都行省之外，乌尔第三王朝的核心行省还包括 16

---

① G. Buccellati, *The Amorites of the Ur III Period*, Naples: Istituto Orientale di Napoli, 1966, pp. 281-282.

② R. Adams, *Heartland of Cities. Surveys of Ancient Settlement and Land Use on the Central Floodplain of the Euphrates*, Chicago: The University of Chicago Press, 1981, p. 269.

③ 2007 年，伊拉克考古队对德莱海姆遗址进行了第一期考古发掘，参见 N. Al-Mutawalli, W. Sallaberger, "The Cuneiform Documents from the Iraqi Excavation at Drehem", *Zeitschrift für Assyriologie und Vorderasiatische Archäologie*, Vol. 107, No. 2 (2017), pp. 151-158.

④ 见文献 OIP 115 1 (S 26 vii).

⑤ 见文献 SAT 3 1998 (IS 3 xii).

个地方行省，这些行省面积大小不一，其地理地位和重要性也各有差异。其中，吉尔苏和温马遗址出土的泥板文献数量都在一万块以上，其次是伊利萨格里格出土了超过一千块泥板，这三个行省出土的文献数量最多。其余的行省出土的文献数量极少，大多数行省的遗址（阿哈、乌鲁姆、普什、库特哈、巴比伦、卡扎鲁、阿皮亚克和马腊德）至今还没有文献资料出土，甚至有些行省的地理位置目前还尚不清楚。除了吉尔苏、温马和伊利萨格里格这三个行省之外，我们对于其他核心行省的内部行政管理以及基本情况一概不知，只能从相关的普兹瑞什达干文献中获取关于这些行省的少量间接信息。

（一）拉伽什—吉尔苏行省

拉伽什—吉尔苏行省位于乌尔第三王朝的最南部，是乌尔第三王朝面积最大的行省，可能有三个城市：吉尔苏、拉伽什、尼那（尼明），其中吉尔苏是这个行省的中心城市（见图2-4）。此外，拉伽什—吉尔苏行省也是乌尔第三王朝最高行政长官"苏卡尔马赫"的驻地，可见其在乌尔第三王朝的重要地位。拉伽什—吉尔苏行省的出土文献几乎都来自吉尔苏遗址，而拉伽什和尼那遗址基本没有出土泥板文献。

吉尔苏遗址位于今伊拉克的泰罗（Tello），这个土丘大约有100多公顷的面积，高约15米。吉尔苏城的保护神是宁吉尔苏，其主要神庙被称为"埃尼努"（e$_2$-ninnu）。吉尔苏遗址的发掘开始于1877年，大概是发掘最早的苏美尔地区的遗址，由法国考古学家德萨尔泽克主持发掘工作，一直持续到1933年。虽然没有留下大型建筑遗址，但是出土的乌尔第三王朝泥板文献有大约一万多块，是我们研究乌尔第三王朝的重要资料。拉伽什遗址位于今伊拉克的阿尔希巴（al-Hiba），是早王朝时期的主要城市，其考古发掘成果也多是早王朝时期的遗迹。[1] 尼那遗址（又称Nigin）位于今伊拉克济伽尔省的苏尔古尔（Surghul），位于阿尔希巴遗址以南约十千米，面积大约有65公顷，平均高约15米。1887年，德国考古学家科尔德维对该地进行过尝试性发掘工作。但在21世纪以前，关于这个遗址的情况很模糊。自2015年起，意大利罗马大学和佩鲁贾大学的联合考古队对

---

[1] R. Matthews, "Girsu and Lagash", in E. M. Meyers, *The Oxford Encyclopedia of Archaeology in the Near East*, Volume 2, Oxford：Oxford University Press, 1996, pp. 408-409.

该遗址进行了系统的考古发掘，①逐渐清晰还原了尼那城以及拉伽什—吉尔苏行省的历史。尼那城的保护神是南塞女神（Nanshe），她的神庙所在地被称为希拉拉（Sirara）。②此外，拉伽什—吉尔苏行省很可能还存在第四个城市基努尼尔（Kinunir）。③

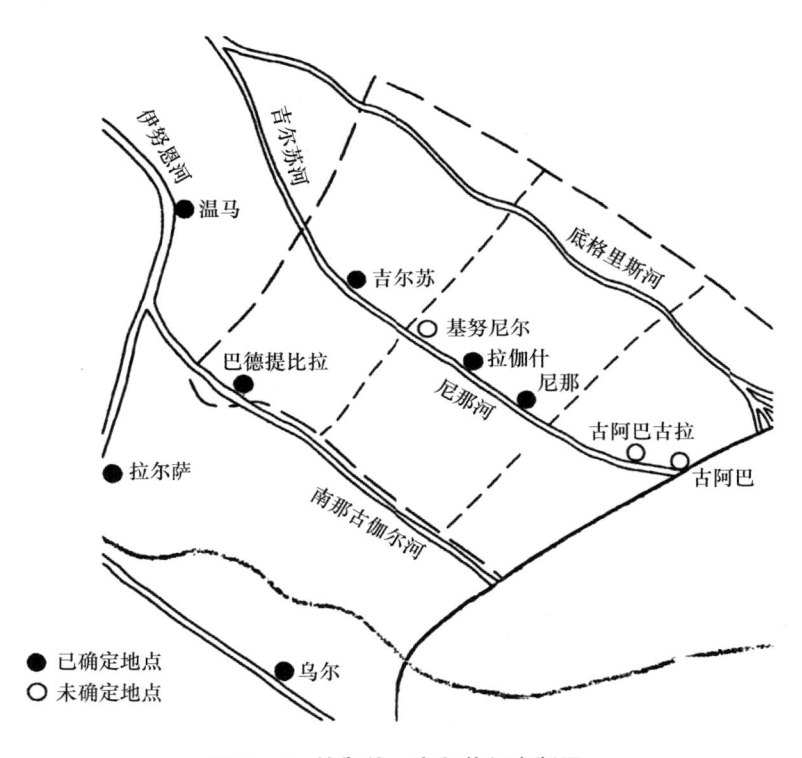

图 2-4 拉伽什—吉尔苏行省版图

资料来源：引自 D. Nadali, A. Polcaro, "The Early Stages of the Sumerian City at Tell Zurghul: New Results from Recent Excavations", *Origini: Prehistory and Protohistory of Ancient Civilizations*, Vol. 39 (2016), p. 85.

---

① D. Nadali, A. Polcaro, L. Verderame, "New Inscriptions of Gudea from Tell Surghul/Niĝin, Iraq", *Zeitschrift für Assyriologie und Vorderasiatische Archäologie*, Vol. 106, No. 1, 2016, pp. 16–21; D. Nadali, A. Polcaro, "Archaeological Discoveries in the Ancient State of Lagash: Results from the Italian Excavations at Tell Zurghul/Nigin in Southern Iraq", *Ash-Sharq*, Vol. 2, No. 1, 2018, pp. 24–49.

② D. O. Edzard, G. Farber, *Répertoire Géographique des Textes Cunéiformes II: Die Orts-und Gewässernamen der Zeit der 3. Dynastie von Ur*, Wiesbaden: Dr. Ludwig Reichert Verlag, 1974, pp. 169–179.

③ D. O. Edzard, G. Farber, *Répertoire Géographique des Textes Cunéiformes II: Die Orts-und Gewässernamen der Zeit der 3. Dynastie von Ur*, Wiesbaden: Dr. Ludwig Reichert Verlag, 1974, pp. 101–103.

拉伽什—吉尔苏行省的最高长官是恩西（总督），在文献中他们被称为"吉尔苏的恩西"。根据文献证据，我们复原拉伽什—吉尔苏行省的五位恩西的继任顺序表。

表 2-3　　　　　　　　　拉伽什—吉尔苏行省总督任期

总督名字	任期时间
卢吉里扎尔（Lu-kirizal）	舒尔吉 28 年—32 年
乌尔兰马（Ur-Lamma）	舒尔吉 33 年—阿马尔辛 2 年
南那孜沙伽尔（Nanna-zishagal）	阿马尔辛 4 年
沙拉卡姆（Sharakam）	阿马尔辛 3 年—6 年
阿拉德南那（Arad-Nanna）[①]	阿马尔辛 7 年—伊比辛 4 年

拉伽什—吉尔苏行省档案是乌尔第三王朝地方行省档案的代表之一，在时间上起于乌尔纳姆时期，[②] 结束于伊比辛 5 年，[③] 与属于中央的王室档案（如普兹瑞什达干和乌尔文献）相互补充。吉尔苏档案与神庙家族有着密切的联系，相比之下，温马的行省档案与神庙家族的联系则要疏远得多。[④] 很可能是由于拉伽什—吉尔苏行省统治的范围过大，所以需要不同的神庙家族来进行管理，而不是直接由行省的行政部门管理。拉伽什—吉尔苏行省的神庙家族大概包括：巴加拉神庙、杜牧孜神庙、加图姆杜格神庙、伊格阿里姆神庙、伊南娜神庙、纳姆哈尼神庙、南塞神庙、宁达尔神庙、宁吉尔苏神庙、宁吉什孜达神庙、宁玛尔神庙和舒尔吉神庙。[⑤] 其中，最大的神庙家族是宁吉尔苏神庙，其次是南塞神庙。所以说，拉伽什—吉

[①]　一般认为，他的名字等同于阿拉德姆（Arad-mu），属于同一个人，他同时兼任乌尔第三王朝的中央最高行政长官"苏卡尔马赫"（sukkal-mah，地位相当于今天的首相或总理）一职。但是也有不同意见，参见 F. Huber, "Au sujet du nom du chancelier d'Ur III, Ir-Nanna ou Ir-mu", *Nouvelles Assyriologiques Brèves et Utilitaires*, 2000/6, p. 10.

[②]　见文献 RA 5 83 AO 03331.

[③]　见文献 TSU 97 (IS 5 xi).

[④]　H. Neumann, "Staatliche Verwaltung und privates Handwerk in der Ur III-Zeit", in A. Bongenaar (ed.), *Interdependency of Institutions and Private Entrepreneurs*, Leiden: NHAII, 2000, p. 119.

[⑤]　K. Maekawa, "The Governor's Family and the 'Temple Households' in Ur III Girsu", in K. Veenhof (ed.), *Houses and Households in Ancient Mesopotamia*, RAI 40, Istanbul: Nederlands Historisch-Archaeologisch Instituut, 1996, pp. 175-176.

尔苏行省的经济属于神庙经济导向性。

（二）温马行省

温马行省（Umma）[①]是仅次于拉伽什—吉尔苏行省的乌尔第三王朝第二大行省，位于尼普尔和吉尔苏之间。温马遗址出土的泥板文献数量与吉尔苏文献不相上下，都是我们研究乌尔第三王朝地方行省制度的重要资料。温马行省是以温马城为中心城市，由许多个其他城市组成，在城市的周围分布着农村和更小的居住区。温马城的保护神是沙拉（Shara）。

温马遗址位于今伊拉克南部的约卡（Tell Jokha），[②]一说位于今伊拉克济伽尔省（Dhi Qar）的乌姆阿尔阿卡里卜（Umm al-Aqarib）地区。[③]早在1854年，欧洲探险家就来过约卡遗址，但是并没有进行过任何发掘工作。20世纪初，许多非法盗挖的温马泥板出现在文物市场，后来陆续被世界各地的收藏机构和私人所收藏。20世纪90年代，伊拉克考古队对约卡遗址进行了抢救性发掘。[④] 2016年，斯洛伐克考古队对约卡遗址进行了系统的考古发掘。[⑤]

温马行省的最高长官是恩西，他负责行省内的各项政治经济活动。温马的经济事务由下设的至少10个经济部门管理，分别管理财政、农业、粮食、动物、皮革、羊毛、船舶、劳动力、金属和森林。[⑥]虽然神庙家族也参与管理，但是与拉伽什—吉尔苏行省的模式不同，温马的神庙家族势力并不是

[①] 有关温马这一名称是苏美尔语还是阿卡德语，学术界存在争议，参见 W. G. Lambert, "The Names of Umma", *Journal of Near Eastern Studies*, Vol. 49, No. 1 (1990), pp. 75 – 80.

[②] V. Bartash, "On the Sumerian City UB-me^{ki}, the Alleged 'Umma'", *Cuneiform Digital Library Bulletin*, 2015/2; T. Bryce, *The Routledge Handbook of The Peoples and Places of Ancient Western Asia: The Near East from the Early Bronze Age to the fall of the Persian Empire*, London and New York: Routledge, 2009, pp. 738 – 739.

[③] 约卡遗址被认为是温马行省的附属地吉沙（Kissa），而其东南部约6.5千米远的乌姆阿尔阿卡里卜遗址，则被认为是真正的温马城遗址，参见 H. O. Almamori, "The Early Dynastic Monumental Buildings At Umm Al-Aqarib", *Iraq*, Vol. 76 (2014), pp. 149 – 187.

[④] S. S. Rumaidh, *Excavations in Chokha: An Early Dynastic Settlement*, Edubba 8, London: Nabu Publications, 2000.

[⑤] D. Hulínek, T. Lieskovský, *Report Archaeological project SAHI-Tell Jokha*, 2016, Bratislava: Slovak Archaeological and Historical Institute, 2016.

[⑥] P. Steinkeller, "Archival Practices in Third Millennium Babylonia: Some General Observation and the Specific Case of the Archives of Umma in Ur III Times", in M. Brosius (ed.), *Archives and Archival Traditions: Concepts of Record-keeping in the Ancient World*, Oxford: Oxford University Press, 2011, pp. 37 – 58.

行省的主要力量。温马行省一共有三位恩西，他们的继承顺序如下：①

表2-4　　　　　　　　　　温马行省总督任期

总督名字	任期时间
乌尔里希（Ur-Lisi）	舒尔吉31年—阿马尔辛8年
阿亚卡拉（Ayakalla）	阿马尔辛8年—舒辛6年
达达加（Dadaga）	舒辛7年—伊比辛2年

温马档案大约始于舒尔吉21年，②结束于伊比辛5年。③与吉尔苏档案有许多的多栏式大文献不同，温马文献多属于短小文献。温马城是温马行省的中心城市或首府，此外还有其他城市和农村。其中，阿皮萨尔（Apisal）是另一个经济上重要的城市，扎巴拉（Zabala）和吉安（KI.AN[ki]）是重要的宗教城市，古埃丁纳（Guedena）和穆什比亚纳（Mušbiana）是小的聚集区。温马行省的三大农业区是达温马（Da-Umma）、阿皮沙尔、古埃丁纳—穆什比亚纳。④需要注意的是，温马行省内有一个特殊的地区或者城市——伽尔沙纳，其具体地理位置不详，它是由国王阿马尔辛的女儿美伊什塔兰及其丈夫舒卡布塔管理，很可能是独立于温马行省的管辖，而属于王室领地。⑤近年来，伽尔沙纳文献陆续被发现

---

① D. Frayne, *Ur III Period* (*2112 - 2004 BC*), The Royal Inscriptions of Mesopotamia Early Periods Volume 3/2 (RIME 3/2), Toronto: University of Toronto Press, 1997, pp. 195, 275, 345, 379; T. Maeda, "Father of Akalla and Dadaga, Governors of Umma", *Acta Sumerologica*, Vol. 12, 1990, p. 71; J. L. Dahl, *The Ruling Family of Ur III Umma: A Prosopographical Analysis of an Elite Family in Southern Iraq 4000 Years Ago*, Publications de l'Institut historique-archéologique néerlandais de Stamboul 108, Leiden: Nederlands Instituut voor het Nabije Oosten, 2007, pp. 55 - 74.

② 见文献 BPOA 7 1745 (S 21).

③ 见文献 SNAT 214 (IS 5 viii).

④ J. L. Dahl, *The Ruling Family of Ur III Umma: A Prosopographical Analysis of an Elite Family in Southern Iraq 4000 Years Ago*, Publications de l'Institut historique-archéologique néerlandais de Stamboul 108, Leiden: Nederlands Instituut voor het Nabije Oosten, 2007, p. 35.

⑤ P. Steinkeller, "On the Location of the Town of GARšana and Related Matters", in D. I. Owen (ed.), *Garšana Studies*, Cornell University Studies in Assyriology and Sumerology 6, Bethesda: CDL Press, 2011, pp. 373 - 390.

和出版，已经出版了 1500 多块泥板，① 形成了乌尔第三王朝新的档案——伽尔沙纳档案，在时间上，起于阿马尔辛 4 年，② 结束于伊比辛 5 年。③

（三）伊利萨格里格

伊利萨格里格（Irisagrig）④ 行省的具体地理位置目前尚存在争议，伊利萨格里格的名称主要出现在普兹瑞什达干文献中。近年来，由于数千块所谓的伊利萨格里格档案的出版，⑤ 为我们研究伊利萨格里格行省提供了直接的文献证据。伊利萨格里格行省可能位于苏美尔地区的中部或北部，处于苏美尔地区和迪亚拉河流域以及埃兰的过渡地带。⑥ 比如，伊利萨格里格文献中记载了大量的阿卡德语人名，还有国王和王室成员巡视伊利萨格里格的记录，这都表明了这一行省的重要程度。甚至文献记载，有的王室成员可能居住在伊利萨格里格。

伊利萨格里格行省由总督（恩西）统治，共历有五位恩西：

表 2–5　　　　　　　　　伊利萨格里格行省总督任期

总督名字	任期时间
卢班达（Lu-banda）	舒尔吉 38 年
南那孜沙伽尔（Nanna-zishagal）	阿马尔辛 2 年
乌尔美斯（Ur-mes）	阿马尔辛 3 年—伊比辛 4 年
达达尼（Dadani）	阿马尔辛 7 年
伊拉鲁姆（Ilallum）	阿马尔辛 8 年

---

① D. I. Owen, R. H. Mayr, *The Garšana Archives*, Cornell University Studies in Assyriology and Sumerology 3, Bethesda: CDL Press, 2007; D. I. Owen (ed.), *Garšana Studies*, Cornell University Studies in Assyriology and Sumerology 6, Bethesda: CDL Press, 2011.

② 见文献 CUSAS 6 1530 (AS 4 ii).

③ 见文献 CUSAS 3 1248 (IS 5 i).

④ 这个地名的读音目前还没有统一，有的学者读其为乌鲁萨里格（Uru-sa$_{12}$-rig$_7^{ki}$），见 I. J. Gelb, *Old Akkadian Writing and Grammar*, Materials for the Assyrian Dictionary 2, Chicago: The University of Chicago Press, 1952, p.21, 有的学者读其为伊利萨格里格（Iri-saĝ-rig$_7^{ki}$ "礼物之城"），见 D. I. Owen, *Cuneiform Texts Primarily from Iri-Saĝ-rig / Āl-Šarrākī and the History of the Ur III Period*, Volume 1: Commentary and Indexes, Nisaba 15, Bethesda: CDL Press, 2013, 其对应的阿卡德语为 Āl-Šarrākī, 意为 "Šarrākū 人们的城市"。

⑤ D. I. Owen, *Cuneiform Texts Primarily from Iri-Saĝ-rig / Āl-Šarrākī and the History of the Ur III Period*, Volume 2: Catalogue and Texts, Nisaba 15, Bethesda: CDL Press, 2013.

⑥ D. I. Owen, *Cuneiform Texts Primarily from Iri-Saĝ-rig / Āl-Šarrākī and the History of the Ur III Period*, Volume 1: Commentary and Indexes, Nisaba 15, Bethesda: CDL Press, 2013, p.45.

（四）其他

上述的行省有文献档案资料，行省档案是我们研究这些行省的第一手文献资料，而对于乌尔第三王朝剩下的 13 个核心行省（西帕尔、阿哈、乌鲁姆、普什、库特哈、巴比伦、基什、卡扎鲁、阿皮亚克、马腊德、伊新、阿达布、舒鲁帕克），至今还没有发现行省档案，虽然有的遗址也已经被发掘（如西帕尔、巴比伦、基什、伊新、阿达布、舒鲁帕克），但是几乎没有出土乌尔第三王朝时期的文献资料，更没有发现行省档案，所以我们对于这些行省的了解仅限于行省总督（恩西）的名字以及关于 bala 税的记录，这些简单的记录来源于普兹瑞什达干档案。从普兹瑞什达干档案关于这些行省总督的记录中，我们可以对这些行省总督进行粗略地、片面地复原与重建。但是需要指出的是，这样的重建结果仅是暂时的，只是根据目前可知的普兹瑞什达干档案，以后随着新文献档案（甚至行省档案）的发现，我们的这些重建也将进一步更新。下列就是我们对这 13 个行省恩西任职时间表的暂时重建（见表 2 - 6）。

表 2 - 6　　　　　　　　　行省总督任期一览表

行省	总督（恩西）	任期
西帕尔	努尔达干（Nur-Dagan）	阿马尔辛 7 年—8 年
阿哈	伊图鲁姆（Iturum） 阿穆尔辛（Amur-Suen） 恩利尔孜沙伽尔（Enlil-zishagal） 达达（Dada）	舒尔吉 30 年 舒尔吉 43 年—46 年 阿马尔辛 7 年—舒辛 2 年 阿马尔辛 8 年—舒辛 6 年
乌鲁姆	乌尔辛（Ur-Suen） 阿拉德南那（Arad-Nanna） 伊布尼伊什库尔（Ibni-Ishkur）	舒尔吉 42 年—阿马尔辛 7 年 舒辛 6 年 ？
普什	阿胡亚（Ahua） 伊吉安纳凯祖（Igi-anna-kezu） 阿胡玛（Ahuma） 卢伽尔库祖（Lugal-kuzu） 杜伊里（Du-ili）	舒尔吉 40 年 舒尔吉 46 年 舒尔吉 47 年—舒辛 6 年 ？ ？

续表

行省	总督（恩西）	任期
库特哈	纳姆孜塔拉（Namzitara） 古地亚（Gudea） 卢丁吉尔拉（Lu-dingira） 皮沙希鲁姆（Pishah-ilum）	舒尔吉45年—阿马尔辛1年 阿马尔辛2年—舒辛2年 伊比辛2年 伊比辛时期
巴比伦	伊图尔伊鲁姆（Itur-ilum） 阿巴（Abba）与阿尔西阿赫（Arshiah） 阿尔西阿赫 穆尔特里（Murteli） 乌纳帕塔尔（Unapatal） 普祖尔图图（Puzur-tutu）	舒尔吉37年—42年 舒尔吉43年—46年 舒尔吉47年—阿马尔辛7年 阿马尔辛8年—9年 舒辛8年 伊比辛2年
基什	乌古拉（Ugula） 阿胡姆巴尼（Ahum-bani） 伊鲁姆巴尼（Ilum-bani）	阿马尔辛3年—4年 阿马尔辛8年 ？
卡扎鲁	伊扎里克（Izariq） 卡拉姆（Kallamu） 舒玛玛（Shu-Mama） 阿皮拉沙（Apilasha） 伊迪迪（Ididi）	舒尔吉33年—34年 舒尔吉43年—46年 舒尔吉47年—阿马尔辛7年 阿马尔辛7年—8年 阿马尔辛8年
阿皮亚克	舒提鲁姆（Shu-Tirum） 沙鲁姆巴尼（Sharrum-bani）	阿马尔辛4年 阿马尔辛5年—7年
马腊德	舒伊里（Shu-ili） 瓦塔鲁姆（Watarum） 里沙努姆（Lishanum） 伊姆里克埃阿（Imlik-Ea） 奈奈（NE-NE）	舒尔吉时期 舒尔吉时期 阿马尔辛4年—7年 阿马尔辛9年—舒辛6年 舒辛8年
伊新	伊什比埃拉（Ishbi-Erra）	
阿达布	哈巴卢吉（Habaluge） 乌尔阿什吉（Ur-Ashgi）	舒尔吉38年—舒辛6年 舒尔吉39年—阿马尔辛1年
舒鲁帕克	乌尔尼伽尔（Ur-nigar） 阿胡亚（Ahua） 卢巴拉萨加（Lu-bala-saga） 乌尔宁库拉（Ur-Ninkura） 库南那（Ku-Nanna）	舒尔吉36年 阿马尔辛1年 阿马尔辛5年—7年 阿马尔辛3年—舒辛4年 舒辛6年—9年

三 核心区管理机制

乌尔第三王朝的行省（内行省）由谁领导？总督（恩西）和将军（沙基那）。乌尔第三王朝采取"平行合作制"的官僚模式来管理核心行省，即在一个行省里由国王任命一位总督管理行省的行政事务，任命一位或多位将军来负责行省的军事事务。总督和将军之间不是隶属关系，而是平等关系，他们都直接隶属于丞相（苏卡尔马赫），并听命于国王，对国王负责。恩西和沙基那是核心行省官僚体系的第一层。

恩西（ensi$_2$），楔形文字符号是"帕泰西"（PA. TE. SI），源于早王朝时期，即苏美尔城邦争霸时期或更早，最初指的是"城邦首领"，和"卢伽尔"（lugal）、"恩"（en）意思相近，具有独立城邦头领的含义。[1] 到阿卡德王国时期，中央集权统治加强，许多原来的独立城邦被合并到阿卡德王国的版图中，原来的城邦头领"恩西"虽然保留了原头衔，但是已经失去了原来的意思，而是变成了"行省总督"的含义。阿卡德王国灭亡之后，两河流域南部一些城邦再度独立，比如拉伽什，它的"恩西"又恢复了独立城邦头领的含义。最后到了乌尔第三王朝，核心行省中的"恩西"含义再次变为"行省总督"。需要注意的是，即使在乌尔第三王朝时期，"恩西"这一称号也有多种指代，在核心行省中指"行省总督"，在外围行省中偶有出现，可能亦指"行省总督"，略带"自治"含义，而在附属国和乌尔第三王朝势力范围之外的独立国家中，"恩西"指的是"独立城邦头领"、甚至有"国王"的意思。

舒尔吉在其统治的第 21 年，对国家的行政体系进行了改革，将行省总督和神庙主管纳入国王的直接控制之下，由国王直接任命这些官吏。这一改革体现在他当年的年名中"恩利尔的手下、战神尼努尔塔在恩利尔与宁利尔神庙发布了一项神谕，宣布乌尔国王舒尔吉主持恩利尔与宁利尔神庙的土地和账目的事宜"[2]。通过这一改革，一是国王将地方行政权收入中央直接控制之下，打破了自早王朝时期以来的城邦独立局面，二是国王将神庙权力纳入中央的实际控制之下，打破了两河流域之前的神庙自主权的传统，为乌尔第三王朝的中央集权统治奠定了基础。

---

[1] T. Jacobsen, "The Term Ensí", *Aula Orientalis*, Vol. 9 (1991), pp. 113 – 121; P. Steinkeller, "On Rulers, Priests and Sacred Marriage: Tracing the Evolution of Early Sumerian Kingship", in K. Watanabe (ed.), *Priests and Officials in the Ancient Near East*, Heidelberg: Universitätsverlag C. Winter, 1999, pp. 103 – 137.

[2] P. Steinkeller, "The Administrative and Economic Organization of the Ur III State: The Core and the Periphery", in M. Gibson and R. D. Biggs (eds.), *The Organization of Power: Aspects of Bureaucracy in the Ancient Near East*, Studies in Ancient Oriental Civilization 46, Chicago: The Oriental Institute of the University of Chicago, 1987, pp. 20 – 21; W. Sallaberger, "Ur III-Zeit", in W. Sallaberger and A. Westenholz (eds.), *Mesopotamien: Akkade-Zeit und Ur III-Zeit*, Orbis Biblicus et Orientalis 160/3, Freiburg: Universitätsverlag, 1999, p. 148.

第二章 核心区 bala 税

乌尔第三王朝的行省总督多来自当地的贵族豪门，他们的职位虽然是由国王任命，但是实际上很多都没有具体任期，而且是世袭。这样的后果是，可能导致行省总督的"离心"倾向，脱离中央独立的倾向蔓延。为了扼制这种不利于中央集权的势头，乌尔中央政府采取总督异地调职的管理方式，防止总督"拥省自重"，从而加强中央集权。甚至在阿马尔辛7年，乌尔中央政府用国王的亲信代替之前的当地贵族，撤换了若干行省的总督。① 乌尔中央政府采取的第二个削弱行省总督权力的政策是"分权"，即在每个行省设立了一名或多名将军，掌管军事事务，与行省总督平级，从而达到制衡总督的目的。② 与总督的出身不同，将军大多是国王身边的亲信，甚至直接就是王子，他们是忠于国王、拥护中央的势力代表。

次于行省总督（恩西）的是神庙管理者"沙布拉"和"萨加"，他们很多都是总督的儿子，属于行省总督家族的亲属，这说明行省之内的神庙体系也被纳入行省行政权的控制之下，失去了其独立性。在行省之下的行政官员里，设有市长或镇长一职（ha-za-num$_2$，哈扎农），负责管理行省内除省会城市之外的小城镇。比如，在温马行省内有吉沙巴市、伽尔沙纳市、马什坎市和纳格苏市的市长等。③ 市长或镇长很可能直接隶属于行省总督，是行省官僚体系的第二层。④ 此外，还有一些具体的官吏名称，比如"牛监"（nu-banda$_3$-gu$_4$，监管行省的神庙土地），⑤ 档案管理员（pisan-

---

① L. Allred, "The Tenure of Provincial Governors: Some Observations", in S. Garfinkle and M. Molina (eds.), *From the 21st Century B. C. to the 21st Century A. D.: Proceedings of the International Conference on Sumerian Studies Held in Madrid 22 – 24 July 2010*, Winona Lake: Eisenbrauns, 2013, pp. 115 – 123.

② 有关乌尔第三王朝的将军（沙基那）情况，参见 A. Goetze, "Šakkanakkus of the Ur III Empire", *Journal of Cuneiform Studies*, Vol. 17, No. 1 (1963), pp. 1 – 31.

③ J. L. Dahl, *The Ruling Family of Ur III Umma: A Prosopographical Analysis of an Elite Family in Southern Iraq 4000 Years Ago*, Publications de l'Institut historique-archéologique néerlandais de Stamboul 108, Leiden: Nederlands Instituut voor het Nabije Oosten, 2007, pp. 33 – 44.

④ 参见 M. Stepien, *From the History of State System in Mesopotamia-The Kingdom of the Third Dynasty of Ur*, Warsaw: Uniwersytetu Warszawskiego i Dyrekcje Instytutu Historycznego, 2009, p. 52. 一说次于行省总督的官僚是神庙主管"沙卜拉"或"萨加"，参见 T. Sharlach, *Provincial Taxation and the Ur III State*, Cuneiform Monographs 26, Leiden and Boston: Brill, 2004, p. 15.

⑤ K. Maekawa, "The Management of Domain Land in Ur III Umma", *Zinbun*, Vol. 22 (1987), pp. 25 – 82; K. Maekawa, "Cereal Cultivation in the Ur III Period", *Bulletin on Sumerian Agriculture*, Vol. 1 (1984), pp. 73 – 96.

dub-ba）、地籍官（sag-sug₅）、粮仓监管（ka-guru₇）、[1] 宝库监管（sar-ra-ab-DU），以及神庙书吏（dub-sar-gu₄）等。

在市长或镇长之下，还设有"长老"（ab-ba）官职，负责更小的村庄事务，是行省官僚体系的第三层，也是乌尔第三王朝的基层官员或一般意义上的"父母官"。

第二节　税收管理

核心行省管理的一个突出特点，是 bala 税及其管理机构的设立。乌尔第三王朝的 bala 税制创立于第二王舒尔吉统治时期（公元前2094—前2047年），一直延续到末王伊比辛统治前期，存在了 50 年左右的时间，经历了乌尔第三王朝的巩固与发展期、繁盛期、衰亡期三个阶段。作为一项联系乌尔第三王朝中央政府与地方政府的经济财政纽带，bala 税制是乌尔第三王朝的经济财政基础，也是乌尔第三王朝中央集权统治的缩影，具有极其重要的意义。

需要指出的是，由于没有出土专门的乌尔第三王朝税收档案，或者财政官员的私人档案，所以我们对乌尔第三王朝赋税的认识，只能来源于零散的经济管理文献，在这些文献中没有"赋税"的专门术语，所以我们只能通过对文献中记载的某些术语含义及其作用的认知之后，再比对今天意义上的赋税概念，从而认定这些术语接近于今天的"赋税"概念，但绝不是说它们的含义就等同于今天的赋税。在这些与赋税相关的术语中，出现最多的、也是最重要的一个术语就是 bala，或者意译为行省税，[2] 或者音译为"巴拉税"[3]，但是为了还原本义，本书保留了楔形文字原文拉丁化 bala 的用法。首先，我们将从 bala 税的课征形式、赋税流向、文献来源与文献格式三个方面来对乌尔第三王朝的 bala 赋税制度进行概括性的介绍。然后，在接下来的章节中，我们将通过对温马行省（见本章第三节）、拉

---

[1] P. Steinkeller, *Sale Documents of the Ur III Period*, Freiburger Altorientalische Studien 17, Stuttgart: Franz Steiner Verlag, 1989, pp. 199–200.

[2] T. Sharlach, *Provincial Taxation and the Ur III State*, Cuneiform Monographs 26, Leiden: Brill, 2004.

[3] 刘昌玉：《乌尔第三王朝行省制度探析》，《社会科学》2017 年第 1 期。

伽什-吉尔苏行省（见本章第四节）和其他行省（见本章第五节）的具体调查研究，详细分析 bala 赋税在各个行省的具体情况，从而窥探出整个乌尔第三王朝的 bala 赋税制度的特征与作用。

一 课征形式

在古代两河流域文明发展的早期，赋税的形式并不是货币税，而是实物税。古代两河流域历史上也是以实物税为主，货币税为辅，直到两河流域历史发展的晚期，即新巴比伦王国时期（公元前626—前539年），才有了明确的货币税。① 所以在乌尔第三王朝，我们所说的赋税都是指实物税。bala 税是其中的一种实物税。具体而言，这里的"实物"都包括哪些内容呢？即乌尔第三王朝 bala 税的课征形式是什么呢？从乌尔第三王朝记载 bala 税的经济文献中（基本上来源于温马文献、吉尔苏文献和普兹瑞什达干文献），我们可以总结出 bala 税的几种主要课征形式，包括：大麦、面粉、芦苇、木材、手工制品、香料、羊毛，还有牲畜（主要是牛、绵羊、山羊，以及少量的驴），另外，劳动力也是一种主要的赋税形式。需要注意的是，拉伽什—吉尔苏行省向中央缴纳的 bala 税形式主要是大麦和面粉，而温马行省向中央缴纳的 bala 税除了大麦和面粉之外，还有芦苇、树木和手工制品，以及一定数量的牲畜。

（一）食料、饮料

食料形式的 bala 税，主要是作为食物供人食用以及作为饲料以喂养牲畜，其具体形式以大麦（še）为主。② 例如，在温马文献中：

---

① I. Schrakamp, P. Paoletti, "Steuer", *Reallexikonder Assyriologie und Vorderasiatischen Archäologie*, Vol. 13 (2011–2013), pp. 163–164.

② 关于乌尔第三王朝的粮食，尤其是大麦，参见 J. M. Renfrew, "Cereals cultivated in Ancient Iraq", *Bulletin on Sumerian Agriculture*, Vol. 1 (1984), pp. 32–44; M. A. Powell, "Sumerian cereal crops", *Bulletin on Sumerian Agriculture*, Vol. 1 (1984), pp. 48–72; K. Maekawa, "Cereal cultivation in the Ur III period", *Bulletin on Sumerian Agriculture*, Vol. 1 (1984), pp. 73–96; H. Brunke, *Essen in Sumer: Metrologie, Herstellung und Terminologie nach Zeugnis der Ur III-zeitlichen Wirtschaftsurkunden*, Geschichtswissenschaften 26, München: Herbert Utz Verlag, 2011. 关于大麦与白银之间的比率关系，参见 E. L. Cripps, "The Structure of Prices in the Neo-Sumerian Economy (I): Barley: Silver Price Ratios", *Cuneiform Digital Library Journal*, No. 2, 2017, pp. 1–44.

BPOA 1 1071 (AS 7 viii, Umma)

7.0.0 še gur	7 古尔①大麦
ša₃-gal gu₄ niga	作为育肥牛的饲料
ki Ur-ᵈIštaran-ta	从乌尔伊什塔兰处
kišib An-na-hi-li-bi	安纳希里比（加印）（收到）
ša₃ bala	作为 bala 税的一部分
iti e₂-iti-6	第 8 月
mu Bi₂-tum-ra-bi₂-umᵏⁱ ba-hul	阿马尔辛 7 年

除了大麦这种常见的 bala 税形式之外，在文献中还记载了小麦（gig）、二粒小麦（ziz₂）、面粉（zi₃）、一种粗面粉（zi₃-gu）、粗粒面粉（dabin）、精面粉（eša）、面包（ninda）、二粒小麦面包（ninda imgaga₃）、大麦片（碾去壳的大麦，ar-za-na）、一种碾去壳的大麦（nig₂-ar₃-ra），这些基本都是供人食用。此外，还有供牲畜食用的饲料，比如麸糠（duh）、秸秆（in-nu）、干草或糠（in-bul₅-bul₅）② 等。其他的食物有：鱼（ku₆）、熏鱼（ku₆-še₆）、植物油（简称 i₃，全称 i₃-geš）、酥油（i₃-nun）、猪油（i₃-nun šah₂ 或 i₃-šah₂）、盐（mun）、奶酪（ga-ar₃）等。需要注意的是，这些食物种类十分繁多，有些术语晦涩难懂，很难对应于今天的某个具体物品。

两河流域的苏美尔人是世界上最早学会酿造啤酒的民族，他们用大麦酿造啤酒。③ 在苏美尔谚语等文学作品中，记载了许多关于啤酒的典故。④ 同

---

① 古尔，古代两河流域容量单位，1 古尔约等于 300 升。

② P. Steinkeller, "AB-tum = èš-tum/iltu", *Nouvelles Assyriologiques Brèves et Utilitaires*, 2001/35, p. 40.

③ L. F. Hartman, A. L. Oppenheim, "On Beer and Brewing Techniques in Ancient Mesopotamia According to the XXIIIrd Tablet of the Series HAR.ra = hubullu", *Journal of the American Oriental Society*, Supplement 10, Baltimore: American Oriental Society, 1950, pp. 1 – 50; W. Röllig, *Das Bier im Alten Mesopotamien*, Berlin: Gesellschaft fiir die Geschichte und Bibliographie des Brauwesens EV, 1970; H. Neumann, "Beer as a Means of Compensation for Work in Mesopotamia During the Ur III Period", in L. Milano (ed.), *Drinking in Ancient Societies: History and Culture of Drinks in the Ancient Near East: Papers of a Symposium held in Rome, May 17 – 19, 1990*, History of the Ancient Near East Studies 6, Padua: Sargon, 1994, pp. 321 – 331; P. Damerow, "Sumerian Beer: The Origins of Brewing Technology in Ancient Mesopotamia", *Cuneiform Digital Library Journal*, No. 2 (2012), pp. 1 – 20. 以及参见刘昌玉《苏美尔啤酒及其酿造技术》，《酿酒科技》2012 年第 7 期。

④ M. Civil, "A Hymn to the Beer Goddess and a Drinking Song", in R. D. Biggs and J. A. Brinkman (eds.), *From the Workshop of the Chicago Assyrian Dictionary: Studies Presented to A. Leo Oppenheim*, Chicago: University of Chicago Press, 1964, pp. 67 – 89.

第二章 核心区 bala 税

样,在两河流域的滚印等艺术品中,也刻画了人们用芦苇管啜吸罐子里的啤酒,这些说明了啤酒以及啤酒文化在古代两河流域文化中的重要地位。啤酒(kaš)作为 bala 税的形式,在文献中出现得不是很多,主要出现在温马文献中。啤酒也有许多种类,按照品级,可以分为普通啤酒(kaš du)和优质啤酒(kaš saga)。还有制作啤酒所需的原料,也是 bala 税的课税形式,这些啤酒原料的术语很难准确翻译,包括 bappir$_2$(或 bappir)和 dida 两种。例如:

Aleppo 334(S 46,Umma)
正面
5 sila$_3$ kaš du　　　　　　　　　　5 希拉①普通啤酒
ki Lugal-ma$_2$-gur$_8$-re-ta　　　　从卢伽尔马古莱处
kišib Ur-^{d}Šul-pa-e$_3$　　　　　乌尔舒尔帕埃加印(接收)
背面
ša$_3$ bala-a　　　　　　　　　　　在缴纳的 bala 税之中
mu Ki-maš^{ki} ba-hul　　　　　　舒尔吉 46 年
印文
Ur-^{d}Šul-pa-e$_3$　　　　　　　　乌尔舒尔帕埃
dub-sar　　　　　　　　　　　　书吏
dumu Lugal-ku$_3$-ga-ni　　　　　卢伽尔库加尼之子

在温马的 bala 文献中,啤酒也经常和面包(ninda)或者面粉(dabin)一起出现。例如下面这篇文献:

BPOA 6789(SS 5,Umma)
正面
0.0.3 kaš du　　　　　　　　　　3 班②普通啤酒
0.0.3 ninda du　　　　　　　　　3 班普通面包
zi-ga didli-ta　　　　　　　　　来自多次的支出

---

① 希拉,古代两河流域容量单位,1 希拉约等于 1 升。
② 班,古代两河流域容量单位,1 班约等于 10 升。

sukkal ka e$_2$-udu	"绵羊房"的信使
背面	
kišib ensi$_2$-ka	（温马）总督加印（接收）
ša$_3$ bala-a	在缴纳的 bala 税之中
mu us$_2$-sa bad$_3$ mar-tu ba-du$_3$	舒辛 5 年
印文	
^{d}Šu-^{d}Suen	舒辛
lugal kala-ga	强大的国王
lugal Uri$_5^{ki}$-ma	乌尔的国王
lugal an-ub-da limmu$_2$-ba	天地四方之王：
A-a-kal-la	阿亚卡拉
ensi$_2$	温马的总督
Umma^{ki}	
arad$_2$-zu	是您的仆人

（二）香料及草本植物

香料（šim）作为 bala 税的课税形式在文献中出现的并不是很多，有的术语的准确含义还存在争议。比如 ^{u2}hu-ri$_2$-um 或 hu-ri$_2$-um 指一种香料，zi-bi$_2$-tum 指一种香料的种子，[①] 这两种香料的具体含义尚不清楚。意思比较明确的是小茴香（^{u2}gamun$_2$ 或 ku-mul）。香料通常取自草本植物，在苏美尔语中一般在其术语前面加限定符 u$_2$ 指代"草本植物"。

除了香料之外，作为 bala 税课税形式的草本植物还有一些蔬菜和豆类。蔬菜包括芥菜（gazi，亦可译为甘草）、芫荽（še-lu$_2$，或胡荽）、洋葱（šum$_2$）、韭葱（za-ha-din 或 ^{šum2}za-ha-din）、水芹菜（za$_3$-hi-li）、一种碱性植物（可能是猪毛菜，naga）[②]。豆类包括大扁豆（gu$_2$-gal，更大的扁豆是 gu$_2$-gal-gal）、小扁豆（gu$_2$-tur）以及一种豆科植物（^{u2}kur）。比如下面一个例子：

[①] K. Maekawa, "Cultivation of legumes and mun-gazi plants in Ur III Girsu", *Bulletin on Sumerian Agriculture*, Vol. 2 (1985), p. 99.

[②] M. Civil, "Feeding Dumuzi's Sheep: The Lexicon as a Source of Literary Inspiration", in F. Rochberg-Halton (ed.), *Language, Literature, and History: Philological and Historical Studies Presented to Erica Reiner*, New Haven: American Oriental Society, 1987, pp. 48 – 49.

第二章 核心区 bala 税

RA 49 91 25（S 39，Umma）

正面：

1.0.0 naga gur	1 古尔碱性植物
aga₃-us₂	为士兵
0.0.3 naga gaz	3 班磨碎的碱性植物
ᵈŠul-gi-ni	为舒尔吉尼
0.1.0 naga aga₃ lugal	1 巴里格①碱性植物为王冠
0.0.1 naga gaz	1 班磨碎的碱性植物
lugal a-tu₅-a	为王家祭酒仪式
0.0.1 naga gaz 0.0.2 naga	1 班磨碎的碱性植物、2 班碱性植物

背面：

Na-hi-da-tum	为纳西达图姆
0.0.1 naga gaz Ku₃-dim₂	1 班磨碎的碱性植物为库蒂姆
0.0.1 naga gaz gu₂ ne-sag	1 班磨碎的碱性植物被放入橱柜
ki Ur-ᵈDumu-zi-da-ta	从乌尔杜牧孜达处
kišib Lugal-ezem ša₃ bala-a	卢伽尔埃孜姆收到了，作为 bala 税的一部分
mu Puzur₄-da-gan ba-du₃	舒尔吉 39 年

（三）芦苇及芦苇制品

芦苇（gi）是古代两河流域十分常见的一种植物，主要生长于幼发拉底河与底格里斯河的岸边，很早就已经被两河流域人们加以利用。芦苇既可以用来编织筛子、不同图案的席子等日用品和篮子等容器，还可作为建筑材料，也可以用来作为吸管饮用啤酒。② 芦苇是乌尔第三王朝 bala 税的主要课税形式之一，尤其在温马文献中有大量的记载，说明了温马行省缴纳芦苇税的数量和比例都是十分庞大的。试举一例：

---

① 巴里格，古代两河流域容量单位，1 巴里格约等于 60 升。
② S. T. Kang, *Sumerian Economic Texts from the Umma Archive: Sumerian and Akkadian Cuneiform Texts in the Collection of the World Heritage Museum of the University of Illinois*, Volume II, Urbana-Chicago-London: University of Illinois Press, 1973, pp. 12 – 13.

UTI 5 3082（AS 8，Umma）
正面：

60 sa gi	60 束芦苇
e$_2$ siskur$_2$-ra	为祭祀房准备
ka e$_2$-gal du$_3$-de$_3$	被放在宫殿门口
ki Šeš-kal-la	从塞什卡拉处
kišib Uš-mu	乌什姆收到了

背面：

ša$_3$ bala-a	作为 bala 税的一部分
mu en Eridu^{ki} ba-hun	阿马尔辛 8 年

除了芦苇之外，温马和吉尔苏文献中还记载了许多芦苇编制成的篮子、筛子（^{gi}ma-an-sim 或 ma-an-sim）、席子（kid 或 ^{gi}kid）等生活用品。这些芦苇做的东西，在苏美尔语中一般在其术语前面加限定符 gi 指代"芦苇制品"。有一些芦苇可能属于不同的品种，在文献中使用了不同的术语，比如 gi-ru-uš 和 ^{gi}su$_7$-su$_7$ 都指一种芦苇，具体是什么品种的芦苇也不清楚。此外，使用芦苇编织而成的篮子，在文献中有非常具体的区分，包括以下的类别：

^{gi}gur-dub	一种鱼篮子
^{gi}hal	一种篮子
^{gi}ha-an	一种宽松编织的芦苇篮子
^{gi}kaskal	旅行（时使用的）篮子
^{gi}kaskal peš$_3$	盛无花果的篮子
^{gi}kaskal siki	盛羊毛的篮子
^{gi}ma-sa$_2$-ab	（祭祀时用的）一种篮子
^{gi}si-ig-da	一种篮子

在文献中，还有一些术语的具体含义尚不清楚，不过它们可能也是指一种芦苇制品，这些术语包括：^{gi}aš-LAGAB，^{gi}giri$_3$-giri$_3$，^{gi}gu-tum，^{gi}gur nag-ta，^{gi}gur pisan，^{gi}gur sal$_4$-la 和 ^{gi}si-da 等。

（四）树木及木制品

古代两河流域南部的苏美尔地区缺乏大型树林，木材多来自周边地区，比如《吉尔伽美什史诗》和《古地亚滚筒铭文》中都有到雪松山（位于今天黎巴嫩）去砍伐雪松，运回苏美尔以修建神庙的记载。由此可见，在乌尔第三王朝，木材是一种十分珍贵的自然资源，也是国家重要的赋税形式之一。在文献中，树木作为 bala 税的课税形式主要指的是原木、木材或木料，以及树枝、树叶等。此外，文献中还记载有许多种类的木制品。在树木和木制品的术语前面，一般都加有限定符 giš（树木、木制品）。这些树含义明确的主要有杨树（^{giš}asal$_2$）、柳树（^{giš}ma-nu）、松树（^{giš}u$_3$-suh$_5$），以及苹果树（^{giš}hašhur）、无花果树（^{giš}peš$_3$）、葡萄藤（^{giš}geštin）、椰枣树（gešimmar 或 ^{giš}gešimmar）等果树，还有一种带刺的树（^{giš}ab-ba）。其中，椰枣树是苏美尔地区的主要果树种类，其果实椰枣（zu$_2$-lum）是两河流域人们的主要食物之一。直到今天，伊拉克也是世界上最重要的椰枣产地之一，其所产的椰枣也是其重要作物。椰枣树的果实椰枣、椰枣树枝（pa gešimmar）、椰枣纤维（mangaga）和叶子（^{giš}ze$_2$-na）也作为 bala 税的课税形式。另外，术语 ^{giš}eme-sig 或 eme-sig 指一种植物（可能是树），nig$_2$-ki-luh 指一种植物的种子。

除了树木的原木或木料之外，许多木制品也作为 bala 税的课税形式。这些木制品包括：木板（^{giš}e$_2$-da）、窄木板（^{giš}mi-ri$_2$-za）、铺板（^{giš}u$_3$）、木条（^{giš}ka-ab 或 ^{giš}kab）、杆（^{giš}dim 或 ^{giš}dim$_2$）、弯棍（^{giš}gam-gam-ma）、撑船杆（^{giš}gi-muš，或译为船舵）、锭子（^{giš}bala，或译为纺锤）、锄（^{giš}al）、水管（kuš$_3$）。另外，术语 ^{giš}dusu 指一种盛土和砖的篮子，^{giš}umbin 指一种船的部件①。还有以下几种树木或者木制品的具体含义未知：^{giš}ka-gal-lum，^{giš}murgu$_2$，^{giš}par$_4$ 和 ^{giš}zi 等。

（五）陶器

两河流域地区尤其是南部的苏美尔地区虽然缺乏树木、金属和石头等自然资源，但是却广泛分布着黏土，人们因地取材，用黏土制成了书写楔形文字的泥板以及建造神庙和房舍的泥砖。在日常生活中，他们用

---

① P. Steinkeller, "The Foresters of Umma: Toward a Definition of Ur III Labor", in M. A. Power (ed.), *Labor in the Ancient Near East*, AOS 68, New Haven: American Oriental Society, 1987, pp. 92 – 93.

黏土烧制成陶器，① 主要是陶罐（dug），不同种类的陶罐作为 bala 税的课税形式。这些陶罐的术语前面一般都加有限定符 dug，包括大陶罐（dug gal）、啤酒罐（^{dug}dida$_2$）、盖碗（^{dug}utul$_2$，或译为大碗），还有一些具体含义不明的陶罐或者容器，包括以下术语：

^{dug}hal	一种陶罐
^{dug}kun-du$_3$	一种容器
^{dug}munu$_4$ u$_3$	一种容器
^{dug}nam-ha-ru-um	一种容器
^{dug}sila$_3$-banda$_3$^{da}	一种容器
^{dug}sila$_3$ bur-zi	一种容器
^{dug}ta$_2$-bil$_3$-tum	一种容器
^{dug}za$_3$-še$_3$-la$_2$	一种容器

（六）皮制品

古代两河流域有大量的牲畜和野生动物，它们除了供宗教祭祀和人们食用之外，其皮毛也作为主要的副产品被制成各种日常用品。皮制品作为 bala 税的课税形式，在文献中记载的并不是很多，主要有两种皮袋或者皮包，^{kuš}a-ga$_2$-la$_2$ 和 ^{kuš}du$_{10}$-gan，其术语前面都加有限定符 kuš 表示"（动物）皮"。例如：

BPOA 7 2092（SS 1，Umma）
正面：

10 ^{kuš}a-ga$_2$-la$_2$	10 个 agala 皮袋
15 ^{kuš}du$_{10}$-gan	15 个 dugan 皮袋
ki A-kal-la-ta	从阿卡拉处
^{d}Šara$_2$-za-me	沙拉扎美
šu ba-ti	收到了

---

① W. Sallaberger, *Der Babylonische Töpfer und Seine Gefässe: Nach Urkunden altsumerischer bis altbabylonischer Zeit sowie Lexikalischen und Literarischen Zeugnissen*, Mesopotamian History and Environment 3, Gent: Universiteit Gent, 1996; R. Moorey, *Ancient Mesopotamian Materials and Industries: The Archaeological Evidence*, Winona Lake: Eisenbrauns, 1999, pp. 141–165.

背面：
ša₃ bala-a   作为 bala 税的一部分
mu ᵈŠu-ᵈSuen lugal   舒辛 1 年

（七）石制品、沥青

古代两河流域南部缺乏石料资源，需要从周边地区进口。两河流域人们除了将石料用于建筑和雕刻之外，在日常生活中也制作和使用大量的石制品。[①] 在乌尔第三王朝的 bala 税文献中，记载了一种石制的磨臼（ⁿᵃ⁴šu-se₃-ga），应该是用来碾磨粮食或者其他物品，不过这种石制品作为 bala 税的课税形式还是比较少见的。除了石制品外，沥青（esir₂）也作为 bala 税的课税形式。比如下面一个例子：

ITT 5 6954（AS 9，Girsu）
正面：
12 ⁿᵃ⁴šu-se₃-ga   12 个石制磨臼
6 naga₄-esir₂   6 个（磨沥青用的）研钵
1 naga₄-geš   1 个（磨草用的）研钵
ki Lu₂-ᵈNin-šubur-ta   从卢宁舒布尔处
背面：
bala-še₃   作为 bala 税
kišib Ur-nig₂   乌尔尼格收到了
giri₃ Ur-ᵈBa-ba₆ šabra   经手人：神庙主管乌尔巴巴
mu en Ga-eš ᵏⁱ ba-hun   阿马尔辛 9 年

（八）金属制品

金属制品作为 bala 税的课税形式在文献中记载的十分少见。[②] 这些金属制品基本上都是铜器，被用作容器或者农具，包括 ᵘʳᵘᵈᵃha-bu₃-da 指

---

① R. Moorey, *Ancient Mesopotamian Materials and Industries: The Archaeological Evidence*, Winona Lake: Eisenbrauns, 1999, pp. 74 – 110.

② H. Limet, *Le travail du métal au pays de Sumer au temps de la III\ᵉ dynastie d'Ur*, Paris: Société d'Édition, 1960; R. Moorey, *Ancient Mesopotamian Materials and Industries: The Archaeological Evidence*, Winona Lake: Eisenbrauns, 1999, pp. 216 – 301.

一种农具（可能是斧子或锄），^{uruda}zi-ir 指一种铜罐，^{uruda}ab-ri$_2$-na 指一种铜器。

（九）羊毛、布料及纺织品

古代两河流域饲养大量的绵羊（udu），羊毛（siki）是重要的副产品，[1] 也是温马行省和拉伽什—吉尔苏行省向中央缴纳的主要 bala 税形式之一。除此之外，一些纺织品（tug$_2$ kal 和^{tug2}uš-bar）以及绳子（eš$_2$）也作为 bala 税的课税形式。

（十）牲畜

古代两河流域是世界上农业的发源地之一，也是最早驯化动物的地区之一。古代两河流域最主要的牲畜是牛（公牛 gu$_4$，母牛 ab$_2$）、羊（包括绵羊 udu 和山羊 maš$_2$-gal）和驴（anše）。其中，牛和驴主要作为役畜，饲养羊主要是为了获取羊肉、羊皮、羊毛、羊奶等。牛羊也是用于宗教祭祀活动的主要献祭动物，这些献祭牛羊一般都是用大麦饲料育肥的（udu niga 和 gu$_4$ niga）。除了成年牛羊之外，还有大量的牛犊（amar）和羊羔（绵羊羔 sila$_4$，山羊羔 maš$_2$）。在乌尔第三王朝的经济文献中，记载了大量的牲畜和野生动物（羚羊、鹿、野羊、野驴和熊等），主要记载动物的经济文献来自普兹瑞什达干，它本身就是乌尔第三王朝的牲畜再分配中心（集散地），于舒尔吉 39 年建立，一直持续到伊比辛 2 年。[2] 另外，温马文献

---

[1] H. Waetzoldt, *Untersuchungen zur Neusumerischen Textilindustrie*, Rome: Istituto per l'Oriente, 1972; H. Waetzoldt, "The Colours and Variety of Fabrics from Mesopotamia during the Ur III Period (2050 BC)", in C. Michel and M.-L. Nosch (eds.), *Textile Terminologies in the Ancient Near East and the Mediterranean from the Third to the First Millennium BC*, Ancient Textiles Series 8, Oxford: Oxbow Books, 2010, pp. 201–209; E. Andersson Strand, M. Cybulska, "Visualising Ancient Textiles-how to make a Textile Visible on the Basis of an Interpretation of an Ur III Text", in M.-L Nosch, H. Koefoed and E. Andersson Strand (eds.), *Textile Production and Consumption in the Ancient Near East: Archaeology, Epigraphy, Iconography*, Ancient Textiles Series 12, Oxford and Oakville: Oxbow Books, 2013, pp. 113–127; R. Firth, "Considering the Finishing of Textiles based on Neo-Sumerian Inscriptions from Girsu", in M.-L. Nosch, H. Koefoed and E. Andersson Strand (eds.), *Textile Production and Consumption in the Ancient Near East: Archaeology, Epigraphy, Iconography*, Ancient Textiles Series 12, Oxford and Oakville: Oxbow Books, 2013, pp. 140–160.

[2] 参见 C. Liu, *Organization, Administrative Practices and Written Documentation in Mesopotamia during the Ur III Period (c. 2112–2004 BC): A Case Study of Puzriš-Dagan in the Reign of Amar-Suen*, Kārum-Emporion-Forum: Beiträge zum Wirtschafts-, Rechts-und Sozialgeschichte des östlichen Mittelmeerraums und Altvorderasiens 3 (KEF 3), Münster: Ugarit-Verlag, 2017.

第二章 核心区 bala 税

中有将近 1/5 的文献是关于牲畜的记载,① 吉尔苏文献中也有不少关于牲畜的记载。

在乌尔第三王朝的 bala 税系统里，牲畜有别于其他的税种。除牲畜之外的 bala 税都是单向的流动，即从地方到中央的流向，地方向中央缴纳 bala 税。而牲畜作为 bala 税则是双向的，既有从地方到中央的流动，也有从中央到地方的流动。普兹瑞什达干文献记载的牲畜都是从中央到地方行省的流向，似乎是作为行省 bala 税的一种补偿或者回馈方式。而温马文献记载了温马向中央缴纳牲畜 bala 税的情况，但是其数量要远远少于从中央流向地方的牲畜。下面两个例子，一个是普兹瑞什达干文献中记载的牲畜从中央到地方的流向，另一个是温马文献中记载的牲畜从地方到中央的流向。

1. 普兹瑞什达干文献：
PPAC 5 1781（AS 7 viii, Drehem）
正面：

160 udu niga	160 只育肥绵羊
sa$_2$-du$_{11}$ lugal	定期的王室供应
bala-a zi-ga	作为 bala 税被支出
ki En-dingir-mu-ta	从恩丁吉尔姆处
Ur-^{d}Li$_9$-si$_4$ ensi$_2$ Umma^{ki}	温马总督乌尔里希

背面：

i$_3$-dab$_5$	收到了
iti šu-eš-ša	第 8 月
mu Hu-uh$_2$-nu-ri^{ki} ba-hul	阿马尔辛 7 年

这篇文献记载了 160 只羊从普兹瑞什达干的官员恩丁吉尔姆处，作为 bala 税（的回馈）被支出给温马的总督乌尔里希。在普兹瑞什达干文献中，还有很多这样的记录。

---

① M. Stepien, *Animal Husbandry in the Ancient Near East: A Prosopographic Study of Third-Millennium Umma*, Bethesda: CDL Press, 1996, p. 16.

2. 温马文献：

BIN 5 80（S 43，Umma）

正面：

83 udu bar-su-ga	83 只已剪羊毛的绵羊
67 sila₄ bar-gal₂	67 只未剪羊毛的绵羊羔
46 maš₂	46 只山羊
zi-ga bala-a	作为 bala 税被缴纳
ša₃ Nibru^ki	到尼普尔

背面：

ki Ba-sa₆-ta	从巴萨处
giri₃ Ur-ni₉-gar kurušda	经手人是育肥师乌尔尼伽尔
mu en ᵈNanna maš-e i₃-pad₃	舒尔吉 43 年

这篇文献记载了 196 只羊从温马行省，作为 bala 税被缴纳给中央（尼普尔），巴萨是温马行省主管牲畜 bala 税的官员（详见本章第三节）。

从乌尔第三王朝的经济文献中，我们知道，乌尔第三王朝中央（乌尔、尼普尔、普兹瑞什达干）的动物主要不是来自内行省（核心区）的 bala 税，而是来自外行省（外围区）的 gun₂ ma-da 税（见第三章）。所以可以说，牲畜并不是 bala 税的主要课税形式，而是中央回馈给地方的主要形式，这些回馈一般发生在行省的 bala 税缴纳期内。它是乌尔第三王朝进行物资再分配的一种主要方式，有利于中央政府加强对地方行省的直接控制。

（十一）白银

两河流域地区不产白银，而是从周边地区（如安纳托利亚高原）进口白银。白银（ku₃-babbar）作为 bala 税的课税形式，依然属于实物税的范畴，但是也与货币税有着密切的关系。[①] 白银的这种 bala 税课税形式，主要被记

[①] 在学术界，对古代两河流域白银的货币功能的讨论由来已久，并且有诸多的争议。对于两河流域后期，尤其是新巴比伦时期的白银货币功能，学术界基本上已经达成了共识，但是对于乌尔第三王朝时期的白银是否具有货币的功能，目前学术界依然没有达成共识。参见 P. Paoletti,"Elusive Silver? Evidence for the Circulation of Silver in the Ur III State", *KASKAL. Rivista di storia, ambienti e culture del Vicino Oriente Antico*, Vol. 5 (2008), pp. 127 - 158；欧阳晓莉《两河流域乌尔第三王朝白银的货币功能探析》，《世界历史》2016 年第 5 期。

录在温马文献和吉尔苏文献中，是温马行省和拉伽什—吉尔苏行省的 bala 税形式之一。另外，在伊利萨格里格文献中也有一些白银充当 bala 税课税形式的记载，其内容与温马文献和吉尔苏文献大抵相同。比如下面这个例子：

JCS 38 37 11（SS 9 x, Irisagrig）

正面：

1 ma-na ku$_3$-babbar　　　　　1 米纳白银

mu bala-a-še$_3$　　　　　　　作为 bala 税

ki Tu-ra-am-i$_3$-li$_2$-ta　　　　从图兰伊里处

Iš-me-ilum u$_3$ Na-ni　　　　　伊什美伊鲁姆和纳尼

背面：

šu ba-ti　　　　　　　　　　收到了

iti nig$_2$-e-ga　　　　　　　　第 10 月

mu ^{d}Šu-^{d}Suen lugal Uri$_5^{ki}$-ma-ke$_4$　　舒辛 9 年

e$_2$ ^{d}Šara$_2$ Umma^{ki}-ka mu-du$_3$

（十二）劳动力或劳役

劳役属于徭役的一种。[①] 徭役指的是政府强迫民众负担的无偿劳动，包括兵役、劳役和杂役。[②] 乌尔第三王朝时期的兵役和杂役情况不明，但是关于劳役的文献记载却十分丰富。劳动力也是 bala 税的课税形式之一，是一种特殊的赋税形式，它征收的不是物，而是人。在乌尔第三王朝的温马文献和吉尔苏文献中，记载有两类劳动力：guruš 和 geme$_2$，前者指男劳动力，后者指女劳动力。[③] 其中，guruš 是一种由政府部门雇佣的按日结算

[①] 关于乌尔第三王朝的劳动力或劳役研究，参见 B. Studevent-Hickman, *The Organization of Manual Labor in Ur III Babylonia*, PhD dissertation, Harvard University, 2006.

[②] 赵德馨主编：《中国经济史辞典》，湖北辞书出版社 1990 年版，第 66—67 页。

[③] 关于 guruš 和 geme$_2$ 的身份，一直是学术界的一个争论问题。20 世纪 60 年代，苏联亚述学家贾科诺夫（Igor Diakonoff）认为 guruš 和 geme$_2$ 的身份是奴隶。70 年代，美国亚述学家格尔布（Ignace Gelb）则认为是半自由的农奴。这一争论持续了十余年。80 年代末，美国亚述学家、哈佛大学教授斯坦因凯勒对 guruš 和 geme$_2$ 这两种劳动力进行了细致深入地研究，支持了格尔布的观点，认为 guruš 和 geme$_2$ 并不是奴隶，而是类似于农奴的性质，具有一定的自由。参见 B. Studevent-Hickman, *The Organization of Manual Labor in Ur III Babylonia*, PhD dissertation, Harvard University, 2006, pp. 11 - 13.

的劳动力,有固定的薪资标准,其工作内容主要是农活,包括挖掘水渠、耕作、耙地、播种、灌溉、收割和运输庄稼作物(主要是大麦)。收获大麦是一个系统的工作,guruš 劳动力使用镰刀收割大麦,其他人将割下的大麦捆成束,然后将这些成捆的大麦运送到打谷场,进行打谷脱皮,最后将大麦粒存放到谷仓,将秸秆用作建筑材料或者直接作为燃料。他们既可以按日被雇佣,也可以按月或者按照实际工作量被雇佣。geme$_2$ 女劳动力分为家用的田地用的,在田地里,她们的主要工作是灌溉,以及在收割大麦之后,将大麦捆成束,并且用篮子和皮袋运输大麦。即使他们的工作一样,geme$_2$ 女工只能拿到 guruš 男工一半的薪资。

乌尔第三王朝时期的人口及社会等级可以分为三类:自由民、半自由民和奴隶。自由民(eren$_2$ 或 dumu-gir$_{15}$)享有完全的公民权,他们一个月需要为国家服劳役半个月,即一年中需要服役半年,另外半年属于自由支配的时间。半自由民(UN-il$_2$)只享有部分的公民权,他们整年都要为国家服役,每个月只有三天时间可以自由支配。这两类人都可以从国家得到粮食配给。[①]

乌尔第三王朝的 bala 劳役主要适用于 eren$_2$ 阶层,他们还可以分为两组,第一组是享有特权的阶层,包括各级官员、各种专业人员和工匠,他们从国家得到土地配额,供私人使用。当他们履行完国家的劳役后,可以继续从事原有的职业,以及管理自己的份地。第二组 eren$_2$ 阶层只享有少量权力,并没有从国家得到份地,他们大多数是没有专业技能的自由劳动者。在服役期间,他们的工作主要集中在农业和建筑工作方面。而在自由时间(每月有 15 天)里,由于没有一技之长,他们还是从事类似的工作,只不过可以从工作中获得工资(a$_2$ hun-ga$_2$),这时的工资往往是他们服役时期获得配给的三倍。[②] 由于 eren$_2$ 阶层的半工半薪特征,即一年只服役半年,所以他们在另外半年的自由时间里可以作为雇佣劳动力继续赚取工资。据吉尔苏文献记载,涉及 bala 税的 eren$_2$ 阶层一般分为两种:一种是

---

① I. J. Gelb, "The Ancient Mesopotamian Ration System", *Journal of Near Eastern Studies*, Vol. 24, 1965, pp. 230 – 243.

② P. Steinkeller, "Archival Practices at Babylonia in the Third Millennium", in M. Brosius (ed.), *Ancient Archives and Archival Traditions*: *Concepts of Record-Keeping in the Ancient World*, Oxford: Oxford University Press, 2003, pp. 44 – 45.

"正在服 bala 劳役"（bala-a gub-ba），另一种是"不在服 bala 劳役"（bala-a tuš-a），这也是 eren₂ 劳动力的工作时期，一半时间是服役期，另一半时间是免役期。① 具体而言，由于处于 bala 服役期的 eren₂ 劳动力都是本地的劳动力，所以在这一时期本地所要雇佣的劳动力只能来自外地（因为本地劳动力正在服役，无法被雇佣）。而当本地劳动力处于免役期时，他们就可以被雇佣。

二 文献概况

乌尔第三王朝的 bala 税证据，主要来自经济管理文献。目前，我们并没有发现专门记录乌尔第三王朝赋税的法律档案和赋税档案，所以我们只能从十余万的经济管理文献中筛选、提取与 bala 税相关的记录。借助于两大楔形文字数据库资源（CDLI 和 BDTNS），我们一共收集了 2881 篇关于 bala 的文献资料，这些文献主要来自温马、吉尔苏、普兹瑞什达干三个遗址。此外，还有少量文献来自伊利萨格里格、尼普尔、乌尔以及不明的来源地。这些文献按照来源地的分布统计如下（见表 2-7）：

表 2-7　　　　　　　　bala 税文献数量及比例统计表

出土遗址	bala 文献数量	比例
温马	1901	66.0%
吉尔苏	477	16.6%
普兹瑞什达干	390	13.5%
伊利萨格里格	49	1.7%
乌尔	19	0.6%
尼普尔	8	0.3%
其他	37	1.3%
共计	2881	100%

从上述统计数据可见，温马的 bala 文献数量是最多的，约占了 2/3。在温马的 bala 文献中，有 1544 篇文献都属于 ša bala-a 文献，约占温马 bala 文

---

① K. Maekawa, "New Texts on the Collective Labor Service of the Erin-People of Ur III Girsu", *Acta Sumerologica*, Vol. 10 (1988), pp. 37-94.

献总量的81.2%。其次是吉尔苏文献,与温马文献不同,吉尔苏文献中的 ša bala-a 文献数量很少,只有21篇,约占吉尔苏 bala 文献总量的4.4%。

温马文献和吉尔苏文献不仅在数量上是最多的,且由于这两种文献都属于行省档案,所以也是我们研究乌尔第三王朝行省经济和地方制度最重要的文献资料来源。与温马文献和吉尔苏文献不同的是,普兹瑞什达干文献不是地方行省档案,虽然普兹瑞什达干的地理位置在尼普尔行省之内,但是其文献并不属于尼普尔的行省档案,而是中央王室档案。普兹瑞什达干文献与温马文献、吉尔苏文献的第二个区别是,普兹瑞什达干文献记载的 bala 税形式基本上都是牲畜,其流向是从中央到地方,即从普兹瑞什达干动物再分配中心或者牲畜牧场流向地方行省,作为地方行省向中央缴纳 bala 税的一种回报或补偿。由于牲畜从中央向地方流动发生在 bala 税的赋税期之内,所以也作为 bala 税体系的一部分。在乌尔第三王朝的经济文献中,关于地方行省统治的文献基本上都来自温马行省和拉伽什—吉尔苏行省,而乌尔第三王朝其余的行省几乎没有文献出土,更没有关于 bala 税的记录,所以我们对于其他行省 bala 税的认识,只能从普兹瑞什达干文献中得到间接证据,而关于这些行省向中央缴纳的 bala 税情况,我们几乎完全不清楚。不过,随着近年来伽尔沙纳文献、[①]伊利萨格里格文献[②]以及其他文献档案[③]的陆续出土与出版问

[①] D. I. Owen, R. H. Mayr, *The Garšana Archives*, Cornell Univeristy Studies in Assyriology and Sumerology Volume 3, Bethesda: CDL Press, 2007; A. Kleinerman, D. I. Owen, *Analytical Concordance to the Garšana Archives*, Cornell Univeristy Studies in Assyriology and Sumerology Volume 4, Bethesda: CDL Press, 2009; D. I. Owen, *Garšana Studies*, Cornell Univeristy Studies in Assyriology and Sumerology Volume 6, Bethesda: CDL Press, 2011.

[②] D. I. Owen, *Cuneiform Texts Primarily from Iri-Saĝrig / Āl-Šarrākī and the History of the Ur III Period*, Nisaba 15, Bethesda: CDL Press, 2013; D. I. Owen, "New Additions to the Iri-Saĝrig/Al-Šarrākī Archives", in P. Corò, E. Devecchi, N. De Zorzi, M. Maiocchi (eds.), *Libiamo ne' lieti calici: Ancient Near Eastern Studies Presented to Lucio Milano on the occasion of his 65th Birthday by Pupils, Colleagues and Friends*, Alter Orient und Altes Testament 346, Münster: Ugarit-Verlag, 2016, pp. 337–362.

[③] 其他档案如西阿雅官员档案、图兰伊里官员档案和乌尔努斯卡官员档案,参见 S. J. Garfinkle, *Entrepreneurs and Enterprise in Early Mesopotamia: A Study of Three Archives from the Third Dynasty of Ur*, Cornell Univeristy Studies in Assyriology and Sumerology Volume 22, Bethesda: CDL Press, 2012. 阿拉德姆官员档案,参见 B. Studevent-Hickman, *Sumerian Texts from Ancient Iraq: From Ur III to 9/11*, Journal of Cuneiform Studies-Supplemental Series 5, Boston: Lockwood Press, 2018. 埃什努那出土文献,参见 H. Frankfort, S. Lloyd, T. Jacobsen, *The Gimilsin Temple and the Palace of the Rulers of Tell Asmar*, Oriental Institute Publications 43, Chicago: The University of Chicago Press, 1940, 不过这些文献只出版了目录,文献材料至今未能完全出版。

世，我们对于乌尔第三王朝其他地方行省的研究也会进一步深化。这里尤其指出，伊利萨格里格文献的出版，为我们初步探讨这个行省的统治情况提供了重要的第一手文献资料。可喜的是，在伊利萨格里格文献中，也要数量可观的 bala 税记录（目前仅发现 49 篇），这些文献的解读不仅丰富了我们对于乌尔第三王朝除了温马、吉尔苏之外的其他地方行省的认识，同时也为我们比较研究乌尔第三王朝的地方制度提供了直接的证据。

通过对上述三个遗址出土的 bala 文献的探讨，我们已经对乌尔第三王朝的 bala 文献有了更为深层的认识。接下来的章节，我们将依据这些研究成果，进一步对乌尔第三王朝的各个行省的 bala 税制度进行深入的探索，尤其是温马行省和拉伽什—吉尔苏行省。

第三节　温马行省的 bala 税

温马行省是仅次于拉伽什—吉尔苏行省的乌尔第三王朝的第二大行省。温马文献的数量是所有乌尔第三王朝出土文献中最多的，这些文献记录的大都是行省内部事务，是我们研究乌尔第三王朝行省管理体系的重要资料。据温马文献记载，温马向中央缴纳 bala 税固定在某月，称为温马 bala 税的纳税期限（简称 bala 税期），在不同的年份，这个 bala 税期所在月份也会有所不同，但是出入不会很大。温马的 bala 税大致跨越了 40 年时间，最早开始于舒尔吉 30 年，[①] 结束于伊比辛 3 年。[②]

一　课征形式

古代两河流域历史晚期，行省向中央政府缴纳的赋税主要以白银或货币为主，而在乌尔第三王朝时期，赋税的形式都是实物税。白银也出现在税赋文献中，但是数量极少。温马行省向中央缴纳的 bala 税有许多种实物，主要包括大麦、面粉、芦苇、木材、手工制品、劳动力和牲畜（其中牛羊最多），羊毛和纺织品数量很少。并不是行省的所有特产都能够充当 bala 赋税形式。与温马的这些非动物实物税一样，劳动力（guruš 或 geme$_2$

---

① 文献 SAT 211（S 30）.
② 文献 L'uomo 48（IS 3 xii d）.

劳役，erin₂ 可能指兵役）也是温马 bala 税重要的课税形式之一。温马文献中有大量劳动力作为 bala 税缴纳到尼普尔或者乌尔的记载，这些劳动力之中有会手艺的工匠，也有普通的劳动者从事粗重工作，比如磨面、装载、拖船等。

温马 bala 税的课税形式根据赋税的流动方向可以分为两个类别：一个是非动物类，bala 税都是从地方行省到中央政府的流动，另一个是动物类，bala 税既有从地方行省到中央政府的流动，又有从中央政府到地方行省的流动，并且以中央→地方的流向为主，中央到地方的赋税流向相当于今天的"税收返还"概念，即中央对地方的税收返还。① 中央的税收返还制度就其性质而言，是一种转移支付，是年年都有的经常性收入返还。或者说，是一种税收补贴制度和税收优惠政策。

通过对温马 bala 文献的整理，我们对温马 bala 税所涉及的课税形式的文献数量进行了分类统计。从而反映出温马 bala 税的课税形式的总体情况（见表 2–8）。

表 2–8　　　　　　　　温马行省 bala 税形式统计表

术语	课税形式	文献数量	所占比例
dabin	粗粒小麦粉	19	1.0%
dug	陶罐器	42	2.1%
duh	麸糠	14	0.7%
esir₂	沥青	20	1.0%
eša	一种精面粉	7	0.4%
ga	牛奶	3	0.2%
geš	树木、木料及木制品	288	14.5%
gi	芦苇及芦苇制品	782	39.4%
i₃/ i₃-nun	植物油、酥油	21	1.1%
kaš	啤酒	83	4.2%
ku₃-babbar	白银	25	1.3%

---

① 参见杜峻峰《税收返还制度》，《学习与研究》1994 年第 10 期；李万慧《"后营改增"时代中国税收返还制度改革方向探索——为税收返还制度正名》，《现代经济探讨》2017 年第 2 期。

续表

术语	课税形式	文献数量	所占比例
ku_6	鱼类	7	0.4%
kuš	皮制品	112	5.6%
nig_2-ar_3-ra	碾去壳的燕麦（小麦）	7	0.4%
ninda	面包	28	1.4%
siki	羊毛	9	0.5%
še	大麦	101	5.1%
šim	香料	8	0.4%
tug_2	布料	6	0.3%
u_2	草本植物	16	0.8%
uruda	铜制品	2	0.1%
zi_3	面粉	35	1.8%
ziz_2	二粒小麦	2	0.1%
zu_2-lum	椰枣	15	0.8%
ma_2	船	11	0.6%
$geme_2$ / guruš	劳动力	147	7.4%
udu / $maš_2$ / gu_4	牲畜	127	6.4%
	其他	49	2.5%
	总计	1986*	100%

* 注意，有的文献记载的课税形式不止一种，而是多种，所以统计的文献数量会比实际数量多。

上述的统计数据表明，温马行省 bala 税的课税形式最多的是芦苇及芦苇制品，[1] 其次是木料及木制品、皮制品等，此外，劳动力和牲畜也是很重要的课税形式，并且具有独特的征收方式。可以肯定的是，这些实物和劳动力都是温马行省本土出产的。温马行省地处两河流域南部的平原地

---

[1] 关于乌尔第三王朝温马行省的芦苇及芦苇制品，参见 H. Waetzoldt, "'Rohr' und dessen Verwendungsweisen anhand der neusumerischen Texte aus Umma", Bulletin on Sumerian Agriculture, Vol. 6, 1992, pp. 125 – 146.

带，靠近底格里斯河及其支流的沼泽地带，盛产芦苇和矮小的灌木林，这些芦苇和灌木具有多重用途，既可以建造房屋，也可以制造芦苇制品或木制品，比如容器、各类工具等小物件。所以说，芦苇和小灌木是温马行省最重要的经济作物。相反，大麦等粮食作物作为 bala 税的课税形式则相对较少。啤酒、植物油、鱼类和其他食物主要是提供给来自各地的信使和旅客，① 他们承担中央政府的任务，虽然这些 bala 税并没有被运到首都，但是其流向也算是从地方到中央。

从温马 bala 文献中，我们可以基本上准确地统计与总结出温马 bala 税课税形式的具体类别。但是也就仅此而已。我们对于温马 bala 税的其他方面，包括课征的对象、征收的方式、税收的具体用途以及税率，则很难从文献中得到准确的直接证据。这是因为，我们目前还没有发现关于 bala 税的专门档案文献和相关法律条文，即没有乌尔第三王朝的赋税档案或者财政档案。目前的温马 bala 文献记录的都是零散的 bala 缴纳情况，并没有总结性的汇总档案。

二 征税对象

征税对象又叫课税对象或征税客体，指税法规定对什么征税，是征税双方权利义务共同指向的客体或标的物，是区别一种税与另一种税的重要标志。② 毋庸置疑，乌尔第三王朝 bala 税的征税对象是各个行省的总督。但是在实际操作过程中，总督只是名义上的征税对象。而实际的征税对象是行省内提供赋税的各个机构负责人。在文献中，他们被标注以 ki PN-ta "来自某人、从某人处、从某人手中"。可惜的是，文献中仅提供了这些 bala 提供者的名字，很少记录他们的家族关系或者职业、名号。为此，我们对于这些人的认识十分有限。

从文献证据看，每个征税对象或 bala 税提供者似乎专门负责一种实物，每个人都负责不同的任务。③ 很有可能，这些提供者本身也是实物的

---

① 例如文献 SAT 3 2085（S 41 v 18）。
② 中国注册会计师协会：《税法》，经济科学出版社 2012 年版，第 9 页。
③ 例如，卢伽尔马古莱（Lugal-magurre）专门负责啤酒（文献 Touzalin 333，S 46），卢伽尔伊提达（Lugal-itida）负责陶器（文献 MVN 14 364，SS 1 viii），阿古（Agu）和塞什阿尼（Sheshani）负责芦苇（Agu，文献 UTI 3 2295，SS1；CM 26 53，--viii）。

生产制作者。例如，阿卡拉（Akalla）主要提供皮制品，他的头衔是 ašgab "皮革工人或皮匠"①。乌尔塔尔卢赫（Ur-TAR.LUH）是林务官员（护林人），专门提供木料。② 卢伽尔沙拉（Lugal-shala）是制陶工人（陶工），提供陶器。③

三 征收官员

温马 bala 税的征收官员一般是由行省的高级官员担任，他们先从 bala 税提供者的手中接收赋税，然后再将这些赋税运往中央机构或者中央管辖的指定目的地，从而完成征税任务。

这些征收官员包括：（1）行省总督。（2）首席神庙管理员（šabra）卢宁舒布尔和卢伽尔埃孜姆。④（3）沙拉神庙的牧牛监管（nu-banda$_3$ gu$_4$ ^{d}Šara$_2$，掌管沙拉神庙的领地）乌尔沙拉。（4）首席档案保管员（pisan-dub-ba）乌尔沙拉及其儿子们。他们都是温马行省的高级官吏或者权贵阶层。其他征税官员还包括：（5）涂油祭司（gudu$_4$），比如穆尼（宁乌拉神庙涂油祭司）、卢伽尔尼拉加雷（尼拉伽尔神庙涂油祭司）。⑤（6）行省总督的直接部下——总督卫队（守卫，aga$_3$-us$_2$），比如卢伽之子阿杜的卫队（aga$_3$-us$_2$ ensi$_2$）。⑥（7）王室侍从或者驯兽师（kuš$_7$，具体含义不明），⑦ 最著名的官员是乌尔尼伽尔和乌尔埃埃。

---

① 文献 Syracuse 40（S 46），Princeton 140（SS 1），RA 49 no. 37（S 42 or AS 6 ix）。关于阿卡拉以及温马行省的皮革制造业，参见 H. Neumann, *Handwerk in Mesopotamien: Untersuchungen zu seiner Organisation in der Zeit der III. Dynastie von Ur*, Berlin: Akademie-Verlag, 1987, pp. 128 – 134.

② 例如文献 MVN 3 231（AS 6 viii）.

③ 例如文献 BIN 3 615（AS 9 viii 26）.

④ 卢宁舒布尔是温马沙拉神庙的主管，卢伽尔埃孜姆是哪个神庙的主管我们不得而知。关于卢伽尔埃孜姆，参见 A. Archi, F. Pomponio, "Tavolette Economiche Neo-Sumeriche dell'Università Pontificia Salesiana", *Vicino Oriente*, Vol. 8（1989），p. 40；R. Mayr, *The Seal Impressions of Ur III Umma*, PhD dissertation, University of Leiden, 1997, pp. 351 – 352.

⑤ 术语 Nig$_2$-lagar 可能是神殿的名字。参见 F. A. M. Wiggerman, "An Unrecognized Synonym of Sumerian *sukkal*, 'Vizier'", *Zeitschrift für Assyriologie und Vorderasiatische Archäologie*, Vol. 78, 1988, pp. 225 – 240.

⑥ 例如文献 Princeton 234, MVN 14 289.

⑦ 这是一个级别非常高的官员，可能仅次于行省总督，参见 T. M. Sharlach, *Provincial Taxation and the Ur III State*, Cuneiform Monographs 26, Leiden and Boston: Brill-Styx, 2004, p. 45, p. 125 note 70.

通过追溯这些征收官员的家族世系关系（印章上的证据），我们可以发现，他们之间存在着密切的联系，可能来自行省的诸多有势力的家族。

这些征收官员（bala 税接收者），有自己专门负责的部门和征税形式。比如，阿古专门负责接收木制品，作为葬礼的供应品。阿图专门负责为"禁忌房"（e₂-uz-ga）这一机构接收木料和木制工具。彼杜加作为温马行省专门负责收 bala 税的官员，负责为普兹瑞什达干的仓库接收芦苇及芦苇制用具。卡什（Kash）专门负责接收粮食，以供给王室卫队（可能是禁军，lugal-ra-us₂-sa）。穆尼专门负责为"牛屠宰房"（e₂-gu₄-gaz，位于普兹瑞什达干）接收木材和陶器。乌马尼为来访者提供啤酒。

四 税收目的地和税收用途

温马行省向中央政府缴纳的 bala 税，一部分被运往首都乌尔、尼普尔、普兹瑞什达干或者乌鲁克，另一部分被运往温马行省内隶属中央政府的军队驻地，供给住在温马的军事机构。比如，据一篇文献记载，[①] 一个芦苇席（作为 bala 税）被征收用来"覆盖将军的盖碗房"（e₂^{dug}utul₂ šagina-ne-ka dul₉-de₃，可能指食堂）。另据一篇文献记载，[②] 啤酒（作为 bala 税）被缴纳给正在拖船的高级士兵（aga₃-us₂）享用。[③]

中央政府的朝臣或者王室成员到温马行省视察，他们的出行费用也是由 bala 税来承担。这些税收主要是为了招待朝臣、王室成员和外国使节。[④] 有时，实物也运往王室成员的代理人那里。例如，芦苇束被支出给王后阿比西姆提的首席神庙管理员卢伽尔马古莱。[⑤] 还有，国王自己的使者（sukkallugal）也代表国王来接收 bala 税。[⑥] 外国使节主要来自马里、

[①] 文献 UTI 6 3806（AS 9 viii）。

[②] 文献 MVN 15 229（AS 9-SS 3）。

[③] 关于术语 aga₃-us₂，参见 T. Gomi, Y. Hirose, K. Hirose, *Neo-Sumerian Administrative Texts of the Hirose Collection*, Potomac: Capital Decisions Limited, 1990, pp. 42–43.

[④] 比如文献 UTI 4 2762（AS 8）。

[⑤] 文献 AAICAB 1/2 pl. 121 1967–1497（AS 1 i）。

[⑥] 文献 MVN 14 419（SS 2），MVN 14 374（SS 2）。

埃布拉、马尔哈西，外国高级官员有巴巴提（王后阿比西姆提之兄①）、胡里巴尔②（杜杜里统治者），这些文献记载的都是小额的 bala 税支出。这些赋税不是支出到首都，而是在温马行省内作为代表中央政府的支出。

（一）在行省内为王室代表所使用

赋税缴纳给王室在行省当地的代表使用的记录，也归为王室档案。这些 bala 税在当地被作为祭祀品用于行省的祭祀活动（代表中央政府或者国王）。大多数在温马行省内的祭祀活动所需的牺牲，都是由国王提供（来自普兹瑞什达干机构），由行省总督负责，有时王室祭祀官员（sagi，"持杯者"）亲自督办（经办人）。③ 行省总督自己也接收 bala 税，在当地代表国王献祭。④ 发往中央的 bala 税，一些用于宗教祭祀活动，在文献中所使用的术语为 suskur$_2$-še$_3$ "作为献祭"。有些 bala 税用于王后主持的献祭仪式（siskur$_2$ nin）⑤、国王主持的献祭仪式（siskur$_2$ lugal）⑥、在星夜举行的献祭活动（siskur$_2$ mul）⑦，以及在果园举行的献祭仪式（siskur$_2$ kiri$_6$ PN, e$_2$-u$_4$-7）⑧。此外，有些 bala 税也可以供给占卜师（maš-šu-gid$_2$-gid$_2$）⑨ 或者驱魔师（maš-maš）⑩，他们虽然在温马行省工作，但是却被认为是中央政府的官员，代表中央政府的利益。

---

① R. M. Whiting, "Tiš-atal of Nineveh and Babati, Uncle of Šu-Sin", *Journal of Cuneiform Studies*, Vol. 28, No. 3 (1976), pp. 173 – 182.

② P. Notizia, "Hulibar, Duhduh (u) NI e la frontiera orientale", in M. G. Biga and M. Liverani (eds.), *ana turri gimilli: studi dedicati al Padre Werner R. Mayer, S. J. da amici e allievi*, Vicino Oriente-Quaderno 5, Rome: Università degli Studi di Roma "La Sapienza", 2010, pp. 269 – 291.

③ W. Sallaberger, *Der kultische Kalender der Ur III-Zeit*, Untersuchungen zur Assyriologie und Vorderasiatischen Archäologie 7/1 – 2, Berlin and New York: Walter de Gruyter, 1993, pp. 230 – 231, 251, 272.

④ 文献 Syracuse 254（S 47 ii）。

⑤ 文献 MVN 14 399（SS 2）。

⑥ 文献 Syracuse 254（S 47 ii）。

⑦ 文献 MVN 14 75（S 38）。

⑧ 文献 MVN 14 124（S 35 vii）。

⑨ 文献 UTI 5 3060（undated）。参见 J. Sasson, "About 'Mari and the Bible'", *Revue d'Assyriologie et d'Archéologie Orientale*, Vol. 92, 1998, p. 116; W. Sallaberger, "Ur III-Zeit", in W. Sallaberger, A. Westenholz, *Mesopotamien: Akkade-Zeit und Ur III-Zeit*, OBO 160/3, Freiburg, Schweiz: Universitätsverlag/Göttingen: Vandenhoeck und Ruprecht, 1999, p. 187.

⑩ 文献 TCNU 544（AS 1）。

（二）发往首都为中央政府所使用

除了供给行省内的王室成员之外，更多的 bala 税则直接被运往首都乌尔（Uri₅ki-še₃）①、乌鲁克②、尼普尔③、普兹瑞什达干（或埃萨格达纳）④、其他行省、王室所辖机构（恩利尔神庙、王家牲畜屠宰场、"禁忌房"（e₂-uz-ga）以及已故国王的纪念堂等。

1. 乌尔

据文献记载，作为 bala 税形式的粮食（饲料）、芦苇和木材被用船从温马运载到乌尔，这是最常见的 bala 纳税方式。⑤ 有的温马文献记载的每次粮食纳税量很少，比如一次运送 19 古尔麦麸到乌尔。⑥ 有的文献记载的数量很大，比如 724 古尔麦麸被运到乌尔。⑦ 在很多情况下，bala 税的征收操作环节不需要经过温马行省总督的直接干预，而是直接从实物赋税所在地被运送到中央的目的地，不需要绕道先到温马行省总督驻地，再运往中央。比如，66 古尔大麦从阿皮沙尔（温马行省的一个城市）的粮仓直接被运到乌尔。⑧ 又如，160 古尔大麦从一个特定的打谷场被运到乌尔。⑨ 在温马文献中，很少关于芦苇和木材船运到乌尔的记载。运送芦苇和木材到乌尔数量最多的一次，发生在舒尔吉 33 年，有 2260 束芦苇和 79 件柳树木料被船运到乌尔。⑩

2. 乌鲁克

乌鲁克是温马行省 bala 税的另一个目的地。但是关于这方面的文献记载很少，可能的原因，一是目前发现的相关文献数量少，可能还有许多相关文献没有被发现和释读，二是温马行省向乌鲁克缴纳的 bala 税本身数量就不多。据一篇文献记载，1920 束芦苇（共 14 捆）、1800 束柳条（共 12

---

① 文献 SAT 2 89（S 34 vii），MVN 16 798（SS 4）。
② 文献 Umma 58（S 46），Syracuse 195（S 48 i），AUCT 3 255（AS 6），UTI 4 2699（SS 3），UTI 4 2833（SS 3）。
③ 文献 Syracuse 30（S 40），Nik 2 193（AS 1 i），CM 26 39（AS 4）。
④ 文献 NYPL 324（S 48），Nebraska 10（AS 1 i）。
⑤ 文献 UTI 5 3370（AS 8），MVN 16 798（SS 4）。
⑥ 文献 MVN 14 409（SS 2）。
⑦ 文献 BIN 5 119（AS 7–8）。
⑧ 文献 MVN 20 162（S45 ii）。
⑨ 文献 AAICAB 2 1935–557（S 47 ii）。
⑩ 文献 MVN 15 162（S 33 viii）。

捆)、212 束杨树条（共 3 捆），从彼杜加处，作为 bala 税被运到乌鲁克，神庙主管杜加之子卢沙拉接收了。①

3. 尼普尔

在温马文献中，很少关于"到尼普尔"（Nibru^{ki}-še$_3$）的记载。从温马运送到尼普尔的 bala 税形式多样，主要包括牲畜②、大麦③、木材及木制品④、芦苇及芦苇制品⑤等。文献中并没有记载这些芦苇及其他物品是如何被使用的。木材及木制品数量不多，一般都存放在尼普尔的仓库里。⑥ 芦苇的数目从几十、几百束⑦到几万束不等。⑧ 其中，运送芦苇数量最多的一年是阿马尔辛 1 年，有 65930 束芦苇从温马行省被运送到尼普尔。例如：

Or 47-49 314（AS 1，Umma）

正面

44330 sa gi	44330 束芦苇
gu-nigin$_2$-ba 18-ta	共 18 捆
21600 sa gi	21600 束芦苇
gu-nigin$_2$-ba 17 sa	共 17 捆

背面

ša$_3$ Nibru^{ki}	（运到）尼普尔
ki Šeš-kal-la-ta	从塞什卡尔处
kišib Bi$_2$-du$_{11}$-ga	彼杜加加印（接收）
mu ^{d}Amar-^{d}Suen lugal	阿马尔辛 1 年

---

① 文献 Umma 58（S 46）。
② 文献 BIN 5 80（S 43），CM 26 3（S 48）。
③ 文献 Fs Lenoble 166 no. 26（S 30 ix），SNAT 293（S 45），SAKF 24（AS 6 iv），YOS 18 123（AS 8 viii-AS 9）。
④ 文献 Nik 2 193（AS 1 i），UTI 4 2621（SS 1 viii），BPOA 7 2921（SS 3），UTI 3 1773（SS 3），BPOA 1 374（SS 4 vi）。
⑤ 文献 BIN 5 84（S 33），Syracuse 30（S 40），BPOA 7 2440（S 47），Rochester 186（S 48），Nik 2 193（AS 1 i），BPOA 7 2858（SS 6）。
⑥ 例如文献 AAICAB 1/1 pl. 48 1911-489（AS 2 xii），OIMA 2630（S 47 xii）。
⑦ 据文献 Umma 52（S 44 xii）记载，300 束芦苇被支出到尼普尔。
⑧ 据文献 UTI 5 3117（S 47 xii）和 UTI 5 3395（S 47 xii）记载，在舒尔吉 47 年，温马运送了至少 20 145 束芦苇到尼普尔。

4. 普兹瑞什达干

许多文献记载了从温马直接发送 bala 税到普兹瑞什达干机构。在这些 bala 税形式中，最多的种类是芦苇及芦苇制品。① 最多一次芦苇被运到普兹瑞什达干发生在阿马尔辛 1 年，有 8735 束芦苇、1007 件木制品以及 57 件芦苇制品②。其次，在阿马尔辛 2 年（或者舒尔吉 45 年），还有 7218 束芦苇被运到普兹瑞什达干。③ 负责温马行省芦苇 bala 税的专职官员叫彼杜加，他是拉阿萨（La'asa）之子。④ 彼杜加可能在一年中有半年时间住在普兹瑞什达干，协助温马总督接收和记录征税情况。此外，运往普兹瑞什达干的 bala 税还有沥青、⑤ 粮食（大麦）⑥ 和木材等。

5. 其他行省

温马行省的 bala 税除了送往首都，也被运送到其他的行省，比如舒鲁帕克⑦、拉伽什—吉尔苏⑧和伊利萨格里格。⑨ 这些活动均发生在舒尔吉统治时期，很可能 bala 税从温马被运送到这些行省之后，被用于当地的祭祀活动。比如：

Nisaba 9 142（S 33 viii，Umma）

正面

20 udu sa$_2$-du$_{11}$ ^{d}Nin-hur-sag	20 只绵羊，作为献给宁胡尔萨格的定期供应
Iri-sag-rig$_7^{ki}$-še$_3$	到伊利萨格里格
ki Lugal-a$_2$-zi-da-ta	从卢伽尔阿孜达处

---

① 比如，文献 Syracuse 434 记载有 3636 束芦苇、2730 束柳条。
② 文献 OIM A02758（AS 1 i），OIM A02747（AS 1 vii），OIM A02670（AS 1 xi），OIM A02751（AS 1 xii）。
③ 文献 SACT 2 148（S 45 or AS 2 xii）。
④ 彼杜加的印章铭文为：Bi$_2$-du$_{11}$-ga dub-sar dumu La-a-sa$_6$ "彼杜加，书吏，拉阿萨之子"，参见文献 SAT 2 285（S 41），Nebraska 10（AS 1 i），SNAT 464（SS 2）。
⑤ 文献 NYPL 324（S 48）。
⑥ 文献 BIN 5 242（S 48）记载 220 古尔粮食船运到普兹瑞什达干。
⑦ 文献 Nik 2200（S 46 ii）记载舒鲁帕克总督的代表卢伽尔埃孜姆（Lugal-ezem lu$_2$ ensi$_2$ Šuruppak^{ki}）从温马总督手中接收 bala 税。
⑧ 文献 AUCT 3218（S 41）记载吉尔苏的代表（lu$_2$ Gir$_2$-su^{ki}）接收啤酒作为 bala 税。
⑨ 文献 Nisaba 9 142（S 33 viii），Syracuse 7（S 48），Aleppo 132（S –）。

Ba-sa₆ i₃-dab₅　　　　　　　　　巴萨接收了
ša₃ bala-a　　　　　　　　　　　在 bala 之中
背面
iti e₂-iti-6　　　　　　　　　　　第 8 月
mu us₂-sa Si-mu-ru-um^ki a-ra₂ 3-kam ba-hul　　舒尔吉 33 年

6. 王室直辖机构/王室经营产业

温马行省缴纳的 bala 税被运送到许多王室直辖机构或王室经营产业，包括尼普尔的恩利尔神庙、王室的牲畜屠宰场以及王室"禁忌房"。

尼普尔的恩利尔神庙（埃库尔神庙）接收来自温马的芦苇、食物、容器和牲畜等形式的 bala 税。据一篇文献记载，136 个鱼筛（^gi hal^ku6）被送到恩利尔神庙，供恩利尔的"第一果"（first-fruits）仪式使用。[1] 另据一篇文献记载，11 个不同的罐子被运送到恩利尔神庙。[2]

牲畜屠宰场（e₂-gu₄-gaz，直译为"屠公牛房"）是乌尔第三王朝重要的机构，可能隶属于中央政府。[3] 从温马被运到牲畜屠宰场的 bala 税，主要形式有芦苇及芦苇制品[4]、羊毛[5]以及陶器（用来装香料或调味品）[6]。据一篇文献记载，[7] 有 660 束芦苇运往普兹瑞什达干的屠宰场。这种赋税缴纳活动发生于阿马尔辛 9 年至伊比辛 1 年。bala 税的接收者或者征税官员主要有，宁乌拉神庙涂油祭司阿卡拉之子穆尼、卢萨加之子书吏伊卡拉[8]等。

---

[1] 术语 nig₂-dab₅ nesag₂ ^dEn-lil₂ e₂ ^dEn-lil₂-ka ba-an-ku₄，见文献 UTI 3 2257（S 48 i）。
[2] 文献 SAT 3 1562（SS 5）。
[3] P. Steinkeller, "Joys of Cooking in Ur III Babylonia", in P. Michalowski (eds.), *On the Third Dynasty of Ur: Studies in Honor of Marcel Sigrist*, Journal of Cuneiform Studies Supplemental Series 1, Boston: American Schools of Oriental Research, 2008, pp. 185–192.
[4] 文献 MVN 14 350（SS 3）。
[5] 文献 PDT 2 1348（SS 4 vi 9）。参见 C. Breniquet, C. Michel (eds.), *Wool Economy in the Ancient Near East and the Aegean: From the Beginnings of Sheep Husbandry to Institutional Textile Industry*, Ancient Textiles Series 17, Oxford and Philadelphia: Oxbow Books, 2014.
[6] 术语 mun-gazi si₃-gi₄-de₃，见文献 UTI 3 2200, UTI 3 2199。关于术语 mun-gazi 指一种香料，参见 K. Maekawa, "Cultivation of legumes and mun-gazi plants in Ur III Girsu", *Bulletin on Sumerian Agriculture*, Vol. 2 (1985), pp. 97–118.
[7] 文献 MVN 14 425（SS 5）。
[8] L. Verderame, G. Spada, "Ikalla, Scribe of (Wool) Textiles and Linen", in S. Garfinkle and M. Molina (eds.), *From the 21st Century B. C. to the 21st Century A. D.: Proceedings of the International Conference on Sumerian Studies Held in Madrid 22–24 July 2010*, Winona Lake: Eisenbrauns, 2013, pp. 425–444.

"禁忌房"的准确地理位置不详，可能位于吐玛尔或者尼普尔[①]，处于中央政府直接管辖之下。在文献中出现的时期是从舒尔吉 33 年直到舒辛 6 年。从温马运送到"禁忌房"的 bala 税形式主要有皮制品、芦苇及芦苇制品、木制品，大多数物品的用途不详。例如，据一篇文献记载，[②] 11 个装盐和香料的皮袋被运往"禁忌房"。

7. 其他属于中央的机构或人员

这些隶属于中央的机构和人员包括：隶属中央的军事机构（军事驻地），代表国王举行的献祭活动，中央派遣到行省的视察官员、外交人员和王室成员，以及已故的王室成员、奠酒祭祀地（ki-a-nag）[③] 王室奠酒仪式（nag lugal，可能在吐玛尔举行）。[④] 这些税收支出数量很少，但是赋税形式种类繁多，包括未加工的芦苇、芦苇席、革制水袋、水桶、沥青、水果等。

五 征收过程

从乌尔第三王朝的劳动力文献中，我们发现，bala 税的征收过程大致分为：收集、装船、拖船（驾船）、卸船、运到指定目的地几个步骤。由于在乌尔第三王朝时期，马和后来流行于中东地区的骆驼还没有被驯化，所以只能使用驴和牛来驮运少量的货物，而对于数量庞大的 bala 税货物，大都通过水运。[⑤]

在乌尔第三王朝的劳动力文献中，有专门的 bala 税运输过程的记载。劳动力是乌尔第三王朝重要的 bala 税形式。乌尔第三王朝已经建立了比较完善的劳动力征用制度，甚至还产生了可能是世界历史上最早的代役制。[⑥]

---

① M. Sigirst, *Drehem*, Bethesda: CDL Press, 1992, pp. 158 – 162.
② 文献 Syracuse 131（S 43）。
③ 文献 Syracuse 130（S 34），MVN 18 492（S 48），UTI 3 2100（AS 5），RA 59 146 FM 14（AS 6），CM 26 55（AS 8），AnOr 7 146（AS 9 viii），AAICAB 1/2 pl. 85 1935 – 513（SS 3），BPOA 2 2247（SS 3 vi）。
④ 文献 CM 26 37（undated），UTI 4 2984（AS 8），MVN 14 372（SS 1），SACT 1 121（SS 3 vi）。
⑤ R. M. Adams, "Shepherds at Umma in the Third Dynasty of Ur: Interlocutors with a World beyond the Scribal Field of Ordered Vision", *Journal of the Economic and Social History of the Orient*, Vol. 49 (2006), pp. 139 – 142.
⑥ M. Stol, "Old Babylonian Corvée (*tupšikkum*)", in T. van den Hout, J. DeRoos (ed.), *Studio Historiae Ardens: Ancient Near Eastern Studies Presented to Philo H. J. Houwink ten Cafe on the Occasion of his 65th Birthday*, Leiden: Nederlands Instituut voor het Habije Oosten, 1995, p. 295.

第二章 核心区 bala 税

居民有义务为总督履行 bala 劳役。总督通过许多方式来使用这些劳动力，用于温马行省的公共项目工程建设，比如开凿水渠、修筑房屋、农业劳动等。由于行省总督也有向中央政府履行劳役的义务，于是他将这些劳动力用于向中央服役的目的。文献表明，许多劳动力在温马服役，但是却代表中央政府服役，其他人则直接到尼普尔和乌尔服劳役。他们在首都的服役期一般持续一月有余。在行省之外的 bala 劳役具有双重功能：一方面，劳动力为行省服 bala 劳役，另一方面，行省用这些劳役作为他们向中央政府缴纳的 bala 劳役。① 我们不清楚到底在一年中，有多少劳动力被送往首都。行省劳动力去首都服劳役的原因，有可能是首都需要大量劳动力，也可能是首都居民免役（豁免），所以需要补充外来的劳役。但是关于这些目前还没有直接的证据。

根据劳动力文献统计，一艘容量为 60 古尔的船上的一个船员，每天可以接收大约 17 希拉粮食（作为工资）；最低工资是每天约 5 希拉粮食。这些文献记载了粮食和芦苇等作为 bala 税形式，从温马用船运到中央，途中所需的路费（劳动力拖船、装船、卸船等费用）也是由行省总督承担。船运文献大多都是记载货物从温马运到尼普尔，很少运到乌尔的记载。

此外，bala 税货物的包装以及船运所产生的费用也是 bala 税体系的一部分。包装的材料也包含在 bala 税中。作为 bala 税运往首都的物品包括：皮条或皮带（用来密封陶器皿），陶器（盛放谷物、面粉和香料），用于测量的容器（^{gi}gur），旅行篮子（^{kuš}a-ga$_2$-la$_2$）②，皮袋（盛放香料或面粉）等。此外，还有用于船运的备用物品，比如船杆、油和芦苇席等。③

---

① 类似的系统参见亚述帝国，参见 N. Postgate, *Taxation and Conscription in the Assyrian Empire*, Rome: Biblical Institute Press, 1974, pp. 239 – 240. 以及罗马的赋税, tributum 既用于指当地税，也指地方向中央缴纳的税。M. Corbier, "City, Territory and Taxation", in J. Rich, A. Wallace-Hadrill (eds.), *City and Country in the Ancient World*, London: Routledge, 1991, p. 124.

② 文献 BPOA 6 1216 (S 48), RA 49 93 37 (AS 6 ix), MVN 16 1386 (AS 7 viii), BPOA 1 1690 (AS 9), BIN 3 341 (AS 9 viii), UTI 4 2939 (SS 1 viii), MVN 16 995 (SS 2), BPOA 2 2184 (SS 3), UTI 5 3335 (SS 4)。

③ 文献 Nik 2 227 (S 38 vi), MVN 14 108 (S 45), MVN 15 61 (S 48 i), AUCT 3 255 (AS 6), Syracuse 201 (AS 6), MCS 3 42 1 BM 113104 (AS 9), UTI 4 2316 (SS 1), JCS 2 186 NBC 2950 (SS 2), Nik 2 226 (SS 4), BCT 2 93 (SS 4), JCS 23 110 3 (SS 5)。

六 税率

温马文献记载的 bala 税都是零散的，没有完整的全年或者一个 bala 月份的所有纳税记录，而零散的记录包括不同的课税形式，每种课税形式是否有各自的税率，还是所有的课税形式都具有统一的税率呢？由于我们没有发现完整的数据资料，所以暂时不能得到准确的答案。据一篇吉尔苏文献记载，[①] 拉伽什—吉尔苏行省的大麦产量约为 99595 古尔，其中有大约 49790 古尔作为 bala 税被缴纳给中央政府，即有将近一半（49.99%，约等于 50%）的大麦被作为 bala 税的课税实物。或者可以这样认为，拉伽什-吉尔苏行省的大麦 bala 税的税率约为 50%。那么，是不是温马行省以及其他行省的大麦 bala 税率也是 50% 呢？这个问题没有直接证据。不过，通过间接证据，我们还是可以计算温马行省 bala 税的大概税率。下面仍然以大麦这种 bala 税形式为例。我们采取的方法是：先计算出温马行省的可耕地，然后计算出温马行省的大麦年产量，最后用温马行省每年缴纳的 bala 大麦税数量，除以大麦年产量，即是温马行省 bala 大麦税的税率。

通过统计出温马行省的可耕地的面积，然后根据这些面积的土地能够出产多少大麦，来推测每年温马行省一共可以出产多少大麦。根据前人研究成果，温马行省的领地面积大约是 1200 布尔（bur_3），其中有一半的土地是可耕地，即 600 布尔是可耕地，另外 600 布尔则是休耕地。[②] 需要指出的是，这 600 布尔的土地并不是温马行省所有的可耕地，而只是处于行省总督直接管辖之下的土地。此外，温马行省之内还包括大量的王室地产（隶属于中央政府），这些土地需要跟行省所控制的土地相区分。另外根据温马文献记载，每布尔的土地每年平均可以出产 30—40 古尔的大麦。那么理论上，600 布尔的土地每年可以出产 18000—24000 古尔大麦。据一篇文献记载，舒尔吉 46 年的大麦总产量是 23444 古尔 232.5 希拉，[③] 这跟我们的估算数值基本吻合，

---

① 文献 CT 7, p. 8 BM 012926（AS 2）。

② K. Maekawa, "The Management of Domain Land in Ur III Umma: A Study of BM 110116", *Zinbun*, Vol. 22 (1987), pp. 25 – 82; P. Steinkeller, "The Foresters of Umma: Towards a Definition of Ur III Labor", in M. A. Powell (ed.), *Labor in the Ancient Near East*, AOS 68, New Haven: American Oriental Society, 1987, pp. 73 – 115. 布尔, 古代两河流域面积单位, 1 布尔约等于 64800 平方米。

③ 文献 UCP 9 – 2 – 1 88（S 46）。

所以 2 万古尔大致是温马行省的大麦年总产量。

既然知道了温马行省总督领地的大麦年产量大约为 2 万古尔，不过这其中到底有多少是作为 bala 赋税被缴纳到了中央，仍然需要文献证据的支持。可惜的是，温马文献中没有关于大麦作为 bala 税的年度总结性文献，温马文献大多是数量较少的大麦作为 bala 税的记载，大麦数量甚至不足 1 古尔，比如 2 巴里格 4 班（等于 16/30 古尔）大麦作为 bala 税，[①] 4 古尔 2 巴里格（合计 7/5 古尔）大麦作为 bala 税，[②] 其中数量较大的是 2565 古尔 1 巴里格 4 班大麦作为 bala 税。[③] 但是这个数目应该也不是温马行省的大麦年总产量，而只是其中的一部分。所以我们只好从没有记载 bala 术语的温马文献中寻找最大数目的大麦支出。目前在已知的温马文献中，关于大麦支出的最大数量是 8700 古尔，[④] 很可能是作为 bala 税，由此可以大概推断，温马行省的大麦 bala 税的税率大概是 44%（8700 除以 20000），这个数字与吉尔苏文献计算的 50% 大体上吻合。综上所述，温马行省的大麦 bala 税的税率也接近 50%。

七　征收时间

理论上讲，乌尔中央政府每年都会草拟一份行省缴纳 bala 税的清单，包括征收的具体实物种类，征收的时间，征收的地点等信息。但是，目前我们并没有在文献中发现这样的征收表单。据普兹瑞什达干文献记载，每个行省被指定在每年的某个特定的月份向中央缴纳 bala 税，这个特定的月份被称为 bala 月。除了拉伽什—吉尔苏行省每年有三至四个 bala 月之外，其余的行省每年只有一个 bala 月，即只需在一个月内向中央政府缴纳 bala 税，有的北方行省（比如巴比伦）每隔三至四年才有一个 bala 月。可见，不同的行省缴纳的 bala 税数量和期限也是有差异的。需要注意的是，每个行省被指定的 bala 月份，基本上是不变的，但是随着时间的推移以及新的统治者的上台，中央政府对每个行省 bala 月份的指定也会发生一些细微的调整。当一年过去之后，第二年这个行省的 bala 月继续轮转，这也是术语 bala "轮转、轮流"

[①] 文献 BCT 2 205 (- - vii)。
[②] 文献 Nisaba 9 66 (AS 5)。
[③] 文献 Fs Lenoble 166 no. 26 (S 30 ix)。
[④] 文献 SNAT 536 (undated)。

的来历。由于受到闰月和各行省月历与中央月历不统一等因素的影响，我们重建温马行省的征收月份显得困难重重。即便如此，根据目前的文献资料，我们大致可以复原大多数年份的温马 bala 月份。

可以肯定的是，温马行省向中央政府缴纳的 bala 税，每年只有一个月属于纳税期。但是有的文献记录跨越了两个月，这里的原因是，征收的过程需要消耗许多天，从温马到乌尔需要大约 4 天时间，从温马到尼普尔或普兹瑞什达干大约需要 7 天时间。所以算上来回时间，从温马到乌尔的纳税总过程至少需要花费 8 天时间（一周左右），从温马到尼普尔或者普兹瑞什达干的纳税过程则至少需要花费半个月时间。如果纳税时间放在 bala 月的月中旬或者中下旬，那么加上路上的时间，完成纳税任务再返回温马行省，很可能时间已经到了下个月了，这也是为什么有些文献会记录温马 bala 月份持续了两个月的缘故。① 普兹瑞什达干文献记载的温马 bala 月份信息比较少，只给出了自舒尔吉 33 年至舒辛 1 年这 26 年中的 9 年 bala 月份（舒尔吉 33、35、46、48 年，阿马尔辛 5、7、8、9 年，舒辛 1 年）。其余的信息来源于温马文献。我们综合普兹瑞什达干文献和温马文献，部分复原了温马行省的 bala 纳税月份（见表 2–9）。

表 2–9　　　　　　　　温马行省 bala 税纳税月份统计表

日期	1月	2月	3月	4月	5月	6月	7月	8月	9月	10月	11月	12月
S 28										温		
S 29												
S 30									温			
S 31									温			
S 32									温			
S 33							温	普				
S 34							温					
S 35						温	普					
S 36							温					

---

① 比如文献 BIN 5 74（S 48），UTI 3 1667（AS 9）。

续表

日期	1月	2月	3月	4月	5月	6月	7月	8月	9月	10月	11月	12月
S 37						温						
S 38						温						
S 39					温							
S 40						温						
S 41					温							
S 42				温								
S 43			普	普								
S 44			温									
S 45	温	普										
S 46	温	普										
S 47	普	温										
S 48	普											温
AS 1	温											
AS 2												温
AS 3												
AS 4												温
AS 5									温	普		
AS 6								温	普			
AS 7								温				
AS 8								温				
AS 9								温				
SS 1						温	普					
SS 2						温						
SS 3						温						
SS 4					温							
SS 5					温							
SS 6					温							
SS 7				温								
SS 8												

续表

日期	1月	2月	3月	4月	5月	6月	7月	8月	9月	10月	11月	12月
SS 9					温							
IS 1				温								
IS 2								温				
IS 3							温					
IS 4						温						

*注：（1）国王名缩写，S = Shulgi（舒尔吉），AS = Amar-Suen（阿马尔辛），SS = Shu-Suen（舒辛），IS = Ibbi-Suen（伊比辛）；（2）普——来源于普兹瑞什达干文献，温——来源于温马文献。

从上述的统计数据中可以看出，乌尔第三王朝时期温马行省的 bala 纳税月份大致经历了三次轮转：第一次是从舒尔吉 28 年至阿马尔辛 1 年，bala 月份从第 10 月至第 1 月依次推进，很多连续三年或两年的 bala 月份保持不变（比如舒尔吉 30—32 年、舒尔吉 33—36 年、舒尔吉 37—38 年、舒尔吉 45—46 年、舒尔吉 47 年——阿马尔辛 1 年）。第二次是从阿马尔辛 2 年至伊比辛 1 年，bala 月份从第 12 月至第 4 月依次递减，其中阿马尔辛 6—9 年连续四年、舒辛 1—3 年和舒辛 4—6 年连续三年的 bala 月份保持不变。第三次是从伊比辛 2 年至 4 年的三年时间里，bala 月份从第 8 月至第 6 月逐年递减。由于温马文献在此后已经没有记录，所以第三次 bala 月份的轮转进行刚刚开始即宣告结束。bala 月份的轮转一方面是中央政府主观意愿制定的花名册，另一方面也反映了乌尔第三王朝月历的变化，以及各个行省和中央政府实行不同的月历，使得月份统一变得不可能，从而导致月份的不同。

第四节　拉伽什—吉尔苏行省的 bala 税

拉伽什—吉尔苏行省是乌尔第三王朝面积最大的行省，也是乌尔第三王朝唯一一个 bala 纳税期多于一个月的行省（每年有二至四个月纳税期）。前面讲过，拉伽什—吉尔苏行省的文献档案基本上出土于吉尔苏遗址，所以我们在讲拉伽什—吉尔苏行省文献时一般只说吉尔苏文献或者吉尔苏档案。吉尔苏档案是最早发掘出土的乌尔第三王朝时期的经济管理文献。早在 19 世纪末,法国考古学家在吉尔苏遗址发掘出土了上万块吉尔苏文献,[1] 为破译苏美尔语以及苏美尔学(Sumerology)的建立提供了文献证据。[2] 吉尔苏文献的记录格式不同于温马文献,吉尔苏的 bala 文献有大量的多栏式文献,记录的内容包括船运粮食到尼普尔、劳动力档案等。

一 课征形式

拉伽什—吉尔苏行省向中央政府缴纳的 bala 税形式种类繁多,包括谷类、牲畜饲料、芦苇及芦苇制品、木材及木制品、皮革及皮革制品、石制品、草本植物、啤酒饮料、香料、椰枣、鱼类、白银、劳动力和牲畜等。这种形式所占文献数量统计见表 2 – 10:

表 2 – 10 **拉伽什—吉尔苏行省 bala 税形式统计表**

术语	课税形式	文献数量
dabin	粗粒小麦粉	16
duh	麸糠	1
esir$_2$	沥青	5
ga	牛奶	1
geš	树木、木料及木制品	9
gi	芦苇及芦苇制品	17
gig	小麦	2
gu$_2$-tur	小扁豆	1
i$_3$/ i$_3$-nun	植物油、酥油	9
kaš	啤酒	19

---

[1] E. de Sarzec, *Découvertes en Chaldée: second volume partie epigraphique et plances*, Paris: Ernest Leroux, 1894; V. Scheil, "Notes d'épigraphie et d'archéologie assyrienne. XI – XVII", *Recueil de Travaux Relatifs à la Philologie et à l'Archéologie Égyptienne et Assyriennes*, Vol. 17 (1895), pp. 27 – 41; F. Thureau-Dangin, "La comptabilité agricole en Chaldée", *Revue d'Assyriologie et d'Archéologie Orientale*, Vol. 3 (1895), pp. 118 – 146; H. de Genouillac, *Textes de l'époque d'Agadé et de l'époque d'Ur (Fouilies d'Ernest de Sarzéc en 1894)*, ITT 2, Paris: Ernest Leroux, 1910.

[2] W. H. Ph. Römer, *Die Sumerologie: Einführung in die Forschung und Bibliographie in Auswahl*, Alter Orient und Altes Testament 262, Münster: Ugarit-Verlag, 1999.

续表

术语	课税形式	文献数量
ku$_3$-babbar	白银	15
ku$_6$	鱼类	7
kuš	皮制品	1
na$_4$	石制品	1
naga	草碱	1
nig$_2$-ar$_3$-ra	碾去壳的燕麦（小麦）	1
nig$_2$-ki-luh	扫帚	4
nig$_2$-šu	一种物品或财产	1
ninda	面包	5
siki	羊毛	4
še	大麦	166
šum$_2$	香料	3
u$_2$	草本植物	4
uruda	铜制品	3
zi$_3$	面粉	16
ziz$_2$	二粒小麦	1
zu$_2$-lum	椰枣	9
ma$_2$	船	26
geme$_2$ / guruš	劳动力	90
erin$_2$	劳动力	11
udu / maš$_2$ / gu$_4$	牲畜	32
	其他	24 [*]
	总计	505

[*] 注：碾去壳的小麦（ar-za-na，1篇）、小麦（gig，1篇）、gur a-bala（2篇）、gur-nag（1篇）、黏土（im，2篇）、秸秆（in-u，1篇）、糖浆（lal$_3$，1篇）、麦芽（munu$_4$，1篇）、草碱（naga，1篇）、木桶板（pa-ku$_5$，2篇）。有的文献记载的课税形式不止一种，所以统计文献的数量会比实际数量多。

在这些课税形式中，最主要的是大麦，记录大麦的文献（166篇）占所有吉尔苏文献的33%，其次是劳动力、牲畜、船、啤酒、芦苇、面粉和白银等。记载 bala 税的吉尔苏文献在数量上远远不及温马文献，但是吉尔苏文献包括大量的多栏式总账目类文献，提供了更为详细的 bala 税记录。

二 征税对象

在前一节我们讲到，乌尔第三王朝 bala 税的征税对象是各个行省的总督。但是在实际操作过程中，总督只是名义上的征税对象，而实际的征税对象是行省内提供赋税的各个机构负责人。在文献中，他们被标注以 ki PN-ta "来自某人、从某人处、从某人手中"。可惜的是，文献中只记录了这些 bala 提供者的名字，很少记录他们的家族关系或者职业。我们对于这些人的认识十分有限。

从文献证据看，每个征税对象或 bala 税提供者似乎有专门的负责领域和物品种类，可能他们同时也是这些物品的生产者或制造者。比如，乌尔阿巴主要提供椰枣①、植物油②、扫帚③、羊毛④等物品，但是从未提供大麦等粮食作物。阿拉姆⑤、卢基纳⑥、乌尔尼伽尔⑦基本上只提供大麦。巴兹基本上只提供大麦和劳动力。⑧ 下面的表格是对几种主要的吉尔苏 bala 课税形式征税对象的统计（见表 2-11）。

---

① 文献 TCTI 2 4266（IS 1），CM 26 122（undated）。
② 文献 P210029（--v），BPOA 2 1937（AS 3 vii），BPOA 1 173（IS 1 i），Nisaba 13 85（SS 7 viii）。
③ 文献 MVN 5 190（SS 7 vi），PPAC 5 1479（AS 8 x）。
④ 文献 TCTI 2 2613（SS 5）。
⑤ 文献 TCTI 2 3781（SS 4 x），MVN 12 451（SS 1 xi），CT 3 pl 5-8 BM 18343（S 44 i），TCTI 2 3382（SS 1 xi）。
⑥ 文献 CM 26 64（S 46 xi），ITT 2 664（AS 8 xi），TEL 149（AS 8 xi），TCTI 2 3400（AS 8 xi），CT 7 pl 22 BM 13138（S 46 iii 24），PPAC 5 326（AS 4），ITT 3 6612（AS 8 xi），TCTI 2 4292（AS 8 xi）。
⑦ 文献 TCTI 2 3857（SS 6 xi），TCTI 2 3906（SS 6 x），TCTI 2 2753（SS 6 viii），TCTI 2 4235（SS 6 x），TCTI 2 4243（SS 7 viii），TCTI 2 4246（SS 6 viii），TEL 169（SS 6 viii），TEL 172（SS 6 ix）。
⑧ 大麦文献：MVN 19 96，ASJ 20 97 1，ASJ 3 164 137，MVN 11 12，ASJ 3 168 153，PPAC 5 1093，CM 26 106，SAT 1 25，MVN 2 18，CT 9 pl 39 BM 14318，Nisaba 10 76，Sumer 23 142，CT 3 pl 44-47 BM 21338，CTPSM 1 46，P234830，TCTI 3 4768，TCTI 2 2670，TCTI 2 3727，Amherst 110，Amherst 112，Amherst 114，DAS 392；劳动力文献：MVN 17 147，OTR 9，MVN 12 95，SAT 1 352，UDT 48，UDT 23，Nisaba 13 10，PPAC 5 195，MVN 12 45，MVN 12 51，MVN 12 54，Nisaba 13 28，OTR 69，PPAC 5 1126，CM 26 104，CM 26 147，MVN 12 47，MVN 12 96，BM Messenger 234，MVN 12 90，MVN 12 123，MVN 12 113，SAT 1 14，MVN 12 109，MVN 12 110，SAT 1 295，BAOM 2 27 37。

表 2–11　拉伽什—吉尔苏行省 bala 税的征收对象统计表

课税形式	征税对象
大麦	阿拉姆（Allamu）、巴兹（Bazi）、恩埃吉阿格（Enekiag）、古地亚（Gudea）、拉玛伊里纳（Lamma-irina）、乌图巴拉之子卢巴巴（Lu-Baba dumu Utu-barra）、卢丁吉尔拉（Lu-dingira）、首席神庙管理员卢丁吉尔拉（Lu-dingira šabra）、巴巴姆之子卢吉什巴莱达（Lu-geshbareda dumu Babamu）、卢基纳（Lu-gina）、卢吉里扎尔（Lu-girizal）、卢卡拉（Lu-kala）、卢宁吉什孜达（Lu-Ningeshzida）、巴兹之子卢宁吉尔苏（Lu-Ningirsu dumu Bazi）、卢伽尔阿马鲁（Lugal-amaru）、卢伽尔古伽尔（Lugal-gugal）、卢伽尔美兰（Lugal-melam）、曼舒姆（Manshum）、纳纳（Nana）、乌尔巴巴（Ur-Baba）、乌尔巴德提比拉（Ur-Badtibira）、乌尔恩利拉（Ur-Enlila）、乌尔吉吉尔（Ur-gigir）、乌尔南塞（Ur-Nanshe）、乌尔尼伽尔（Ur-nigar）、乌尔萨加（Ur-saga）
椰枣	阿巴古拉（Abbagula）、阿古（Agu）、巴哈尔（Bahar）、乌尔阿巴（Ur-abba）、乌尔尼格（Ur-nig）
白银	阿吉（Agi）、阿伊里（A-ili）、安库（Anku）、阿拉德（Arad）、卢基努尼尔（Lu-Kinunir）、卢乌图（Lu-Utu）、乌尔巴巴（Ur-Baba）、乌尔古恩纳（Ur-guenna）、乌尔兰马（Ur-Lamma）、乌尔南塞（Ur-Nanshe）、乌尔舒尔帕埃（Ur-Shulpae）
牲畜	因提丹（Imtidam）、卢巴巴（Lu-Baba）、卢卡尔卡尔（Lu-kalkal）、纳拉姆伊里（Naram-ili）、乌努戴内（Unudene）、乌尔阿巴（Ur-abba）、乌尔埃伽尔（Ur-egal）
粗面粉（dabin）	乌尔伊吉孜巴拉之子卢古拉（Lu-gula dumu Ur-Igizibara）、卢马尔萨（Lu-marsa）、巴兹之子卢宁吉尔苏（Lu-Ningirsu dumu Bazi）、乌尔伊格阿里姆（Ur-Igalim）、乌尔努恩伽尔（Ur-Nungal）、乌图姆（Utumu）
芦苇	卡亚姆之子卢宁吉尔苏（Lu-Ningirsu dumu Kaamu）、卢伽尔库加尼（Lugal-kugani）、卢伽尔内萨格（Lugal-nesag）、阿达之子曼舒姆（Manshum dumu Ada）、纳姆马赫（Nammah）、乌尔梅斯（Ur-mes）
劳动力（guruš）	阿卡拉（Akala）、阿拉德姆（Aradmu）、巴兹（Bazi）、古地亚（Gudea）、伊尼姆巴巴伊达布（Inim-Baba-idab）、纳姆之子卢里扎尔（Lu-girizal dumu Namu）、卢卡拉（Lu-kala）、卢宁吉尔苏（Lu-Ningirsu）、卢乌什基纳（Lu-ushgina）、纳姆马赫（Nammah）、尼古鲁姆（Nigurum）、乌尔巴巴（Ur-Baba）、乌尔巴德提比拉（Ur-Badtibira）、乌尔吉吉尔（Ur-gigir）、乌尔尼伽尔（Ur-nigar）、乌尔舒什巴巴（Ur-Shush-Baba）

吉尔苏文献保存了关于税收来源地的丰富信息。以大麦为例，作为 bala 税的大麦主要来源于拉伽什—吉尔苏行省的谷仓或粮仓（i$_3$-dub）、地

块或片区（的粮仓）（a-ša₃）①、磨坊（e₂-kikken₂）②、仓库或储藏室（ga₂-nun）等。

拉伽什—吉尔苏行省的粮仓类型十分繁多，分布在该省的不同地区，来自粮仓的 bala 税多发生在每年的 7—11 月间，包括如下种类（见表 2-12）：

表 2-12　　　　拉伽什—吉尔苏行省的粮仓种类一览表

术语	汉译	例子
i₃-dub a-ba-al-la-ta	干燥粮仓	Nisaba 10 25（S 47 ix）
i₃-dub a-gibil₄-ta	新粮仓	SNAT 161（IS 2）
i₃-dub e₂-gibil₄-le	新房粮仓	TCTI 3 4768（AS 9 x）
i₃-dub a-ša₃ gibil-ta	新地粮仓	TCTI 2 4168（SS 9 vii）
i₃-dub a-ša₃ du₁₀-gal₂	皮包片区粮仓	MVN 12 319（AS 1）
i₃-dub a-ša₃ hub₂-e-gar-ra-ta	堆积区粮仓	Hermitage 3 16（S 45 viii）
i₃-dub a-ša₃ lahtan₂-ta③	啤酒桶片区粮仓	MVN 17 53（IS 2 vi）
i₃-dub a-ša₃ ᵈNin-tu-ta	宁图神庙区粮仓	TCTI 2 4271（IS 1 x）
i₃-dub a-ša₃ su₃-GAN₂ gu-la-ta	大冶金材料粮仓	ITT 2 2748（IS 3 x）
i₃-dub a-ša₃ ᵍⁱˢtir ma-nu	柳条弓片区粮仓	TEL 182（IS 1）
i₃-dub a-ša₃ ᵈŠul-gi-zi-kalam-ma-ta	舒尔吉孜卡兰马片区粮仓	MVN 11 12（S 44 ix）
i₃-dub ambar sur-ra	半沼泽地粮仓	SAT 1 392（S 45 ix）
i₃-dub a-ša₃ ambar sur-ra	半沼泽地片区粮仓	OTR 25（S 45 viii）
i₃-dub bara₂-si-ga	神龛粮仓	BAOM 2 27 37（S 47 vii）

---

① 包括：（1）a-ša₃ duruₓ（U₃）-a-du₁₀-ga-ta "有利灌溉区块"，文献 TCTI 2 4304（IS 1 iv）；（2）a-ša₃ iri-ni u₃ lugal-nam-tar-re-da "其城及命运之主区块"，文献 SNAT 161（IS 2）；（3）a-ša₃ ᵈNin-gir₂-su-siskur-zi-da-ᵈNanše-ta "南塞真正祝福的宁吉尔苏区块"，文献 HLC 36（pl. 14）（S 46 ix）。

② W. R. Brookman, *The Umma Milling Industry: Studies in Neo-Sumerian Texts*, PhD dissertation, University of Minnesota, 1984; A. Uchitel, "Daily Work at Sagdana Millhouse", *Acta Sumerologica*, Vol. 6 (1984), pp. 75–98.

③ A. Salonen, *Die Hausgeräte der Alten Mesopotamier nach sumerisch-akkadischen Quellen*, Teil II: *Gefässe*, Helsinki: Suomalaisen Kirjallisuuden Kirjapaino Oy Helsinki, 1966, p. 206.

续表

术语	汉译	例子
i_3-dub du_6-sa-ba-ra	网状土堆粮仓	TUT 177（S 45 xi）
i_3-dub e_2-$duru_5$ elam-e-ne-ta	埃兰农村粮仓	MVN 12 57（S 46 viii）
i_3-dub e_2-$duru_5$ en-na-ta	祭司农村粮仓	PPAC 5 644（S 47）
i_3-dub Inim-^{d}Inanna-ta	伊宁伊南娜粮仓	SAT 1 14（S 46 xi）
i_3-dub e_2-$duru_5$ Inim-^{d}Inanna-ta	伊宁伊南娜农村粮仓	Nisaba 13 10（S 46 xi）
i_3-dub e_2 ^{d}Nin-mar^{ki}-ka sipa	宁玛尔神庙粮仓	CT 3 pl. 20 BM 016366（IS 1）
i_3-dub igi-gal_2 ^{d}Nanše-ta	南塞所见粮仓	MVN 2 65（S 42 x）
i_3-dub Inim-ma-DINGIR-ta	伊宁马伊鲁姆粮仓	MVN 12 45（S 46 viii）
i_3-dub a-$ša_3$ Inim-ma-DINGIR	伊宁马伊鲁姆片区粮仓	PPAC 5 195（-- viii）
i_3-dub Inim-ma-^{d}Ia_3	伊宁马亚粮仓	OTR 69（S 46 viii）
i_3-dub a-$ša_3$ Inim-ma-DINGIR-ta	伊宁马伊鲁姆片区粮仓	ASJ 10 92 5（-- viii）
i_3-dub ka-mar-ri_2-ta	运货车头粮仓	CM 26 147（S 46 viii）
i_3-dub KA suhuš gu-la	大地基粮仓	ASJ 2 12 28（-- vii）
i_3-dub $Muš_2$-ar-mu-na-gub-ba-ta	穆沙尔姆纳古巴粮仓	Nisaba 10 76（S 47 xi）
i_3-dub $Nigin_6^{ki}$-ta	尼那粮仓	MVN 17 147（S 45 vii）
i_3-duba-$ša_3$ ^{d}Nin-gir_2-su-a_2-zi-da-^{d}Nanše-ta	宁吉尔苏阿孜达南塞片区粮仓	MVN 2 72（S 46 x）
i_3-dub ^{d}Nin-hur-sag	宁胡尔萨格粮仓	UDT48（S 46 x）
i_3-dub ^{d}Nin-hur-sag-lu_2-ku_3-nun-ta	宁胡尔萨格卢库努恩粮仓	PPAC 5 1093（S 46 ix）
i_3-dub e_2-$duru_5$ ^{d}Nin-hur-sag-lu_2-ku_3-nun-ta	宁胡尔萨格卢库努恩农村粮仓	CM 26 106（S 46 ix）
i_3-dub lu_2-ku_3-nun-ta	卢库努恩粮仓	SAT 1 295（S 46 xi）
i_3-dub Pu_2-šu-i-ne-ta	普舒伊奈粮仓	TCTI 2 2584（IS 1 ix）
i_3-dub sahar-dub-ba	泥土粮仓	TCTI 2 3910（IS 2）
i_3-dub sipa da-ta	牧羊人粮仓	HLC 216（pl. 14）（S 45）
i_3-dub sipa da-ri_2	不朽的牧羊人粮仓	HLC 184（pl. 13）（S 45 xi）
i_3-dub ^{giš}tir-gibil-ta	新弓粮仓	CTPSM 1 70（SS 2 xi）
i_3-dub ukken-ne_2-gaba-ta	犁装粮仓	CM 26 103（-- x）
i_3-dub Uru_{11}^{ki}-ta	乌鲁城粮仓	HLC 320（pl. 131）（AS 3 xi）

储藏室（ga$_2$-nun）① 区别于粮仓（i$_3$-dub），② 作为吉尔苏 bala 税的另一个重要来源，很可能是储存除粮食之外的其他食物或物品。储藏室主要包括以下种类：ga$_2$-nun giš-ta 和 ga$_2$-nun-mah-ta（见表 2-13）。

表 2-13　　　　　拉伽什—吉尔苏行省的储藏室种类一览表

术语	汉译	例子
ga$_2$-nun bala-a-ri	对面的储藏室	PPAC 5 307（----）
ga$_2$-nun giš-ta	植物储藏室	SAT 1 372（-- iii）
ga$_2$-nun mah	大的储藏室	TCTI 2 3451（AS 8 vi）
ga$_2$-nun ^{d}Nin-gir$_2$-su a$_2$ zi-da ^{d}Nanše-ta	南塞所保护的宁吉尔苏的储藏室	MVN 11 117（S 47 ix）
ga$_2$-nun sanga-ta	神庙管理员的储藏室	OTR 17（-- viii）

三　征收官员

同温马行省类似，拉伽什—吉尔苏行省的 bala 税征收工作也是由专门的征收官员负责。从文献的印文中我们知道，这些征收官员的职位非常显赫，他们大都是拉伽什—吉尔苏行省的权贵阶层，既有宗教领域的祭司和神庙管理员，也有世俗领域的各类高级官员。根据职位的不同，我们将这些 bala 征税官员分为以下几类：

（一）御前侍卫

御前侍卫（gu-za-la$_2$"手持王座之人"）这一职位的具体含义尚不清楚，他们很可能是中央政府派遣的巡视员之类的官员，代表国王或者中央政府的利益。例如，御前侍卫乌尔宁吉尔苏（Ur-Ningirsu gu-za-la$_2$）征收大麦 bala 税。③

---

① J. G. Westenholz, "Intimations of Mortality", in S. Graziani (ed.), *Studi sul Vicino Oriente Antico dedicati alla memoria di Luigi Cagni*, Napoli: Istituto Universitario Orientale, 2000, pp. 1179-1201.

② A. Salonen, *Agricultura Mesopotamica nach sumerisch-akkadischen Quellen*, Helsinki: Suomalaisen Kirjallisuuden Kirjapaino Oy Helsinki, 1968, p. 282; A. Salonen, *Die Hausgeräte der Alten Mesopotamier nach sumerisch-akkadischen Quellen*, Teil II: *Gefässe*, Helsinki: Suomalaisen Kirjallisuuden Kirjapaino Oy Helsinki, 1966, p. 206.

③ 文献 MVN 6 465（S 32 ix）。

（二）神庙管理员

这一职业仅次于首席神庙管理员或者主管（šabra），[1] 一个神庙可以有多位神庙管理员，负责具体的神庙事务。比如乌鲁神庙的管理员阿巴卡拉（其父杜杜也是该神庙的管理员），[2] 南塞神庙管理员乌尔埃宁努（其父阿拉姆则是该神庙的首席管理员 šabra），[3] 伊南娜神庙的管理员乌尔兰马（卢宁吉尔苏之子），[4] 他们主要负责征收大麦形式的 bala 税。

（三）涂油祭司

比如某神庙涂油祭司（gudu$_4$）阿图之子卢伽尔埃利都征收大麦。[5]

（四）牲畜育肥师

比如牲畜育肥师（kurušda）卡亚姆（Kaamu）征收牲畜形式的 bala 税，[6] 他同时也作为征收大麦 bala 税的经办人（giri$_3$）。[7] 此外，阿拉姆（Allamu）[8]、卢卡拉（Lu-Kala）[9] 和卢米尔扎（Lu-mirza）[10] 也征收大麦形式的 bala 税。

（五）牧官

比如"纳卡布图姆"机构[11]的牧羊人或牧官（sipa na-gab$_2$-tum）伊里姆之子卡亚姆征收牲畜 bala 税。[12]

---

[1] J. Hernández, "The Role of the Sagga in Ur III Based on the Puzriš-Dagān Texts", in L. Feliu, et al（eds.）, *Time and History in the Ancient Near East*: *Proceedings of the 56th Recontre Assyriologique Internationale at Barcelona 26 – 30 July 2010*, Winona Lake: Eisenbrauns, 2013, pp. 689 – 704.

[2] Abba-kala sanga Uru$_{11}$^{ki}, Abba-kala dumu Dudu sanga Uru$_{11}$, 文献 TCTI 3 4768（AS 9 x）。

[3] Ur-Eninnu sanga ^{d}Nanshe（dumu Allamu šabra），文献 Amherst 112（AS 9 x）。

[4] Ur-Lamma sanga ^{d}Inana（dumu Lu-Ningirsu），文献 Amherst 110（AS 9 x）。

[5] Lugal-Eridu dumu Atu gudu$_4$［DN］，文献 MVN 5 172（SS 1 xi）。

[6] Kaamu kurušda, 文献 Fs Foster 192 – 194（AS 3）。

[7] giri$_3$ Kaamu kurušda, 文献 MVN 12 506（IS 1 iii）。

[8] Allamu kurušda, 文献 PPAC 5 254（S 41 – S 42 i）。

[9] Lu-kala kurušda, 文献 MVN 12 307（S 48 xi）。F. Pomponio, "Lukalla of Umma", *Zeitschrift für Assyriologie und Vorderasiatische Archäologie*, Vol. 82（1992）, pp. 169 – 179.

[10] Lu-mirza kurušda, 文献 MVN 4 49（S 48 viii）。

[11] M. Hilgert, *Cuneiform Texts from the Ur III Period in the Oriental Institute*, Volume 2: *Drehem Administrative Documents from the Reign of Amar-Suena*, Oriental Institute Publications 121, Chicago: The Oriental Institute, 2003, p. 43; H. Brunke, "The *Nakabtum*: An Administrative Superstructure for the Storage and Distribution of Agricultural Products", *KASKAL. Rivista di storia, ambienti e culture del Vicino Oriente Antico*, Vol. 5（2008）, pp. 111 – 126.

[12] Kaamu dumu Ili-mu sipa na-gab$_2$-tum, 文献 SNAT 60（S 48 ix）。

第二章　核心区 bala 税

（六）牧牛校尉监督官、监督官

比如监督官（nu-banda₃）穆祖（乌尔乌图之子），① 乌尔伊格阿里姆，② 乌尔宁埃布伽尔③征收大麦 bala 税。此外，牧牛校尉监督官（nu-banda₃-gu₄）乌尔丁吉尔拉也作为征收官员征收大麦 bala 税。④

（七）商人、商务官员

比如商人（dam-gar₃）⑤埃基之子乌尔萨加⑥、商人乌尔泰什之子乌尔巴巴⑦征收白银形式的 bala 税。

在吉尔苏文献中，除了这些带有职位的人名之外，大多数征收官员都只有一个人名，没有职位信息，所以我们不清楚这些官员的社会地位和详细信息。

四　赋税运输

在吉尔苏文献中，有大量的船运文献，基本上都属于阿马尔辛 8 年的文献，记载大麦或其他谷类被运往尼普尔的内容。这些文献提供了丰富的 bala 税运输过程的记录，记载了正在服 bala 劳役的劳动力装船（ma₂-a si-ga）、拖船（ma₂ gid₂-da）、卸船的经过，船上装着向中央缴纳的 bala 税货物，由水路运往中央。这些船运文献大致分为两类：bala-še₃（作为 bala 税）类别和 ma₂ bala-a gub-ba（正在服 bala 劳役的船）类别。⑧ bala-še₃ 文献有的只是列举了不同容量的船的数量。比如：

---

① Muzu nu-banda₃, Muzu dumu Ur-Utu, 文献 MVN 11 17 (S 45 ix)。
② Ur-Igalim nu-banda₃, 文献 PPAC 5 1276 (S 45 x)。
③ Ur-Ninebgal nu-banda₃, 文献 ASJ 3 168 153 (S 45 vii)。
④ Ur-dingira nu-banda₃-gu₄, 文献 TCTI 2 3702 (IS 1 vii)。
⑤ D. C. Snell, *Ledgers and Prices: Early Mesopotamian Merchant Accounts*, Yale Near Eastern Researches 8, New Haven and London: Yale University Press, 1982; H. Neumann, "Handel und Händler in der Zeit der III. Dynastie von Ur", *Altorientalische Forschungen*, Vol. 6 (1979), pp. 15–67; S. J. Garfinkle, "Merchants and State Formation in Early Mesopotamia", in S. C. Melville and A. L. Slotsky (eds.), *Opening the Tablet Box: Near Eastern Studies in Honor of Benjamin R. Foster*, Culture and History of the Ancient Near East 42, Leiden and Boston: Brill, 2010, pp. 185–202.
⑥ Ur-saga dumu Eki dam-gar₃, 文献 CM 26 118 (AS 6 v)。
⑦ Ur-Baba dumu Ur-teš dam-gar₃, 文献 ASJ 3 167 149 (S 45 v)。
⑧ 参见本章"第二节 税收管理"之"二 文献概况"。

CM 26 98（AS 8 x 25，Girsu）

正面

22 ma$_2$ 60 gur	22 只（容量为）60 古尔的船
1 ma$_2$ 40 gur	1 只（容量为）40 古尔的船
1 ma$_2$ 30 gur	1 只（容量为）30 古尔的船
1 ma$_2$ 20 gur	1 只（容量为）20 古尔的船

背面

bala-še$_3$	作为 bala 税（役）
giri$_3$ Lugal-ušumgal šeš Tul$_2$-ta	经办人为图尔塔之兄弟卢伽尔乌舒姆伽尔
iti amar-a-a-si u$_4$ 25 ba-zal	第 8 月，第 25 日
mu en Eridu^{ki} ba-hun	阿马尔辛 8 年

有的 bala-še$_3$ 文献不仅列举了船的数量和容量，而且还记载了船所运的货物种类。比如：

CM 26 99（AS 8 x 7，Girsu）

正面

7 ma$_2$ 60 gur	7 只（容量为）60 古尔的船
1 ma$_2$ 40 gur	1 只（容量为）40 古尔的船
ma$_2$ zi$_3$-da ma$_2$ ninda	这些是装载面粉的船以及装载面包的船
1 ma$_2$ 60 mun-gazi	1 只（容量为）60（古尔）装载 mun-gazi（农作物）的船
1 ma$_2$ geme$_2$ ba-a-u$_3$	1 只装载女劳力的船
1 ma$_2$ 60 gur	1 只（容量为）60 古尔的船
1 ma$_2$ 40 gur	1 只（容量为）40 古尔的船
nig$_2$ geš-kin-ti ba-a-gar	装上工匠的东西（工具）

背面

1 ma$_2$ 30 i$_3$ zu$_2$-lum	1 只（容量为）30 古尔装载植物油和椰枣的船
1 ma$_2$ šandana bala	1 只装载服 bala 劳役的果园工人的船
bala-še$_3$	（这些船）作为 bala 服役
iti amar-a-a-si u$_4$ 7 ba-zal	第 10 月，第 7 日
mu en Eridu^{ki} ba-hun	阿马尔辛 8 年

第二章 核心区 bala 税

第二类船文献 ma₂ bala-a gub-ba 类别，列举的是正在服 bala 劳役的船。这些文献格式十分有规则，列举了船的数量和容量，以及所装载的货物或劳动力种类。比如：

TCTI 3 6457（AS 8 v 26，Girsu）

正面

21 ma₂ 60 gur gu₂ e₂-bappir	21 只（容量为）60 古尔至啤酒房
3 ma₂ ZUM e₂-bappir	3 只 ZUM 船至啤酒房
1 ma₂ e₂-kišib-ba šim	1 只船至啤酒麦芽仓库
8 ma₂ ugula kikken₂-me	8 只船由磨坊工监督
10 ma₂ gi ᵍⁱˢma-nu	10 只船装芦苇和"马努"树木
3 ma₂ erin₂-na	3 只船载劳动力
1 ma₂ mun-gazi	1 只船装"蒙伽孜"农产品
1 ma₂ i₃ zu₂-lum	1 只船装植物油和椰枣
1 ma₂ zi₃ eša	1 只船装精面粉
2 ma₂ ninda	2 只船装面包
1 ma₂ ra-gaba Unug ᵏⁱ	1 只船装（来自）乌鲁克的骑使
4 ma₂ dug sila₃	4 只船装陶罐
2 ma₂ gu₄ udu	2 只船载牛和羊
1 ma₂ gir₄-še-sa	1 只船装烘烤大麦的烤炉
8 ma₂ aga₃-us₂ ki sukkal-mah	8 只船载"大苏卡尔"的士兵
8 ma₂ aga₃-us₂ ki I₃-lal₃-lum	8 只船载伊拉鲁姆的士兵
3 ma₂ sipa ur-gi₇-ra	3 只船载"吉拉"狗的牧人
1 ma₂ sipa ur-mah	1 只船载"大狗"的牧人
1 ma₂ šandana bala	1 只船载服 bala 劳役的园丁

背面

10 ma₂ ninda geš-rum	10 只船装"吉什鲁姆"面包
8 ma₂ siki Uri₅ᵏⁱ-še₃	8 只船装到乌尔的羊毛
1 ma₂ ᵍⁱˢbanšur	1 只船装桌子
1 ma₂ gal za-hum	1 只船装金属盆
1 ma₂ sipa si₂-si₂	1 只船载野驴的牧人
1 ma₂ udu ša₃ e₂-gal	1 只船装到王宫的绵羊
2 ma₂ zi₃ si-ga	2 只船装粗制面粉

1 ma₂ kaš sa₂-du₁₁ šagina		1只船装啤酒，作为给将军的定期供应	
2 ma₂ kas₄ giri₃ ᵈNanna-kam		2只船载使节，经办人是南那卡姆	
šu-nigin₂ 100-la₂-2 ma₂ hi-a		共计有98只船	
ma₂ bala-a gub-ba		（这些）船是正在服 bala 劳役	
u₄ 26-kam		第26日	
iti munu₄-gu₇		第5月	
mu en Eriduᵏⁱ ba-hun		阿马尔辛8年	

这些文献为我们提供了丰富的船运货物信息，间接反映了拉伽什—吉尔苏行省的经济富饶程度，同时也揭露了拉伽什—吉尔苏行省的 bala 课税之重。我们将这些船运文献统计总结如下（见表2-14）。

表2-14　　　　　　　拉伽什—吉尔苏行省的船文献统计表

日期	船数量	格式	文献
—	38	ma₂ bala-a gub-ba	TCTI 3 6443
—	194*	ma₂ še bala-še₃／ ša₃-bi-ta	HLC 384（pl. 145）
--x 29	46 +［x］	ma₂ bala-a gub-ba	TEL 15
--xi 12	40	bala-a gub-ba	TCTI 2 2785
--xii 17	60	ma₂ bala-a gub-ba	TCTI 2 2772
AS 7 xi	5	bala-še₃	CT 10 pl. 50 BM 12248
AS 8 iii	35	ma₂ gu₄ bala-e-de₃	Nisaba 18 91
AS 8 iv 25	3	bala-še₃	CM 26 101
—	98	ma₂ bala-a gub-ba	ITT 2 1007
AS 8 v 7	98	ma₂ bala-a gub-ba	TCTI 3 6421
AS 8 v 20	98	ma₂ bala-a gub-ba	ITT 2 927
AS 8 v 21	98	ma₂ bala-a gub-ba	CM 26 95
AS 8 v 22	98	ma₂ bala-a gub-ba	TCTI 22797
AS 8 v 23	98	ma₂ bala-a gub-ba	TCTI 3 6459
AS 8 v 26	98	ma₂ bala-a gub-ba	TCTI 3 6457
AS 8 v 27	98	ma₂ bala-a gen-na	PPAC 5 723

续表

日期	船数量	格式	文献
AS 8 v 28	98	ma$_2$ bala-a gub-ba	ITT 2 916
AS 8 vi 25	103	ma$_2$ bala-a gub-ba	CM 26 96
AS 8 x 7	14	bala-še$_3$	CM 26 99
AS 8 x 25	25	bala-še$_3$	CM 26 98
AS 8 xi 29	91	ma$_2$ bala-a gub-ba	ITT 2 922
AS 8 xii [n]	60 + [x]	ma$_2$ bala-a gub-ba	TCTI 3 6454
AS 8 xii 19	60	bala gub-ba	CM 26 97
AS 8 xii 29	60	bala-a gub-ba	TCTI 3 6434
AS 9 xi 6	36	ma$_2$ bala-a gub-ba	SNAT 122

* 179 只船作为装载 bala 大麦的船。

劳动力拖船到尼普尔，这些船是服 bala 劳役的船。船上所装载的货物以谷类为主，以及少量木材。[①] 例如：

ITT 3 6128（AS 8 xi，Girsu）

正面

31 guruš u$_4$ 13-še$_3$	31 个劳动力，工作 13 天
ma$_2$ kuš bala-še$_3$ gid$_2$-da	拖船，这些皮船在服 bala 劳役
Nibru^{ki}-še$_3$	（驶往）尼普尔

背面

dumu dab$_5$-ba-me	他们是被选中的子民
giri$_3$ U$_2$-da	经办人是乌达
dumu ^{d}Nin-gir$_2$-su-ka-i$_3$-sa$_6$	宁吉尔苏卡伊萨之子
iti še-sag$_{11}$-ku$_5$	第 11 月
mu en Eridu^{ki} ba-hun	阿马尔辛 8 年

[①] 文献 CM 26 94，CT 7 13165，SAT 1 372（gi 芦苇），CM 26 123（guruš 劳动力），CM 26 93（guruš 劳动力），ITT 3 6128（guruš 劳动力），CM 26 94（še 大麦），SAT 1 453（šum$_2$-sikil 葱类蔬菜），TCTI 2 4322（še 大麦）。

此外，一篇文献详细记载了60古尔1巴里格4班4希拉的大麦，作为牛羊的饲料，从吉尔苏被运到了尼普尔，由乌尔辛经办。[①] 当然，也有少量文献记载了作为bala税的货物被运往乌尔。[②]

五 税收用途

拉伽什—吉尔苏行省所缴纳的bala税主要用于三个目的：祭祀活动、喂养牲畜以及官员食用。这些bala税一般是从拉伽什—吉尔苏行省运往乌尔或者尼普尔。

（一）祭祀活动

作为祭祀活动的bala税形式主要是牲畜和一些供品，比如椰枣被献给南塞神（^{d}Nanše）、天神安的神位（ki An-na）、恩利尔神庙（e_2^{d}En-lil$_2$），以及恩利尔的定期供应（sa$_2$-du$_{11}$^{d}En-lil$_2$-la$_2$）。牛羊等牲畜也主要作为牺牲献祭，提供给节日庆典（eš$_3$-eš$_3$-še$_3$，gu$_4$udu eš$_3$-eš$_3$-še$_3$）、众神的定期供应（sa$_2$-du$_{11}$ dingir-re-ne）、神庙的神职人员的定期供给（sa$_2$-du$_{11}$ še-ba giri$_3$-se$_3$-ga gu-ru-ru）等。牲畜也提供脂肪（udu i$_3$）、腊肉（udu niga mu-du-lum）等bala税形式。还有，大麦被运到南塞神庙（e_2^{d}Nanše）、宁达尔神庙（e_2^{d}Nin-dar-a）、舒尔吉神庙（e_2^{d}Šul-gi）和迦图姆杜格神庙（e_2 ba-ga-ra$_2$ e_2^{d}Ga$_2$-tum$_3$-dug$_3$）等。比如：

TCTI 2 2670（AS 9 x，Girsu）

正面

2.4.0 še gur lugal	2古尔4巴里格王室大麦
erin$_2$ bala gub-ba	为正在服bala劳役的劳动力
0.0.3 5 sila$_3$ dumu Ba-uš$_2$-me	3班5希拉大麦，为巴乌什美的人们
e_2^{d}Nin-dar-a	运到宁达尔神庙
še sanga^{d}Dumu-zi	这些是杜牧孜神庙主管的大麦
i$_3$-dub e_2-gibil$_4$-le	来自"新房"粮仓

背面

ki Ba-zi-ta	从巴兹处

---

① 文献CM 26 73（SS 8 ii – iii）。
② 文献MVN 12 506（še大麦），TCTI 2 4304（še大麦），CM 26 66（šum$_2$-sikil葱类蔬菜）。

第二章 核心区 bala 税

Lugal-iri-da	卢伽尔伊里达
šu ba-ti	收到了
iti amar-a-a-si	第 10 月
mu en ^{d}Nanna Kar-zi-da ba-hun	阿马尔辛 9 年

（二）牲畜的饲料

作为牲畜饲料的 bala 税形式主要是粮食，[①] 以大麦最为普遍，也有小麦，作为牛、绵羊、山羊和驴的饲料。比如：

RTC 305（S 44 vi – xii, Girsu）
正面
第一栏

747. 2. 0 3 2/3 sila$_3$ duh gur lugal	747 古尔 2 巴里格 3 $\frac{2}{3}$ 希拉（尺寸）王室麦麸
7746 5/6 geme$_2$ u$_4$ 1-še$_3$	7746 $\frac{5}{6}$ 个工作日，女劳动力
30 gu$_2$ 26 ma-na ^{giš}ma-nu	30 塔兰特 26 米纳柳条
13220 sa gi	13220 束芦苇
si-i$_3$-tum	这些是剩余的
iti a$_2$-ki-ti	第 6 月
mu Si-mu-ru-um^{ki} Lu-lu-bu-um^{ki} a-ra$_2$ 10-la$_2$-1-kam-aš ba-hul-a	舒尔吉 44 年
1800 še gur	1800 古尔大麦
40 gig gur	40 古尔小麦
ša$_3$-gal gu$_4$ udu maš anše	作为牛、绵羊、山羊和驴的饲料
1. 3. 0 gur še-ba mar-tu-ne	1 古尔 3 巴里格大麦，是阿摩利人的配给
iti še-sag$_{11}$-ku$_5$	第 12 月
1800 še gur	1800 古尔大麦
40 gig gur	40 古尔小麦
ša$_3$-gal gu$_4$ udu maš anše	作为牛、绵羊、山羊和驴的饲料
1. 3. 0 gur še-ba mar-tu-ne	1 古尔 3 巴里格大麦，是阿摩利人的配给

[①] 文献 CM 26 73（SS 8 ii – iii），MVN 17 61（S 48 xi）。

iti diri še-sag₁₁-ku₅	闰 12 月
第二栏	
[……] da [……]	……
še [……]	大麦，……
nig₂-sa₁₀ gu₄ udu [……] -a-ka	为牛、羊等交易的饲料
211. 4. 3 3 sila₃ gur še kaš ninda	211 古尔 4 巴里格 3 班 3 希拉大麦、啤酒、面包
4351 sa gi	4351 束芦苇
12 2/3 gu₂ ᵍⁱˢma-nu	12 $\frac{2}{3}$ 塔兰特柳条
Na-ap-ta₂-num₂ nu-gu₇-a u₃ u₄-de₃ gid₂-da u₄ 1-kam	延期的一天纳普塔努姆没有喂养
1049. 1. 0 duh gur	1049 古尔 1 巴里格麦麸
duh-bi bala-ka	作为 bala 税的麦麸
iti še-sag₁₁-ku₅ u₃ iti diri še-sag₁₁-ku₅	第 12 月和闰 12 月
šu-nigin₂ 1 guru₇ 205. 0. 3 3 sila₃ še gur ᵈŠul-gi-ra	共计：1 筒仓 205 古尔 3 班 3 希拉舒尔吉（尺寸）大麦
šu-nigin₂ 80. 0. 0 gig gur	共计：80 古尔小麦
še-bi 1 guru₇ 375. 0. 3 3 sila₃ gur	其（换算）大麦（额）为 1 筒仓 375 古尔 3 班 3 希拉
šu-nigin₂ 1796. 3. 0 3 2/3 sila₃ duh gur	共计：1796 古尔 3 巴里格 3 $\frac{2}{3}$ 希拉麦麸
背面	
第一栏	
šu-nigin₂ 7746 5/6 geme₂ u₄ 1-še₃	共计：7746 $\frac{5}{6}$ 个工作日，女劳动力
šu-nigin₂ 43 gu₂ 6 ma-na ᵍⁱˢma-nu	共计：43 塔兰特 6 米纳柳条
šu-nigin₂ 17571 sa gi	共计：17571 束芦苇
sag-nig₂-gur₁₁-ra-kam	这些是借记
ša₃-bi-ta	从这些中：
2750. 1. 1 6 2/3 sila₃ še gur	2750 古尔 1 巴里格 1 班 6 $\frac{2}{3}$ 希拉大麦
diri nig₂-kas₇-ak	（之前）账目的剩余
iti a₂-ki-ti	第 6 月

mu Si-mu-ru-um^{ki} Lu-lu-bu-um^{ki} a-ra$_2$-10-la$_2$-1-kam-aš ba-hul	舒尔吉 44 年
3. 3. 5 5 sila$_3$ gig gur	3 古尔 3 巴里格 5 班 5 希拉小麦
e$_2$-kišib-ba-ka ba-an-ku$_4$	被送到储存室
giri$_3$ Lu$_2$-^{d}Utu ugula kikken	经办人是磨坊监管卢乌图
252. 0. 2 duh gur	252 古尔 2 班麦麸
^{d}Šul-gi-a-a-mu	为舒尔吉阿亚姆
〔…〕	
第二栏	
〔…〕 duh gur	……古尔麦麸
mu-DU	带来
la$_2$-ia$_3$ 1217. 1. 2 6 1/3 sila$_3$ še gur	赤字：1217 古尔 1 巴里格 2 班 6 $\frac{1}{3}$ 希拉大麦
1254. 2. 4 3 2/3 duh gur	1254 古尔 2 巴里格 4 班 3 $\frac{2}{3}$ 希拉麦麸
7746 5/6 geme$_2$ u$_4$ 1-še$_3$	7746 $\frac{5}{6}$ 个工作日，女劳动力
43 gu$_2$ 6 ma-na ^{giš}ma-nu	43 塔兰特 6 米纳柳条
9371 sa gi	9371 束芦苇
la$_2$-ia$_3$-am$_3$	是赤字
nig$_2$-kas$_7$-ak	这是吉尔苏总督乌尔兰马的 bala 税账目
bala Ur-^{d}Lamma ensi$_2$ Gir$_2$-su^{ki}	从第 12 月
iti še-sag$_{11}$-ku$_5$-ta	
iti diri še-sag$_{11}$-ku$_5$-še$_3$	到闰 12 月
iti 2-kam	共 2 个月
bala〔…〕	……bala 税
mu Si-mu-ru-um^{ki} Lu-lu-bu-um^{ki} a-ra$_2$-10-la$_2$-1-kam-aš ba-hul	舒尔吉 44 年

（三）人员食用

作为官员及其他人员食物来源的 bala 税形式主要是大麦。根据不同的用途和对象，这些食用大麦主要包括以下的类别（见表 2-15）：

103

表 2-15　　拉伽什—吉尔苏行省的食用大麦术语统计表

术语	汉译
ma₂-luh₅ lu₂ mar-sa bala tuš-a	服完 bala 劳役的军用仓库工人和水手（的食物）
ša₃-gal ma₂-lah₅ bala-še₃ ma₂ gid₂-da	正在拖船服 bala 劳役的水手的食物
ša₃-gal dumu dab₅-ba bala dub-ba	被带来服 bala 劳役的劳动力的食物
ša₃-gal dumu dab₅-ba bala dub-ba bala tuš-a-še₃	被带来服 bala 劳役以及服完 bala 劳役的劳动力的食物
ša₃-gal erin₂ bala gub-ba e₂-kurušda	育肥师房服 bala 劳役的军队的食物
ša₃-gal erin₂ bala gub-ba e₂-sukkal	使节房服 bala 劳役的军队的食物
ša₃-gal erin₂ bala gub-ba erin₂ gi-zi-me	服 bala 劳役的"吉孜"军队的食物
ša₃-gal erin₂ bala tuš-a erin₂ gi-zi-la₂	服完 bala 劳役的"吉孜"军队的食物
ša₃-gal eirn₂ bala-a e₂-gu-za-la₂	服 bala 劳役的"持王座"官员的食物
ša₃-gal erin₂ ša₃-gu₄ bala gub-ba	服 bala 劳役的"牛心"军队的食物
ša₃-gal erin₂ še tur-ra bala gub-ba eš₃ didli	供圣地服 bala 劳役的军队食用的"小的"大麦
ša₃-gal lu₂ azlag bala gub-ba-še₃	服 bala 劳役的漂洗工的食物
ša₃-gal lu₂ mar-sa bala gub-ba	服 bala 劳役的军用仓库工人的食物
še a-ša₃ bala-a ka-naga u₃ gir₂-du₃-a-ka	服 bala 劳役的建筑工人的大麦
še-ba aga₃-us₂ dumu Nigin₆ᵏⁱ	尼那的士兵的大麦配给
še-ba dumu dab₅-ba	带来的人们的大麦配给
še-ba giri₃-se₃-ga ša₃ e₂-gal	王宫服务人员的大麦配给
še-ba mar-sa	军用仓库工人的大麦配给

六　税率

根据目前的文献证据，我们无法知道所有 bala 课税形式的税率，只能间接推算出大麦这一种 bala 税形式的税率大约是 50%。其他的课税形式是否也和大麦是相等的税率，我们不得而知。

我们推算拉伽什—吉尔苏行省大麦 bala 税的税率的方法是：首先知道拉伽什—吉尔苏行省的大麦年产总量，然后知道每年该行省向中央缴纳的大麦 bala 税的数量，最后用后者除以前者，就是拉伽什—吉尔苏行省大麦 bala 税的税率。首先，关于拉伽什—吉尔苏行省的大麦年产量，在吉尔苏文献中可以找到某些年份的相关证据，即阿马尔辛 2 年拉伽什—吉尔苏行

第二章 核心区 bala 税

省的大麦产量为 27 筒仓 2395 古尔 5 班 2 希拉（即 99595 古尔 5 班 2 希拉，约为 99595 古尔或者 10 万古尔）。例如：

CT 7，pl. 8，BM 012926（AS 2，Girsu）
正面
第一栏

23 guru$_7$ ^{d}Šul-gi-ra 1866.0.4 7 sila$_3$ še gur	23 舒尔吉标准筒仓①1866 古尔 4 班 7 希拉大麦
še GAN$_2$-gu$_4$	是"公牛"地（生产）的大麦
1902.0.2 gur	1902 古尔 2 班（大麦）
še a-sag-us$_2$	是"次于优等"大麦
še gibil	（当年）新大麦
3 guru$_7$ 2226.4.4 5 sila$_3$ gur	3 筒仓 2226 古尔 4 巴里格 4 班 5 希拉（大麦）
še sumun	是陈大麦
šu-nigin$_2$ 27 guru$_7$ 2395.0.5 2 sila$_3$ gur	共计：27 筒仓 2395 古尔 5 班 2 希拉（大麦）
sag-nig$_2$-gur$_{11}$-ra-kam	这些是可用自产
ša$_3$-bi-ta	从其中
13 guru$_7$ 2990.2.4 1 1/2 sila$_3$ gur	13 筒仓 2990 古尔 2 巴里格 4 班 1$\frac{1}{2}$ 希拉（大麦）

第二栏

zi-ga bala-a	作为 bala 税被支出
3 guru$_7$ 1670.3.1 5 1/3 sila$_3$ gur	3 筒仓 1670 古尔 3 巴里格 1 班 5$\frac{1}{3}$ 希拉（大麦）
ša$_3$ Gir$_2$-su^{ki}	在吉尔苏
1 guru$_7$ 2842.3.0 7 sila$_3$ gur	1 筒仓 2842 古尔 3 巴里格 7 希拉（大麦）
gu$_2$ i$_7$ Unug^{ki}-ka	在乌鲁克河口
3 guru$_7$ 526.2.2 gur	3 筒仓 526 古尔 2 巴里格 2 班（大麦）

---

① 古代两河流域容量单位，1 筒仓等于 3600 古尔（约等于 1080000 升）。

ša Gu$_2$-ab-ba^{ki}　　　　　　　　　　　　在古阿巴

sa$_2$-du$_{11}$ še-ba　　　　　　　　　　　　作为大麦的定期供应

1 guru$_7$ 1673. 4. 1 1 sila$_3$ 15 gin$_2$ gur　　1 筒仓 1673 古尔 4 巴里格 1 班 1 希拉 15 舍客勒（大麦）

še GAN$_2$ apin-a　　　　　　　　　　　　是犁地的大麦

117. 3. 0 gur　　　　　　　　　　　　　　117 古尔 3 巴里格（大麦）

še GAN$_2$ bala-a　　　　　　　　　　　　是"分裂"地的大麦

86. 2. 0 gur　　　　　　　　　　　　　　86 古尔 2 巴里格（大麦）

še amar gu$_4$ apin　　　　　　　　　　　是耕犁的公牛崽的大麦

背面

第一栏

2220. 0. 0 gur　　　　　　　　　　　　　2220 古尔（大麦）

[…] gur　　　　　　　　　　　　　　　……古尔（大麦）

303 + . 1. 4 […] apin　　　　　　　　　303 + 古尔 1 巴里格 4 班（大麦）（……犁）

še […] GAN$_2$ bala-a　　　　　　　　　是"分裂"地的大麦

24 guru$_7$ 121 + . 2. 2 3 2/3 sila$_3$ gur　　24 筒仓 131 + 古尔 2 巴里格 2 班 3 $\frac{2}{3}$ 希拉（大麦）

nig$_2$ Zi-zi-mu　　　　　　　　　　　　是孜孜姆的财产

4 guru$_7$ gur　　　　　　　　　　　　　4 筒仓（大麦）

še ^{d}En-lil$_2$-la$_2$　　　　　　　　　　是（献给）恩利尔的大麦

šu-nigin$_2$ 28 guru$_7$ 3066. 2. 2 3 2/3 sila$_3$ gur　共计：28 筒仓 3066 古尔 2 巴里格 2 班 3 $\frac{2}{3}$ 希拉（大麦）

zi-ga　　　　　　　　　　　　　　　　被支出

diri 1 guru$_7$ 666. 1. 3 1 2/3 sila$_3$ gur　　剩余：1 筒仓 666 古尔 1 巴里格 3 班 1 $\frac{2}{3}$ 希拉（大麦）

第二栏

nig$_2$-kas$_7$-ak še nigin-ba　　　　　　　全部大麦的平衡账目

ša$_3$ Gir$_2$-su^{ki}　　　　　　　　　　　在吉尔苏

mu ^{d}Amar-^{d}Suen lugal-e Ur-bi$_2$-lum^{ki}　阿马尔辛 2 年

mu-hul

另一种方法是，根据可耕地计算，拉伽什—吉尔苏行省的神庙土地在舒尔吉 41 年为 3114 布尔，在舒尔吉 47 年为 3192 布尔。[1] 平均而言，1 布尔土地可生产 30 古尔大麦，那么吉尔苏的神庙土地的大麦产量是 93420—95760 古尔之间，这个数字正好跟文献中直接记载的大麦产量基本吻合。由于在拉伽什—吉尔苏行省的经济中，神庙经济占据主导地位，所以神庙土地也是该行省的最主要可耕地。由此，我们大概可以推测，拉伽什—吉尔苏行省的年大麦产量在 10 万古尔左右。

接下来，我们需要从文献证据中寻找拉伽什—吉尔苏行省一年需要向中央缴纳的大麦 bala 税总量。从上述的文献中，我们知道了有 13 筒仓 2990 古尔 2 巴里格 4 班 1$\frac{1}{2}$希拉（即 49790 古尔 2 巴里格 4 班 1$\frac{1}{2}$希拉，约为 49790 古尔或者近 5 万古尔）大麦作为 bala 税被缴纳（zi-ga bala-a）给乌尔中央政府。所以说，拉伽什—吉尔苏行省的大麦 bala 税的税率大约为 49.99%（或者一半 50%）。

七 征收时间

拉伽什—吉尔苏行省的 bala 纳税期有别于乌尔第三王朝的其他行省，不是每年一个月，而是二至四个月，划分为两"季"[2]。许多吉尔苏文献提到，较早的纳税季（bala dub-sag）和较晚的纳税季（bala egir）。拉伽什—吉尔苏行省为什么有如此多的纳税任务呢？这可能跟拉伽什—吉尔苏行省的大小有关，因为它是乌尔第三王朝最大的行省，但是具体的原因不详。据一篇文献（MVN 9 124）记载，拉伽什—吉尔苏行省的 bala 月份是每年四个月，即第 1、2、6、7 月，第 1、2 月为第一季（bala dub-sag 较早的纳税期），第 6、7 月为第二季（bala egir 较晚的纳税期）。表示两季 bala 的术语还有：bala-bi 1-am$_3$（它的纳税期是一个月）和 bala-bi 2-am$_3$（它的纳税期是两个月）。

---

[1] K. Maekawa, "The Governor's Family and the 'Temple Households' in Ur III Girsu", in K. Veenhof (ed.), *Houses and Households in Ancient Mesopotamia*, RAI 40, Istanbul: Nederlands Historisch-Archaeologisch Instituut, 1996, p. 176.

[2] W. W. Hallo, "A Sumerian Amphictyony", *Journal of Cuneiform Studies*, Vol. 14 (1960), p. 93. T. M. Sharlach, *Provincial Taxation and the Ur III State*, Cuneiform Monographs 26, Leiden and Boston: Brill-Styx, 2004, p. 67.

下面，我们根据普兹瑞什达干文献中关于吉尔苏总督从普兹瑞什达干接收 bala 动物的月份，以及吉尔苏文献中向中央缴纳 bala 税的月份进行合并统计。需要注意的是，吉尔苏的月历和普兹瑞什达干月历之间存在差异，所以有些月份可能对应不上，我们应该以吉尔苏的月历为准，以普兹瑞什达干的月历为参照（见表 2-16）。

表 2-16　　拉伽什—吉尔苏行省 bala 税纳税月份统计表

日期	1月	2月	3月	4月	5月	6月	7月	8月	9月	10月	11月	12月
S 27								吉				
S 28												
S 29												
S 30												
S 31			吉									
S 32			吉						吉		吉	吉
S 33										吉	吉	吉
S 34					吉				吉		吉	吉
S 35		吉	吉	吉	吉				吉	吉/普		
S 36												
S 37				吉		吉		吉		吉	吉	吉
S 38		吉		吉								
S 39												
S 40												
S 41							普	普	普			普
S 42			吉							吉	吉	吉/普
S 43	吉							吉				吉
S 44	吉			普	普	普			吉	吉	吉	
S 45	吉			普	吉/普		吉	吉	吉	吉	吉	
S 46	吉		吉	吉	吉	吉	吉	吉	吉	吉		吉
S 47	吉		普	普	吉		吉	吉	吉	吉/普	普	

108

续表

日期	1月	2月	3月	4月	5月	6月	7月	8月	9月	10月	11月	12月
S 48						吉	吉	吉	吉	普	吉/普	普
AS 1		吉						吉/普	吉	普		吉
AS 2	吉		吉	吉/普	吉/普		吉	吉	普	吉		
AS 3	吉		吉/普	吉/普	吉		吉/普				吉/普	
AS 4	吉/普	普					吉		普		吉	吉
AS 5	普				吉/普		吉	普				吉
AS 6	吉				吉	吉	普			吉		
AS 7										吉	吉	吉/普
AS 8			吉	吉	吉	吉	普			吉	吉	吉/普
AS 9						吉	普	普		吉	吉	吉/普
SS 1					吉			吉	吉	吉	吉/普	吉/普
SS 2		吉						吉	吉	吉/普	吉/普	吉/普
SS 3			吉	吉	吉			吉				
SS 4	普						吉	吉	吉			
SS 5					吉			普	吉	普	普	
SS 6								吉	吉	吉	吉	
SS 7						吉		吉				
SS 8	吉	吉	吉			吉						
SS 9	吉					吉		吉		吉		吉
IS 1	吉		吉	吉		吉	吉		吉			
IS 2	吉				吉	吉		吉				
IS 3										吉	吉	

*注：（1）国王名缩写，S = Shulgi（舒尔吉），AS = Amar-Suen（阿马尔辛），SS = Shu-Suen（舒辛），IS = Ibbi-Suen（伊比辛）；（2）普——普兹瑞什达干文献，吉——吉尔苏文献。

第五节 其他行省的 bala 税

前面我们提到，行省档案对于我们认识 bala 税至关重要，也是研究 bala 税的直接证据。目前，除了拉伽什—吉尔苏行省档案和温马行省档案之外，其他行省的档案文献几乎没有发现。① 所以，我们对于其他行省 bala 税的认识，只能从代表中央政府的普兹瑞什达干文献寻找间接证据。在普兹瑞什达干文献中，记载了几乎每个行省从中央政府接收 bala 动物的情况，这些 bala 动物并不是这些行省向中央政府缴纳的，而是在他们的 bala 月份（纳税期）时，即他们向中央政府缴纳 bala 税（非动物形式）之后，又从中央政府接收动物作为其纳税的补偿或者回报。这些从中央到地方流向的动物，也是 bala 赋税体系的一部分。这可以看成是一种税收返还（政府补助）或者税收补贴制度。

普兹瑞什达干机构的动物种类繁多，以家养牲畜为主，包括牛、羊、驴等，每种牲畜又根据其喂养饲料级别、年龄、颜色、来源地、身体条件等特性划分为若干具体的种类，比如 udu u$_2$ "食草的绵羊" 和 udu niga "食大麦的绵羊（育肥绵羊）"；gu$_4$ mu-1 "生长一年的牛"、gu$_4$ mu-2 "生长两年的牛"、gu$_4$ mu-3 "生长三年的牛" 等。普兹瑞什达干机构的动物除了少量来自核心行省，其余大多数来源于外围行省（见下一章）。

一 bala 税负责官员

中央政府直辖的普兹瑞什达干机构，设有专门负责 bala 动物管理的部门和官员。这些官员可以分为两类，一类是支出官员，一类是接收官员，bala 税大概的流转过程如下（见图 2-5）：

支出官员 → 接收官员 → 行省总督或神庙主管

图 2-5 bala 税流转过程示意图

支出官员一般是由普兹瑞什达干机构的中心部门官员及部分分支部门的官员担任，他们或者将 bala 动物直接支付给行省总督或者神庙主管，完成 bala 税收补贴过程，或者先将 bala 动物转运给接收官员，再由接收官员支付

---

① 伊利萨格里格行省档案是近几年才陆续出版的，但是关于 bala 税的文献寥寥无几，只有 30 多篇，不足以构成研究所需的样本。尼普尔和乌尔档案则更少记载 bala 税的情况。

给行省总督或者神庙主管。需要注意的是，根据普兹瑞什达干文献证据表明，这些支出官员处理bala税收返还只是他们众多工作之一，他们还有其他处理动物的工作，而接收官员一般都是专门处理负责bala动物的部门官员，他们的部门隶属于中心部门，属于普兹瑞什达干机构的分支部门之一。

担任bala动物的支出官员包括：纳拉姆伊里、恩利拉（专门处理牛）、纳萨、阿胡尼、伊宁沙拉之子卢丁吉尔拉、舒伊丁、阿巴萨加、舒尔吉阿亚姆、因塔埃阿和沙拉卡姆。担任bala动物的接收官员包括：卡亚姆、贝里阿祖、乌什姆、卢巴巴、卢萨加、南那玛巴、阿哈尼舒、杜加、卢伽尔阿马尔库和乌尔库努纳。

二 行省bala纳税期花名册

依据普兹瑞什达干文献，我们可以理清乌尔第三王朝核心行省bala纳税期大多数年份和月份，但是并不能包括所有的年月信息。从残缺的文献中我们发现，在乌尔第三王朝时期，中央政府已经制定过这样的花名册，由于bala月份随着年度的不同也会发生变化，所以这种行省bala纳税月份花名册也是每年一更新，记录这一年每个月的bala纳税行省。目前，我们发现了一些纳税期花名册档案。比如下面这篇残缺文献列举了阿马尔辛4年第1—4月的bala纳税行省，只可惜该文献残缺，未能保存阿马尔辛4年全年bala月份及其对应的纳税行省信息。

JCS 14 113 21（AS 4 i – v）
正面
iti maš-da$_3$-gu$_7$ 第1月
iti ses-da-gu$_7$ 第2月
bala ensi$_2$ Gir$_2$-su^{ki} （是）吉尔苏行省总督的bala税纳税月份
iti u$_5$-bi$_2$-gu$_7$ 第3月
bala ensi$_2$ Adab^{ki} （是）阿达布行省总督的bala税纳税月份
iti ki-siki ^{d}Nin-a-zu   第4月
bala ensi$_2$ Ka-[zal-lu]^{ki} （是）卡扎鲁行省总督的bala税纳税月份
（剩余残缺）
背面
（开头残缺）

bala ensi₂ Gir₂-su₂^ki　　　　　　　（是）吉尔苏行省总督的 bala 税纳税月份

mu En-mah-gal-an-na en
^dNanna ba-hun　　　　　　　　　阿马尔辛 4 年

有的文献不仅列举了 bala 纳税行省及其对应的 bala 月份信息，还提供了税收形式与数量，以及税收的用途等有用的信息。比如下面一篇阿马尔辛 5 年的文献：

Hermitage 3 249（AS 5 i-viii）
正面
25 u₈ 40 maš₂　　　　　　　　　　25 只母绵羊、40 只山羊
eš₂-eš₃ u₄-7 iti u₄ 5 ba-zal　　　　　为第七日节，在第 5 日
bala ^dŠara₂-kam　　　　　　　　　作为沙拉卡姆的 bala 税
iti maš-da₃-gu₇　　　　　　　　　　第 1 月
40 udu 2 sila₄ ki-gi₄-a　　　　　　　40 只公绵羊、2 只用于占卜的绵羊羔
20 u₈ 30 maš₂　　　　　　　　　　20 只母绵羊、30 只山羊
eš₂-eš₃ u₄ 30 ba-zal　　　　　　　　为第 30 日节庆
bala Ha-ba-lu₅-ge ensi₂ Adab^ki　　作为阿达布总督哈巴卢吉的 bala 税
iti ses-da-gu₇　　　　　　　　　　　第 2 月
28 udu 18 u₈ 15 maš₂-gal
5 ud₅　　　　　　　　　　　　　　28 只公绵羊、18 只母绵羊、15 只公山羊
　　　　　　　　　　　　　　　　　5 只母山羊
eš₂-eš₃ u₄ 15 ba-zal　　　　　　　　为第 15 日节庆
3 udu niga sa₂-du₁₁ ^dEn-ki ur₃-ra　3 只食大麦绵羊，为护佑恩基的定期供应
bala ^dŠara₂-kam　　　　　　　　　作为沙拉卡姆的 bala 税
iti ezem ^dNin-a-zu　　　　　　　　第 5 月
3 udu niga sa₂-du₁₁ ^dEn-ki ša₃
Uri₅^ki-ma　　　　　　　　　　　　3 只食大麦绵羊，为乌尔恩基的定期供应
背面
13 udu［…］　　　　　　　　　　　13 只绵羊
bala［…］mu［x］u₄ Aš₂-nun^ki-
ma-kam　　　　　　　　　　　　　作为埃什努那……的 bala 税
iti a₂-ki-ti　　　　　　　　　　　　　第 6 月
3 udu niga sa₂-du₁₁ ^dEn-ki　　　　3 只食大麦绵羊，为恩基的定期供应

112

第二章 核心区 bala 税

bala ^{d}Šara$_2$-kam ensi$_2$ Gir$_2$-su^{ki}	作为吉尔苏总督沙拉卡姆的 bala 税
iti šu-eš$_5$-ša	第 8 月
ki Na-lu$_5$-ta	从纳鲁处
Lu$_2$-^{d}Ba-ba$_6$ i$_3$-dab$_5$	卢巴巴收到了
mu En-unu$_6$-e ba-hun	阿马尔辛 5 年

此外，还有一篇文献记录了库特哈、吉尔苏、普斯、基什、乌鲁姆等行省的 bala 纳税月份。①

SAT 3 2030（--vi-ix）
正面
（开头残缺）

bala ensi$_2$ Gu$_2$-du$_8$-a^{ki}	库特哈行省总督的 bala 税
iti a$_2$-ki-ti	（在）第 6 月
75 gu$_4$ niga 34 gu$_4$	75 头育肥牛、34 头（普通）牛
bala ensi$_2$ Gu$_2$-du$_8$-a^{ki}	库特哈行省总督的 bala 税
iti ezem ^{d}Šul-gi	（在）第 7 月
67 gu$_4$ niga 33 gu$_4$	67 头育肥牛、33 头（普通）牛
bala ensi$_2$ Gir$_2$-su^{ki}	吉尔苏行省总督的 bala 税
iti šu-eš-ša	（在）第 8 月
26 gu$_4$ niga 2 gu$_4$	26 头育肥牛、2 头（普通）牛
bala Igi-an-na-ke$_4$-zu	（普斯行省总督）伊吉安纳克祖的 bala 税
iti ezem mah	（在）第 9 月
[x] +8 gu$_4$ niga 7 gu$_4$	8+ 头育肥牛、7 头（普通）牛
bala ensi$_2$ Kiš^{ki} [xxx]	基什行省总督（和）乌鲁姆行省总督
Urum$_2$^{ki}-še$_3$	的 bala 税

（其余破损残缺）

---

① P. Steinkeller, "On the Reading and Location of the Toponyms ÚRxÚ. KI and A. HA. KI", *Journal of Cuneiform Studies*, Vol. 32 (1980), pp. 23–33; M. W. Green, "Urum and Uqair", *Acta Sumerologica*, Vol. 8 (1986), pp. 77–83; D. I. Owen, "The Ensis of Gudua", *Acta Sumerologica*, Vol. 15 (1993), pp. 131–152.

上述这些文献中，文献 JCS 14 113 21 很可能是乌尔第三王朝时期所编制的行省 bala 纳税月份花名册，这样的花名册在理论上应该每年由中央政府编制与公布，一般可能会在前一年末制定出来，公布并且发放给各个需要纳税的行省，来年一开始即刻实行。但是十分遗憾的是，我们目前所能发现的这类花名册档案只有这一篇。此外，诸如文献 Hermitage 3 249 和 SAT 3 2030 这样记录多个月份的多个行省的纳税情况，也是我们复原 bala 纳税月份的重要证据。当然，我们能够利用的档案基本上是记载一个月一个行省的 bala 纳税情况，由于大多数普兹瑞什达干 bala 文献都保留了月名，对应上行省的 bala 纳税记录，即可以对行省 bala 纳税月份进行整体的复原与重建。

下列表格就是在对普兹瑞什达干文献统计整理的基础上，我们对乌尔第三王朝所有涉及行省 bala 纳税月份和年份的暂时重建（见表 2 - 17）。

表 2 - 17　　　乌尔第三王朝内行省 bala 税纳税月份统计表

日期	1月	2月	3月	4月	5月	6月	7月	8月	9月	10月	11月	12月
S 33			卡				温					
S 34							卡					
S 35						温			吉			
S 41					巴		吉	吉	吉			吉
S 42			马									吉
S 43			普					姆				
S 44		普/温	提/巴	吉	吉	吉		X				
S 45				吉	吉		库		尔			
S 46	温	巴/普/提	马	布/基								
S 47		普	吉	吉	布/埃		库			卡	吉	吉
S 48						库				吉	吉	吉/温
AS 1					布	库	舒	吉/姆/尼		吉		
AS 2	巴		布	吉	吉	库	舒		吉			
AS 3	X	格/Y	吉	吉			吉		库/尔/克	X	吉/卡	
AS 4	吉	吉		马			X		X/吉/苏		基	

续表

日期	1月	2月	3月	4月	5月	6月	7月	8月	9月	10月	11月	12月
AS 5	吉	布	皮	卡	吉	埃		吉	温	X/巴/西		普
AS 6						吉			舒		巴/提	
AS 7		布	马	卡	西/X	埃/IS	库	温		尔	巴/提/普	吉
AS 8				卡	西/卡		吉	舒/温	舒/基	X	巴	吉
AS 9	卡		马				吉	吉/温	舒		巴	吉
SS 1							温		埃		吉	吉
SS 2			西					埃	布/埃	吉	吉	吉
SS 3			西					埃	巴		马	
SS 4	吉											
SS 5	格							吉		吉	吉	
SS 6					普/姆				马			
SS 7	西											
SS 8	巴/西					巴						
SS 9	西					埃	巴		格			
IS 1	西					埃	巴				格	
IS 2							巴		基	马/格		

缩写表示：（1）国王名缩写，S = Shulgi（舒尔吉），AS = Amar-Suen（阿马尔辛），SS = Shu-Suen（舒辛），IS = Ibbi-Suen（伊比辛）；（2）行省缩写，阿达布（布）、阿皮亚克（皮）、巴比伦（巴）、吉尔苏（吉）、基什（基）、卡扎鲁（卡）、库特哈（库）、马腊德（马）、尼普尔（尼）、普斯（普）、舒鲁帕克（舒）、提威（提）、温马（温）、乌尔（尔）、乌鲁克（克）、乌鲁姆（姆）、西帕尔（西）、伊利萨格里格（格）、伊新（新）。埃什努那（埃）、苏萨（苏）、伊西姆舒尔吉（IS）、不详（X）。

在关于乌尔第三王朝赋税文献中，记载 bala 税的文献数量是最多的，内涵的信息量也是最大的。通过对这些文献资料的整理与分析，我们可以大致复原乌尔第三王朝的核心行省赋税制度的运转形式及其特色。首先，核心区 bala 税的课税形式是大麦、面粉、芦苇、木材、手工制品、香料、羊毛以及劳动力等实物。其中，拉伽什—吉尔苏行省缴纳的 bala 税以大麦为主，而温马行省缴纳的 bala 税以芦苇及芦苇制品、木料及木制品为主。其次，bala 税的一大特色是税收返还制度，即核心行省向中央缴纳大麦、面粉、芦苇、木材、手工制品、香料、羊毛以及劳动力等实物，而中央政府从普兹瑞什达干机构交付牲畜给纳税行省，作为补偿或返还。再次，bala 税的征税对象名义上是各个行省的总督，实际上是行省内负责税收的专门机构，并且不同的机构负责不同的课税形式。bala 税的一部分被运往首都乌尔、宗教中心尼普尔、中央直辖机构普兹瑞什达干、王室成员常住地乌鲁克等，另一部分被运往行省内隶属于中央政府的军队驻地，供给中央军队、王室成员、中央官员以及外国使节。最后，bala 税的征收方式主要是通过船运，其过程大致分为：收集、装船、托船、卸船、运到目的地等步骤。bala 税的征收比例大约占每个行省年财政收入的一半。除了拉伽什-吉尔苏行省每年有两季（多个月）作为缴税时间外，其他行省每年有固定的月份作为缴税时间，且各个行省的缴税月份呈现规律性变化，中央政府每年会制定各个行省的缴税月份，使每个月都有行省向中央缴纳 bala 税，从而保证中央财政收入的稳定性。

乌尔第三王朝的核心区（核心行省）是王朝最重要的一级地方行政区划，乌尔中央政府通过实行 bala 税制，直接从核心行省征收赋税，既保证了中央政府的稳定财政收入，又加强了中央对地方的直接控制，体现了乌尔第三王朝中央集权统治的特点。

第三章　外围区 gun₂ ma-da 税

乌尔第三王朝的行政区划分为三个部分：核心区、外围区和附属国。其中，核心区向中央政府缴纳 bala 税，赋税形式多种多样，包括大麦、芦苇、面粉、木材、手工制品、劳动力和牲畜等，而外围区向中央政府缴纳 gun₂ ma-da 税，以牲畜作为课税形式，这种牲畜税由普兹瑞什达干机构负责管理，牲畜的用途是作为尼普尔诸神庙的献祭品，以及供外国使节和军事人员食用。外围区（外省）税和核心区（内省）税一同构成了乌尔第三王朝的行省税收体系，是乌尔中央政府加强对地方直接控制的一种强有力措施，也是乌尔第三王朝中央集权统治在经济方面的体现。

接下来，我们首先从地理范围、行政区划、经济结构以及性质和作用等角度，来介绍外围区的概况，然后追溯原始文献与术语记录，通过对原始文献资料的整理与分析，进一步探讨外围区 gun₂ ma-da 税的征税对象、税率、征税时限与拖欠税收等情况。

第一节　外围区概况

乌尔第三王朝的外围区，又称军事缓冲区和防御区，与核心区相对。从乌尔第三王朝的行省制度来看，核心区作为内省，而外围区就是外省。

一　地理范畴

在地理范围上，核心区主要分布在两河流域的南部地区，以及迪亚拉河流域少部分区域，是古代两河流域传统上所说的苏美尔—阿卡德之地。而外围区顾名思义，应该是在核心区的外围，即围绕着核心的环形区域。

具体而言，外围区主要分布在底格里斯河的东部地区，从东北部的扎格罗斯山脉一直延伸至东南部的埃兰地区，比如萨布姆（Sabum）、苏萨和阿丹顿（Adamdun），① 甚至有可能向南延伸至波斯湾沿岸的帕西美（Pashime），② 而在北部地区一直延伸至阿淑尔和乌尔比隆（Urbilum，今Erbil），一共大概包括90个地区。③ 由此，外围区在地理版图上，构成了一个对乌尔第三王朝核心区从北部到东部及东南部的环形包围圈（见图3-1）。在外围区的外部，还有一个更大的包围圈，即乌尔第三王朝的附属国体系（见第四章）。

由于文献资料的缺乏，我们对乌尔第三王朝的外围区的认识程度远远不及核心区，我们只能大概确定外围区的整体地理范畴，但是对于每一个地区的具体地理位置，目前看来还很难定位。另外，对于外围区政治经济的具体情况，我们更是知之甚少，仅有的文献资料来源仅是普兹瑞什达干文献和王室铭文等间接证据，而几乎没有来自这些外围区遗址的考古发掘成果。④

作为乌尔第三王朝的军事防御区或缓冲区，外围区向中央政府缴纳 gun₂ ma-da 税，基本都是以牲畜的形式缴纳，缴税的目的地是普兹瑞什达干各机构。外围区的军事性质已经被学界大多数学者们所认可，只是在关于外围区的所属性质以及行政特征方面，在学界存在一些争议。大致有两种不同的见解，以美国密歇根大学米哈沃夫斯基为主的观点认为，外围区是乌尔第三王朝未合并的领土或势力范围，其作用是乌尔第三王朝的缓冲

---

① P. Michalowski, "Observations on 'Elamites' and 'Elam' in Ur III Times", in P. Michalowski (ed.), *On the Third Dynasty of Ur: Studies in Honor of Marcel Sigrist*, The Journal of Cuneiform Studies Supplemental Series Volume 1, Boston: American Schools of Oriental Research, 2008, pp. 114-121.

② P. Steinkeller, "The Question of Marhaši: A Contribution to the Historical Geography of Iran in the Third Millennium B. C.", *Zeitschrift für Assyriologie und Vorderasiatische Archäologie*, Vol. 72 (1982), pp. 241-242.

③ P. Steinkeller, "The Administrative and Economic Organization of the Ur III State", in McG. Gibson, R. Biggs (eds.), *The Organization of Power: Aspects of Bureaucracy in the Ancient Near East*, Studies in Ancient Oriental Civilization 46, Chicago: The Oriental Institute of the University of Chicago, 1987, p. 28, 该文称有90个地区；T. Maeda, "The Defence Zone during the Rule of the Ur III Dynasty", *Acta Sumerologica*, Vol. 14 (1992), pp. 165-172, 列举了89个地区。D. Patterson, *Elements of the Neo-Sumerian Military*, PhD dissertation, University of Pennsylvania, 2018, 列有96个地区。

④ 迪亚拉和哈明（Hamrin）地区有一些考古发掘，很少有乌尔第三王朝的遗迹，参见 D. Patterson, *Elements of the Neo-Sumerian Military*, PhD dissertation, University of Pennsylvania, 2018, p. 27。

第三章 外围区 gun₂ ma-da 税

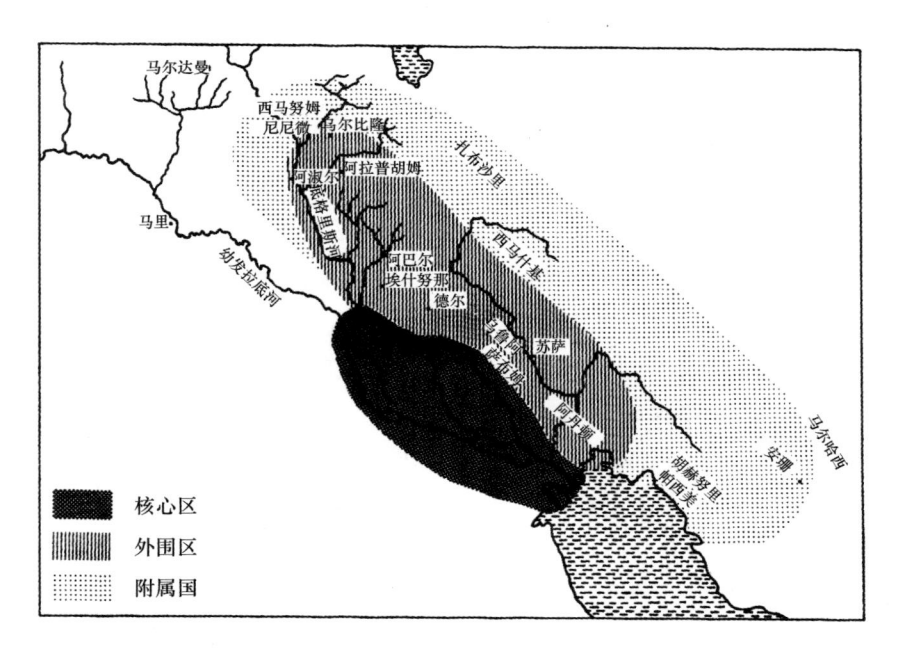

图 3-1 乌尔第三王朝外围区版图

资料来源：引自 P. Steinkeller, "The Administrative and Economic Organization of the Ur III State: the Core and the Periphery", in McG. Gibson, R. Biggs (eds.), *The Organization of Power Aspects of Bureaucracy in the Ancient Near East*, Chicago: The Oriental Institute of the University of Chicago, 1987, p. 31.

区或者缓冲带（buffer zone），作为乌尔国家抵御外来入侵的防线以及对外军事征服的集结待命地区；[①] 而以美国哈佛大学斯坦因凯勒为主的观点则认为，外围区是乌尔第三王朝的固有领土或者已经合并的领土，和核心区一样，都属于乌尔第三王朝的地方行省，所不同的是，外围区属于乌尔国家的自治行省，其独立性要强于核心区，并且具有军事防御和军事驻地的性质，类似于罗马时期的 *limes*。[②] 笔者支持后一种观点，并且认为外围区

[①] P. Michalowski, "Foreign Tribute to Sumer during the Ur III Period", *Zeitschrift für Assyriologie und Vorderasiatische Archäologie*, Vol. 68 (1978), p. 46.

[②] P. Steinkeller, "The Administrative and Economic Organization of the Ur III State: The Core and the Periphery", in M. Gibson and R. D. Biggs (eds.), *The Organization of Power: Aspects of Bureaucracy in the Ancient Near East*, Studies in Ancient Oriental Civilization 46, Chicago: The Oriental Institute of the University of Chicago, 1987, pp. 26-29.

是一种直属于乌尔中央政府的具有军事防御性质的地方行政机构，这有点类似于我国古代的卫所制度。①

二 行政组织

在行政组织上，根据行政区域大小以及管辖的范围不同，外围区可以划分为三类：第一类是大型地区，由将军（或军事总督）负责管理，少数由总督负责管理；第二类是中型地区，由高级军尉负责管理，一般是每个军尉需向中央缴纳两头牛和20只羊的税额；第三类是小型地区，由低级军尉负责管理，一般每个军尉需向中央缴纳一头牛和10只羊的税额。需要注意的是，前两类地区的管理者都是该地区的最高军事和行政长官，而第三类地区的管理者是隶属于前两类最高长官的低级官员。

首先，我们需要解决以下问题：乌尔第三王朝到底有多少个外省？这个问题目前几乎无法回答。另外一个问题是：外省总共包括多少个地区或者城市？这个问题目前有了暂时的答案。有的学者认为是89个，②有的学者认为是90个，③有的学者认为是96个。④由于新的文献依然不时出现，所以属于外围区的地区数量也在不时更新，我们认为属于外围区的地区或者城市大概有100个。这些地区以及文献出处暂时列举如下（见表3-1）：⑤

---

① 关于我国古代的卫所制度，可参见顾诚《隐匿的疆土：卫所制度与明帝国》，光明日报出版社2012年版；李新峰《明代卫所政区研究》，北京大学出版社2016年版；毛亦可《清代卫所归并州县研究》，社会科学文献出版社2018年版。

② T. Maeda, "The Defence Zone during the Rule of the Ur III Dynasty", *Acta Sumerologica*, Vol. 14 (1992), pp. 165–172.

③ P. Steinkeller, "The Administrative and Economic Organization of the Ur III State: The Core and the Periphery", in M. Gibson and R. D. Biggs (eds.), *The Organization of Power: Aspects of Bureaucracy in the Ancient Near East*, Studies in Ancient Oriental Civilization 46, Chicago: The Oriental Institute of the University of Chicago, 1987, pp. 19–41.

④ D. Patterson, *Elements of the Neo-Sumerian Military*, PhD dissertation, University of Pennsylvania, 2018, pp. 375–376.

⑤ 注意，这些地名有的可能指附属国，或者在某个时期内是附属国，这里的列举只是暂时性的。

第三章 外围区 gun₂ ma-da 税

表 3-1 　　　　　　　乌尔第三王朝外围区统计表

编号	地区汉译	地区	编号	地区汉译	地区
1	阿比巴纳	Abibana	25	加布拉什	Gablash
2	阿丹顿	Adamdun	26	伽尔奈奈	Garnene
3	阿加孜	Agaz	27	哈布拉	Habura
4	阿拉美	Arame	28	哈尔西	Harshi
5	阿尔曼	Arman	29	哈马孜	Hamazi
6	阿拉普胡姆	Arraphum	30	希比拉特	Hebilat
7	阿淑尔	Ashur	31	胡比乌姆	Hubium
8	阿瓦尔	Awal	32	胡布尼	Hubni
9	阿扎曼	Azaman	33	胡普姆	Hupum
10	巴比	Babi	34	胡尔提	Hurti
11	巴鲁埃	Balue	35	伊巴尔	Ibbal
12	巴尔曼	Barman	36	因纳巴	Innaba
13	比达顿	Bidadun	37	伊西姆舒尔吉	Ishim-Shulgi
14	达尔图姆	Daltum	38	伊西姆舒辛	Ishim-Shu-Suen
15	达西比韦	Dashibiwe	39	伊舒姆	Ishum
16	达什提	Dashti	40	伊舒尔	Ishur
17	德尔	Der	41	卡库拉图姆	Kakkulatum
18	德尔—吉孜	Der-KI.ZI	42	卡拉哈尔	Karahar
19	杜尔埃布拉	Dur-Ebla	43	基马什①	Kimash
20	杜尔马什	Durmash	44	基什加提	Kishgati
21	埃巴尔	Ebal	45	吉斯马尔	Kismar
22	埃杜鲁舒尔吉	Eduru-Shulgi	46	卢卢布	Lullubu
23	埃鲁特	Erut	47	马哈祖姆	Mahazum
24	埃什努那	Eshnuna	48	马尔曼	Marman

---

① D. Potts, "Adamšah, Kimaš and the miners of Lagaš", in H. D. Baker, E. Robson and G. Zolyomi (eds.), *Your Praise is Sweet: A Memorial Volume for Jeremy Black from Students, Colleagues and Friends*, London: British Institute for the Study of Iraq, 2010, pp. 248-249.

续表

编号	地区汉译	地区	编号	地区汉译	地区
49	马什堪阿比	Mashkan-abi	73	希乌米	Si'ummi
50	马什堪加埃什	Mashkan-gaesh	74	舒阿希	Shu'ahi
51	马什堪卡拉图姆	Mashkan-kallatum	75	舒伊尔胡姆	Shu'irhum
52	马什堪沙鲁姆	Mashkan-sharrum	76	舒尔吉南那	Shulgi-Nanna
53	马什堪乌舒里	Mashkan-ushuri	77	舒尔吉乌图	Shulgi-Utu
54	奈贝尔阿马尔辛	Neber-Amar-Suen	78	舒恩提	Shunti
55	奈贝鲁姆	Neberum	79	舒姆提乌姆	Shumtium
56	尼达拉什韦	NIdarashwe	80	舒尔布	Shurbu
57	尼希	NI. HI	81	苏萨	Susa
58	尼姆孜乌姆	Nimzium	82	舒辛伊杜格	Shu-Suen-idug
59	尼尼微①	Ninua	83	塔布拉拉	Tablala
60	努伽尔	Nugar	84	塔布拉	Tabra
61	帕西美	Pashime	85	泰尔加	Terga
62	皮伊尔	PI'il	86	提兰	Tiran
63	普赫兹伽尔	Puhzigar	87	图图布	Tutub
64	普特沙达尔	Putshadar	88	乌尔比隆	Urbilum
65	普图里乌姆	Puttulium	89	乌尔古哈拉姆	Urguhalam
66	拉比	Rabi	90	乌鲁阿	Urua
67	萨布姆	Sabum	91	瓦努姆	Wanum
68	萨拉奈韦	SallaNEwe	92	亚阿米什	Ya'amish
69	沙米	Shami	93	扎巴巴	Zababa
70	沙尼达特	Shanidat	94	扎图姆	Zatum
71	塞希尔	Sheshil	95	孜比莱	Zibire
72	塞提尔沙	Shetirsha	96	孜姆达尔	Zimudar

① 关于乌尔第三王朝时期的尼尼微，参见 R. M. Whiting, "Tiš-atal of Nineveh and Babati, Uncle of Šu-Sin", *Journal od Cuneiform Studies*, Vol. 28（1976）, pp. 173 - 182; R. L. Zettler, "Tišatal and Nineveh at the End of the 3rd Millennium BCE", in A. K. Guinan, et al（eds.）, *If a Man Builds a Joyful House: Assyriological Studies in Honor of Erle Verdun Leichty*, Cuneiform Monographs 31, Leiden and Boston: Brill, 2006, pp. 503 - 514.

第三章　外围区 gun₂ ma-da 税

外省依据面积大小不同，较大的外省由将军（šagina）或总督（ensi₂）负责管理，较小的外省由高级军尉负责管理。每个外省不仅包括一个主要城市，作为该行省的首府以及最高长官的驻地，还包括若干个更小的、依附于首府的小城市或者村庄，由低级军尉负责管理。例如，阿比巴纳（Abibana）行省的首府是阿比巴纳城，此外还有卡库拉图姆（Kakkulatum）和普赫兹伽尔（Puhzigar）两座附属小城。阿比巴纳行省的将军是伊里布姆（Iribum），其子阿胡尼是高级军尉，后来继承其父的将军一职。卡库拉图姆和普赫兹伽尔由低级军尉负责管理。根据文献记载，首府阿比巴纳大约有1200名士兵，而卡库拉图姆和普赫兹伽尔分别只有900名和300名驻军。① 另一个例子是关于将军尼里达伽尔（Niridagal）的行省，其行省的名字和首府不详，这个外围行省包括两个附属小城：伽尔内内（Garnene）和塔卜拉拉（Tablala）。② 我们知道，大多数外省的最高长官都是将军，而也有一些外省是由总督负责管理，比如阿丹顿、哈马孜、萨布姆、西穆卢姆、苏萨以及乌鲁阿。

三　内部管理

在官制方面，外围区的最高长官由乌尔国王直接任命，比如扎里克既是阿淑尔的将军，也是阿淑尔的总督，后来又被调任为苏萨的总督。③ 这说明，外省的官员也可以随时随地进行调动。在一些外省，将军或者总督一职是世袭的，儿子在继承父亲的将军或者总督职位之前，一般先担任军尉（nu-banda₃），比如上文中所提到的阿比巴纳行省的将军伊里布姆及其子阿胡尼，阿胡尼在其父伊里布姆担任将军时，他担任的是军尉一职，作为其父的副手，后来才继承其父担任将军一职。另外一个例子是，阿拉普胡姆（Arraphum）的将军哈西帕塔尔（Haship-atal）及其

---

① 文献 PDT 15（S 47），YBC 3635（AS 2），CT 32 pl. 19 - 22（IS 2）.
② 文献 SACT 1 65（S 48），SET 10（AS 5）.
③ W. W. Hallo, "Zāriqum", *Journal of Near Eastern Studies*, Vol. 15（1956），pp. 220 - 225; R. Kutscher, "A Note on the Early Careers of Zariqum and Šamši-illat", *Revue d'Assyriologie et d'Archéologie Orientale*, Vol. 73（1979），p. 81; P. Michalowski, "Aššur during the Ur III Period", in O. Drewnowska（ed.）, *Here & There Across the Ancient Near East: Studies in Honour of Krystyna Lyczkowska*, Warszawa: Agade, 2009, pp. 149 - 156.

子普祖尔舒尔吉。① 外省的将军或者总督直属于乌尔第三王朝中央政府的最高行政长官"苏卡尔马赫"（sukkal-mah）。"苏卡尔马赫"派遣"苏卡尔"（sukkal）到外围区全权代表其进行巡视和监督工作。②

由于缺乏文献证据，我们对于外围区的经济结构和经济地位知之甚少。虽然外围区具有明显的军事防御和驻军性质，但是外围区的官民很可能也是从中央政府获取土地配给，不过他们的主业可能不是从事农耕业，而是畜牧业。在地理上，外围区没有大河流经，无法开展灌溉农业，这一地带处于200—400毫米等降雨量线之间，被称为"二态区域"③，是旱地农业和游牧业的过渡地带，牧场的面积要大于耕地的面积。外围区畜牧业的发展也为 gun_2 ma-da 税的缴纳提供了可能，这些可以从普兹瑞什达干的文献中找到相关证据。

第二节 文献与术语

乌尔第三王朝的外围区 gun_2 ma-da 税的文献资料的唯一来源，是普兹瑞什达干的王室档案。在上一章我们提到，核心区 bala 税的文献资料来源主要包括普兹瑞什达干的王室档案，以及吉尔苏、温马和伊利萨格里格等行省的地方档案。地方行省的档案文献是研究行省税的最直接的证据，王室档案则是间接证据来源。由于乌尔第三王朝外围区及其城市的具体地理位置尚不明确，没有关于这些外围区的考古发掘成果，更没有来自这些外围区出土的原始文献资料，所以我们目前所能依靠的有关乌尔第三王朝外围区的文献资料，只有普兹瑞什达干的王室档案，也是属于间接的资料证据。这些普兹瑞什达干文献主要记载的是，外围区向中央政府（由普兹瑞什达干机构代理）缴纳 gun_2 ma-da 税，在文献中只是简单提到外围区的名称，有的文献还提到外围区的将军或者总督的名字。除此之外，文献中很少再有其他更为详细的证据。同时，在普兹瑞什达干文献，关于外围区税的术语一直存在争议，主

---

① 文献 PDT 16（AS 5），JCS 31, pp. 166 – 167（AS 8）.

② M. Stepien, *From the History of State System in Mesopotamia*: *The Kingdom of the Third Dynasty of Ur*, Warsaw: Zaklad Graficzny UW, 2009, p. 71.

③ M. B. Rowton, "Dimorphic Structure and Topology", *Oriens Antiquus*, Vol. 15（1976）, pp. 17 – 31.

第三章 外围区 gun₂ ma-da 税

要是对 gun₂ ma-da 和 gun₂ 这两种术语形式的讨论。

一 术语 gun₂ ma-da

在赋税术语表示方面，同核心区赋税统一使用 bala 这一个术语不同的是，外围区赋税的术语表示比较复杂。一般意义上，我们都把外围区的赋税叫作 gun₂ ma-da 税，认为 gun₂ ma-da 是外围区赋税的唯一表达形式。可是事实并非如此，外围区税的术语可能还应该包括 gun₂（赋税）、mu-DU（带来、贡入）或 mu-DU lugal〔为国王贡入，与 erin₂ GN（某地区军队）、ša₃ GN（在某地）、šu-gid₂ 或 udu 连用〕这几种形式。因为从文献证据中我们知道，gun₂ ma-da 这个术语只是在舒辛统治第 3 年才开始使用，并且成为表示外围区赋税的固定表达形式，而其他几种术语主要是用于舒辛统治第 3 年之前的时期，并没有固定统一的使用规则，至少我们目前还没有发现这种规律。

苏美尔语术语 gun₂ ma-da 直译为"地区税"，其中 gun₂（或 gu₂，gu₂-un）的普通意思是"税、赋税"，而 ma-da 的意思是"地区、以外的地区"，主要指的是乌尔第三王朝核心区之外的地区。在乌尔第三王朝的年名（比如舒尔吉第 37 年、第 48 年、舒辛第 7 年）[①] 中，多次出现有 ma-da 的记载，指的是"外国、反叛之地、被征服地区"[②]。所以 ma-da 的意思可能指的是处于乌尔国家之外的平原地区，相对于高山地区而言（kur），属于乌尔第三王朝的敌对地区。[③] 由此可见，单纯从语义学角度，我们不能

[①] 舒尔吉统治第 37 年的年名是 mu ᵈNanna u₃ ᵈŠul-gi lugal-e bad₃ ma-da mu-du₃，"南那和国王舒尔吉建造地区墙（长城）之年"，缩写形式是 mu bad₃ ma-da ba-du₃，"地区墙被建造之年"。舒尔吉统治第 48 年的年名是 mu Ha-ar-šiᵏⁱ Ki-mašᵏⁱ Hu-ur₅-tiᵏⁱ u₃ ma-da-bi u₄ 1-bi ba-hul，"哈尔西、基马什、胡尔提及其地区在一天之内被毁之年"。舒辛统治第 7 年的年名是 mu ma-da Za-ab-ša-liᵏⁱ ba-hul，"扎布沙里地区被毁之年"。参见 D. Frayne, *Ur III Period（2112－2004 BC）*, The Royal Inscriptions of Mesopotamia Early Periods Volume 3/2（RIME 3/2）, Toronto: University of Toronto Press, 1997, pp. 106－110, 293.

[②] F. R. Kraus, "Provinzen des neusumerischen Reiches von Ur", *Zeitschrift für Assyriologie und Vorderasiatische Archäologie*, Vol. 51（1955）, p. 66.

[③] H. Limet, "Étude sémantique de ma. da, kur, kalam", *Revue d'Assyriologie et d'Archéologie Orientale*, Vol. 72（1978）, pp. 1－11; H. Limet, "L'étrangere dans la société sumérienne", in D. O. Edzard（ed.）, *Gesellschaftsklassen im Alten Zweistromland und in den angrenzenden Gebieten-XVI-II. Rencontre assyriologique internationale, München, 29. Juni bis 3. Juli 1970*, München: Verlag der Baberyischen Akademie der Wissenschaften, 1972, pp. 123－138.

很清楚地解释外围区税的真正含义，因为如果直接根据两个术语 ma-da 以及 gun$_2$ 的苏美尔语本义来理解，那么我们应该将其解释为"外国税、被征服地区的赋税"的含义，但是事实并非如此。所以，我们只能从外围区税的性质来理解，即这种赋税与军事机构或者军队（erin$_2$）[1] 有着密切的联系，这种赋税的缴纳人是具有军事性质的团体或者个人，要么是将军（šagina）、军尉（nu-banda$_3$）、军士或者"负责60人军官"（ugula-geš$_2$-da）等，要么是普通的士兵（erin$_2$）或者卫兵（aga-us$_2$），这些人都驻扎在乌尔第三王朝的外围区之内，所以从这个角度出发去理解这种赋税，我们可以比较真实地还原外围区税的内涵与特征。

术语 gun$_2$ ma-da 最早出现于舒辛统治第 3 年，[2] 结束于伊比辛统治第 2 年，[3] 大概一共经历了 10 年时间。目前我们只发现有八篇记载 gun$_2$ ma-da 的文献，全部来自普兹瑞什达干。[4] 例如，舒辛 3 年的一篇 gun$_2$ ma-da 文献记载了 1 头牛和 10 只羊作为外围区 gun$_2$ ma-da 税，从德尔地区的军尉扎里亚手中，尼里达伽尔作为监督官，被普兹瑞什达干机构的总管因塔埃阿接收了。这篇文献如下：

SA 4（SS 3 xi 13）

正面

1 gu$_4$ niga   1 头牛

---

[1] M. Sigrist, "Erín-un-íl", *Revue d'Assyriologie et d'Archéologie Orientale*, Vol. 73（1979）, pp. 101 – 120; K. Maekawa, "The erín-People of Lagash in Ur III Times", *Revue d'Assyriologie et d'Archéologie Orientale*, Vol. 70（1976）, pp. 9 – 44; A. Salonen, *Agricultura Mesopotamica nach sumerisch-akkadischen Quellen*, Helsinki: Suomalaisen Kirjallisuuden Kirjapaino Oy Helsinki, 1968, pp. 366 – 371.

[2] 文献 P235549（SS 3 x 23）.

[3] 文献 CT 32 pl. 19 – 22 BM 103398（IS 2 iv 29）.

[4] 文献 P235549（SS 3 x 23）, SA 4（SS 3 xi 13）, UTI 4 2378（SS 4 iv）, AUCT 3 198（SS 6/8 ix 13）, RA 9 54 AM 14（pl. 7）（SS 7 iii 25）, CHEU 6（SS 7 viii 13）, AnOr 7 44（SS 7 xi 2）, CT 32 pl. 19 – 22 BM 103398（IS 1 x – IS 2 iv 29）。注意，gun$_2$ ma-da 这个术语除了出现在乌尔第三王朝的普兹瑞什达干档案之外，还出现在早王朝时期的埃布拉文献（gu$_2$-ma-da, ARET 4 11, ARET 3 535）、古巴比伦时期文学文献（eš$_3$ gu$_2$ ma-da-ka me-te-bi, ETCSL 2.04.02.03 Shulgi C; gun$_2$ ma-da ge-en-gen$_6$-ne$_2$-de$_3$, ETCSL 3.01.01 Letter from Aradmu to Shulgi about Apillasha）、中巴比伦时期的词表文献（gun$_2$ ma-da ki-in-gi uri = MIN MIN *šu-me-ri u ak-ka-di-i*, TBER pl. 55, AO 017664）、新亚述王铭（gu$_2$ ma-da-tu$_2$ anše-kur-ra-meš la$_2$-at 一种税和马的贡赋, RIMA 3.0.102.014, ex. 01）。

第三章 外围区 gun₂ ma-da 税

8 udu u₂	8 只食草绵羊
1 maš₂-gal u₂	1 只食草山羊
1 sila₄	1 只羊羔
Za-li-a nu-banda₃ lu₂ BAD₃.AN^ki	来自德尔地区负责人的军尉扎里亚
ugula Nir-i₃-da-gal₂	尼里达伽尔是监督官
背面	
gun₂ ma-da	作为 gun₂ ma-da 税
u₄ 13-kam	第 13 日
mu-DU	带来
In-ta-e₃-a i₃-dab₅	因塔埃阿收到了
giri₃ Nu-ur₂-^dSuen dub-sar	经办人是书吏努尔辛
iti ezem Me-ki-gal₂	第 11 月
mu ^dŠu-^dSuen lugal Si-ma-num₂^ki mu-hul	舒辛 3 年
左侧	
1 gu₄ 10 udu	1 头牛、10 只羊

记载 gun₂ ma-da 税最详细的文献是伊比辛 2 年的一份长长的文献，列举了若干个外省的地区（包括阿比巴纳、卡库拉图姆、伊西姆舒尔吉、图图布、基什加提、孜姆达尔、布赫兹伽尔、马什堪乌舒里、普特沙达尔、马什堪阿比）[①] 及其缴纳的 gun₂ ma-da 的数额，对于我们认识 gun₂ ma-da 税具有重要的作用。这份文献列举如下：

CT 32 pl. 19 – 22 BM 103398（IS 1 x，IS 2 iv 29）
正面
第一栏

1 gu₄ u₂	1 头食草牛
A-hu-ni dumu I-ri-bu-um	（来自）伊里布姆之子阿胡尼
1 gu₄ u₂	1 头食草牛
Nu-ur₂-Eš₁₈-tar₂ nu-banda₃ A-bi₂-ba-na^ki	（来自）阿比巴纳的军尉努尔埃什塔尔

---

① D. I. Owen, "Ur III Geographical and Prosopographical Notes", in G. D. Young, M. W. Chavalas and R. E. Averbeck（eds.）, *Crossing Boundaries and Linking Horizons: Studies in Honor of Michael C. Astour on His 80th Birthday*, Bethesda: CDL Press, 1997, pp. 367 – 398.

1 gu$_4$ u$_2$	1 头食草牛
Na-bi$_2$-^{d}Suen nu-banda$_3$ Gag-gu-la-tum^{ki}	（来自）卡库拉图姆的军尉纳比辛
ugula A-hu-ni dumu I-ri-bu-um	监督官是伊里布姆之子阿胡尼
1 gu$_4$ u$_2$	1 头食草牛
A-gu-a-ni nu-banda$_3$ I-šim-^{d}Šul-gi^{ki}	（来自）伊西姆舒尔吉的军尉阿古阿尼
ugula Se-lu-uš-^{d}Da-gan	监督官是塞卢什达干
2 ab$_2$ u$_2$ mu gu$_4$ niga 1-še$_3$	2 头食草母牛，代替 1 头食大麦公牛
Bar-ra	（来自）巴尔拉
1 gu$_4$ u$_2$	1 头食草牛
Ša-lim-a-hu-um	（来自）沙里玛胡姆
nu-banda$_3$ Tu-tu-ub^{ki}-me-eš$_2$	（他们）都是图图布的军尉
ugula Lu$_2$-^{d}Nanna Maš-kan$_2$-a-bi$_2^{ki}$	监督官是玛什堪阿比的卢南那
1 gu$_4$ u$_2$ Šu-Ma-ma	1 头食草牛，（来自）舒玛玛
1 gu$_4$ u$_2$ Dam-qum	1 头食草牛，（来自）达姆库姆
nu-banda$_3$ Ki-iš-ga-ti^{ki}-me-eš$_2$	（他们）都是基什加提的军尉
ugula Se-lu-uš-^{d}Šul-gi	监督官是塞卢什舒尔吉
gun$_2$ mu ^{d}I-bi$_2$-^{d}Suen lugal	作为伊比辛 1 年的 gun$_2$ 税
10 gu$_4$ u$_2$	10 头食草牛
100 udu u$_2$	100 只食草羊
Se-lu-uš-^{d}Da-gan	（来自）塞卢什达干
1 gu$_4$ u$_2$	1 头食草牛
10 udu u$_2$	10 只食草羊
I$_3$-li$_2$-tab-ba	（来自）伊里塔巴
2 gu$_4$ u$_2$	2 头食草牛
20 udu u$_2$	20 只食草羊
[⋯] -a	（来自）（某某）阿
第二栏	
1 gu$_4$ u$_2$	1 头食草牛
10 udu u$_2$	10 只食草羊
Puzur$_4$-a-bi-ih	（来自）普祖尔阿比赫
1 gu$_4$ u$_2$	1 头食草牛
10 udu u$_2$	10 只食草羊
^{d}Šul-gi-i$_3$-li$_2$	（来自）舒尔吉伊里

第三章 外围区 gun₂ ma-da 税

1 gu₄ u₂	1 头食草牛
10 udu u₂	10 只食草羊
I₃-li₂-se₂-li₂	（来自）伊里舍里
1 gu₄ u₂	1 头食草牛
10 udu u₂	10 只食草羊
Nu-ur₂-ᵈIškur	（来自）努尔阿达德
1 gu₄ u₂	1 头食草牛
10 udu u₂	10 只食草羊
A-gu-a-ni	（来自）阿古阿尼
1 gu₄ u₂	1 头食草牛
10 udu u₂	10 只食草羊
Za-ri₂-iq	（来自）扎里克
1 gu₄ u₂	1 头食草牛
10 udu u₂	10 只食草羊
Za-a-num₂	（来自）扎亚努姆
1 gu₄ u₂	1 头食草牛
10 udu u₂	10 只食草羊
I₃-li₂-tab-ba	（来自）伊里塔巴
2 gu₄ u₂	2 头食草牛
20 udu u₂	20 只食草羊
Ši-ha-lum	（来自）西哈卢姆
nu-banda₃-me-eš₂	（他们）都是军尉
17 gu₄ u₂	17 头食草牛
135 udu u₂	135 只食草绵羊
35 maš₂-gal u₂	35 只食草山羊
erin₂ I-šim-ᵈŠul-giᵏⁱ	（来自）伊西姆舒尔吉的军队
ugula Se-lu-uš-ᵈDa-gan	监督官是塞卢什达干
2 gu₄ u₂	2 头食草牛
20 udu u₂	20 只食草羊
第三栏	
Lu₂-ᵈNanna Zi-mu-darᵏⁱ	（来自）孜姆达尔的卢南那
1 gu₄ u₂	1 头食草牛
10 udu u₂	10 只食草羊
Di-ku₅-i₃-li₂	（来自）迪库伊里

1 gu₄ u₂	1 头食草牛
10 udu u₂	10 只食草羊
Puzur₄-ha-ia₃	（来自）普祖尔哈亚
1 gu₄ u₂	1 头食草牛
10 udu u₂	10 只食草羊
I-ku-mi-šar	（来自）伊库米沙尔
nu-banda₃-me-eš₂	（他们）都是军尉
1 gu₄ u₂	1 头食草牛
10 udu u₂	10 只食草羊
ugula-geš₂-da-bi 20-me-eš₂	（来自）20人的军士
4 gu₄ u₂	4 头食草牛
27 udu u₂	27 只食草绵羊
3 maš₂-gal u₂	3 只食草山羊
erin₂ Ša-mi^{ki}	（来自）沙米的军队
2 gu₄ u₂	2 头食草牛
20 udu u₂	20 只食草羊
Lu₂-^dNin-šubur nu-banda₃	（来自）军尉卢宁舒布尔
3 gu₄ u₂	3 头食草牛
25 udu u₂	25 只食草绵羊
5 maš₂-gal u₂	5 只食草山羊
erin₂ Tum-ba-al^{ki}	（来自）图姆巴尔的军队
ugula Lu₂-^dNanna Zi-mu-dar^{ki}	监督官是孜姆达尔的卢南那
2 gu₄ u₂	2 头食草牛
20 udu u₂	20 只食草羊
A-hu-ni dumu I-ri-bu-um	（来自）伊里布姆之子阿胡尼
1 gu₄ u₂	1 头食草牛
10 udu u₂	10 只食草羊
第四栏	
Nu-ur₂-Eš₁₈-tar₂ nu-banda₃	（来自）军尉努尔埃什塔尔
2 gu₄ u₂	2 头食草牛
35 udu u₂	35 只食草绵羊
5 maš₂-gal u₂	5 只食草山羊
erin₂ A-bi₂-ba-na^{ki}	（来自）阿比巴纳的军队

第三章 外围区 gun$_2$ ma-da 税

1 gu$_4$ u$_2$	1 头食草牛
10 udu u$_2$	10 只食草羊
Na-bi$_2$-^{d}Suen nu-banda$_3$	（来自）军尉纳比辛
1 gu$_4$ u$_2$	1 头食草牛
10 udu u$_2$	10 只食草羊
erin$_2$ Bu-uh$_2$-zi-gar$_3^{ki}$	（来自）布赫兹伽尔的军队
3 gu$_4$ u$_2$	3 头食草牛
25 udu u$_2$	25 只食草绵羊
5 maš$_2$-gal u$_2$	5 只食草山羊
erin$_2$ Gag-gu-la-tum^{ki}	（来自）卡库拉图姆的军队
ugula A-hu-ni dumu I-ri-bu-um	监督官是伊里布姆之子阿胡尼
2 gu$_4$ u$_2$	2 头食草牛
13 udu u$_2$	13 只食草绵羊
7 maš$_2$-gal u$_2$	7 只食草山羊
Amar-Ma-ma nu-banda$_3$	（来自）军尉阿马尔玛玛
1 gu$_4$ u$_2$	1 头食草牛
10 udu u$_2$	10 只食草羊
erin$_2$ Maš-kan$_2$-u$_2$-šu-ri^{ki}	（来自）马什堪乌舒里的军队
ugula Kur-bi-la-ak	监督官是库尔比拉克
2 gu$_4$ u$_2$	2 头食草牛
20 udu u$_2$	20 只食草羊
Hu-um-zum	（来自）胡姆祖姆
1 gu$_4$ u$_2$	1 头食草牛
10 udu u$_2$	10 只食草羊
Za-a-num$_2$	（来自）扎亚努姆
1 gu$_4$ u$_2$	1 头食草牛
10 udu u$_2$	10 只食草羊
AN-［...］	（来自）安（某某）
背面	
第一栏	
1 gu$_4$ u$_2$	1 头食草牛
10 udu u$_2$	10 只食草羊
Ar-ši-ah	（来自）阿尔西阿赫
nu-banda$_3$-me-eš$_2$	（他们）都是军尉

1 gu₄ u₂	1 头食草牛
10 udu u₂	10 只食草羊
ugula-geš₂-da-bi 20-me-eš₂	（来自）20 人的军士
4 gu₄ u₂	4 头食草牛
34 udu u₂	34 只食草绵羊
6 maš₂-gal u₂	6 只食草山羊
erin₂ Pu-ut-ša-dar^ki	（来自）普特沙达尔的军队
ugula Hu-um-zum	监督官是胡姆祖姆
2 gu₄ u₂	2 头食草牛
20 udu u₂	20 只食草羊
Se-lu-uš-^dŠul-gi	（来自）塞卢什舒尔吉
1 gu₄ u₂	1 头食草牛
10 udu u₂	10 只食草羊
Šu-Ma-ma	（来自）舒玛玛
1 gu₄ u₂	1 头食草牛
10 udu u₂	10 只食草羊
Dam-qum	（来自）达姆库姆
nu-banda₃-me-eš₂	（他们）都是军尉
8 gu₄ u₂	8 头食草牛
61 udu u₂	61 只食草绵羊
19 maš₂-gal u₂	19 只食草山羊
erin₂ Ki-iš-ga-ti^ki	（来自）基什加提的军队
ugula Se-lu-uš-^dŠul-gi	监督官是塞卢什舒尔吉
2 gu₄ u₂	2 头食草牛
20 udu u₂	20 只食草羊
mu Tu-tu-ub^ki-še₃	以图图布的名义
Lu₂-^dNanna	（来自）卢南那
1 gu₄ u₂	1 头食草牛
10 udu u₂	10 只食草羊
Ša-lim-a-hu-um	（来自）沙里玛胡姆
1 gu₄ u₂	1 头食草牛
10 udu u₂	10 只食草羊
第二栏	

第三章　外围区 gun₂ ma-da 税

Bar-ra	（来自）巴尔拉
1 gu₄ u₂	1 头食草牛
10 udu u₂	10 只食草羊
La-qi₃-ip	（来自）拉齐普
nu-banda₃-me-eš₂	（他们）都是军尉
6 gu₄ u₂	6 头食草牛
47 udu u₂	47 只食草绵羊
13 maš₂-gal u₂	13 只食草山羊
erin₂ Tu-tu-ub^ki	（来自）图图布的军队
8 gu₄ u₂	8 头食草牛
65 udu u₂	65 只食草绵羊
15 maš₂-gal u₂	15 只食草山羊
erin₂ Maš-kan₂-a-bi₂^ki	（来自）马什堪阿比的军队
ugula Lu₂-^dNanna Maš-kan₂-a-bi₂^ki	监督官是马什堪阿比的卢南那
giri₃ Dingir-sukkal lu₂-kin-gi₄-a lugal	经办人是王室使节丁吉尔苏卡尔
u₃ Suhuš-ki-in kurušda	和育肥师苏胡什金
121 gu₄ 1110 udu	（总共）121 头牛、1110 只羊
gun₂ ma-da	作为 gun₂ ma-da 税
2 gu₄ u₂ mu gu₄ niga 1-še₃	2 头食草牛，代替 1 头食大麦牛
10 udu u₂	10 只食草羊
Lu₂-^dNanna	（来自）卢南那
mu Maš-kan₂-a-bi₂^ki-še₃	以马什堪阿比的名义
giri₃ Dingir-sukkal lu₂-kin-gi₄-a lugal	经办人是王室使节丁吉尔苏卡尔
u₃ Suhuš-ki-in kurušda	和育肥师苏胡什金
2 gu₄ 10 udu	（总共）2 头牛、10 只羊
maš₂-da-ri-a ezem-mah	作为献给"大节日"庆典的王室税
mu-DU lugal nu-ub-tuku	没有为国王带来
第三栏	
šu-nigin₂ 121 gu₄ u₂	共计 121 头食草公牛
šu-nigin₂ 2 ab₂ u₂	共计 2 头食草母牛
šu-nigin₂ 1007 udu u₂	共计 1007 只食草绵羊
šu-nigin₂ 113 maš₂-gal u₂	共计 113 只食草山羊
123 gu₄ 1120 udu	总共 123 头牛、1120 只羊

ša₃-bi-ta	在它们之中：
50 gu₄ u₂	50 头食草牛
312 udu u₂	312 只食草绵羊
40 maš₂-gal u₂	40 只食草山羊
30 gu₄ 352 udu	共计 30 头牛、352 只羊
A-ba-ᵈEn-lil₂-gin₇ i₃-dab₅	阿巴恩利尔金收到了
30 gu₄ u₂	30 头食草牛
187 udu u₂	187 只食草绵羊
23 maš₂-gal u₂	23 只食草山羊
30 gu₄ 210 udu	共计 30 头牛、210 只羊
Puzur₄-ᵈEn-lil₂ i₃-dab₅	普祖尔恩利尔收到了
30 gu₄ u₂	30 头食草牛
187 udu u₂	187 只食草绵羊
23 maš₂-gal u₂	23 只食草山羊
30 gu₄ 210 udu	共计 30 头牛、210 只羊
ᵈŠul-gi-i₃-li₂ i₃-dab₅	舒尔吉伊里收到了
10 gu₄ u₂	10 头食草牛
63 udu u₂	63 只食草绵羊
8 maš₂-gal u₂	8 只食草山羊
10 gu₄ 71 udu	共计 10 头牛、71 只羊
Nu-ur₂-ᵈIškur i₃-dab₅	努尔阿达德收到了
第四栏	
[…]	
[x] udu u₂	x 只食草绵羊
[x] maš₂-gal u₂	x 只食草山羊
e₂-kurušda ᵈEn-lil₂-la₂-še₃	为恩利拉的育肥房
157	总共 157 只牲畜
Inim-ᵈNanna-zu šabra i₃-dab₅	首席神庙管理员伊宁南那祖收到了
[x] ab₂ u₂	x 头食草母牛
[x] +2 gu₄	（共计）2+ 头牛
Ur-ku₃-nun-na i₃-dab₅	乌尔库努纳收到了
[x] gu₄ u₂	x 头食草牛
[x] ša₃ gun₂-na	……在 gun₂ 税中

第三章 外围区 gun₂ ma-da 税

[x] +1 gu₄ （共计）1+头牛
Lu₂-ᵈBa-ba₆ i₃-dab₅ 卢巴巴收到了
ki-bi-gi₄-a 因塔埃阿的平衡账目
In-ta-e₃-a
iti u₅-bi₂ᵐᵘšᵉⁿ-gu₇ 第3月
mu en ᵈInana Unugᵏⁱ maš₂-e i₃-pad₃ 伊比辛2年
左侧
u₄ 29-kam giri₃ ᵈNanna-ma-ba dub-sar 第29日，经办人是书吏南那玛巴

  可以肯定的是，应该还存在有更多的 gun₂ ma-da 文献，只是目前还没有被我们所知，它们很可能被藏在某个博物馆或者私人手中还没有被解读，或者甚至还被深埋在伊拉克的某个土丘之下等待发掘出土。由于样本数量很少，目前我们对于 gun₂ ma-da 文献的认识只能是片面的，得出的结论也只是暂时的。

  由于记载 gun₂ ma-da 术语的普兹瑞什达干文献目前我们仅仅发现了八篇，而这肯定不是所有的关于乌尔第三王朝外围区 gun₂ ma-da 税的文献数量，加之记载 gun₂ ma-da 术语的文献都是从舒辛3年才开始的。所以，这里就出现了几个疑惑：在舒辛3年之前是否存在外围区 gun₂ ma-da 税呢？如果存在的话，这种赋税是使用什么术语记载的？围绕这些问题，我们讨论以下几个有可能表示外围区税的术语，这些术语是在舒辛3年 gun₂ ma-da 术语出现之前表示外围区税概念的，但是它们的内涵与外延也有着严格的规定。

二 术语 gun₂

  苏美尔语术语 gun₂ 的基本含义是"赋税、贡赋"。gun₂（或写作 gu₂-un 或者 gu₂）有三种意思：一是表示核心区中的地方税，主要适用于行省之内，二是表示外围区 gun₂ ma-da 税的前身或者缩写形式，三是表示附属国的贡税。这一章我们只讨论第二种情况。

  在乌尔第三王朝的经济文献中，记载 gun₂ 的文献常常容易和记载 gun₂ ma-da 的文献相混淆，甚至有的学者还认为 gun₂ 就是 gun₂ ma-da 的缩写形式

以及前身。① 当然，这种观点遭到了很多学者的反对，他们认为 gun₂ 和 gun₂ ma-da 是两个不同含义的术语，使用的范围也不尽相同，只是在特殊情况下，比如表示牲畜税没有被缴纳（"发送"，nu-mu-DU②）时，两者可以混用，③即 gun₂ 可以作为 gun₂ ma-da 的缩写形式存在。试看下面一个例子：

TAD 66（SS 9，Drehem）

正面

10 gu₄ u₂   10 头食草牛

gun₂ Zaq-tum^ki   作为扎克图姆的 gun₂（ma-da）税

ugula Šeš-kal-la   塞什卡拉是监督官

nu-mu-DU   没有缴纳（带来）

背面

mu ᵈŠu-ᵈSuen lugal Uri₅^ki-ma-ke₄   舒辛 9 年

e₂ ᵈŠara₂ Umma^ki-ka mu-du₃

为了更为清晰地区分 gun₂ 和 gun₂ ma-da 这两个术语的使用范围和具体含义，我们需要遵循以下四条标准：④ 第一，被带来的 gun₂ 形式不局限于牲畜。第二，被带来的 gun₂ 来自比 gun₂ ma-da 外围区更大的地区或者国家。第三，当地的统治者担任运输者或者监督官。第四，术语 gun₂ 在舒辛 3 年之后依然被使用。

三　术语 mu-DU 或 mu-DU lugal

在舒辛统治第 3 年之前，外围区的赋税并没有一个固定的术语，而是

---

① P. Steinkeller, "The Administrative and Economic Organization of the Ur III State: The Core and the Periphery", in M. Gibson and R. D. Biggs (eds.), *The Organization of Power: Aspects of Bureaucracy in the Ancient Near East*, Studies in Ancient Oriental Civilization 46, Chicago: The Oriental Institute of the University of Chicago, 1987, p. 31.

② 亦可写作 nu-mu-de₆ 或者 nu-mu-tum₂。参见 T. Maeda, "The Defense Zone during the Rule of the Ur III Dynasty", *Acta Sumerologica*, Vol. 14 (1992), p. 140.

③ T. Maeda, "The Defense Zone during the Rule of the Ur III Dynasty", *Acta Sumerologica*, Vol. 14 (1992), pp. 139–140; D. Patterson, *Elements of the Neo-Sumerian Military*, PhD dissertation, University of Pennsylvania, 2018, p. 364.

④ T. Maeda, "The Defense Zone during the Rule of the Ur III Dynasty", *Acta Sumerologica*, Vol. 14 (1992), p. 140.

第三章　外围区 gun₂ ma-da 税

使用"带来、贡入"的泛指术语 mu-DU 或者 mu-DU lugal（为国王带来、贡入）。① 术语 mu-DU 直译为"带来"，其中符号 mu 是动词前缀，DU 是动词词干。关于符号 DU 的具体读音，目前大致有两种观点，一种观点认为符号 DU 读作 tum₂ 或者 de₆ "带来"②，另一种观点认为符号 DU 读作 ku_x "进入、贡入"③。

在普兹瑞什达干文献中，术语 mu-DU④ 主要用来表示牲畜从乌尔国家各地以及外国被带到普兹瑞什达干王室牲畜中心，被中心总管所接收，然后进行再分配，有的牲畜被转运（i₃-dab₅）给中心机构下属分支机构，有的牲畜直接从中心机构被支出（ba-zi）至其最终目的地。最早的 mu-DU 接收文献出现在舒尔吉第 29 年，⑤ 属于普兹瑞什达干机构建立之前的早期文献或者舒尔吉西姆提文献，一直到舒尔吉第 42 年，接收官员包括：⑥

舒库布姆	Šu-ku₈-bu-um，	舒尔吉 29 年—32 年
阿比拉图姆	A₂-bi₂-la-tum，	舒尔吉 33 年
贝利杜	Be-li₂-du₁₀，	舒尔吉 33 年—37 年
阿比里亚	A₂-bi₂-li₂-a，	舒尔吉 38 年—42 年
阿比拉图姆	A₂-bi₂-la-tum，	舒尔吉 43 年—45 年
乌尔卢伽尔埃丁卡	Ur-ᵈLugal-edin-ka，	舒尔吉 45 年—47 年

---

① T. Gomi, "Über mu. tù. lugal：'Eingebrachtes für den König' in den neusumerischen Viehverwaltungsurkunden aus Drehim", *Orient*, Vol. 11 (1975), pp. 1 – 14.

② T. Maeda, "Bringing (mu-túm) livestock and the Puzrish-Dagan organization in the Ur III dynasty", *Acta Sumerologica*, Vol. 11 (1989), pp. 69 – 111. 注意，tum₂ 用于未完成时单数形式，而 de₆ 用于完成时单数形式，参见 D. O. Edzard, *Sumerian Grammar*, Leiden and Boston：Brill, 2003, p. 78.

③ J. Krecher, "DU = ku_x (-r) eintreten, hineinbringen", *Zeitschrift für Assyriologie und Vorderasiatische Archäologie*, Vol. 77 (1987), pp. 7 – 21；J. Bauer, "DU = ku_x (-dr), eintreten, hineinbringen'?", *Zeitschrift für Assyriologie und Vorderasiatische Archäologie*, Vol. 94 (2004), pp. 16 – 17.

④ 在舒辛时期主要使用 mu-DU lugal 术语。T. Maeda, "Bringing (mu-túm) livestock and the Puzrish-Dagan organization in the Ur III dynasty", *Acta Sumerologica*, Vol. 11 (1989), p. 94.

⑤ 文献 OIP 115 16 (S 29 xi)。

⑥ T. B. Jones, J. W. Snyder, *Sumerian Economic Texts from the Third Ur Dynasty：A Catalogue and Discussion of Documents from Various Collections*, Minneapolis：University of Minnesota Press, 1961, pp. 203 – 208；F. Weierhäuser, *Die königlichen Frauen der III. Dynastie von Ur*, Göttinger Beiträge zum Alten Orient 1, Göttingen：Universitätsverlag Göttingen, 2008, pp. 31 – 105；J. Wang, Y. Wu, "A Research on the Incoming (mu-túm) Archive of Queen Šulgi-simti's Animal Institution", *Journal of Ancient Civilizations*, Vol. 26 (2011), pp. 41 – 60.

普兹瑞什达干机构于舒尔吉第 39 年建立之后，最早的 mu-DU 接收文献（由机构总管接收）出现在舒尔吉第 43 年，当时的接收官员即机构总管是一位匿名官员。[①] 这篇最早的 mu-DU 接收文献如下：

MVN 13 516（S 43 i 1，Drehem）
正面
1 ^{munus}aš$_2$-gar$_3$ niga 1 sila$_4$　　　　　1 只食大麦山羊羔、1 只绵羊羔
I-šar-pa$_2$-dan　　　　　　　　　　　（来自）伊沙尔帕丹
3 amar maš-da$_3$ A-hu-ni　　　　　　3 只羚羊羔，（来自）阿胡尼
3 amar maš-da$_3$ E$_2$-lu$_2$　　　　　　　3 只羚羊羔，（来自）埃鲁
1 amar maš-da$_3$ I-šar-^{d}Šul-gi　　　1 只羚羊羔，（来自）伊沙尔舒尔吉
2 amar maš-da$_3$ U$_2$-u$_2$-mu nu-banda$_3$　2 只羚羊羔，（来自）军尉乌乌姆
背面
2 amar maš-da$_3$ Šar-ru-um-ba-ni　　2 只羚羊羔，（来自）沙鲁姆巴尼
mu-DU　　　　　　　　　　　　　　带来，（匿名官员接收了）
iti maš-da$_3$-gu$_7$　　　　　　　　　　第 1 月
mu en ^{d}Nanna maš-e i$_3$-pad$_3$　　　舒尔吉 43 年
左侧
u$_4$ 1-kam　　　　　　　　　　　　　第 1 日

普兹瑞什达干机构的几位 mu-DU 接收官员都是该机构的中心总管，他们分别是匿名官员（舒尔吉 43 年）、纳萨（舒尔吉 47 年—阿马尔辛 1 年）[②]、阿巴萨加（阿马尔辛 1 年—9 年）、卢伽尔阿马尔库（阿马尔辛 8

[①] 有的学者怀疑这位匿名官员就是纳萨，参见 Y. Wu, "The Anonymous Nasa and Nasa of the Animal Center during Šulgi 44 – 48 and the Wild Camel (gú-gur5), Hunchbacked Ox (gur 8-gur 8), ubi, habum and the Confusion of the Deer (lulim) with Donkey (anše) or šeg 9", *Journal of Ancient Civilizations*, Vol. 25（2010），pp. 1 – 20.

[②] 注意，在舒尔吉 43 年至 47 年之间，也有纳萨的 mu-DU 接收文献，但是记录格式不同（ki PN-ta），比如文献 Rochester 12（S 43 v）、OIP 115 257（S 43 ix，S 44 iii，S 46 viii）、P235343（S 43 xi）、Nisaba 8 122（S 44）、SAT 2 363（S 44 i，S 45 i）、MVN 5 96（S 44 i，S 45 i）、BPOA 6 39（S 44 ii-S 45 ii）、TRU 105（S 44 ii-S 45 ii）等。从舒尔吉第 43—47 年，共有三种 mu-DU 接收文献，一是匿名官员接收，二是纳萨接收，三是阿比拉图姆接收（舒尔吉西姆提档案）。

年)、因塔埃阿（阿马尔辛 9 年——伊比辛 2 年）。① 最早出现 mu-DU 接收官员的文献如下：

StOr 9 - 1 24（pl. 7）（S 47 i 3, Drehem）

正面

1 sila₄ A-hu-wa-qar	1 只羊羔，（来自）阿胡瓦卡尔
1 sila₄ Ma-ba-ne-a	1 只羊羔，（来自）玛巴内亚
1 sila₄ Ur-ᵈNanna	1 只羊羔，（来自）乌尔南那
1 sila₄ Zu-bi-a	1 只羊羔，（来自）祖比亚
1 sila₄ Ku-ru-ub-Er₃-ra	1 只羊羔，（来自）库鲁布埃拉
1 sila₄ A₂-bi₂-li₂-a	1 只羊羔，（来自）阿比里亚
1 sila₄ Ku-ru-ub-ᵈIškur	1 只羊羔，（来自）库鲁布阿达德
1 sila₄ Hal-i₃-lum	1 只羊羔，（来自）哈里鲁姆
nu-banda₃-me	（他们）都是军尉

背面

1 sila₄ 1 amar maš-da₃	1 只羊羔、1 只羚羊崽
A₂-bi₂-li₂-a ku₃-gal₂	（来自）运河检查官阿比里亚
2 amar maš-da₃ zabar-dab₅	2 只羚羊崽，（来自）"扎巴尔达布"官员
1 amar az Ur-ᵈSuen	1 只熊崽，（来自）乌尔辛
1 sila₄ Lu₂-ᵈNin-šubur	1 只羊羔，（来自）卢宁舒布尔
1 sila₄ Da-da u₃-kul	1 只羊羔，（来自）"乌库尔"官员达达
mu-DU Na-sa₆ i₃-dab₅	带来，纳萨收到了
iti maš-da₃-gu₇	第 1 月
mu us₂-sa Ki-maškⁱ ba-hul	舒尔吉 47 年

左侧

u₄ 3-kam	第 3 日

大约在舒辛 3 年，普兹瑞什达干机构总管因塔埃阿开始大规模的接收

---

① C. Tsouparoupoulo, "A Reconstruction of the Puzriš-Dagan Central Livestock Agency", *Cuneiform Digital Library Journal*, 2013/2; C. Liu, *Organization, Administrative Practices and Written Documentation in Mesopotamia during the Ur III Period*（c. 2112 – 2004 BC）: *A Case Study of Puzriš-Dagan in the Reign of Amar-Suen*, Kārum-Emporion-Forum: Beiträge zum Wirtschafts-, Rechts-und Sozialgeschichte des östlichen Mittelmeerraums und Altvorderasiens 3（KEF 3）, Münster: Ugarit-Verlag, 2017, pp. 15 – 227.

mu-DU lugal（为国王带来的）牲畜（舒辛 3 年 7 月 16 日[①]—伊比辛 2 年 8 月 26 日[②]），取代了之前的 mu-DU 牲畜，[③] 这是舒辛 3 年的一次重大的税制改革。最早由因塔埃阿接收的 mu-DU lugal 文献如下：

BIN 3 233（SS 3 vii 16，Drehem）

正面

1 sila$_4$ Iš-me-Er$_3$-ra	1 只绵羊羔，（来自）伊什美埃拉
1 sila$_4$ Šu-dam-ki-na	1 只绵羊羔，（来自）舒达姆基纳
1 sila$_4$ Šu-Er$_3$-ra	1 只绵羊羔，（来自）舒埃拉
1 ^{munus}aš$_2$-gar$_3$ niga dumu Kur-giri$_3$-ni-še$_3$	1 只食大麦山羊羔，（来自）库尔基里尼塞之子
u$_4$ 16-kam	第 16 日

背面

mu-DU lugal	为国王带来
In-ta-e$_3$-a	因塔埃阿
i$_3$-dab$_5$	收到了
giri$_3$ Nu-ur$_2$-^{d}Suen dub-sar	经办人是书吏努尔辛
iti ezem^{d}Šul-gi	第 7 月
mu Si-ma-num$_2$^{ki} ba-hul	舒辛 3 年

左侧

4 udu	4 只羊

这些被带来或进贡而来的牲畜（mu-DU）来自许多地区，有的来自乌尔第三王朝的核心区，有的来自外围区，有的甚至来自附属国，所以 mu-DU 只是表示"带来、进入"的泛指称呼，当然这些"带来"或者"贡

[①] 文献 BIN 3 233（SS 3 vii 16）.
[②] 文献 NYPL 13（IS 2 viii 26）.
[③] 注意，普兹瑞什达干中心总管接收 mu-DU lugal 牲畜其实最早在舒尔吉 48 年已经开始，由总管纳萨接收（Ontario 1 53，Nisaba 8 25），在阿马尔辛时期也有少量的 mu-DU lugal 接收文献，SumRecDreh 14（AS 2 iv 23），Fs Levine 115 – 119，148ff.（AS 2 xi），P235015（AS 5 ii 2），P406796（AS 5 vi 1），BRM 3 50（AS 5 viii），BRM 3 31（AS 5 xi），Amorites 18（AS 5 xii 1 – 29），由中心总管阿巴萨加接收。但是这种接收活动并不是常规的操作，只是偶尔的行为，只有到了舒辛 3 年开始，中心总管才开始大规模、常规性接收 mu-DU lugal 牲畜。

入"的牲畜都带有"贡税"的意思。例如，在阿马尔辛统治时期，普兹瑞什达干机构的总管阿巴萨加一共接收了大约两万多只动物，其中有1300多头牛、13000多只绵羊、近6000只山羊，还有1000只左右的野生动物（比如羚羊、鹿、野山羊、熊等），这些动物来自各个地区，包括乌尔第三王朝的核心区、外围区和附属国，作为缴纳给中央政府的赋税或者贡物。[①] 其中，就包括有外围区 gun₂ ma-da 税。

在舒辛第3年之前，还没有一个固定的术语用来表示外围区税。不过，我们可以根据文献中所记载的牲畜数量特征以及牲畜的来源地，判断这些牲畜到底是不是属于外围区税。通过对相关文献的分析，我们发现，表示外围区 gun₂ ma-da 税前身的术语有 gun₂ "赋税"、erin₂ GN "地区的军事（税）"、ša₃ GN "在某地（的税）"、šu-gid₂ "转手（税）"和 udu "绵羊（税）"，它们在文献中都与术语 mu-DU "带来"连用。

因此，我们在讨论外围区 gun₂ ma-da 税的时候，不能仅仅关注含有 gun₂ ma-da 术语的文献，也要关注其他可能属于 gun₂ ma-da 税的文献，即便是 gun₂ ma-da 术语没有出现，也要关注 mu-DU 文献和 mu-DUlugal 文献。下面，我们将具体讨论外围区的 gun₂ ma-da 税情况。

第三节　外围区 gun₂ ma-da 税的征收

外围区 gun₂ ma-da 税的课税形式只有牲畜，主要是牛和羊，羊又细分为绵羊和山羊，有成年羊和羊羔之分。另外，根据牛羊的饲料级别，也可以分为食大麦（育肥）牛羊和食草（普通）牛羊。由于目前我们并没有发现外围区的地方档案，所以只能从普兹瑞什达干的中央档案中获得间接证据。关于外围区 gun₂ ma-da 税的征收，下面主要从征税对象、征税时限、税收拖欠以及税率和税额等方面开展论述。

一　征税对象

乌尔第三王朝外围区 gun₂ ma-da 税的征税对象应该是各个外围区（外

---

① C. Liu, *Organization, Administrative Practices and Written Documentation in Mesopotamia during the Ur III Period (c. 2112 – 2004 BC): A Case Study of Puzriš-Dagan in the Reign of Amar-Suen*, Kārum-Emporion-Forum: Beiträge zum Wirtschafts-, Rechts-und Sozialgeschichte des östlichen Mittelmeerraums und Altvorderasiens 3 (KEF 3), Münster: Ugarit-Verlag, 2017, pp. 161 – 162.

省），具体而言，是各个外省的军事人员，所征收的税额多少依据于每个军事人员的级别和地位身份的高低，上到该外省的最高长官将军或者总督，下至普通的士兵。这些外围区游离于乌尔第三王朝核心区的周边地区，在传统上并不属于"苏美尔和阿卡德之地"，被看作是"外国"的范畴。乌尔中央政府向外围区征收 gun₂ ma-da 税，体现了乌尔第三王朝已将外围区纳入王朝的领土范围之内，属于被合并的地区。向中央政府缴纳 gun₂ ma-da 税的军事人员居住在外围区，通过税收这一经济手段加强了他们同乌尔中央政府的联系和认同感。

从普兹瑞什达干文献中，我们只知道许多属于外省的地名，它们可能是一些外省的主城市或者首府，也可能是一些外省的附属城市或者城镇。从文献中，我们可以理清部分外省的建构。普兹瑞什达干文献中所记载的这些地名是不是都属于外围区？以及有的地名是否属于附属国范畴？由于我们对于其中相当一部分地名的具体地理位置不清楚，所以对其到底是外围区还是附属国的判断也只是暂时的。如何判定一个地区是属于外围区还是属于附属国，大致有以下几个标准：一是这个地区的大致地理位置如果清楚的话，则容易判断其所属；二是从这些地区向中央缴纳的赋税形式以及税率来判定；三是从这些赋税所使用的术语来判定，如果直接使用了 gun₂ ma-da 的术语（当然是发生在舒辛 3 年之后），那么可以直接判定该地区属于外围区范畴。但是由于目前我们所能得到的 gun₂ ma-da 文献数量太少，我们只能判定这少数文献中的地名是属于外围区范畴。然而，对于舒辛 3 年之前的 gun₂ ma-da 税文献（使用其他术语）中所记载的地名，我们需要谨慎对待以及考证其属性。同时，还有一个问题需要注意，就是一个地区可能在某个阶段是属于乌尔第三王朝的外围区，而在另一个阶段则属于其附属国的范畴，对于这种属性的变化我们也需要注意甄别。

上文提到，记载 gun₂ ma-da 的文献目前一共只发现有八篇，这八篇文献中所记载的地名肯定属于外围区范畴，这些文献对于我们准确认识乌尔第三王朝的外围区 gun₂ ma-da 税具有相当重要的意义。所以，我们首先将这八篇文献列举如下（见表 3-2）：

第三章 外围区 gun₂ ma-da 税

表 3-2　　　　　　　　　gun₂ ma-da 文献统计分析表

文献/日期	地区	牲畜 牛	牲畜 羊	征税对象 军尉 (nu-banda₃)	征税对象 军士 (ugula-geš₂)	征税对象 军队/士兵 (erin₂)	监督官 (ugula)
MVN 8 222 (SS--)	伊舒姆	[8]	[220]	瓦祖姆舒尔吉			瓦祖姆舒尔吉
		4	180			erin₂	
P235549 (SS 3 x 23)	利布里		24		aga₃-us₂ lu₂		塔希沙塔尔
SA 4 (SS 3 xi 13)	德尔	1	10	扎里亚			尼里达伽尔
AUCT 3 198 (SS 6/8 ix 13)	舒辛伊杜格	[x] [x]	[x] [x]	南那伊吉杜 [...]			南那伊吉杜
		[x]	[33 +]			erin₂	
	达尔图姆	1 —	10 5	卢伽尔埃孜姆 伊沙尔里比			塔希沙塔尔
RA 9 54 AM 14 (pl. 7) (SS 7 iii 25)	普图里乌姆	—	10	沙鲁姆巴尼			伊布尼舒尔吉
		—	80			erin₂	
CHEU 6 (SS 7 viii 13)	乌尔比隆	30 1 1 1 1 1 1 [x]	240 1 1 1 1 1 1 [x]	乌纳帕塔尔 沙拉亚 达塞 吉布拉塔古 哈纳姆 埃尼某某 [...] [...]			乌纳帕塔尔
		70	—			erin₂	
	塞提尔沙	1	—	塔希塞恩			阿拉德姆
		4	—			erin₂	
AnOr 7 44 (SS 7 xi 2)	阿扎曼	6 1 1 1	80 10 10 10	塔班达拉赫 泰舒普塞拉赫 其妻阿杜 乌孜			塞卢什达干

143

续表

文献/日期	地区	牲畜 牛	牲畜 羊	征税对象 军尉 (nu-banda$_3$)	征税对象 军士 (ugula-geš$_2$)	征税对象 军队/士兵 (erin$_2$)	监督官 (ugula)
CT 32 pl. 19–22 BM 103398 (IS 2 iv 29)	伊西姆舒尔吉	10	100	塞卢什达干			塞卢什达干
		1	10	伊里塔巴			
		2	20	某某阿			
		1	10	普祖尔阿比赫			
		1	10	舒尔吉伊里			
		1	10	伊里茨里			
		1	10	努尔阿达德			
		1	10	阿古阿尼			
		1	10	扎里克			
		1	10	扎亚努姆			
		1	10	伊里塔巴			
		2	20	伊吉哈鲁姆			
		17	170			erin$_2$	
	沙米	2	20	卢南那			卢南那
		1	10	迪库伊里			
		1	10	普祖尔哈亚			
		1	10	伊库米沙尔			
		1	10		20-me-eš$_2$		
		4	40			erin$_2$	
	图姆巴尔	2	20	卢宁舒布尔			
		3	30			erin$_2$	
	阿比巴纳	2	20	阿胡尼			伊里布姆之子阿胡尼
		1	10	努尔埃什塔尔			
		4	40			erin$_2$	
	普赫兹伽尔	1	10	纳比辛			
		1	10			erin$_2$	
	卡库拉图姆	3	30			erin$_2$	
	马什堪乌舒里	2	20	阿马尔玛玛			库尔比拉克
		1	10			erin$_2$	
	普特沙达尔	2	20	胡姆祖姆			
		1	10	扎亚努姆			
		1	10	安某某			
		1	10	阿尔西阿赫			

第三章　外围区 gun₂ ma-da 税

续表

文献/日期	地区	牲畜 牛	牲畜 羊	征税对象 军尉 (nu-banda₃)	征税对象 军士 (ugula-geš₂)	征税对象 军队/士兵 (erin₂)	监督官 (ugula)
CT 32 pl. 19-22 BM 103398 (IS 2 iv 29)	普特沙达尔	1	10		20-me-eš₂		胡姆祖姆
		4	40		ensi₂		
	基什加提	2	20	塞卢什舒尔吉			塞卢什舒尔吉
		1	10	舒玛玛			
		1	10	达姆库姆			
		8	80			erin₂	
	图图布	2	20	卢南那			卢南那
		1	10	沙里玛胡姆			
		1	10	巴尔拉			
		1	10	拉齐普			
		6	60			erin₂	
	马什堪阿比	8	80			erin₂	

从上述统计表格中，我们可以得出以下结论：第一，外围区 gun₂ ma-da 税的牛羊固定比例是 1∶10。第二，gun₂ ma-da 税的征税对象包括军尉（高级军尉很可能就是该外省的将军）、军士和军队的士兵。第三，gun₂ ma-da 税所涉及的地区有伊舒姆、利布里、德尔、舒辛伊杜格、达尔图姆、普图里乌姆、乌尔比隆、塞提尔沙、阿扎曼、伊西姆舒尔吉、沙米、图姆巴尔、阿比巴纳、普赫兹伽尔、卡库拉图姆、马什堪乌舒里、普特沙达尔、基什加提、图图布和马什堪阿比。目前我们至少可以肯定，这些地区是属于外围区范畴。从这些地名出发，我们可以从普兹瑞什达干文献中搜集与这些地名有关的舒辛 3 年之前的其他文献，并且通过比较分析来判定在舒辛 3 年之前的外围区 gun₂ ma-da 税情况。我们以普图里乌姆为例，分析一下舒辛 3 年之前和之后的 gun₂ ma-da 税缴纳情况。

普图里乌姆的军队缴纳的 gun₂ ma-da 税数量，大致固定在 8 牛头和 80 只羊。在第三篇文献（舒辛 7 年）中，出现了术语 gun₂ ma-da，而在第一篇文献（舒尔吉 48 年）和第二篇文献（阿马尔辛 8 年）中，没有使用固定的表示赋税的术语，只是使用了 ša₃ Pu-tu-li-um^ki "在普图里乌姆" 以及 erin₂ Pu-ut-tu-li-um^ki "普图里乌姆的军队" 的泛指术语，但是我们可以确定，这两篇文献也是关于普图里乌姆 gun$_2$ ma-da 税的记载。接下来，我们将从 gun$_2$ ma-da 税的纳税期与税率角度来进一步分析外围区税的特征。

表 3-3　　　　　　　　普图里乌姆 gun$_2$ ma-da 税缴纳情况

文献 AUCT 1 743 （S 48 ix 19）	12 gu$_4$ ša$_3$ Pu-tu-li-um^{ki} mu-DU Na-sa$_6$ i$_3$-dab$_5$	12 头牛 在普图里乌姆 带来，纳萨接收了
文献 Nisaba 30 46 （AS 8 iii 13）	8 gu$_4$ erin$_2$ Pu-ut-tu-li-um^{ki} ugula Hu-ba-a mu-DU Lugal-amar-ku$_3$ i$_3$-dab$_5$	8 头牛 （来自）普图里乌姆的军队 胡巴亚是监督官 带来，卢伽尔阿马尔库接收了
文献 RA 9 54 AM 14（pl. 7） （SS 7 iii 25）	72 udu u$_2$ 8 maš$_2$-gal u$_2$ erin$_2$ Pu-ut-tu-li-um^{ki} ugula Ib-ni-^{d}Šul-gi gun$_2$ ma-da mu-DU In-ta-e$_3$-a i$_3$-dab$_5$	72 只食草绵羊、8 只食草山羊 （来自）普图里乌姆的军队 伊布尼舒尔吉是监督官 作为 gun$_2$ ma-da 税 带来，因塔埃阿接收了

二　征收期限与税率

乌尔第三王朝的外围区 gun$_2$ ma-da 税是一种固定税，一般的征收期限是一年一缴纳，属于一种年税。每个外省缴纳的时间主要集中在每年的 9 月中旬到 12 月中旬，即每年的秋冬季节。选择这样的季节发送牲畜税到乌尔，可能是考虑到了气候变化的因素，[①] 但是这仅仅是我们的猜测，目前没有直接证据可以证明。

虽然 gun$_2$ ma-da 税的征收时间是固定的，但是并不是每个外省都能完成纳税的任务，有一些外省也会拖欠缴纳赋税，在文献中使用 nu-mu-DU 的术语，表示"没有带来"。这些拖欠的税额一般会在第二年被补交上。比如以下的例子，分别提到提兰（Tiran）、阿尔曼（Arman）和扎克图姆

[①] P. Steinkeller, "The Administrative and Economic Organization of the Ur III State: The Core and the Periphery", in M. Gibson and R. D. Biggs (eds.), *The Organization of Power: Aspects of Bureaucracy in the Ancient Near East*, Studies in Ancient Oriental Civilization 46, Chicago: The Oriental Institute of the University of Chicago, 1987, p. 26.

第三章 外围区 gun₂ ma-da 税

（Zaqtum）拖欠 gun₂ ma-da 税的情况。这三个地区拖欠的赋税情况列举如表 3-4：

表 3-4　　　提兰、阿尔曼和扎克图姆拖欠 gun₂ ma-da 税情况

提兰 文献 TAD 54 （undated）	1 gu₄ niga 18 udu maš₂ hi-a gun₂ Ti-ra-an^ki ugula Šar-ru-um-ba-ni nu-mu-DU	1 头食大麦的牛、18 只绵羊或山羊 作为提兰的 gun₂（ma-da）税 沙鲁姆巴尼是监督官 没有带来
阿尔曼 文献 Trouvaille 50 （SS 9）	3 gu₄ niga erin₂ Ar-ma-an^ki nu-mu-DU ugula A₂-pi-la-ša	3 头食大麦的牛 作为阿尔曼军队的（gun₂ ma-da 税） 没有带来 阿皮拉沙是监督官
扎克图姆 文献 TAD 66 （SS 9）	1 gu₄ u₂ gun₂ Zaq-tum^ki ugula Šeš-kal-la nu-mu-DU	1 头食草的牛 作为扎克图姆的 gun₂（ma-da）税 塞什卡拉是监督官 没有带来

上文我们提到，乌尔第三王朝的外围区 gun₂ ma-da 税的税率大致是牛和羊维持在 1∶10 的固定比例范围，至于到底是缴纳多少的税额，还需要从文献证据中寻求解答，不同级别、不同社会地位的群体所缴纳的税额也是不同的。从文献中我们已经知道，向中央政府缴纳 gun₂ ma-da 税的征收对象包括：将军（šagina）、军尉（nu-banda₃）、军士或者"负责 60 人军官"（ugula-geš₂-da）、军队士兵（erin₂）。每个级别的纳税人所要缴纳的 gun₂ ma-da 税额在不同的年份基本上是不变的，中央政府可能已经提前为每个外省不同级别的纳税人制定了详细明确的固定纳税额度。

通过对这些不同级别纳税者的分析，我们可以得知，他们缴纳 gun₂ ma-da 税的额度分别为（见表 3-5）：[①]

[①] P. Steinkeller, "The Administrative and Economic Organization of the Ur III State: The Core and the Periphery", in M. Gibson and R. D. Biggs (eds.), *The Organization of Power: Aspects of Bureaucracy in the Ancient Near East*, Studies in Ancient Oriental Civilization 46, Chicago: The Oriental Institute of the University of Chicago, 1987, p. 30.

表 3 – 5　　　　　　　　　gun₂ ma-da 税缴纳额度一览表

牛	羊	等价的白银	纳税者职务
10	100	200 舍客勒	将军（兼任监督官）
2	20	40 舍客勒	高级军尉
1	10	20 舍客勒	低级军尉
1/20	1/2	1 舍客勒	军士（每人）
1/300	1/30	12 舍客勒	士兵（每人）

由于乌尔第三王朝的外围区与附属国的界线并不是十分清楚，加之舒辛 3 年之前的外围区税没有固定的 gun₂ ma-da 术语，所以我们对于这两个区域也很难准确区分。从文献证据中，我们大致得出一个规律来，即外围区税的特点，一是牛羊的比例基本维持在 1∶10 的区间内，二是外围区所缴纳的牲畜税的数量总体上不是很大，每个外省每年缴纳的牲畜数量大致维持在几十到几百之间，几乎没有上千的。而附属国向中央政府缴纳的牲畜数量往往很庞大，在几千到几万之间，这也是我们区分一个地区到底是属于外围区还是附属国的一个有效的方法。在下一章中，我们将就乌尔第三王朝的附属国及其赋税情况进行探讨。

第四章　附属国 gun$_2$ 税

乌尔第三王朝是中央集权制国家，在其对外征服战争中，有一些国家附属于乌尔第三王朝，成为其附属国或者卫星国。据乌尔第三王朝的普兹瑞什达干王室档案记载，附属国经常向乌尔中央政府派遣使节（lu$_2$-kin-gi$_4$-a），并且向乌尔中央缴纳赋税，这些赋税有一个统一的术语 gun$_2$，所以我们将附属国税称为 gun$_2$ 税，其原义为"地区税、外国税"，其赋税形式基本上只有牲畜，以牛和羊为主，且数量庞大。附属国 gun$_2$ 税基本只被记录在普兹瑞什达干的王室文献中，在有的文献中，术语 gun$_2$ 也会被省略。目前我们所发现的记录附属国 gun$_2$ 税的文献也不是很多，这对于我们全面认识和研究乌尔第三王朝的附属国 gun$_2$ 税提出了很大的挑战。

第一节　附属国概况

乌尔第三王朝的三层势力范围包括核心区、外围区和附属国，其中前两个属于乌尔第三王朝已被合并的领土和行政区，是乌尔第三王朝的行省机构，它们和乌尔的中央政府之间是地方与中央的关系。然而，附属国属于乌尔第三王朝未被合并的地区，它和乌尔中央政府之间属于附属国与宗主国的关系。在舒辛3年之前，外围区和附属国的概念和范畴很难界定，因此判断一个地区到底是外围区还是附属国，一是从它们所缴纳的赋税形式（gun$_2$ ma-da 和 gun$_2$）来判断，这种判断只能适应舒辛3年税制改革之后；二是从乌尔第三王朝的王室铭文以及普兹瑞什达干的王室档案中所记载的"外国使节"（lu$_2$-kin-gi$_4$-a）和"恩西"（ensi$_2$）

这些术语中推断。当然，这种区分法也不是绝对的，比如"外国使节"不仅可以表示来自附属国的使节，也可以表示来自其他独立国家的使节。如何区分乌尔第三王朝的附属国和独立国家，这是一个比较困难的问题。我们只能结合各种资料的记载，尤其是结合文献中所记载的地名的大概地理位置的判断，并且依据乌尔第三王朝各位国王的对外征服战争和领土扩张的记载，来综合考证外围区、附属国和独立国家之间的大致界限。

从地理范围上看，乌尔第三王朝的附属国肯定比其外围区还要靠外，处于更外层的一环。附属国紧邻西部叙利亚地区边界的是古勃拉和埃布拉，以幼发拉底河为界的是马里和图图尔，[①] 位于底格里斯河上游北部边界的是阿巴尔尼乌姆、马尔达曼和西马努姆，[②] 位于东部的边界是西马什基，[③] 位于东南部的边界是安珊和马尔哈西，位于南部的边界是马干。概括而言，乌尔第三王朝的附属国范围，东到伊朗高原，西至地中海沿岸，南抵波斯湾沿岸的马干（今阿曼）以及马尔哈西（今伊朗的法尔斯省 Fars 或马克冉 Mekran），北达两河流域北部的库尔德地区。

通过对乌尔第三王朝王室铭文以及普兹瑞什达干王室档案的考察，依据文献中记录各附属国所所带术语形式不同，我们可以搜集到的附属国见表 4–1。

在这些可能的附属国中，有一些是介于附属国和独立国家之间，我们对其认识尚存在争议。比如，马里、马尔哈西、埃布拉、古勃拉（毕布罗

---

① T. M. Sharlach, "Beyond Chronology: The *šakkanakkus* of Mari and the Kings of Ur", in W. W. Hallo and I. Winter (eds.), *Proceedings of the XLVᵉ Rencontre Assyriologique Internationale. Part II: Seals and Seal Impressions*, Bethesda: CDL Press, 2001, pp. 59–70.

② P. Michalowski, "The Bride of Simanum", *Journal of the American Oriental Society*, Vol. 95, No. 4 (1975), pp. 716–719; T. Maeda, "The Defense Zone during the Rule of the Ur III Dynasty", *Acta Sumerologica*, Vol. 14 (1992), p. 148; T. Potts, *Mesopotamia and the East*, Oxford: Oxford University Committee for Archaeology, 1995, p. 140.

③ P. Steinkeller, "On the Identity of the Toponym LÚ. Su (. A)", *Journal of the American Oriental Society*, Vol. 108 (1988), pp. 197–202; P. Steinkeller, "New Light on Šimaški and Its Rulers", *Zeitschrift für Assyriologie und Vorderasiatische Archäologie*, Vol. 97 (2007), pp. 215–232; P. Steinkeller, "On the Dynasty of Šimaški: Twenty Years (or so) After", in M. Kozuh, et al (eds.), *Extraction & Control: Studies in Honor of Matthew W. Stolper*, Studies in Ancient Oriental Civilization 68, Chicago: The Oriental Institute of the University of Chicago, 2014, pp. 287–296.

斯）和马干，这些国家或地区很有可能是独立的国家，它们和乌尔第三王朝之间并不是附属关系，而是对等的外交关系。乌尔第三王朝的统治者们对这些附属国和独立国家采取了多种外交手段，比如联姻、赠送外交礼物等。

表 4–1　　　　　　　　乌尔第三王朝附属国统计表

类别	国家和地区名单
带 lu_2-kin-gi_4-a 术语	阿巴尔尼乌姆（Abarnium） 安珊（Anshan） 布伊尔（Bu'ir） 达里巴（Dariba） 杜杜里（Duduli） 埃布拉（Ebla） 吉吉比努姆（Gigibinum） 哈布拉（Habura） 哈尔西（Harshi） 亚布鲁（Iabru） 亚布拉特（Iabrat） 亚布图姆（Iabtium） 伊吉伽尔某某（Igi-gal-［x-x］） 因布（Inbu） 库米（Kumu） 库布拉（Kubla） 马干（Magan） 马里（Mari） 马尔达马尼（Mardamani） 马尔哈西（Marhashi） 西马努姆（Simanum） 沙胡安（Shahuan） 西马什基（Shimashgi） 舒达埃（Shudae） 图图尔（Tutul） 乌勒（U'ul） 乌尔比隆（Urbilum） 乌尔凯什（Urkesh） 孜达尼乌姆（Zidanium）

续表

类别	国家和地区名单
带 gun$_2$ 术语	阿丹顿（Adamdun） 安珊（Anshan） 埃布拉（Ebla） 马干（Magan） 马尔哈西（Marhashi） 萨布姆（Sabum） 苏萨（Susa） 提兰（Tiran） 乌鲁阿（Urua） 扎克图姆（Zaqtum） 孜姆达尔（Zimudar）

资料来源：T. Maeda, "The Defense Zone during the Rule of the Ur III Dynasty", *Acta Sumerologica*, Vol. 14 (1992), pp. 143-149; D. I. Owen, "Syrians in Sumerian Sources from the Ur III Period", *Bibliotheca Mesopotamica*, Vol. 25 (1992), p. 117; P. Steinkeller, "The Historical Background of Urkesh and the Hurrian Beginnings in Northern Mesopotamia", in G. Buccellati and M. Kelly-Buccellati (eds.), *Urkesh / Mozan Studies 3*: *Urkesh and the Hurrians Studies in Honor of Lloyd Cotsen*, Bibliotheca Mesopotamica 26, Malibu: Undena Publications, 1998, pp. 75-98.

此外，还有一些地区或国家是介于附属国和外围区之间，具有两者的特征，比如阿丹顿、孜姆达尔、萨布姆和苏萨。这些地区或国家向乌尔中央缴纳 gun$_2$ 税，征税对象是军队，这一点和外围区税的情况相似，然而这些地区或国家缴纳的牲畜数量极大，这一点又和外围区税的情况不同，而且它们缴纳的赋税在文献中从未使用过 gun$_2$ ma-da 的术语。综合考虑，我们还是认为这些存有争议的地区或国家应该属于乌尔第三王朝的附属国，而不是外围区。或者存在这样一种情况，即它们在一个时间段里属于外围区，在另一个时间段里则属于附属国，它们与乌尔第三王朝的关系不是固定不变的。

第二节 术语与文献概况

乌尔第三王朝附属国税的术语是 gun$_2$，等同于 gu$_2$，也可以写成 gu$_2$-na 和 gu$_2$-un，分别在 gun$_2$（gu$_2$）的后面加上了 na 或 un 符号如表 4-2[①]。

[①] 注意，苏美尔语 gu$_2$ 是一个多义词，有许多个意思。在乌尔第三王朝文献中，gu$_2$ 的意思主要有："（河）岸、（河）边""脖子""小扁豆""（表示一种重量单位）"等。在文献中，要根据上下文以及文献内容，区分这些不同的含义。

第四章 附属国 gun₂ 税

表4-2　　　　　　　乌尔第三王朝附属国税术语不同写法

楔形文字	转写
	gun₂ 或 gu₂
	gu₂-na
	gu₂-un
	gun₂ ma-da

由于 gun₂ 和外围区税 gun₂ ma-da 很容易被混淆，有的学者认为这两个术语指的是同一种税，认为 gun₂ 是 gun₂ ma-da 的缩写形式。① 其实不然，在上一章中我们讲过，术语 gun₂ 作为 gun₂ ma-da 的缩写形式是有条件的，并不是所有的 gun₂ 都是 gun₂ ma-da 的缩写形式。如果符合下面条件之一者，gun₂ 指的就是附属国税，而不是 gun₂ ma-da 的缩写形式：

（1）不限于牲畜；
（2）来源地大于外围区；
（3）本地统治者作为赋税运送者或者监督官；
（4）gun₂ 术语出现在舒辛之后。

这里我们只是为了区分附属国税和外围区税，即区分 gun₂ 和 gun₂ ma-da 两个术语，其文献来源是普兹瑞什达干的王室档案和乌尔的王室铭文。不过，在乌尔第三王朝的行省（内省）档案中，比如在吉尔苏文献和温马文献中，也有关于 gun₂ 术语的记载，这些文献中所记载的 gun₂ 术语指的并不是附属国税或者外围区税，而是泛指"赋税"的概念，和具体的税目连用。② 对此，我们需要注意区分。比如，下面这篇温马文献：

---

① P. Steinkeller, "The Administrative and Economic Organization of the Ur III State: The Core and the Periphery", in M. Gibson and R. D. Biggs (eds.), *The Organization of Power: Aspects of Bureaucracy in the Ancient Near East*, Studies in Ancient Oriental Civilization 46, Chicago: The Oriental Institute of the University of Chicago, 1987, p. 25.

② T. M. Sharlach, *Provincial Taxation and the Ur III State*, Cuneiform Monographs 26, Leiden and Boston: Brill-Styx, 2004, pp. 28-29, 279-280.

CM 26 23（AS 9，Umma）

正面

21 guruš u₄ 2-še₃	21 个劳动力，工作 2 天
nig₂ gu₂-na bala-ta	来自 bala 税的（劳动力）
tak₄-a ma₂-a ga₂-ra	上船返回
ša₃ Tum-malₓ（TUR₃）ki-ke₄	在吐玛尔
ugula Lugal-iti-da	监督官是卢伽尔伊提达

背面

inim Lu₂-kal-la-ta	来自卢卡拉的命令
kišib ᵈŠara₂-kam	沙拉卡姆收到了
mu en ᵈNanna Kar-zi-da ba-hun	阿马尔辛 9 年

目前，我们发现有 37 篇文献记载有 gun₂ 术语，通过对这些文献的内容进行分析之后，我们认为，其中只有 14 篇文献记载的是乌尔第三王朝的附属国 gun₂ 税，其余文献中记载的 gun₂ 术语指的不是附属国 gun₂ 税，而是其他的含义。这 14 篇附属国 gun₂ 税文献，基本上都来自普兹瑞什达干的王室经济文献以及乌尔的王室铭文。我们将 gun₂ 文献统计如下（见表 4 - 3）：

表 4 - 3　　　　　　包含术语 gun₂ 的文献统计表

文献来源	属于附属国税文献数量	总文献数量
普兹瑞什达干	11	15 *
乌尔	2	2
尼普尔	1	2
吉尔苏	0	5 **
温马	0	11
不详	0	2
共计	14	37

注 *：gu₂ Li-pi₂-i₃-sa kurušda，文献 PDT 2 1156（S 44 iv）．gu₂ šu-a-gi-na，文献 PDT 1 166（AS 5 v 25），可能指 gun₂ ma-da，后面加 erin₂ Ar-ra-ap-hu-umki，牲畜数量是 20 头牛、240 只羊。

**：文献 ITT 2776（SS 8 xi）：600 še gur，gu₂ ma₂-gan-še₃，ki ensi₂ Gir₂-suki-ta，Bu₃-u₂-du šu ba-ti "600 古尔大麦，运送到马干的边界，从吉尔苏的总督处，布乌杜收到了"，这里的 gu₂ 并不是指附属国税，而是"岸边、边界、边"的意思。

154

其次，这14篇文献的具体内容统计如下（见表4-4）：

表4-4　　　　　　　附属国 gun₂ 税文献统计分析表

附属国	日期	文献	来自
阿丹顿（ša₃ gu₂ A-dam-dun^ki）*	S 47 ix	PDT 1 18	普兹瑞什达干
阿丹顿（gu₂ A-dam-dun^ki）	S 47 ix 30	ZA 68 42 Smith 475	普兹瑞什达干
阿丹顿（gu₂ YN，erin₂ A-dam-dun^ki）	AS 8，AS 9 viii 26	StOr 9-1 30 (pl. 11)	普兹瑞什达干
苏萨（gu₂ Šušin^ki）	无	AUCT 2 364	普兹瑞什达干
苏萨（gu₂ Šušin^ki）	S 46 vii 8	CST 124	普兹瑞什达干
苏萨（gu₂ Šušin^ki）	S 48 vii 12	OIP 115 343	普兹瑞什达干
苏萨（ša₃ gu₂ Šušin^ki）	IS 2 iii 3	BCT 1 117	普兹瑞什达干
孜姆达尔（gu₂ Zi-mu-dar^ki）	AS 7 x	ZA 68 40 YBC 6805	普兹瑞什达干
孜姆达尔（gu₂-un gudu₄ eš₃ didli Zi-mu-dar^ki）	AS 4 iii 2	ZA 68 37 NVBT 1628	普兹瑞什达干
萨布姆（ša₃ gu₂ Sa-bu-um^ki）	AS 1 viii 3	AUCT 2 179	普兹瑞什达干
乌鲁阿（gu₂ iri-ki ᵈŠul-gi-ad-mu ensi₂ Urua^ki）	SS 7 ix 14	TCL 2 5515	普兹瑞什达干
埃布拉（gu₂ lu₂ Eb-la^ki）	S 46 iii 1	TMH NF 1-2 313	尼普尔？
安珊（gu₂-un An-ša-an^ki）	SS	RIME 3/2.01.04.06	乌尔
马尔哈西（Mar-ha-ši^ki-ta gu₂-un-še₃）	IS	RIME 3/2.01.05.04	乌尔

注*：或者拼写为 A-dam-šah₂^ki，参见 P. Steinkeller,"Puzur-Inšušinak at Susa: A Pivotal Episode of Early Elamite History Revonsidered", in K. De Graef, J. Tavernier (eds.), *Susa and Elam, Archaeological, Philological, Historical and Geographical Perspectives: Proceedings of the International Congress Held at Ghent University, December 14-17, 2009*, Leiden and Boston: Brill, 2013, p. 296; D. Potts, "Adamšah, Kimaš and the miners of Lagaš", in H. D. Baker, E. Robson and G. Zolyomi (eds.), *Your Praise is Sweet: A Memorial Volume for Jeremy Black from Students, Colleagues and Friends*, London: British Institute for the Study of Iraq, 2010, pp. 245-254.

简而言之，目前我们发现记载乌尔第三王朝附属国 gun₂ 税的文献数量，同外围区 gun₂ ma-da 税文献的数量一样稀少。这大概有两个原因，一是附属国税和外围区税文献本身就比较少，缴纳的次数也有限，不能和内省的 bala 税文献相比；二是还有大量的附属国税和外围区税文献没有被发现，或者是已经出土的却还没有被释读出版，或者是依然还没有被发掘出土。因此，目前我们对于乌尔第三王朝附属国 gun₂ 税的探讨，只能借助仅有的文献资料，我们得出的结论也仅仅是暂时的。

第三节　附属国 gun₂ 税解析

乌尔第三王朝附属国 gun₂ 税的课税形式不限于牛羊等牲畜，还包括陶器①、大麦②、白银③、木制品④。gun₂ 税的征税对象是乌尔第三王朝的附属国。gun₂ 税的税率目前由于资料缺乏，尚不清楚。gun₂ 税的纳税期限大致为一年一缴纳，但是由于文献资料的缺乏，我们无法进行更为深入的研究。gun₂ 税的目的地是乌尔中央，主要是普兹瑞什达干的动物管理中心。附属国缴纳的 gun₂ 牲畜税数量极大，这些牲畜被运送到普兹瑞什达干机构之后，首先被机构的总管接收，然后分配给其他分支负责官员，或者直接将牲畜发送到最终目的地，比如用于宗教祭祀活动，发送给王室成员、军队士兵或外交使节等。

根据目前我们所能掌握的文献证据，并不是所有的附属国都有向乌尔中央缴纳 gun₂ 税的记录留下来。目前的文献中，只记载了部分的附属国向乌尔中央缴纳 gun₂ 税的情况，这些附属国包括：阿丹顿、苏萨、孜姆达尔、提兰、萨布姆、乌鲁阿、扎克图姆、埃布拉、安珊及马尔哈西 10 个国家。我们根据这 10 个附属国的纳税特征、地理位置、身份性质等因素，将其分为以下四类：第一，阿丹顿、苏萨、萨布姆和乌鲁阿属于埃兰地区（今伊朗）缴纳 gun₂ 税数量巨大的附属国。第二，安珊和马尔哈西属于埃兰地区及其周边地区（也属于今伊朗）缴纳 gun₂ 税的附属国，但是关于它们纳税的记录都是在王室铭文中记录，在经济文献没有记载。第三，埃布拉的身份介于附属国和独立国王之间。第四，孜姆达尔、提兰和扎克图姆的身份介于附属国和外围区之间，更有可能是属于外围区范畴。

一　阿丹顿、苏萨、萨布姆、乌鲁阿

阿丹顿、苏萨、萨布姆和乌鲁阿这四个地名同时出现在许多乌尔第三

---

① 文献 ZA 68 40 YBC 6805（AS 7 x，Drehem）。
② 文献 ITT 2 776（SS 8 xi，Girsu）。
③ 文献 TCL 2 5515（SS 7 ix 14，Drehem）。
④ 文献 TMH NF 1 - 2 313（S 46 iii 1，Nippur）。

第四章 附属国 gun_2 税

王朝的吉尔苏文献中。据这些文献记载，大量的粮食作为路资从拉伽什—吉尔苏行省被支出给许多来自这四个国家的使节。比如：

ABTR 10（--viii，Girsu）
正面

5 $sila_3$ zi_3-gu	5 希拉粗制面粉
Da-da-ni u_3-kul	给"乌库尔"官员达达尼
5 $sila_3$ Šu-na-a šeš-ba	5 希拉面粉，给他的兄弟舒纳亚
^{u2}Urua$^{a.ki}$-ta du-ni	当他们去乌鲁阿时
0.0.2 zi_3 u_4 2-kam $ša_3$-iri	2 班面粉，于第 2 日，在城里
0.0.1 zi_3 kaskal-$še_3$	1 班面粉，在旅途中
Ba-za-mu aga_3-us_2-gal	给上等士兵巴扎姆
u_3 I-dara$_3$-ki-li_2 šeš-ni	和他的兄弟伊达拉基里
Sa-bu-um^{ki}-ta du-ni	当他们去萨布姆时
2 $sila_3$ zi_3 Šu-^{d}Utu lu_2-kas_4	2 希拉面粉，给信使舒乌图
5 $sila_3$ zi_3 A_2-bi_2-li_2-a aga_3-us_2-gal	5 希拉面粉，给上等士兵阿比里亚

背面

Šušin^{ki}-ta du-ni	当他们去苏萨时
0.0.2 zi_3 u_4 2-kam $ša_3$-iri	2 班面粉，于第 2 日，在城里
0.0.1 zi_3 kaskal-$še_3$	1 班面粉，在旅途中
Gu-ub-^{d}Utu sukkal	给使节古布乌图
u_3 Arad$_2$-^{d}Nanna aga_3-us_2-gal	和上等士兵阿拉德南那
A-dam-dun^{ki}-$še_3$ du-ni	当他们去阿丹顿时
0.0.1 5 $sila_3$ zi_3 u_4 3-kam	1 班 5 希拉面粉，于第 3 日
Da-gu-nir aga_3-us_2-gal	给上等士兵达古尼尔
0.0.1 5 $sila_3$ zi_3 u_4 3-kam	1 班 5 希拉面粉，于第 3 日
Šu-^{d}Utu sukkal	给使节舒乌图
Šušin^{ki}-ta du-ni	当他们去苏萨时
0.0.1 zi_3 u_4 2-kam	1 班面粉，于第 2 日
A-hu-du$_{10}$ u_3-kul	给"乌库尔"官员阿胡杜
^{u2}Urua$^{a.ki}$-ta du-ni	当他去乌鲁阿时

左侧

iti ezem-^{d}Ba-ba_6	第 8 月

157

（一）阿丹顿

阿丹顿（A-dam-dun^{ki}）① 向乌尔中央缴纳的 gun$_2$ 税，见于文献中的只有舒尔吉 47 年和阿马尔辛 8—9 年这两个时间段，处于乌尔国王统治末年。在舒尔吉 47 年，阿丹顿向乌尔中央缴纳 gun$_2$ 税，共有 7200 头牛、1331 只绵羊、62 只山羊，它们都是活牲，以及 225 只被屠宰的羊，这些牲畜被纳萨接收。其中，225 只被屠宰的羊在另一篇吉尔苏文献中被再次提到，并且交代了其用途，它们的皮被运送到皮毛加工场，其骨肉被运到仓库保存。第一篇文献是纳萨的接收文献，列举如下：

ZA 68 42 Smith 475（S 47 ix 30）

7200 gu$_4$	7200 头牛
1331 udu	1331 只绵羊
62 maš$_2$	62 只山羊
udu-ti-la	活牲
225 udu ba-ug$_7$	225 只绵羊，被屠宰
gun$_2$ A-dam-dun^{ki}	是阿丹顿的 gun$_2$ 税
ki U$_{18}$-ba-a-ta	从乌巴亚处
……	
mu-DU	带来
Na-sa$_6$ i$_3$-dab$_5$	纳萨收到
iti ezem-mah	第 9 月
mu us$_2$-sa Ki-maš^{ki} ba-hul	舒尔吉 47 年
u$_4$ 30-kam	第 30 日

第二篇文献是纳萨的支出文献，列举如下：

PDT 1 18（S 47 ix, Drehem）

225 udu	225 只绵羊

---

① M. Civil, "'Adamdun,' the Hippopotamus, and the Crocodile", *Journal of Cuneiform Studies*, Vol. 50（1998）, pp. 11 – 14.

第四章 附属国 gun$_2$ 税

ba-ug$_7$	被屠宰
ša$_3$ gun$_2$ A-dam-dun^{ki}	含在阿丹顿 gun$_2$ 税中
kuš-bi giš-kin-ti ba-an-ku$_4$	皮被带到皮毛加工场
ad$_6$-bi e$_2$-kišib-ba-še$_3$ ba-an-ku$_4$	骨肉被带到了储存室
ki Na-sa$_6$-ta ba-zi	从纳萨手中,被支出
iti ezem-mah	第 9 月
mu us$_2$-sa Ki-maš^{ki} ba-hul	舒尔吉 47 年

在阿马尔辛 9 年,阿丹顿再一次向乌尔中央缴纳了多达 1200 只羊(其中包括 1100 只绵羊和 100 只山羊)的 gun$_2$ 税,并且是由阿丹顿的军队缴纳,这一点类似于外围区的军事税性质。不仅如此,在这一年,阿丹顿还补缴了前一年拖欠的 1200 只绵羊的 gun$_2$ 税,由阿丹顿的恩西乌巴亚亲自监督运送。这篇文献列举如下:

StOr 9 – 1 30 (pl. 11) (AS 8, AS 9 viii 26, Drehem)	
1200 udu gun$_2$ mu en Eridu^{ki} ba-hun	1200 只绵羊,是阿马尔辛 8 年的 gun$_2$ 税
1100 udu 100 maš$_2$-gal	1100 只绵羊、100 只山羊
gun$_2$ mu en ^{d}Nanna Kar-zi-da ba-hun	是阿马尔辛 9 年的 gun$_2$ 税
erin$_2$ A-dam-dun^{ki}	来自阿丹顿的军队
giri$_3$ Dan-^{d}Šul-gi ra-gaba	由骑使丹舒尔吉亲自经办
ugula U$_{18}$!(UR)-ba-a①	乌巴亚监督
……	
u$_4$ 26-kam	第 26 日
mu-DU	带来
In-ta-e$_3$-a i$_3$-dab$_5$	因塔埃阿收到了
giri$_3$ ^{d}Nanna-ma-ba dub-sar	记账经办人是书吏南那玛巴

---

① 注意,这个符号 U$_{18}$ 由两个符号 URU 和 MIN 组成,人名 U$_{18}$-ba-a 在其他文献中被证明是阿丹顿的恩西,有的文献是 U$_{19}$-ba-a,其中 U$_{19}$ 的符号又被读作 ri$_2$ 或者 uru,所以有的学者把这个人名读作 Ri$_2$-ba-a,我们认为应该读作 U$_{19}$-ba-a,与 U$_{18}$-ba-a 呼应。而该文献中的 ur-ba-a 中的 ur 符号很可能是现代释读者的错误,因为 ur 和 uru(u$_{19}$)的符号有些类似,由于我们无法得到该文献的原始图片,所以这里只是推测。关于这个人名,参见 R. Zadok, "Elamites and Other Peoples from Iran and the Persian Gulf Region in Early Mesopotamian Sources", *Iran*, Vol. 32 (1994), pp. 34 – 37.

iti šu-eš₅-ša 第 8 月
mu en ᵈNanna Kar-zi-da ba-hun 阿马尔辛 9 年

还有一些 mu-DU 文献，记载了阿丹顿运送牲畜到普兹瑞什达干牲畜中心，这些文献中并没有出现 gun₂ 的术语，但是很可能也是指附属国 gun₂ 税。这些文献记录的不仅有牲畜，而且还包括木制品（giš）①和羊毛（si-ki）②，主要出现于舒尔吉 33—34 年（见表 4-5）。阿丹顿向乌尔中央缴纳的牲畜 gun₂ 税主要集中在每年的第 8 月至第 9 月。

表 4-5 附属国阿丹顿纳税统计分析表

日期	文献	牛	羊	术语（汉译）	
S 33 xi	AOAT 240 80 6		44（死牲）	nam-ra-ak An-ša-anᵏⁱ	安珊的战利品
				ki Ur-ᵍⁱˢgigir ensi₂ A-dam-dunᵏⁱ-ta	从阿丹顿的总督乌尔吉吉尔处
				giri₃ Ab-ba-na-ka	经办人是阿巴纳卡
				udu-bi su-su-dam	偿还了其绵羊
				ugu₂ Na-ra-am-i₃-li₂-ka i₃-im-gal₂	置于纳拉姆伊里的平衡账目的开头
S 44 viii 17	AnOr 7 148		2	U₁₉-ba-a ensi₂ A-dam-dunᵏⁱ mu-DU	阿丹顿的总督乌巴亚带来
S 44----	TRU 24		[x]	U₁₉-ba-a ensi₂ A-dam-dunᵏⁱ [mu-DU]	阿丹顿的总督乌巴亚带来
S 45 xii 6	Amorites 6	30 +	1740	ša₃ A-dam-dunᵏⁱ	在阿丹顿
				ugula U₁₉-ba-a	监督官是乌巴亚
				mu-DU	带来
S 46 viii	Nik 2 483		6190	šu-gid₂	转手
				ki U₁₉-ba-a ensi₂ A-dam-dunᵏⁱ-ta	从阿丹顿的总督乌巴亚处
				Na-sa₆ i₃-dab₅	纳萨接收了
				giri₃ Bu₃-u₂-daᵏⁱ	经办人是布乌达（人）

① 文献 SumRecDreh 4（S 34 xii），TRU 384（S 43 vi）.
② 文献 Rochester 8（S 33 vi）.

续表

日期	文献	牛	羊	术语	术语（汉译）
S 46 viii	TRU 107		384（死牲）	ki U$_{19}$-ba-a ensi$_2$ A-dam-dun^{ki}-ta	从阿丹顿的总督乌巴亚处
				mu-DU	带来
				Na-sa$_6$ i$_3$-dab$_5$	纳萨接收了
S 46 viii	PDT 1 39			384 kuš udu	384 张绵羊皮
				384 ad$_6$ udu	384 腔绵羊肉
				ša$_3$ udu A-dam-dun^{ki}	在阿丹顿的绵羊之中
				giri$_3$ Gid$_2$-da-ki šeš U$_{19}$-ba-a	经办人是乌巴亚之兄弟基德达吉
				ki Na-sa$_6$-ta	从纳萨处
				e$_2$-kišib-ba-še$_3$	被送到储存室
				ba-an-ku$_4$	
S 47 iv 25	Anavian 59（u.）ASJ 9 318 13		1	U$_{19}$-ba-a ensi$_2$ A-dam-dun^{ki}	阿丹顿的总督乌巴亚
				mu-DU	带来
				Na-sa$_6$ i$_3$-dab$_5$	纳萨接收了
undated	SACT 1 189	20 2	210 20	mu A-dam-dun^{ki}-še$_3$	以阿丹顿之名
				mu Hu-bu-um^{ki}-še$_3$	以胡布姆之名
				U$_3$-ba-a	乌巴亚
				…… ša$_3$-bi-ta	……从其中

阿丹顿缴纳的 gun$_2$ 税中的牲畜数量差异很大，每次缴纳的数量从 1 只羊（文献 ASJ 9 318 13）到 6190 只羊（Nik 2 483）不等。这些作为 gun$_2$ 税的牲畜不仅包括活牲，而且还有死牲（44 只死羊，文献 AOAT 240 806；384 只死羊，文献 TRU 107）。值得注意的是，在一次阿丹顿与胡布姆一起缴纳 gun$_2$ 税的文献中（SACT 1 189），作为 gun$_2$ 税的牛和羊的比例大致是 1∶10，这个比例关系恰好符合外围区 gun$_2$ ma-da 税的特征，所以很可能的解释是，这两个地区处于乌尔第三王朝的附属国和外围区之间，或者不同时期它们的身份会发生变化，一个阶段属于乌尔第三王朝的附属国，另一个阶段则作为外围区。不过，这也只是我们的推测，由于缺乏足够的文献证据，我们对于这一问题也无法做出更为可信的结论。

（二）苏萨

苏萨（Šušin[ki]）处于埃兰与两河流域的中间位置，在乌尔第三王朝时期介于核心区、外围区和附属国三者角色之间，政治地位比较特殊。① 苏萨向乌尔中央缴纳的是 gun_2 税，主要集中在每年的第 7 月，我们并没有发现苏萨向乌尔中央缴纳 gun_2 ma-da 税，却发现有缴纳 bala 税的记录。② 从这一点可以看出，苏萨至少在某个时间段属于乌尔第三王朝的附属国。苏萨向乌尔中央缴纳的作为 gun_2 税的牲畜数量众多，其中一次缴纳的数量是 55 头牛和 1814 只羊。试举一例：

CST 124（S 46 vii 8，Drehem）

……

51 gu_4 4 ab_2	51 头公牛、4 头母牛
1380 udu	1380 只公绵羊
334 u_8	334 只母绵羊
86 $maš_2$-gal	86 只山羊
14 $sila_4$ ga	14 只绵羊崽
gun_2 Šušin[ki]	作为苏萨的 gun_2 税
……	
mu-DU	带来，（匿名官员收到了）
iti ezem[d]Šul-gi	第 7 月
mu Ki-maš[ki] u_3 Hu-ur$_5$-ti[ki] ba-hul	舒尔吉 46 年
u_4 8-kam	第 8 日

此外，苏萨缴纳给乌尔中央的 gun_2 税大都用于乌尔的宗教祭祀活动，以及支付给外交使节等官员。比如，作为苏萨 gun_2 税的一只绵羊被献祭给

---

① W. W. Hallo, "Zāriqum", Journal of Near Eastern Studies, Vol. 15, No. 4 (1956), pp. 220 – 225；P. Michalowski, "Aššur during the Ur III Period", in O. Drewnowska (ed.), Here & There Across the Ancient Near East：Studies in Honour of Krystyna Lyczkowska, Warszawa：Agade, 2009, pp. 149 – 156.

② bala Za-ri$_2$-iq ensi$_2$ Šušin[ki]，文献 AAICAB 1/4 Bod S 322（AS 4 ix 24），PDT 1 557（AS 4 i-xii）. Za-ri$_2$-iq ensi$_2$ Šušin[ki] mu-DU，文献 RT 37 134（AS 4 vi）. Be-li$_2$-a-ri$_2$-ik ensi$_2$ Šušin[ki]，文献 SACT 1 189（undated）.

乌尔纳姆的祭酒仪式。

OIP 115 343（S 48 vii 12，Drehem）
1 udu ki-a-nag Ur-^{d}Nanna　　　　　　　1 只绵羊，献祭给乌尔纳姆的祭酒仪式
ša$_3$ mu-DU gun$_2$ Šušin^{ki}　　　　　　包含在苏萨带来的 gun$_2$ 税中
……
u$_4$ 12-kam　　　　　　　　　　　　　第 12 日
ki Na-sa$_6$-ta ba-zi　　　　　　　　　从纳萨处，支出
iti ezem^{d}Šul-gi　　　　　　　　　　第 7 月
mu Ha-ar-ši^{ki} Hu-ur$_5$-ti^{ki} Ki-maš^{ki} u$_3$
ma-da-bi aš-a ba-hul　　　　　　　　舒尔吉 48 年

（三）萨布姆

萨布姆（Sa-bu-um^{ki}）① 在乌尔第三王朝经济文献中出现得较少，只有一篇文献记载萨布姆向乌尔中央缴纳的 gun$_2$ 税，作为 gun$_2$ 税形式的牲畜被献祭给神庙以及供外国使节食用。如下所示：

AUCT 2 179（AS 1 viii 3，Drehem）
……
1 gu$_4$ 2 udu 1 maš$_2$ ^{d}En-lil$_2$　　　　1 头牛、2 只绵羊、1 只山羊，献给恩利尔神
1 gu$_4$ 2 udu 1 maš$_2$ ^{d}Nin-lil$_2$　　　　1 头牛、2 只绵羊、1 只山羊，献给宁利尔神
1 gu$_4$ Nin-šuba$_3$ lu$_2$-kas$_4$　　　　　1 头牛，供给使节宁舒巴
ša$_3$ gun$_2$ Sa-bu-um^{ki}　　　　　　　这些是萨布姆 gun$_2$ 税的一部分
……
u$_4$ 3-kam　　　　　　　　　　　　　第 3 日
ki Na-sa$_6$-ta ba-zi　　　　　　　　　从纳萨处，支出
iti šu-eš$_5$-ša　　　　　　　　　　　第 8 月
mu ^{d}Amar-^{d}Suen ba-hul　　　　　　阿马尔辛 1 年

---

① D. O. Edzard, G. Farber, *Répertoire Géographique des Textes Cunéiformes II：Die Orts-und Gewässernamen der Zeit der 3. Dynastie von Ur*, Wiesbaden：Dr. Ludwig Reichert Verlag, 1974, pp. 159 - 161；K. De Graef, "Annus Simaškensis：L'Usage des Noms d'Année Pendant la Période Simaškéenne (ca. 1930 - 1880 AV. Notre Ère) à Suse", *Iranica Antiqua*, Vol. 43 (2008), p. 79.

此外，萨布姆还出现普兹瑞什达干的 mu-DU 文献中，不过文献中并没有出现 gun_2 术语，所以很可能在 mu-DU 文献中，从萨布姆"被带来"的牲畜也是作为 gun_2 税的形式。在 mu-DU 文献中，记载了普兹瑞什达干机构总管纳萨接收了来自萨布姆"进贡"的 29 头牛。例如：

AUCT 1 743（S 48 ix 19，Drehem）

$30\text{-}la_2\text{-}1\ gu_4$	29 头牛
$ša_3\ Sa\text{-}bu\text{-}um^{ki}$	作为萨布姆（gun_2 税）的一部分
$u_4\ 20\text{-}la_2\text{-}1\text{-}kam$	第 19 日
mu-DU	带来
$ki\ Na\text{-}sa_6\text{-}ta$	从纳萨处
$^dEn\text{-}lil_2\text{-}la_2\ i_3\text{-}dab_5$	恩利拉收到了
iti ezem-mah	第 9 月
$mu\ Ha\text{-}ar\text{-}ši^{ki}\ u_3\ Ki\text{-}maš^{ki}\ ba\text{-}hul$	舒尔吉 48 年

另据一篇 ba-zi 文献记载，萨布姆军队带来的 600 只羊从总管阿巴萨加处支出，被用于宗教仪式。很有可能，萨布姆的 gun_2 税也可以由军队负责缴纳。比如：

JCS 32 172 2（AS 4 vi 22，Drehem）

正面

$600\ udu\ gi_6$	600 只黑色绵羊
$a\text{-}ri\text{-}a\ ^dNin\text{-}hur\text{-}sag\ Iri\text{-}sag\text{-}rig_7^{ki}$	献祭给伊利萨格里格的宁胡尔萨格的 a-ri-a 仪式
$ša_3\ mu\text{-}DU\ erin_2\ Sa\text{-}bu\text{-}um^{ki}$	这些是由萨布姆军队带来的一部分
$Arad_2\text{-}mu\ maškim$	阿拉德姆是监督官

背面

$u_4\ 22\text{-}kam$	第 22 日
$ki\ Ab\text{-}ba\text{-}sa_6\text{-}ga\text{-}ta\ ba\text{-}zi$	从阿巴萨加处，支出
$iti\ a_2\text{-}ki\text{-}ti$	第 6 月
$mu\ En\text{-}mah\text{-}an\text{-}an\ en\ ^dNanna\ ba\text{-}hun$	阿马尔辛 4 年

左侧

600	（共计）600（只羊）

（四）乌鲁阿

乌鲁阿[①]在乌尔第三王朝文献中出现得也极少，文献中提到乌鲁阿的恩西给乌尔中央带来白银，作为 gun_2 税。如下所示：

TCL 2 5515（SS 7 ix 14，Drehem）

1 ma-na ku_3-babbar	1 米纳白银
gun_2 iri-ki	作为"城市" gun_2 税
^{d}Šul-gi-gi-ad-mu $ensi_2$ Urua^{ki}	由乌鲁阿的恩西舒尔吉基德姆
……	
mu-DU	带来
Lu_2-dingir-ra	卢丁吉尔拉
šu ba-ti	收到了
$ša_3$ Nibru^{ki}	在尼普尔

其他记载乌鲁阿的文献没有提到 gun_2 术语，但是也可能是属于附属国税范畴。这些文献大多是属于接收（mu-DU）文献或者支出（ba-zi）文献。我们将其归纳如下（见表4-6）：

表4-6　　　　　　　附属国乌鲁阿纳税统计分析表

日期	文献	牛	羊	术语	
S 40 ii 29	JCS 35 185 3		821	Urua^{ki}-ta	从乌鲁阿
				mu-DU	带来
S 45 vi 30	MVN 13 517	2	148	$erin_2$ Urua^{ki}	由乌鲁阿的军队
				mu-DU a_2-ki-ti	带来为阿基图节日
S 46 vi	PDT 2 781		1974	šu-gid_2 udu Urua^{ki}	作为乌鲁阿的 šu-gid 羊
				ki Mi-it-har $kuš_7$-ta	从驯兽师米特哈尔处
				mu-DU	带来
				Ur-ku_3-nun-na i_3-dab_5	乌尔库努纳收到

---

① P. Steinkeller, "The Question of Marhaši: A Contribution to the Historical Geography of Iran in the Third Millennium B. C.", *Zeitschrift für Assyriologie und Vorderasiatische Archäologie*, Vol. 72, 1982, pp. 244–246.

续表

日期	文献	牛	羊	术语	
AS 6 ix 13	SAT 2 914	3	180	A-bi₂-si₂-im-ti mu-DU erin₂ Urua^ki ki Ab-ba-sa₆-ga-ta ba-zi	为阿比西姆提 带来，由乌鲁阿的军队 从阿巴萨加处，支出
AS 6 xi	PDT 1 234		15	šu-gid₂ lu₂ Urua^ki ki ᵈŠul-gi-zi-mu-ta mu-DU Ab-ba-sa₆-ga i₃-dab₅	作为乌鲁阿的 šu-gid 羊 从舒尔吉孜姆处 带来 阿巴萨加收到
AS 8 ix 18	TRU 126	3	180	erin₂ Urua^ki ugula ᵈŠul-gi-zi-mu mu-DU Ab-ba-sa₆-ga i₃-dab₅	由乌鲁阿的军队 监督官是舒尔吉孜姆 带来 阿巴萨加收到

二 安珊、马尔哈西

安珊①和马尔哈西②这两个伊朗地区的地名，出现在乌尔第三王朝的王室铭文和年名中，乌尔对这两个国家的政策是兼容并蓄，一方面采取政治联姻和互派使节的和平友好方式，另一方面也与这两个国家进行战争。在战争之后，这两个国家表示臣服，成为乌尔第三王朝的附属国，也向乌尔缴纳 gun₂ 税。

在乌尔第三王朝舒尔吉的年名中，曾提到安珊和马尔哈西的地名，比如在舒尔吉18年，乌尔王室和马尔哈西进行了政治联姻。另外，比如在舒尔吉30年，乌尔和安珊进行了政治联姻，但是在舒尔吉34年，乌尔和安珊爆发战争，可能是联姻没有满足双方利益。

舒尔吉18年：mu Li₂-wir-mi-ta₂-šu dumu-munuslugal nam-nin Mar-ha-ši^ki-še₃ ba-il₂
国王的女儿利维尔米塔苏被提升为马尔哈西的王后之年

---

① E. Reiner, "The Location of Anšan", *Revue d'Assyriologie et d'archéologie orientale*, Vol. 67 (1973), pp. 57–62; D. T. Potts, *The Archaeology of Elam: Formation and Transformation of an Ancient Iranian State*, Cambridge: Cambridge University Press, 2004, pp. 130–157.

② P. Steinkeller, "The Question of Marhaši: A Contribution to the Historical Geography of Iran in the Third Millennium B.C.", *Zeitschrift für Assyriologie und Vorderasiatische Archäologie*, Vol. 72 (1982), pp. 246–263.

第四章 附属国 gun_2 税

舒尔吉 30 年：mu dumu-munus lugal ensi₂ An-ša-an^{ki}-ke₄ ba-an-tuku/du
　　　　　　国王的女儿嫁给安珊恩西之年
舒尔吉 34 年：mu An-ša-an^{ki} ba-hul
　　　　　　安珊被毁之年

安珊和马尔哈西向乌尔中央缴纳 gun_2 税的情况并没有记录在现已发现的经济文献中。反而，在乌尔第三王朝的王室铭文中，有安珊和马尔哈西向乌尔缴纳 gun_2 税的相关记录，但是，这些记录都是伴随着乌尔对这两个国家的征服战争而产生的，它们可能是作为战败国的赔偿或者战利品之类的形式。其中，安珊向乌尔中央缴纳 gun_2 税的铭文位于舒辛统治时期，如下所示：

RIME 3/2.01.04.06（SS，Ur）

ᵈŠu-ᵈSuen	舒辛
lugal kala-ga	强大的国王
lugal Uri₅^{ki}-ma	乌尔之王
lugal an-ub-da limmu₂-ba-ke₄	天地四方之王
u₄ ma-da Za-ab-ša-li^{ki}	当扎布沙里地区
u₃ ma-da ma-da	和西马什基诸地区
Šimašgi^{ki}-ka	
mu-hul-a	被（他）毁灭时
maš₂-gal	山羊
gu₂-un An-ša-an^{ki}-na	作为安珊的 gun_2 税
mu-un-tum₂-ma-na	他们带来给他（舒辛）
dam-ši-lum-bi	他们为他立了一尊雕像
mu-na-an-dim₂	
nam-ti-la-ni-še₃	为他祈祷生命长久
a mu-na-ru	献给他（某位神）

此外，马尔哈西也向乌尔中央缴纳 gun_2 税，其记录列举如下：

RIME 3/2.01.05.04（IS，Ur）

ᵈNanna amar banda₃^{da} An-na	为南那，安神的冲动牧牛人
en dumu sag ᵈEn-lil₂-la₂	主人，恩利尔的长子

167

lugal-a-ni-ir	他的主人
^{d}I-bi$_2$-^{d}Suen	伊比辛
dingir kalam-ma-na	他的国家的神
lugal kala-ga	强大的国王
lugal Uri$_5^{ki}$-ma	乌尔之王
lugal an-ub-da limmu$_2$-ba-ke$_4$	天地四方之王
ur gun$_3$-a Me-luh-ha^{ki}	他的有斑点的麦鲁哈"狗"
Mar-ha-ši^{ki}-ta	来自马尔哈西
gu$_2$-un-še$_3$ mu-na-ab-tum$_2$-ma-ni	由他们带来，作为 gun$_2$ 税
dam-ši-lum-bi	他制造了它的复制品
mu-dim$_2$	
nam-ti-la-ni-še$_3$	为了他的生命长久
a mu-na-ru	他（伊比辛）把它献给他（南那）
ur gun$_3$-a-ba	关于这只有斑点的"狗"
he$_2$-dab$_5$	"抓住他"
mu-bi-im	是它的名字

这两篇王室铭文只是分别提到了安珊和马尔哈西向乌尔第三王朝缴纳 gun$_2$ 税，是作为歌颂国王业绩的组成部分。我们从中只知道来自安珊的 gun$_2$ 税形式是山羊，来自马尔哈西的 gun$_2$ 税形式是有斑点的麦鲁哈"狗"（可能是雕刻品）。然而，王铭中并没有提到 gun$_2$ 税的细节内容，比如这些赋税的目的地、纳税期限、税率等内容，所以我们无法对安珊和马尔哈西的 gun$_2$ 税进行更为细致的研究。

三 埃布拉

埃布拉[①]位于今天叙利亚境内，距离乌尔第三王朝的核心区十分遥远，所以它与乌尔第三王朝的关系很可能是介于附属国和独立国家之间。在普

---

① M. A. Astour, "An Outline of the History of Ebla (Part 1)", in C. H. Gordon and G. A. Rendsburg (eds.), *Eblaitica*: *Essays on the Ebla Archives and Eblaite Language*, Vol. 3, Winona Lake: Eisenbrauns, 1992, pp. 3 – 82; M. A. Astour, "An Reconstruction of the History of Ebla (Part 2)", in C. H. Gordon (ed.), *Eblaitica*: *Essays on the Ebla Archives and Eblaite Language*, Vol. 4, Winona Lake: Eisenbrauns, 2002, pp. 57 – 195; A. Archi, *Ebla and Its Archives*: *Texts, History, and Society*, Studies in Ancient Near Eastern Records 7, Boston and Berlin: Walter de Gruyter, 2015.

第四章 附属国 gun₂ 税

兹瑞什达干文献中，记载有埃布拉统治者的使节祖里姆①、伊孜因达干、库尔比拉克②、伊里达干③、埃祖恩达干④这些官员的名字，他们和马里、乌尔舒的"人"（使节）一同从普兹瑞什达干机构接收牲畜。例如：

Hermitage 3 194（P211503，AS 1 xii 29，Drehem）

正面

1 maš₂-gal niga I₃-li₂-ᵈDa-gan lu₂ Eb-laᵏⁱ	1 只食大麦山羊，给埃布拉人（使节）伊里达干
1 maš₂-gal niga Bu-du-ur₂ lu₂ Ur-šuᵏⁱ	1 只食大麦山羊，给乌尔舒人（使节）布杜尔
1 maš₂-gal niga Iš-me-ᵈDa-gan lu₂ Ma-ri₂ᵏⁱ	1 只食大麦山羊，给马里人（使节）伊什美达干
giri₃ Lugal-inim-gi-na sukkal	经办人是信使卢伽尔伊宁基纳

背面

Arad₂-mu maškim	阿拉德姆是全权监督官
iti u₄ 30-la₂-1 ba-zal	第 29 日过去了
ki A-hu-ni-ta	从阿胡尼处
ba-zi	支出
iti še-sag₁₁-ku₅	第 12 月
mu ᵈAmar-ᵈSuen lugal	阿马尔辛 1 年

---

① Zu-ri₂-um lu₂ Eb-laᵏⁱ，文献 AAICAB 1/2 pl. 144 1971 - 363（S 46 iii 7），MMFM 2005 20 3（S 46 ix）. Zu-ri-im lu₂-kin-gi₄-a lu₂ Eb-laᵏⁱ，文献 AJSL 39 65（S 46），MCS 7 19 Liv 51 63 51（S 46 ii 28）。

② I-zi-in-ᵈDa-gan, Kur-bi-la-ak, lu₂ Eb-laᵏⁱ-me-eš₂，文献 Amorites 21（SS 6 ix 14）。

③ I₃-li₂-ᵈDa-gan lu₂ Eb-laᵏⁱ，文献 P424375（AS 1 ii 14），JCS 57 28 4（AS 1 ii 23），Ebla 1975 - 1985 289 K（AS 1 ii 26），PDT 1 594（AS 1 iii 4），Hermitage 3 194（AS 1 xii 29），MVN 15 360（AS 2 iii 13），BPOA 7 2916（AS 2 iv 14），LAOS 1 28（AS 2 v 16），JCS 7 104 SLAM 61：1927（AS 2 v 20），CST 254（AS 2 vi 3），TRU 305（AS 2 vi 4），P453367（AS 2 vi 5），Ebla 1975 - 1985 287 A（AS 2 vi 8），JCS 7 105 NBCT 01593（AS 2 viii），CST 468（AS 6 iv 1），MVN 13 635（AS 6 iv 5），TRU 344（AS 6 iv 6），JCS 7 104 Smith College 473（AS 6 iv 9），Hirose 231（AS 6 iv 23），MVN 11 146（AS 6 iv 26），Fs Hallo 182（AS 2 vii 21），Hermitage 3 317（AS 6 viii 10），CDLJ 2012/1 4. 38（AS 6 viii 29）. I₃-li₂-ᵈDa-gan lu₂-kin-gi₄-a Me-gu-um ensi₂ Eb-laᵏⁱ，文献 Ebla 1975 - 1985 267（AS 7 v 21）. I₃-li₂-ᵈDa-gan lu₂-kin-gi₄-a lu₂ Eb-laᵏⁱ，文献 Ontario 1 32（S 44 iii 13）。

④ E-zu-un-ᵈDa-gan lu₂ Eb-laᵏⁱ，文献 Ebla 1975 - 1985 287 B（SS 3 iii 6）。

关于埃布拉向乌尔中央缴纳 gun$_2$ 税的记录，目前我们只发现了一篇相关文献。而且，埃布拉缴纳的 gun$_2$ 税形式不是牲畜，而是木制品。这篇可能来自尼普尔的文献列举如下：

TMH NF 1-2 313（S 46 iii 1，Nippur?）

正面

500 ^{giš}ilar rig$_2$-ti-a-lum	500个"里格提亚鲁姆"木制弓
500 ^{giš}kab$_2$-kul rig$_2$-ti-a-lum	500个"里格提亚鲁姆"木制容器
gun$_2$ lu$_2$ Eb-la^{ki}	作为埃布拉的 gun$_2$ 税
giri$_3$ Zu-ri$_2$-im lu$_2$-na	经办人是（埃布拉）使节祖里姆

背面

u$_3$ Lugal-pa-e$_3$	和卢伽尔帕埃
mu-DU	带来
DINGIR-ba-ni	伊鲁姆巴尼
šu ba-ti	收到了
iti u$_5$-bi$_2$-gu$_7$ u$_4$ 1-kam	第3月，第1日
mu Ki-maš^{ki} ba-hul	舒尔吉46年

四 孜姆达尔

孜姆达尔（Zi-mu-dar^{ki}）地区①大致位于埃兰地区，它与乌尔第三王朝的距离相对不远，根据它向乌尔中央缴纳赋税的种类与数量，我们推断孜姆达尔很可能介于乌尔第三王朝的附属国和外围区之间，或者是它在一个时期属于外围区，另一个时期属于附属国。根据乌尔纳姆的王室铭文记载，乌尔纳姆曾经驻军在库提和孜姆达尔。②

---

① D. R. Frayne, "The Zagros Campaigns of the Ur III Kings", *The Canadian Society for Mesopotamian Studies*, Vol. 3 (2008), p. 36. 注意，还有两篇文献记载了提兰（Ti-ra-an^{ki}，文献 TAD 54）、扎克图姆（Zaq-tum^{ki}，文献 TAD 66）向乌尔中央缴纳的 gun$_2$ 税没有带来（nu-mu-DU），这里的 gun$_2$ 是 gun$_2$ ma-da 的缩写形式，所以提兰和扎克图姆向乌尔缴纳的不是附属国税，而是外围区税，详细介绍见上一章。

② a-na bi$_2$-in-ak-bi, ma-da Gu-tim-um^{ki} Zi-mu-dar^{ki} sig-ba ugnim ki ba-ni-tag, 文献 RIME 3/2.01.01.30.

第四章 附属国 gun₂ 税

孜姆达尔向乌尔中央缴纳的 gun₂ 税，既包括牲畜，也包括其他产品。当赋税是牲畜时，孜姆达尔负责缴纳 gun₂ 税的是涂油祭司（gudu₄），[1] 税收的目的地是缴纳给王后阿比西姆提。例如：

ZA 68 37 NVBT 1628（AS 4 iii 2，Drehem）
正面

8 gu₄ 2 ab₂	8 头公牛、2 头母牛
gu₂-un gudu₄ eš₃didli Zi-mu-dar^ki	作为孜姆达尔诸神殿的涂油祭司的 gun₂ 税
ugula Šu-i₃-li₂	监督官是舒伊里
A-bi₂-si₂-im-ti ba-na-šum₂	献给阿比西姆提
giri₃ Er₃-ra-ba-ni kurušda	经办人是育肥师埃拉巴尼
mu-DU lugal-ta	来自王室带来
šu ur₃-dam	被抹掉

背面

u₄ 2-kam	第 2 日
iti u₅-bi₂-gu₇	第 3 月
mu En-mah-gal-an-na en^d Nanna ba-hun	阿马尔辛 4 年

除了牲畜形式的 gun₂ 税之外，孜姆达尔也向乌尔中央缴纳其他产品的 gun₂ 税，比如陶罐，试举一例：

ZA 68 40 YBC 6805（AS 7 x，Drehem）
正面

955 ^dug gur₄-gur₄ geštin	955 个藤制容器[2]
160 ^dug dal geštin	160 个藤制测量器皿[3]
gun₂ Zi-mu-dar^ki	作为孜姆达尔的 gun₂ 税

---

[1] D. Charpin, *Le Clergé d'Ur au Siècle d'Hammurabi（XIXe-XVIIIe Siècles av. J.-C.）*, Genève-Paris: Librairie Droz, 1986, pp. 252-257.

[2] M. A. Powell, "Metron Ariston: Measure as a Tool for Studying Beer in Ancient Mesopotamia", in L. Milano (ed.), *Drinking in Ancient Societies: History and Culture of Drinks in the Ancient Near East*, HANES 6, Padova: Sargon srl, 1994, pp. 102-103.

[3] A. Salonen, *Die Hausgeräte der Alten Mesopotamier nach sumerisch-akkadischen Quellen, Teil II: Gefässe*, Helsinki: Suomalaisen Kirjallisuuden Kirjapaino Oy Helsinki, 1966, pp. 108, 179.

ki Nin-ga₂-ta	从宁伽处
背面	
I-šar-kur-ba-šum	伊沙尔库尔巴舒姆
šu ba-ti	收到了
iti ezem An-na	第10月
mu Hu-uh₂-nu-ri^ki ba-hul	阿马尔辛7年

孜姆达尔的统治者是将军或军事总督，名叫卢南那。① 孜姆达尔向乌尔中央缴纳赋税的活动是由军队负责，而且牛和羊的比例接近于外围区 gun₂ ma-da 税的 1∶10。所以很有可能，在舒尔吉时期和阿马尔辛前期，孜姆达尔作为乌尔第三王朝的外围区，而在阿马尔辛统治后期成为其附属国。比如下面两篇文献的对比（见表 4-7）：

表 4-7　　　　　　　　附属国孜姆达尔纳税统计分析表

日期	文献	牛	羊	术语	
S 47 xi 28	OrSP 18 pl. 4 12	11 +	130	erin₂ Zi-mu-dar^ki mu-DU Na-sa₆ i₃-dab₅	由孜姆达尔的军队 带来 纳萨接收
AS 2 xi	Fs Levine 115-119 148ff	15	150	erin₂ Zi-mu-dar^ki ugula Zi-qur₂-i₃-li₂ mu-DU lugal Ab-ba-sa₆-ga i₃-dab₅	由孜姆达尔的军队 监督官是孜库尔伊里 为国王带来 阿巴萨加接收

由于关于乌尔第三王朝的附属国 gun₂ 税的文献记录数量过于稀少，我们很难对这种赋税有更为深入的认识和研究。要进一步研究附属国、外围区、独立国家向乌尔中央的朝贡，需要整理所有的普兹瑞什达干出土的记载牲畜的 mu-DU 文献，对 mu-DU 的"进贡者"或者"携带者、运送者"的身份及其时间段进行综合的研究。

---

① Lu₂-^dNanna šagina Zi-mu-dar^ki，文献 UET 3 75（SS 1 i, Ur），NATN 776（SS 1, Nippur）。

第五章　王室 maš-da-ri-a 税

乌尔第三王朝作为中央集权制的国家，乌尔王室是一个庞大的群体和权力机构，这个群体的成员有的担任政府官职，其他成员独立于政府之外，作为一个拥有特殊权力的群体存在。王室成员的日常开销和衣食住行通过地方上缴的赋税维持，这种赋税被称为王室税，其苏美尔语术语是 maš-da-ri-a。顾名思义，王室税也是乌尔第三王朝地方向中央缴纳的一种赋税类目，和之前我们讲过的核心区 bala 税、外围区 gun_2 ma-da 税以及附属国 gun_2 税不同的是，王室税的目的和受益者不是整个乌尔中央政府，而仅是乌尔的王室成员，也包括国王自身。

王室税由行省和神庙管理者缴纳，作为一种国家税（中央税），由特定职业的人员（如商人）缴纳给国王（尤其是为了庆祝乌尔的节日）。此外，温马阿亚卡拉档案中提到了这种税的税率。在普兹瑞什达干文献中，有关于神庙中的首席神庙主管（šabra）和神庙管理员（sanga）与总督（$ensi_2$）缴纳牲畜的记载。这种赋税主要是用于祭祀节日中，在国家王室管理下，履行他们的祭祀庆典任务。在舒辛 3 年的税制改革之后，王室税用于乌尔的三大国家节日中，这表明乌尔作为国家祭祀中心的特殊地位。从经济角度看，这三大节日可能有更重要的作用。首先，我们介绍一下乌尔第三王朝的王室概况。

第一节　乌尔第三王朝王室概况

乌尔第三王朝共有五位国王（lugal）：乌尔纳姆[1]、舒尔吉[2]、阿马尔辛[3]、舒辛和伊比辛。[4] 国王一般有多名妻子，在一个时期国王只有一位王后（nin），其他的都称为"卢库尔"（lukur），[5] 相当于王妃。每位国王有许多儿女，分别是王子（dumu lugal）和公主（dumu-munus lugal）。这些是乌尔第三王朝王室成员的基本组成部分。[6] 除此之外，比如像公主的丈夫（也即驸马），王后的父母、兄弟姐妹等外戚，以及王子与公主的乳母（um-me-ga-la$_2$）和保姆（um-me-da）[7] 等人员，也可以算作是王室成员的组成部分。

---

[1] S. N. Kramer, "The Death of Ur-Nammu and His Descent to the Netherworld", *Journal of Cuneiform Studies*, Vol. 21 (1967), pp. 104 – 122; S. N. Kramer, "The Death of Ur-Nammu", in M. Mori, H. Ogawa, M. Yoshikawa (eds.), *Near Eastern Studies: Dedicated to H. I. H. Prince Takahito Mikasa on the Occasion of His Seventy-Fifth Birthday*, Wiesbaden: Otto Harrassowitz, 1991, pp. 193 – 214.

[2] W. Horowitz, P. J. Watson, "The Ascent of Shulgi and the Death of Shulgi", *Acta Sumeriologica*, Vol. 13 (1991), pp. 411 – 413; P. Michalowski, "The Death of Shulgi", *Orientalia Nova Series*, Vol. 46 (1977), pp. 220 – 225.

[3] P. Michalowski, "Amar-Su'ena and the Historical Tradition", in M. de Jong Ellis (ed.), *Essays on the Ancient Near East in Memory of Jacob Joel Finkelstein*, Hamden: Archon Books, 1977, pp. 155 – 157.

[4] A. Falkenstein, "Ibbisîn-Ishbi'erra", *Zeitschrift für Assyriologie und Vorderasiatische Archäologie*, Vol. 49 (1950) 59 – 79; T. Jacobsen, "The Reign of Ibbisin", *Journal of Cuneiform Studies*, Vol. 7 (1953), pp. 36 – 47.

[5] T. M. Sharlach, "Priestesses, Concubines, and the Daughters of Men: Disentangling the Meaning of the Word lukur in Ur III Times", in P. Michalowski (ed.), *On the Third Dynasty of Ur: Studies in Honor of Marcel Sigrist*, Journal of Cuneiform Studies Supplemental Series 1, Boston: American Schools of Oriental Research, 2008, pp. 177 – 184. 关于乌尔第三王朝的王室妇女研究，参见 P. Michalowski, "Royal Women of the Ur III Period, Part I: the wife of Šulgi", *Journal of Cuneiform Studies*, Vol. 28 (1976), pp. 169 – 172; P. Michalowski, "Royal women of the Ur III period, Part II: Geme-Ninlila", *Journal of Cuneiform Studies*, Vol. 31 (1979), pp. 171 – 176; P. Michalowski, "Royal Women of the Ur III Period, Part III", *Acta Sumeriologica*, Vol. 4 (1982), pp. 129 – 142; P. Steinkeller, "More on the Ur III Royal Wives", *Acta Sumeriologica*, Vol. 3 (1981), pp. 77 – 92.

[6] H. Limet, "Le Rôle du Palais dans l'Économie Néo-Sumérienne", in E. Lipinski (ed.), *State and Temple Economy in the Ancient Near East, I: Proceedings of the International Conference Organized by the Katholieke Universiteit Leuven from the 10th to the 14th of April 1978*, Orientalia Lovaniensia Analecta 5, Leuven: Departement Orientalistiek, 1979, pp. 235 – 248.

[7] 参见刘昌玉《古代两河流域的乳母与保姆》，《妇女与性别史研究》第 2 辑，2017 年。

第五章　王室 maš-da-ri-a 税

在第一章我们讲过，乌尔第三王朝的王位继承以及五位国王之间的世系关系，这是一个至今仍然没有彻底解决的问题。尤其是关于阿马尔辛、舒辛和伊比辛三人之间的关系问题，在学术界有许多争议。同时，围绕着乌尔国王们所引起的乌尔王室成员的世系问题，也是困扰学者们的难题。在这些问题中，有三个问题最为典型：第一，乌图赫伽尔和乌尔纳姆是兄弟关系吗？第二，阿比西姆提是舒尔吉的妻子，还是阿马尔辛的妻子？第三，伊比辛的父亲是谁？第一个问题，我们目前只发现了一篇文献提到这俩人之间的关系，这篇文献提到 šeš-a-ni（他的兄弟），① 可惜的是，该文献有部分残缺（其中表示"兄弟"的术语 šeš 在文献中部分残缺），最重要的"关系"部分则是学者的恢复。第二个问题，没有直接的文献证据记录阿比西姆提是谁的妻子，她在阿马尔辛时期和舒辛时期的文献中都出现过，在舒辛时期的文献中，阿比西姆提被称为"王后"（nin），而在阿马尔辛时期的文献中，她没有用这个称号。② 因此，可能是在舒辛时期，她成为了王太后。另据古巴比伦时期的两个相互印证的证据（阿比西姆提的兄弟巴巴提的印章铭文）表明，阿比西姆提是舒辛的母亲。③ 从一篇文献中所记载的一个人名：舒辛—瓦利德—舒尔吉（Shu-Suen-walid-Shulgi），直译为"舒尔吉所生的舒辛"，可以推断出，舒辛应该是舒尔吉的儿子。④ 第三个问题，目前没有任何证据表明谁是伊比辛的父亲。在学术界一般认为，在舒尔吉统治时期的文献中所记载的"国王的儿子"（dumu lugal）指的是舒尔吉的儿子，在阿马尔辛时期文献中所记载的"国王的儿子"（du-mu lugal）指的是阿马尔辛的儿子，以此类推。

根据文献证据，我们统计乌尔第三王朝国王的妻子们如下（见表 5 - 1）：⑤

---

① C. Wilcke, "Zum Königtum in der Ur III-Zeit", in P. Garelli (ed.), *Le palais et la royauté* (*Archéologie et Civilisation*): *XIXe Rencontre Assyriologique Internationale Organisée par le Groupe François Thureau-Dangin*, *Paris*, *29 juin-2 juillet 1971*, Paris: Librairie Orientaliste Paul Geuthner S. A., 1974, pp. 177 - 232.

② 文献 UTI 3 2003 (AS 9), MVN 16 713 (SS 4), MVN 16 916 (SS 3)。

③ 文献 RIME 3/2.1.4.33; PDT 2 1200 (SS 7 i – iii)。

④ D. I. Owen, "On the Patronymy of Šu-Suen", *Nouvelles Assyriologiques Brèves et Utilitaires* 2001/17, pp. 19 - 20.

⑤ D. Frayne, *Ur III Period* (*2112 - 2004 BC*), The Royal Inscriptions of Mesopotamia Early Periods Volume 3/2 (RIME 3/2), Toronto: University of Toronto Press, 1997, pp. xxxvii - xxxix, 85 - 87.

表 5-1　　　　　　　　乌尔第三王朝王妻统计表

国王（lugal）	王后（nin）	其他妻子（王妃，lukur）
乌尔纳姆	瓦塔尔图姆（Watartum）	
舒尔吉	塔兰乌兰（Taram-Uram）* 吉美辛（Geme-Suen） 舒尔吉西姆提（Shulgi-simti） 阿玛特辛（Amat-Suen）	埃阿尼莎（Ea-nisha） 吉美宁利拉（Geme-Ninlila） 美埃阿（ME-Ea，西马特埃阿 Simat-Ea） 宁卡拉（Ninkalla） 舒库尔图姆（Shuqurtum）
阿马尔辛	阿比西姆提（Abi-simti）	普祖尔乌沙（Puzur-usha） 乌达德孜纳特（Udad-zenat） 扎甘比（Zaga-AN-bi）
舒辛	库巴图姆（Kubatum）	塔昆马图姆（Takun-matum）① 提亚马特巴什提（Tiamat-bashti）②
伊比辛	吉美恩利拉（Geme-Enlila）	

资料来源：D. Frayne, *Ur III Period* (2112 – 2004 BC), The Royal Inscriptions of Mesopotamia Early Periods Volume 3/2 (RIME 3/2), Toronto：University of Toronto Press, 1997, pp. xxxvii – xxxix, 85 – 87. D. Frayne, *Ur III Period* (2112 – 2004 BC), The Royal Inscriptions of Mesopotamia Early Periods Volume 3/2 (RIME 3/2), Toronto：University of Toronto Press, 1997, pp. xxxvii – xl.

这些国王的妻子们很多都不是乌尔国内的，而是来自外国和外族，很可能是通过政治联姻的方式进入乌尔王室。在她们之中，塔兰乌兰来自马里，舒尔吉西姆提和阿比西姆提来自埃什努那。有的王后或王妃本身是王宫的侍女或者保姆，后来被新国王看上后成为王后，比如舒辛的王后库巴图姆，原先是阿马尔辛时期的王室保姆，很可能是专门服侍王子舒辛的，舒辛继位后被封为王后。

国王的儿女们数量也非常多，大概有 100 名。王子们在年轻时，参与国家的军事事务，很多王子被国王任命为行省的将军，掌握一个地区的军事。公主们则是更多地作为一种政治工具，成为国王实现对内对外统治的一枚枚棋子，被嫁给外国的君主或王子，或者被嫁给乌尔国内的权贵，乌尔国王们通过与这些人联姻加强中央集权。③ 根据文献证据，我们统计乌尔第三王朝国王的儿女

---

① G. Frame, "A New Wife for Šu-Sîn", *Annual Review of the RIM Project*, Vol. 2 (1984), p. 3.
② SUHUŠ-kīn, P. Steinkeller, "More on the Ur III Royal Wives", *Acta Sumerologica*, Vol. 3 (1981), p. 84.
③ J. Klein, "Šeleppūtum a hitherto Unknown Ur III Princess", *Zeitschrift für Assyriologie und Vorderasiatische Archäologie*, Vol. 80 (1990), p. 26; N. Schneider, "Die Königskinder des Herrscherhauses von Ur III", *Orientalia, Nova Series*, Vol. 12 (1943), pp. 185 – 191.

第五章 王室 maš-da-ri-a 税

们如下（见表5-2）：

表5-2　　乌尔第三王朝国王儿女统计表

国王（lugal）	王子（dumu lugal）	公主（dumu-munus lugal）
乌尔纳姆		恩尼尔伽尔安娜（En-nirgal-ana）
舒尔吉	阿马尔达姆（Amar-Damu） 达干杜尼（Dagan-DUni） 埃什塔尔伊尔舒（Eshtar-ilshu） 埃泰尔普达干（Etel-pu-Dagan） 卢杜加（Lu-duga） 卢伽尔阿孜达（Lugal-azida） 卢南那（Lu-Nanna） 卢苏孜达（Lu-Sunzida） 纳比恩利尔（Nabi-Enlil） 纳比乌姆（Nabium） 纳迪（Na-DI） 普祖尔埃什塔尔（Puzur-Eshtar） 舒恩利尔（Shu-Enlil） 舒埃什塔尔（Shu-Eshtar） 乌尔尼伽（Ur-nigar） 乌尔辛（Ur-Suen）	巴卡尔图姆（Baqartum） 达达古（Dadagu） 恩尼尔孜安娜（En-nirzi-ana） 恩乌布尔孜安娜（En-uburzi-ana） 利维尔米塔舒（Liwwir-mittashu） 宁图尔图尔姆（Nin-TUR.TUR-mu） 佩斯图尔图尔（Pesh-TUR.TUR） 西马特恩利尔（Simat-Enlil） 西马特埃什塔尔（Simat-Eshtar） 沙特苏恩（Shat-Suen） 沙特舒尔吉（Shat-Shulgi） 图兰舒尔吉（Taram-Shulgi）
阿马尔辛	阿胡尼（Ahuni） 阿拉德南那（Arad-Nanna） 阿米尔舒尔吉（Amir-Shulgi） 巴姆（Bamu，巴亚姆 Bayamu） 达达（Dada） 伊比伊什塔兰（Ibbi-Ishtaran） 伊宁南那（Inim-Nanna） 卢舒尔吉（Lu-Shulgi） 曼舒姆（Manshum） 纳比舒尔吉（Nabi-Shulgi） 南那玛巴（Nanna-maba） 舒尔吉拉玛（Shulgi-rama） 舒辛（Shu-Suen） 舒-舒尔吉（Shu-Shulgi） 乌尔巴巴（Ur-Baba） 乌尔恩利拉（Ur-Enlila） 乌尔伊什塔兰（Ur-Ishtaran） 乌尔宁苏（Ur-Ninsun） 乌尔萨加（Ur-saga）	恩马赫伽尔安娜（En-mahgal-ana） 恩尼尔伽尔安娜（En-nirgal-ana） 吉美埃安娜（Geme-Eanna） 吉美南娜（Geme-Nanna） 宁海杜（Nin-hedu） 宁利莱马娜格（Ninlile-manag） 宁利尔图库尔提（Ninlil-tukulti） 帕吉娜娜（Pakinana） 西马特伊什塔兰（Simat-Ishtaran） 沙特玛米（Shat-Mami） 塞莱普图姆（Shelepputum） 塔丁埃什塔尔（Taddin-Eshtar） 泰辛玛玛（Tesin-Mamma） 卢伽尔马古莱之妻 乌尔尼伽尔之子卢南那之妻 沙鲁姆巴尼之妻
舒辛		吉美宁利拉（Geme-Ninlila） 沙特埃拉（Shat-Erra） 塔布尔哈图姆（Tabur-Hattum）

续表

国王（lugal）	王子（dumu lugal）	公主（dumu-munus lugal）
伊比辛		玛美图姆（Mammetum） 舒尔吉西姆提（Shulgi-simti）
其他不详	阿胡威尔（Ahu-Wer） 阿图（Atu） 卢伽尔埃孜恩（Lugal-ezen） 卢乌图（Lu-Utu） 纳比辛（Nabi-Suen） 普祖尔宁苏（Puzur-Ninsuna） 普祖尔辛（Puzur-Suen）	玛玛尼莎（Mamma-nisha） 宁埃加莱西（Ninegale-si）

在所列王子中，卢南那是苏萨（Susa）、孜姆达尔（Zimudar）和纳格苏（Nagsu）的将军（šagina）。① 普祖尔埃什塔尔也是将军（šagina）。② 舒恩利尔是纳萨乌鲁克和德尔的将军。③ 乌尔尼伽尔是乌鲁克的将军（Ur-ni$_9$-gar šagina Unug^{ki}）。④ 乌尔辛是乌鲁克和德尔的将军（Ur-^{d}Suen šagina Unu^{ki}-ga u$_3$ BAD$_3$.AN^{ki}）。⑤ 达达是扎巴兰的将军（Da-da šagina Zabala$_3$^{ki}）。⑥ 乌尔萨加是将军（Ur-sa$_6$-ga šagina）。⑦ 在所列的公主中，沙特舒尔吉是阿摩利人阿布亚姆提（Abya-muti）之妻。⑧ 恩马赫伽尔安娜是南那神庙的最高女祭司（En-mah-gal-an-na en ^{d}Nanna）。⑨ 吉美埃安娜是"苏卡尔马赫"阿拉德之子的妻子，即阿拉德的儿媳（Geme$_2$-e$_2$-an-na e$_2$-gi$_4$-a

---

① 文献 RA 19 40 18（--v），TCL 2 5488（S 46 iv），TIM 6 36（S 46 iii）。
② 文献 Nisaba 22 74（--ix），StOr 9 - 1 22（pl.6）（S 44 v 9），OrSP 47 - 49 126（IS 2 vi），TRU 342（IS 2 v 20）。
③ 文献 BRM 3 52（S--）。关于德尔，参见 P. Verkinderen, "Les toponymes bàd^{ki} et bàd. an^{ki}", *Akkadica*, Vol. 127（2006），pp. 109 - 122。
④ 文献 AUCT 2 299（--iv-ix），Nik 2 466（S 43 vi 21），Princeton 2 1（S 43 v），UTI 4 2489（SS 3），NYPL 375（SS 4 vii）。
⑤ 文献 BIN 5 316（----），RIME 3/2 p. 189 E3/2.1.2.96（undated）。
⑥ 文献 AUCT 1 26（AS 3 viii-xii），SAT 3 1181（SS 1 xii），TCTI 2 4267（IS 2 i-iv），UET 3 272（--x-xii）。
⑦ 文献 RA 65 19 1（S 7），RTC 278（S 7），MVN 6 7（S 9 i），BIN 3 418（S 46 ii），DoCu 600（--i），HLC 92（pl. 88）（----）。
⑧ 文献 TRU 267（S 46 viii 5）。
⑨ D. Frayne, *Ur III Period*（2112 - 2004 BC），The Royal Inscriptions of Mesopotamia Early Periods Volume 3/2（RIME 3/2），Toronto：University of Toronto Press, 1997, p. 237.

第五章　王室 maš-da-ri-a 税

Arad₂-mu sukkal-mah)。① 宁海杜是将军哈西帕塔尔之妻（Nin-he₂-du₇ e₂-gi₄-a Ha-ši-pa₂-tal）。②

上述统计列表中提到了舒辛作为舒尔吉的儿子，在继任国王之前，担任重要官职，但是文献中并没有提到阿马尔辛和伊比辛在称王之前的事迹。③ 关于乌尔第三王朝王室家族的世系关系，目前我们还没有完全掌握。尤其是关于各国王的儿女们的长幼序列，几乎没有文献指出，我们无法对此做出判断。不过，有些普兹瑞什达干文献中列举了一长串国王的儿女名字，作为牲畜的接收人，这个列举可能是按照长幼排列的，比如：

CTMMA 1 17（AS 4 vii 1，Drehem）: obv. Col. 1 line 5-Col. 2 line 17，rev. Col. 2 line 16－20

1 gu₄ niga	1 头食大麦牛
3 udu niga gu₄-e-us₂-sa	3 只"次于牛级别"食大麦绵羊
7 udu	7 只绵羊
Ta₂-din-Eš₁₈-tar₂	给塔丁埃什塔尔
1 gu₄ niga	1 头食大麦牛
2 udu niga gu₄-e-us₂-sa	2 只"次于牛级别"食大麦绵羊
1 udu 2 maš₂-gal	1 只绵羊、2 只山羊
ᵈNin-lil₂-tu-kul-ti	给宁利尔图库尔提
1 gu₄ niga	1 头食大麦牛
2 udu niga gu₄-e-us₂-sa	2 只"次于牛级别"食大麦绵羊
1 udu 2 maš₂-gal	1 只绵羊、2 只山羊
Geme₂-ᵈNanna	给吉美南娜
1 gu₄ niga	1 头食大麦牛

---

① 文献 OIP 121 9（AS 2 xii）。
② 文献 TRU 110（S 47 xii 4）。另外，宁海杜也是"苏卡尔马赫"之妻（Nin-he₂-du₇ dam sukkal-mah），见文献 ASJ 9 126 57（----），以及卢南那之妻（Nin-he₂-du₇ dam Lu₂-ᵈNanna），见文献 P234825（SS 3 iv）。
③ C. Wilcke, "Zum Königtum in der Ur III-Zeit", in P. Garelli (ed.), *Le palais et la royauté* (Archéologie et Civilisation): *XIXe Rencontre Assyriologique Internationale Organisée par le Groupe François Thureau-Dangin, Paris, 29 juin-2 juillet 1971*, Paris: Librairie Orientaliste Paul Geuthner S. A., 1974, pp. 177－232; J. Boese, W. Sallaberger, "Apil-Kin von Mari und die Könige der III. Dynastie von Ur", *Altorientalische Forschungen*, Vol. 23（1996），pp. 24－39.

2 udu niga gu$_4$-e-us$_2$-sa	2 只"次于牛级别"食大麦绵羊
1 udu 2 maš$_2$-gal	1 只绵羊、2 只山羊
Pa$_4$-ki-na-na	给帕吉娜娜
1 gu$_4$ niga	1 头食大麦牛
2 udu niga gu$_4$-e-us$_2$-sa	2 只"次于牛级别"食大麦绵羊
1 udu 2 maš$_2$-gal	1 只绵羊、2 只山羊
Ša-at-^{d}Ma-mi	给沙特玛米
1 gu$_4$ niga	1 头食大麦牛
2 udu niga gu$_4$-e-us$_2$-sa	2 只"次于牛级别"食大麦绵羊
1 udu 2 maš$_2$-gal	1 只绵羊、2 只山羊
Nin-he$_2$-du$_7$	给宁海杜
1 gu$_4$ niga	1 头食大麦牛
2 udu niga gu$_4$-e-us$_2$-sa	2 只"次于牛级别"食大麦绵羊
1 udu 2 maš$_2$-gal	1 只绵羊、2 只山羊
Geme$_2$-E$_2$-an-na	给吉美埃安娜
1 gu$_4$ niga 2 udu niga [gu$_4$-e-us$_2$-sa]	1 头食大麦牛、2 只"次于牛级别"食大麦绵羊
1 udu 2 maš$_2$-gal	1 只绵羊、2 只山羊
Te-ze$_2$-en$_6$-Ma-ma	给泰辛玛玛
1 gu$_4$ niga 2 udu niga gu$_4$-e-us$_2$-sa	1 头食大麦牛、2 只"次于牛级别"食大麦绵羊
1 udu 2 maš$_2$-gal	1 只绵羊、2 只山羊
dam Lugal-ma$_2$-gur$_8$-re	给卢伽尔马古莱之妻
1 gu$_4$ niga 2 udu niga gu$_4$-e-us$_2$-sa	1 头食大麦牛、2 只"次于牛级别"食大麦绵羊
1 udu 2 maš$_2$-gal	1 只绵羊、2 只山羊
ME-^{d}Ištaran	给西马特伊什塔兰
1 gu$_4$ niga 2 udu niga gu$_4$-e-us$_2$-sa	1 头食大麦牛、2 只"次于牛级别"食大麦绵羊
2 udu 1 maš$_2$-gal	2 只绵羊、1 只山羊
dam Šar-ru-um-ba-ni	给沙鲁姆巴尼之妻
1 gu$_4$ niga 2 udu niga gu$_4$-e-us$_2$-sa	1 头食大麦牛、2 只"次于牛级别"食大麦绵羊
2 udu 1 maš$_2$-gal	2 只绵羊、1 只山羊

第五章　王室 maš-da-ri-a 税

dam Lu₂-ᵈNanna dumu Ur-ni₉-gar	给乌尔尼伽尔之子卢南那之妻
dumu-munus lugal-me	她们都是国王的女儿
……	
u₄ 1-kam	第 1 日
ki Ab-ba-sa₆-ga-ta	从阿巴萨加处
ba-zi	支出
iti ezemᵈŠul-gi	第 7 月
mu En-mah-gal-an-na en ᵈNanna ba-hun	阿马尔辛 4 年

这篇文献中所列举的 12 位公主：塔丁埃什塔尔、宁利尔图库尔提、吉美南娜、帕吉娜娜、沙特玛米、宁海杜、吉美埃安娜、泰辛玛玛、卢伽尔马古莱之妻（匿名）、西马特伊什塔兰、沙鲁姆巴尼之妻（匿名）、乌尔尼伽尔之子卢南那之妻（匿名），很可能是按照年龄从低到高的顺序排列。至少可以肯定，她们在阿马尔辛 4 年都已经长大成人，有三位明确已经嫁为人妻，只是她们的名字可能是由于已经出嫁了，所以在文献中只提到夫家名字，不再提女方名字。①

乌尔第三王朝的王室成员虽然隶属乌尔中央政府，但是他们的日常生活和开销有特定的供应渠道，这一渠道即是王室 maš-da-ri-a 税。不同于之前我们讲过的行省税和附属国税，王室税是一种专门为乌尔王室提供的赋税类目，在舒辛 3 年改革之后逐渐成为一种供应乌尔的几大节日庆典的特殊税目。下面，我们还需要探究一下王室税的术语以及文献概况。

第二节　术语与文献概况

乌尔第三王朝的王室税的苏美尔语术语是 maš₍₂₎-da-ri₍₆₎-a，直译为"以山羊羔带路或引领"，其中术语 maš 或 maš₂ 直译为"山羊"，引申为

---

① 注意，虽然在舒辛 7 年、伊比辛 2 年有两篇温马文献（文献 PPAC 5 478，STA 16）提到了卢伽尔马古莱的妻子是阿玛卡拉（Ama-kal-la dam Lugal-ma₂-gur₈-re），但是这里的卢伽尔马古莱很可能是重名现象。

"费用、利息、税"①，术语 da-ri 意为"以……引领"②。这一术语可以写成共 4 种不同的形式（见表 5-3）。

表 5-3　　　　　　　　　　王室税术语形式

𒈩𒁕𒊑𒀀	maš-da-ri-a
𒈦𒁕𒊑𒀀	maš₂-da-ri-a
𒈩𒁕𒊑𒀀	maš-da-ri₆-a
𒈦𒁕𒊑𒀀	maš₂-da-ri₆-a

这些不同形式的术语出现在不同时期、不同地点的文献中，似乎有一定的规律存在。目前为止，根据 CDLI 的统计数据（截至 2021 年 1 月 1 日），我们共发现有 573 件记录王室税的文献，在时间分布上历经早王朝 IIIb（ED IIIb）、阿卡德王朝（OAkk）、拉伽什第二王朝（Lagash II）、乌尔第三王朝（Ur III）、古巴比伦（OB）共五个时期，每个时期所使用的王室税术语略有不同。我们将这些文献的具体统计分列如下（见表 5-4）。

从上面所列表格中，我们可以大致总结出一些规律：术语 maš-da-ri-a 主要用于早王朝和乌尔第三王朝时期，术语 maš₂-da-ri-a 主要用于阿卡德王朝、乌尔第三王朝以及古巴比伦时期，术语 maš₍₂₎-da-ri₆-a 仅用于乌尔第三王朝时期。

---

① M. Hudson, "How Interest Rates Were Set, 2500 BC-1000 AD: Máš, tokos and fœnus as Metaphors for Interest Accruals", *Journal of the Economic and Social History of the Orient*, Vol. 43 (2000), pp. 132-161.

② G. J. Selz, "Maš-da-ri-a und Verwandtes. Ein Versuch über da-ŕi 'an der Seite führen': ein zusammengesetztes Verbum und einige nominale Ableitungen", *Acta Sumerologica*, Vol. 17 (1995), pp. 251-274; G. J. Selz, "Schrifterfindung als Ausformung eines reflexiven Ziechensystems", *Wiener Zeitschrift für die Kunde des Morgenlandes*, Vol. 90 (2000), p. 195.

第五章　王室 maš-da-ri-a 税

表 5-4　　　　　王室税术语不同时期文献分布统计表

术语形式	文献总数	ED Ⅲb	OAkk	Lagash Ⅱ	Ur Ⅲ	OB
maš-da-ri-a	233	82	10	9	132	
maš$_2$-da-ri-a	253	12	92		119	30*
maš-da-ri$_6$-a	30				30	
maš$_2$-da-ri$_6$-a	57				57	
共计	573	94	102	9	338	30

注：* 有 1 篇文献（Syria 12 234 8 + Syria 13 236 11）来自中巴比伦时期。

此外，根据上表的统计数据，目前为止我们共发现有 338 件乌尔第三王朝时期的王室税文献，它们是我们研究乌尔第三王朝王室税的第一手资料来源和直接证据。这些文献主要出土于普兹瑞什达干（PD）、吉尔苏（G）、温马（U）、乌尔（Ur）、尼普尔（N）和伊利萨格里格（Iri）六个遗址。每个遗址出土的文献数量统计如下（见表 5-5）：

表 5-5　　　乌尔第三王朝王室税术语不同遗址出土文献分布统计表

术语形式	文献总数	PD	G	U	Ur	N	Iri	不详
maš-da-ri-a	132	7	81	3	3		35	3
maš$_2$-da-ri-a	119	51	10	18	31	3	1	5
maš-da-ri$_6$-a	30		1	27	1			1
maš$_2$-da-ri$_6$-a	57	1		56				
共计	338	59	92	104	35	3	36	9

术语 maš-da-ri-a（使用 maš 符号）主要用于吉尔苏文献和伊利萨格里格文献中，术语 maš$_2$-da-ri-a（使用 maš$_2$ 符号）主要用于普兹瑞什达干文献、乌尔文献和温马文献中，maš-da-ri$_6$-a 和 maš$_2$-da-ri$_6$-a 这两种带 ri$_6$ 符号的术语基本只用于温马文献中。这体现了不同地区在使用这一术语上的区域特色和倾向性。由此可见，在乌尔第三王朝时期，王室税被记录在至少 6 个地区（行省、出土遗址）的文献中，共分为两类：第一类是中央王室档案，包括乌尔文献、普兹瑞什达干文献和尼普尔文献，第二类是地方行省文献，包括温马文献、吉尔苏文献、伊利萨格里格文献。按照王室税文

献数量多少，可以将其排列如下（见表5-6）：

表5-6 乌尔第三王朝王室税文献统计分析表

出土遗址	文献数量	所占比例
温马	104	30.8%
吉尔苏	92	27.2%
普兹瑞什达干	59	17.4%
乌尔	35	10.3%
伊利萨格里格	36	10.7%
尼普尔	3	0.9%
不详	9	2.7%
共计	338	100%

这些文献是我们研究乌尔第三王朝王室税的唯一直接证据和资料来源。其中，普兹瑞什达干文献、乌尔文献和尼普尔文献主要记载各地缴纳给中央的王室税情况，而温马文献、吉尔苏文献和伊利萨格里格文献主要记载本行省缴纳王室税的情况。

第三节 王室税的征收

乌尔第三王朝王室税的征收包括：课税形式、征收对象（税收来源）、税收用途（目的）、征税官员、征税期限、税率等一系列要素。由于文献证据的缺乏，我们无法对每一项征收过程进行细致详细的考究，只能依据目前文献所记载的证据信息，来大致考察乌尔第三王朝王室税的征收过程。

王室税的课税形式主要以牲畜（牛和羊）为主。此外，还有其他形式，包括啤酒（kaš）、面包（ninda）、酥油（奶油，i_3-nun）、奶酪（ga-ar_3）、植物油（i_3-giš）、羊毛（siki）、兽皮（kuš）、大麦（še）、芦苇（gi）、芦苇篮子（^{gi}gur-dub）、沥青（$esir_2$）、布料（纺织品，tug_2）、椰枣（zu_2-lum）、苹果（^{giš}hašhur）、无花果（$^{giš}peš_3$）、面粉（zi_3）、粗面粉（dabin）、精面粉（eša）、洋葱（$^{giš}šum_2$）、熏鱼（ku_6-$še_6$）、鱼类（ku_6）、

第五章 王室 maš-da-ri-a 税

鸟类（mušen）、[1] 战车构件（gab₂-il₂）、白银（ku₃-babbar）、黄金（ku₃-sig₁₇）、戒指（har）、碗（ma-al-tum）、篮子（giri₃-lam）、劳动力（guruš）等，这体现了王室税的征收范围之广泛。此外，不同的征收对象征收不同形式的王室税。

一 征收对象

王室税的征收对象包括牧牛人、牧羊人，来源于外围区和附属国。

（一）牧牛人

据普兹瑞什达干的中央王室档案记载，牧牛人（unu₃）向中央缴纳王室税，[2] 其课税形式是酥油（奶油，i₃-nun）、奶酪（ga-ar₃），[3] 作为牛的副产品，这些赋税被运送到仓库（e₂-kišib-ba-še₃）。例如：

Ontario 1 7（S 43 xii, Drehem）
正面

37 unu₃ libir	37 个年长的牧牛人
2 sila₃ i₃-nun-ta	（每人带）2 希拉酥油（奶油）
2 sila₃ ga-ar₃-ta	（每人带）2 希拉奶酪
šu-nigin₂ 0. 1. 1 4 sila₃ i₃-nun	共计 1 巴里格 1 班 4 希拉酥油
šu-nigin₂ 0. 1. 1 4 sila₃ ga-ar₃	共计 1 巴里格 1 班 4 希拉奶酪
maš₂-da-ri-a unu₃-e-ne	作为牧牛人（缴纳的）王室税

背面

e₂-kišib-ba-še₃	被送入仓库
ba-an-ku₄	
iti še-sag₁₁-ku₅	第 12 月

---

[1] A. Salonen, *Vögel und Vogelfang im Alten Mesopotamien*, Helsinki: Suomalainen Tiedeakatemia, 1973; E. Von der Osten-Sacken, *Untersuchungen zur Geflügelwirtschaft im Alten Orient*, Orbis Biblicus et Orientalis 272, Fribourg and Göttingen: Academic Press Fribourg and Vandenhoeck & Ruprecht Göttingen, 2015.

[2] 关于术语 unu₃ "牧牛人"，参见 H. Waetzoldt, "Das Amt des Utullu", in G. Van Driel, et al (eds.), *Zikir Šumim: Assyriological Studies Presented to F. R. Kraus on the Occasion of his Seventieth Birthday*, Leiden: E. J. Brill, 1982, pp. 386–397.

[3] R. K. Englund, "Regulating Dairy Productivity in the Ur Ⅲ Period", *Orientalia, Nova Series*, Vol. 64 (1995), pp. 377–429.

mu en ᵈNanna maš₂-e i₃-pad₃　　　舒尔吉 43 年

王室税是一种每年征收的赋税，即年税，缴纳的时间多为年末，即每年的第 12 月。目前已知的文献记录的都是舒尔吉统治时期。① 王室税具有固定的税额以及 10% 的固定税率。这些奶油和乳酪提供给那些在宫殿中居住的人，和在尼那和古阿巴的吉尔苏驿站中的人。还有一些可能缴纳给行省总督。

（二）牧羊人

除了牧牛人（unu₃）缴纳酥油和奶酪的王室税形式之外，牧羊人（sipa）② 或者牧羊机构缴纳绵羊和山羊作为王室税，由普兹瑞什达干的机构总管代表王室接管，③ 然后转运（i₃-dab₅）给专门的负责官员舒埃拉，④ 再由舒埃拉转运给努尔辛，⑤ 由努尔辛转运给乌尔辛⑥或者直接支出至其目的地⑦。这种王室税主要发生在从舒尔吉 48 年至阿马尔辛 7 年期间，具体的缴纳月份多为每年的第 12 月，每次缴纳的绵羊和山羊数量大致保持在 60 只到 100 只不等，绵羊和山羊的比例大致为 3∶1。例如，普兹瑞什达干机构总管阿巴萨加转运给舒埃拉。

---

① 文献 BJRL 64 110 62（S 40 xii, 31 unu₃ libir），Ontario 1 7（S 43 xii, 37 unu₃ libir），MVN 8 145（S 44 i – xiid, 37 unu₃ libir），MVN 13 559（S 44 i – v, 38 unu₃ libir）．

② R. M. Adams, "Shepherds at Umma in the Third Dynasty of Ur: Interlocutors with a World beyond the Scribal Field of Ordered Vision", *Journal of the Economic and Social History of the Orient*, Vol. 49（2006），pp. 133 – 169.

③ 53 只绵羊、8 只山羊，见文献 NABU 2018/41 2（S 48 x）：带来，纳萨接收（mu-DU Na-sa₆ i₃-dab₅）。

④ 64 只绵羊、23 只山羊，见文献 OrSP 47 – 49 22（AS 2 xii）：舒埃拉接收，从阿巴萨加处支出（Šu-Er₃-ra i₃-dab₅，ki Ab-ba-sa₆-ga-ta ba-zi）；63 只绵羊、17 只山羊，见文献 AUCT 1 455（AS 4 xii）：从阿巴萨加处，舒埃拉接收（ki Ab-ba-sa₆-ga-ta, Šu-Er₃-ra i₃-dab₅）；63 只绵羊、13 只山羊，见文献 Nik 2 505（AS 5 xii）：从阿巴萨加处，舒埃拉接收（ki Ab-ba-sa₆-ga-ta, Šu-Er₃-ra i₃-dab₅）。

⑤ 6 只绵羊、4 只山羊，见文献 TRU 85（AS 6 xii）：从舒埃拉处，努尔辛接收（ki Šu-Er₃-ra-ta, Nu-ur₂-ᵈSuen i₃-dab₅）。

⑥ 1 只绵羊，见文献 BIN 3 270（AS 6 xii）：从努尔辛处，乌尔辛接收（ki Nu-ur₂-ᵈSuen-ta, Ur-ᵈSuen i₃-dab₅）。

⑦ 11 只绵羊，见文献 OIP 121 504（AS 7 i-xii）：从努尔辛处支出（ki Nu-ur₂-ᵈSuen-ta ba-zi）．

第五章　王室 maš-da-ri-a 税

AUCT 1 455（AS 4 xii，Drehem）
正面
63 udu   63 只绵羊
17 maš$_2$ 17 只山羊
maš$_2$-da-ri-a sipa-e-ne   是牧羊人缴纳的王室税
ki Ab-ba-sa$_6$-ga-ta   从阿巴萨加处
Šu-Er$_3$-ra   舒埃拉
背面
i$_3$-dab$_5$ 接收了
iti še-sag$_{11}$-ku$_5$ 第 12 月
mu En-mah-gal-an-na en ^{d}Nanna ba-hun   阿马尔辛 4 年
左侧
80   （共计：）80（只羊）

（三）外围区和附属国

乌尔第三王朝的王室税来源于外围区和附属国，课税形式是牲畜，以牛为主。由于相关文献的缺乏，目前只有来自西穆卢姆（Simurum）[①] 和乌尔比隆（Urbilum）这两个附属国缴纳王室税的记录，都发生在舒尔吉统治时期。而在阿马尔辛、舒辛和伊比辛统治时期，我们并没有发现来自外围区和附属国向乌尔缴纳王室税的记录。乌尔比隆向乌尔王室缴纳的王室税如下所示：

BIN 3 18（S 47 i，Drehem）
正面
1 gu$_4$ 1 头公牛
Ša-da-zi lu$_2$ Ur-bi$_2$-lum^{ki} 由乌尔比隆人沙达孜

[①] 文献 TCL 2 5502（S 41 vii-xii）。S. J. Garfinkle, "The Economy of Warfare in Southern Iraq at the End of the Third Millennium BC", in H. Neumann, et al (eds.), *Krieg und Frieden im Alten Vorderasien: 52e Rencontre Assyriologique Internationale International Congress of Assyriology and Near Eastern Archaeology Münster, 17.-21. Juli 2006*, Alter Orient und Altes Testament 401, Münster: Ugarit-Verlag, 2014, p. 358; D. R. Frayne, "On the Location of Simurrum", in G. D. Young, M. W. Chavalas and R. E. Averbeck (eds.), *Crossing Boundaries and Linking Horizons: Studies in Honor of Michael C. Astour on His 80th Birthday*, Bethesda: CDL Press, 1997, pp. 243–270.

7 gu₄	7头公牛
3 ab₂	3头母牛
maš-da-ri-a	是乌尔比隆地区缴纳的王室税
ma-da Ur-bi₂-lum^ki-ka	
背面	
mu-DU lugal	带来
Be-li₂-a-zu i₃-dab₅	贝里阿祖接收了
giri₃ Lu₂-^dNanna sagi	经办人是持杯者卢南那
iti maš-da₃-gu₇	第1月
mu us₂-sa Ki-maš^ki ba-hul	舒尔吉47年

二 王室税的目的地

关于王室税的用途或者目的地，顾名思义是王室成员或者王宫。然而，在普兹瑞什达干的中央王室档案中，则很少出现"送往王宫"（e₂-gal-la ku₄-ra）这样的术语，而这一术语基本上只被使用于地方档案中。同术语 mu-DU（带来）的改革为术语 mu-DU lugal（为国王带来）一样，王室税的基本术语 maš₂-da-ri-a，在很多情况下使用 maš₂-da-ri-a lugal "为国王的王室税"。在普兹瑞什达干档案中，有提到王室税的目的地信息，主要分为两类：一类是王后（nin），[1] 另一类是神庙最高女祭司（en，国王的女儿们），主要是月神南那神庙的最高女祭司，也有乌鲁克的伊南娜神庙最高女祭司。[2] 这里的月神南那神庙有的位于乌尔第三王朝首都乌尔，[3] 有的是位于卡尔孜达（Karzida）[4] 或者加埃什（Gaeš）[5] 的南那神庙，具体的纳税月份大致为每年的第1月或第10月。例如，牲畜作为王室税从乌尔被支出给位于加埃什的南那神庙中：

---

[1] 术语 maš₂-da-ri-a nin-še₃，见文献 SET 104（AS 8 x），Ontario 1 3（SS 4 xii 5-SS 5 iv 15）。

[2] 术语 maš₂-da-ri-a lugal, ki en ^dInana-še₃, ša₃ Unu^ki-ga，见文献 OIP 121 376（AS 5 i 1）。

[3] 术语 maš₂-da-ri-a lugal ki en ^dNanna-še₃, ša₃ Uri₅^ki-ma，见文献 MVN 2 164（AS 9 x 7），AA-ICAB 1/2 pl. 118 1954–208（SS 7 ix 7）。

[4] 术语 mu maš₂-da-ri-a en ^dNanna Kar-zi-da-še₃，见文献 AUCT 3 326（AS 7 viii）。

[5] 术语 maš₂-da-ri-a（lugal）ki en ^dNanna-še₃ ša₃ Ga-eš^ki，见文献 Ontario 1 82（AS 9 i 5），RSO 83 346 20（SS 1 x），JCS 52 42 45（SS 7 i 8），Kyoto 46（SS 9 i 7），BPOA 6 111（IS 2 x 11），PDT 2 1213（IS 2 x 11）。

第五章 王室 maš-da-ri-a 税

Kyoto 46（SS 9 i 7，Drehem）
正面
6 udu niga　　　　　　　　　　　6 只食大麦绵羊
13 udu u$_2$　　　　　　　　　　13 只食草绵羊
1 sila$_4$　　　　　　　　　　　　1 只绵羊羔
maš$_2$-da-ri-a lugal　　　　　　作为给国王的王室税
ki en ^{d}Nanna-še$_3$　　　　　　送入加埃什的南那神庙最高女祭司处
ša$_3$ Ga-eš$_5^{ki}$
giri$_3$ ^{d}Suen-a-bu-šu sagi　　经办人是"持杯者"辛阿布舒
背面
u$_4$ 7-kam　　　　　　　　　　　第 7 日
ki A-ba-^{d}En-lil$_2$-gin$_7$-ta　　从阿巴恩利尔金处
ba-zi　　　　　　　　　　　　　　支出
ša$_3$ Uri$_5^{ki}$-ma　　　　　　在乌尔
giri$_3$ Ur-^{d}Šul-gi-ra šar$_2$-ra-ab-du　经办人是"沙拉布杜"乌尔舒尔吉拉
iti še-sag$_{11}$-ku$_5$　　　　　　第 1 月
mu ^{d}Šu-^{d}Suen lugal Uri$_5^{ki}$-ma-ke$_4$
e$_2$ ^{d}Šara$_2$ Umma^{ki}-ka mu-du$_3$　　舒辛 9 年

在乌尔档案中，除了三篇文献属于舒尔吉和阿马尔辛时期之外，[①] 其余文献都属于伊比辛统治时期，从伊比辛第 1 年到第 12 年，集中于第 4—8 年。由于普兹瑞什达干文献、吉尔苏文献、温马文献和伊利萨格里格文献在伊比辛 2 年左右都停止记录，所以乌尔文献档案成为我们研究伊比辛 2 年之后的乌尔第三王朝赋税制度的唯一资料来源。

乌尔档案中并没有提到王室税的来源，只提到了王室税的目的地，包括：这些赋税被送到"国王之地"（ki lugal-še$_3$）[②]、"王后之地"（ki nin-še$_3$）[③] 或

[①] 文献 UET 3 60（S 40 vii），UET 3 65（S 45 x），UET 3 275（AS 9）。
[②] 术语 maš$_2$-da-ri-a ki lugal-še$_3$，见文献 UET 9 1114（undated），UET 3 102（IS 4 x），UET 3 118（IS 5 i 27），UET 3 141（IS 5 ix 15），UET 3 154（IS 6 vii 28），UET 3 411（IS 7 xii 28）。
[③] 术语 ki lugal-še$_3$/ ki nin-še$_3$ maš$_2$-da-ri-a，见文献 UET 9 993（--viii），UET 3 96（IS 4 vii），UET 3 99（IS 4 viii 7），UET 3 100（IS 4 viii 12）。

者"女祭司（国王的女儿）之地"（ki en-na-še₃）[①]，这些"之地"指的是王室成员在王宫中的居所。其中，在大多数文献中并没有提到王后的具体名字，有的文献提到了王后指的是舒尔吉西姆提[②]或者吉美恩利拉[③]。例如：

UET 3 100（IS 4 viii 12）

正面

60 mušen	60 只鸟
1 giri₃-lam zu₂-lum 0.0.1-ta	1 个盛 1 班椰枣的篮子
3 giri₃-lam ᵍⁱˢUR₂xA.NA nig₂-gal 0.0.1-ta	3 个盛 1 班"乌拉纳"（植物）的篮子
ki lugal-še₃	送入国王之地
2 giri₃-lam zi₂-lum 0.0.1-ta	2 个盛 1 班椰枣的篮子

背面

1 giri₃-lam ᵍⁱˢUR₂xA.NA nig₂-gal	1 个盛 1 班"乌拉纳"（植物）的篮子
ki nin-še₃	送入王后之地
maš₂-da-ri-a u₄ 12-kam	作为王室税，第 12 日
iti ezem ᵈŠul-gi	第 8 月
mu En-am-gal-an-na en ᵈInana ba-hun	伊比辛 4 年

三　拉伽什—吉尔苏行省

从乌尔第三王朝的地方行省档案，主要是吉尔苏、温马和伊利萨格里格行省的档案中，我们发现，乌尔第三王朝的核心区或者内省也是王室税的主要征收对象。核心行省缴纳的王室税主要由行省总督负责，或者由其亲自经办（giri₃ ensi₂），或者加印证明（kišib ensi₂），[④] 或者直接使用"行

---

① 术语 maš₂-da-ri-a ki en-na-še₃，见文献 UET 9 958（undated），UET 3 1563（--i）。
② 术语 ki nin-še₃/ ki ᵈŠul-gi-si₂-im-ti-še₃ maš₂-da-ri-a，见文献 UET 9 1004（--vii）。
③ 术语 maš₂-da-ri-a ki Geme₂-ᵈEn-lil₂-la₂ nin-še₃，见文献 UET 3 379（IS 5 ix 2）。
④ 术语 maš-da-ri-a lugal-（še₃）e₂-gal-la ba-ku₄，kišib ensi₂，见文献 PPAC 5 1730（--xid），MVN 12 80（S 46 x）；术语 maš-da-ri-a（ki）lugal-še₃（giri₃ ensi₂/ kišib ensi₂），见文献 ASJ 3 167 148（S 45 v），PPAC 5 1215（S 46 ii），PPAC 5 1109（AS 3 iv），BAOM 2 32 76（AS 4 vi），RTC 429（SS 9 v）；术语 maš-da-ri-a ᵈŠara₂-kam e₂-gal-la ba-a-de₆ ša₃ Nibruᵏⁱ，见文献 TCTI 2 3262（AS 7 iv）。

第五章 王室 maš-da-ri-a 税

省总督（缴纳）的王室税"（maš-da-ri-a ensi₂-ka）的术语①。

据吉尔苏文献记载，拉伽什—吉尔苏行省有沉重的王室税负担。王室税由行省总督负责征收，并且被带到王宫（e₂-gal-la ba-an-ku₄）②或者"国王之地"（ki lugal-še₃）③，这些王室之地不仅位于首都乌尔，有的还位于乌鲁克、尼普尔和尼那等地王室驻地。

其中，拉伽什—吉尔苏行省缴纳的王室税被运送到王宫，例如：

Amherst 22（S 48 xid, Girsu）
正面
130 ᵍⁱˢšum₂-sikil　　　　　　　130 筐大蒜
ma₂-u₄-zal-la　　　　　　　　装入船上
e₂-gal-la ba-an-ku₄　　　　　被送入王宫
maš-da-ri-a lugal　　　　　　作为给国王的王室税
背面
giri₃ Ur-bad₃-tibirₓ（KU）-ra　经办人是乌尔巴德提比拉
iti diri še-sag₁₁-ku₅　　　　　闰 11 月
mu Ha-ar-šiᵏⁱ ba-hul　　　　　舒尔吉 48 年

此外，拉伽什—吉尔苏行省缴纳的王室税被运送到"王后之地"，例如：

Nisaba 17 99（S 46 viii, Girsu）
正面
5 dug dida 0.0.5 imgaga₃ kaš 0.0.3　　5 个王家罐子盛 5 班麦芽和 3
lugal-ta　　　　　　　　　　　　　　班制造啤酒的二粒大麦
10 dug dida saga kaš 0.0.3-ta　　　　10 个罐子盛 3 班优质制造啤酒麦芽

---

① 术语 maš-da-ri-a ensi₂-ka e₂-gal-la ba-an-ku₄（ša₃ Unugᵏⁱ），见文献 MDP 10 p. 21（AS 3 xid），SAT 1 66（AS 4 i）。
② 术语 maš-da-ri-a e₂-gal-（še₃），见文献 CTPSM 1 176（--iii），BM Messenger 206（UN--x），TEL 1（AS 7 v）；术语 maš-da-ri-a e₂-gal-la ku₄-ra / e₂-gal-la ba-an-ku₄ maš-da-ri-a lugal，见文献 PPAC 5 922（undated），UNT 101（UN 2 x），MVN 11 118（S 46 iv），Amherst 22（S 48 xid）。
③ 术语 maš-da-ri-a ki lugal-še₃，见文献 Nisaba 17 66（S 44 xii），Nisaba 17 99（S 46 viii）；术语 maš-da-ri-a ki lugal-še₃ ša₃ Nigin₆ᵏⁱ，见文献 OTR 197（--xi）。

191

ki nin-a-na-ta	从王后处
背面	
maš-da-ri-a lugal-še₃	作为王室税给国王
giri₃ Ur-ᵈIg-alim	经办人是乌尔伊格阿里姆
iti ezem ᵈBa-ba₆	第 8 月
mu Ki-mašᵏⁱ ba-hul	舒尔吉 46 年

拉伽什—吉尔苏行省缴纳的王室税有的被运送到王宫后，直接交付给王后。① 有的文献中没有提到王后的具体名字，有的文献中直接提到王后就是舒尔吉西姆提。例如：

Orient 16 90 132（S 46 iv，Girsu）

正面	
4 ᵍⁱˢhašhur duru₅ lugal	4 筐王家新鲜苹果
6 dusu zu₂-lum 2 lugal-ta	6 个王家篮子盛 2 希拉椰枣
ki Ga-mu-ta	从加姆处
5 dusu zu₂-lum 2-ta	5 个篮子盛 2 希拉椰枣
背面	
ki Ur-ᵈBa-ba₆-ta	从乌尔巴巴处
maš-da-ri-a nin-a-še₃	作为给王后的王室税
e₂-gal-la ba-an-ku₄	被送入王宫
iti šu-numun	第 4 月
mu us₂-sa Ur-bi₂-lumᵏⁱ ba-hul	舒尔吉 46 年

除了由行省总督直接负责之外，拉伽什—吉尔苏行省缴纳的王室税也可以由神庙管理员负责经办，② 许多牲畜作为王室税，其饲料（比如大麦）

---

① 术语 maš-da-ri-a nin-a-še₃ e₂-gal-la ba-an-ku₄，见文献 Orient 16 90 132（S 46 iv），PPAC 5 1416（AS 4 i）；术语 ki ᵈŠul-gi-si₂-im-tum-še₃ maš-da-ri-a，见文献 UET 9 1022（--vii）。

② 术语 maš-da-ri-a šabra，见文献 PPAC 5 1246（AS 8 xi）；术语 ša₃-gal gu₄ maš-da-ri-a Nibruᵏⁱ-še₃ e-du-du，见文献 MVN 6 287（S 43 ii-viii）；术语 ša₃-gal gu₄ maš-da-ri-a kaskal-la i₃-ra，见文献 ITT 2 737（IS 1 i-xii）。

也是王室税的一部分，由行省内的神庙提供。①

四　温马行省

同拉伽什—吉尔苏行省类似的是，温马行省也有沉重的王室税负担。温马行省缴纳的王室税是由行省总督亲自负责。② 在温马总督阿亚卡拉时期，其妻子宁希莉娅也负责缴纳王室税，③ 她可能是代替或者协助其丈夫承担此项任务。例如：

BPOA 7 2379（SS 4 vii, Umma）
正面

1 gu$_4$	1 头牛
2 udu bar-gal$_2$	2 只未脱毛绵羊
3 sila$_4$ bar-gal$_2$	3 只未脱毛绵羊羔
5 maš$_2$	5 只山羊
maš$_2$-da-ri-a	作为王室税
nin Zabala$_3$^{ki}-še$_3$ gen-na	送入扎巴拉的王后处

背面

2 sila$_4$ bar-gal$_2$ babbar	2 只白色未脱毛绵羊羔
maš$_2$-da-ri-a nin	作为给王后的王室税
giri$_3$ Nin$_9$-hi-li$_2$-a	经办人是宁希莉娅
ki Uš-mu-ta	从乌什姆处
kišib ensi$_2$-ka	（温马）总督加印（接收）
iti nin-eš$_3$	第 7 月
mu us$_2$-sa Si-<…>	舒辛 4 年

---

① 例如：文献 ITT 2 737（IS 1 i-xii, Girsu）。
② 术语 maš-da-ri$_6$-a lugal, kišib ensi$_2$-ka, 见文献 MVN 11 Y（S 35），BIN 5 4（S 42），AR RIM 4 18 4（S 43）；术语 maš$_2$-da-ri$_6$-a giri$_3$ ensi$_2$, 见文献 P235452（AS 5 i）；术语 maš$_2$-da-ri$_6$-a ensi$_2$-ka, 见文献 Nisaba 26 99（undated），NYPL 367（AS 4）；术语 maš-da-ri$_6$-a ki ensi$_2$-ta, 见文献 Ontario 2 218（AS 5）。
③ 术语 maš$_2$-da-ri$_6$-a Nin$_9$-hi-li$_2$-a, 见文献 Nisaba 24 17（SS 4 vii）；术语 maš-da-ri-a nin, gi-ri$_3$ Nin$_9$-hi-li$_2$-a, ki Uš-mu-ta, kišib ensi$_2$-ka, 见文献 BPOA 7 2379（SS 4 vii）。其中，宁希莉娅是温马总督阿亚卡拉之妻（Nin$_9$-hi-li$_2$-a dam A-a-kal-la ensi$_2$ Umma^{ki}-ka），见文献 BPOA 6 547。

温马总督主要是从两名官员手中接收王室税,然后再负责运送给王室成员,一名官员是卡什(其印章中的名字为恩卡什),他是乌尔伊什塔兰之子,[①] 另一名官员是安纳希里比,他的身份是育肥师。[②] 这些作为王室税形式的牲畜,被运送到尼普尔、普兹瑞什达干或者吐玛尔。例如:

UTI 4 2599 (AS 8 iv, Umma)

正面

1 sila₄	1 只绵羊羔
maš₂-da-ri₆-a lugal	作为给国王的王室税
ša₃ Nibru^ki	在尼普尔
ki An-na-hi-li-bi-ta	从安纳希里比处

背面

kišib ensi₂-ka	(温马)总督加印(接收)
iti nesag	第 4 月
mu en Eridu^ki ba-hun	阿马尔辛 8 年

温马行省缴纳的王室税有一部分被运送给王后,包括舒尔吉的妻子宁卡拉、[③] 阿马尔辛的妻子阿比西姆提,[④] 以及加埃什的南那神庙最高女祭

[①] 术语 maš₂-da-ri₆-a lugal (Umma^ki-še₃), ki Kas₄-ta, kišib ensi₂-ka, 见文献 RA 101 40 8 (AS 2), BPOA 6 1057 (AS 3), ViOr 8/1 85 (AS 3), BPOA 6 1344 (AS 4)。关于恩卡什的印章铭文,参见文献 MVN 14 292 (SS 1):En-kas₄ dub-sar dumu Ur-^dIštaran "恩卡什,书吏,乌尔伊什塔兰之子"。

[②] 术语 maš₂-da-ri₆-a lugal (ša₃ Nibru^ki/ ša₃ E₂-te-na-ka / ša₃ Tum-mal^ki), ki An-na-hi-li-bi-ta, kišib ensi₂-ka, 见文献 UTI 4 2599 (AS 8 iv), MVN 16 1568 (AS 8 v), UTI 5 3228 (AS 8 viii)。关于安纳希里比的身份,一说是认为他是育肥师,也是乌图吉之子,参见文献 BPOA 1 1071 (AS 7 viii):An-na-hi-li-bi kurušda dumu ^dUtu-ge₅;一说是认为他可能是王室信使 (An-na-hi-li-bi lu₂-kin-gi₄-a lugal, 文献 BIN 5 107, SS 3)。

[③] 术语 maš-da-ri₆-a Nin₍₉₎-kal-la, 见文献 OrNS 55 134 (S 41), YNER 8 19 (AS 6)。宁卡拉是舒尔吉的"卢库尔",参见 F. Weiershäuser, *Die königlichen Frauen der III. Dynastie von Ur*, Göttinger Beiträge zum Alten Orient 1, Göttingen:Universitätsverlag Göttingen, 2008, pp. 211 – 216.

[④] 术语 maš₂-da-ri-a A-bi₂-si₂-im-ti nin, ša₃ Zabala₃^ki, ki PN-ta kišib ensi, 见文献 MVN 16 916 (SS 3);术语 maš₂-da-ri-a nin, 见文献 MVN 14 598 (AS 8)。

司①（国王的女儿）。这些王室税的缴纳也是由行省总督直接负责。比如：

MVN 16 916（SS 3，Umma）
正面
1 gu$_4$　　　　　　　　　1 头牛
10-la$_2$-1 udu bar-gal$_2$　　9 只未脱毛的绵羊
1 sila$_4$ bar-gal$_2$　　　　1 只未脱毛的绵羊羔
maš$_2$-da-ri-a　　　　　作为王室税
A-bi$_2$-si$_2$-im-ti nin　　　给王后阿比西姆提
背面
ša$_3$ Zabala$_3$^{ki}　　　　在扎巴拉
ki Uš-mu-ta　　　　　　从乌什姆处
kišib ensi$_2$　　　　　　（温马）总督加印（接收）
mu Si-ma-num$_2$^{ki} ba-hul　舒辛 3 年

需要注意的是，温马行省缴纳的王室税并不是都被运送到了中央的王室机构，而是有一些直接被运送到温马的沙拉神庙中，以及温马行省所辖的阿皮沙尔的沙拉神庙中，②用于献祭沙拉神所使用。比如：

OrSP 6 59 Wengler 44（--iv，Umma）
8 u$_8$　　　　　　　　　8 只母绵羊
1 udu giš-du$_3$-a　　　　1 只带斑点公绵羊
1 maš$_2$ gaba　　　　　1 只成年公山羊
maš$_2$-da-ri-a　　　　　作为王室税
^{d}Šara$_2$　　　　　　　给温马的沙拉神
ša$_3$ Umma^{ki}
iti nesag　　　　　　　第 4 月

---

① 术语 maš$_2$-da-ri$_6$-a en Ga-eš^{ki} hun-ga$_2$，giri$_3$ lu$_2$-kin-gi$_4$-a，ki Uš-mu-ta，kišib ensi$_2$-ka，见文献 Nisaba 9 51（AS 9）。
② 术语 i$_3$ kaš lu$_2$ maš$_2$-da-ri$_6$-a-ke$_4$-ne ^{d}Šara$_2$ A-pi$_4$-sal$_4$^{ki}，见文献 Princeton 1 281（AS 7），SAT 2 1035（AS 7 i-xii），BPOA 1 446（AS 8），BPOA 7 2411（SS 2）。

五 伊利萨格里格行省

伊利萨格里格行省向乌尔中央缴纳的王室税，由行省总督直接负责，①发生在从阿马尔辛 7 年②到伊比辛 3 年③。

Nisaba 15 592（IS 1 v，Irisagrig）
正面

1 gu$_4$ mu-2	1 头两年生牛
maš-da-ri-a ensi$_2$ im-ma	是总督（缴纳的）王室税
ki U$_2$-tul$_2$-Ma-ma-ta	从乌图尔玛玛处
1 gu$_4$ mu-2	1 头两年生牛
maš-da-ri-a ensi$_2$ im-ma	是总督（缴纳的）王室税

背面

ki Ur-^{d}Gu$_3$-de$_2$-a-ta	从乌尔古地亚处
Ba-a-ga kurušda	育肥师巴亚加
i$_3$-dab$_5$	收到了
iti ezem-a-bi	第 5 月
mu ^{d}I-bi$_2$-^{d}Suen lugal	伊比辛 1 年

伊利萨格里格行省缴纳的王室税被运送到尼普尔，献给王后阿比西姆提和库巴图姆，由行省总督亲自经办。比如：

Nisaba 15 366（SS 6 vii，Irisagrig）
正面

240 dusu zu$_2$-lum 0.0.1 5 sila$_3$-ta	240 个容量为盛 1 班 5 希拉椰枣的篮子
20 hašhur PA-ur nu-eš$_3$ hašhur 0.0.1 5 sila$_3$-ta	20 个容量为盛 1 班 5 希拉苹果的篮子
maš-da-ri-a lugal	给国王的王室税
120 dusu zu$_2$-lum 0.0.1 5 sila$_3$-ta	120 个容量为盛 1 班 5 希拉椰枣的篮子

---

① 术语 maš-da-ri-a ensi$_2$ im-ma，见文献 Nisaba 15 592（IS 1 v），Nisaba 15 622（IS 1 viii）。
② 文献 Nisaba 15 55（AS 7 x）。
③ 文献 Nisaba 15 949（IS 3 viii）。

第五章 王室 maš-da-ri-a 税

maš-da-ri-a	作为王室税
背面	
A-bi₂-si₂-im-ti u₃ Ku-ba-tum	（给）阿比西姆提和库巴图姆
ša₃ Nibru^ki	在尼普尔
giri₃ ensi₂	经办人是（伊利萨格里格行省）总督
iti ezem ^d Šul-gi	第 7 月
mu ^d Šu-^d Suen lugal Uri₅^ki-ma-ke₄	
na-ru₂-a mah ^d En-lil₂ ^d Nin-lil₂-ra	舒辛 6 年
mu-ne-du₃	

在伊利萨格里格行省缴纳王室税的过程中，王室信使代表乌尔王室作为税收的征税人，可以理解为王室征税使。行省不仅要提供王室税，而且还要提供食物给这些王室信使，供他们在运送途中食用，供给的食物包括面包、啤酒、鱼肉、蔬菜等。担任王室征税使的有古加努姆[1]、舒尔吉萨图尼[2]、舒尔吉巴尼[3]、努尔埃什塔尔[4]等。下面以舒尔吉萨图尼为例：

Nisaba 15 730（IS 2 ii 29）：13-15，25-27

1 sila₃ tu₇ 1 ku₆	1 希拉汤、1 条鱼
^d Šul-gi-sa-tu-ni lu₂-kin-gi₄-a lugal	为王家使节舒尔吉萨图尼
u₄ gu₄ maš-da-ri-a-še₃ im-gen-na-a	当他去（管理）作为王室税的牛时
……	
zi-ga	支出
iti ^giš apin	第 2 月
mu en ^d Inana Unu^ki-ga maš₂-e in-pad₃	伊比辛 2 年

---

[1] Gu-ga-nu-um lu₂-kin-gi₄-a lugal u₄ gu₄ udu maš₂-da-ri-a BAD₃.AN^ki-ta e₂-gal-še₃ mu-la-ha-a，文献 Nisaba 15 1159（IS 2 ix 6）。

[2] ^d Šul-gi-sa-tu-ni lu₂-kin-gi₄-a lugal u₄ kaš maš-da-ri-a-še₃ im-gen-na-a，文献 Nisaba 15 887（IS 2），Nisaba 15 727（IS 2 ii 12, gu₄），Nisaba 15 730（IS 2 ii 29, gu₄）。

[3] ^d Šul-gi-ba-ni lu₂-kin-gi₄-a lugal u₄ gu₄ maš-da-ri-a-še₃ im-gen-na-a，文献 Nisaba 15 738（IS 2 ii）。

[4] Nu-ur₂-Eš₁₈-tar₂ lu₂-kin-gi₄-a lugal u₄ maš-da-ri-a a₂-ki-ti im-gen-na-a，文献 Nisaba 15 691（IS 2 i 4）。

第四节　王室税的变革

从舒辛 3 年开始，同外围区税一样，舒辛对王室税也进行了重要的变革。据普兹瑞什达干文献记载，作为牲畜的王室税被用于乌尔的三大节日庆典时，在舒辛 3 年之前是以 mu-DU 加节日的术语用法，而在舒辛 3 年之后，中性的 mu-DU 加节日的用法被取消，取而代之的是 maš-da-ri-a 加乌尔的这三大节日，分别是哀悼节（er$_2$-su$_3$-a）、播种大麦阿基图节（a$_2$-ki-ti šu-numun-na）、收割大麦阿基图节（a$_2$-ki-ti še-sag$_{11}$-ku$_5$）。[①] 根据普兹瑞什达干文献记载，mu-DU 加节日和 mas-da-ri-a 加节日的统计如下（见表 5 - 7）：

表 5 - 7　　　　　　　王室税加乌尔三大节日统计表

节日	形式	文献出处
er$_2$-su$_3$-a	mu-DU er$_2$-su$_3$-a	Nik 2 449（S 43 iv 5），UDT 110（AS 1 x 9），PDT 1 450（AS 4 ix），TCL 2 5504（AS 5 x 9），CTNMC 11（AS 5 x 18）
	maš-da-ri-a er$_2$-su$_3$-a	OIP 121 429（AS 9 x 11），P406807（SS 5 x 13），AnOr 7 108（SS 9 x）
a$_2$-ki-ti šu-numun-na	mu-DU a$_2$-ki-ti šu-nu-mun-na	OIP 115 174（S 44 vi-S 46 vi），AAICAB 1/4 Bod S 587（S 46），Princeton 2 89（S 47 v 30），CT-MMA 1 17（AS 4 vii 1），Nisaba 30 37（AS 6 vi 25），MVN 13 477（AS 9 vii），PDT 2 959（undated），UDT 91（undated）
	maš-da-ri-a a$_2$-ki-ti šu-numun-na	JAOS 33 175 8（SS 3vii 1），MVN 15 129（SS 3 vii 29），Kyoto 36（SS 5 viii 22），AUCT 1 637（undated）

[①] J. Bidmead, *The Akītu Festival: Religious Continuity and Royal Legitimation in Mesopotamia*, Gorgias Dissertations Near Eastern Studies 2, Piscataway: Gorgias Press, 2002; M. Cohen, *The Cultic Calendars of the Ancient Near East*, Bethesda: CDL Press, 1993, pp. 140 - 160; A. Pitts, *The Cult of the Deified King in Ur III Mesopotamia*, PhD dissertation, University of Pennsylvania, 2015, pp. 106 - 109.

第五章 王室 maš-da-ri-a 税

续表

节日	形式	文献出处
a₂-ki-ti še-sag₁₁-ku₅	mu-DU a₂-ki-ti še-sag₁₁-ku₅	SET 1 (S 44 ii 23), TRU 27 (S 44 iii), MVN 5 98 (S 44 iii 2), PDT 1 433 (S 45 i 26), CDLJ 2012/1 4.07 (S 46 i), NYPL 196 (S 46 i 6), AUCT 2 175 (S 48 i 5), AUCT 327 (AS 3 i 5), TCL 2 5508 (AS 4 i 6), Amorites 18 (AS 5 xii), P218050 (AS 7 ii 3), AUCT 3 307 (AS 8 i 30), MVN 13 396 (SS 1 ii 16), PDT 1 597 (SS 2 ii 7), MVN 15 274 (SS 3 iv 9)
	maš-da-ri-a a₂-ki-ti še-sag₁₁-ku₅	SAT 3 1483 (SS 4 iii 28), NYPL 374 (IS 2 i), AAICAB 1/1 pl. 57 1924-516 (undated), BPOA7 2350 (undated)

很显然，这些作为王室税的牲畜都是被用于乌尔的这三个节日中。在文献中，还记录有节日的地点"在乌尔"或"在加埃什"。如果运送动物发送到乌尔的节日庆祝，它们应该在节日举办之前到达。为舒辛 2 年或 4 年"盛大节日"（ezem-mah）征收的王室税，实际上是在舒辛 5 年初才到达普兹瑞什达干。例如：

HUCA 29 74 3 (SS 2-5, Drehem)

正面

1 gu₄ niga	1 头食大麦牛
10 udu u₂	10 只食草绵羊
Lum-ma šabra	给首席神庙管理员卢玛
maš₂-da-ri-a ezem-mah	作为献给"盛大节日"的王室税
mu ᵈŠu-ᵈSuen lugal Uri₅ᵏⁱ-ma-ke₄ ma₂-dara₃ ᵈEn-ki-ka bi₂-in-du₈	舒辛 2 年
2 gu₄ niga 20 udu u₂	2 头食大麦牛、20 只食草绵羊
Di-ku₅-i₃-li₂	给迪库伊里
maš₂-da-ri-a ezem-mah	作为献给"盛大节日"的王室税
mu ᵈŠu-ᵈSuen lugal Uri₅ᵏⁱ-ma-ke₄ bad₃ mar-tu Mu-ri-iq-ti-id-ni-im mu-du₃	舒辛 4 年

199

背面

maš₂-da-ri-a ezem-mah	作为献给"盛大节日"的王室税
u₄ 1-kam	第 1 日
mu-DU	带来
In-ta-e₃-a i₃-dab₅	因塔埃阿收到了
giri₃ ᵈNanna-ma-ba dub-sar	经办人是书吏南那玛巴
iti maš-da₃-gu₇	第 1 月
mu us₂-sa ᵈŠu-ᵈ Suen lugal Uri₅ᵏⁱ-ma-ke₄ bad₃ mar-tu Mu-ri-iq-ti-id-ni-im mu-du₃	舒辛 5 年

左侧

3 gu₄ 30 udu	（共计：）3 头牛、30 只绵羊

因此，乌尔的节日庆典不依赖当前的供应，而是有一定的资金来供应节日。王室税用于乌尔的南那、宁伽尔（Ningal）、杜乌尔（Du'ur），用于"舒尔吉的王座"，用于王室成员，用于高官、外国使节。在节日期间，有如下支出：王室税被缴纳给南那神庙祭司之地，在乌尔或者在加埃什，在阿基图节日房。所以，南那神庙最高女祭司也作为王室税的接收者。

需要注意的是，除了普兹瑞什达干之外的其他文献，比如乌尔文献、温马文献、吉尔苏文献和伊利萨格里格文献，也有 maš-da-ri-a 术语加节日的记载。下面表格是对各个文献中 maš-da-ri-a 术语加节日情况的统计（见表 5-8）：

表 5-8　　　　　　　　　王室税加各个节日文献统计分析表

mas-da-ri-a + 节日	文献种类	文献出处（日期）
er₂-su₃-a	普兹瑞什达干	OIP 121 429（AS 9 x 11），P406807（SS 5 x 13），AnOr 7 108（SS 9 x 1 – 30，gešbun₂ er₂-su₃-a）
	乌尔	UET 9 1120（undated），UET 3 103（IS 4 x），UET 3 186（IS 7 vii），UET 3 412（IS 7 x）

续表

maš-da-ri-a + 节日	文献种类	文献出处（日期）
ezem-mah	普兹瑞什达干	AUCT 2 185（AS 5 x），HUCA 29 74 3（SS 2－5），RA 49 87 5（SS 5 i 20），CST 434（SS 5 ix 24），PPAC 4 115（SS 5 xi），AUCT 3 13（SS 9 x），PPAC 4 119（SS 9 xi 6），BIN 3 591（IS 1 xi 2），CT 32 pl. 19－22 BM 103398（SS 2 iv 29）
	吉尔苏	PPAC 5 12（--ix），MVN 11 106（AS 3 xi-AS 4 x），MVN 12 414（AS 5），ITT 2 3410（AS 7），ITT 2 4108（AS 8），ITT 5 6986（AS 8），ITT 3 5552（AS 8ix），PPAC 5 201（AS 8 ix），BM Messenger 267（AS 9 ix），TEL 270（SS 1，šа$_3$ Uri$_5$^{ki}-ma），MVN 2 174（SS 1 ix），MVN 13 734（SS 2 x），TEL 5（SS 2 x），TCTI 2 2569（SS 3 vi），ITT 2 3483（SS 8 x），DAS 388（SS 8）e$_2$-gal-la ba-an-ku$_4$，SNAT 29（S 45 ix），ABTR 4（AS 2），ITT 3 6160（AS 6），PPAC 5 1441（SS 4 xii）
	伊利萨格里格	Nisaba 15 55（AS 7 x），Nisaba 15 290（SS 4 x）
	温马	Princeton 1 565（S 43），P275033（AS 6），UTI 6 3688（AS 6），MVN 16 684（AS 8 i-vi），BPOA 7 1674（AS 8 vi-x），Santag 6 327（SS 9 xi）
še-sag$_{11}$-ku$_5$	温马	TCL 5 5671（S 45 i-S 46 iv），Nisaba 6 20（S 48 i），Tavolette 24（AS 7 i），BPOA 1 1691（AS 8），BRM 3 47（AS 8 i-x），MVN 4 138（SS 2 i），UTI 6 3680（SS 3 i）
šu-numun	温马	BPOA 1 1184（SS 2 viii）
a$_2$-ki-ti	吉尔苏	ITT 5 6959（--iv 15-v 14），ITT 5 6756（--vii），MVN 12 414（AS 5），DAS 29（AS 7 iii），Nisaba 18 87（SS 3 vi），TEL 73（SS 5 vi），RA 62 5 4（SS 6 vii），ITT 2 3757（SS 7），DAS 388（SS 8），TUT 276（IS 5 vii）
	温马	CST 530（undated），MVN 16 715（undated），AAICAB 1/1 pl. 20 1911-163（SS 5）
a$_2$-ki-ti še-sag$_{11}$-ku$_5$	普兹瑞什达干	SAT 3 1483（SS 4 iii 28），NYPL 374（IS 2 i）
	乌尔	UET 3 380（IS 5 vii），SAT 3 2024（IS 8 i）
	伊利萨格里格	Nisaba 15 372（SS 6 xii）
	温马	UTI 6 3692（AS 8），BPOA 7 1586（AS 8 i），BCT 2 82（SS 8 vi-SS 9 i）

续表

maš-da-ri-a + 节日	文献种类	文献出处（日期）
a₂-ki-ti šu-numun-na	普兹瑞什达干	JAOS 33 175 8（SS 3 vii 1），MVN 15 129（SS 3 vii 29），Kyoto 36（SS 5 viii 22）
	乌尔	UET 9 1120（undated），UET 3 186（IS 7 vii）
	吉尔苏	ITT 5 6922（AS 8），ITT 3 6167（SS 1 vi）
	伊利萨格里格	Nisaba 15 514（SS 9 vi 30-vii 30）
	温马	ArOr 62 238 I 867（S 41 vi），AAS 149（S 43，vi），UTI 3 2209（AS 7 vi），UTI 4 2371（SS 4 vii）
ezem 3-a-ba	温马	SNAT 403（AS 8），Nisaba 26 2（SS 7-8），ZA 95 191（SS 7-IS 1）

在舒辛3年之前，很多文献中也有maš-da-ri-a术语加节日的记录。从阿马尔辛到伊比辛时期，均有类似的支出。但是，王室税作为一种节日税，只是舒辛3年之后的事。在阿马尔辛时期，来自外围区的王室税有相同的目的，因此能够在乌尔节日时被使用，这些不同的王室税是否有共同的特征呢？或者说，就像从舒辛3年开始，这些被带到普兹瑞什达干的标有mu-DU的动物，转变为标有mu-DU lugal的动物一样，这些mu-DU加节日名字的动物是否也是作为王室税？关于这些问题，由于缺乏直接的文献证据，我们暂时对此保持关注。

第六章　神庙 zag-u 税

什一税（Tithe）作为中世纪欧洲最重要的税种之一，并非起源于欧洲，而是起源于古代两河流域地区。与中世纪什一税同教堂密切有关相似，古代两河流域的 zag-u 税也同神庙密切相关。在两河流域文明早期，zag-u 税就被缴纳给神庙，作为神庙税收的最重要组成部分。从这一层面上讲，最早的 zag-u 税是一种宗教税。① 首先，我们来介绍一下乌尔第三王朝的神庙和宗教祭祀概况。

第一节　神庙体系概况

神庙是古代两河流域重要的建筑形式之一，也是古代两河流域人们日常生活中的重要宗教祭祀场所，即宗教生活的中心。神庙的苏美尔语为 e_2，对应的阿卡德语为 *bītum*，本义是"房子"，用于指"神的房子"时即为神庙。神庙里"居住"（供奉）着众多的神，主神的神像立于主神殿之上。在古代两河流域，一个神庙除了供奉一位主神之外，还可以供奉其他神位。所以说，一般比较大的主要神庙里都供奉着多位神灵；此外，一位神也可以被供奉在多个神庙中，比如月神南那既被供奉在首都乌尔的神庙

[①] 在古代两河流域，zag-u 税除了作为宗教赋税之外，也同时具有世俗赋税的性质，不过这方面的文献证据要远远少于宗教税的记录，主要见于古亚述文献中。在著名的古亚述贸易中，来自亚述的商人需将其贸易收入的 1/10 作为什一税缴纳给安纳托利亚当地的统治者，这些赋税形式主要是作为商品的纺织品，而不是作为货币功能的白银。参见 J. G. Dercksen, *Old Assyrian Institutions*, *MOS Studies 4*, PIHANS 98, Leiden: Nederlands Instituut voor het Nabije Oosten, 2004, p. 173；这种形式的什一税有别于宗教赋税，而是一种贸易税或者商品进口税性质。国王和其他王室成员一般作为世俗什一税的接收者。另外，中国古代农业赋税的"十一而税"传统也带有世俗税的特征。

里，也被供奉在加埃什或者卡尔孜达的神庙里。乌尔第三王朝的神数量众多，见于文献中的有数百个，主要的神包括恩利尔、宁利尔、南那（辛）、伊南娜、恩基、安、伊什库尔、伊什塔兰、南塞、宁伽尔、宁苏、尼努尔塔和乌图等。[①]

一般而言，一个城市有一位主神以及为这位主神所建造的神庙。许多神庙都有自己的名字，比如尼普尔的主神恩利尔的神庙叫作"埃库尔"（e₂-kur，直译为"山之房"），埃利都的主神恩基的神庙叫作"埃阿布祖"（e₂-abzu，直译为"地下之房"），吉尔苏主神宁吉尔苏的神庙叫作"埃尼努"（e₂-ninnu，直译为"五十房"），以及乌鲁克的安神和伊南娜神的神庙叫作"埃安纳"（e₂-an-na，直译为"天之房"）等。[②] 目前已知最早的神庙遗址是埃利都的恩基神庙，大约处于公元前5千纪晚期至前4千纪早期。古代两河流域的神庙在后来发展演变成为独具特色的"塔庙"（ziggurat）形式，并且一直是古代两河流域的特有神庙形式。其中，最著名的塔庙是乌尔第三王朝时期位于乌尔的塔庙（The Great Ziggurat at Ur），始建于乌尔第三王朝的建立者乌尔纳姆时期，长210英尺、宽150英尺、高100英尺，在新巴比伦时期由国王那波尼德重新修建，遗址至今尚存（位于今伊拉克的纳西里耶）。

在古代两河流域，神庙一直具有特殊的重要地位，其作用不仅局限于城市或城邦的宗教生活方面，而且也影响着城市的社会和经济生活，包括农业生产、商品交易、赋税征收、对外贸易等方面，被称为神庙经济。[③] 在苏美尔城邦时期，神庙独立于城邦政治之外，具有自主与自治权力。到乌尔第三王朝时期，中央集权统治加强，神庙被收归国有，神庙经济被纳

---

① 关于乌尔第三王朝的神，参见 W. Sallaberger, *Der kultische Kalender der Ur III-Zeit*, Untersuchungen zur Assyriologie und Vorderasiatischen Archäologie 7/1 – 2, Berlin and New York: Walter de Gruyter, 1993; M. Such-Gutiérrez, *Beiträge zum Pantheon von Nippur im 3. Jahrtausend*, Rome: Herder Libreria editrice, 2003.

② A. R. George, *House Most High: The Temples of Ancient Mesopotamia*, Mesopotamian Civilizations 5, Winona Lake: Eisenbrauns, 1993; D. O. Edzard, "The Names of the Sumerian Temples", in I. L. Finkel and M. J. Geller (eds.), *Sumerian Gods and Their Representations*, Cuneiform Monographs 7, Groningen: Styx Publications, 1997, pp. 159 – 165.

③ R. L. Sterba, "The Organization and Management of the Temple Corporations in Ancient Mesopotamia", *Academy of Management Review*, Vol. 1 (1976), pp. 17 – 19.

第六章 神庙 zag-u 税

入乌尔国家经济之中。① 比如，舒尔吉在其统治的第 21 年的年名如下：②

mu ^{d}Nin-urta ensi$_2$-gal ^{d}En-lil$_2$-la$_2$-ke$_4$ e$_2$ ^{d}En-lil$_2$ ^{d}Nin-lil$_2$-la$_2$-ke$_4$ eš-bar-kin ba-an-du$_{11}$-ga ^{d}Šul-gi lugal Uri$_5^{ki}$-ma-ke$_4$ gan$_2$ nig$_2$-ka$_9$ ša$_3$ e$_2$ ^{d}En-lil$_2$ ^{d}Nin-lil$_2$-la$_2$-ke$_4$ si bi$_2$-sa$_2$-a

恩利尔的土地管理员尼努尔塔在恩利尔和宁利尔神庙发布神谕：乌尔国王舒尔吉掌管恩利尔和宁利尔神庙的土地、账目和日常事务。

这一事件表明，舒尔吉已经将神庙收归中央政府直接管辖，弱化了宗教管理，加强了国家的行政管理。神庙失去了独立性，成为中央政府或者地方行省势力的组成部分。

在神庙管理方面，乌尔第三王朝的统治者借鉴阿卡德王国的做法，任命国王的女儿（即公主）担任神庙的最高女祭司（苏美尔语：en），作为神庙的最高领导者。③ 乌尔第三王朝的统治者任命其女儿担任神庙的最高女祭司，列举如下：

舒尔吉 15 年： mu En-nir-zi-an-na en ^{d}Nanna maš$_2$-e i$_3$-pad$_3$
　　　　　　　恩尼尔孜安娜被选为南那神庙最高女祭司之年
舒尔吉 17 年： mu En-nir-zi-an-na en ^{d}Nanna ba-hun-ga$_2$
　　　　　　　恩尼尔孜安娜被任命为南那神庙最高女祭司之年
舒尔吉 28 年： mu en Eridu^{ki}-ga ba-hun-ga$_2$
　　　　　　　埃利都（恩基神庙）的最高女祭司被任命之年
舒尔吉 43 年： mu En-ubur-zi-an-na en ^{d}Nanna maš-e i$_3$-pad$_3$
　　　　　　　恩乌布尔孜安娜被选为南那神庙最高女祭司之年
阿马尔辛 3 年： mu En-mah-gal-an-na en ^{d}Nanna maš-e i$_3$-pad$_3$
　　　　　　　恩马赫伽尔安娜被选为南那神庙最高女祭司之年
阿马尔辛 4 年： mu En-mah-gal-an-na en ^{d}Nanna ba-hun

---

① K. Maekawa, "The 'Temples' and the 'Temple Personnel' of Ur III Girsu-Lagash", in K. Watanabe (ed.), *Priests and Officials in the Ancient Near East: Papers of the Second Colloquium on the Ancient Near East-The City and its Life held at the Middle Eastern Culture Center in Japan (Mitaka, Tokyo) March 22 – 24, 1996*, Heidelberg: Universitätsverlag C. Winter, 1999, pp. 61 – 102.

② D. Frayne, *Ur III Period (2112 – 2004 BC)*, The Royal Inscriptions of Mesopotamia Early Periods Volume 3/2 (RIME 3/2), Toronto: University of Toronto Press, 1997, pp. 102 – 103.

③ 王献华：《皇族"恩图"女祭司与阿卡德帝国的治理》，《中山大学学报》（社会科学版）2016 年第 5 期。

阿马尔辛5年： mu En-unu₆-gal ᵈInana Unug^(ki) ba-hun
恩马赫伽尔安娜被任命为南那神庙最高女祭司之年
恩乌努伽尔（安娜）被任命为乌鲁克的伊南娜神庙最高女祭司之年

阿马尔辛8年： mu en Eridu^(ki) ba-hun①
埃利都（恩基神庙）最高女祭司被任命之年

阿马尔辛9年： mu En-ᵈNanna-ᵈAmar-ᵈSuen-ra-ki-ag₂ en ᵈNanna Kar-zi-da-ka ba-hun
恩南那阿马尔辛拉吉阿格被任命为卡尔孜达的南那神庙最高女祭司之年

伊比辛2年： mu en ᵈInana maš₂-e i₃-pad₃
伊南娜神庙最高女祭司被选出之年

伊比辛4年： mu En-am-gal-an-na en ᵈInana ba-hun
恩阿姆伽尔安娜被任命为伊南娜神庙最高女祭司之年

伊比辛10年： mu En-nir-si₃-an-na en ᵈNanna maš₂-e i₃-pad₃
恩尼尔希安娜被选为南那神庙最高女祭司之年

伊比辛11年： mu En-nam-ti-ᵈI-bi₂-ᵈSuen-ka-še₃ kiri₃-šu-gal₂ x-unu en ᵈEn-ki-ka maš₂-e i₃-pad₃
恩纳姆提伊比辛卡塞被选为恩基神庙最高女祭司之年

在具体事务方面，乌尔第三王朝神庙的管理是由一系列管理人员或者官员负责，首席管理官员被称为"沙布拉"（šabra）②，其他管理人员包括"萨加"（sanga）③、"乌什加"（uš-ga）、"吉尔希加"（gir₃-sig₁₀-ga）④、神庙厨师"恩吉孜"（engiz）⑤、"古杜"祭司（gudu₄）⑥、"埃莱

---

① 这位最高女祭司的名字从其他文献资料中可以得到，即恩努奈阿马尔辛拉吉阿格（En-nune-Amar-Suenra-kiag），参见 N. Schneider, *Die Zeitbestimmungen der Wirtschaftsurkunden von Ur III*, Analecta Orientalia 13, Rome: Pontificio Instituto Biblico, 1936, p. 29.

② M. Sigrist, *Drehem*, Bethesda: CDL Press, 1992, pp. 219 – 221; W. Sallaberger, "Ur III-Zeit", in W. Sallaberger, A. Westenholz (eds.), *Mesopotamien: Akkade-Zeit und Ur III-Zeit*, OBO 160/3, Freiburg, Schweiz: Universitätsverlag / Göttingen: Vandenhoeck und Ruprecht, 1999, pp. 194 – 195.

③ M. Sigrist, *Drehem*, Bethesda: CDL Press, 1992, pp. 218 – 219.

④ K. Maekawa, "The Agricultural Texts of Ur III Lagash of the British Museum (V)", *Acta Sumerologica*, Vol. 9 (1987), pp. 96 – 97.

⑤ D. Charpin, *Le Clergé d'Ur au Siècle d'Hammurabi (XIXe-XVIIIe Siècles av. J.-C.)*, Genève-Paris: Librairie Droz, 1986, pp. 381 – 382.

⑥ D. Charpin, *Le Clergé d'Ur au Siècle d'Hammurabi (XIXe-XVIIIe Siècles av. J.-C.)*, Genève-Paris: Librairie Droz, 1986, pp. 252 – 257.

什"祭司（ereš）① 等。

第二节 术语与文献

在古代两河流域的楔形文字文献中，什一税的术语一般包括两类：一类是苏美尔语术语，一类是阿卡德语术语。苏美尔语的什一税术语为 za_3-u，或者 zag-u，出现在公元前 3 千纪的苏美尔语文献中，其中符号 za_3 或 zag 本义是"边、边界"，符号 u 即"十"之义。这个术语主要用于乌尔第三王朝时期，这也是目前已知的世界上最早的关于 zag-u（如图 6-1）税的证据，记载于乌尔第三王朝的第二位国王舒尔吉在位时期，而最晚的关于 zag-u 税的楔形文字文献证据见于马其顿亚历山大大帝统治时期（公元前 331—前 323 年），前后跨越近两千年时间。② 阿卡德语的什一税术语大致有三个，第一个术语为 ešrētum，见于公元前 2 千纪的古巴比伦文献和古亚述文献，亦见于叙利亚地区的乌加里特文献。注意，在古亚述文献中一般拼写为 išrātum 或者 ušrātum，是 ešrētum 形式的变形，体现了亚述地区的特色。第二个术语为 ešrû，见于公元前 1 千纪的新巴比伦时期文献和古波斯文献中，其变体为 išrum，亦见于古巴比伦文献。第三个术语为 ma'šaru，只见于乌加里特文献，很少出现。

在两河流域早期的苏美尔文献中，zag-u 税的证据比较匮乏，但是在两河流域后期的阿卡德语文献中，关于什一税的记载变得越来越丰富，同时也越来越详细。在乌尔第三王朝的文献中，目前我们共发现有 49 件记录 zag-u 术语的文献，在时间上从舒尔吉 30 年③至伊比辛 8 年④，分别

图 6-1 zag-u 税对应的楔形文字

---

① P. Steinkeller, "On Rulers, Priest and Sacred Marriage: Tracing the Evolution of Early Sumerian Kingship", in K. Watanabe (ed.), *Priests and Officials in the Ancient Near East*, Heidelberg: Winter, 1999, pp. 120 – 121; N. Brisch, "The Priestess and the King: The Divine Kingship of Šū-Sîn of Ur", *Journal of the American Oriental Society*, Vol. 126 (2006), pp. 165 – 168.

② E. Salonen, *Über den Zehnten im alten Mesopotamien: Ein Beitrag zur Geschichte der Besteuerung*, Helsinki: Suomalaisen Kirjallisuuden Kirjapaino Oy Helsinki, 1972, pp. 9 – 11.

③ 文献 MVN 7 347 (S 30 viii, Girsu)。

④ 文献 UET 3 250 (IS 8 viii, Ur)。

来源于普兹瑞什达干、乌尔、温马、吉尔苏和尼普尔五个遗址，具体的文献数量和所占比例统计如下（见表6-1）：

表6-1　　　　　　乌尔第三王朝 zag-u 文献统计表

出土遗址	文献数量	所占比例
乌尔	16	33%
普兹瑞什达干	8	16%
温马	17	35%
吉尔苏	3	6%
尼普尔	3	6%
其他	2	4%
共计	49	100%

注意，在这49件 zag-u 文献中，只有26件文献记录的是 zag-u 赋税缴纳给神庙或者神庙祭司，可以肯定它们指的是一种什一税。其余23件文献中所记录的 zag-u 术语很可能只是指数字"十分之一"的概念，而不是指一种税。这26件可以肯定是 zag-u 税的文献统计如下（见表6-2）。接下来，我们对于乌尔第三王朝 zag-u 税的探讨都是基于这些文献资料。

表6-2　　　　　乌尔第三王朝神庙 zag-u 税统计分析表

来自	文献日期	赋税形式	献给
普兹瑞什达干	MVN 11 215（AS 8 vii 14）	牲畜	伊南娜神庙 en 祭司
	PDT 1 203（AS 8 ix 29）	牲畜	伊南娜神庙 en 祭司
	AUCT 1 497（AS 8 xii 20）	牲畜	伊南娜神庙 en 祭司
	JCS 52 43 47（SS 8 vii 2）	牲畜	伊南娜神庙 en 祭司
	P464910（SS 8 vii 12）	牲畜	伊南娜神庙 en 祭司
	AUCT 3 194（IS 2 x 2）	牲畜	伊南娜神庙 en 祭司

第六章 神庙 zag-u 税

续表

来自	文献日期	赋税形式	献给
温马	MVN 18 745（undated）	不清楚	伊南娜神庙
	MVN 11 Y（S 35）	牲畜	宁乌拉神庙 egi-zi 祭司
	BPOA 1 1018（AS 5 xii）	鱼类	带入王宫
	BPOA 1 885（AS 7）	牲畜，羊毛	吉安的沙拉神庙 lu$_2$-mah 祭司
	MVN 16 906（AS 8）	牲畜，羊毛	沙拉神庙 lu$_2$-mah 祭司
	SET 139（SS 2）	牲畜	宁乌拉神庙 egi-zi 祭司
	CST 741（SS 5 iv）	芦苇制品	恩利尔神庙
乌尔	UET 3 1755（undated）	纺织品	南那神庙
	UET 9 1072（undated）	可耕地（gan$_2$）	宁伽尔神庙
	UET 3 1770（--xii）	羊毛、木制品	宁伽尔神庙
	UET 3 61（S 41）	石制品	南那神庙
	UET 3 1777（AS 9 vi）	羊毛、植物油、木制品	宁伽尔神庙
	UET 3 25（SS 1）	牲畜	南那神庙
	UET 3 1368（IS 1）	可耕地	宁伽尔神庙
	UET 3 1087（IS 2）	无花果	宁伽尔神庙
	UET 3 2（IS 2 x）	大麦	宁伽尔神庙
	UET 3 365（IS 3 i-xi）	青铜制品	宁伽尔神庙
	UET 3 91（IS 3 x）	椰枣	南那神庙
	UET 3 250（IS 8 viii）	牲畜	宁伽尔神庙
不清楚	TLB 3 152（undated）	大麦	南那神庙

从上述统计表中，我们知道，乌尔第三王朝的 zag-u 税资料主要来自三个遗址的文献：普兹瑞什达干、温马和乌尔。普兹瑞什达干文献主要记录阿马尔辛 8 年的 zag-u 税缴纳情况，温马文献零散记载了从舒尔吉时期到舒辛时期的 zag-u 税，乌尔文献主要集中于伊比辛时期的 zag-u 税记录。普兹瑞什达干文献记载的 zag-u 税形式只有牲畜，温马文献记载的 zag-u 税

209

形式除了牲畜之外，还有羊毛和芦苇，乌尔文献记载的 zag-u 税形式种类多样，包括牲畜、羊毛、木制品、青铜制品、大麦、无花果、椰枣等。在 zag-u 税的目的地记载方面，普兹瑞什达干文献记载的 zag-u 税都是献给伊南娜神庙，温马文献记载的 zag-u 税主要的目的地是宁乌拉神庙和温马的保护神沙拉的神庙，乌尔文献记载的 zag-u 税都是献给乌尔的保护神南那的神庙或者其妻宁伽尔的神庙。

第三节　神庙 zag-u 税的征收

在乌尔第三王朝，zag-u 税的赋税形式主要包括：牲畜、鱼类、大麦、无花果、椰枣、纺织品、芦苇制品、石制品等。[①] 其中，最主要的赋税形式是牲畜，包括牛、绵羊和山羊。它们被用作神庙祭祀仪式的献祭品，以及神庙管理人员的日常食用需求。zag-u 税形式多种多样，没有一个固定的赋税形式，这体现了 zag-u 税诞生伊始朴素粗简的特色。

zag-u 税最早可以追溯到公元前 3 千纪的苏美尔文明时期。虽然目前已知最早的 zag-u 税证据，见于乌尔第三王朝的第二位国王舒尔吉统治时期，但是很可能，并不是舒尔吉创立了 zag-u 税，而是在舒尔吉统治之前，甚至在乌尔第三王朝之前，随着神庙的产生，zag-u 税就已经在两河流域产生了。zag-u 税的产生很可能要追溯到两河流域文明的伊始，即大约公元前 3200 年楔形文字的发明以及苏美尔城邦国家的诞生时期。一般而言，zag-u 税的目的地是神庙，它与神庙有着密切的关系，故被认为是一种神庙税或宗教赋税类型。据楔形文字文献记载，大量的物品作为 zag-u 税的课税形式，被缴纳给各大神庙，奉献给诸多神灵，这些神主要包括：乌鲁克的保护神伊南娜、乌尔的保护神南那及其妻宁伽尔、温马的保护神沙拉及其妻宁乌拉，其中沙拉神和宁乌拉是夫妻神，南那神和宁伽尔也是夫妻神。这些文献的出处来源也有所不同，其详细情况列举如下：

[①] 关于古代两河流域的 zag-u 税，参见 E. Salonen, *Über den Zehnten im Alten Mesopotamien：Ein Beitrag zur Geschichte der Besteuerung*, Helsinki：Suomalaisen Kirjallisuuden Kirjapaino Oy Helsinki, 1972；刘昌玉、应俊《欧洲什一税源于古代两河流域》，《中国社会科学报》2018 年 10 月 29 日。

表 6-3　　　　　　　　　　　神庙 zag-u 税贡献的主要神

神名	祭司	文献来源
伊南娜（Inana）	en	普兹瑞什达干
沙拉（Shara）	lu$_2$-mah	温马
宁乌拉沙拉之妻（Ninurra）	egi-zi	温马
南那（Nanna）		乌尔
宁伽尔南那之妻（Ningal）		乌尔

据普兹瑞什达干文献记载，乌尔第三王朝的 zag-u 税被缴纳给伊南娜神庙的最高女祭司（en）。这些 zag-u 税的赋税形式都是牲畜，文献中提到这些作为 zag-u 税的牲畜是从普兹瑞什达干的机构总管阿巴萨加或者因塔埃阿手中，最终被支出给伊南娜神庙的最高女祭司。很显然，阿巴萨加或者因塔埃阿并不是 zag-u 税的真正来源地，而只是扮演了中转地的角色，他们从 zag-u 税的真正来源地先接收了牲畜，然后再将其支出。此外，在时间上，这些 zag-u 税的缴纳大多是发生在阿马尔辛第 8 年和舒辛第 8 年。下面，以阿马尔辛第 8 年阿巴萨加支出的 zag-u 税牲畜为例：

PDT 1 203（AS 8 ix 29，Drehem）
正面

1 u$_8$ niga^d Inana	1 只食大麦母绵羊，为伊南娜
^{d}En-lil$_2$-zi-ša$_3$-gal$_2$ maškim	恩利尔孜沙伽尔是总监
1 udu	1 只绵羊
1 sila$_4$	1 只绵羊羔
1 maš$_2$	1 只山羊羔
zag-u en ^{d}Inana	作为什一税，为伊南娜神庙最高女祭司
Lugal-ku$_3$-zu maškim	卢伽尔库祖是总监
ša$_3$ mu-DU-ra-ta	从这些带来的之中

背面

u$_4$ 29-kam	第 29 日
ki Ab-ba-sa$_6$-ga-ta	从阿巴萨加处
ba-zi	支出
giri$_3$ Da-a-a-ti dub-sar	经办人是书吏达亚亚提

古代两河流域乌尔第三王朝赋税制度研究

iti ezem-mah　　　　　　　　　　第 9 月
mu en Eridu^{ki} ba-hun　　　　　阿马尔辛 8 年
左侧
4 udu　　　　　　　　　　　　　（共计：）4 只羊

据乌尔文献记载，乌尔第三王朝的 zag-u 税缴纳给南那及其妻宁伽尔两位神。这些 zag-u 税形式包括纺织品、羊毛、木制品、石制品、青铜制品、香料、牲畜、无花果、大麦、椰枣等诸多种类。在时间上，zag-u 税缴纳给首都乌尔的主神南那及其妻宁伽尔，主要见于伊比辛 1 年至 3 年的乌尔文献。不过，据舒尔吉 41 年的一篇乌尔文献记载，磨石作为 zag-u 税被缴纳给乌尔主神南那，例如：

UET 3 61（S 41，Ur）
正面
1 ^{na4}kikkin šu-se$_3$-ga babbar$_2$①　　　　1 个白色的"舒塞加"磨石
a-ru-a　　　　　　　　　　　　　　　　　奉献供品
zag-u ^{d}Nanna　　　　　　　　　　　　　作为 zag-u 税，为南那（神庙）
Ba-a-a i$_3$-dab$_5$　　　　　　　　　　　　巴亚亚收到了
背面
mu us$_2$-sa e$_2$ Puzur$_4$-iš-^{d}Da-gan ba-du$_3$
　　　　　　　　　　　　　　　　　　　　舒尔吉 41 年
mu us$_2$-sa-bi

在文献中并没有提到 zag-u 税的来源地，但是多次提到，这些 zag-u 税在被送到乌尔的南那神庙或者宁伽尔神庙之后，被作为供品（a-ru-a）奉献给神。② 此外，拉伽什—吉尔苏行省的一些土地作为 zag-u 税被缴纳给宁伽尔神庙，作为神庙土地。③ zag-u 税被缴纳给南那或宁伽尔神庙的记录，多见于伊比辛统治时期的文献。比如：

---

① 关于术语 šu-se$_3$-ga，参见 E. Prang, "Das Archiv des Imgûa", *Zeitschrift für Assyriologie und Vorderasiatische Archäologie*, Vol. 66（1976）, p. 19.
② I. J. Gelb, "The Arua Institution", *Revue d'Assyriologie et d'archéologie orientale*, Vol. 66（1972）, pp. 1-32.
③ 文献 UET 9 1072（undated）。

第六章 神庙 zag-u 税

UET 3 91（IS 3 x，Ur）
正面
2.4.0 zu₂-lum gur　　　　　　　　2 古尔、4 巴里格椰枣
a-ru-a Ur-šu-mu-gi₄　　　　　　　是乌尔舒姆吉的奉献供品
0.2.0 zu₂-lum gur　　　　　　　　2 巴里格椰枣
zag-u e₂ ᵈNanna-ka　　　　　　　作为（给）南那神庙的 zag-u 税
ki ᵈŠu-ᵈSuen-an-dul₃-ta　　　　　从舒辛安杜尔处
背面
Lu₂-sukkal　　　　　　　　　　　卢苏卡尔
šu ba-an-ti　　　　　　　　　　　收到了
iti ezem-mah　　　　　　　　　　第 10 月
mu Si-mu-ru-umᵏⁱ ba-hul　　　　　伊比辛 3 年
印文
Lu₂-sukkal　　　　　　　　　　　卢苏卡尔
dub-sar　　　　　　　　　　　　书吏
dumu Lugal-a-ni-sa₆　　　　　　　卢伽尔阿尼萨之子

zag-u 税除了被缴纳给中央属性的神（乌鲁克的伊南娜、乌尔的南那）之外，地方行省也向当地神庙缴纳 zag-u 税，供当地神庙所用。比如，据温马文献记载，乌尔第三王朝的 zag-u 税被缴纳给温马保护神沙拉神庙的"卢马赫"祭司（lu₂-mah）以及沙拉之妻宁乌拉神庙的"埃吉孜"祭司（egi-zi）。①

沙拉神庙的"卢马赫"祭司作为 zag-u 税接收者的例子如下：

BPOA 1 885（AS 7，Umma）
正面
1 gu₄ mu-1　　　　　　　　　　　1 头一年生公牛
1 dur₃ giš　　　　　　　　　　　　1 头耕地的幼年公驴

---

① P. Steinkeller, "The Priestess égi-zi and Related Matters", in Y. Sefati, et al (eds.), "An Experienced Scribe Who Neglects Nothing": Ancient Near Eastern Studies in Honor of Jacob Klein, Bethesda: CDL Press, 2005, pp. 301–310.

1 udu bar-gal₂	1 只长有羊毛的绵羊
3 udu bar-su-ga	3 只剪掉羊毛的绵羊
1 ud₅	1 只母山羊
4 ma-na siki	4 米纳羊毛
zag-u-še₃	作为 zag-u 税
lu₂-mah i₃-dab₅	"卢马赫"祭司收到了
背面	
mu-DU ᵈŠara₂ KI.ANᵏⁱ	带来给基安的沙拉（神庙）
giri₃ Ur-dun	经办人是乌尔顿
mu Hu-uh₂-nu-riᵏⁱ ba-hul	阿马尔辛 7 年

沙拉之妻宁乌拉神庙的"埃吉孜"祭司作为 zag-u 税接收者的例子如下：

SET 139（SS 2，Umma）
正面

6 maš₂	6 只山羊
zag-u-še₃	作为 zag-u 税
egi-zi ᵈNin-ur₄-ra-ke₄ i₃-dab₅	宁乌拉神庙"埃吉孜"祭司接收了
ki Ša₃-ku₃-ge-ta	从沙库吉处
背面	
mu ma₂ ᵈEn-ki ba-ab-du₈	舒辛 2 年

zag-u 税在征收之后，一般都被储存在神庙区或者神庙附近地区。作为 zag-u 税的大麦、芝麻和椰枣等农产品被储存在仓库中，而这些仓库也隶属于神庙。zag-u 税的缴税地点一般是神庙的主门口，征收来的 zag-u 税在此登记入库。zag-u 税的征收不仅限于两河流域本土，也涉及两河流域的周围地区以及与两河流域发生对外贸易的地区。

古代两河流域 zag-u 税的纳税人囊括了几乎所有的自由民阶层，他们将自己收入和财产的 1/10 缴纳给神庙。这些纳税人包括：国王及其他王室成员，各级世俗与宗教官员，各种职业的自由民，城市或地区为单位的集体纳税人。国王一方面作为 zag-u 税的接收者，另一方面也作为 zag-u 税

第六章 神庙 zag-u 税

的纳税人，他需要将王室财产缴纳给神庙，体现了君权神授的思想。国王缴纳的 zag-u 税到底是神庙的强制要求，还是出于国王的自愿，我们尚且不知。但是从整个两河流域历史来看，神庙势力和王权的斗争与矛盾一直没有中断，作为具有至高无上权力的国王，时刻都会受到神庙势力的牵制与影响，而 zag-u 税就是一个很好的牵制工具。作为 zag-u 税纳税人的各级世俗与宗教官员主要包括维齐尔、行省总督、神庙主管等。与我们对纳税人十分清楚相比，我们关于收税人的具体信息的认识却十分模糊。由于 zag-u 税主要是被缴纳给各个神庙，所以神庙理所当然应该作为其收税人或者接收者，但是在文献中却没有记录具体的接收者。自新巴比伦王国开始，zag-u 税收税人的信息才逐渐丰富起来。新巴比伦文献记载有一个特定的阿卡德语术语 ša muhhi ešrû，直译为"什一税接收者"，明确了收税人的存在。据新巴比伦文献记载，zag-u 税的收税人是神庙的服务人员，他们作为 zag-u 税的直接接收者，最终的收税人应该是神庙主管，甚至是国王。由于相关文献的缺乏，我们对于乌尔第三王朝神庙 zag-u 税的探讨并不是系统的，所得出的结论也只是暂时的。

第七章　赋税制度与国家治理

乌尔第三王朝是古代两河流域的中央集权制国家。前文提到，乌尔第三王朝的主要税收种类有核心行省 bala 税、外围行省 gun$_2$ma-da 税、附属国 gun$_2$ 税、王室 maš$_2$-da-ri-a 税和神庙 zag-u 税。税制是乌尔第三王朝统治者实现其国家治理的重要措施和手段，从第二位国王舒尔吉时期的税制建立与革新，到第三位国王阿马尔辛时期的税制微调与修正，再到第四位国王舒辛时期的激进税制政策，乌尔国家的治理经历了由主动进取到被动冒失的演变。

首王乌尔纳姆统治时期处于国家巩固与统一时期，末王伊比辛统治时期国家领土不断减少，最后可能只剩首都及其附近的弹丸之地，加之这两位国王统治时期的现存文献数量很少，而更多的文献集中于第二王舒尔吉统治中后期，以及第三王阿马尔辛和第四王舒辛时期这大约 50 年的时间。这三位国王在位时期，实行了多次赋税变革，不仅影响了乌尔第三王朝的财政政策的执行与经济政策的制定，更加体现了乌尔第三王朝的国家治理模式与特征，为我们重新认识人类文明早期的国家构建提供了直接的证据和重要的参考。通过对原始楔形文字档案文献的整理与分析，以舒尔吉、阿马尔辛和舒辛这三位国王的税制动态演变为主线，接下来我们来探讨乌尔第三王朝的国家治理模式及其纵向演变过程。

第一节　舒尔吉时期的赋税制度

乌尔第三王朝的第二位国王舒尔吉一共在位 48 年，是古代两河流域历史上统治时间最长的君主之一。他的统治大致可以分为两个阶段，从在位第 1 年至第 20 年作为前一阶段，主要致力于国内建设和休养生息，从其第 21 年征服德尔起，直到第 48 年作为后一阶段，主要是组织对外战争和领土扩张，并且逐渐确立了乌尔第三王朝的统治区域和势力范围，所以一般认为，舒尔吉才是乌尔第三王朝的"真正缔造者"[1]。同时，在其统治时期，舒尔吉进行了一系列卓有成效的改革，被称为"舒尔吉改革"[2]。其内容包括：国王神化（自第 20 年）[3]、驻军（第 20 年）、重组神庙体系（第 21 年）、统一北部和南部的行政管理、建立普兹瑞什达干再分配中心和 bala 税制度、建立官僚等级制度和书吏学校、文字改革、经济管理文献新的记录格式和类型、统一度量衡、创制国家月历。舒尔吉改革在时间上基本都发生在其统治的第 20 年之后，通过这些改革措施，尤其是税制方面，舒尔吉逐步建立起中央集权的国家治理模式。

舒尔吉在其统治时期，建立了核心行省税、外围行省税、神庙税和王室税，加强了乌尔中央政府对地方的直接控制，体现了乌尔第三王朝统治初期的国家治理举措。

一　建立神庙 zag-u 税制

由于神庙经济收归国有，结束神庙势力独立于中央政府的传统，导致神庙的经济来源失去了保障，为了更加有效地管理神庙经济，舒尔吉建立了相应的神庙税收制度，即 zag-u 税制。从早王朝时期的城邦并立开始，神庙权力凌驾于世俗权力之上，或者独立于世俗权力，在每个城邦里，最高的世俗统治者被称为恩西（ensi$_2$）、卢伽尔（lugal）或者恩（en），他们是城邦主神所委任的城邦实际统治者，但是城邦的宗教事务归神庙管理，

---

[1] M. Stepien, *From the History of State System in Mesopotamia: The Kingdom of the Third Dynasty of Ur*, Warszawa: Instytut Historyczny, Uniwerstytet Warszawski, 2009, p. 16; J. L. Dahl, *The Ruling Family of Ur III Umma: A Prosopographical Analysis of an Elite Family in Southern Iraq 4000 Years Ago*, Publications de l'Institut historique-archéologique néerlandais de Stamboul 108, Leiden: Nederlands Instituut voor het Nabije Oosten, 2007, p. 15.

[2] 注意，目前我们并没有发现关于舒尔吉改革的法律法规档案或者明确的汇编文献，而是从零散的经济管理文献和年名等记录中推测与归纳出来的。参见 W. Sallaberger, "Ur III-Zeit", in P. Attinger, M. Wäfler (eds.), *Mesopotamien: Akkade-Zeit und Ur III-Zeit*, Orbis Biblicus et Orientalis 160/3, Freiburg: Universitätsverlag, 1999, p. 148.

[3] J. DuPont, *Divine Kingship in the Third Dynasty of Ur: Methods of Legitimizing Royal Authority in Ancient Mesopotamia*, MA thesis, Central Michigan University, 2012; A. Pitts, *The Cult of the Deified King in Ur III Mesopotamia*, PhD dissertation, University of Pennsylvania, 2015.

不受世俗统治者的制约。随着乌尔第三王朝的建立，舒尔吉在其统治的第 21 年的年名中记载，恩利尔的土地管理员尼努尔塔在恩利尔和宁利尔神庙发布神谕：乌尔国王舒尔吉掌管恩利尔和宁利尔神庙的土地、账目和日常事务。① 这一事件表明，舒尔吉已经将神庙收归中央政府直接管辖，弱化了宗教管理，加强了国家的行政管理。神庙失去了独立性，成为中央政府或者地方行省的组成部分。

目前已知最早的 zag-u 税证据是舒尔吉 35 年的一份温马文献，记录了有 29 只山羊缴纳给宁乌拉神庙的 egi-zi 女祭司作为 zag-u 税。② zag-u 税主要是向神庙缴纳的税目，涉及的神庙包括乌尔的南那神庙③、宁伽尔神庙④、宁乌拉神庙⑤，以及乌鲁克的伊南娜神庙⑥。可见，zag-u 税是地方向中央缴纳的一种赋税，其税收来源应该是地方行省，比如吉尔苏和温马。

zag-u 税的课税形式包括鱼类、洋葱、椰枣、无花果、大麦、植物油等食物，以及布料、羊毛、石制品（磨石^{na4}kin$_2$、红玉髓^{na4}gug）、芦苇及芦苇制品和牲畜。舒尔吉在其统治时期，通过神庙税的创建，将神庙纳入乌尔第三王朝的直接管辖和统治之下，加强了中央集权统治的基础。

二 建立王室税制

王室税的苏美尔语术语有 maš-da-ri$_6$-a、maš-da-ri-a、maš$_2$-da-ri-a，及 maš$_2$-da-ri$_6$-a 四种形式。作为一种王室税，由行省和神庙管理者缴纳给乌尔的王室成员（包括国王）。

最早的王室税证据，见于舒尔吉 24 年的温马文献,⑦ 记载了财宝和牲

---

① D. Frayne, *Ur III Period* (2112–2004 BC), The Royal Inscriptions of Mesopotamia Early Periods Volume 3/2（RIME 3/2）, Toronto: University of Toronto Press, 1997, pp. 102–103.
② 文献 MVN 11 Y（S 35, Umma）. 此外，一份舒尔吉 30 年的吉尔苏记载了 816 条鱼被"带来"，乌尔达姆经办，军尉（nu-banda$_3$）接收了其他的十分之一（文献 MVN 7 347）。
③ 文献 TLB 3 152（undated）, UET 3 1755（undated）, UET 3 61（S 41）, UET 3 25（SS 1）, UET 3 91（IS 3 x）。
④ 文献 UET 9 1072（undated）, UET 3 1770（undated）, UET 3 1777（AS 9 vi）, UET 3 1368（IS 1）, UET 3 1087（IS 2）, UET 3 2（IS 2 x）, UET 3 365（IS 3 i-xi）, UET 3 250（IS 8 viii）。
⑤ 文献 MVN 11 Y（S 35）, SET 139（SS 2）。
⑥ 文献 PDT 1 203（AS 8 ix 29）, AUCT 1 497（AS 8 xii 20）, SET 140（SS 2）, JCS 52 43 47（SS 8 vii 2）, AUCT 3 194（IS 2 x 2）。
⑦ 文献 MVN 4 137（S 24 xi, Umma）。

畜作为首席警卫（gal₅-la₂-gal）的王室税，这种警卫可能是王室服务人员。此后，自舒尔吉 27 年开始，温马文献主要记载的是缴纳给国王的王室税。① 吉尔苏文献记载了王室税被运送到王宫（给王后或国王）。② 自舒尔吉 40 年起，普兹瑞什达干的王室档案开始记载牧牛人的王室税被运送到仓库。③ 可见，为了满足王室成员的日常生活需要，舒尔吉建立了专门供给王室成员的赋税体系，使得王室机构的基本开销有了制度保障。

三 革新核心行省税制

如果说神庙税和王室税的建立，主要为了加强对神庙的控制以及巩固王室的统治，是舒尔吉税制的前奏，那么核心行省税（bala）的建立则是乌尔第三王朝国家治理的典范与关键的改革措施。由于早王朝时期属于苏美尔城邦并立阶段，并没有中央政府和地方政府的划分，所以行省并不存在。阿卡德王国虽然是统一的国家，建立了两河流域历史上最早的行省制，但是在经济方面并没有建立行省税，且因现存相关文献数量过少，无法判断其赋税制度的概貌。目前，我们发现最早的 bala 税证据是舒尔吉 25 年的温马文献，记载了 40 捆芦苇作为牲畜的饲料，由伊宁沙拉缴纳，沙拉伊祖收到了。④ 最早的吉尔苏 bala 文献记载于舒尔吉 27 年，据文献记载，乌尔萨加缴纳 2 古尔大麦给卢恩利尔。⑤ 温马行省和拉伽什—吉尔苏行省是向乌尔中央政府缴纳 bala 税最重要的两个行省，每个行省每年有一个月时间作为 bala 税的缴纳期限，拉伽什—吉尔苏行省是唯一的例外，每年有二至四个月时间，并且分为前半季（bala dub-sag）和后半季（bala egir）。拉伽什—吉尔苏行省缴纳的大麦 bala 税约占该行省大麦总产量的 50%，⑥ 大麦 bala 税的税率约为 1/2，可能其他 bala 税形式的税率也是这个标准。

---

① maš-da-ri₆-a lugal 或者 maš-da-ri-a lugal。
② maš₂-da-ri-a e₂-gal-la ba-an-ku₄，maš₂-da-ri-a nin-a-še₃ e₂-gal-la ba-an-ku₄，maš₂-da-ri-a lugal e₂-gal-la ba-ku₄。
③ maš₂-da-ri-a unu₃-e-ne e₂-kišib-ba-še₃ ba-an-ku₄。
④ 文献 BPOA 1 1249（S 25 iv, Umma）。
⑤ 文献 P500110（S 27 viii, Girsu）。
⑥ 文献 CM 26 112（undated）。

舒尔吉继承了阿卡德王国所创的行省制，建立了乌尔第三王朝的内外二元行省制，内省（核心区或核心行省）向乌尔中央缴纳 bala 税，由总督（恩西）和将军（沙基纳）负责，总督主要出自当地权贵阶层，主管行省的行政事务，将军是国王委派，许多由王室成员担任，主管行省的军事事务，总督和将军之间属于平级关系，权力相互制约。[①] 外省（外围区或外围行省）向乌尔中央政府缴纳 gun_2 ma-da 税，一般是由将军负责，具有军事税的性质。[②] 舒尔吉在其统治的第 39 年，在尼普尔行省内的普兹瑞什达干建立了一个大型的动物再分配中心，该中心虽然位于尼普尔行省，却是隶属于中央政府的机构。随着普兹瑞什达干机构的建立，核心行省 bala 税经历了一个重要的革新，即建立了国家主导的税收补偿或者税收返还制度。地方行省将大麦、面粉、芦苇、木材和劳动力以 bala 税形式缴纳给乌尔中央之后，可以从中央接收牛羊等牲畜，作为 bala 税的返还或者补偿，而这一过程也在行省 bala 纳税期之内进行，属于行省 bala 税体系的组成部分。

在舒尔吉统治时期，属于乌尔国家形态的初创阶段，舒尔吉通过建立神庙税、王室税和行省税，在国内巩固了中央集权的统治，加强了中央政府对地方势力的直接控制，体现了国家建立初期的治理措施，为阿马尔辛时代的繁荣奠定了物质基础。

第二节　阿马尔辛时期的赋税制度

阿马尔辛是乌尔第三王朝的第三位国王，共在位 9 年时间（公元前 2046—前 2038 年）。在其统治时期，乌尔第三王朝不管是在政治方面，还是在经济和文化方面都达到了繁盛时期。[③] 在政治上，阿马尔辛在前任舒尔吉对外征服的基础上，不断扩大乌尔国家的控制范围，核心区、外围区和附属国逐渐趋于稳定。在阿马尔辛统治的 9 年时间里，一共发

[①] 刘昌玉：《乌尔第三王朝行省制度探析》，《社会科学》2017 年第 1 期。

[②] T. Maeda, "The Defense Zone during the Rule of the Ur III Dynasty", *Acta Sumerologica*, Vol. 14 (1992), pp. 135–172.

[③] 关于乌尔第三王朝阿马尔辛的统治，参见 C. Liu, *Organization, Administrative Practices and Written Documentation in Mesopotamia during the Ur III Period（c. 2112 – 2004 BC）: A Case Study of Puzriš-Dagan in the Reign of Amar-Suen*, KEF 3, Münster: Ugarit-Verlag, 2017.

第七章 赋税制度与国家治理

生了三次对外战争，分别是对乌尔比隆（第 2 年）、沙什卢姆（第 6 年）和胡赫努里（第 7 年）；有三位神庙最高祭司被重新任命，分别是乌尔的南那神庙、乌鲁克的伊南娜神庙和卡尔孜达的南那神庙，这体现了国家对神庙控制的加强。在经济方面，已发现的阿马尔辛时期的经济管理文献数量是最多的，要远远超过其他乌尔第三王朝国王统治时期的文献数量。同时，乌尔国家的跨区域贸易活动繁荣，向东远及印度河流域的麦鲁哈地区，向西到达东地中海沿岸的埃布拉，甚至埃及，都成为乌尔第三王朝的对外贸易对象。这一切都反映了阿马尔辛统治时期的繁荣局面。透过这种繁荣现象，我们需要对阿马尔辛时期的诸项经济政策进行剖析，尤其是税制方面对乌尔第三王朝国家治理的影响。

不过，在阿马尔辛统治时期，社会矛盾与社会危机也时有发生，他改变了舒尔吉时期的许多机构与政策，任免了一大批中央和地方官吏。例如，尼普尔行省的总督在舒尔吉时期被乌尔麦麦（Ur-meme）家族所控制，但是到了阿马尔辛时期，乌尔麦麦及其家族成员失去了尼普尔行省的统治权，直到舒辛继位之后，乌尔麦麦家族才恢复了尼普尔行省的总督职位。[①] 再如，阿马尔辛在其统治第 8 年废黜了温马总督乌尔里希（Ur-Lisi），改由乌尔里希的兄弟阿亚卡拉（Ayakala）担任，这可能是因为乌尔里希对阿马尔辛的统治不满。[②] 此外，伊利萨格里格行省的总督乌尔美斯（Ur-mes）几乎同时被废黜，他从阿马尔辛 3 年起一直担任伊利萨格里格行省的总督，[③] 而在阿马尔辛 7 年，[④] 被达达尼（Dadani）和伊拉鲁姆（Ilalum）取代，[⑤] 直到舒辛继位后，乌尔美斯才恢复了伊利萨格里格行省总督之职。[⑥] 除了对地方行省机构的官吏进行任免之外，阿马尔辛还对普兹瑞什达干中

[①] W. W. Hallo, "The House of Ur-Meme", *Journal of Near Eastern Studies*, Vol. 31 (1972), pp. 87–95; R. Zettler and M. T. Roth, "The Genealogy of the House of Ur-Me-me: a Second Look", *Archiv für Orientforschung*, Vol. 31 (1984), pp. 1–9.

[②] 乌尔里希担任温马总督的最后日期是阿马尔辛 8 年第 8 月（文献 PDT 2 1240），阿亚卡拉担任温马总督的开始日期是阿马尔辛 8 年第 9 月（文献 MVN 16 627）。参见 M. Stepien, "The Economic Status of Governors in Ur III Times: An Example of the Governor of Umma", *Journal of Cuneiform Studies*, Vol. 64 (2012), p. 29.

[③] 文献 AOAT 240 81 7 (AS 3 ii)。

[④] 文献 YOS 4 76 (AS 7 v)。

[⑤] Da-da-ni, 见文献 AUCT 2 277 (AS 8 ix); I_3-lal_3-lum, 见文献 JCS 14 110 12 (AS 8 xi 9)。

[⑥] 文献 BPOA 6 79 (SS 1 iii 25)。

央直辖机构的官吏进行了任免与更换，新任了许多专职官吏，[1] 比如主管支出牲畜给王室成员的图兰达干（Turam-Dagan，阿马尔辛4—6年）、乌塔米沙兰（Uta-misharam，阿马尔辛5—9年）和塔希沙塔尔（Tahishatal，阿马尔辛6年至舒辛3年），纳卡布图姆（Nakabtum）分支机构的官员舒玛玛（Shu-Mama，阿马尔辛6—8年）、祖巴加（Zubaga，阿马尔辛8年至舒辛1年）和伊吉恩利尔塞（Igi-Enlilshe，阿马尔辛8年至舒辛1年），专门负责牛牲的官员乌尔图尔（Ur-tur，阿马尔辛5—9年），专门负责驴牲的官员努尔辛（Nur-Suen，阿马尔辛6—8年），以及专门负责bala税的官员卢萨加（Lu-saga，阿马尔辛6—9年）等。阿马尔辛新成立了许多分工细致的分支部门，由不同的分支部门支出牲畜至其最终目的地，体现了机构运转分工的专业化。据普兹瑞什达干文献记载，在阿马尔辛时期，关于普兹瑞什达干机构中心部门的支出（ba-zi）文献数量明显减少，而转运（i_3-dab_5）给分支部门的文献数量明显增多。[2] 另在阿马尔辛8年，普兹瑞什达干文献的记录格式发生了明显变化，即在大多数文献的末尾（位于交易活动之后、月名和年名之前），增加了经办人$giri_3$的名字，[3] 这很可能是阿马尔辛新设的一个专门记录王室档案的机构。

阿马尔辛统治时期，乌尔税制趋于稳定，只有略微的调整。首先，阿马尔辛确定了外围行省税（gun_2ma-da）的形式及税率，即缴纳牛和羊的固定比例为1∶10。[4] 这一固定赋税比例的设置，规范了外围行省税的征收和管理，有利于加强乌尔中央对外围行省的控制。阿马尔辛时期的税制更

---

[1] C. Liu, *Organization, Administrative Practices and Written Documentation in Mesopotamia during the Ur III Period* (*c. 2112 – 2004 BC*)*: A Case Study of Puzriš-Dagan in the Reign of Amar-Suen*, KEF 3, Münster: Ugarit-Verlag, 2017, pp. 407 – 408.

[2] C. Liu, *Organization, Administrative Practices and Written Documentation in Mesopotamia during the Ur III Period* (*c. 2112 – 2004 BC*)*: A Case Study of Puzriš-Dagan in the Reign of Amar-Suen*, KEF 3, Münster: Ugarit-Verlag, 2017, p. 12.

[3] M. Hilgert, *Cuneiform Texts from the Ur III Period in the Oriental Institute*, Volume 2: *Drehem Administrative Documents from the Reign of Amar-Suena*, Oriental Institute Publications 121, Chicago: The Oriental Institute, 2003, pp. 24 – 25.

[4] P. Steinkeller, "The Administrative and Economic Organization of the Ur III State: The Core and the Periphery", in M. Gibson, R. D. Biggs (eds.), *The Organization of Power: Aspects of Bureaucracy in the Ancient Near East*, Chicago: The Oriental Institute of the University of Chicago, 1987, p. 25.

加注重实用性。① 例如，在其统治时期，牲畜税的用途发生了明显改变，即由舒尔吉时期中央政府所征收的牲畜更多地用于宗教祭祀活动，转变为阿马尔辛时期牲畜更多地被支出给"厨房"、王室成员、高级官吏和外交使节等实用性目的，同样也从侧面反映了阿马尔辛意图削弱宗教势力，加强世俗或者王权的重要性。

其次，记录地方向中央缴纳牲畜税的文献格式有所变化。在普兹瑞什达干文献中，牲畜税被统一记录为 mu-DU（直译为"带来"，引申为"进贡"之义），这些从乌尔第三王朝各地"进贡"的牲畜，被普兹瑞什达干机构的中心总管所接收，然后再进行重新分配。② 自舒尔吉第 26 年开始，在文献中出现了术语 mu-DU lugal，意为"带来给国王"或者"进贡给王室"③。不过，直到舒尔吉最后一年（第 48 年），记录普兹瑞什达干机构中心总管接收 mu-DU lugal 牲畜的文献格式才出现。④ 这种文献记录格式在阿马尔辛时期成为常规记录。术语格式"进贡给王室"（mu-DU lugal）的出现，反映了乌尔第三王朝对王室的重视，体现了乌尔王权的加强，以及王室成员对征税活动的直接管理。阿马尔辛在其统治时期，尝试建立由普兹瑞什达干机构中心总管接收 mu-DU lugal 牲畜的常规性操作。例如，在阿马尔辛 2 年，中心总管阿巴萨加（Abba-saga）接收了 1223 只"进贡给王室"的牲畜和野生动物，包括 81 头牛、1 只鹿（lulim）、47 只野鹿（šeg$_9$-bar）、1054 只羊、23 只羚羊和 17 只熊。⑤ 在阿马尔辛 5 年，中心总管阿巴萨加接收了 11520 只"进贡给王室"的牲畜和野生动物，包括 471 头牛、26 只鹿（lulim）、2 只野驴或马（si$_2$-si$_2$）、11004 只羊、2 只羚羊和 15 只熊。⑥ 另据普兹瑞什达干文献记载，从阿马尔辛 5 年开始，有关从地方向中央"进贡"牲畜的文献格式"mu-DU ＋人名"逐渐被一种泛称格

---

① M. Hilgert, *Cuneiform Texts from the Ur III Period in the Oriental Institute*, Volume 2: *Drehem Administrative Documents from the Reign of Amar-Suena*, Oriental Institute Publications 121, Chicago: The Oriental Institute, 2003, pp. 15 – 16.

② T. Maeda, "Bringing (mu-túm) Livestock and the Puzurish-Dagan Organization in the Ur III Dynasty", *Acta Sumerologica*, Vol. 11 (1989), pp. 69 – 107.

③ 文献 OIP 115 1（S 26 vii）。

④ mu-DU lugal Na-sa$_6$ i$_3$-dab$_5$, 见文献 Nisaba 8 25（S 48 vi）。

⑤ 文献 Fs Levine 115 – 119, 148ff.（AS 2 xi）。

⑥ 文献 BRM 3 50（AS 5 viii）。

式 ša₃ mu-DU-ra-ta（从带来的之中）所取代，即中央档案不再记录每个"进贡者"的名字，而是采用一种统称的方式略去。这一文献格式的取代过程历经了三年有余，直到阿马尔辛 8 年才最终完成。[①] 其原因很可能与乌尔中央机构的政策变化有关：第一，在阿马尔辛时期，进贡者人数太多，中央机构难以全部将其记录下来。第二，在阿马尔辛时期，乌尔国家更加注重纳税数额与时间等要素，而对"进贡者"信息并不特别关心。第三，在阿马尔辛时期，术语 ša₃ mu-DU-ra-ta 已经逐渐成为一种固定文献记录格式，即一种新的范式。

最后，阿马尔辛对牧业税进行了调整，并且加强了对王室卫队的控制与管理。乌尔第三王朝的牧业税（šu-gid₂），建立于舒尔吉统治时期。[②] 这是中央政府向牧人（牧羊人、牧牛人等）机构征收牲畜的一种税制，作为牧业税的牲畜可能是一种未育肥的牲畜，以青草或秸秆（干草）喂养，其肉质量低下，属于中等品级的牲畜。这些牲畜显然不是献给神庙的，而是供人食用，由中央牧业部门负责管理。牧业税的纳税期一般是在每年的 5 月至 12 月。在舒尔吉统治第 43 年，作为牧业税的牲畜一般是缴纳给王室"厨房"或者中央牲畜屠宰场进行宰杀加工。[③] 而在舒尔吉 45 年，作为牧业税的牲畜被支付给中央牲畜屠宰场进行屠宰加工后，分派给 aga₃-us₂ 军事人员。[④] 到阿马尔辛统治第 6 年，作为牧业税的牲畜被缴纳给中央牲畜屠宰场进行屠宰加工后，不再分派给 aga₃-us₂ 军事人员，而是分派给 gar₃-du 王室卫队。[⑤] 阿马尔辛建立 gar₃-du 卫队，取代了舒尔吉所创建的 aga₃-

---

[①] M. Hilgert, *Cuneiform Texts from the Ur III Period in the Oriental Institute*, Volume 2: *Drehem Administrative Documents from the Reign of Amar-Suena*, Oriental Institute Publications 121, Chicago: The Oriental Institute, 2003, pp. 20 – 21.

[②] M. Sigirst, *Drehem*, Bethesda: CDL Press, 1992, pp. 40 – 42.

[③] L. B. Allred, *Cooks and Kitchen: Centralized Food Production in Late Third Millennium Mesopotamia*, PhD thesis, Johns Hopkins University, 2006, pp. 61 – 66.

[④] mu aga₃-us₂-e-ne-še₃，见文献 AUCT 1 314, Hermitage 3 140, SACT 1 138, AAICAB 1/2 pl. 101 1937 – 048, MVN 4 118。参见 L. B. Allred, *Cooks and Kitchen: Centralized Food Production in Late Third Millennium Mesopotamia*, PhD thesis, Johns Hopkins University, 2006, pp. 57 – 61。

[⑤] 苏美尔语术语"gar₃-du"特指一类军事人员，级别低于军尉（nu-banda₃），受军尉的直接统治，其职能是保护阿马尔辛及其随从的防卫安全，参见 M. Hilgert, *Cuneiform Texts from the Ur III Period in the Oriental Institute*, Volume 2: *Drehem Administrative Documents from the Reign of Amar-Suena*, Oriental Institute Publications 121, Chicago: The Oriental Institute, 2003, pp. 21 – 24。

us₂ 卫队系统。在阿马尔辛统治第 7 年，许多将军发誓效忠于乌尔中央，[①] 这种发誓仪式是阿马尔辛确立王权威信和确保国王统治地位的必要行为，也很可能与军队或宫廷发生危机、从而迫使阿马尔辛重建卫队系统有关。直到舒辛继位之后，aga₃-us₂ 卫队系统才得以恢复。

阿马尔辛不仅对乌尔国家的官吏进行了大范围任免，还对税制进行了部分调整，阿马尔辛时期的税制调整出于巩固乌尔国家统治的目的，是乌尔第三王朝统治中期在经济方面进行国家治理的集中体现。

第三节 舒辛时期的赋税制度

舒辛是乌尔第三王朝的第四位国王，共在位 9 年时间（公元前 2037—前 2029 年），是乌尔第三王朝由盛而衰的转折时期。在其统治第 3 年，为了防御北方游牧民族阿摩利人的渗入，舒辛下令建造了阿摩利长城，[②] 标志着乌尔第三王朝在对外政策上由主动进攻转为被动防御，[③] 成为王朝由盛而衰的重要转折点。舒辛在其统治时期改变了阿马尔辛时期的许多政策，尤其是在其统治第 3 年对税制进行了许多革新。通过一系列的税制革新措施，舒辛试图挽救乌尔第三王朝的衰落趋势，但是成效甚微。

舒辛建立了具体的王室税名目。王室税作为一种向王室成员缴纳的赋税种类，由行省和神庙管理者缴纳给国王和其他王室成员，主要用于重要的宗教或世俗目的，比如奉献于乌尔的南那神庙、宁伽尔神庙和杜乌尔神

---

① D. Patterson, *Elements of the Neo-Sumerian Military*, PhD dissertation, University of Pennsylvania, 2018, pp. 345 – 353.

② 由于阿摩利人大量涌入两河流域南部，他们一方面能够担任乌尔第三王朝的重要官职，另一方面也对乌尔国家的统治构成了很大的威胁。为了防止阿摩利人的不断南下，舒辛在其统治第 3 年决定修建一条长城。舒辛派沙鲁姆巴尼（Sharrum-bani）担任筑城的监工，他后来被巴巴尼（Babani）取代。到舒辛 4 年，阿摩利长城修建完成，这一年的年名是：mu ᵈŠu-ᵈSuen lugal Uri₅ᵏⁱ-ma-ke₄ bad₃ mar-tu Mu-ri-iq-ti-id-ni-im mu-du₃ "乌尔国王舒辛建造了名称为'穆里克提德尼姆'的阿摩利长城之年"，参见 D. Frayne, *Ur III Period (2112 – 2004 BC)*, The Royal Inscriptions of Mesopotamia Early Periods Volume 3/2（RIME 3/2），Toronto: University of Toronto Press, 1997, pp. 290 – 292.

③ M. Silver, "Climate Change, the Mardu Wall, and the Fall of Ur", in O. Drewnowska and M. Sandowicz eds., *Fortune and Misfortune in the Ancient Near East: Proceedings of the 60th Recontre Assyriologique Internationale Warsaw, 21 – 25 July 2014*, Winona Lake: Eisenbrauns, 2017, pp. 271 – 295.

庙，献于"舒尔吉的王座"，用于王室成员、高官和外国使节消费等。在舒辛3年之前，献给国家三大节日庆典的赋税来自多种税目，在文献中统一使用泛指贡赋的"mu-DU＋节日"术语。而从舒辛3年开始，在文献记录中取消了这一用法，代之以特指王室税的"maš$_{(2)}$-da-ri-a＋节日"术语。[①] 在国家节日庆典期间，王室税被缴纳给在乌尔或者在加埃什的南那神庙祭司之后，先是被存放于为阿基图（a$_2$-ki-ti）节日庆典的储备房中。[②] 所以，南那神庙祭司在这里作为王室税的接收者。

舒辛在其统治第3年建立了具体的外围行省税名目，使用 gun$_2$ ma-da 这一术语特指外围行省税。[③] gun$_2$ ma-da 这个术语直译为"地区税"，它不是 gun$_2$ 税的延伸，而是特指一种具体的赋税名目。在舒辛3年之前，外围行省向中央缴纳的贡赋名目繁多，在文献中记录的术语也不尽统一，主要包括 gu$_2$ GN "（某地的）贡赋"、erin$_2$ GN "（某地的）军事人员"、ša$_3$ GN "在某地"、šu-gid$_2$ "转手"、udu GN "（某地的）羊"等术语。以牲畜这一课税形式为例，缴纳牛和羊的比例基本上维持在1∶10左右的固定比例。外围行省税发生变化的原因，很可能与舒辛3年阿摩利长城的修建有关。政治与军事局势的变化，迫使舒辛必须对乌尔第三王朝的外围行省采取更有力的经济措施，体现了乌尔国家意在加强对外围行省的控制。舒辛统治时期的对外政策，一改之前的主动进攻，转为被动的防御，这不仅体现在政治和军事方面，也体现在诸如王室税和外围行省税变化这些经济方面。

乌尔第三王朝的外围行省和附属国的政治变动，不仅可以从王室税和外围行省税的直接证据中体现出来，而且在普兹瑞什达干文献中也能找到间接证据。据普兹瑞什达干文献记载，在舒辛3年，mu-DU 文献记录格式也发生了重要的变化，表现为机构中心总管因塔埃阿（Intaea）开始大量接收 mu-DU lugal（为国王进贡）牲畜，[④] 而非之前的 mu-DU（普通"进

---

① 这里的"节日"指乌尔王朝的三大国家节日：a$_2$-ki-ti šu-numun、a$_2$-ki-ti še-sag$_{11}$-ku$_5$ 和 ezem-mah（在舒辛3年第10月之前为 er-su-a），参见 M. Cohen, *The Cultic Calendars of the Ancient Near East*, Bethesda：CDL Press, 1993, pp. 140-160。

② 关于阿基图节，参见刘健《古代两河流域新年礼俗、观念及其政治功能的演进》，《贵州社会科学》2017年第10期。

③ T. Maeda, "Bringing (mu-túm) Livestock and the Puzrish-Dagan Organization in the Ur III Dynasty", *Acta Sumerologica*, Vol. 11 (1989), pp. 98-99。

④ mu-DU lugal In-ta-e$_3$-a i$_3$-dab$_5$，见文献 BIN 3 233 (SS3 vii 16), NYPL 13 (IS 2 viii 26)。

第七章 赋税制度与国家治理

贡")牲畜。由于这些"进贡"的牲畜大多来源于乌尔第三王朝的外围行省和附属国,所以舒辛在其统治第三年特意将这一类"进贡"贴上了"(为)国王"的标签,旨在突出乌尔王室及中央政府的重要性,进一步加强中央对外围行省和附属国的控制。

根据温马行省文献记载,舒辛时期的核心行省 bala 税发生了一些变化。在舒辛 3—4 年,温马行省向乌尔中央提供的牲畜饲料数量明显增加。相应地,在舒辛 3 年,乌尔中央向已经缴纳了 bala 税的地方行省补偿的牲畜数量也迅速增加。[①] 这两种变化绝非巧合,而是存在某种联系。一方面,可能是因为乌尔国家出现了社会危机,为了缓和与稳定地方行省,乌尔中央加大了对行省税补偿和返还的力度;另一方面,因为在舒辛 3 年修建阿摩利长城需要大量税收,乌尔中央加大了对核心行省 bala 税的征收力度,进而导致中央对地方行省税补偿力度的相应增加。

乌尔第三王朝的税制是舒尔吉、阿马尔辛和舒辛三位国王进行国家治理的经济方面体现,经历了由盛而衰、由主动到被动的演变过程。舒尔吉设立了一系列新的赋税名目,继承发展了一些自阿卡德王朝乃至早王朝时期已经存在的赋税种类,并且对其进行了革新。舒尔吉时期的税制处于乌尔第三王朝的始创阶段,也是乌尔国家治理的初始时期,为乌尔第三王朝的巩固与发展奠定了经济基础,这些经济举措也影响了乌尔第三王朝的政治和军事政策,以国王神化为特色的中央集权统治以及核心行省、外围行省和附属国的三重地方治理模式逐渐建立起来。

阿马尔辛时期的税制多是对舒尔吉时期税制的修正和微调。在阿马尔辛统治时期,乌尔第三王朝的国家治理趋于完善,国家政治和经济发展进入繁盛时期。内外政治处于对乌尔第三王朝有利的局面,阿马尔辛没有必要采取大刀阔斧式的激进赋税措施,而是更多以小修小补为特征的税制微调。值得注意的是,在阿马尔辛统治后期,由于社会矛盾的加剧等因素,乌尔第三王朝的统治出现了危机,为了应对突如其来的不利局面,阿马尔辛一改统治前期的温和治理模式,实施了比较激进的经济措施。最终,他采用这种挽救式的税制革新未能取得良效。继阿马尔辛之后,乌尔第三王

---

① T. Sharlach, *Provincial Taxation and the Ur III State*, Cuneiform Monographs 26, Leiden: Brill, 2004, pp. 352 – 353.

朝由盛而衰，在国家治理方面也开始由主动变为被动。

舒辛时期的税制，特别是舒辛统治第三年的税制变化，是在特定政治背景下的被动举措。舒辛意图摆脱困境，对王室税、核心行省税和外围行省税等进行了冒进的变革，一方面使得乌尔国家的税制逐渐趋于明晰化和专业化，为后来的巴比伦和亚述赋税制度的完善奠定了基础，另一方面这一时期名目繁多的税种也给乌尔第三王朝的灭亡埋下了隐患。

简而言之，乌尔第三王朝存在短短百余年，是古代两河流域中央集权统治的较早尝试者，统治者通过征收各种类型的赋税来增加国家财政收入，乌尔第三王朝税制的建立与变动，受到内外多重因素的影响，与当时的社会历史发展有着密切的关联。自舒尔吉统治的初创期，到阿马尔辛统治的繁荣期，再到舒辛统治的转折期，乌尔第三王朝的统治者尝试人类早期文明的国家治理模式，利用赋税来调节国家经济的发展，以经济手段来达到治理国家的目的，这是人类历史上最早利用赋税的杠杆作用来调节国家经济政策的例证之一，对于后来的两河流域历史发展乃至整个西亚文明的演进具有重要的引导和借鉴价值。

结　　语

乌尔第三王朝存在的短短一百余年时间（公元前2112—前2004年），是两河流域的苏美尔人从城邦体制尝试向区域性帝国体制过渡的一个关键时期。乌尔第三王朝建立在驱逐外族势力（阿卡德人、库提人）入侵的基础上，继阿卡德王国之后，再一次完成了对两河流域南部的统一。在政治和军事方面，乌尔第三王朝的统治者采取战争（对外征服）与和平（政治联姻）两种政治手腕，不断扩张和巩固王朝的势力范围，建立了核心区、外围区、附属国三层政治势力模式。在经济方面，乌尔第三王朝统治者们不仅积极开展对外贸易，发展国内经济，将神庙经济收归国有，而且还为此制定了详细的税收政策，细化了每种赋税的内容，构成了乌尔第三王朝完整的赋税体系，成为乌尔第三王朝国家治理的重要体现，同时对于乌尔第三王朝的兴衰也具有十分重要的引导作用。

通过以上各章对乌尔第三王朝赋税制度的梳理和研究，我们对这一重要问题的内容有了一个较为全面的认知，并且发现乌尔第三王朝的各种赋税制度在课税形式、征收对象、征收方式、赋税用途、赋税账目记录等诸方面具有一些突出的特点。

第一，乌尔第三王朝相较两河流域后来的历史而言，其赋税种类较少且征收区域相对零散，很多税种尚未创立，还没有形成比较完善的赋税体系。乌尔第三王朝处于古代两河流域文明发展的早期阶段，是两河流域文明从城邦体制向帝国体制的过渡阶段，统治者在政治军事方面的不断对外扩张，亟须相应的经济措施出台，尤其为了加强中央集权统治，加强中央对地方的经济管理，而赋税就是一种比较有效的经济措施。乌尔第三王朝是许多赋税的初创时期，统治者虽然沿用了许多前朝的税种，比如王室maš-da-ri-a税，也创立了一些新的税种，比如核心行省bala税、外围行省

gun₂ ma-da 税以及神庙 zag-u 税等，但是在总体上依然比较零散，没有形成一个完善的赋税体系，很多税种在当时还没有创立，比如农业税、关税、增值税、商品税、人头税等，这体现了早期两河流域文明发展的原始朴素特征。

第二，乌尔第三王朝赋税的课税形式多种多样，每种赋税具有相对固定的课税形式。核心行省 bala 税的课税形式种类繁多，比如大麦、小麦、面包、面粉等食物，牲畜饲料、芦苇及芦苇制品、木材及木制品、石材及石制品、布料及纺织品、牲畜和劳动力等。而且，不同的行省缴纳的 bala 税形式也各具特色，比如温马行省以芦苇及芦苇制品为主，拉伽什—吉尔苏行省主要的 bala 税课税形式是大麦和面粉，这体现了不同地方行省的特产和因地制宜的原则。外围行省 gun₂ ma-da 税的课税形式仅限于牛和羊等牲畜。附属国 gun₂ 税的课税形式除了牲畜之外，还包括大麦、白银、木制品、陶器等形式。如同核心行省 bala 税，王室 maš-da-ri-a 税的课税形式种类也十分繁多，以牲畜为主，还包括大麦、面粉、面包等食物，芦苇及芦苇制品，布料等纺织品，啤酒等饮料，苹果、无花果、洋葱等蔬菜水果，以及黄金、白银、羊毛和劳动力等形式，几乎囊括了古代两河流域所出产的各类物产。神庙 zag-u 税的课税形式也类似于王室税，以牲畜为主，还包括大麦、无花果、椰枣、纺织品、芦苇制品等物产。可以说，除了外围区 gun₂ ma-da 税的课税形式仅限于牲畜之外，其余税种的课税形式多种多样，体现了古代两河流域的农业和手工业领域的方方面面，如同一部古代两河流域的经济物产史。

第三，乌尔第三王朝赋税的征收对象相对比较固定，且服务于国家的政治目的和中央集权的统治政策。bala 税的征收对象是乌尔第三王朝的核心行省（或称内省），由行省总督亲自负责赋税的缴纳工作，并且设有专门的税务官员。gun₂ ma-da 税的征收对象是乌尔第三王朝的外围区（即外省），由外围区的将军负责，具有军事税的性质。gun₂ 税的征收对象是乌尔第三王朝的附属国，由于目前相关文献资料匮乏，我们对这一税目的认识还不够全面。以上三个税种分别对应于乌尔第三王朝的三重地方机构——核心区、外围区和附属国，乌尔中央政府通过不同的赋税制度，对这三重地方政区进行分而治之的有效管辖和控制。此外，王室税的征收对象包括牧羊人和牧牛人的专门机构，来源于乌尔第三王朝的外围区。神庙

结　语

zag-u 税的征收对象尚不清楚，但是很可能也来自乌尔第三王朝的外围区或者附属国。上述税种的共同特点是，这些赋税都是从乌尔第三王朝的地方向中央流动，即地方向中央纳税，是乌尔第三王朝统治者加强中央集权统治的重要经济举措。乌尔第三王朝的统治者通过赋税的杠杆作用，将地方行省和附属国的物产源源不断地运往王朝的中心，并且通过税收补偿的方式分配给地方部分的物产（以 bala 牲畜为主），以此来加强王朝内部物产的有序运转，达到直接控制各级地方势力的最终目的。

第四，乌尔第三王朝每种赋税具有固定的记录模式和文献出处，体现了乌尔第三王朝严格的账目记录和审核制度。同一税种也会使用不同的术语来记录，术语之间的差异体现了不同时期、不同地区的记录习惯和特征。比如，王室税的术语就有四种类型：（1）maš-da-ri-a 型、（2）maš$_2$-da-ri-a 型、（3）maš-da-ri$_6$-a 型、（4）maš$_2$-da-ri$_6$-a 型。其中，第一种类型 maš-da-ri-a 型主要被用于早王朝时期和乌尔第三王朝，第二种类型 maš$_2$-da-ri-a 型主要用于阿卡德王国、乌尔第三王朝和古巴比伦王国时期，第三种类型 maš-da-ri$_6$-a 型和第四种类型 maš$_2$-da-ri$_6$-a 型都是仅用于乌尔第三王朝时期。在乌尔第三王朝的经济文献中，第一种类型主要被用于吉尔苏文献和伊利萨格里格文献，第二种类型主要被用于普兹瑞什达干文献、乌尔文献和温马文献中，第三种类型和第四种类型主要被用于温马文献中。这样的书写记录并非只是不同书吏（记账员）的行为习惯，而是不同地区的相关规定和人为制定的政策所致。

第五，乌尔第三王朝的赋税制度进行过多次改革，并且税制改革与乌尔第三王朝的国家治理之间关系密切。这也暗示了乌尔第三王朝赋税制度的不固定性。乌尔第三王朝的赋税制度并不是自始至终一成不变的，而是经历了多次的税制改革，这些赋税改革，一方面是新国王继位的主动改革措施，另一方面也是统治者为了应对不断变化的政治、经济、军事和外交政策，不得已而做出的赋税改革举措。税制改革作为乌尔第三王朝统治者实现其国家治理意愿的重要举措和手段之一，从第二位国王舒尔吉开始，历经第三位国王阿马尔辛，直到第四位国王舒辛统治时期，统治者进行税制改革的步伐从未停止。可以说，税制改革从一个方面可以映射出乌尔第三王朝兴衰的历史变迁。具体而言，在舒尔吉统治时期，处于乌尔第三王朝的国家初创阶段和巩固时期，舒尔吉建立了一系列赋税名目，包括核心行省 bala 税、王室税和神庙 zag-u 税，加强了乌尔中央政府对地方的直接控制，体现了乌尔第三王朝中央集权的统治特征。尤其是，在舒尔吉统治的第 39 年，随着大型牲畜集散中心——普兹瑞什达干机构的建立，bala 税经历了一个重要的改革，即舒尔吉建立了以国家为主导的税收补偿或者税收返还制度，不仅地方行省向中央缴纳 bala 税，而且中央也针对地方行省的纳税进行适当的不同形式的返还或者补偿，以此建立起中央和地方之间的某种平衡，体现了乌尔中央政府对经济的调控作用以及王朝建立初期的国家治理措施。在阿马尔辛统治时期，乌尔第三王朝达到鼎盛，但是王朝内外依然存在诸多矛盾和不稳定因素，为了应对这些变化，阿马尔辛国王一共进行了两次税制改革。在第一次税制改革中，阿马尔辛对行省税进行了微调，统一了外围行省的税率，规定了牛羊缴纳的比例为 1∶10。而且，这次税制改革更加注重实用性。在第二次税制改革中，阿马尔辛对 mu-DU 术语及其相关文献的记录进行了改革，并且对行省税进行了更为细化的改革，设立了专门负责 bala 税的官员机构。在舒辛统治时期，乌尔第三王朝由盛而衰，统治者的税制改革也由主动进取转为被动防御。以舒辛统治第 3 年的税制改革最为突出和彻底，舒辛建立了具体的王室税名目，对王室税的性质和功能进行了改革，并且建立了具体的外围行省赋税名目，正式设立了 gun_2 ma-da 税。舒辛 3 年的税制改革，是继舒尔吉建立赋税制度以来，乌尔第三王朝的统治者对赋税制度进行的最大的一次改革运动，体现了乌尔第三王朝在晚期的国家治理特征。

第六，乌尔第三王朝的赋税基本上都属于实物税，还没有产生人头税。虽然白银也作为课税形式之一，但是在乌尔第三王朝时期，它更可能是作为实物税的形式，并不具有货币的功能。乌尔第三王朝征收赋税的依据，是财产而非人身，这有利于保证国家财政收入的稳定。乌尔第三王朝赋税的征收，依据各级地方机构物产的多寡和特产的种类，徭役的摊派多服务于赋税的征收环节，作为赋税制度的一部分存在，根本没有严格意义上的人头税。乌尔第三王朝的土地和财产，名义上属于国王和王朝的保护神所有，以财产作为征税的依据和标准，可以确保乌尔国家在社会发展过程中依然获得较为稳定的财政收入，有利于国家治理各个方针政策的执行。乌尔第三王朝的实物税，依据纳税地区的物产，因地制宜地规定纳税形式，比如吉尔苏和温马分别向中央缴纳大麦和芦苇形式的 bala 税，而后

结　语

中央以牲畜形式的 bala 税返还给这两个地方行省，这些牲畜大多来源于乌尔第三王朝的外围行省和附属国，以 gun$_2$ ma-da 税或者 gun$_2$ 税的形式被缴纳到乌尔中央，通过中央的税收返还制度，不同的物产进行地区间的交流与互换，在稳定国家财政收入的基础上，尽可能实现乌尔第三王朝内部各个地区之间的资源互补与物产交流。

第七，赋税和徭役比较沉重，体现了中央集权统治对地方行省和被征服地区的剥削和压迫。实物和徭役是国家经济和财政收入的基础。从总体上讲，乌尔第三王朝的赋税征收比例是比较高的，其中核心行省 bala 税的税率大约是 50%，即地方行省约一半的收入要作为税收缴纳给中央政府，这种超高比例的赋税压力，直接被地方政府转移到普通劳动者身上，同时也隐含了地方行省的不稳定因素。外围行省的情况也不容乐观，带有军事性质的 gun$_2$ ma-da 税，将赋税压力转移到军事人员身上，这类人员既要承担战时从军作战的义务，又要在闲时从事农牧业生产，履行向乌尔中央缴纳牲畜税的义务。相比于外围区，乌尔第三王朝的附属国向乌尔中央缴纳的牲畜数量大得惊人。比如，在舒尔吉 47 年，阿丹顿一次性就向乌尔中央缴纳了 7200 头牛和 1618 只羊。埃布拉于舒尔吉 46 年，向乌尔中央缴纳了 1000 件木制品，孜姆达尔于阿马尔辛 7 年，向乌尔中央缴纳了 1115 件藤制器皿。这些沉重的赋税不仅加重了乌尔地方政府的负担，也带来的负面效应。劳役是乌尔第三王朝赋税的课税形式之一，也是赋税制度的重要组成要素。乌尔第三王朝的劳役负担同样十分沉重，以自由民为例，他们虽然享有完全的自由权，但是需要在一年中服半年劳役，即一年里有一半的时间用来服劳役。半自由民则需要整年为国家服役。乌尔第三王朝的沉重赋税也可以从文学作品中得到体现。据一则古代两河流域的谚语记载，人们最害怕的就是征税者。[①]

第八，乌尔第三王朝没有成文的赋税法，赋税的税率和纳税期限并不完全统一。尽管乌尔第三王朝的建立者乌尔纳姆颁布了目前已知最早的法典《乌尔纳姆法典》[②]，说明乌尔第三王朝有法制传统，但是在该法典中，我们并没有发现与赋税相关的条文和规定。截至目前，我们也没有发现乌

[①] S. Bertman, *Handbook to Life in Ancient Mesopotamia*, Oxford: Oxford University Press, 2003, p. 179.

[②] M. T. Roth, *Law Collections from Mesopotamia and Asia Minor*, Atlanta: Scholars Press, 1995, pp. 13 – 22.

尔第三王朝专门记载赋税法令和条文的相关文献。因此，乌尔第三王朝赋税的征收，很可能要依据各地的习惯或者国王的诏令。以核心行省 bala 税为例，中央政府在前一年需要制定来年每个月的 bala 税缴纳行省的名单和顺序，以期地方行省提前知晓自己的具体纳税期限。这些都说明，在乌尔第三王朝时期，至少应该存在类似于赋税管理和决策的专门机构，这样的机构组织应该直接听命于国王，或者由国王直接管理。我们尚不清楚是否存在赋税管理决策机构制定赋税规则的记录，但是至少已经具有习惯法的性质，只是还没有发展到成文法。不过，需要指出的是，在乌尔第三王朝的文献中，尤其是在温马文献中，已经明确记载征税人的相关术语（enku 或者 en-ku$_3$），说明了在当时已经有了专门的征收官员和机构，拥有"征收人"职业身份是官员包括库南那、乌尔巴巴、乌尔吉吉尔、乌尔玛米、乌尔宁伽尔、乌尔乌图和乌尔辛等。

　　乌尔第三王朝的赋税制度是古代两河流域早期历史发展中赋税制度的典型代表，不仅体现了早期两河流域文明经济制度的特征，而且对于两河流域后来的历史发展，尤其是赋税制度的演变，具有重要的影响和启示。作为古代两河流域赋税制度发展的重要阶段，乌尔第三王朝赋税制度扮演着承上启下的角色。乌尔第三王朝的统治者利用赋税来调节国家经济的发展，以经济手段来达到治理国家的目的，这是人类历史上最早的利用赋税的杠杆作用来调节国家经济政策的例子之一，对于后来的两河流域历史发展具有重要的引导和借鉴价值。乌尔第三王朝的赋税制度，一方面表现出其内容的广泛性，另一方面又在其起源、发展演变、征收形式、征收对象、赋税目的等诸多方面存在明显的独特性。乌尔第三王朝赋税制度与国家治理有密切关系，反映了经济基础与上层建筑之间密切的互动关系。乌尔第三王朝的赋税制度，始终都是为乌尔第三王朝的上层建筑服务，一直与乌尔第三王朝的对内中央集权统治和对外军事扩张有着密不可分的关系。乌尔第三王朝的赋税制度与古代两河流域历史发展密切相关，其许多税种在王朝灭亡之后的两河流域历史中，继续被延续使用，并且进行了演变和新的发展。

　　综上所述，乌尔第三王朝的赋税制度是一个内容广泛的统一体，是乌尔第三王朝的政治、经济和文化发展高度凝聚的结果，也是古代两河流域文明历史发展长河中的光辉杰作，深入研究这一问题，无疑对于研究古代

结　语

两河流域乃至古代世界的政治史、经济史和文明史，都具有极为重要的意义。我们对于这一问题的研究并没有彻底结束，随着既有材料的重新解读，尤其是新的考古发掘以及新资料的出土与整理，学界会不断取得新的研究成果，许多目前的困惑和谜团也将陆续被解开。我们对此满怀期待，并将不懈努力。

附　录

附录一　古代两河流域历史框架

时期	朝代	时间	时期	时间
	巴比伦尼亚			亚述
古苏美尔时期	早王朝	约公元前3200—前2350年		
	早王朝Ⅰ期	约公元前2900—前2700年		
	早王朝Ⅱ期	约公元前2700—前2600年		
	早王朝Ⅲa期	约公元前2600—前2500年		
	早王朝Ⅲb期	约公元前2600—前2350年		
	阿卡德王国	公元前2334—前2154年		
	库提王朝	约公元前2210—前2119年		
新苏美尔时期	拉伽什第二王朝（古地亚王朝）	约公元前2200—前2110年		
	乌鲁克第五王朝	公元前2119—前2112年		
	乌尔第三王朝	公元前2112—前2004年		

续表

时期	巴比伦尼亚		亚述	
	朝代	时间	时期	时间
古巴比伦时期	伊新王朝	公元前 2017—前 1794 年		
	拉尔萨王朝	公元前 2025—前 1763 年	古亚述／阿淑尔城邦	约公元前 2000—前 1809 年
	巴比伦第一王朝／古巴比伦王国	公元前 1894—前 1595 年	上美索不达米亚王国	公元前 1809—前 1741 年
中巴比伦时期	巴比伦第二王朝／海国王朝	公元前 1732—前 1460 年	米坦尼王国	约公元前 1500—前 1335 年
	巴比伦第三王朝／加喜特王朝	公元前 1570—前 1157 年		
	巴比伦第四王朝／伊新第二王朝	公元前 1156—前 1025 年	中亚述	约公元前 1400—前 1050 年
	巴比伦第五王朝	公元前 1024—前 1004 年		
	巴比伦第六王朝	公元前 1003—前 984 年		
	巴比伦第七王朝	公元前 983—前 978 年		
	巴比伦第八王朝	公元前 977—前 941 年		
	巴比伦第九王朝	公元前 940—前 732 年	新亚述	公元前 934—前 612 年
	亚述统治时期	公元前 731—前 627 年		
新巴比伦时期	巴比伦第十王朝／新巴比伦王国	公元前 626—前 539 年		

资料来源：A. L. Oppenheim, *Ancient Mesopotamia*, Chicago and London: The University of Chicago Press, 1964; G. Roux, *Ancient Iraq*, Middlesex: Penguin Books, 1966; M. Van de Mieroop, *A History of the Ancient Near East (ca. 3000 – 323 BC)*, Malden: Blackwell Publishing, 2004; D. O. Edzard, *Geschichte Mesopotamiens: Von den Sumerern bis zu Alexander dem Großen*, München: Verlag C. H. Beck, 2004.

附录二 乌尔第三王朝年名

国王	年	年名（楔文原文）	年名（中文译文）
乌尔纳姆	l	mu Ur-^{d}Nammu lugal	乌尔纳姆称王之年
	b*	mu en ^{d}Nanna maš-e ba-pad$_3$-da	南那神庙最高女祭司被选中之年
	c	mu KIB. KIB še Lagaš^{ki} giš bi$_2$-ra-a	拉伽什的大麦打谷之年
	d		驱逐库提人之年
	e/i		"乌尔城墙"首次始建之年
	e/ii		埃利都的恩基神庙、库阿尔的宁苏神庙和乌尔的伊南娜—宁库努纳神庙被建之年
	f		乌尔纳姆到尼普尔巡游之年
	g	mu e$_2$ ^{d}Nanna ba-du$_3$-a	南那神庙始建之年
	h	mu Ur-^{d}Nammu lugal-e sig-ta IGI. NIM-še$_3$ gir$_3$ si bi$_2$-sa$_2$-a	国王乌尔纳姆从下到上检修"道路"之年
	h/i		马干恢复与乌尔贸易之年
	h/ii		《乌尔纳姆法典》颁布之年
	h/iii		新的领土合并到乌尔王国之年
	i	mu en ^{d}Inana Unug^{ki}-a dumu Ur-^{d}Nammu lugal-a maš-e ba-pad$_3$-da	乌鲁克的伊南娜神庙最高女祭司、乌尔纳姆的后裔被选中之年
	j	mu ^{giš}gigir^d Nin-lil$_2$ ba-dim$_2$-ma	宁利尔的战车被制造之年
	k	mu e$_2$ ^{d}Nin-sun$_2$ Uri$_5^{ki}$-a ba-du$_3$-a	乌尔的宁苏神庙被建之年
	l	mu e$_2$ ^{d}En-lil$_2$-la$_2$ ba-du$_3$-a	恩利尔神庙被建之年
	m	mu I$_7$. EN. EREN$_2$. NUN ba-al	伊图尔温伽尔水渠被挖掘之年
	n	mu nin-dingir ^{d}Iškur maš-e pad$_3$-da	伊什库尔神庙的"宁丁吉尔"祭司被选中之年

续表

国王	年	年名（楔文原文）	年名（中文译文）
乌尔纳姆	o	mu uš e₂ ᵈNin-gublaga ki ba-a-gar	宁古布拉加神庙的地基被立之年
	p	mu bad₃ Uri₅ᵏⁱ-ma ba-du₃-a	"乌尔城墙"被建之年
	q	mu I₇-a-ᵈNin-tu ba-al	阿宁图水渠被挖掘之年
	r		乌尔纳姆在迪亚拉地区的远征；乌尔纳姆之死
舒尔吉	1	mu Šul-gi lugal	舒尔吉称王之年
	2	mu Šul-gi lugal Uri₅ᵏⁱ-ma-ke₄ ᵍⁱˢgu-za za-gin₃ ᵈEn-lil₂-ra i₃-na-ku₄-ra	乌尔国王舒尔吉为恩利尔进献青金石神座之年
	3	mu e₂-muhaldim ᵈNin-šubur ba-du₃-a	宁舒尔神庙的厨房被建之年
	4		（不清楚）
	5	mu uš e₂ ᵈNin-urta ki ba-a-gar	尼努尔塔神庙的地基被立之年
	6	mu BAD₃. GAL. ANᵏⁱ ki-bi-gi₄-a	德尔被毁之年
	6a	mu us₂-sa uš e₂ ᵈNin-urta ki-a bi₂-gar	尼努尔塔神庙的地基被立之次年
	7	mu gir₃ Nibruᵏⁱ si bi₂-sa₂-a	尼普尔道路被铺设之年
	7a	mu lugal-e Uri₅ᵏⁱ-ta	国王从乌尔而来之年
	8	mu ma₂ ᵈNin-lil₂-la₂ ba-du₈	宁利尔的船被补漏缝之年
	9	mu ᵈNanna Kar-zi-da e₂-a ba-ku₄	卡尔孜达的南那被带入神庙之年
	10	mu e₂-hur-sag lugal ba-du₃	国王的"山房"被建之年
	11	mu ᵈIštaran BAD₃. GAL. ANᵏⁱ e₂-a ba-ku₄	德尔的伊什塔兰被带入神庙之年
	12	mu Nu-ᵘᵐᵘˢmuš-da Ka-zal-luᵏⁱ e₂-a ba-ku₄	卡扎鲁的努姆什达被带入神庙之年
	12a	mu lugal Ba-gara₂ e₂-a-na ku₄-ra	"巴加拉"的王（宁吉尔苏）被带入神庙之年
	13	mu e₂-hal-bi lugal ba-du₃	国王的"冰房"被建之年
	13a	mu lugal Ba-gara₂ e₂-a ku₄-ra us₂-sa	"巴加拉"的王（宁吉尔苏）被带入神庙之次年
	14	mu ᵈNanna Nibruᵏⁱ e₂-a ba-ku₄	尼普尔的南那被带入神庙之年
	15	mu En-nir-zi-an-na en ᵈNanna maš₂-e i₃-pad₃	恩尼尔孜安娜被选为南那神庙最高女祭司之年
	16	mu na₂ ᵈNin-lil₂-la₂ ba-dim₂	宁利尔的"床"被建之年

续表

国王	年	年名（楔文原文）	年名（中文译文）
舒尔吉	17	mu En-nir-zi-an-na en ^{d}Nanna ba-hun-ga$_2$	恩尼尔孜安娜被任命为南那神庙最高女祭司之年
	18	mu Li$_2$-wir-mi-ta-šu dumu-lugal nam-nin Mar-ha-ši^{ki} ba-il$_2$	国王的女儿利维尔米塔苏被提升为马尔哈西的王后之年
	19	mu EZENxKASKAL^{ki} ki-bi ba-ab-gi$_4$	埃金卡斯卡尔被毁之年
	20	mu dumu Uri$_5^{ki}$-ma lu$_2$-giš-gid$_2$-še$_3$ KA ba-ab-kešda	乌尔公民被征召为长矛兵之年
	20a	mu ^{d}Nin-hur-sag-ga$_2$ nu-tur e$_2$-a-na ba-an-ku$_4$	努图尔的宁胡尔萨格被带入神庙之年
	21	mu ^{d}Nin-urta ensi$_2$-gal ^{d}En-lil$_2$-la$_2$-ke$_4$ e$_2$ ^{d}En-lil$_2$ ^{d}Nin-lil$_2$-la$_2$-ke$_4$ eš-bar-kin ba-an-du$_{11}$-ga ^{d}Šul-gi lugal Uri$_5^{ki}$-ma-ke$_4$ gan$_2$ nig$_2$-kas$_7$ šuku e$_2$ ^{d}En-lil$_2$ ^{d}Nin-lil$_2$-la$_2$-ke$_4$ si bi$_2$-sa$_2$-a	恩利尔的重要"土地管理员"尼努尔塔在恩利尔和宁利尔神庙发布圣谕：乌尔国王舒尔吉整顿恩利尔和宁利尔神庙的土地和账目
	21a	mu BAD$_3$. AN^{ki} ba-hul	德尔被毁之年
	22	mu us$_2$-sa BAD$_3$. AN^{ki} ba-hul	德尔被毁之次年
	23	mu ^{d}Šul-gi lugal-e a$_2$-mah ^{d}En-lil$_2$ sum-ma-ni […]	恩利尔授予国王舒尔吉最高权力
	24	mu Kara$_2$-har^{ki} ba-hul	卡拉哈尔被毁之年
	25	mu Si-mu-ru-um^{ki} ba-hul	西穆卢姆被毁之年
	26	mu Si-mu-ru-um^{ki} a-ra$_2$ 2-kam-ma-aš ba-hul	西穆卢姆第二次被毁之年
	27	mu Ha-ar-ši^{ki} ba-hul	哈尔西被毁之年
	28	mu en Eridu^{ki}-ga ba-hun-ga$_2$	埃利都的最高女祭司被任命之年
	29	mu us$_2$-sa en Eridu^{ki}-ga ba-hun-ga$_2$	埃利都的最高女祭司被任命之次年
	30	mu dumu-munus lugal ensi$_2$ An-ša-an^{ki}-ke$_4$ ba-tuku	国王的女儿嫁给安珊恩西之年
	31	mu Kara$_2$-har^{ki} a-ra$_2$ 2-kam-ma-aš ba-hul	卡拉哈尔第二次被毁之年
	32	mu Si-mu-ru-um^{ki} a-ra$_2$ 3-kam-ma-aš ba-hul	西穆卢姆第三次被毁之年
	33	mu us$_2$-sa Si-mu-ru-um^{ki} a-ra$_2$ 3-kam-ma-aš ba-hul	西穆卢姆第三次被毁之次年

续表

国王	年	年名（楔文原文）	年名（中文译文）
舒尔吉	34	mu An-ša-an^{ki} ba-hul	安珊被毁之年
	35	mu us$_2$-sa An-ša-an^{ki} ba-hul	安珊被毁之次年
	36	mu ^{d}Nanna Kar-zi-da^{ki} a-ra$_2$ 2-kam-aš e$_2$-a ba-ku$_4$	卡尔孜达的南那第二次进入神庙之年
	37	mu bad$_3$ ma-da ba-du$_3$	（乌尔）国家的长墙被建之年
	38	mu us$_2$-sa mu bad$_3$ ma-da ba-du$_3$	（乌尔）国家的长墙被建之次年
	39	mu e$_2$ Puzur$_4$-iš-^{d}Da-gan-na ba-du$_3$	普兹瑞什达干被建之年
	40	mu us$_2$-sa e$_2$ Puzur$_4$-iš-^{d}Da-gan-na ba-du$_3$	普兹瑞什达干被建之次年
	41	mu us$_2$-sa e$_2$ Puzur$_4$-iš-^{d}Da-gan-na ba-du$_3$ mu us$_2$-sa-a-bi	普兹瑞什达干被建之次年的次年
	42	mu Ša-aš-ru^{ki} ba-hul	沙什卢姆被毁之年
	43	mu En-ubur-zi-an-na en ^{d}Nanna maš-e i$_3$-pad$_3$	恩乌布尔孜安娜被选为南那神庙最高女祭司之年
	44	mu Si-mu-ru-um^{ki} u$_3$ Lu-lu-bi^{ki} a-ra$_2$ 10-la$_2$-1-kam-aš ba-hul	西穆卢姆和卢卢布第九次被毁之年
	45	mu ^{d}Šul-gi nita kala-ga lugal Uri$_5^{ki}$-ma lugal an-ub-da-limmu$_2$-ba-ke$_4$ Ur-bi$_2$-lum^{ki} Si-mu-ru-um^{ki} Lu-lu-bu^{ki} u$_3$ Kara$_2$-har^{ki}-ra aš-eš šu du$_{11}$-ga šu-tibir-ra im-mi-ra	强大的男人、乌尔之王、四方之王舒尔吉同时征服乌尔比隆、西穆卢姆、卢卢布和卡拉哈尔之年
	46	mu ^{d}Šul-gi nita kala-ga lugal Uri$_5^{ki}$-ma lugal an-ub-da-limmu$_2$-ba-ke$_4$ Ki-maš^{ki} Hu-ur$_5$-ti^{ki} u$_3$ ma-da-bi u$_4$-aš-a mu-hul	强大的男人、乌尔之王、四方之王舒尔吉在同一天摧毁基马什、胡尔提及其地区之年
	47	mu ^{d}Šul-gi nita kala-ga lugal Uri$_5^{ki}$-ma lugal an-ub-da-limmu$_2$-ba-ke$_4$ Ki-maš^{ki} Hu-ur$_5$-ti^{ki} u$_3$ ma-da-bi u$_4$ aš-a mu-hul-a mu us$_2$-sa-a-bi	强大的男人、乌尔之王、四方之王舒尔吉在同一天摧毁基马什、胡尔提及其地区之次年
	48	mu Ha-ar-ši^{ki} Ki-maš^{ki} Hu-ur$_5$-ti^{ki} u$_3$ ma-da-bi u$_4$-aš-a ba-hul	哈尔西、基马什、胡尔提及其地区在同一天被毁之年

续表

国王	年	年名（楔文原文）	年名（中文译文）
阿马尔辛	1	mu ^{d}Amar-^{d}Suen lugal	阿马尔辛称王之年
	2	mu Ur-bi$_2$-lum^{ki} ba-hul	乌尔比隆被毁之年
	3	mu ^{d}gu-za ^{d}En-lil$_2$-la$_2$ ba-dim$_2$	恩利尔的神座被制造之年
	3a	mu En-mah-gal-an-na en ^{d}Nanna maš$_2$-e i$_3$-pad$_3$	恩马赫伽尔安娜被选为南那神庙最高女祭司之年
	4	mu En-mah-gal-an-na en ^{d}Nanna ba-hun	恩马赫伽尔安娜被任命为南那神庙最高女祭司之年
	5	mu En-unu$_6$-gal ^{d}Inana Unug^{ki} ba-hun	恩乌努伽尔（安娜）被任命为乌鲁克的伊南娜神庙最高女祭司之年
	6	mu Ša-aš-ru-um^{ki} a-ra$_2$ 2-kam ba-hul	沙什卢姆第二次被毁之年
	6a	mu Ša-aš-ru^{ki} ba-hul	沙什卢姆被毁之年
	7	mu Hu-uh$_2$-nu-ri^{ki} ba-hul	胡赫努里被毁之年
	8	mu en Eridu^{ki} ba-hun	埃利都的最高女祭司被任命之年
	9	mu En-^{d}Nanna-^{d}Amar-^{d}Suen-ra-ki-ag$_2$ en ^{d}Nanna Kar-zi-da-ka ba-hun	恩南那阿马尔辛拉吉阿格被任命为卡尔孜达的南那神庙最高女祭司之年
舒辛	1	mu ^{d}Šu-^{d}Suen lugal	舒辛称王之年
	2	mu ^{d}Šu-^{d}Suen lugal Uri$_5^{ki}$-ma-ke$_4$ ma$_2$ dara$_3$-abzu ^{d}En-ki in-dim$_2$	乌尔之王舒辛为恩基建造"阿布祖野山羊"船之年
	3	mu ^{d}Šu-^{d}Suen lugal Uri$_5^{ki}$-ma-ke$_4$ Si-ma-num$_2^{ki}$ mu-hul	乌尔之王舒辛摧毁西马努姆之年
	4	mu ^{d}Šu-^{d}Suen lugal Uri$_5^{ki}$-ma-ke$_4$ bad$_3$ mar-tu Mu-ri-iq-ti-id-ni-im mu-du$_3$	乌尔之王舒辛建造阿摩利长城"疏远提德努姆"之年
	5	mu us$_2$-sa ^{d}Šu-^{d}Suen lugal Uri$_5^{ki}$-ma-ke$_4$ bad$_3$ mar-tu Mu-ri-iq-ti-id-ni-im mu-du$_3$	乌尔之王舒辛建造阿摩利长城"疏远提德努姆"之次年
	6	mu ^{d}Šu-^{d}Suen lugal Uri$_5^{ki}$-ma-ke$_4$ na-ru$_2$-a mah ^{d}En-lil$_2$ ^{d}Nin-lil$_2$-ra mu-ne-du$_3$	乌尔之王舒辛为恩利尔和宁利尔建造圣碑之年
	7	mu ^{d}Šu-^{d}Suen lugal Uri$_5^{ki}$-ma-ke$_4$ ma-da Za-ab-ša-li^{ki} mu-hul	乌尔之王舒辛摧毁扎布沙里地区之年
	8	mu ^{d}Šu-^{d}Suen lugal Uri$_5^{ki}$-ma-ke$_4$ ma$_2$-gur$_8$ mah ^{d}En-lil$_2$ ^{d}Nin-lil$_2$-ra mu-ne-dim$_2$	乌尔之王舒辛为恩利尔和宁利尔建造圣船"马古尔"之年
	9	mu ^{d}Šu-^{d}Suen lugal Uri$_5^{ki}$-ma-ke$_4$ e$_2$ ^{d}Šara$_2$ Umma^{ki} mu-du$_3$	乌尔之王舒辛建造温马的沙拉神庙之年

附　录

续表

国王	年	年名（楔文原文）	年名（中文译文）
伊比辛	1	mu ^{d}I-bi$_2$-^{d}Suen lugal	伊比辛称王之年
	2	mu en ^{d}Inana maš$_2$-e i$_3$-pad$_3$	伊南娜神庙最高女祭司被选中之年
	3	mu ^{d}I-bi$_2$-^{d}Suen lugal Uri$_5^{ki}$-ma-ke$_4$ Si-mu-ru-um^{ki} mu-hul	乌尔之王伊比辛摧毁西穆卢姆之年
	4	mu En-am-gal-an-na en ^{d}Inana ba-hun	恩阿姆伽尔安娜被任命为伊南娜神庙最高女祭司之年
	5	mu Tu-ki-in-PA-mi-ig-ri-ša dumu-munus lugal ensi$_2$ Za-ab-ša-li^{ki}-ke$_4$ ba-an-tuku	扎布沙里恩西迎娶（乌尔）国王女儿图金哈提米格丽莎之年
	6	mu ^{d}I-bi$_2$-^{d}Suen lugal Uri$_5^{ki}$-ma-ke$_4$ Nibru^{ki} Uri$_5^{ki}$-ma bad$_3$ gal-bi mu-du$_3$	乌尔之王伊比辛建造尼普尔和乌尔的宏伟城墙之年
	7	mu us$_2$-sa ^{d}I-bi$_2$-^{d}Suen lugal Uri$_5^{ki}$-ma-ke$_4$ Nibru^{ki} Uri$_5^{ki}$-ma bad$_3$ gal-bi mu-du$_3$	乌尔之王伊比辛建造尼普尔和乌尔的宏伟城墙之次年
	8	mu us$_2$-sa ^{d}I-bi$_2$-^{d}Suen lugal Uri$_5^{ki}$-ma-ke$_4$ Nibru^{ki} Uri$_5^{ki}$-ma bad$_3$ gal-bi mu-du$_3$-a mu us$_2$-sa-bi	乌尔之王伊比辛建造尼普尔和乌尔的宏伟城墙之次年的次年
	9	mu ^{d}I-bi$_2$-^{d}Suen lugal Uri$_5^{ki}$-ma-ke$_4$ Hu-uh$_2$-nu-ri KA.BAD ma-da An-ša-an^{ki}-še$_3$ a$_2$-dugud ba-ši-in-gin […] -ra-gin$_7$ a$_2$-mah si$_3$-bi sa bi$_2$-in-gar	乌尔之王伊比辛带领重装军队进军胡赫努里，安珊地区的"开口"，如……一样，将其包围，用网将其抓住
	10	mu En-nir-si$_3$-an-na en ^{d}Nanna maš$_2$-e in-pad$_3$	恩尼尔希安娜被选为南那神庙最高女祭司之年
	11	mu En-nam-ti-^{d}I-bi$_2$-^{d}Suen-ka-še$_3$ kiri$_3$ šu-gal$_2$ x-unu en ^{d}En-ki-ka maš$_2$-e i$_3$-pad$_3$	恩纳姆提伊比辛卡塞被选为恩基神庙最高女祭司之年
	12	mu ^{d}I-bi$_2$-^{d}Suen lugal Uri$_5^{ki}$-ma-ke$_4$ gu-za an ^{d}Nanna-ra mu-na-dim$_2$	乌尔之王伊比辛为南那建造神座之年
	13	mu us$_2$-sa ^{d}I-bi$_2$-^{d}Suen lugal Uri$_5^{ki}$-ma-ke$_4$ gu-za an ^{d}Nanna-ra mu-na-dim$_2$	乌尔之王伊比辛为南那建造神座之次年
	14	mu ^{d}I-bi$_2$-^{d}Suen lugal Uri$_5^{ki}$-ma-ke$_4$ Šušin^{ki} A-dam-dun^{ki} ma-da A-wa-an^{ki}-ka u$_4$-gin$_7$ ŠID bi$_2$-in-gi$_4$ u$_4$-AŠ-a mu-un-GAM u$_3$ en-bi LU$_2$xKAR-a mi-ni-in-dab$_5$-ba-a	乌尔之王伊比辛席卷苏萨、阿丹顿和阿万地区，在一天内使他们投降，将他们的统帅作为俘虏抓获之年

243

续表

国王	年	年名（楔文原文）	年名（中文译文）
伊比辛	15	mu ^{d}I-bi$_2$-^{d}Suen lugal Uri$_5^{ki}$-ma-ra ^{d}I-nana-a ša$_3$-ki-ag$_2$-ga$_2$-ni dalla mu-un-na-an-e$_3$-a	南那通过仁慈之心，使乌尔之王伊比辛壮丽前行之年
	16	mu ^{d}I-bi$_2$-^{d}Suen lugal Uri$_5^{ki}$-ma-ke$_4$ ^{d}Nanna-ar ^{d}Nun-me-te-an-na mu-na-dim$_2$	乌尔之王伊比辛为南那制造"王子，天之装饰"之年
	17	mu ^{d}I-bi$_2$-^{d}Suen lugal Uri$_5^{ki}$-ma-ra mar-tu a$_2$-IM-ulu$_3$ ul-ta uru^{ki} nu-zu gu$_2$ im-ma-na-na-ga$_2$-ar	南方边界的阿摩利人，自古至今没有城市，向乌尔之王伊比辛屈服之年
	18	mu ^{d}I-bi$_2$-^{d}Suen lugal Uri$_5^{ki}$-ma-ke$_4$ ^{d}Nin-lil$_2$ u$_3$ ^{d}Inana-ra e$_2$ šutum$_2$-ku$_3$ mu-ne-du$_3$	乌尔之王伊比辛为宁利尔和伊南娜建造华丽的储藏房之年
	19	mu us$_2$-sa ^{d}I-bi$_2$-^{d}Suen lugal Uri$_5^{ki}$-ma-ke$_4$ ^{d}Nin-lil$_2$ u$_3$ ^{d}Inana-ra e$_2$ šutum$_2$-ku$_3$ mu-ne-du$_3$	乌尔之王伊比辛为宁利尔和伊南娜建造华丽的储藏房之次年
	20	mu ^{d}I-bi$_2$-^{d}Suen lugal Uri$_5^{ki}$-ma En-lil$_2$-le me-lam$_2$-a-ni kur-kur-ra bi$_2$-in-dul$_4$	恩利尔使乌尔之王伊比辛的可怕光辉笼罩周边土地之年
	21	mu ^{d}I-bi$_2$-^{d}Suen lugal Uri$_5^{ki}$-ma-ke$_4$ ^{d}Nin-igi-zi-bar-ra balag ^{d}Inana-ra mu-na-dim$_2$	乌尔之王伊比辛为伊南娜建造"宁伊吉孜巴拉"竖琴之年
	22	mu ^{d}I-bi$_2$-^{d}Suen lugal Uri$_5^{ki}$-ma-ke$_4$ a-ma-ru nig$_2$-du$_{11}$-ga dingir-re-ne-ke$_4$ za$_3$-an-ki im-suh$_3$-suh$_3$-a Uri$_5^{ki}$ URUxUD^{ki} tab-ba bi$_2$-in-ge-en	乌尔之王伊比辛加固被诸神下令的洪水以及整个世界的震动所毁坏的乌尔城和乌鲁乌德城之年
	23	mu ^{d}I-bi$_2$-^{d}Suen lugal Uri$_5^{ki}$-ma-ra ugu$_2^{ku}$-bi-dugudkur-bi mu-na-e-ra	外国人给乌尔之王伊比辛带来一只"蠢猴"之年
	24	mu [⋯] bi$_2$-ra	（乌尔或伊比辛被击败之年？）

* 这里单独的字母表示年份不详。"数字+字母"表示该年名的另一种写法。

资料来源：D. Frayne, *Ur III Period* (*2112 - 2004 BC*), RIME 3/2, Toronto：University of Toronto Press, 1997; RIME 3/2; M. Sigrist, T. Gomi, *The Comprehensive Catalogue of Published Ur III Tablets*, Bethesda：CDL Press, 1991.

附录三 乌尔第三王朝月名

I. 普兹瑞什达干月名

普兹瑞什达干月名（舒辛3年及之前）

月份	语义符	汉译
1	iti maš-da$_3$/ku$_3$-gu$_7$	食羚羊月/食圣羊月
2	iti ses-da/šah$_2$-ku$_3$-gu$_7$	食"赛思达"猪月/食圣猪月
3	iti u$_5$-bi$_2$ $^{(mušen)}$-gu$_7$	食"乌比"鸟月
4	iti ki-siki ^{d}Nin-a-zu	宁阿祖的羊毛地月
5	iti ezem ^{d}Nin-a-zu	宁阿祖节月
6	iti a$_2$-ki-ti	阿基图节月
7	iti ezem ^{d}Šul-gi	舒尔吉节月
8	iti šu-eš$_{(5)}$-ša	"三只手"月
9	iti ezem mah	盛大节月
10	iti ezem An-na	安节月
11	iti (ezem) $^{(d)}$Me-ki-gal$_2$	美吉伽尔节月
12	iti še-sag$_{(11)}$-ku$_5$	大麦收割月

普兹瑞什达干月名（舒辛3年之后）

月份	语义符	汉译
1	iti še-sag$_{(11)}$-ku$_5$	大麦收割月
2	iti maš-da$_3$/ku$_3$-gu$_7$	食羚羊月/食圣羊月
3	iti ses-da/šah$_2$-ku$_3$-gu$_7$	食"赛思达"猪月/食圣猪月
4	iti u$_5$-bi$_2$ $^{(mušen)}$-gu$_7$	食"乌比"鸟月
5	iti ki-siki ^{d}Nin-a-zu	宁阿祖的羊毛地月
6	iti ezem ^{d}Nin-a-zu	宁阿祖节月
7	iti a$_2$-ki-ti	阿基图节月

续表

I. 普兹瑞什达干月名

普兹瑞什达干月名（舒辛 3 年之后）

月份	语义符	汉译
8	iti ezem ^{d}Šul-gi	舒尔吉节月
9	iti ezem ^{d}Šu-^{d}Suen	舒辛节月
10	iti ezem mah	盛大节月
11	iti ezem An-na	安节月
12	iti（ezem）$^{(d)}$Me-ki-gal$_2$	美吉伽尔节月

II. 乌尔月名

月份	语义符	汉译
1	iti še-sag$_{(11)}$-ku$_5$	大麦收割月
2	iti maš-da$_3$/ku$_3$-gu$_7$	食羚羊月／食圣羊月
3	iti ses-da/šah$_2$-ku$_3$-gu$_7$	食"赛思达"猪月／食圣猪月
4	iti u$_5$-bi$_2$$^{(mušen)}$-gu$_7$	食"乌比"鸟月
5	iti ki-siki ^{d}Nin-a-zu	宁阿祖的羊毛地月
6	iti ezem ^{d}Nin-a-zu	宁阿祖节月
7	iti a$_2$-ki-ti	阿基图节月
8	iti ezem ^{d}Šul-gi	舒尔吉节月
9	iti šu-eš$_{(5)}$-ša	"三只手"月
10	iti ezem mah	盛大节月
11	iti ezem An-na	安节月
12	iti（ezem）$^{(d)}$Me-ki-gal$_2$	美吉伽尔节月

III. 尼普尔月名

月份	语义符	汉译
1	iti bara$_2$-za$_3$-gar	圣座月
2	iti gu$_4$-si-su	公牛角月
3	iti sig$_4$-（g）a	泥砖月
4	iti šu-numun	播种月
5	iti ne-ne-gar	放火月
6	iti kin ^{d}Inana	伊南娜工作月
7	iti du$_6$-ku$_3$	圣丘月

续表

III. 尼普尔月名

月份	语义符	汉译
8	iti apin-du$_8$-a	犁耕月
9	iti gan-gan-e$_3$	"甘甘埃"月
10	iti ku$_3$ ab-e$_3$	"库阿布埃"月
11	iti udru^{duru5}	"乌德鲁"月
12	iti še-sag$_{(11)}$-ku$_5$	大麦收割月

IV. 吉尔苏月名

吉尔苏月名(舒尔吉12年及之前)

1	iti GAN$_2$-maš	灌溉地月
2	iti gu$_4$-ra$_2$-bi$_2$-mu$_2$-mu$_2$	公牛生长月
3	iti ezem^{d}Li$_9$-si$_4$	里希节月
4	iti šu-numun	播种月
5	iti munu$_4$-gu$_7$	食麦芽月
6	iti ezem ^{d}Dumu-zi	杜牧孜节月
7	iti UR	"乌尔"月
8	iti ezem^{d}Ba-ba$_6$	巴巴节月
9	iti mu-šu-du$_7$	"穆舒杜"月
10	iti amar-a-a-si	安置牛仔月
11	iti še-sag$_{(11)}$-ku$_5$	大麦收割月
12	iti še-il$_2$-la	大麦生长月

吉尔苏月名(舒尔吉12年之后)

1	iti GAN$_2$-maš	灌溉地月
2	iti gu$_4$-ra$_2$-bi$_2$-mu$_2$-mu$_2$	公牛生长月
3	iti ezem^{d}Li$_9$-si$_4$	里希节月
4	iti šu-numun	播种月
5	iti munu$_4$-gu$_7$	食麦芽月
6	iti ezem ^{d}Dumu-zi	杜牧孜节月
7	iti ezem ^{d}Šul-gi	舒尔吉节月

续表

IV. 吉尔苏月名

吉尔苏月名（舒尔吉 12 年之后）

月份	语义符	汉译
8	iti ezem ^{d}Ba-ba$_6$	巴巴节月
9	iti mu-šu-du$_7$	"穆舒杜"月
10	iti amar-a-a-si	安置牛仔月
11	iti še-sag$_{(11)}$-ku$_5$	大麦收割月
12	iti še-il$_2$-la	大麦生长月

V. 温马月名

温马月名（舒尔吉 30 年之前）

月份	语义符	汉译
1	iti še-sag$_{(11)}$-ku$_5$	大麦收割月
2	iti sig$_4$ ^{giš}i/u$_3$-šub-ba-gar	砖模铺砖月
3	iti še-kar-ra-gal$_2$-la	大麦入市月
4	iti nesag	第一果月
5	iti dal	占卜师月
6	iti šu-numun	播种月
7	iti min$_{(3)}$-eš$_3$	双神殿月
8	iti e$_2$-iti-6	六个月神庙月
9	iti ^{d}Li$_9$-si$_4$	里希月
10	iti UR	"乌尔"月
11	iti Pa$_{4/5}$-u$_2$-e	（神）帕乌埃月
12	iti ^{d}Dumu-zi	杜牧孜月

温马月名（舒尔吉 30 年—阿马尔辛 6 年）

月份	语义符	汉译
1	iti še-sag$_{(11)}$-ku$_5$	大麦收割月
2	iti sig$_4$ ^{giš}i/u$_3$-šub-ba-gar	砖模铺砖月
3	iti še-kar-ra-gal$_2$-la	大麦入市月
4	iti nesag	第一果月
5	iti dal	占卜师月
6	iti šu-numun	播种月
7	iti min$_{(3)}$-eš$_3$	双神殿月

续表

V. 温马月名

温马月名（舒尔吉30年—阿马尔辛6年）

月份	语义符	汉译
8	iti e$_2$-iti-6	六个月神庙月
9	iti ^{d}Li$_9$-si$_4$	里希月
10	iti ezem ^{d}Šul-gi	舒尔吉节月
11	iti Pa$_{4/5}$-u$_2$-e	（神）帕乌埃月
12	iti ^{d}Dumu-zi	杜牧孜月

温马月名（阿马尔辛7年—舒辛2年）

月份	语义符	汉译
1	iti še-sag$_{(11)}$-ku$_5$	大麦收割月
2	iti sig$_4$ ^{giš}i/u$_3$-šub-ba-gar	砖模铺砖月
3	iti še-kar-ra-gal$_2$-la	大麦入市月
4	iti nesag	第一果月
5	iti dal	占卜师月
6	iti šu-numun	播种月
7	iti ezem ^{d}Amar-^{d}Suen	阿马尔辛节月
8	iti e$_2$-iti-6	六个月神庙月
9	iti ^{d}Li$_9$-si$_4$	里希月
10	iti ezem ^{d}Šul-gi	舒尔吉节月
11	iti Pa$_{4/5}$-u$_2$-e	（神）帕乌埃月
12	iti ^{d}Dumu-zi	杜牧孜月

温马月名（舒辛3年之后）

月份	语义符	汉译
1	iti še-sag$_{(11)}$-ku$_5$	大麦收割月
2	iti sig$_4$ ^{giš}i/u$_3$-šub-ba-gar	砖模铺砖月
3	iti še-kar-ra-gal$_2$-la	大麦入市月
4	iti nesag	第一果月
5	iti dal	占卜师月
6	iti šu-numun	播种月
7	iti min$_{(3)}$-eš$_3$	双神殿月

续表

V. 温马月名

温马月名（舒辛 3 年之后）

月份	语义符	汉译
8	iti e$_2$-iti-6	六个月神庙月
9	iti ^{d}Li$_9$-si$_4$	里希月
10	iti ezem ^{d}Šul-gi	舒尔吉节月
11	iti Pa$_{4/5}$-u$_2$-e	（神）帕乌埃月
12	iti ^{d}Dumu-zi	杜牧孜月

VI. 伊利萨格里格月名

伊利萨格里格月名（Owen）

月份	语义符	汉译
1	iti šu-gar-ra	任务完成月
2	iti ^{giš}apin	犁耕月
3	iti kir$_{11}$-si-ak	调整母绵羊羔月
4	iti ezem ^{d}Li$_9$-si$_4$	里希节月
5	iti ezem a-bi	阿比节月
6	iti gi-sig-ga	削芦苇月
7	iti ezem ^{d}Šul-gi	舒尔吉节月
8	iti nig$_2$ ^{d}En-lil$_2$-la$_2$	恩利尔财产月
9	iti ezem a-dara$_4$	野山羊节月
10	iti nig$_2$-e-ga	"埃加"财产月
11	iti ezem An-na	安节月
12	iti še-sag$_{(11)}$-ku$_5$	大麦收割月

伊利萨格里格月名（Ozaki）

月份	语义符	汉译
1	iti šu-gar-ra	任务完成月
2	iti šu-gar-gal	任务圆满完成月
3	iti ^{giš}apin	犁耕月
4	iti ezem^{d}Li$_9$-si$_4$	里希节月
5	iti ezem a-bi	阿比节月
6	iti gi-sig-ga	削芦苇月

续表

VI. 伊利萨格里格月名

伊利萨格里格月名（Ozaki）

月份	语义符	汉译
7	iti ezem ^{d}Šul-gi	舒尔吉节月
8	iti nig$_2$ ^{d}En-lil$_2$-la$_2$	恩利尔财产月
9	iti kir$_{11}$-si-ak	调整母绵羊羔月
10	iti nig$_2$-e-ga	"埃加"财产月
11	iti ezem a-dara$_4$	野山羊节月
12	iti še-sag$_{(11)}$-ku$_5$	大麦收割月

VII. 阿达布月名

1	iti šu-gar-ra	任务完成月
2	—	
3	iti a$_2$-ki-ti	阿基图月
4	iti ku$_3$ ab-e$_3$	"库阿布埃"月
5	iti ga$_2$-udu-ur$_4$	绵羊房丰收月
6	iti ezem ^{d}Dumu-zi	杜牧孜节月
7	—	
8	—	
9	iti ezem ^{d}Šuba$_3$-nun-na	舒巴努纳节月
10	iti ezem ^{d}Nin-mug	宁姆格节月
11	iti še-sag$_{(11)}$-ku$_5$	大麦收割月
12	iti du$_6$-ku$_3$	圣丘月

VIII. 伽尔沙纳月名（同乌尔月名）

1	iti še-sag$_{(11)}$-ku$_5$	大麦收割月
2	iti maš-da$_3$/ku$_3$-gu$_7$	食羚羊月/食圣羊月
3	iti ses-da/šah$_2$-ku$_3$-gu$_7$	食"赛思达"猪月/食圣猪月
4	iti u$_5$-bi$_2$$^{(mušen)}$-gu$_7$	食"乌比"鸟月
5	iti ki-siki ^{d}Nin-a-zu	宁阿祖的羊毛地月
6	iti ezem ^{d}Nin-a-zu	宁阿祖节月
7	iti a$_2$-ki-ti	阿基图节月

251

续表

月份	VIII. 伽尔沙纳月名（同乌尔月名） 伊利萨格里格月名（Ozaki）语义符	汉译
8	iti ezem ᵈŠul-gi	舒尔吉节月
9	iti šu-eš₍₅₎-ša	"三只手"月
10	iti ezem mah	盛大节月
11	iti ezem An-na	安节月
12	iti（ezem）⁽ᵈ⁾Me-ki-gal₂	美吉伽尔节月

资料来源：H. Hunger, "Kalender", *Reallexikonder Assyriologie und Vorderasiatischen Archäologie*, Vol. 5（1976 - 1980）, pp. 297 - 303; R. M. Whiting, "Some Observations on the Drehem Calendar", *Zeitschrift für Assyriologie und Vorderasiatische Archäologie*, Vol. 69（1979）, pp. 6 - 33; T. Gomi, "The Calendars of Ur and Puzriš-Dagān in the Early Ur-III Period", *Acta Sumeriologica*, Vol. 1（1979）, pp. 1 - 11; F. Pomponio, "The Reichskalender of Ur III in the Umma Texts", *Zeitschrift für Assyriologie und Vorderasiatische Archäologie*, Vol. 79（1989）, pp. 10 - 13; W. Sallaberger, *Der kultische Kalender der Ur III-Zeit*, Untersuchungen zur Assyriologie und Vorderasiatischen Archäologie 7/1, Berlin and New York: Walter de Gruyter, 1993, pp. 7 - 11; M. Cohen, *The Cultic Calendars of the Ancient Near East*, Bethesda: CDL Press, 1993, pp. 23 - 224; M. Such-Gutiérrez, "Der Kalendar von Adab im 3. Jahrtausend", in L. Feliu, et al（eds.）, *Time and History in the Ancient Near East: Proceedings of the 56th Recontre Assyriologique Internationale at Barcelona 26 - 30 July 2010*, Winona Lake: Eisenbrauns, 2013, pp. 325 - 340.

附录四　度量衡单位对照

重量单位

名称			进制	现代重量
苏美尔语	英译	汉译		
še	grain	麦	1 še	约 0.046 克
gin₂	shekel	舍客勒	180 še	约 8.3 克
ma-na	mina	米纳	60 gin₂	约 500 克
gu₂	talent	塔兰特	60 ma-na	约 30 千克

长度单位

名称			进制	现代长度
苏美尔语	英译	汉译		
šu-si	finger	指	1 šu-si	约 1.66 厘米
kuš₃	cubit	库比特	20 šu-si	约 33 厘米
gi	reed	里德	6 kuš₃	约 3 米
ninda			12 kuš₃	约 6 米
gar-du	cord	考德	2 gi	约 6 米
eš₂			10 gar-du	约 60 米
uš			6 eš₂	约 360 米
danna			30 uš	约 11 千米

续表

面积单位

名称			进制	现代面积
苏美尔语	英译	汉译		
sar	garden	加顿	1 sar	约36平方米
iku	field	场	100 sar	约3600平方米
bur$_3^{iku}$		布尔	18 iku	约64800平方米
bur$_3$'u^{iku}		布尔乌	10 bur$_3^{iku}$	约648000平方米
šar$_2^{iku}$		沙尔	6 bur$_3$'u^{iku}	约3.8平方千米
šar$_2$'u^{iku}		沙尔乌	10 šar$_2^{iku}$	约38平方千米

容积单位

名称			进制	现代容积
苏美尔语	英译	汉译		
gin$_2$	shekel	舍客勒		
sila$_3$	quart	希拉	60 gin$_2$	约1升
ban$_2$	seah	班	10 sila$_3$	约10升
nigida / barig		巴里格	6 ban$_2$	约60升
gur	Kor	古尔	5 nigida / barig	约300升
guru$_7$	grain-heap	筒仓	3600 gur	约1080000升

资料来源：J. Høyrup, *Lengths, Widths, Surfaces: A Portrait of Old Babylonian Algebra and Its Kin*, New York: Springer, 2002.

附录五　动物（牲畜）的种类与级别

种类	公		母	
牛	gu₄	公牛	ab₂	母牛
	gu₄ niga	食大麦公牛	ab₂ niga	食大麦母牛
	gu₄ niga sag-gu₄	头牛级食大麦公牛	—	—
	gu₄ u₂	食草公牛	ab₂ u₂	食草母牛
	gu₄ mu-1	一年生公牛	ab₂ mu-1	一年生母牛
	gu₄ mu-2	二年生公牛	ab₂ mu-2	二年生母牛
	gu₄ mu-3	三年生公牛	ab₂ mu-3	三年生母牛
	—	—	ab₂ mah₂	成年（产奶）母牛①
	amar gu₄ mu-1	一年生公牛崽	—	—
	amar gu₄ mu-2	二年生公牛崽	—	—
	amar gu₄	公牛崽	amar ab₂	母牛崽
	amar gu₄ ga	吃奶公牛崽	—	—
	gu₄ amar ga	吃奶公牛崽	ab₂ amar ga	吃奶母牛崽
	gu₄ gun₃-a	斑点公牛	ab₂ gun₃-a	斑点母牛
	gu₄ giš-du₃	育种公牛	—	—
	gu₄ a-am	家野混杂公牛	ab₂ a-am	家野混杂母牛
	amar gu₄ a-am	家野混杂公牛崽	—	—
	amar gu₄ a-am ga	吃奶家野混杂公牛崽	—	—

---

① 现实中不存在 gu₄ mah（成年产奶公牛）这一种类，参见文献 OB Nippur Ura 03（P461397），OIP 11 37 + 46，MSL 9 41（V1 + V19），MSL 8/1 82（V9 + V36 + V42 + V52）（P227892），ED Animals A（P499080），MEE 3 p. 47 - 56（P010677）。

续表

种类	公		母	
牛	am gu$_4$	野生公牛	am ab$_2$	野生母牛
	gu$_4$ mar-tu	阿摩利公牛	ab$_2$ mar-tu	阿摩利母牛
	gu$_4$ apin	耕牛	—	—
	gu$_4$ giš	役牛	—	—
	amar peš	幼牛	—	—
	amar peš ga	吃奶幼牛	—	—
	amar peš gun$_3$-a	斑点幼牛	—	—
	amar peš am	野生幼牛	—	—
	amar peš a-am ga	吃奶野生幼牛	—	—
	amar peš mu-1	一年生幼牛	—	—
绵羊	udu	公绵羊	u$_8$	母绵羊
	gukkal	肥尾公绵羊（短宽）	u$_8$ gukkal / U$_8$ + HUL$_2$	肥尾母绵羊（短宽）
	udu kun-gid$_2$	肥尾公绵羊（长）	u$_8$ kun-gid$_2$	长尾母绵羊（长）
	udu gal-tab-bu-um	肥尾公绵羊（超大）	u$_8$ gal-tab-bu-um	肥尾母绵羊（超大）
	udu a-lum	长尾公绵羊	u$_8$ a-lum	长尾母绵羊
	udu LU$_2$.SU.(A^{ki})	西马什基公绵羊	u$_8$ LU$_2$.SU.(A^{ki})	西马什基母绵羊
	udu lu$_2$-ulu$_3$-um	卢卢布公绵羊	u$_8$ lu$_2$-ulu$_3$-um	卢卢布母绵羊
	udu Ša-ru-mi-um	沙鲁米姆公绵羊	u$_8$ Ša-ru-mi-um	沙鲁米姆母绵羊
	udu a-udu hur-sag	家野混杂公绵羊	u$_8$ a-udu hur-sag	家野混杂母绵羊
	udu hur-sag	野生公绵羊	u$_8$ hur-sag	野生母绵羊
	udu niga sig$_5$	优等食大麦公绵羊	u$_8$ niga sig$_5$	优等食大麦母绵羊
	udu niga sig$_5$-us$_2$	次等食大麦公绵羊	u$_8$ niga sig$_5$-us$_2$	次等食大麦母绵羊
	udu niga 3-kam-us$_2$	三等食大麦公绵羊	u$_8$ niga 3-kam-us$_2$	三等食大麦母绵羊
	udu niga 4-kam-us$_2$	四等食大麦公绵羊	u$_8$ niga 4-kam-us$_2$	四等食大麦母绵羊
	udu niga	食大麦公绵羊	u$_8$ niga	食大麦母绵羊
	udu niga gu$_4$-e-us$_2$-sa	次牛等食大麦公绵羊	u$_8$ niga gu$_4$-e-us$_2$-sa	次牛等食大麦母绵羊
	udu u$_2$	食草公绵羊	u$_8$ u$_2$	食草母绵羊
	sila$_4$	公绵羊羔	kir$_{11}$	母绵羊羔

续表

种类	公		母	
绵羊	sila$_4$ ga	吃奶公绵羊羔	kir$_{11}$ ga	吃奶母绵羊羔
	sila$_4$ gaba	半断奶公绵羊羔	kir$_{11}$ gaba	半断奶母绵羊羔
	sila$_4$ gub	断奶公绵羊羔	kir$_{11}$ gub	断奶母绵羊羔
	udu giš-du$_3$	育种公绵羊	u$_8$ giš-du$_3$	育种母绵羊
	—	—	u$_8$ sila$_4$ nu$_{(2)}$-a	怀孕母绵羊
	—	—	u$_8$ sila$_4$ du$_3$-a	受孕母绵羊
	udu babbar$_{(2)}$	白色公绵羊	u$_8$ babbar$_{(2)}$	白色母绵羊
	udu gi$_6$	黑色公绵羊	u$_8$ gi$_6$	黑色母绵羊
	udu si$_4$	红色公绵羊	u$_8$ si$_4$	红色母绵羊
	udu sig$_{17}$	黄色公绵羊	u$_8$ sig$_{17}$	黄色母绵羊
	udu gun$_3$-a	斑点公绵羊	u$_8$ gun$_3$-a	斑点母绵羊
	udu bar-gal$_2$	带毛公绵羊	u$_8$ bar-gal$_2$	带毛母绵羊
	udu bar-su-ga	剪毛公绵羊	u$_8$ bar-su-ga	剪毛母绵羊
	sila$_4$ aš-ur$_4$	第一次脱毛公绵羊	kir$_{11}$ aš-ur$_4$	第一次脱毛母绵羊
	udu si-2-la$_2$	第二次脱毛公绵羊	u$_8$ si-2-la$_2$	第二次脱毛母绵羊
山羊	maš$_2$-gal	公山羊	ud$_5$	母山羊
	maš$_2$-gal a-dara$_4$	家野混杂公山羊	ud$_5$ a-dara$_4$	家野混杂母山羊
	dara$_4$ nita$_2$	野生公山羊	dara$_4$ munus	野生母山羊
	maš$_2$-gal LU$_2$.SU.(A^{ki})	西马什基公山羊	ud$_5$ LU$_2$.SU.(A^{ki})	西马什基母山羊
	maš$_2$-gal Ma$_2$-gan$^{(ki)}$	马干公山羊	ud$_5$ Ma$_2$-gan$^{(ki)}$	马干母山羊
	maš$_2$	公山羊羔	^{munus}aš$_2$-gar$_3$	母山羊羔
	maš$_2$ ga	吃奶公山羊羔	^{munus}aš$_2$-gar$_3$ ga	吃奶母山羊羔
	—	—	ud$_5$ maš$_2$ nu$_{(2)}$-a	怀孕母山羊
	—	—	ud$_5$ maš$_2$ du$_3$-a	受孕母山羊
	maš$_2$-gal niga sig$_5$	优等食大麦公山羊	ud$_5$ niga sig$_5$	优等食大麦母山羊
	maš$_2$-gal niga sig$_5$-us$_2$	次等食大麦公山羊	ud$_5$ niga sig$_5$-us$_2$	次等食大麦母山羊
	maš$_2$-gal niga 3-kam-us$_2$	三等食大麦公山羊	ud$_5$ niga 3-kam-us$_2$	三等食大麦母山羊
	maš$_2$-gal niga 4-kam-us$_2$	四等食大麦公山羊	ud$_5$ niga 4-kam-us$_2$	四等食大麦母山羊
	maš$_2$-gal niga	食大麦公山羊	ud$_5$ niga	食大麦母山羊
	maš$_2$-gal niga gu$_4$-e-us$_2$-sa	次牛等食大麦公山羊	ud$_5$ niga gu$_4$-e-us$_2$-sa	次牛等食大麦母山羊
	maš$_2$-gal u$_2$	食草公山羊	ud$_5$ u$_2$	食草母山羊

续表

种类	公		母	
驴	dusu$_2$ nita$_2$	公驴	dusu$_2$ munus	母驴
	dusu$_2$ nita$_2$ amar ga	吃奶公驴崽	dusu$_2$ munus amar ga	吃奶母驴崽
	dusu$_2$ nita$_2$ mu-1	一年生公驴	dusu$_2$ munus mu-1	一年生母驴
	dusu$_2$ nita$_2$ mu-2	二年生公驴	dusu$_2$ munus mu-2	二年生母驴
	—	—	dusu$_2$ munus mah$_2$	成年（产奶）母驴
	amar dusu$_2$ nita$_2$	公驴崽	—	—
	amar dusu$_2$ nita$_2$ mu-1	一年生公驴崽	—	—
	dur$_3$	公驴驹	eme$_6$	母驴驹
	amar dur$_3$	公驴驹崽	amar eme$_6$	母驴驹崽
	amar dur$_3$ ga	吃奶公驴驹	amar eme$_6$ ga	吃奶母驴驹
	^{anše}kunga$_2$ nita$_2$	公野驴（或骡）	^{anše}kunga$_2$ munus	母野驴
	^{anše}kunga$_2$ nita$_2$ mu-1	一年生公野驴	^{anše}kunga$_2$ munus mu-1	一年生母野驴
	^{anše}kunga$_2$ nita$_2$ mu-2	二年生公野驴	^{anše}kunga$_2$ munus mu-2	二年生母野驴
	^{anše}kunga$_2$ nita$_2$ mu-3	三年生公野驴	^{anše}kunga$_2$ munus mu-3	三年生母野驴
	^{anše}si$_2$-si$_2$ nita$_2$	公马	^{anše}si$_2$-si$_2$ munus	母马
	^{anše}si$_2$-si$_2$ nita$_2$ mu-1	一年生公马	^{anše}si$_2$-si$_2$ munus mu-1	一年生母马
	^{anše}si$_2$-si$_2$ nita$_2$ mu-2	二年生公马	^{anše}si$_2$-si$_2$ munus mu-2	二年生母马
	^{anše}si$_2$-si$_2$ nita$_2$ babbar	白色公马	^{anše}si$_2$-si$_2$ munus babbar	白色母马
	amar ^{anše}si$_2$-si$_2$ nita$_2$ ga	吃奶公马崽*	amar ^{anše}si$_2$-si$_2$ munus ga	吃奶母马崽
	anše eden-na nita$_2$	草原公驴	anše eden-na munus	草原母驴
鹿	lulim nita$_2$	公牡鹿	lulim munus	母牡鹿
	lulim nita$_2$ niga	食大麦公牡鹿	lulim munus niga	食大麦母牡鹿
	lulim nita$_2$ u$_2$	食草公牡鹿	—	—
	lulim nita$_2$ mu-1	一年生公牡鹿	lulim munus mu-1	一年生母牡鹿
	lulim nita$_2$ mu-2	二年生公牡鹿	lulim munus mu-2	二年生母牡鹿
	lulim nita$_2$ mu-3	三年生公牡鹿	lulim munus mu-3	三年生母牡鹿
	amar lulim nita$_2$ ga	吃奶公牡鹿崽	amar lulim munus ga	吃奶母牡鹿崽
	šeg$_9$-bar nita$_2$	公黇鹿	šeg$_9$-bar munus	母黇鹿

续表

种类	公		母	
鹿	šeg₉-bar nita₂ niga	食大麦公鼦鹿	šeg₉-bar munusniga	食大麦母鼦鹿
	šeg₉-bar nita₂ mu-1	一年生公鼦鹿	šeg₉-bar munus mu-1	一年生母鼦鹿
	šeg₉-bar nita₂ mu-2	二年生公鼦鹿	šeg₉-bar munus mu-2	二年生母鼦鹿
	amar šeg₉-bar nita₂	公鼦鹿崽	amar šeg₉-bar munus	母鼦鹿崽
	amar šeg₉-bar nita₂ ga	吃奶公鼦鹿崽	amar šeg₉-bar munus ga	吃奶母鼦鹿崽
羚羊	maš-da₃ (nita₂)	（公）羚羊	maš-da₃ munus	母羚羊
	amar maš-da₃ (nita₂)	（公）羚羊崽	amar maš-da₃ munus	母羚羊崽
	maš-da₃ niga	食大麦羚羊	—	—
	maš-da₃ hur-sag	野生羚羊	—	—
	amar maš-da₃ hur-sag	野生羚羊崽	—	—
熊	az	熊	—	—
	amar az	熊崽	—	—

资料来源：绵羊、山羊类参见 W. Heimpel, "Zu den Bezeichnungen von Schafen und Ziegen in den Drehem-und Ummatexten", *Bulletin on Sumerian Agriculture*, Vol. 7 (1993), pp. 115 – 160; P. Steinkeller, "Sheep and goat terminology in Ur III sources from Drehem", *Bulletin on Sumerian Agriculture*, Vol. 8 (1995), pp. 49 – 70; M. Stepien, *Animal Husbandry in the Ancient Near East: A Prosopographic Study of Third-Millennium Umma*, Bethesda: CDL Press, 1996; 牛类参见：W. Heimpel, "Plow animal inspection records from Ur III Girsu and Umma", *Bulletin on Sumerian Agriculture*, Vol. 8 (1995), pp. 71 – 171; M. Stol, "Old Babylonian cattle", *Bulletin on Sumerian Agriculture*, Vol. 8 (1995), pp. 173 – 213; 驴类参见 K. Maekawa, "The Ass and the Onager in Sumer in the Late Third Millennium B. C.", *Acta Sumerologica*, Vol. 1 (1979), pp. 35 – 62; J. Zarins, "The Domesticated Equidae of Third Millennium B. C. Mesopotamia", *Journal of Cuneiform Studies*, Vol. 30 (1978), pp. 3 – 17; 驴、鹿、熊类参见 C. Mittermayer, *Die Entwicklung der Tierkopfzeichen: Eine Studie zur syro-mesopotamischen Keilschriftpaläographie des 3. und frühen 2. Jahrtausends v. Chr.*, Alter Orient und Altes Testament 319, Münster: Ugarit-Verlag, 2005.

附录六 缩写词

AAICAB	J.-P. Grégoire, *Archives Administratives et Inscriptions Cunéiformes*: *Ashmolean Museum Bodleian Collection Oxford*, I/1-4 (Paris, 1996–2002)
AAS	J.-P. Grégoire, *Archives administratives sumériennes* (Paris 1970)
ABTR	W. R. Arnold, *Ancient-Babylonian temple records in the Columbia University library* (New York, 1896)
Aegyptus	*Aegyptus*: *Rivista italiana di Egittologia e di Papirologia*
Aevum	*Aevum*
Akkadica	*Akkadica. Périodiquebimestriel de la Fondation Assyriologique Georges Dossin*
Aleppo	M. Touzalin, *L'Administration palatiale à l'époque de la troisième dynastie d'Ur*: *Textes inédits du Musée d'Alep* (Thèse de doctorat de troisième cycle soutenue à l'Université de Tours, 1982)
Amherst	Th. G. Pinches, *The Amherst Tablets. Part I*: *Texts of the Period extending to and including the reign of Bur-Sin* (London, 1908)
AnOr	*Analecta Orientalia*
AnOr 1	N. Schneider, *Die Drehem-und Djoha-Urkunden*: *Der Strassburger Universitäts- und Landesbibliothek* (Roma, 1931)
AnOr 7	N. Schneider, *Die Drehem-und Djohatexte*: *Im Kloster Montserrat* (Barcelona) (Roma, 1932)
ArOr	*Archiv Orientalni*
AR RIM	*Annual Review of the Royal Inscriptions of Mesopotamia Project*
ASJ	*Acta Sumerologica*
Atiqot	*Journal of the Israel Department of Antiquities*
AUCT	*Andrews University Cuneiform Texts*
AUCT 1	M. Sigrist, *Neo-Sumerian Account Texts in the Horn Archaeological Museum*, Volume 1 (Berrien Springs, 1984)

续表

AUCT 2	M. Sigrist, *Neo-Sumerian Account Texts in the Horn Archaeological Museum*, Volume 2 (Berrien Springs, 1988)
AUCT 3	M. Sigrist, *Neo-Sumerian Account Texts in the Horn Archaeological Museum*, Volume 3 (Berrien Springs, 1988)
AuOr	*Aula Orientalis*
Babyloniaca	*Babyloniaca: Études de philologie assyrobabylonienne*
BAOM	*Bulletin of the Ancient Orient Museum*
BBVO	*Berliner Beiträge zum Vorderer Orient*
BBVO 11	R. L. Zettler, *The Ur III Temple of Inanna at Nippur: The Operation and Organization of Urban Religious Institutions in Mesopotamia in the Late Third Millennium B. C.* (Berlin, 1992)
BCT	Catalogue of cuneiform tablets in Birmingham City Museum
BCT 1	P. J. Watson, *Neo-Sumerian Texts from Drehem* (Warminster, 1986)
BCT 2	P. J. Watson, *Neo-Sumerian Texts from Umma and Other Sites* (Warminster, 1993)
BIN	Babylonian Inscriptions in the Collection of J. B. Nies
BIN 3	C. E. Keiser, *Neo-Sumerian Account Texts from Drehem* (New Haven and London, 1971)
BIN 5	G. G. Hackman, *Temple Documents of the Third Dynasty of Ur from Umma* (New Haven and London, 1937)
BJPL	*Bulletin of the John Rylands Library*
BM Messenger	M. Sigrist, *Messenger Texts from the British Museum* (Ann Arbor, 1990)
BMC Roma	Bollettino dei Musei Comunali di Roma
BPOA	Biblioteca del Proximo Oriente Antiguo
BPOA 1	T. Ozaki, M. Sigrist, *Ur III Administrative Tablets from the British Museum*. Part One (Madrid, 2006)
BPOA 2	T. Ozaki, M. Sigrist, *Ur III Administrative Tablets from the British Museum*. Part Two (Madrid, 2006)
BPOA 6	M. Sigrist, T. Ozaki, *Neo-Sumerian Administrative Tablets from the Yale Babylonian Collection*. Part One (Madrid, 2009)
BPOA 7	M. Sigrist, T. Ozaki, *Neo-Sumerian Administrative Tablets from the Yale Babylonian Collection*. Part Two (Madrid, 2009)
BRM	Babylonian Records in the Library of J. Pierpont Morgan

续表

BRM 3	C. E. Keiser, *Cuneiform Bullae of the Third Millennium B. C.* (New Haven, 1914)
CDLB	*Cuneiform Digital Library Bulletin*
CDLJ	*Cuneiform Digital Library Journal*
CDLN	*Cuneiform Digital Library Notes*
CHEU	G. Contenau, *Contribution à l'histoire économique d'Umma* (Paris, 1915)
CM	Cuneiform Monographs
CM 26	T. M. Sharlach, *Provincial taxation and the Ur III state* (Leiden, 2004)
CST	T. Fish, *Catalogue of Sumerian Tablets in the John Rylands Library* (Manchester 1932)
CT	Cuneiform Texts from Babylonian Tablets in the British Museum
CT 9	L. W. King, *Cuneiform Texts from Babylonian Tablets, &c., in the British Museum, Part IX* (*CT* 9) (London, 1900)
CT 32	L. W. King, *Cuneiform Texts from Babylonian Tablets, &c., in the British Museum, Part XXXII* (*CT* 32) (London, 1912)
CTPSM	Cuneiform Texts in the Collection of the Pushkin State Museum of Fine Arts
CTPSM 1	B. Perlov, Y. Saveliev, *Cuneiform Texts in the Collection of the Pushkin State Museum of Fine Arts. I. Administrative Texts from Tello from the Ur III Period* (Moscow, 2014)
CUSAS	Cornell University Studies in Assyriology and Sumerology
CUSAS 16	S. J. Garfinkle, H. Sauren, M. Van De Mieroop, *Ur III Tablets from the Columbia University Library* (Bethesda, 2010)
CUSAS 39	J. Dahl, *Ur III Texts in the Schøyen Collection, Manuscripts in the Schøyen Collection. Cuneiform Texts XIII* (University Park, 2019)
CUSAS 40	M. Sigrist, T. Ozaki, *Tablets from the Irisaĝrig Archive* (University Park, 2019)
DAS	B. Lafont, *Documents Administratifs Sumériens, provenant du site de Tello et conservés au Musée du Louvre* (Paris, 1985)
Dissertation Cooper	M. Cooper, *Studies in Neo-Sumerian Administrative Procedures*, Ph. D. Diss., (University of Minnesota, 1979)
DoCu	J.-M. Durand, *Documents cunéiformés de la IVe Section de l'École pratique des Hautes Etudes*, vol. 1: *catalogue et copies cunéiformés* (Geneva, 1982)
Frühe Schrift	H. Nissen, P. Damerow, R. Englund, *Frühe Schrift und Techniken der Wirtschaftsverwaltung im alten Vorderen Orient* (Berlin, 1990)

Fs Hruška	L. Vacín (ed.), $U_4\ du_{11}$-ga-ni sá mu-ni-ib-du_{11}. Ancient Near Eastern Studies in Memory of Blahoslav Hruška (Dresden, 2011)
Fs Klengel	J. M. Córdoba (ed.), Actas del I Symposium Internacional" Una década de estudios sobre el Oriente antiguo (1986-1996)". Homenaje al Prof. Dr. Horst Klengel, ISIMU 1 (Madrid, 1998)
Fs Leichty	A. K. Guinan, et al. (eds.), If a Man Builds a Joyful House: Assyriological Studies in Honor of Erle Verdun Leichty (Leiden, 2006)
Fs Lenoble	V. Rondot, F. Alpi, F. Villeneuve (eds.), La pioche et la plume. Autour du Soudan, du Liban et de la Jordanie. Hommages archéologiques à Patrice Lenoble (Paris, 2011)
Fs Sigrist	P. Michalowski (ed.), On the Third Dynasty of Ur: Studies in Honor of Marcel Sigrist (Boson, 2008)
Fs Součková-Siegelová	Š. Velhartická (ed.), Audiasfabulasveteres. Anatolian Studies in Honor of Jana Součková-Siegelová (Leiden, 2016)
Georgica	M. Civil, The Farmer's Instructions. A Sumerian Agricultural Manual, Aula Orientalis-Supplementa 5 (Sabadell, 1994)
Hirose	T. Gomi, Y. Hirose, K. Hirose, Neo-Sumerian Administrative Texts of the Hirose Collection (Potomac, 1990)
HSS	Harvard Semitic Series
HSS 4	M. I. Hussey, Sumerian Tablets in the Harvard Semitic Museum (II) from the Time of the Dynasty of Ur (Cambridge, 1915)
HUCA	Hebrew Union College Annual
IOS	Israel Oriental Studies
ITT	Inventaire des Tablettes de Telloconservées au Musée Impérial Ottoman
ITT 2	H. de Genouillac, Textes de l'Époque d'Agadé et de l'Époque d'Ur (Paris, 1910)
ITT 3	H. de Genouillac, Textes de l'Époque d'Ur (Paris, 1912)
ITT 5	H. de Genouillac, Époque Présargonique, Époque d'Agadé, Époque d'Ur (Paris, 1921)
JANES	Journal of the Ancient Near Eastern Society
JAOS	Journal of the American Oriental Society
JCS	Journal of Cuneiform Studies
JNES	Journal of Near Eastern Studies
JRAS	Journal of the Royal Asiatic Society of Great Britain and Ireland

续表

JSOR	*Journal of the Society of Oriental Research*
Kyoto	Y. Nakahara, *The Sumerian Tablets in the Imperial Library of Kyoto* (Tokyo 1928)
LAOS	Leipziger Altorientalische Studien
LAOS 1	M. P. Streck (ed.), *Die Keilschrifttexte des Altorientalischen Instituts der Universität Leipzig* (Wiesbaden, 2011)
L'uomo	G. Pettinato, *L'uomocominciò a scrivere. Iscrizioni cuneiformi della Collezione-Michail* (Milan, 1997)
MCS	Manchester Cuneiform Studies
MDP	Mémoires de la Délégation en Perse
MDP 10	V. Scheil, *Textes Élamites-Sémitiques. Quatrième Série* (Paris, 1908)
MVN	Materiali per il Vocabulario Neosumerico
MVN 1	G. Pettinato, H. Waetzoldt, *La collezione Schollmeyer*, Materiali per il Vocabolario Neosumerico 1 (Rome, 1974)
MVN 2	H. Sauren, *Wirtschaftsurkunden des Musée d'Art et d'Histoire in Genf*, Materiali per il Vocabolario Neosumerico 2 (Rome, 1975)
MVN 3	D. I. Owen, *The John Frederick Lewis Collection*, Materiali per il Vocabolario Neosumerico 3 (Rome, 1975)
MVN 4	L. Cagni, G. Pettinato, *La collezione del Pontificio Istituto Biblico-Rome. La collezione della Collegiata dei SS. Pietro e Orso-Aosta*, Materiali per il Vocabolario Neosumerico 4 (Rome, 1976)
MVN 5	E. Sollberger, *The Pinches Manuscript*, Materiali per il Vocabolario Neosumerico 5 (Rome, 1978)
MVN 6	G. Pettinato, *Testi economici di Lagaš del Museo di Istanbul. Parte I: La. 7001 – 7600*, Materiali per il Vocabolario Neosumerico 6 (Rome, 1977)
MVN 7	G. Pettinato, S. A. Picchioni, *Testi economici di Lagash del Museo di Istanbul. Parte II: La. 7601 – 8200*, Materiali per il Vocabolario Neosumerico 7 (Rome, 1978)
MVN 8	D. Calvot, G. Pettinato, S. A. Picchioni, F. Reschid, *Textes économiques du Selluš-Dagan du Musée du Louvre et du College de France* (D. Calvot); *Testi economici dell'Iraq Museum Baghdad* (G. Pettinato-S. A. Picchioni-F. Reschid), Materiali per il Vocabolario Neosumerico 8 (Rome, 1979)
MVN 9	D. C. Snell, *The E. A. Hoffman Collection and Other American Collections*, Materiali per il Vocabolario Neosumerico 9 (Rome, 1979)
MVN 10	J. -P. Grégoire, *Inscriptions et archives administratives cunéiformes-Ie Partie*, Materiali per il Vocabolario Neosumerico 10 (Rome, 1981)

续表

MVN 11	D. I. Owen, *Selected Ur III Texts from the Harvard Semitic Museum*, Materiali per il Vocabolario Neosumerico 11 (Rome, 1982)
MVN 12	T. Gomi, *Wirtschaftstexte der Ur III-Zeit aus dem British Museum*, Materiali per il Vocabolario Neosumerico 12 (Rome, 1982)
MVN 13	M. Sigrist, D. I. Owen, G. D. Young, *The John Frederick Lewis Collection-Part II*, Materiali per il Vocabolario Neosumerico 13 (Rome, 1984)
MVN 14	F. Yildiz, H. Waetzoldt, H. Renner, *Die Umma-Texte aus den Archäologischen Museen zu Istanbul. Nr. 1 - 600*, Materiali per il Vocabolario Neosumerico 14 (Rome, 1988)
MVN 15	D. I. Owen, *Neo-Sumerian Texts from American Collections*, Materiali per il Vocabolario Neosumerico 15 (Rome, 1991)
MVN 16	H. Waetzoldt, F. Yildiz, *Die Umma-Texte aus den Archäologischen Museen zu Istanbul. Band II. Nr. 601 - 1600*, Materiali per il Vocabolario Neosumerico 16 (Rome, 1994)
MVN 17	G. Pettinato, *Testi economici Neo-Sumerici del British Museum (BM 12230-BM 12390)*, Materiali per il Vocabolario Neosumerico 17 (Rome, 1993)
MVN 18	M. Molina, *Tablillas administrativas neosumerias de la Abadía de Montserrat (Barcelona) . Copias Cuneiformes*, Materiali per il Vocabolario Neosumerico 18 (Rome, 1993)
MVN 20	F. D'Agostino, *Testi amministrativi della III Dinastia di Ur dal Museo Statale Ermitage San Pietroburgo-Russia*, Materiali per il Vocabolario Neosumerico 20 (Rome, 1997)
MVN 21	N. Koslova, *Neusumerische Verwaltungstexte aus Umma aus der Sammlung der Ermitage zu St. Petersburg-Rußland*, Materiali per il Vocabolario Neosumerico 21 (Rome, 2000)
MVN 22	M. Molina, *Testi amministrativi neosumerici del British Museum. BM 13601 - 14300*, Materiali per il Vocabolario Neosumerico 22 (Rome, 2003)
NABU	*Nouvelles Assyriologiques Brèves et Utilitaires*
NATN	D. l. Owen, *Neo-Sumerian Archival Texts primarily from Nippur* (Winona Lake, 1982)
Nebraska	N. W. Forde, Nebraska Cuneiform Texts of the Sumerian Ur III Dynasty (Lawrence, 1967)
Nik 2	M. Nikol'skij, *Dokumenty chozjajstvennoj otcetnosti drevnejšej epochi Chaldei iz sobranija N. P. Lichaceva cast' II*: *Epoch dinastii Agade i epocha dinastii Ura*, *Drevnosti Vostocnya* 5 (Moskou, 1915)

续表

Nisaba	Nisaba：Studi Assiriologici Messinesi
Nisaba 3/1	M. E. Milone, G. Spada, M. Capitani, *Umma Messenger Texts in the British Museum, Part Two (UMTBM 2). Girsu Messenger Texts in the British Museum* (Messina, 2003)
Nisaba 6	F. al-Rawi, F. D'Agostino, *Neo-Sumerian Administrative Texts from Umma kept in the British Museum. Part One (NATU I)* (Messina, 2005)
Nisaba 9	M. Molina, M. Such-Gutiérrez, *Neo-Sumerian Administrative Texts in the British Museum. BM 107926 – 108315* (Messina, 2005)
Nisaba 11	F. al-Rawi, L. Verderame, *Documenti amministrativi neo-sumerici da Umma conservati al British Museum (NATU II)* (Messina, 2006)
Nisaba 13	P. Notizia, *Testi amministrativi Neo-Sumerici da Girsu nel British Museum (BM 98119-BM 98240)* (Messina, 2006)
Nisaba 15	D. I. Owen, *Cuneiform Texts Primarily from Iri-Saǧrig/Āl-Šarrākī and the History of the Ur III Period. 2. Catalogue and Texts* (Bethesda, 2013)
Nisaba 17	F. Pomponio, L. Verderame, *Neo-Sumerian Girsu Texts of Barley and Cereal Products, kept in the British Museum (with an Appendix by E. Santagati, and Cylinder Seal Impresions by S. Altavilla)* (Messina, 2007)
Nisaba 18	A. Anastasi, F. Pomponio, *Neo-Sumerian Girsu Texts of Various Contents kept in the British Museum (with an Appendix of Stefania Altavilla)* (Messina, 2009)
Nisaba 23	F. al-Rawi, L. Verderame, *Neo-Sumerian Administrative Texts from Umma kept in the British Museum. Part Three (NATU III)* (Messina, 2009)
Nisaba 24	F. al-Rawi, F. D'Agostino, J. Taylor, *Neo-Sumerian Administrative Texts from Umma kept in the British Museum, Part Four (NATU IV)* (Messina, 2009)
Nisaba 26	F. al-Rawi, F. Gorello, P. Notizia, *Neo-Sumerian Administrative Texts from Umma kept in the British Museum. Part Five (NATU V)* (Messina, 2013)
Nisaba 31	B. Foster, S. Alivernini, A. Greco, *Sargonic Texts from Umma in the Oriental Institute of the University of Chicago. Neo – Sumerian administrative texts from the Géjou Collection kept in the Brisith Museum* (Messina, 2019)
Nisaba 32	P. Notizia, *Neo – Sumerian Administrative Texts from the Rosen Collection* (Messina, 2019)
Nisaba 33	T. Ozaki, *The Lost and the Found. Cuneiform Collections Rediscovered* (Messina, 2020)
NYPL	H. Sauren, *Les tablettes cunéiformes de l'époque d'Ur des collections de la New York Public Library*, Publications de l'Institut Orientaliste de Louvain 19 (Louvain, 1978)

续表

OBO	OrbisBiblicus et Orientalis
OBO 200	H. Keel-Leu, B. Teissier, *Die vorderasiatischen Rollsiegel der Sammlungen "Bibel + Orient" der Universität Freiburg Schweiz*, Orbis Biblicus et Orientalis 200 (Göttingen, 2004)
OIP	Oriental Institute Publications
OIP 115	M. Hilgert, *Cuneiform Texts from the Ur III Period in the Oriental Institute, Vol. 1: Drehem Administrative Documents from the Reign of Šulgi*, Oriental Institute Publications 115 (Chicago, 1998)
OIP 121	M. Hilgert, *Cuneiform Texts from the Ur III Period in the Oriental Institute, Vol. 2: Drehem Administrative Documents from the Reign of Amar-Suena*, Oriental Institute Publications 121 (Chicago, 2003)
OLP	*Orientalia Lovaniensia Periodica*
OLZ	*Orientalistische Literaturzeitung*
OMRO	*Oudheidkundige Mededelingen uit het Rijksmuseum van Oudheden te Leiden*
Ontario 1	M. Sigrist, *Neo-Sumerian Texts from the Royal Ontario Museum. I. The Administration at Drehem* (Bethesda, 1995)
Ontario 2	M. Sigrist, *Neo-Sumerian Texts from the Royal Ontario Museum. II. Administrative Texts Mainly from Umma* (Bethesda, 2004)
Orient	*Orient. Report of the Society for Near Eastern Studies in Japan*
OrNS	*Orientalia*, NS = *Nova Series*
OrSP	*Orientalia*, SP = *Series Prior*
OTR 3	R. Lau, *Old Babylonian Temple Records*, Columbia University Oriental Studies 3 (New York, 1906)
P	Cuneiform Digital Library Initiative, Number
PDT 1	M. Çig, H. Kizilyay, A. Salonen, *Die Puzriš-Dagan-Texte der Istanbuler Archäologischen Museen Teil I: Nrr. 1-725* (Helsinki, 1954)
PDT 2	F. Yildiz, T. Gomi, *Die Puzriš-Dagan-Texte der Istanbuler Archäologischen Museen II: Nr. 726 – 1379*, Freiburger Altorientalische Studien 16 (Stuttgart, 1988)
PPAC	Periodic Publications on Ancient Civilisations
PPAC 4	T. Ozaki, M. Sigrist, *Tablets in Jerusalem: Sainte-Anne and Saint-Étienne* (Changchun, 2010)
PPAC 5	M. Sigrist, T. Ozaki, *Administrative Ur III Texts in the British Museum (AUTBM)* (Changchun, 2013)

续表

Prima del'alfabeto	F. M. Fales, *Prima dell'alfabeto La storia della scrittura attraverso test icuneiformi inediti* (Venice, 1989)
Princeton 1	M. Sigrist, *Tablettes du Princeton Theological Seminary. Époque d'Ur III*, Occasional Publications of the Samuel Noah Kramer Fund 10 (Philadelphia, 1990)
Princeton 2	M. Sigrist, *Tablets from the Princeton Theological Seminary. Ur III Period. Part 2*. Occasional Publications of the Samuel Noah Kramer Fund 18 (Philadelphia, 2005)
RA	*Revue d'Assyriologie et d'Archéologie Orientale*
RIME	The Royal Inscriptions of Mesopotamia, Early Periods
RIME 3/2	D. Frayne, *Ur III Period (2112 – 2004 BC)*, RIME 3/2 (Toronto-Buffalo-London, 1997)
Rochester	M. Sigrist, *Documents from Tablet Collections in Rochester*, New York (Bethesda, Maryland 1991)
RSO	*Rivistadegli Studi Orientali*
RTC	F. Thureau-Dangin, *Recueil des tablettes chaldéennes* (Paris, 1903)
SA	C. -F. Jean, *Shumer et Akkad, contribution a l'histoire de la civilisation dans la Basse-Mésopotamie* (Paris, 1923)
SACT 1	S. T. Kang, *Sumerian Economic Texts from the Drehem Archive, Sumerian and Akkadian Cuneiform Texts in the Collection of the World Heritage Museum of the University of Illinois I* (Urbana-Chicago-London, 1972)
SACT 2	S. T. Kang, *Sumerian Economic Texts from the Umma Archive, Sumerian and Akkadian Cuneiform Texts in the Collection of the World Heritage Museum of the University of Illinois II* (Urbana-Chicago-London, 1973)
SAKF	K. Oberhuber, *Sumerische und akkadische Keilschriftdenkmäler des Archäologischen Museums zu Florenz* (Innsbruck, 1958 – 1960)
Santag 6	N. Koslova, *Ur III-Texte der St. Petersburger Eremitage*, Santag 6 (Wiesbaden, 2000)
Santag 7	T. Ozaki, *Keilschrifttexte aus japanischen Sammlungen*, Santag 7 (Wiesbaden, 2002)
SAT 1	M. Sigrist, *Texts from the British Museum*, Sumerian Archival Texts 1 (Bethesda, 1993)
SAT 2	M. Sigrist, *Texts from the Yale Babylonian Collections. I*, Sumerian Archival Texts 2 (Bethesda, 2000)
SAT 3	M. Sigrist, *Texts from the Yale Babylonian Collections. II*, Sumerian Archival Texts 3 (Bethesda, 2000)

续表

SET	T. B. Jones, J. W Snyder, *Sumerian Economic Texts from the Third Ur Dynasty* (Minneapolis, 1961)
SNAT	T. Gomi, S. Sato, *Selected Neo-Sumerian Administrative Texts from the British Museum* (Chiba, 1990)
South Dakota	N. W. Forde, *Neo-Sumerian texts from South Dakota University, Luther and Union Colleges* (Lawrence, 1987)
STA	E. Chiera, *Selected Temple Accounts (from Telloh, Yokha and Drehem)* (Philadelphia, 1922)
StOr	Studia Orientalia
StOr 9 - 1	A. Holma, A. Salonen, *Some Cuneiform Tablets from the Time of the Third Ur Dynasty (Holma Collection Nos. 11 - 39)*, Studia Orientalia 9/1 (Helsinki, 1940)
STU	C. L. Bedale, *Sumerian tablets from Umma in the John Rylands Library* (New York, 1915)
Syracuse	M. Sigrist, *Textes Économiques Néo-Sumeriens de l'Université de Syracuse*, ERC 29 (Paris, 1983)
TAD	S. Langdon, *Tablets from the Archives of Drehem* (Paris, 1911)
Tavolette	G. Boson, *Tavolette cuneiformisumere, degliarchivi di Drehem e di Djoha, dell'Ultima Dinastia di Ur*, Publicazioni della Università Catholica del Sacro Cuore 2 (Milan, 1936)
TCBI 2	F. Pomponio, M. Stol, A. Westenholz, *Tavolette cuneiformi di varia provenienza delle collezioni della Banca d'Italia* (Rome, 2006)
TCL	Textes cunéiformes, Musées du Louvre
TCL 2	H. de Genouillac, *Tablettes de Drehem publiées avec inventaire et tables*, Textes Cunéiformes-Musée du Louvre 2 (Paris, 1911)
TCL 5	H. de Genouillac, *Textes économiques d'Oumma à l'époque d'Our*, Textes Cunéiformes du Musée du Louvre 5 (Paris, 1922)
TCNU	A. Archi, F. Pomponio, G. Bergamini. *Testi Cuneiformi Neo-Sumerici da Umma, NN. 0413 - 1723. Catalogo del Museo Egizio di Torino. Serieseconda. Collezioni 8.* (Torino, 1995)
TCS 1	E. Sollberger, *The Business and Administrative Correspondence under the Kings of Ur*, Texts from Cuneiform Sources 1 (Locust Valley, 1966)
TCTI 2	B. Lafont, F. Yildiz, *Tablettes cunéiformes de Tello au Musée d'Istanbul, datant de l'époque de la IIIe Dynastie d'Ur. Tome II. ITT II/1, 2544 - 2819, 3158 - 4342, 4708 - 4714*, PIHANS 77 (Leiden, 1996)

续表

TCUR	L. Boulay, *Mémoire sur des Tablettes de la 3e Dynastie d'Ur à Rouen* (Rouen, 1920)
TEL	C. Virolleaud, M. Lambert, *Tablettes écomomiques de Lagash* (Paris, 1968)
TJA	E. Szlechter, *Tablettesjuridiques et administratives de la IIIe Dynastie d'Ur et de la Ière dynastie de Babylone, conservées au Musée de l'Université de Manchester, à Cambridge, au Musée Fitzwilliam, à l'Institut d'Études Orientales et à l'Institut d'Egyptologie* (Paris, 1963)
TLB	Tabulae Cuneiformes a F. M. Th. de Liagre Böhl collectae
TLB 3	W. W. Hallo, *Sumerian Archival Texts*, Tabulae Cuneiformes a F. M. Th. de Liagre Böhl Collectae, Leidae Conservatae 3 (Leiden, 1963)
TMH NF 1 – 2	A. Pohl, *Rechts- und Verwaltungsurkunden der III. Dynastie von Ur*, Neue Folge 1 – 2 (Leipzig, 1937)
TRU	L. Legrain, *Le temps des rois d'Ur*, Bibliothèque de l'École des Hautes Études 199 (Paris, 1912)
TSU	H. Limet, *Textes sumériens de la IIIe dynastie d'Ur*, Documents du Proche Orient Ancien-Épigaphie 1 (Gembloux, 1973)
TUT	G. Reisner, *Tempelurkunden aus Telloh* (Berlin, 1901)
UCP 9 – 2	H. Lutz, *Sumerian Temple Records of the Late Ur Dynasty*, University of California Publications in Semitic Philology 9/2, 1 – 2 (Berkeley, 1928)
UDT	J. Nies, *Ur Dynasty Tablets. Texts Chiefly from Tello and Drehem Written during the Reigns of Dungi, Bur-Sin, Gimil-Sin and Ibi-Sin* (Leipzig, 1920)
UET	Ur Excavations Texts
UET 3	L. Legrain, *Business Documents of the Third Dynasty of Ur*, Ur Excavations Texts 3 (London, 1937)
UET 9	D. Loding, *Economic Texts from the Third Dynasty*, Ur Excavations Texts 9 (Pennsylvania-London, 1976)
Umma	G. Contenau, *Umma sous la dynaste d'Ur* (Paris, 1916)
UNT	H. Waetzoldt, *Untersuchtungen zur neusumerischen Textilindustrie* (Rome, 1972)
UTI 3	F. Yildiz, T. Gomi, *Die Umma-Texte aus den Archäologischen Museen zu Istanbul. Band III* (*Nr. 1601 – 2300*) (Bethesda, 1993)
UTI 4	T. Gomi, F. Yildiz, *Die Umma-Texte aus den Archäologischen Museen zu Istanbul. Band IV* (*Nr. 2301 – 3000*) (Bethesda, 1997)
UTI 5	F. Yildiz, T. Ozaki, *Die Umma-Texte aus den Archäologischen Museen zu Istanbul. Band V* (*Nr. 3001 – 3500*) (Bethesda, 2000)

续表

UTI 6	F. Yildiz, T. Ozaki, *Die Umma-Texte aus den Archäologischen Museen zu Istanbul. Band VI* (*Nr. 3501 – 3834*) (Bethesda, 2001)
VDI	*Vestnik drevnej istorii*
ViOr	*Vicino Oriente. Annuario dell'Istituto di Studi del Vicino Oriente, Università di Roma*
YNER	Yale Near Eastern Researches
YNER 8	D. C. Snell, *Ledgers and Prices: Early Mesopotamian Merchant Accounts*, Yale Near Eastern Researches 8, (New Haven-London, 1982)
YOS	Yale Oriental Series, Babylonian Texts
YOS 4	C. E. Keiser, *Selected Temple Documents of the Ur Dynasty*, Yale Oriental Series 4 (New Haven, 1919)
YOS 15	A. Goetze, *Cuneiform Texts from Various Collections*, Yale Oriental Series 15 (New Haven-London, 2009)
YOS 18	D. C. Snell, C. Lager, *Economic Texts from Sumer*, Yale Oriental Series 18 (New Haven-London, 1991)
ZA	*Zeitschrift für Assyriologie und Vorderasiatische Archäologie*

附录七　原始档案目录

(1) 核心区 bala 税档案
i. 来自普兹瑞什达干档案

AAICAB 1/2 pl. 95 1935 – 548	AUCT 1 208
AAICAB 1/2 pl. 112 1937 – 629	AUCT 1 209
AAICAB 1/4 Bod S 322	AUCT 1 277
Aegyptus 17 58 121	AUCT 1 449
AION 69 119 – 122 1	AUCT 1 483
AJSL 38 141	AUCT 1 653
Akkadica 13 28	AUCT 1 683
AnOr 1 16	AUCT 1 772
AnOr 1 27	AUCT 2 18
AnOr 7 92	AUCT 2 35
AnOr 7 257	AUCT 2 190
AnOr 7 346	AUCT 2 254
AOAT 240 81 7	AUCT 2 260
ArOr 25 557 4	AUCT 2 263
ASJ 9 255 38	AUCT 2 270
ASJ 12 44 17	AUCT 2 297
ASJ 19 211 31	AUCT 2 353
AUCT 1 10	AUCT 2 383
AUCT 1 49	AUCT 2 401
AUCT 1 50	AUCT 3 1
AUCT 1 51	AUCT 3 6
AUCT 1 66	AUCT 3 66
AUCT 1 151	AUCT 3 67

附　录

AUCT 3 105
AUCT 3 109
AUCT 3 177
AUCT 3 413
Babyloniaca 7 75 5
Babyloniaca 8 pl. 11 HG 11
BCT 1 39
BCT 1 75
BIN 3 198
BIN 3 219
BIN 3 241
BIN 3 258
BIN 3 340
BIN 3 343
BIN 3 353
BIN 3 373
BIN 3 392
BIN 3 393
BIN 3 394
BIN 3 463
BIN 3 494
BIN 3 540
BIN 3 559
BIN 3 586
BIN 3 593
BIN 3 602
BJRL 64 112 72
BPOA 6 18
BPOA 6 173
BPOA 6 711
BPOA 6 737
BPOA 7 2560
BPOA 7 2618
BPOA 7 2746

BPOA 7 2907
BRM 3 150
BRM 3 156
CM 26 1
CM 26 61
CM 26 107
CM 26 108
CM 26 109
CM 26 138
CM 26 139
CM 26 140
CM 26 141
CM 26 142
CST 301
CST 335
CST 341
CST 362
CST 386
CST 418
CST 452
CST 454
CST 508
CT 32 pl. 12 BM 103426
CTMMA 1 10
CUSAS 16 292
CUSAS 40 511
DIA 78.064
DMNS A440.07
DoCu 128
Hermitage 3 117
Hermitage 3 249
Hermitage 3 264
Hermitage 3 305
Hermitage 3 343

273

Hermitage 3 347	KM 89315
Hermitage 3 355	LoC 27
Hermitage 3 356	MCS 1 45 BM 103400
Hermitage 3 359	MCS 7 16 HSM 8221
Hermitage 3 398	MMFM 2005 14 1
Hermitage 3 432	MVN 1 113
Hermitage 3 557	MVN 1 133
Hermitage 3 558	MVN 3 307
Hermitage 3 559	MVN 3 344
JANES 8 43 2	MVN 5 106
JANES 9 23 7	MVN 5 112
JAOS 126 166 – 167	MVN 8 98
JCS 14 107 1	MVN 8 99
JCS 14 107 2	MVN 8 139
JCS 14 107 4	MVN 8 149
JCS 14 107 5	MVN 9 174
JCS 14 108 3	MVN 10 144
JCS 14 109 7	MVN 10 172
JCS 14 109 8	MVN 10 222
JCS 14 109 9	MVN 11 147
JCS 14 110 10	MVN 11 153
JCS 14 110 12	MVN 11 178
JCS 14 110 13	MVN 11 195
JCS 14 111 14	MVN 11 211
JCS 14 111 15	MVN 13 30
JCS 14 112 16	MVN 13 122
JCS 14 112 17	MVN 13 124
JCS 14 113 21	MVN 13 128 = 829
JCS 14 114 22	MVN 13 367
JCS 35 129 1	MVN 13 385
JCS 57 27 3	MVN 13 391
KM 89111	MVN 13 408
KM 89145	MVN 13 443
KM 89256	MVN 13 482

MVN 13 532	Nisaba 33 620
MVN 13 585	Nisaba 33 1075
MVN 13 653	Nisaba 33 1124
MVN 13 690	NYPL 287
MVN 13 694	NYPL 348
MVN 13 764	OIP 121 34
MVN 13 854	OIP 121 364
MVN 13 873	OIP 121 587
MVN 15 99	OIP 121 589
MVN 15 101	Ontario 1 40
MVN 15 134	Ontario 1 59
MVN 15 146	Ontario 1 73
MVN 15 170	Ontario 1 95
MVN 15 186	Ontario 1 173
MVN 15 258	Orient 16 54 48
MVN 15 343	OrSP 47–49 60
MVN 17 23a & b	OrSP 47–49 62
MVN 18 631	OrSP 47–49 81
MVN 21 266	OrSP 47–49 111
Nebraska 36	OrSP 47–49 485
Nik 2 502	P235916
Nik 2 518	P275032
Nisaba 8 9	PDT 1 136
Nisaba 8 42	PDT 1 174
Nisaba 8 119	PDT 1 205
Nisaba 8 120	PDT 1 211
Nisaba 8 134	PDT 1 243
Nisaba 30 79	PDT 1 342
Nisaba 33 116	PDT 1 417
Nisaba 33 201	PDT 1 424
Nisaba 33 366	PDT 1 425
Nisaba 33 410	PDT 1 438
Nisaba 33 552	PDT 1 446
Nisaba 33 610	PDT 1 477

PDT 1 516	Princeton 2 367
PDT 1 557	RA 9 42 SA 17（pl. 1）
PDT 1 607	RA 9 49 SA 125（pl. 3）
PDT 1 629	RA 9 49 SA 129（pl. 4）
PDT 1 641	RA 9 49 SA 134（pl. 4）
PDT 2 806	RA 9 51 SA 182（pl. 5）
PDT 2 886	RA 9 52 AM 13（pl. 6）
PDT 2 960	RA 9 54 SA 223
PDT 2 1097	RA 79 27 21
PDT 2 1122	Ripon 2
PDT 2 1161	Rochester 1
PDT 2 1197	Rochester 53
PDT 2 1216	RSO 9 472 P368
PDT 2 1240	RT 37 136 r
PPAC 4 124	RTC 298
PPAC 4 180	SACT 1 70
PPAC 4 240	SACT 1 182
PPAC 5 1677	SACT 1 194
PPAC 5 1694	Santag 7 159
PPAC 5 1771	SAT 2 428
PPAC 5 1775	SAT 2 495
PPAC 5 1781	SAT 2 758
Princeton 1 9	SAT 2 785
Princeton 1 13	SAT 2 902
Princeton 1 88	SAT 2 1002
Princeton 1 89	SAT 2 1016
Princeton 1 93	SAT 2 1104
Princeton 1 102	SAT 2 1122
Princeton 2 35	SAT 2 1173
Princeton 2 68	SAT 2 1176
Princeton 2 72	SAT 3 1761
Princeton 2 85	SAT 3 1876
Princeton 2 117	SAT 3 1882
Princeton 2 300	SAT 3 1883

附　录

SAT 3 1885	TCL 2 5589
SAT 3 1927	TCUR 19
SAT 3 1998	TIM 6 50
SAT 3 2030	TLB 3 26
SAT 3 2132	TLB 3 27
SET 11	TLB 3 28
SET 57	TLB 3 58
SET 58	TLB 3 149
SET 68	Trouvaille 3
SET 93	Trouvaille 26
SET 105	Trouvaille 29
SET 108	Trouvaille 31
SET 116	Trouvaille 32
SET 129	Trouvaille 71
SM 1911. 10. 030	Trouvaille 73
SM 1911. 10. 066	Trouvaille 79
SumTemDocs 19	TRU 13
SumTemDocs 24	TRU 36
Syracuse 327	TRU 49
Syracuse 336	TRU 116
Syracuse 476	TRU 117
TAD 40	TRU 194
TAD 50	TRU 293
TAD 53	TRU 294
Tavolette 143	TRU 357
TCL 2 4691	TUT 60
TCL 2 5482	UCP 9 – 2 – 2 50
TCL 2 5489	UDT 127
TCL 2 5492	UDT 154
TCL 2 5501	USC 6634
TCL 2 5507	YOS 4 64
TCL 2 5514	YOS 4 69
TCL 2 5544	YOS 4 73
TCL 2 5577	YOS 4 74

YOS 4 75

YOS 4 76

YOS 4 78

ZA 107 182 no. 24

ii. 来自吉尔苏档案

AAICAB 1/3 pl. 191 – 192 Bod A 37

Amherst 69

Amherst 110

Amherst 112

Amherst 114

ASJ 2 12 28

ASJ 2 13 31

ASJ 3 164 137

ASJ 3 164 139

ASJ 3 166 144

ASJ 3 167 149

ASJ 3 168 153

ASJ 3 168 155

ASJ 3 169 156

ASJ 3 170 158

ASJ 3 172 167

ASJ 9 328 5

ASJ 9 345 19

ASJ 10 88 2

ASJ 10 92 5

ASJ 11 140 67

ASJ 13 227 72

ASJ 15 127 96

ASJ 20 97 1

ASJ 20 99 2

Atiqot 4 pl. 5 – 6 8

AUCT 2 16

AUCT 2 272

AuOr 17 – 18 224 24

AuOr 17 – 18 225 27

AuOr 17 – 18 227 34

Babyloniaca 8 pl. 11 HG 9

BAOM 2 26 25

BAOM 2 27 37

BAOM 2 30 56

BCT 2 49

BM Messenger 234

BPOA 1 8

BPOA 1 104

BPOA 1 173

BPOA 1 202

BPOA 1 250

BPOA 1 320

BPOA 2 1846

BPOA 2 1909

BPOA 2 1937

BPOA 2 1943

BSA 3 40 1

CDLJ 2015/3 2. 22

CDLJ 2015/3 2. 24

CM 26 59

CM 26 64

CM 26 65

CM 26 66

CM 26 67

CM 26 68

CM 26 69

CM 26 70

CM 26 71

CM 26 73

CM 26 74

CM 26 75

CM 26 76

CM 26 77	CM 26 131
CM 26 78	CM 26 132
CM 26 79	CM 26 133
CM 26 93	CM 26 134
CM 26 94	CM 26 135
CM 26 95	CM 26 143
CM 26 96	CM 26 144
CM 26 97	CM 26 147
CM 26 98	CM 26 148
CM 26 99	CM 26 149
CM 26 101	CST 29
CM 26 103	CST 33
CM 26 104	CST 881 +
CM 26 105	CT 3 pl. 5 – 8 BM 018343
CM 26 106	CT 3 pl. 20 BM 016366
CM 26 110	CT 3 pl. 26 BM 018958
CM 26 112	CT 3 pl. 27 – 30 BM 019027
CM 26 113	CT 3 pl. 40 – 43 BM 021336
CM 26 114	CT 3 pl. 44 – 47 BM 021338
CM 26 115	CT 7 pl. 8 BM 012926
CM 26 116	CT 7 pl. 22 BM 013138
CM 26 117	CT 7 pl. 45 BM 017767
CM 26 118	CT 9 pl. 39 BM 014318
CM 26 119	CT 9 pl. 46 BM 021348
CM 26 120	CT 10 pl. 30 – 31 BM 014612
CM 26 121	CT 10 pl. 48 BM 019067
CM 26 122	CT 10 pl. 50 BM 012248
CM 26 123	CTPSM 1 46
CM 26 124	CTPSM 1 70
CM 26 125	CUSAS 16 169
CM 26 127	DAS 23
CM 26 128	DAS 182
CM 26 129	DAS 187
CM 26 130	DAS 196

DAS 370	ITT 3 5001
DAS 384	ITT 3 5044
DAS 392	ITT 3 5070
DAS 394	ITT 3 5365
From the 21st Century BC p. 217	ITT 3 5412
Fs Foster 192 – 194	ITT 3 6031
Hermitage 3 16	ITT 3 6128
HLC 20（pl. 40）	ITT 3 6294
HLC 36（pl. 14）	ITT 3 6554
HLC 71（pl. 82）	ITT 3 6612
HLC 104（pl. 94）	ITT 5 6705
HLC 128（pl. 98）	ITT 5 6760
HLC 141（pl. 18）	ITT 5 6776
HLC 184（pl. 13）	ITT 5 6804
HLC 216（pl. 14）	ITT 5 6811
HLC 282（pl. 127）	ITT 5 6878
HLC 303（pl. 129）	ITT 5 6954
HLC 320（pl. 131）	ITT 5 8214
HLC 340（pl. 36）	ITT 5 9584
HLC 362（pl. 137）	ITT 5 9816
HLC 384（pl. 145）	ITT 5 10013
ICP varia 17	JSOR 13 179 47
ITT 2 631	LAOS 1 16
ITT 2 641	LAOS 1 36
ITT 2 649	MVN 2 4
ITT 2 664	MVN 2 5
ITT 2 714	MVN 2 18
ITT 2 914	MVN 2 65
ITT 2 916	MVN 2 72
ITT 2 922	MVN 2 81
ITT 2 927	MVN 2 89
ITT 2 1007	MVN 2 194
ITT 2 2748	MVN 2 221
ITT 2 4216	MVN 4 49

MVN 5 171	MVN 12 51
MVN 5 172	MVN 12 54
MVN 5 190	MVN 12 57
MVN 5 273	MVN 12 59
MVN 6 15	MVN 12 65
MVN 6 45	MVN 12 90
MVN 6 216	MVN 12 95
MVN 6 221	MVN 12 96
MVN 6 244	MVN 12 109
MVN 6 261	MVN 12 110
MVN 6 329	MVN 12 113
MVN 6 353	MVN 12 123
MVN 6 362	MVN 12 145
MVN 6 465	MVN 12 270
MVN 7 95	MVN 12 307
MVN 7 353	MVN 12 319
MVN 7 398	MVN 12 451
MVN 9 77	MVN 12 455
MVN 9 125	MVN 12 456
MVN 9 130	MVN 12 500
MVN 9 131	MVN 12 506
MVN 11 6	MVN 13 242
MVN 11 12	MVN 17 53
MVN 11 17	MVN 17 61
MVN 11 31	MVN 17 83
MVN 11 70	MVN 17 147
MVN 11 75	MVN 19 63
MVN 11 80	MVN 19 96
MVN 11 101	MVN 22 152
MVN 11 117	MVN 22 176
MVN 11 130	MVN 22 288
MVN 11 135	NATN 402
MVN 12 45	Nisaba 7 14
MVN 12 47	Nisaba 7 26

Nisaba 10 26	P205835
Nisaba 10 76	P210029
Nisaba 13 10	P234819
Nisaba 13 28	P234830
Nisaba 13 84	P235256
Nisaba 13 85	P377883
Nisaba 17 45	P500110
Nisaba 18 71	PPAC 4 179
Nisaba 18 91	PPAC 5 86
Nisaba 18 107	PPAC 5 195
Nisaba 33 63	PPAC 5 227
Nisaba 33 370	PPAC 5 244
Nisaba 33 748	PPAC 5 254
Nisaba 33 828	PPAC 5 292
Nisaba 33 853	PPAC 5 298
Nisaba 33 882	PPAC 5 307
Nisaba 33 889	PPAC 5 311
Nisaba 33 921	PPAC 5 326
Nisaba 33 932	PPAC 5 331
Nisaba 33 1009	PPAC 5 378
Nisaba 33 1040	PPAC 5 644
OMRO 66 54 19	PPAC 5 659
Ontario 2 90	PPAC 5 723
Orient 16 85 127	PPAC 5 893
OTR 9	PPAC 5 951
OTR 17	PPAC 5 952
OTR 25	PPAC 5 985
OTR 69	PPAC 5 1054
OTR 83	PPAC 5 1056
OTR 84	PPAC 5 1093
OTR 91	PPAC 5 1123
OTR 129	PPAC 5 1126
OTR 213	PPAC 5 1276
OTR 254	PPAC 5 1479

PPAC 5 1571	STA 13
PPAC 5 1638	Sumer 23 142
PPAC 5 1641	TCTI 2 2584
PPAC 5 1756	TCTI 2 2613
Princeton 1 566	TCTI 2 2670
Princeton 2 270	TCTI 2 2696
RA 10 63 12	TCTI 2 2715
RA 62 6 7	TCTI 2 2742
RTC 305	TCTI 2 2753
RTC 333	TCTI 2 2772
RTC 336	TCTI 2 2782
RTC 341	TCTI 2 2785
RTC 420	TCTI 2 2794
Santag 6 16	TCTI 2 2797
SAT 1 14	TCTI 2 2813
SAT 1 25	TCTI 2 3227
SAT 1 26	TCTI 2 3273
SAT 1 77	TCTI 2 3285
SAT 1 146	TCTI 2 3329
SAT 1 180	TCTI 2 3345 + 3395
SAT 1 194	TCTI 2 3382
SAT 1 270	TCTI 2 3400
SAT 1 283	TCTI 2 3411
SAT 1 295	TCTI 2 3451
SAT 1 352	TCTI 2 3492
SAT 1 372	TCTI 2 3702
SAT 1 392	TCTI 2 3727
SAT 1 453	TCTI 2 3781
SNAT 60	TCTI 2 3796 + 3801
SNAT 101	TCTI 2 3808
SNAT 122	TCTI 2 3836
SNAT 161	TCTI 2 3857
SNAT 174	TCTI 2 3865
SNAT 186	TCTI 2 3871

TCTI 2 3882	TCTI 3 6454
TCTI 2 3884	TCTI 3 6457
TCTI 2 3892	TCTI 3 6459
TCTI 2 3901	TCTI 3 6644
TCTI 2 3904	TEL 9
TCTI 2 3905	TEL 15
TCTI 2 3906	TEL 17
TCTI 2 3910	TEL 108
TCTI 2 3971	TEL 117
TCTI 2 3988	TEL 149
TCTI 2 4038	TEL 169
TCTI 2 4075	TEL 172
TCTI 2 4122	TEL 182
TCTI 2 4157	TEL 244
TCTI 2 4168	TEL 246
TCTI 2 4219	TEL 284
TCTI 2 4235	TIM 6 3
TCTI 2 4241	TLB 3 10
TCTI 2 4243	TLB 3 145
TCTI 2 4246	TLB 3 146
TCTI 2 4254	TUT 17
TCTI 2 4255	TUT 80
TCTI 2 4258	TUT 94
TCTI 2 4260	TUT 100
TCTI 2 4266	TUT 118
TCTI 2 4271	TUT 142
TCTI 2 4287	TUT 170
TCTI 2 4292	TUT 171
TCTI 2 4304	TUT 172
TCTI 2 4322	TUT 177
TCTI 3 4768	TUT 199
TCTI 3 6421	TUT 272
TCTI 3 6434	TUT 290
TCTI 3 6443	TUT 299

UDT 23
UDT 48
UDT 51
UDT 97
YOS 18 124

iii. 来自伊利萨格里格档案

CUSAS 40 385
CUSAS 40 388
CUSAS 40 523
CUSAS 40 598
CUSAS 40 628
CUSAS 40 657
CUSAS 40 919
CUSAS 40 1069
CUSAS 40 1586
CUSAS 40 1896
JCS 38 37 11
JCS 38 45 15
JCS 38 49 17
JCS 38 50 18
JCS 38 56 22
JCS 38 60 24
JCS 38 61 25
JCS 38 63 27
JCS 38 73 36
Nisaba 15 56
Nisaba 15 180
Nisaba 15 189
Nisaba 15 191
Nisaba 15 199
Nisaba 15 303
Nisaba 15 427
Nisaba 15 633
Nisaba 15 636
Nisaba 15 675
Nisaba 15 676
Nisaba 15 677
Nisaba 15 678
Nisaba 15 831
Nisaba 15 859
Nisaba 15 865
Nisaba 15 900
Nisaba 15 906
Nisaba 15 907
Nisaba 15 914
Nisaba 15 933
Nisaba 15 979
Nisaba 15 1034
Nisaba 15 1055
Nisaba 15 1085
Nisaba 15 1100
Nisaba 15 1128
Nisaba 15 1134
P274591
P500108

iv. 来自尼普尔档案

BBVO 11 279 6N–T366
BBVO 11 288 6N–T479
BE 3/1 118
MVN 3 323
NATN 453
NRVN 1 184
P325399
TCBI 2/2 11

v. 来自温马档案

AAICAB 1/1 pl. 18 1911–146
AAICAB 1/1 pl. 19 1911–154
AAICAB 1/1 pl. 20 1911–167

AAICAB 1/1 pl. 21 1911 – 173
AAICAB 1/1 pl. 23 1911 – 183
AAICAB 1/1 pl. 27 1911 – 196
AAICAB 1/1 pl. 31 1911 – 216
AAICAB 1/1 pl. 40 1911 – 232
AAICAB 1/1 pl. 56 1923 – 429
AAICAB 1/1 pl. 63 – 64 1924 – 665
AAICAB 1/1 pl. 73 1924 – 685
AAICAB 1/1 pl. 75 1924 – 694
AAICAB 1/1 pl. 75 1924 – 696
AAICAB 1/2 pl. 85 1935 – 513
AAICAB 1/2 pl. 86 1935 – 516
AAICAB 1/2 pl. 86 1935 – 518
AAICAB 1/2 pl. 111 1937 – 93
AAICAB 1/2 pl. 121 1967 – 1497
AAICAB 1/2 pl. 129 1971 – 301
AAICAB 1/2 pl. 133 1971 – 323
AAICAB 1/2 pl. 135 1971 – 332
AAICAB 1/2 pl. 146 1971 – 369
AAICAB 1/2 pl. 152 1971 – 390
AAICAB 1/2 pl. 167 1975 – 297
AAICAB 1/2 pl. 169 1978 – 145
AAICAB 1/3 pl. 222 Bod S 179
AAICAB 1/3 pl. 232 Bod S 224
AAICAB 1/3 pl. 241 Bod S 276
AAICAB 1/4 Bod S 335
AAICAB 1/4 Bod S 357
AAICAB 1/4 Bod S 380
AAICAB 1/4 Bod S 383
AAICAB 1/4 Bod S 384
AAICAB 1/4 Bod S 386
AAICAB 1/4 Bod S 388
AAICAB 1/4 Bod S 437
AAICAB 1/4 Bod S 444

AAICAB 1/4 Bod S 485
AAICAB 1/4 Bod S 501
AAICAB 1/4 Bod S 518
AAICAB 1/4 Bod S 520
AAICAB 1/4 Bod S 522
AAICAB 1/4 Bod S 526
AAICAB 1/4 Bod S 534
AAICAB 1/4 Bod S 545
AAICAB 1/4 Bod S 568
AAS 65
AAS 107
AAS 112
AAS 115
AAS 116
AAS 129
AAS 130
AAS 156
Aegyptus 26 163 12
Aevum 36 228 1
Akkadica 135/1 100 – 101 14
Akkadica 138 160 – 162 4
Akkadica 138 168 – 175 8
Aleppo 9
Aleppo 50
Aleppo 53
Aleppo 54
Aleppo 58
Aleppo 60
Aleppo 62
Aleppo 63
Aleppo 66
Aleppo 67
Aleppo 77
Aleppo 78

附　录

Aleppo 79	Aleppo 130
Aleppo 80	Aleppo 131
Aleppo 85	Aleppo 132
Aleppo 86	Aleppo 133
Aleppo 89	Aleppo 134
Aleppo 90	Aleppo 135
Aleppo 91	Aleppo 136
Aleppo 93	Aleppo 137
Aleppo 94	Aleppo 141
Aleppo 95	Aleppo 143
Aleppo 96	Aleppo 146
Aleppo 97	Aleppo 150
Aleppo 99	Aleppo 151
Aleppo 100	Aleppo 160
Aleppo 101	Aleppo 183
Aleppo 102	Aleppo 261
Aleppo 103	Aleppo 269
Aleppo 104	Aleppo 307
Aleppo 107	Aleppo 327
Aleppo 108	Aleppo 328
Aleppo 109	Aleppo 330
Aleppo 110	Aleppo 332
Aleppo 112	Aleppo 333
Aleppo 113	Aleppo 334
Aleppo 115	Aleppo 335
Aleppo 116	Aleppo 375
Aleppo 117	Aleppo 391
Aleppo 118	Aleppo 421
Aleppo 119	Aleppo 428
Aleppo 120	Aleppo 498
Aleppo 121	Aleppo 501
Aleppo 126	AnOr 1 50
Aleppo 128	AnOr 1 54
Aleppo 129	AnOr 1 61

AnOr 1 66
AnOr 1 91
AnOr 1 120
AnOr 1 147
AnOr 1 148
AnOr 1 150
AnOr 1 159
AnOr 1 167
AnOr 1 168
AnOr 1 199
AnOr 1 226
AnOr 1 250
AnOr 1 270
AnOr 7 146
AnOr 7 236
AnOr 7 247
AnOr 7 248
AnOr 7 328
AR RIM 5 39 322
AR RIM 7 26 17
AR RIM 7 32 20
ArOr 62 247 I 878
ASJ 7 126 31
ASJ 9 252 31
ASJ 15 77 3
ASJ 16 111 17
ASJ 19 213 38
ASJ 19 217 47
Atiqot 4 pl. 15 30
Atiqot 4 pl. 17 34
AUCT 2 327
AUCT 3 218
AUCT 3 219
AUCT 3 221

AUCT 3 223
AUCT 3 255
AUCT 3 374
AUCT 3 423
AUCT 3 474
AuOr 8 84 9
AuOr 8 84 10
Babyloniaca 8 pl. 5 Pupil 13
Babyloniaca 8 pl. 5 Pupil 16
BCT 1 129
BCT 2 16
BCT 2 91
BCT 2 93
BCT 2 127
BCT 2 151
BCT 2 186
BCT 2 195
BCT 2 205
BCT 2 225
BIN 3 341
BIN 3 381
BIN 3 383
BIN 3 401
BIN 3 406
BIN 3 433
BIN 3 535
BIN 3 543
BIN 3 545
BIN 3 549
BIN 3 615
BIN 5 4
BIN 5 74
BIN 5 75
BIN 5 76

BIN 5 77	BPOA 1 675
BIN 5 78	BPOA 1 684
BIN 5 79	BPOA 1 685
BIN 5 80	BPOA 1 733
BIN 5 82	BPOA 1 765
BIN 5 83	BPOA 1 768
BIN 5 84	BPOA 1 795
BIN 5 85	BPOA 1 847
BIN 5 87	BPOA 1 861
BIN 5 154	BPOA 1 923
BIN 5 171	BPOA 1 927
BIN 5 291	BPOA 1 982
BIN 5 345	BPOA 1 1014
BJRL 64 107 49	BPOA 1 1016
BMC Roma 8 10 3	BPOA 1 1021
BPOA 1 374	BPOA 1 1045
BPOA 1 376	BPOA 1 1057
BPOA 1 377	BPOA 1 1071
BPOA 1 475	BPOA 1 1072
BPOA 1 480	BPOA 1 1079
BPOA 1 485	BPOA 1 1088
BPOA 1 503	BPOA 1 1097
BPOA 1 513	BPOA 1 1108
BPOA 1 524	BPOA 1 1115
BPOA 1 528	BPOA 1 1118
BPOA 1 554	BPOA 1 1125
BPOA 1 576	BPOA 1 1126
BPOA 1 588	BPOA 1 1140
BPOA 1 606	BPOA 1 1151
BPOA 1 607	BPOA 1 1163
BPOA 1 615	BPOA 1 1166
BPOA 1 627	BPOA 1 1167
BPOA 1 640	BPOA 1 1176
BPOA 1 667	BPOA 1 1191

BPOA 1 1211	BPOA 1 1668
BPOA 1 1230	BPOA 1 1677
BPOA 1 1240	BPOA 1 1684
BPOA 1 1249	BPOA 1 1687
BPOA 1 1267	BPOA 1 1690
BPOA 1 1276	BPOA 1 1692
BPOA 1 1280	BPOA 1 1703
BPOA 1 1283	BPOA 1 1706
BPOA 1 1323	BPOA 1 1709
BPOA 1 1324	BPOA 1 1712
BPOA 1 1337	BPOA 1 1713
BPOA 1 1338	BPOA 1 1720
BPOA 1 1341	BPOA 1 1768
BPOA 1 1379	BPOA 1 1777
BPOA 1 1382	BPOA 1 1778
BPOA 1 1387	BPOA 2 1814
BPOA 1 1393	BPOA 2 1831
BPOA 1 1433	BPOA 2 1867
BPOA 1 1448	BPOA 2 1872
BPOA 1 1452	BPOA 2 1912
BPOA 1 1472	BPOA 2 1986
BPOA 1 1488	BPOA 2 1992
BPOA 1 1492	BPOA 2 1993
BPOA 1 1507	BPOA 2 2013
BPOA 1 1527	BPOA 2 2023
BPOA 1 1539	BPOA 2 2024
BPOA 1 1574	BPOA 2 2036
BPOA 1 1582	BPOA 2 2041
BPOA 1 1613	BPOA 2 2043
BPOA 1 1619	BPOA 2 2054
BPOA 1 1639	BPOA 2 2056
BPOA 1 1650	BPOA 2 2059
BPOA 1 1652	BPOA 2 2070
BPOA 1 1657	BPOA 2 2072

BPOA 2 2075	BPOA 2 2372
BPOA 2 2086	BPOA 2 2374
BPOA 2 2087	BPOA 2 2404
BPOA 2 2089	BPOA 2 2406
BPOA 2 2096	BPOA 2 2418
BPOA 2 2109	BPOA 2 2428
BPOA 2 2119	BPOA 2 2443
BPOA 2 2127	BPOA 2 2449
BPOA 2 2137	BPOA 2 2450
BPOA 2 2157	BPOA 2 2461
BPOA 2 2164	BPOA 2 2491
BPOA 2 2167	BPOA 2 2497
BPOA 2 2184	BPOA 2 2507
BPOA 2 2190	BPOA 2 2510
BPOA 2 2195	BPOA 2 2511
BPOA 2 2198	BPOA 2 2533
BPOA 2 2210	BPOA 2 2589
BPOA 2 2221	BPOA 2 2635
BPOA 2 2223	BPOA 2 2638
BPOA 2 2227	BPOA 2 2640
BPOA 2 2244	BPOA 6 12
BPOA 2 2258	BPOA 6 129
BPOA 2 2259	BPOA 6 135
BPOA 2 2261	BPOA 6 167
BPOA 2 2275	BPOA 6 197
BPOA 2 2295	BPOA 6 220
BPOA 2 2296	BPOA 6 223
BPOA 2 2299	BPOA 6 232
BPOA 2 2304	BPOA 6 242
BPOA 2 2310	BPOA 6 243
BPOA 2 2325	BPOA 6 244
BPOA 2 2344	BPOA 6 246
BPOA 2 2345	BPOA 6 248
BPOA 2 2349	BPOA 6 262

BPOA 6 271	BPOA 6 789
BPOA 6 274	BPOA 6 822
BPOA 6 276	BPOA 6 825
BPOA 6 285	BPOA 6 837
BPOA 6 318	BPOA 6 845
BPOA 6 326	BPOA 6 846
BPOA 6 327	BPOA 6 855
BPOA 6 333	BPOA 6 883
BPOA 6 349	BPOA 6 895
BPOA 6 351	BPOA 6 958
BPOA 6 368	BPOA 6 966
BPOA 6 375	BPOA 6 1014
BPOA 6 391	BPOA 6 1017
BPOA 6 393	BPOA 6 1018
BPOA 6 398	BPOA 6 1058
BPOA 6 403	BPOA 6 1059
BPOA 6 416	BPOA 6 1088
BPOA 6 434	BPOA 6 1103
BPOA 6 440	BPOA 6 1108
BPOA 6 449	BPOA 6 1120
BPOA 6 458	BPOA 6 1129
BPOA 6 463	BPOA 6 1135
BPOA 6 470	BPOA 6 1169
BPOA 6 471	BPOA 6 1173
BPOA 6 498	BPOA 6 1199
BPOA 6 506	BPOA 6 1203
BPOA 6 511	BPOA 6 1216
BPOA 6 521	BPOA 6 1227
BPOA 6 548	BPOA 6 1228
BPOA 6 611	BPOA 6 1233
BPOA 6 749	BPOA 6 1266
BPOA 6 755	BPOA 6 1285
BPOA 6 761	BPOA 6 1294
BPOA 6 763	BPOA 6 1315

BPOA 6 1337	BPOA 7 1914
BPOA 6 1373	BPOA 7 1918
BPOA 6 1381	BPOA 7 1953
BPOA 6 1397	BPOA 7 1960
BPOA 6 1402	BPOA 7 1961
BPOA 6 1408	BPOA 7 1965
BPOA 6 1425	BPOA 7 1971
BPOA 6 1447	BPOA 7 1984
BPOA 6 1460	BPOA 7 2015
BPOA 6 1467	BPOA 7 2034
BPOA 6 1474	BPOA 7 2040
BPOA 6 1489	BPOA 7 2045
BPOA 6 1506	BPOA 7 2050
BPOA 6 1513	BPOA 7 2060
BPOA 6 1532	BPOA 7 2061
BPOA 7 1547	BPOA 7 2078
BPOA 7 1564	BPOA 7 2092
BPOA 7 1619	BPOA 7 2100
BPOA 7 1694	BPOA 7 2109
BPOA 7 1699	BPOA 7 2134
BPOA 7 1706	BPOA 7 2160
BPOA 7 1712	BPOA 7 2172
BPOA 7 1757	BPOA 7 2176
BPOA 7 1781	BPOA 7 2179
BPOA 7 1783	BPOA 7 2182
BPOA 7 1809	BPOA 7 2187
BPOA 7 1822	BPOA 7 2216
BPOA 7 1827	BPOA 7 2222
BPOA 7 1876	BPOA 7 2294
BPOA 7 1877	BPOA 7 2312
BPOA 7 1878	BPOA 7 2341
BPOA 7 1884	BPOA 7 2353
BPOA 7 1899	BPOA 7 2382
BPOA 7 1913	BPOA 7 2440

BPOA 7 2459	CHEU 21
BPOA 7 2460	CHEU 45
BPOA 7 2474	CHEU 56
BPOA 7 2476	CM 26 2
BPOA 7 2482	CM 26 3
BPOA 7 2487	CM 26 6
BPOA 7 2507	CM 26 12
BPOA 7 2518	CM 26 13
BPOA 7 2524	CM 26 15
BPOA 7 2539	CM 26 16
BPOA 7 2540	CM 26 17
BPOA 7 2541	CM 26 20
BPOA 7 2546	CM 26 21
BPOA 7 2547	CM 26 22
BPOA 7 2549	CM 26 23
BPOA 7 2567	CM 26 24
BPOA 7 2575	CM 26 26
BPOA 7 2577	CM 26 27
BPOA 7 2590	CM 26 30
BPOA 7 2615	CM 26 31
BPOA 7 2664	CM 26 32
BPOA 7 2754	CM 26 33
BPOA 7 2819	CM 26 34
BPOA 7 2837	CM 26 35
BPOA 7 2858	CM 26 36
BPOA 7 2859	CM 26 37
BPOA 7 2900	CM 26 38
BPOA 7 2921	CM 26 39
BRM 3 139	CM 26 40
CDLB 2016/1 2.3.1	CM 26 41
CDLJ 2003/1 no. 1	CM 26 42
CDLJ 2009/2 2.4	CM 26 43
CDLJ 2009/6 1	CM 26 44
CDLJ 2011/2	CM 26 45

CM 26 46	CST 802
CM 26 47	CST 874
CM 26 48	CUSAS 16 279
CM 26 49	CUSAS 39 63
CM 26 50	CUSAS 39 74
CM 26 51	CUSAS 39 156
CM 26 52	CUSAS 39 215
CM 26 53	CUSAS 40 527
CM 26 54	CUSAS 40 724
CM 26 55	CUSAS 40 926
CM 26 56	CUSAS 40 1056
CM 26 57	CUSAS 40 1224
CM 26 58	CUSAS 40 1309
CM 26 60	CUSAS 40 1480
CM 26 126	CUSAS 40 1709
CM 26 136	CUSAS 40 1802
CST 381	CUSAS 40 1906
CST 525	Dissertation Cooper p. 73
CST 562	DoCu 305
CST 578	Frühe Schrift 13. 13
CST 581	Fs Freydank p. 208 SIL 46
CST 584	Fs Hruška 85
CST 586	Fs Klengel 161 3
CST 587	Fs Leichty 285 14
CST 623	Fs Leichty 286 15
CST 629	Fs Lenoble 160 no. 1
CST 659	Fs Lenoble 161 no. 5
CST 702	Fs Lenoble 164 no. 16
CST 703	Fs Lenoble 164 no. 18
CST 704	Fs Lenoble 166 no. 26
CST 727	Fs Lenoble 166 no. 27
CST 729	Fs Lenoble 168 no. 34
CST 730	Fs Sigrist 31 no. 16
CST 731	Fs Součková – Siegelová 417 9

Georgica 1. 2. 1
Georgica 1. 2. 2
Georgica 3. 11
Hirose 10
Hirose 345
Hirose 347
Hirose 393
HUCA 29 83 10
HUCA 29 93 17
IOS 6 39 P 1
JANES 21 72 5
JCS 2 185 NBC 3084
JCS 2 185 PTS 0453
JCS 2 186 NBC 2950
JCS 2 186 YBC 12536
JCS 2 187 PTS 1213
JCS 2 190 YBC 12534
JCS 2 191 NBC 3221
JCS 2 191 PTS 1210
JCS 2 191 YBC 12539
JCS 2 192 NBC 0948
JCS 2 192 NBC 2070
JCS 2 192 NBC 2963
JCS 2 192 PTS 0630
JCS 2 192 PTS 0986
JCS 2 193 NBC 2031
JCS 2 194 NBC 3208
JCS 2 196 NBC 1856
JCS 2 196 PTS 1339
JCS 2 198 YBC 12523
JCS 2 198 YBC 12541
JCS 23 69 2
JCS 23 110 3
JCS 25 176

JCS 28 209 2
JCS 28 209 4
JCS 28 210 6
JCS 28 212 13
JCS 28 212 14
JCS 28 214 21
JCS 28 214 22
JCS 28 223 53
JCS 28 224 54
JCS 35 178 3
JCS 35 206 3
JCS 35 207 4
JCS 38 245
JCS 39 124 12
JCS 40 113 5
JCS 52 47 66
JCS 52 50 79
JCS 52 51 87
JCS 52 52 91
JCS 52 53 96
JCS 52 123
JCS 54 12 81
JCS 54 15 92
JNES 50 255 – 280
JRAS 1939 32
JSOR 12 39 20
JSOR 12 40 23
L'uomo 48
L'uomo 56
LAOS 1 9
LAOS 1 11
MCS 1 54 BM 105430
MCS 3 42 1 BM 113104
MCS 3 42 2 BM 113149

附　录

MCS 3 42 6 BM 113163	MVN 11 Y
MCS 3 43 8 BM 105546	MVN 13 6
MCS 3 43 9 BM 105567	MVN 13 33
MCS 3 43 10 BM 105485	MVN 13 143
MCS 3 43 15 BM 105550	MVN 13 144
MCS 3 43 17 BM 105409	MVN 13 145
MCS 3 44 20 BM 105380	MVN 13 156
MCS 3 44 21 BM 112976	MVN 13 168
MCS 3 87 BM 105534	MVN 13 228
MCS 3 93 BM 113155	MVN 13 355
MCS 6 19 BM 112990	MVN 13 379
MCS 8 96 BM 111750	MVN 13 603
MVN 1 62	MVN 13 614
MVN 1 199	MVN 13 618
MVN 1 204	MVN 13 637
MVN 1 232	MVN 13 699
MVN 1 238	MVN 13 754
MVN 1 239	MVN 13 758
MVN 2 354	MVN 13 860
MVN 3 231	MVN 14 11
MVN 3 239	MVN 14 12
MVN 3 301	MVN 14 13
MVN 3 312	MVN 14 16
MVN 4 25	MVN 14 18
MVN 4 146	MVN 14 30
MVN 4 168	MVN 14 31
MVN 4 183	MVN 14 32
MVN 4 258	MVN 14 40
MVN 4 267	MVN 14 41
MVN 5 9	MVN 14 42
MVN 5 10	MVN 14 51
MVN 5 59	MVN 14 53
MVN 9 186	MVN 14 55
MVN 10 230	MVN 14 70

MVN 14 71	MVN 14 323
MVN 14 72	MVN 14 350
MVN 14 73	MVN 14 353
MVN 14 75	MVN 14 356
MVN 14 87	MVN 14 359
MVN 14 90	MVN 14 361
MVN 14 93	MVN 14 364
MVN 14 98	MVN 14 372
MVN 14 99	MVN 14 373
MVN 14 100	MVN 14 374
MVN 14 101	MVN 14 375
MVN 14 103	MVN 14 377
MVN 14 108	MVN 14 385
MVN 14 115	MVN 14 388
MVN 14 122	MVN 14 399
MVN 14 124	MVN 14 406
MVN 14 131	MVN 14 408
MVN 14 139	MVN 14 411
MVN 14 156	MVN 14 414
MVN 14 178	MVN 14 416
MVN 14 210	MVN 14 418
MVN 14 213	MVN 14 419
MVN 14 216	MVN 14 421
MVN 14 218	MVN 14 422
MVN 14 229	MVN 14 423
MVN 14 230	MVN 14 425
MVN 14 284	MVN 14 426
MVN 14 289	MVN 14 433
MVN 14 291	MVN 14 437
MVN 14 296	MVN 14 440
MVN 14 298	MVN 14 441
MVN 14 311	MVN 14 442
MVN 14 317	MVN 14 445
MVN 14 321	MVN 14 461

附　录

MVN 14 463	MVN 16 808
MVN 14 466	MVN 16 819
MVN 14 476	MVN 16 821
MVN 14 478	MVN 16 829
MVN 14 481	MVN 16 833
MVN 14 485	MVN 16 843
MVN 14 488	MVN 16 845
MVN 14 501	MVN 16 856
MVN 14 507	MVN 16 875
MVN 14 508	MVN 16 881
MVN 14 513	MVN 16 886
MVN 14 516	MVN 16 890
MVN 14 525	MVN 16 924
MVN 14 526	MVN 16 945
MVN 14 533	MVN 16 982
MVN 14 534	MVN 16 995
MVN 14 535	MVN 16 1004
MVN 14 539	MVN 16 1005
MVN 14 597	MVN 16 1006
MVN 15 35	MVN 16 1009
MVN 15 61	MVN 16 1010
MVN 15 92	MVN 16 1012
MVN 15 108	MVN 16 1032
MVN 15 176	MVN 16 1042
MVN 15 229	MVN 16 1059
MVN 15 334	MVN 16 1060
MVN 16 634	MVN 16 1062
MVN 16 635	MVN 16 1067
MVN 16 652	MVN 16 1080
MVN 16 715	MVN 16 1088
MVN 16 732	MVN 16 1095
MVN 16 786	MVN 16 1096
MVN 16 803	MVN 16 1097
MVN 16 806	MVN 16 1098

MVN 16 1099	MVN 16 1250
MVN 16 1106	MVN 16 1251
MVN 16 1114	MVN 16 1256
MVN 16 1122	MVN 16 1262
MVN 16 1134	MVN 16 1266
MVN 16 1135	MVN 16 1267
MVN 16 1136	MVN 16 1270
MVN 16 1137	MVN 16 1278
MVN 16 1138	MVN 16 1281
MVN 16 1143	MVN 16 1295
MVN 16 1144	MVN 16 1302
MVN 16 1150	MVN 16 1315
MVN 16 1151	MVN 16 1316
MVN 16 1154	MVN 16 1332
MVN 16 1155	MVN 16 1339
MVN 16 1167	MVN 16 1347
MVN 16 1179	MVN 16 1356
MVN 16 1188	MVN 16 1361
MVN 16 1189	MVN 16 1364
MVN 16 1193	MVN 16 1370
MVN 16 1198	MVN 16 1373
MVN 16 1200	MVN 16 1383
MVN 16 1202	MVN 16 1386
MVN 16 1203	MVN 16 1389
MVN 16 1204	MVN 16 1396
MVN 16 1209	MVN 16 1406
MVN 16 1213	MVN 16 1407
MVN 16 1215	MVN 16 1411
MVN 16 1219	MVN 16 1413
MVN 16 1223	MVN 16 1419
MVN 16 1229	MVN 16 1423
MVN 16 1230	MVN 16 1425
MVN 16 1235	MVN 16 1440
MVN 16 1245	MVN 16 1441

MVN 16 1442	MVN 18 506
MVN 16 1445	MVN 18 556
MVN 16 1447	MVN 18 669
MVN 16 1451	MVN 18 672
MVN 16 1452	MVN 18 731
MVN 16 1453	MVN 18 733
MVN 16 1454	MVN 20 9
MVN 16 1471	MVN 20 24
MVN 16 1473	MVN 20 26
MVN 16 1474	MVN 20 30
MVN 16 1480	MVN 20 37
MVN 16 1490	MVN 20 61
MVN 16 1496	MVN 20 100
MVN 16 1498	MVN 20 106
MVN 16 1501	MVN 20 152
MVN 16 1508	MVN 21 6
MVN 16 1509	MVN 21 36
MVN 16 1510	MVN 21 167
MVN 16 1516	MVN 21 173
MVN 16 1558	MVN 21 199
MVN 16 1560	MVN 21 201
MVN 16 1569	MVN 21 203
MVN 16 1572	MVN 21 205
MVN 16 1583	MVN 21 250
MVN 16 1590	MVN 21 259
MVN 16 1597	MVN 21 260
MVN 18 384	MVN 21 317
MVN 18 419	NABU 1995/64
MVN 18 450	NABU 1996/131
MVN 18 459	NABU 2018/59 3
MVN 18 471	NABU 2020/47 3
MVN 18 474	Nebraska 10
MVN 18 478	Nik 2 119
MVN 18 492	Nik 2 180

Nik 2 183	Nisaba 9 85
Nik 2 185	Nisaba 9 89
Nik 2 186	Nisaba 9 92
Nik 2 187	Nisaba 9 110
Nik 2 188	Nisaba 9 114
Nik 2 193	Nisaba 9 117
Nik 2 199	Nisaba 9 123
Nik 2 200	Nisaba 9 142
Nik 2 214	Nisaba 9 165
Nik 2 215	Nisaba 9 166
Nik 2 216	Nisaba 9 177
Nik 2 226	Nisaba 9 178
Nik 2 227	Nisaba 9 198
Nik 2 228	Nisaba 9 215
Nik 2 229	Nisaba 9 237
Nik 2 230	Nisaba 9 250
Nik 2 233	Nisaba 9 262
Nik 2 234	Nisaba 9 265
Nik 2 235	Nisaba 9 266
Nik 2 278	Nisaba 9 271
Nik 2 310	Nisaba 9 304
Nik 2 321	Nisaba 9 307
Nik 2 403	Nisaba 9 310
Nik 2 428	Nisaba 9 342
Nik 2 431	Nisaba 9 344
Nisaba 3/1 78	Nisaba 13 69
Nisaba 6 9	Nisaba 15 1123
Nisaba 6 20	Nisaba 15 1129
Nisaba 9 20	Nisaba 23 13
Nisaba 9 21	Nisaba 23 26
Nisaba 9 25	Nisaba 23 43
Nisaba 9 35	Nisaba 23 53
Nisaba 9 66	Nisaba 23 64
Nisaba 9 78	Nisaba 23 68

Nisaba 23 70	Nisaba 33 379
Nisaba 23 86	Nisaba 33 569
Nisaba 23 122	Nisaba 33 1114
Nisaba 23 141	NYPL 23
Nisaba 24 9	NYPL 42
Nisaba 24 24	NYPL 73
Nisaba 24 27	NYPL 81
Nisaba 24 28	NYPL 188
Nisaba 26 2	NYPL 191
Nisaba 26 34	NYPL 302
Nisaba 26 94	NYPL 324
Nisaba 31 23	NYPL 342
Nisaba 31 30	NYPL 363
Nisaba 31 36	NYPL 385
Nisaba 31 51	OBO 200 no. 97
Nisaba 31 63	OLP 20 18
Nisaba 31 71	OLP 20 21 2
Nisaba 31 75	Ontario 2 7
Nisaba 31 82	Ontario 2 38
Nisaba 31 129	Ontario 2 79
Nisaba 31 140	Ontario 2 201
Nisaba 31 155	Ontario 2 222
Nisaba 32 20	Ontario 2 224
Nisaba 32 152	Ontario 2 301
Nisaba 32 166	Ontario 2 327
Nisaba 32 222	Ontario 2 336
Nisaba 32 229	Ontario 2 365
Nisaba 32 236	Ontario 2 377
Nisaba 32 247	Ontario 2 385
Nisaba 33 92	Ontario 2 388
Nisaba 33 108	Ontario 2 398
Nisaba 33 145	Ontario 2 487
Nisaba 33 162	Ontario 2 493
Nisaba 33 276	Orient 16 58 57

Orient 16 63 73	P234883
Orient 16 63 75	P234918
Orient 16 68 88	P234970
Orient 16 72 101	P234977
Orient 55 152 8	P234982
Orient 55 152 9	P235032
Orient 55 157 no. 2	P235046
Orient 55 157 – 158 no. 3	P235073
Orient 55 158 – 159 no. 4	P235087
Orient 55 166 no. 13	P235355
OrNS 68 111 2	P235358
OrSP 47 – 49 172	P235370
OrSP 47 – 49 176	P235373
OrSP 47 – 49 177	P235380
OrSP 47 – 49 194	P235480
OrSP 47 – 49 195	P235482
OrSP 47 – 49 195a	P235486
OrSP 47 – 49 233	P235553
OrSP 47 – 49 238	P235556
OrSP 47 – 49 262	P235613
OrSP 47 – 49 297	P250472
OrSP 47 – 49 300	P250546
OrSP 47 – 49 316	P250644
OrSP 47 – 49 330	P250654
OrSP 47 – 49 333	P250761
OrSP 47 – 49 336	P253724
OrSP 47 – 49 348	P313083
OrSP 47 – 49 377	P341911
OrSP 47 – 49 456	P341915
OrSP 47 – 49 476	P341918
OrSP 47 – 49 477	P341926
P109310	P341932
P143176	P341937
P210030	P341959

P341967	Princeton 1 152
P341985	Princeton 1 170
P341991	Princeton 1 195
P342001	Princeton 1 214
P342031	Princeton 1 223
P342050	Princeton 1 225
P342105	Princeton 1 226
P413899	Princeton 1 227
P423656	Princeton 1 228
P424382	Princeton 1 231
P424388	Princeton 1 232
P424390	Princeton 1 234
P469841	Princeton 1 236
P497531	Princeton 1 241
P500131	Princeton 1 244
PDT 2 1346	Princeton 1 253
PDT 2 1348	Princeton 1 375
PDT 2 1367	Princeton 1 376
PDT 2 1372	Princeton 1 532
PPAC 4 147 & 148	Princeton 2 161
PPAC 4 167	Princeton 2 192
PPAC 4 169	Princeton 2 315
PPAC 4 171	Princeton 2 335
PPAC 4 200	Princeton 2 336
PPAC 5 485	Princeton 2 339
PPAC 5 514	Princeton 2 347
PPAC 5 1083	Princeton 2 350
Prima del' alfabeto 32	Princeton 2 355
Princeton 1 134	Princeton 2 376
Princeton 1 140	Princeton 2 407
Princeton 1 142	Princeton 2 418
Princeton 1 148	Princeton 2 445
Princeton 1 149	RA 8 156 AO 5649
Princeton 1 150	RA 25 22 AF 2

RA 49 91 25	Santag 6 89
RA 49 93 37	Santag 6 96
RA 59 146 FM 14	Santag 6 235
RA 98 7 9	Santag 6 252
Rochester 186	Santag 6 263
RSO 83 349 36	Santag 6 264
RSO 83 350 42	Santag 6 266
SA 158	Santag 6 269
SACT 1 118	Santag 6 273
SACT 1 121	Santag 6 275
SACT 2 93	Santag 6 278
SACT 2 113	Santag 6 298
SACT 2 155	Santag 6 320
SACT 2 179	Santag 6 357
SACT 2 180	Santag 6 374
SACT 2 184	Santag 6 375
SACT 2 186	Santag 7 22
SACT 2 188	Santag 7 25
SACT 2 190	Santag 7 75
SACT 2 194	Santag 7 76
SACT 2 198	Santag 7 85
SACT 2 205	SAT 2 11
SACT 2 214	SAT 2 12
SACT 2 272	SAT 2 27
SAKF 20	SAT 2 37
SAKF 24	SAT 2 61
SAKF 45	SAT 2 64
SAKF 72	SAT 2 88
SAKF 78	SAT 2 89
SAKF 84	SAT 2 133
Santag 6 24	SAT 2 141
Santag 6 38	SAT 2 165
Santag 6 56	SAT 2 175
Santag 6 88	SAT 2 193

SAT 2 263	SAT 2 646
SAT 2 285	SAT 2 695
SAT 2 291	SAT 2 836
SAT 2 304	SAT 2 846
SAT 2 324	SAT 2 886
SAT 2 330	SAT 2 934
SAT 2 338	SAT 2 957
SAT 2 357	SAT 2 961
SAT 2 365	SAT 2 992
SAT 2 369	SAT 2 1072
SAT 2 381	SAT 2 1077
SAT 2 386	SAT 2 1091
SAT 2 395	SAT 2 1144
SAT 2 467	SAT 3 1195
SAT 2 470	SAT 3 1214
SAT 2 482	SAT 3 1304
SAT 2 488	SAT 3 1312
SAT 2 496	SAT 3 1343
SAT 2 503	SAT 3 1347
SAT 2 506	SAT 3 1362
SAT 2 520	SAT 3 1379
SAT 2 530	SAT 3 1388
SAT 2 544	SAT 3 1395
SAT 2 554	SAT 3 1405
SAT 2 569	SAT 3 1412
SAT 2 570	SAT 3 1416
SAT 2 572	SAT 3 1418
SAT 2 578	SAT 3 1421
SAT 2 580	SAT 3 1424
SAT 2 593	SAT 3 1429
SAT 2 594	SAT 3 1432
SAT 2 599	SAT 3 1433
SAT 2 600	SAT 3 1434
SAT 2 634	SAT 3 1435

SAT 3 1442	SAT 3 2085
SAT 3 1454	SAT 3 2086
SAT 3 1455	SAT 3 2122
SAT 3 1460	SAT 3 2138
SAT 3 1461	SAT 3 2145
SAT 3 1467	SAT 3 2178
SAT 3 1471	SDSU 4
SAT 3 1473	SET 130
SAT 3 1475	SET 241
SAT 3 1485	SET 274
SAT 3 1489	SET 283
SAT 3 1491	Smithsonian 21
SAT 3 1524	SNAT 25
SAT 3 1555	SNAT 285
SAT 3 1562	SNAT 293
SAT 3 1664	SNAT 377
SAT 3 1666	SNAT 400
SAT 3 1667	SNAT 425
SAT 3 1669	SNAT 428
SAT 3 1671	SNAT 430
SAT 3 1674	SNAT 439
SAT 3 1728	SNAT 447
SAT 3 1742	SNAT 464
SAT 3 1819	SNAT 484
SAT 3 1907	SNAT 504
SAT 3 1936	SNAT 537
SAT 3 1995	SNAT 539
SAT 3 2047	South Dakota 48
SAT 3 2059	STA 3
SAT 3 2064	STA 23
SAT 3 2071	STA 31
SAT 3 2075	Syracuse 7
SAT 3 2083	Syracuse 9
SAT 3 2084	Syracuse 30

Syracuse 40	Tavolette 207
Syracuse 50	Tavolette 311
Syracuse 85	TCL 5 5665
Syracuse 101	TCL 5 5667
Syracuse 108	TCL 5 5670
Syracuse 127	TCL 5 5671
Syracuse 130	TCL 5 6038
Syracuse 131	TCL 5 6057
Syracuse 132	TCNU 520
Syracuse 143	TCNU 588
Syracuse 162	TCNU 589
Syracuse 167	TCNU 634
Syracuse 174	TCNU 635
Syracuse 177	TCNU 685
Syracuse 192	TCNU 709
Syracuse 195	TCNU 720
Syracuse 201	TCUR 6
Syracuse 215	TJA pl. 56 IOS 28
Syracuse 220	TLB 3 37
Syracuse 243	UCP 9 – 2 – 1 26
Syracuse 244	UCP 9 – 2 – 1 33
Syracuse 245	UCP 9 – 2 – 1 57
Syracuse 254	UCP 9 – 2 – 1 73
Syracuse 260	UCP 9 – 2 – 1 77
Syracuse 272	UCP 9 – 2 – 2 63
Syracuse 355	UCP 9 – 2 – 2 105
Syracuse 432	UCP 9 – 2 – 2 106
Syracuse 433	UCP 9 – 2 – 2 113
Syracuse 434	UCP 9 – 2 – 2 121
Tavolette 8	Umma 10
Tavolette 10	Umma 21
Tavolette 21	Umma 22
Tavolette 60	Umma 24
Tavolette 84	Umma 27

Umma 46	UTI 3 1860
Umma 58	UTI 3 1871
Umma 60	UTI 3 1898
Umma 67	UTI 3 1909
Umma 73	UTI 3 1913
Umma 92	UTI 3 1914
Umma 98	UTI 3 1915
Umma 102	UTI 3 1919
UTI 3 1601	UTI 3 1920
UTI 3 1603	UTI 3 1922
UTI 3 1604	UTI 3 1924
UTI 3 1606	UTI 3 1926
UTI 3 1614	UTI 3 1927
UTI 3 1620	UTI 3 1934
UTI 3 1626	UTI 3 1940
UTI 3 1634	UTI 3 1963
UTI 3 1645	UTI 3 1965
UTI 3 1657	UTI 3 1970
UTI 3 1663	UTI 3 1973
UTI 3 1667	UTI 3 1981
UTI 3 1675	UTI 3 2011
UTI 3 1695	UTI 3 2012
UTI 3 1698	UTI 3 2036
UTI 3 1715	UTI 3 2090
UTI 3 1757	UTI 3 2100
UTI 3 1773	UTI 3 2105
UTI 3 1774	UTI 3 2146
UTI 3 1784	UTI 3 2199
UTI 3 1790	UTI 3 2200
UTI 3 1807	UTI 3 2205
UTI 3 1818	UTI 3 2210
UTI 3 1820	UTI 3 2216
UTI 3 1833	UTI 3 2221
UTI 3 1840	UTI 3 2222

附　录

UTI 3 2227	UTI 4 2500
UTI 3 2230	UTI 4 2502
UTI 3 2239	UTI 4 2503
UTI 3 2243	UTI 4 2507
UTI 3 2257	UTI 4 2511
UTI 3 2295	UTI 4 2513
UTI 4 2314	UTI 4 2521
UTI 4 2316	UTI 4 2522
UTI 4 2320	UTI 4 2526
UTI 4 2326	UTI 4 2529
UTI 4 2328	UTI 4 2532
UTI 4 2330	UTI 4 2536
UTI 4 2335	UTI 4 2541
UTI 4 2394	UTI 4 2549
UTI 4 2405	UTI 4 2552
UTI 4 2406	UTI 4 2565
UTI 4 2408	UTI 4 2571
UTI 4 2418	UTI 4 2572
UTI 4 2422	UTI 4 2579
UTI 4 2427	UTI 4 2586
UTI 4 2431	UTI 4 2593
UTI 4 2434	UTI 4 2596
UTI 4 2439	UTI 4 2611
UTI 4 2442	UTI 4 2621
UTI 4 2448	UTI 4 2623
UTI 4 2451	UTI 4 2625
UTI 4 2452	UTI 4 2626
UTI 4 2457	UTI 4 2631
UTI 4 2458	UTI 4 2637
UTI 4 2474	UTI 4 2640
UTI 4 2484	UTI 4 2644
UTI 4 2495	UTI 4 2656
UTI 4 2496	UTI 4 2664
UTI 4 2497	UTI 4 2667

UTI 4 2670	UTI 4 2945
UTI 4 2671	UTI 4 2948
UTI 4 2672	UTI 4 2954
UTI 4 2678	UTI 4 2966
UTI 4 2679	UTI 4 2972
UTI 4 2691	UTI 4 2974
UTI 4 2695	UTI 4 2976
UTI 4 2699	UTI 4 2984
UTI 4 2701	UTI 4 2991
UTI 4 2707	UTI 5 3009
UTI 4 2709	UTI 5 3029
UTI 4 2714	UTI 5 3033
UTI 4 2731	UTI 5 3034
UTI 4 2741	UTI 5 3038
UTI 4 2742	UTI 5 3042
UTI 4 2752	UTI 5 3053
UTI 4 2761	UTI 5 3060
UTI 4 2762	UTI 5 3082
UTI 4 2780	UTI 5 3086
UTI 4 2798	UTI 5 3116
UTI 4 2804	UTI 5 3122
UTI 4 2806	UTI 5 3137
UTI 4 2813	UTI 5 3143
UTI 4 2815	UTI 5 3154
UTI 4 2825	UTI 5 3189
UTI 4 2827	UTI 5 3238
UTI 4 2831	UTI 5 3266
UTI 4 2833	UTI 5 3296
UTI 4 2923	UTI 5 3335
UTI 4 2928	UTI 5 3348
UTI 4 2929	UTI 5 3350
UTI 4 2930	UTI 5 3356
UTI 4 2934	UTI 5 3370
UTI 4 2939	UTI 5 3420

UTI 5 3428	ViOr 8/1 38
UTI 6 3524	ViOr 8/1 39
UTI 6 3528	ViOr 8/1 40
UTI 6 3530	ViOr 8/1 41
UTI 6 3532 + 3552	YNER 8 2
UTI 6 3541	YNER 8 9
UTI 6 3545	YOS 4 66
UTI 6 3559	YOS 4 102
UTI 6 3571 + 3576	YOS 4 142
UTI 6 3586	YOS 4 250
UTI 6 3596	YOS 4 292
UTI 6 3609	YOS 4 323
UTI 6 3622	YOS 15 187
UTI 6 3634	YOS 15 203
UTI 6 3646	YOS 18 110
UTI 6 3649	YOS 18 123

vi. 来自乌尔档案

UTI 6 3655	
UTI 6 3657	MVN 3 233
UTI 6 3664	MVN 13 119
UTI 6 3665	MVN 13 414
UTI 6 3674	MVN 13 727
UTI 6 3679	SAT 3 2008
UTI 6 3806	SAT 3 2010
UTI 6 3807	UET 3 107
UTI 6 3813	UET 3 110
UTI 6 3814	UET 3 113
UTI 6 3819	UET 3 122
UTI 6 3821	UET 3 128
UTI 6 3823	UET 3 136
UTI 6 3831	UET 3 137
VDI 1976/3 110 – 111	UET 3 138
ViOr 8/1 33	UET 3 158
ViOr 8/1 34	UET 3 188
ViOr 8/1 35	UET 3 841

UET 3 1111
UET 9 1135

vii. 来自其他档案

AAICAB 1/2 pl. 101 1937 – 045
AUCT 3 479
Babyloniaca 8 pl. 6 Pupil 23
BCT 2 118
BCT 2 283
BCT 2 295
CUSAS 40 812
CUSAS 40 857
CUSAS 40 1511
JCS 14 113 18
JCS 14 113 20
JCSSS 5 12
MDP 10 22 3
MDP 10 22 4
MDP 10 71 121
MDP 28 505
MVN 3 165
MVN 8 230
MVN 13 137
MVN 13 212
MVN 13 765
MVN 15 28
MVN 15 288
P253739
P342005
P342056
P342116
P342138
P423655
SAKF 26
SAKF 52
SAKF 70
SAKF 89
SAKF 109
Syracuse 463
TSU 31
YOS 4 236

（2）外围区 gun_2 ma – da 税档案

AnOr 7 44
AUCT 3 198
CDLI Literary 397（Shulgi C）
CHEU 6
CT 32 pl. 19 – 22 BM 103398
MVN 8 222
P235549
RA 9 54 AM 14（pl. 7）
SA 4
UTI 4 2378

（3）附属国 gun_2 税档案

ASJ 3 50 1
AUCT 2 179
AUCT 2 364
AUCT 3 458
BCT 1 117
BPOA 1 760
BPOA 2 1863
BPOA 6 307
BPOA 7 2312
CDLJ 2012/1 3. 09
CM 26 23
CST 124
Fs Hruška 165 7
ITT 2 776

OIP 115 343
Ontario 2 348
OTR 5
P235532

（4）王室 maš-da-ri-a 税档案
AAICAB 1/1 pl. 20 1911 – 163
AAICAB 1/1 pl. 57 1924 – 516
AAICAB 1/2 pl. 118 1954 – 208
AAS 149
AAS 150
AAS 151
ABTR 4
Akkadica 135/1 74 – 76 1
Amherst 22
AnOr 7 108
AR RIM 4 18 4
AR RIM 8 53 5
ArOr 62 238 I 867
ASJ 3 167 148
ASJ 9 329 6
AUCT 1 182
AUCT 1 225
AUCT 1 455
AUCT 1 637
AUCT 2 185
AUCT 2 308
AUCT 3 13
AUCT 3 326
Babyloniaca 8 pl. 11 HG 9
BAOM 2 32 76
BAOM 2 39 114
BBVO 11 268 5N – T633
BCT 2 71

BCT 2 82
BIN 3 18
BIN 3 270
BIN 3 591
BIN 5 4
BIN 5 61
BJRL 64 110 62
BM Messenger 206
BM Messenger 267
BM Messenger 271
BPOA 1 218
BPOA 1 446
BPOA 1 830
BPOA 1 1184
BPOA 1 1691
BPOA 1 1779
BPOA 2 1895
BPOA 6 111
BPOA 6 925
BPOA 6 944
BPOA 6 954
BPOA 6 1057
BPOA 6 1344
BPOA 6 1361
BPOA 7 1586
BPOA 7 1674
BPOA 7 2350
BPOA 7 2379
BPOA 7 2399
BPOA 7 2411
BPOA 7 2530
BPOA 7 2563
BRM 3 15
BRM 3 47

CST 29
CST 434
CST 530
CT 9 pl. 29 BM 020011
CT 32 pl. 16 – 18 BM 103399
CT 32 pl. 19 – 22 BM 103398
CTPSM 1 86
CTPSM 1 176
CUSAS 40 14
CUSAS 40 116
CUSAS 40 145
CUSAS 40 158
CUSAS 40 374
CUSAS 40 418
CUSAS 40 461
CUSAS 40 663
CUSAS 40 732
CUSAS 40 984
CUSAS 40 1031
CUSAS 40 1116
CUSAS 40 1275
CUSAS 40 1450
CUSAS 40 1737
CUSAS 40 1744
DAS 29
DAS 388
HSS 4 52
HUCA 29 74 3
ITT 2 737
ITT 2 878
ITT 2 3410
ITT 2 3483
ITT 2 3757
ITT 2 4108

ITT 2 4175
ITT 3 5552
ITT 3 6160
ITT 3 6167
ITT 5 6756
ITT 5 6922
ITT 5 6959
ITT 5 6986
JAOS 33 175 8
JCS 11 77
JCS 52 42 45
Kyoto 35
Kyoto 36
Kyoto 46
L'uomo 59
LAOS 1 36
MCS 4 21 18
MDP 10 p. 21
MVN 2 164
MVN 2 174
MVN 3 258
MVN 4 137
MVN 4 138
MVN 6 287
MVN 8 145
MVN 8 234
MVN 11 106
MVN 11 118
MVN 11 165
MVN 11 166
MVN 11 AA
MVN 11 Y
MVN 12 80
MVN 12 359

MVN 12 414	Nisaba 15 581
MVN 13 122	Nisaba 15 592
MVN 13 559	Nisaba 15 622
MVN 13 734	Nisaba 15 629
MVN 14 504	Nisaba 15 691
MVN 14 598	Nisaba 15 727
MVN 15 129	Nisaba 15 730
MVN 16 634	Nisaba 15 736
MVN 16 684	Nisaba 15 738
MVN 16 715	Nisaba 15 739
MVN 16 744	Nisaba 15 887
MVN 16 823	Nisaba 15 942
MVN 16 916	Nisaba 15 949
MVN 16 925	Nisaba 15 1159
MVN 16 1208	Nisaba 17 66
MVN 16 1568	Nisaba 17 99
MVN 17 104	Nisaba 18 87
NABU 1989/95 2	Nisaba 23 67
NABU 2018/41 2	Nisaba 24 17
NATN 416	Nisaba 26 2
NATN 569 + 798	Nisaba 26 99
NATN 580	Nisaba 33 264
Nik 2 505	Nisaba 33 400
Nisaba 6 20	Nisaba 33 944
Nisaba 9 51	Nisaba 33 986
Nisaba 9 260	Nisaba 33 1003
Nisaba 11 1	NYPL 55
Nisaba 15 55	NYPL 367
Nisaba 15 90	NYPL 374
Nisaba 15 290	OIP 115 491
Nisaba 15 366	OIP 121 376
Nisaba 15 372	OIP 121 429
Nisaba 15 514	OIP 121 504
Nisaba 15 515	OLZ 17 241

OMRO 66 47 13
Ontario 1 3
Ontario 1 7
Ontario 1 82
Ontario 2 218
Orient 16 90 132
OrNS 55 134
OrSP 6 59 Wengler 44
OrSP 47 – 49 22
OrSP 47 – 49 197
OTR 175
OTR 197
P206453
P235034
P235452
P275033
P406807
P453234
PDT 1 298
PDT 1 381
PDT 1 522
PDT 2 1213
PDT 2 1321
PPAC 4 115
PPAC 4 119
PPAC 4 238
PPAC 5 82
PPAC 5 198
PPAC 5 201
PPAC 5 226
PPAC 5 610
PPAC 5 922
PPAC 5 1109
PPAC 5 1215

PPAC 5 1246
PPAC 5 1303
PPAC 5 1416
PPAC 5 1441
PPAC 5 1730
Princeton 1 281
Princeton 1 290
Princeton 1 565
Princeton 2 370
Princeton 2 414
Princeton 2 458
RA 49 87 5
RA 62 5 4
RA 62 5 5
RA 101 40 8
RSO 83 346 20
RTC 429
SAKF 47
Santag 6 327
Santag 7 97
SAT 1 66
SAT 2 148
SAT 2 190
SAT 2 249
SAT 2 1035
SAT 3 1483
SAT 3 1713
SAT 3 2024
SET 104
SNAT 29
SNAT 260
SNAT 403
STA 7
Tavolette 24

附　录

TCBI 2/2 1	UET 3 373
TCL 2 5502 = 5503	UET 3 379
TCL 5 5667	UET 3 380
TCL 5 5671	UET 3 411
TCTI 2 2569	UET 3 412
TCTI 2 2761	UET 3 1208
TCTI 2 3262	UET 3 1211
TCTI 2 3627	UET 3 1444
TCTI 2 3660	UET 3 1563
TCTI 2 4046	UET 9 354
TEL 1	UET 9 905
TEL 5	UET 9 958
TEL 73	UET 9 993
TEL 270	UET 9 1004
TLB 3 37	UET 9 1022
TRU 85	UET 9 1060
TUT 276	UET 9 1114
UDT 91	UET 9 1120
UET 3 60	UNT 71
UET 3 65	UNT 101
UET 3 96	UTI 3 2128
UET 3 97	UTI 3 2130
UET 3 99	UTI 3 2209
UET 3 100	UTI 4 2371
UET 3 102	UTI 4 2599
UET 3 103	UTI 4 2658
UET 3 118	UTI 5 3228
UET 3 141	UTI 6 3680
UET 3 154	UTI 6 3688
UET 3 186	UTI 6 3692
UET 3 245	ViOr 8/1 85
UET 3 248	YNER 8 15
UET 3 258	YNER 8 19
UET 3 275	YOS 4 56

YOS 4 207
YOS 4 270
ZA 95 191

（5）神庙 zag-u 税档案

AnOr 1 168
AnOr 7 164
AUCT 1 497
AUCT 3 194
BPOA 1 885
BPOA 1 1018
CST 741
Fs Součková-Siegelová 410 4
JCS 52 43 47
MVN 6 84
MVN 7 347
MVN 11 141
MVN 11 215
MVN 11 Y
MVN 16 906
MVN 16 1092
MVN 16 1187
MVN 18 745
MVN 22 119
NATN 860
NATN 862
NATN 865

P429870
P464910
PDT 1 203
PDT 2 911
Princeton 1 531
Santag 6 40
SAT 3 2039
SET 139
SET 140
TLB 3 152
UET 3 2
UET 3 25
UET 3 61
UET 3 91
UET 3 250
UET 3 341
UET 3 365
UET 3 1087
UET 3 1193
UET 3 1368
UET 3 1755
UET 3 1770
UET 3 1777
UET 9 456
UET 9 962
UET 9 1072
UTI 4 2983

资料来源：美国加利福尼亚大学洛杉矶分校、英国牛津大学和德国马克斯·普朗克历史科学研究所的"楔形文字数字图书馆计划"（Cuneiform Digital Library Initiative，简称 CDLI），https：//cdli. ucla. edu/；西班牙马德里高等科学研究院的"新苏美尔语文献数据库"（西班牙语：Base de Datos de Textos Neo – Sumerios，简称 BDTNS，英语：Database of Neo – Sumerian Texts），http：//bdtns. filol. csic. es/。截至日期：2021 年 1 月 1 日。

参考文献
（按照作者姓氏首字母顺序）

一 外文参考书目

Adams, R., *Heartland of Cities, Surveys of Ancient Settlement and Land Use on the Central Floodplain of the Euphrates*, Chicago: University of Chicago Press, 1981.

Ahmed, K. M., *The Beginning of Ancient Kurdistan (c. 2500 – 1500 BC): a historical and cultural synthesis*, PhD dissertation, Universiteit Leiden, 2012.

Algaze, G., *The Uruk World System*, Chicago, 1993.

Alivernini, S., *La Struttura Amministrativa del Mar-sa nella Documentazione della III Dinastia di Ur*, Alla Rivista Degli Studi Orientali, Nuova Serie 86, Pisa and Roma: Fabrizio Serra Editore, 2013.

Allred, L., *Cooks and Kitchens: Centralized Food Production in Late Third Millennium Mesopotamia*. PhD thesis. Baltimore: Johns Hopkins University, 2006.

Alster, B., *Proverbs of Ancient Sumer: The World's Earliest Proverb Collections*, Volume I-II, Bethesda: CDL Press, 1997.

Alster, B., *Wisdom of Ancient Sumer*, Bethesda: CDL Press, 2005; J. Black, et al., *The Literature of Ancient Sumer*, Oxford: Oxford University Press, 2004.

AndelsonR. V. (ed.), *Land-Value Taxation Around the World*, The American Journal of Economics and Society Supplement 59/5, Malden: Blackwell, 2000.

Andersson, J., *Kingship in the Early Mesopotamian Onomasticon 2800 – 2200 BCE*, Studia Semitica Upsaliensia 28, Uppsala: Uppsala Universitet, 2012.

Archi, A., *Ebla and Its Archives: Texts, History, and Society*, Studies in Ancient

Near Eastern Records 7, Boston and Berlin: Walter de Gruyter, 2015.

Asher-Greve, J. M., *Frauen in altsumerischer Zeit*, Bibliotheca Mesopotamica 18, Malibu: Undena Publications, 1985.

Bahrani, Z., *Women of Babylon: Gender and Representation in Mesopotamia*, London: Routledge, 2001.

Bertman, S., *Handbook to Life in Ancient Mesopotamia*, Oxford: Oxford University Press, 2003.

Bidmead, J., *The Akītu Festival: Religious Continuity and Royal Legitimation in Mesopotamia*, Gorgias Dissertations Near Eastern Studies 2, Piscataway: Gorgias Press, 2002.

Bienkowski, P., Millard A. (eds.), *Dictionary of the Ancient Near East*, Philadelphia: University of Pennsylvania Press, 2000.

Black, J., *The Literature of Ancient Sumer*, Oxford: Oxford University Press, 2004.

Black, J., Green, A., *Gods, Demons and Symbols of Ancient Mesopotamia: An Illustrated Dictionary*, Austin: University of Texas Press, 1992.

Breniquet, C., Michel C. (eds.), *Wool Economy in the Ancient Near East and the Aegean: From the Beginnings of Sheep Husbandry to Institutional Textile Industry*, Ancient Textiles Series 17, Oxford and Philadelphia: Oxbow Books, 2014.

Brookman, W. R., *The Umma Milling Industry: Studies in Neo-Sumerian Texts*, PhD dissertation, University of Minnesota, 1984.

Brunke, H., *Essen in Sumer: Metrologie, Herstellung und Terminologienach Zeugnis der Ur III-zeitlichen Wirtschaftsurkunden*, Geschichtswissenschaften 26, München: Herbert Utz Verlag, 2011.

Bryce, T. R., *The Routledge Handbook of the Peoples and Places of Ancient Western Asia: The Near East from the Early Bronze Age to the Fall of the Persian Empire*, London and New York: Routledge, 2009.

Bryce, T. R., *Ancient Syria: A Three Thousand Year History*, Oxford: Oxford University Press, 2014.

Buccellati, G., *The Amorites of the Ur III Period*, Naples: Istituto Orientale di

Napoli, 1966.

Castellino, G., *Two Shulgi Hymns (B, C)*, Studi semitici 42, Rome: Istituto di studi del Vicino Oriente, Universita, 1972.

Caubet, A., Pouyssegur, P., *The Origins of Civilization, The Ancient Near East*, Paris: Finest/Terrail, 1998.

Charpin, D., *Le Clergé d'Ur au Siècle d'Hammurabi (XIXe-XVIIIe Siècles av. J.-C.)*, Genève-Paris: Librairie Droz, 1986.

Charvát, P., *Mesopotamia before History*, London and New York: Routledge, 2005.

Chavalas, M. W., Hayes, J. L. (eds.), *New Horizons in the Study of Ancient Syria*, Bibliotheca Mesopotamica 25, Malibu: Undena Publications, 1992.

Çig, M., Kizilyay, H., Salonen, A., *Die Puzris-Dagan-Texte der Istanbuler Archäologischen Museen Teil I: Nrr. 1 – 725*, Helsinki: Suomalaisen Kirjallisuuden Kirjapaino Oy Heldinki, 1954.

Cline, E. H., Graham, M. W., *Ancient Empires: From Mesopotamia to the Rise of Islam*, Cambridge: Cambridge University Press, 2011.

Cohen, M., *The Cultic Calendars of the Ancient Near East*, Bethesda: CDL Press, 1993.

Cohen, M., *Festivals and Calendars of the Ancient Near East*, Bethesda: CDL Press, 2015.

Crawford, H., *Sumer and the Sumerians*, Melbourne: Cambridge University Press, 2004.

D'Agostino, F., Pomponio, F., *Umma Messenger Texts in the British Museum, Part One (UMTBM 1)*, Nisaba 1, Messina: Dipartimento di Scienze dell'Antichità dell'Università degli Studi di Messina, 2002.

Dahl, J. L., *The Ruling Family of Ur III Umma: A Prosopographical Analysis of an Elite Family in Southern Iraq 4000 Years ago*, PIHANS 108, Leiden: Nederlands Instituutvoor het Nabije Oosten, 2007.

DeBlois, L., Van der Spek, R. J., *An Introduction to the Ancient World*, London and New York: Routledge, 1997.

De Boer, R., *Amorites in the Early Old Babylonian Period*, PhD dissertation, Universiteit Leiden, 2014.

Dercksen, J. G., *Old Assyrian Institutions*, MOS Studies 4, PIHANS 98, Leiden: Nederlands Instituut voor het Nabije Oosten, 2004.

DeGenouillac, H., *Textes de l'époque d'Agadé et de l'époque d'Ur (Fouilies d'Ernest de Sarzéc en 1894)*, ITT 2, Paris: Ernest Leroux, 1910.

DeGraef, K., Tavernier J. (eds.), *Susa and Elam. Archaeological, Philological, Historical and Geographical Perspectives: Proceedings of the International Congress held at Ghent University, December 14 – 17, 2009*, Leiden and Boston: Brill, 2013.

DeSarzec, E., *Découvertes en Chaldée: second volume partieepigraphique et plances*, Paris: Ernest Leroux, 1894.

DuPont, J., *Divine Kingship in the Third Dynasty of Ur: Methods of Legitimizing Royal Authority in Ancient Mesopotamia*, MA thesis, Central Michigan University, 2012.

Edzard, D. O., *Gudea and His Dynasty*, The Royal Inscriptions of Mesopotamia Early Periods, Volume 3/1 (RIME 3/1), Toronto-Buffalo-London: University of Toronto Press, 1997.

Edzard, D. O., *Geschichte Mesopotamiens: Von den Sumerern bis zu Alexander dem Großen*, München: Verlag C. H. Beck, 2004.

Edzard, D. O., Farber, G., *Répertoire Géographique des Textes Cunéiformes II: Die Orts-und Gewässernamen der Zeit der 3. Dynastie von Ur*, Wiesbaden: Dr. Ludwig Reichert Verlag, 1974.

Englund, R. K., *Organisation und Verwaltung der Ur III-Fischerei*, Berliner Beiträge zum Vorderen Orient 10, Berlin: Dietrich Reimer Verlag, 1990.

Falkenstein, A., *Die neusumerischen Gerichtsurkunden*, Munich: Verlag der Bayerischen Akademie der Wissenschaften, 1956 – 1957.

Finkel, I., Taylor, J., *Cuneiform*, London: British Museum, 2015.

Fitzgerald, M. A., *The Rulers of Larsa*, PhD dissertation, Yale University, 2002.

Flückiger-Hawker, E., *Urnamma of Ur in Sumerian Literary Tradition*, Orbis Biblicus et Orientalis 166, Fribourg/Göttingen: University Press/Vandenhoeck & Ruprecht, 1999.

Foster, B. R., *Umma in the Sargonic Period*, Hamden: Archon Books, 1982.

Foster, B. R., *From Distant Days: Myths, Tales, and Poetry of Ancient Mesopotamia*, Bethesda: CDL Press, 1995.

Foster, B. R., Foster, K. P., *Civilizations of Ancient Iraq*, Princeton and Oxford: Princeton University Press, 2009.

Frankfort, H., Lloyd, S., Jacobsen, T., *The Gimilsin Temple and the Palace of the Rulers of Tell Asmar*, Oriental Institute Publications 43, Chicago: The University of Chicago Press, 1940.

Frayne, D., *Sargonic and Gutian Periods (2334 – 2113 BC)*, The Royal Inscriptions of Mesopotamia Early Periods, Volume 2, Toronto-Buffalo-London: University of Toronto Press, 1993.

Frayne, D., *Ur III Period (2112 – 2004 BC)*, The Royal Inscriptions of Mesopotamia Early Periods, Volume 3/2, Toronto-Buffalo-London: University of Toronto Press, 1997.

Frayne, D., *Presargonic Period (2700 – 2350 BC)*, The Royal Inscriptions of Mesopotamia Early Periods, Volume 1, Toronto-Buffalo-London: University of Toronto Press, 1998.

Garfinkle, S., *Entrepreneurs and Enterprise in Early Mesopotamia: A Study of three Archives from the Third Dynasty of Ur*, Cornell University Studies in Assyriology and Sumerology 22, Bethesda: CDL Press, 2012.

Garfinkle, S., Johnson J. C. (eds.), *The growth of an Early State in Mesopotamia: Studies in Ur III administration Proceedings of the First and Second Ur III Workshops at the 49th and 51st Rencontre assyriologique internationale, London July 10, 2003 and Chicago July 19, 2005*, BPOA 5, Madrid: Consejo Superior de Investigaciones Cientificas, 2005.

Garfinkle, S., Molina M. (eds.), *From the 21st Century B. C. to the 21st Century A. D.: Proceedings of the International Conference on Sumerian Studies Held in Madrid 22 – 24 July 2010*, Winona Lake: Eisenbrauns, 2013.

Gelb, I. J., *Old Akkadian Writing and Grammar*, Materials for the Assyrian Dictionary 2, Chicago: The University of Chicago Press, 1952.

George, A. R., *House Most High: The Temples of Ancient Mesopotamia*, Mesopotamian Civilizations 5, Winona Lake: Eisenbrauns, 1993.

Glassner, J. -J., *Chroniques mésopotamiennes*, Paris: Les Belles Lettres, 1993.

Gomi, T., Hirose, Y., Hirose, K., *Neo-Sumerian Administrative Texts of the Hirose Collection*, Potomac: Capital Decisions Limited, 1990.

Gong, Y., *Die Namen der Keilschriftzeichen*, Alter Orient und Altes Testament 268, Münster: Ugarit-Verlag, 2000.

Greco, A., *Garden administration in the Ĝirsu Province during the Neo-Sumerian period*, BPOA 12, Madrid: Consejo Superior de Investigaciones Científicas, 2015.

Hall, M. G., *A Study of the Sumerian Moon-God, Nann/Su'en*, PhD dissertation, University of Pennsylvania, 1985.

Hallo, W. W., *The Ensi's of the Ur III Dynasty*, PhD dissertation, University of Chicago, 1953.

Hallo, W. W., *Early Mesopotamian Royal Titles: A Philologic and Historical Analysis*, New Haven: American Oriental Society, 1957.

Hallo, W. W., Simpson, W. K., *The Ancient Near East. A History*, Belmont: Wadsworth / Thomson, 1998.

Halloran J. A. (ed.), *Sumerian Lexicon: A Dictionary Guide to the Ancient Sumerian Language*, Los Angeles: Logogram Publishing, 2006.

Hilgert, M., *Cuneiform Texts from the Ur III Period in the Oriental Institute, Volume 1: Drehem Administrative Documents from the Reign of Šulgi*, Oriental Institute Publications 115, Chicago: The Oriental Institute, 1998.

Hilgert, M., *Akkadisch in der Ur III-Zeit*, IMGULA 5, Münster: Rhema, 2002.

Hilgert, M., *Cuneiform Texts from the Ur III Period in the Oriental Institute, Volume 2: Drehem Administrative Documents from the Reign of Amar-Suena*, Oriental Institute Publications 121, Chicago: The Oriental Institute, 2003.

Höflmayer F. (ed.), *The Late Third Millennium in the Ancient Near East: Chronology, C14, and Climate Change*, Oriental Institute Seminars 11, Chicago: The Oriental Institute of the University of Chicago, 2017.

Horsnell, M. J., *The Year-Names of the First Dynasty of Babylon*, I-II, McMaster: McMaster University Press, 1999.

Høyrup, J., *Lengths, Widths, Surfaces: A Portrait of Old Babylonian Algebra and Its Kin*, New York: Springer, 2002.

Hrouda, B., *Isin-Išan BahriyatIII: Die Ergebnisse der Ausgrabungen 1983 – 1984*, Bayerische Akademie der Wissenschaften 94, Munich: C. H. Beck Verlag, 1987.

Hulínek, D., Lieskovský, T., *Report Archaeological project SAHI-Tell Jokha, 2016*, Bratislava: Slovak Archaeological and Historical Institute, 2016.

Hunger, H., *Spätbabylonische Texte aus Uruk*, I, Berlin: Gebr. Mann Verlag, 1976.

Hunt, C., *The History of Iraq*, Westport and London: Greenwood Press, 2005.

Jacobsen, T., *The Sumerian King List*, Assyriological Studies 11, Chicago: The Oriental Institute of the University of Chicago, 1939.

Jacobsen, T., *The Harps That Once…: Sumerian Poetry in Translation*, New Haven and London: Yale University Press, 1987.

Jean, C.-F., *Šumer et Akkad: Contribution a l'histoire de la civilisation dans la Basse-Mésopotamie*, Paris: Librairie Orientaliste Paul Geuthner, 1923.

Jones T. B. (ed.), *The Sumerian Problem*, New York: John Wiley, 1969.

Jones, T. B., Snyder, J. W., *Sumerian Economic Texts from the Third Ur Dynasty: A Catalogue and Discussion of Documents from Various Collections*, Minneapolis: University of Minnesota Press, 1961.

Kamil, A., *L'archive d'Esidum, un entrepreneur du temps des rois d'Ur (XXIe s. av. J.-C.): d'après les textes cunéiformes inédits conservés au musée de Suleymaniyeh (Kurdistan irakien)*, PhD dissertation, École doctorale d'Histoire de l'Université Paris 1 Panthéon-Sorbonne (Paris), 2015.

Kang, S. T., *Sumerian Economic Texts from the Umma Archive: Sumerian and Akkadian Cuneiform Texts in the Collection of the World Heritage Museum of the University of Illinois*, Volume II, Urbana-Chicago-London: University of Illinois Press, 1973.

Keiser, C. E., *Patesi's of the Ur Dynasty*, New Haven: Yale University Press, 1919.

King, L. W., *A History of Sumer and Akkad*, New York: Greenwood Press, 1968.

Kleber, K., *Tempel und Palast: Die Beziehungen zwischen dem König und dem Eanna-Tempel im spätbabylonischen Uruk*, Alter Orient und Altes Testament 358, Münster: Ugarit-Verlag, 2008.

Kleinerman, A., Owen, D. I., *Analytical Concordance to the Garšana Archives*, Cornell University Studies in Assyriology and Sumerology 4, Bethesda: CDL Press, 2009.

Klengel, H., *Syria 3000 to 300 B. C. : A Handbook of Political History*, Berlin: Akademie Verlag, 1992.

Klinkott, H., Kubisch S., Müller-Wollermann, R. (eds.), *Geschenke und Steuern, Zölle und Tribute: Antike Abgabenformen in Anspruch und Wirklichkeit*, Culture and History of the Ancient Near East 29, Leiden and Boston: Brill, 2007.

Kramer, S. N., *The Sumerians: Their History, Culture, and Character*, Chicago and London: The University of Chicago Press, 1963.

Kramer, S. N., *The Sacred Marriage Rite: Aspects of Faith, Myth, and Ritual in Ancient Sumer*, Bloomington: Indiana University Press, 1969.

Kramer, S. N., *Sumerian Mythology: A Study of Spiritual and Literary Achievement in the Third Millennium B. C.*, Philadelphia: University of Pennsylvania Press, 1972.

Kramer, S. N., *History Begins at Sumer: Thirty-Nine Firsts in Man's Recorded History*, Philadelphia: The University of Pennsylvania Press, 1981.

Kuhrt, A., *The Ancient Near East c. 3000 – 330 BC*, 2 volumes, New York: Routledge, 1995.

Kuiper K. (ed.), *Mesopotamia: The World's Earliest Civilization*, New Work: Britannica Educational Publishing, 2011.

Lamberg-Karlovsky, C. C., Sabloff, J. A., *Ancient Civilizations: The Near East and Mesoamerica*, Illinois: Waveland Press, 1979.

Langdon, S., *Tablets from the Archives of Drehem*, Paris: Librairie Paul Geuthner, 1911.

Laursen, S., Steinkeller, P., *Babylonia, the Gulf Region and the Indus: Archaeological and Textual Evidence for Contact in the Third and Early Second Millennia BC*, Mesopotamian Civilizations 20, Winona Lake: Eisenbrauns, 2017.

Lehmann, U., *^{d}Šára-ì-sa$_6$ und Ur-ba-gára: Untersuchungen zu den Verwaltungstexten der neusumerischen Lagaš II-Periode aus Ĝirsu*, AOAT 430, Münster:

Ugarit-Verlag, 2016.

Leick, G., *Who's Who in the Ancient Near East*, London and New York: Routledge, 1999.

Leick, G., *Historical Dictionary of Mesopotamia*, Lanham and Toronto and Plymouth: The Scarecrow Press, 2010.

Limet, H., *Le travail du métal au pays de Sumer au temps de la IIIe dynastie d'Ur*, Paris: Société d'Édition, 1960.

Liu, C., *Organization, Administrative Practices and Written Documentation in Mesopotamia during the Ur III Period (c. 2112 – 2004 BC): A Case Study of Puzriš-Dagan in the Reign of Amar-Suen*, Kārum-Emporion-Forum: Beiträge zum Wirtschafts-, Rechts-und Sozialgeschichte des östlichen Mittelmeerraums und Altvorderasiens 3 (KEF 3), Münster: Ugarit-Verlag, 2017.

Liverani, M., *The Ancient Near East: History, Society and Economy*, London and New York: Routledge, 2014.

Lönnqvist, M., *Between Nomadism and Sedentism: Amorites from the Perspective of Contextual Archaeology*, Helsinki: Juutiprint, 2000.

Mallowan, M., *Early Mesopotamia and Iran*, London: Thames and Hudson, 1965.

Martin, W. J., *Tribut und Tributleistungen bei den Assyrien*, Studia Orientalia 8/1, Helsinki: Societas Orientalis Fennica, 1936.

Matthews, R. J., *Cities, Seals and Writing: Archaic Seal Impressions from Jemdet Nasr and Ur*, Berlin: Gebr. Mann, 1993.

Mayr, R., *The Seal Impressions of Ur III Umma*, PhD dissertation, University of Leiden, 1997.

McIntosh, J. R., *Ancient Mesopotamia: New Perspectives*, Santa Barbara: ABC-CLIO, 2005.

McNeil, R. C., *The "Messenger Texts" of the Third Ur Dynasty*, PhD dissertation, University of Pennsylvania, 1971.

Michalowski, P., *The Royal Correspondence of Ur*, PhD dissertation, Yale University, 1976.

Michalowski, P., *Letters from Early Mesopotamia*, Atlanta: Scholars Press, 1993.

Michalowski, P., *The Correspondence of the Kings of Ur: An Epistolary History* of an Ancient Mesopotamian Kingdom, Mesopotamian Civilizations 15, Winona Lake: Eisenbrauns, 2011.

Mittermayer, C., *Die Entwicklung der Tierkopfzeichen: Eine Studie zursyro-mesopotamischen Keilschriftpaläographie des 3. und frühen 2. Jahrtausends v. Chr.*, Alter Orient und Altes Testament 319, Münster: Ugarit-Verlag, 2005.

Moorey, R., *Ancient Mesopotamian Materials and Industries: The Archaeological Evidence*, Winona Lake: Eisenbrauns, 1999.

Mynarova, J., Alivernini, S. (eds.), *Economic Complexity in the Ancient Near East, Management of Resources and Taxation (Third-Second Millennium BC)*, Prague: Charles University, 2020.

Nemet-Nejat, K. R., *Daily Life in Ancient Mesopotamia*, Peabody: Hendrickson Publishers, 1998.

Neumann, H., *Handwerk in Mesopotamien: Untersuchungen zu seiner Organisation in der Zeit der III. Dynastie von Ur*, Berlin: Akademie-Verlag, 1987.

Nissen, H. J., *The Early History of the Ancient Near East 9000 – 2000 B. C.*, Chicago: The University of Chicago Press, 1988.

Oppenheim, A. L., *Catalogue of the Cuneiform Tablets of the Wilberforce Eames Babylonian Collection in the New York Public Library: Tablets of the Time of the Third Dynasty of Ur*, New Haven: American Oriental Society, 1948.

Oppenheim, A. L., *Ancient Mesopotamia*, Chicago and London: The University of Chicago Press, 1964.

Ouyang, X., *Monetary Role of Silver and Its Administration in Mesopotamia during the Ur III Period (c. 2112 – 2004 BCE): A Case Study of the Umma Province*, BPOA 11, Madrid: CSIC, 2013.

Owen, D. I., *Garšana Studies*, Cornell University Studies in Assyriology and Sumerology 6, Bethesda: CDL Press, 2011.

Owen, D. I., *Cuneiform Texts Primarily from Iri-Saĝrig/Āl-Šarrākī and the History of the Ur III Period*, Nisaba 15/1-2, Bethesda: CDL Press, 2013.

Owen, D. I., Mayr, R. H., *The Garšana Archives*, Cornell University Studies in Assyriology and Sumerology 3, Bethesda: CDL Press, 2007.

Paoletti, P., *Der König und sein Kries: Das staatliche Schatzarchiv der*

III. Dynastie von Ur, Biblioteca del Proximo Oriente Antiguo 10, Madrid: Consejo Superior de Investigaciones Cientificas, 2012.

Patterson, D., *Elements of the Neo-Sumerian Military*, PhD dissertation, Harvard University, 2018.

Pitts, A., *The Cult of the Deified King in Ur III Mesopotamia*, PhD dissertation, University of Pennsylvania, 2015.

Pollock, S., *Ancient Mesopotamia: The Eden that Never Was*, Cambridge: Cambridge University Press, 1999.

Postgate, N., *Taxation and Conscription in the Assyrian Empire*, Rome: Biblical Institute Press, 1974.

Postgate, N., *Early Mesopotamia: Society and Economy at the Dawn of History*, London and New York: Routledge, 1992.

Potts, D. T., *Mesopotamia and the East*, Oxford: Oxford University Committee for Archaeology, 1995.

Potts, D. T., *The Archaeology of Elam: Formation and Transformation of an Ancient Iranian State*, Cambridge: Cambridge University Press, 2004.

Powell M. A. (ed.), *Labor in the Ancient Near East*, AOS 68, New Haven: American Oriental Society, 1987.

Reichel, C., *Political Changes and Cultural Continuity in the Palace of the Rulers at Eshnunna (Tell Asmar): From the Ur III Period to the Isin-Larsa Period (CA. 2070 – 1850 B. C.)*, PhD dissertation, University of Chicago, 2001.

Röllig, W., *Das Bier im Alten Mesopotamien*, Berlin: Gesellschaft für die Geschichte und Bibliographie des Brauwesens EV, 1970.

Römer, W. H. Ph., *Die Sumerologie: Einführung in die Forschung und Bibliographie in Auswahl*, Alter Orient und Altes Testament 262, Münster: Ugarit-Verlag, 1999.

Römer, W. H. Ph., *Die Zylinderinschriften von Gudea*, Alter Orient und Altes Testament 376, Münster: Ugarit-Verlag, 2010.

Rost, S., *Watercourse Management and Political Centralization in Third-Millennium B. C. Southern Mesopotamia: A Case Study of the Umma Province of the Ur III Period (2112 – 2004 B. C.)*, PhD dissertation, Stony Brook University, 2015.

Roth, M. T., *Law Collections from Mesopotamia and Asia Minor*, Atlanta: Scholars Press, 1995.

Roux, G., *Ancient Iraq*, Middlesex: Penguin Books, 1966 (1992).

Rumaidh, S. S., *Excavations in Chokha: An Early Dynastic Settlement*, Edubba 8, London: Nabu Publications, 2000.

Sallaberger, W., *Der kultische Kalender der Ur III-Zeit*, Untersuchungen zur Assyriologie und Vorderasiatischen Archäologie 7/1-2, Berlin and New York: Walter de Gruyter, 1993.

Sallaberger, W., *Der Babylonische Töpfer und Seine Gefässe: Nach Urkunden altsumerischer bis altbabylonischer Zeitsowie Lexikalischen und Literarischen Zeugnissen*, Mesopotamian History and Environment 3, Gent: Universiteit Gent, 1996.

Sallaberger, W., Westenholz, A., *Mesopotamien: Akkade-Zeit und Ur III-Zeit*, OBO 160/3, Freiburg, Schweiz: Universitätsverlag / Göttingen: Vandenhoeck und Ruprecht, 1999.

Salonen, A., *Die Hausgeräte der Alten Mesopotamiernach sumerisch-akkadischen Quellen, Teil II: Gefässe*, Helsinki: Suomalaisen Kirjallisuuden Kirjapaino Oy Helsinki, 1966.

Salonen, A., *Agricultura Mesopotamica nach sumerisch-akkadischen Quellen*, Helsinki: Suomalaisen Kirjallisuuden Kirjapaino Oy Helsinki, 1968.

Salonen, A., *Vögel und Vogelfang im Alten Mesopotamien*, Helsinki: Suomalainen Tiedeakatemia, 1973.

Salonen, E., *Über den Zehnten im alten Mesopotamien: Ein Beitragzur Geschichte der Besteuerung*, Helsinki: Suomalaisen Kirjallisuuden Kirjapaino Oy Helsinki, 1972.

Samet, N., *The Lamentation over the Destruction of Ur*, Mesopotamian Civilizations 18, Winona Lake: Eisenbrauns, 2014.

Schneider, N., *Die Zeitbestimmungen der Wirtschaftsurkunden von Ur III*, Analecta Orientalia 13, Rome: Pontificio Instituto Biblico, 1936.

Sharlach, T. M., *Provincial Taxation and the Ur III State*, Cuneiform Monographs 26, Leiden and Boston: Brill-Styx, 2004.

Sharlach, T. M., *An Ox of One's Own: Royal Wives and Religion at the Court of the Third Dynasty of Ur*, Studies in Ancient Near Eastern Records 18, Berlin and Boston: Walter de Gruyter GmbH, 2017.

Sigrist, M., *Isin Year Names*, Berrien Springs: Andrews University Press, 1988.

Sigrist, M., *Larsa Year Names*, Berrien Springs: Andrews University Press, 1990.

Sigrist, M., *Drehem*, Bethesda: CDL Press, 1992.

Sigrist, M., Damerow, P., *Mesopotamian Yearnames: Neo-Sumerian and Old Babylonian Date Formulae*, Potomac: Capital Decisions Ltd., 1991.

Sigrist, M., Gomi, T., *The Comprehensive Catalogue of Published Ur III Tablets*, Bethesda: CDL Press, 1991.

Sigrist, M., Ozaki, T., *Neo-Sumerian Administrative Tablets from the Yale Babylonian Collection*, Part 1 – 2, Madrid: Consejo Superior de Investigaciones Científicas, 2009.

Snell, D. C., *Ledgers and Prices: Early Mesopotamian Merchant Accounts*, Yale Near Eastern Researches 8, New Haven and London: Yale University Press, 1982.

Snell, D. C., *Life in the Ancient Near East 3100 – 332 B. C. E.*, New Haven: Yale University Press, 1997.

Snell, D. C. (ed.), *A Companion to the Ancient Near East*, Malden: Blackwell Publishing, 2005.

Steible, H., *Die Altsumerischen Bau-und Weihinschriften*, Freiburger Altorientalische Studien 5/1-2, Stuttgart: Franz Steiner Verlag, 1982.

Steible, H., *Die Neusumerischen Bau-und Weihinschriften: Teil 2 Kommentar zu den Gudea-Statuen Inschriften der III. Dynastie von Ur Inschriften der IV. und "V." Dynastie von Uruk Varia*, Freiburger Altorientalische Studien 9/2, Stuttgart: Franz Steiner Verlag, 1991.

Steinkeller, P., *Sale Documents of the Ur III Period*, Freiburger Altorientalische Studien 17, Stuttgart: Franz Steiner Verlag, 1989.

Steinkeller, P., *History, Texts and Art in Early Babylonia: Three Essays*, Studies in Ancient Near Eastern Records 15, Boston and Berlin: Walter de Gruyter, 2017.

Steinkeller, P., Hudson M. (eds.), *Labor in the Ancient World*, *Volume V in a series sponsored by the Institute for the Study of Long-term Economic Trends and the International Scholars Conference on Ancient Near Eastern Economies. A Colloquium held at Hirschbach (Saxony), April 2005*, Dresden: Islet-Verlag, 2015.

Steinkeller, P., Postgate, J. N., *Third-Millennium Legal and Administrative Texts in the Iraq Museum, Baghdad*, Mesopotamian Civilizations 4, Winona Lake: Eisenbrauns, 1992.

Stepien, M., *Animal Husbandry in the Ancient Near East: A Prosopographic Study of Third-Millennium Umma*, Bethesda: CDL Press, 1996.

Stepien, M., *From the History of State System in Mesopotamia-The Kingdom of the Third Dynasty of Ur*, Warsaw: Department of Graphic Design, University of Warsaw, 2009.

Studevent-Hickman, B., *The Organization of Manual Labor in Ur III Babylonia*, PhD dissertation, Harvard University, 2006.

Studevent-Hickman, B., *Sumerian Texts from Ancient Iraq: From Ur III to 9/11*, Journal of Cuneiform Studies-Supplemental Series 5, Boston: Lockwood Press, 2018.

Such-Gutiérrez, M., *Beiträge zum Pantheon von Nippur im 3. Jahrtausend*, Rome: Herder Libreria editrice, 2003.

Tinney S. (ed.), *Pennsylvania Sumerian Dictionary B*, Philadelphia: University Museum, 1984.

Tsouparopoulou, C., *The Material Face of Bureaucracy: Writing, Sealing and Archiving Tablets for the Ur III State at Drehem*, PhD dissertation, University of Cambridge, 2008.

Tsouparopoulou, C., *The Ur III Seals Impressed on Documents from Puzriš-Dagan (Drehem)*, HSAO 16, Heidelberg: Heidelberger Orientverlag, 2015.

Vacin, L., *Šulgi of Ur: Life, Deeds, Ideology and Legacy of a Mesopotamian Ruler as Reflected Primarily in Literary Texts*, PhD dissertation, University of London, 2011.

Van de Mieroop, M., *A History of the Ancient Near East (ca. 3000 – 323 BC)*,

Malden: Blackwell Publishing, 2004.

Von der Osten-Sacken, E., *Untersuchungen zur Geflügelwirtschaft im Alten Orient*, Orbis Biblicus et Orientalis 272, Fribourg and Göttingen: Academic Press Fribourg and Vandenhoeck & Ruprecht Göttingen, 2015.

Vulliet, F. H., *Le Personnel Cultuel à l'Époque Néo-Sumérienne (ca. 2160 – 2003 av. J.-C.)*, BPOA 14, Madrid: Consejo Superior de Investigaciones Científicas, 2019.

Waetzoldt, H., *Untersuchungen zur Neusumerischen Textilindustrie*, Rome: Istituto per l'Oriente, 1972.

Walker, C. B. F., *Reading the Past: Cuneiform*, Berkeley and Los Angeles: University of California Press, 1987.

Wang, X., *The Metamorphosis of Enlil in Early Mesopotamia*, Alter Orient und Altes Testament 385, Münster: Ugarit-Verlag, 2011.

Weiershäuser, F., *Die königlichen Frauen der III. Dynastie von Ur*, Göttinger Beiträge zum Alten Orient 1, Göttingen: Universitätsverlag Göttingen, 2008.

Widell, M., *The Administrative and Economic Ur III texts from the City of Ur*, Piscataway: Gorgias Press, 2003.

Wilcke, C., *Isin-Išan Bahriyat III*, Bayerische Akademie der Wissenschaften 94, München: Verlag der Bayerischen Akademie der Wissenschaften, 1987.

Woolley, L., *Ur Excavations at Ur*, London: Ernest Benn Ltd, 1954.

Wu, Y., *A Political History of Eshnunna, Mari and Assyria during the Early Old Babylonian Period (from the end of Ur III to the death of Šamši-Adad)*, Changchun: Institute of History of Ancient Civilizations Northeast Normal University, 1994.

Zettler, R. L., *The Ur III Temple of Inanna at Nippur: The Operation and Organization of Urban Religious Institutions in Mesopotamia in the Late Third Millennium B. C.*, Berlin: Dietrich Reimer Verlag, 1992.

二 外文参考论文

Adams, R. M., "Shepherds at Umma in the Third Dynasty of Ur: Interlocutors with a World beyond the Scribal Field of Ordered Vision", *Journal of the Eco-*

nomic and Social History of the Orient, Vol. 49 (2006).

Alivernini, S., "The Ur III Field Surveying Texts: Measurement Techniques and Officials in Charge in the City of Girsu", *Journal of Cuneiform Studies*, Vol. 66 (2014).

Alivernini, S., "Mathematical Aspects of Earth-Moving Linked to Hydraulic Works in Ur III Umma", *Iraq*, Vol. 80 (2018).

Alivernini, S., "Management of Resources and Taxation in an Early Mesopotamian Empire: the Case of the Third Dynasty of Ur", in Mynarova, J., Alivernini, S. (eds.), *Economic Complexity in the Ancient Near East, Management of Resources and Taxation (Third-Second Millennium BC)*, Prague: Charles University, 2020.

Allred, L., "The Tenure of Provincial Governors: Some Observations", in S. Garfinkle and M. Molina (eds.), *From the 21st Century B. C. to the 21st Century A. D.: Proceedings of the International Conference on Sumerian Studies Held in Madrid 22 – 24 July 2010*, Winona Lake: Eisenbrauns, 2013.

Almamori, H. O., "The Early Dynastic Monumental Buildings At Umm Al-Aqarib", *Iraq*, Vol. 76 (2014).

Al-Mutawalli, N., Sallaberger, W., "The Cuneiform Documents from the Iraqi Excavation at Drehem", *Zeitschrift für Assyriologie und Vorderasiatische Archäologie*, Vol. 107, No. 2 (2017).

Andersson Strand, E., Cybulska, M., "Visualising Ancient Textiles-how to make a Textile Visible on the Basis of an Interpretation of an Ur III Text", in M. -L. Nosch, H. Koefoed and E. Andersson Strand (eds.), *Textile Production and Consumption in the Ancient Near East: Archaeology, Epigraphy, Iconography*, Ancient Textiles Series 12, Oxford and Oakville: Oxbow Books, 2013.

Archi, A., "Ebla and Eblaite", in C. H. Gordon, G. A. Rendsburg and N. H. Winter (eds.), *Eblaitica: Essays on the Ebla Archives and Eblaite Language, Volume I*, Winona Lake: Eisenbrauns, 1987.

Archi, A., "In Search of Armi", *Journal of Cuneiform Studies*, Vol. 63 (2011).

Archi, A., Biga, M. G., "A Victory over Mari and the Fall of Ebla", *Journal of Cuneiform Studies, Vol. 55 (2003).

Archi, A., Pomponio, F., "Tavolette Economiche Neo-Sumeriche dell' Università Pontificia Salesiana", *Vicino Oriente*, Vol. 8 (1989).

Astour, M. A., "An Outline of the History of Ebla (Part 1)", in C. H. Gordon and G. A. Rendsburg (eds.), *Eblaitica: Essays on the Ebla Archives and Eblaite Language*, Vol. 3, Winona Lake: Eisenbrauns, 1992.

Astour, M. A., "An Reconstruction of the History of Ebla (Part 2)", in C. H. Gordon (ed.), *Eblaitica: Essays on the Ebla Archives and Eblaite Language*, Vol. 4, Winona Lake: Eisenbrauns, 2002.

Bachvarova, M. R., "Sumerian Gala Priests and Eastern Mediterranean Returning Gods: Tragic Lamentation in Cross-Cultural Perspective", in A. Suter (ed.), *Lament: Studies in the Ancient Mediterranean and Beyond*, Oxford: Oxford University Press, 2008.

Bär, J., "Tributdarstellungen in der Kunst des Alten Orients", in H. Klinkott, S. Kubisch and R. Müller-Wollermann (eds.), *Geschenke und Steuern, Zölle und Tribute: Antike Abgabenformen in Anspruch und Wirklichkeit*, Culture and History of the Ancient Near East 29, Leiden and Boston: Brill, 2007.

Bartash, V., "On the Sumerian City UB-me^{ki}, the Alleged 'Umma'", *Cuneiform Digital Library Bulletin*, 2015/2.

Bauer, J., "DU = ku$_x$ (-dr), eintreten, hineinbringen '?'", *Zeitschrift für Assyriologie und Vorderasiatische Archäologie*, Vol. 94 (2004).

Becker, A., "Neusumerische Renaissance? Wissenschaftsgeschichtliche Untersuchungen zur Philologie und Archäologie", *Baghdader Mitteilungen*, Vol. 16 (1985).

Beckman, G. M., "Foreigners in the Ancient Near East", *Journal of the American Oriental Society*, Vol. 133, No. 2 (2013).

Benati, G., "Re-modeling Political Economy in Early 3rd Millennium BC Mesopotamia: Patterns of Socio-Economic Organization in Archaic Ur (Tell al-Muqayyar, Iraq)", *Cuneiform Digital Library Journal*, 2015/2.

Biggs, R. D., "The Šu-Suen Year 9 sa$_2$-du$_{11}$ ku$_5$-ra$_2$ Flour Dossier from Puzris-Dagan", in Y. Heffron, A. Stone and M. Worthington (eds.), *At the Dawn of History. Ancient Near Eastern Studies in Honour of J. N. Postgate*, Winona Lake: Eisenbrauns, 2017.

Boese, J., Sallaberger, W., "Apil-kin von Mari und die Könige der III. Dynastie von Ur", *Altorientalische Forschungen*, Vol. 23 (1996).

Boivin, O., "Agricultural Economy and Taxation in the Sealand I Kingdom", *Journal of Cuneiform Studies*, Vol. 68 (2016).

Borrelli, N., "Water environments in Ur III Ĝirsu/Lagaš: from natural setting to economic resource", *Water History*, Vol. 12 (2020).

Bramanti, A., "The Scepter (ĝidru) in Early Mesopotamian Written Sources", *KASKAL: Rivista di storia, ambienti e culture del Vicino Oriente Antico*, Vol. 14 (2017).

Brisch, N., "The Priestess and the King: The Divine Kingship of Šū-Sîn of Ur", *Journal of the American Oriental Society*, Vol. 126 (2006).

Brunke, H., "The *Nakabtum*: An Administrative Superstructure for the Storage and Distribution of Agricultural Products", *KASKAL. Rivista di storia, ambienti e culture del Vicino Oriente Antico*, Vol. 5 (2008).

Brunke, H., "On the Role of Fruit and Vegetables as Food in the Ur III Period", in L. Milano (ed.), *Paleonutrition and Food Practices in the Ancient Near East towards a Multidisciplinary Approach*, History of the Ancient Near East, Monographs 14, Padova: S. A. R. G. O. N. Editrice e Libreria, 2014.

Burke, A. A., "Amorites, Climate Change, and the Negotiation of Identity at the End of the Third Millennium B. C.", in F. Höflmayer (ed.), *The Late Third Millennium in the Ancient Near East: Chronology, C14, and Climate Change*, Oriental Institute Seminars 11, Chicago: The Oriental Institute of the University of Chicago, 2017.

Carroué, F., "La Chronologie Interne du Règne de Gudea, Partie I", *Acta Sumerologica*, Vol. 19 (1997).

Chambers, H., "Ancient Amphictyonies, Sic et Non", in W. W. Hallo (ed.), *Scripture in Context III*, Winona Lake: Eisenbrauns, 1983.

Chambon, G., "Apišal, un Royaume du Nord-Ouest", in E. Cancik-Kirschbaum and N. Ziegler (eds.), *Entre les fleuves-I: Untersuchungen zur histo-*

rischen Geographie Obermesopotamiens im 2. Jahrtausend V. Chr, Berliner Beiträge zumVorderen Orient 20, Gladbeck: PeWe-Vrlag, 2009.

Charpin, D., Ziegler, N., "Mekum, Roi d'Apišal", *MARI, Annales de Recherches Interdisciplinaires*, Vol. 8 (1997).

Civil, M., "A Hymn to the Beer Goddess and a Drinking Song", in R. D. Biggs and J. A. Brinkman (eds.), *From the Workshop of the Chicago Assyrian Dictionary: Studies Presented to A. Leo Oppenheim*, Chicago: University of Chicago Press, 1964.

Civil, M., "Enlil and Ninlil: The Marriage of Sud", *Journal of the American Oriental Society*, Vol. 103, No. 1 (1983).

Civil, M., "On Some Texts Mentioning Ur-Namma", *Orientalia, Nova Series*, Vol. 54 (1985).

Civil, M., "Feeding Dumuzi's Sheep: The Lexicon as a Source of Literary Inspiration", in F. Rochberg-Halton (ed.), *Language, Literature, and History: Philological and Historical Studies Presented to Erica Reiner*, New Haven: American Oriental Society, 1987.

Civil, M., "'Adamdun,' the Hippopotanus, and the Crocodile", *Journal of Cuneiform Studies*, Vol. 50 (1998).

Civil, M., "Remarks on ad-gi$_4$ (A. K. A. 'Archaic Word List C' or 'Tribute')", *Journal of Cuneiform Studies*, Vol. 65 (2013).

Clapham, J. H., "Tithe Surveys As a Source of Agrarian History", *The Cambridge Historical Journal*, Vol. 1 (1924).

Corbier, M., "City, Territory and Taxation", in J. Rich, A. Wallace-Hadrill (eds.), *City and Country in the Ancient World*, London: Routledge, 1991.

Cripps, E. L., "The Structure of Prices in the Neo-Sumerian Economy (I): Barley: Silver Price Ratios", *Cuneiform Digital Library Journal*, 2017/2.

Cripps, E. L., "The Structure of Prices in the Ur III Economy: Cults and Prices at the Collapse of the Ur III State", *Journal of Cuneiform Studies*, Vol. 71 (2019).

Dahl, J. L., "Revisiting Bala: Reviewed Works, Provincial Taxation and the Ur III State by Tonia M. Sharlach", *Journal of the American Oriental Society*,

Vol. 126 (2006).

Damerow, P., "Sumerian Beer: The Origins of Brewing Technology in Ancient Mesopotamia", *Cuneiform Digital Library Journal*, 2012/2.

De Graef, K., "Annus Simaškensis: L'Usage des Noms d'Année Pendant la Période Simaškéenne (ca. 1930–1880 AV. Notre Ère) à Suse", *Iranica Antiqua*, Vol. 43 (2008).

De Graef, K., "Dual power in Susa: Chronicle of a transitional period from Ur III via Šimaški to the Sukkalmas", *Bulletin of the School of Oriental and African Studies*, Vol. 75, No. 3 (2012).

De Zorzi, N., "The Death of Utu-hegal and Other Historical Omens", *Journal of Cuneiform Studies*, Vol. 68 (2016).

De J. Ellis, M., "Taxation in Ancient Mesopotamia: The History of the Term miksu", *Journal of Cuneiform Studies*, Vol. 26 (1974).

Edzard, D. O., "The Names of the Sumerian Temples", in I. L. Finkel and M. J. Geller (eds.), *Sumerian Gods and Their Representations*, Cuneiform Monographs 7, Groningen: Styx Publications, 1997.

Englund, R. K., "Administrative Timekeeping in Ancient Mesopotamia", *Journal of the Economic and Social History of the Orient*, Vol. 31 (1988).

Englund, R. K., "Hard Work-Where Will It Get You? Labor Management in Ur III Mesopotamia", *Journal of Near Eastern Studies*, Vol. 50 (1991).

Englund, R. K., "Regulating Dairy Productivity in the Ur III Period", *Orientalia, Nova Series*, Vol. 64 (1995).

Englund, R. K., "Equivalency Values and the Command Economy of the Ur III Period in Mesopotamia", in J. K. Papadopoulos and G. Urton (eds.), *The Construction of Value in the Ancient World*, Los Angeles: Cotsen Institute of Archaeology, University of California, Los Angeles, 2012.

Edzard, D., "Puzriš-Dagān—Silluš-Dagān", *Zeitschrift für Assyriologie und Vorderasiatische Archäologie*, Vol. 63 (1973).

Falkenstein, A., "Ibbisîn-Ishbi'erra", *Zeitschrift für Assyriologie und Vorderasiatische Archäologie*, Vol. 49 (1950).

Fink, S., "Battle and War in the Royal Self-Representation of the Ur III Period", in T. R. Kämmerer, M. Koiv and V. Sazonov (eds.), *Kings, Gods and People: Establishing Monarchies in the Ancient World*, Alter Orient und Altes Testament 390/4, Münster: Ugarit-Verlag, 2016.

Firth, R., "Considering the Finishing of Textiles based on Neo-Sumerian Inscriptions from Girsu", in M. -L. Nosch, H. Koefoed and E. Andersson Strand (eds.), *Textile Production and Consumption in the Ancient Near East: Archaeology, Epigraphy, Iconography*, Ancient Textiles Series 12, Oxford and Oakville: Oxbow Books, 2013.

Firth, R., "Synchronization of the Drehem, Nippur and Umma Calendars During the Latter Part of Ur III", *Cuneiform Digital Library Journal*, 2016/1.

Foster, B. R., "Management and Administration in the Sargonic Period", in M. Liverani (ed.), *Akkad: The First World Empire*, Padova: Sargon srl, 1993.

Frame, G., "A new wife for Šu-Sîn", *Annual Review of the RIM Project*, Vol. 2 (1984).

Frayne, D. R., "On the Location of Simurrum", in G. D. Young, M. W. Chavalas and R. E. Averbeck (eds.), *Crossing Boundaries and Linking Horizons: Studies in Honor of Michael C. Astour on His 80th Birthday*, Bethesda: CDL Press, 1997.

Frayne, D. R., "The Zagros Campaigns of the Ur III Kings", *The Canadian Society for Mesopotamian Studies*, Vol. 3 (2008).

Francfort, H. -P., Tremblay, X., "Marhaši et la Civilisation de l'Oxus", *Iranica Antiqua*, Vol. 45 (2010).

Garcia-Ventura, A., "Ur III Studies: Bibliography 1997 – 2014", *Studia Orientalia*, Vol. 3 (2015).

Garfinkle, S. J., "SI. A-a and His Family: the Archive of a 21st Century (BC) Entrepreneur", *Zeitschrift für Assyriologie und Vorderasiatische Archäologie*, Vol. 93, No. 2 (2003).

Garfinkle, S. J., "Was the Ur III State Bureaucratic? Patrimonialism and Bureaucracy in the Ur III Period", in S. J. Garfinkle and J. C. Johnson (eds.), *The Growth of an Early State in Mesopotamia: Studies in Ur III Administration. Proceedings of the First and Second Ur III Workshops at the 49th and 51st*

Rencontre Assyriologique Internationale, London July 10, 2003 and Chicago July 19, 2005, BPOA 5, Madrid: Consejo Superior de Investigaciones Científicas, 2008.

Garfinkle, S. J., "Merchants and State Formation in Early Mesopotamia", in S. C. Melville and A. L. Slotsky (eds.), *Opening the Tablet Box: Near Eastern Studies in Honor of Benjamin R. Foster*, Culture and History of the Ancient Near East 42, Leiden and Boston: Brill, 2010.

Garfinkle, S. J., "The Economy of Warfare in Southern Iraq at the End of the Third Millennium BC", in H. Neumann, et al (eds.), *Krieg und Frieden im AltenVorderasien: 52e Rencontre Assyriologique Internationale International Congress of Assyriology and Near Eastern Archaeology Münster, 17. – 21. Juli 2006*, Alter Orient und Altes Testament 401, Münster: Ugarit-Verlag, 2014.

Garfinkle, S. J., "The House of Ur-saga: Ur III Merchants in Their Non-Institutional Context", in J. Mas and P. Notizia, *Working at Home in the Ancient Near East*, Oxford: Archaeopress, 2020.

Gelb, I. J., "The Ancient Mesopotamian Ration System", *Journal of Near Eastern Studies*, Vol. 24 (1965).

Gelb, I. J., "The Arua Institution", *Revue d'Assyriologie et d'Archéologie Orientale*, Vol. 66 (1972).

Glassner, J.-J., "Les Temps de l'Histoire en Mésopotamie", in A. de Pury (ed.), *Israël Construit son Histoire*, Paris: Monde de la Bible, 1996.

Glassner, J.-J., "L'abdication de Šulgi", in K. Kleber, G. Neumann and S. Paulus (eds.), *Grenzüberschreitungen. Studien zur Kulturgeschichte des Alten Orients: Festschrift für Hans Neumann zum 65. Geburtstag am 9. Mai 2018*, Dubsar 5, Münster: Zaphon, 2018.

Goetze, A., "Šakkanakkus of the Ur III Empire", *Journal of Cuneiform Studies*, Vol. 17 (1963).

Gomi, T., "Über mu. tù. lugal: 'Eingebrachtes für den König' in den neusumerischen Viehverwaltungsurkunden aus Drehim", *Orient*, Vol. 11 (1975).

Gomi, T., "The Calendars of Ur and Puzriš-Dagān in the Early Ur-III Period", *Acta Sumeriologica*, Vol. 1 (1979).

Green, M. W., "Early Sumerian Tax Collectors", *Journal of Cuneiform Studies*, Vol. 36 (1984).

Green, M. W., "Urum and Uqair", *Acta Sumerologica*, Vol. 8 (1986).

Hallo, W. W., "Zāriqum", *Journal of Near Eastern Studies*, Vol. 15, No. 4 (1956).

Hallo, W. W., "Gutium (Qutium)", *Reallexikon der Assyriologie und Vorderasiatischen Archäologie*, Vol. 3 (1957 – 1971).

Hallo, W. W., "A Sumerian Amphictyony", *Journal of Cuneiform Studies*, Vol. 14 (1960).

Hallo, W. W., "The House of Ur-Meme", *Journal of Near Eastern Studies*, Vol. 31, No. 2 (1972).

Hallo, W. W., "Women of Sumer", in D. Schmandt-Besserat (ed.), *The Legacy of Sumer: Invited lectures on the Middle East at the University of Texas at Austin*, Bibliotheca Mesopotamica 4, Malibu: Undena Publications, 1976.

Hallo, W. W., "Simurrum and the Hurrian Frontier", *Revue Hittite et Asianique*, Vol. 36 (1978).

Hammer, E., "The City and Landscape of Ur: An Aerial, Satellite, and Ground Reassessment", *Iraq*, Vol. 81 (2019).

Hartman, L. F., Oppenheim, A. L., "On Beer and Brewing Techniques in Ancient Mesopotamia According to the XXIIIrd Tablet of the Series HAR. ra = hubullu", *Journal of the American Oriental Society*, Supplement 10, Baltimore: American Oriental Society, 1950.

Heeßel, N. P., "Būr-Sîn or Amar-Su-ena: Was There a "Historical Omen" of Būr-Sîn of Isin?" *Journal of Cuneiform Studies*, Vol. 68 (2016).

Heimpel, W., "Zu den Bezeichnungen von Schafen und Ziegen in den Drehem- und Ummatexten", *Bulletin on Sumerian Agriculture*, Vol. 7 (1995).

Heimpel, W., "Plow animal inspection records from Ur III Girsu and Umma", *Bulletin on Sumerian Agriculture*, Vol. 8 (1995).

Heine, Peter., "Kochen in Mesopotamien. Ein kulturgeschichtlicher Versuch", in K. Kleber, G. Neumann and S. Paulus (eds.), *Grenzüberschreitungen. Studien zur Kulturgeschichte des Alten Orients: Festschrift für Hans Neumann zum*

65. *Geburtstag am 9. Mai 2018*, Dubsar 5, Münster: Zaphon, 2018.

Heltzer, M., "Zum Steuersystem in Ugarit (pilku-ubdy und Ähnliches)", in H. Hirsch and H. Hunger (eds.), *Vorträge gehalten auf der 28. Rencontre Assyriologique Internationale in Wien 6. - 10. Juli 1981*, Horn: Verlag Ferdinand Berger & Söhne Gesellschaft M. B. H., 1982.

Hernández, J., "The Role of the Sagga in Ur III Based on the Puzriš-Dagān Texts", in L. Feliu, et al (eds.), *Time and History in the Ancient Near East: Proceedings of the 56th RecontreAssyriologique Internationale at Barcelona 26 - 30 July 2010*, Winona Lake: Eisenbrauns, 2013.

Horowitz, W., Watson, P. J., "The Ascent of Shulgi and the Death of Shulgi", *Acta Sumeriologica*, Vol. 13 (1991).

Huber, F., "Ausujet du nom du chancelier d'Ur III, Ir-Nanna ou Ir-mu", *Nouvelles Assyriologiques Brèves et Utilitaires*, 2000/6.

Huber, P. J., "Astronomical dating of Babylon I and Ur III", *Monographic Journals of the Near East*, Vol. 41 (1982).

Huber, P. J., "Astronomical Evidence for the Long and against the Middle and Short Chronologies", in P. Åström (ed.), *High, Middle or Low? Acts of an International Colloquium on Absolute Chronology held at the University of Gothenburg 20th-22nd August 1987*, Göteborg: Paul Äströms Förlag, 1987 - 1989.

Hudson, M., "How Interest Rates Were Set, 2500 BC-1000 AD: Máš, tokos and fœnus as Metaphors for Interest Accruals", *Journal of the Economic and Social History of the Orient*, Vol. 43 (2000).

Hudson, M., "Mesopotamia and Classical Antiquity", in R. V. Andelson (ed.), *Land-Value Taxation Around the World*, The American Journal of Economics and Society Supplement 59/5, Malden: Blackwell, 2000.

Hunger, H., "Kalender", *Reallexikonder Assyriologie und Vorderasiatischen Archäologie*, Vol. 5 (1976 - 1980).

Jacobsen, T., "The Reign of Ibbisin", *Journal of Cuneiform Studies*, Vol. 7 (1953).

Jacobsen, T., "The Term Ensí", *Aula Orientalis*, Vol. 9 (1991).

Kalla, G., "Date Palms, Deer/Gazelles and Birds in Ancient Mesopotamia and

Early Byzantine Syria, A Christian Iconographic Scheme and Its Sources in the Ancient Orient", in T. A. Bacs, A. Bollok and T. Vida (eds.), *Across the Mediterranean-Along the Nile: Studies in Egyptology, Nubiology and Late Antiquity Dedicated to László Török on the Occasion of His 75th Birthday*, Budapest: Institute of Archaeology, Research Centre for the Humanities, Hungarian Academy of Sciences and Museum of Fine Arts, 2018.

Klein, J., "Šulgi and Gilgameš: Two Brother-Peers (Šulgi O)", in B. L. Eichler (ed.), *Kramer Anniversary Volume: Cuneiform Studies in Honor of Samuel Noah Kramer*, Alter Orient und Altes Testament 25, Kevelaer: Verlag Butzon &Bercker and Neukirchen-Vluyn: Neukirchener Verlag, 1976.

Klein, J., "From Gudea to Šulgi: Continuity and Change in Sumerian Literary Tradition", in H. Behrens, D. Loding and M. T. Roth (eds.), *DUMU-E$_2$-DUB-BA-A: Studies in Honor of Åke W. Sjöberg*, Occasional Publications of the Samuel Noah Kramer Fund 11, Philadelphia: The University Museum, 1989.

Klein, J., "Šeleppūtum, a Hitherto Unknown Ur III Princess, *Zeitschrift für Assyriologie und Vorderasiatische Archäologie*, Vol. 80 (1990).

Klein, J., "Šulgi and Išmedagan: Originality and Dependence in Sumerian Royal Hymnology", in J. Klein and A. Skaist (eds.), *Bar-Ilan Studies in Assyriology dedicated to Pinhas Artzi*, Ramat Gan: Bar-Ilan University Press, 1990.

Koslova, N., Vizirova, E., "Organization of Animal Husbandry in Sumer: the Case of Girsu at the End of the Third Millennium B. C.", *Vestnik drevnej istorii*, Vol. 79, No. 4 (2019).

Kramer, S. N., "The Death of Ur-Nammu and his Descent to the Netherworld", *Journal of Cuneiform Studies*, Vol. 21 (1967).

Kramer, S. N., "The death of Ur-Nammu", in M. Mori et al (eds.), *Near Eastern Studies Dedicated to H. I. H. Prince Takahito Mikasa*, Bulletin of the Middle Eastern Culture Center in Japan 5, Wiesbaden: Otto Harrassowitz, 1991.

Kraus, F. R., "Zur Chronologie der Könige Ur-Nammu und Šulgi von Ur", *Orientalia Nova Series*, Vol. 20 (1951).

Kraus, F. R., "Provinzen des neusumerischen Reiches von Ur", *Zeitschrift für*

Assyriologie und Vorderasiatische Archäologie, Vol. 51（1955）.

Krecher, J., "DU = ku$_x$（-r）eintreten, hineinbringen", *Zeitschrift für Assyriologie und Vorderasiatische Archäologie*, Vol. 77（1987）.

Kudrinski, M., "The Sumerogram KUR：Logogram or Determinative?" *Journal of Cuneiform Studies*, Vol. 69（2017）.

Kupper, J.-R., "Roi et šakkanakku", *Journal of Cuneiform Studies*, Vol. 21（1967）.

Kutscher, R., "A Note on the Early Careers of Zariqum and Šamši-illat", *Revue d'Assyriologie et d'Archéologie Orientale*, Vol. 73（1979）.

Lafont, B., "Zabar. dab$_5$ et le culte d'après les textes de Drehem", *Revue d'Assyriologie et d'Arché Ologieorientale*, Vol. 77（1983）.

Lafont, B., "zabar-dab$_5$, zab/mardabbum", *Nouvelles Assyriologiques Brèves et Utilitaires*, 1987/94.

Lafont, B., "L'avènement de Shu-Sin", *Revue d'Assyriologie et d'Archéologie Orientale*, Vol. 88（1994）.

Lafont, B., "The Army of the Kings of Ur：The Textual Evidence", *Cuneiform Digital Library Journal*, 2009/5.

Lafont, B., "Male and Female Professions in Sumer at the End of the IIIrd Millennium BC", *Orient*, Vol. 51（2016）.

Lafont, B., "Game of Thrones：the Years when Šu-Sin Succeeded Amar-Su'en in the Kingdom of Ur", in L. Feliu, F. Karahashi and G. Rubio（eds.）, *The First Ninety Years：A Sumerian Celebration in Honor of Miguel Civil*, SANER 12, Berlin：De Gruyter, 2017.

Lambert, W. G., "The Names of Umma", *Journal of Near Eastern Studies*, Vol. 49, No. 1（1990）.

Limet, H., "L'étranger dans la société sumérienne", in D. O. Edzard（ed.）, *Gesellschaftsklassen im Alten Zweistromland und in den angrenzenden Gebieten-XVIII. Rencontre assyriologique internationale, München, 29. Juni bis 3. Juli 1970*, München：Verlag der Babyerischen Akademie der Wissenschaften, 1972.

Limet, H., "Étude sémantique de ma. da, kur, kalam", *Revue d'Assyriologie et d'Archéologie Orientale*, Vol. 72（1978）.

Limet, H., "Le Rôle du Palais dans l'Économie Néo-Sumérienne", in E. Lipinski (ed.), *State and Temple Economy in the Ancient Near East*, I: *Proceedings of the International Conference organized by the Katholieke Universiteit Leuven from the 10th to the 14th of April 1978*, Orientalia Lovaniensia Analecta 5, Leuven: Departement Orientalistiek, 1979.

Liu, C., "A Note on the Regular Offering to Ninlil at Tummal", *Cuneiform Digital Library Notes*, 2014/6.

Liu, C., "Notes on Elamites and the date of three Drehem texts", *Cuneiform Digital Library Notes*, 2014/17.

Liu, C., "An Ur III Tablet from Southwestern University", *Aula Orientalis*, Vol. 32, No. 1 (2014).

Liu, C., "Idadu, son of the governor of Egula", *Nouvelles Assyriologiques Bréves et Utilitaires* 2015/90.

Liu, C., "Šulgi 45 or Amar-Suen 2: an ambiguous Ur III Year Name", *Nouvelles Assyriologiques Bréves et Utilitaires* 2015/63.

Liu, C., "Aba-saga's Activities during the Reign of Sulgi in the Ur III Dynasty", *Journal of Ancient Civilizations*, Vol. 31 (2016).

Liu, C., "Lu-Nanna son of Ur-niĝar and Lu-Nanna from Hamazi not the same person", *Nouvelles Assyriologiques Bréves et Utilitaires* 2017/63.

Liu, C., "On a personal name Kiššer in Ur III source", *Nouvelles Assyriologiques Bréves et Utilitaires* 2017/32.

Maeda, T., "Bringing (mu-túm) livestock and the Puzrish-Dagan organization in the Ur III dynasty", *Acta Sumerologica*, Vol. 11 (1989).

Maeda, T., "Father of Akalla and Dadaga, Governors of Umma", *Acta Sumerologica*, Vol. 12 (1990).

Maeda, T., "The Defense Zone during the Rule of the Ur III Dynasty", *Acta Sumerologica*, Vol. 14 (1992).

Maeda, T., "Bal-ensí in the Drehem Texts", *Acta Sumerologica*, Vol. 16 (1994).

Maeda, T., "Šà-bal-a in Umma Tablets: Bal duty of the Ensí of Umma", *Acta Sumerologica*, Vol. 17 (1995).

Maekawa, K., "Agricultural Production in Ancient Sumer", *Zinbun*, Vol. 13 (1974).

Maekawa, K., "The erín-People of Lagash in Ur III Times", *Revue d'Assyriologie et d'Archéologie Orientale*, Vol. 70 (1976).

Maekawa, K., "The Ass and the Onager in Sumer in the Late Third Millennium B. C.", *Acta Sumerologica*, Vol. 1 (1979).

Maekawa, K., "Cereal Cultivation in the Ur III Period", *Bulletin on Sumerian Agriculture*, Vol. 1 (1984).

Maekawa, K., "Cultivation of legumes and mun-gazi plants in Ur III Girsu", *Bulletin on Sumerian Agriculture*, Vol. 2 (1985).

Maekawa, K., "The Agricultural Texts of Ur III Lagash of the British Musuem (Ⅲ)", *Acta Sumerologica*, Vol. 8 (1986).

Maekawa, K., "Agricultural Texts of Ur III Lagash of the British Museum (Ⅳ)", *Zinbun*, Vol. 21 (1986).

Maekawa, K., "The Agricultural Texts of Ur III Lagash of the British Musuem (Ⅴ)", *Acta Sumerologica*, Vol. 9 (1987).

Maekawa, K., "The Management of Domain Land in Ur III Umma", *Zinbun*, Vol. 22 (1987).

Maekawa, K., "New Texts on the Collective Labor Service of the Erin-People of Ur III Girsu", *Acta Sumerologica*, Vol. 10 (1988).

Maekawa, K., "The Governor's Family and the 'Temple Households' in Ur III Girsu", in K. Veenhof (ed.), *Houses and Households in Ancient Mesopotamia*, RAI 40, Istanbul: Nederlands Historisch-Archaeologisch Instituut, 1996.

Maekawa, K., "The 'Temples' and the 'Temple Personnel' of Ur III Girsu-Lagash", in K. Watanabe (ed.), *Priests and Officials in the Ancient Near East: Papers of the Second Colloquium on the Ancient Near East-The City and its Life held at the Middle Eastern Culture Center in Japan (Mitaka, Tokyo) March 22 – 24, 1996*, Heidelberg: Universitätsverlag C. Winter, 1999.

Marchesi, G., "Ur-Nammâ (k) 's Conquest of Susa", in K. De Graef and J. Tavernier (eds.), *Susa and Elam. Archaeological, Philological, Historical and Geographical Perspectives: Proceedings of the International Congress Held at*

Ghent University, December 14 - 17, 2009, MDP 58, Leiden and Boston: Brill, 2013.

Matthews, R., "Girsu and Lagash", in E. M. Meyers, *The Oxford Encyclopedia of Archaeology in the Near East*, Volume 2, Oxford: Oxford University Press, 1996.

Michalowski, P., "The Bride of Simanum", *Journal of the American Oriental Society*, Vol. 95, No. 4 (1975).

Michalowski, P., "Royal women of the Ur III period, Part I: the wife of Šulgi", *Journal of Cuneiform Studies*, Vol. 28 (1976).

Michalowski, P., "Amar-Su'ena and the Historical Tradition", in M. de Jong Ellis (ed.), *Essays on the Ancient Near East in Memory of Jacob Joel Finkelstein*, Hamden: Archon Books, 1977.

Michalowski, P., "Durum and Uruk During the Ur III Period", *Mesopotamia*, Vol. 12 (1977).

Michalowski, P., "The death of Šulgi", *Orientalia Nova Series*, Vol. 46 (1977).

Michalowski, P., "Foreign Tribute to Sumer during the Ur III Period", *Zeitschrift für Assyriologie und Vorderasiatische Archäologie*, Vol. 68 (1978).

Michalowski, P., "Royal women of the Ur III period, Part II: Geme-Ninlila", *Journal of Cuneiform Studies*, Vol. 31 (1979).

Michalowski, P., "Royal Women of the Ur III Period-Part III", *Acta Sumerologica*, Vol. 4 (1982).

Michalowski, P., "Third Millennium Contacts: Observations on the Relationships between Mari and Ebla", *Journal of the American Oriental Society*, Vol. 105, No. 2 (1985).

Michalowski, P., "Charisma and Control: On Continuity and Change in Early Mesopotamian Bureaucratic Systems", in McG. Gibson and R. D. Biggs (eds.), *The Organization of Power: Aspects of Bureaucracy in the Ancient Near East*, Studies in Ancient Oriental Civilization 46, Chicago: The Oriental Institute of the University of Chicago, 1987.

Michalowski, P., "Iddin-Dagan and his Family", *Zeitschrift für Assyriologie und Vorderasiatische Archäologie*, Vol. 95 (2005).

Michalowski, P., "Love or Death? Observations on the Role of the Gala in Ur III Ceremonial Life", *Journal of Cuneiform Studies*, Vol. 58 (2006).

Michalowski, P., "The Mortal Kings of Ur: A Short Century of Divine Rule in Ancient Mesopotamia", in N. Brisch (ed.), *Religion and Power: Divine Kingship in the Ancient World and Beyond*, Oriental Institute Seminars 4, Chicago: The Oriental Institute of the University of Chicago, 2007.

Michalowski, P., "Observations on 'Elamites' and 'Elam' in Ur III Times", in P. Michalowski (ed.), *On the Third Dynasty of Ur: Studies in Honor of Marcel Sigrist*, The Journal of Cuneiform Studies Supplemental Series Volume 1, Boston: American Schools of Oriental Research, 2008.

Michalowski, P., "Aššur during the Ur III Period", in O. Drewnowska (ed.), *Here & There Across the Ancient Near East: Studies in Honour of Krystyna Lyczkowska*, Warszawa: Agade, 2009.

Michalowski, P., "On the Names of Some Early Ancient Near Eastern Royal Women and on a Seal Impression from Karum Kanesh", in S. Dönmez (ed.), *Veysel Donbaz'a Sunulan Yazılar DUB. SAR É. DUB. BA. A: Studies Presented in Honour of Veysel Donbaz*, Istanbul: Ege Publications, 2010.

Michalowski, P., "The Steward of Divine Gudea and His Family in Ur IIIGirsu", in B. J. Collins and P. Michalowski (eds.), *Beyond Hatti: A Tribute to Gary Beckman*, Atlanta: Lockwood Press, 2013.

Michalowski, P., "Networks of Authority and Power in Ur III Times", in S. Garfinkle and M. Molina (eds.), *From the 21st Century B. C. to the 21st Century A. D. : Proceedings of the International Conference on Sumerian Studies Held in Madrid 22 - 24 July 2010*, Winona Lake: Eisenbrauns, 2013.

Michalowski, P., "News of a Mari Defeat from the Time of King Šulgi", *Nouvelles Assyriologiques Brèves et Utilitaires*, 2013/23.

Michalowski, P., "Of Bears and Men: Thoughts on the End of Šulgi's Reign and on the Ensuing Succession", in D. S. Vanderhooft and A. Winitzer (eds.), *Literature as Politics, Politics as Literature: Essays on the Ancient Near East in Honor of Peter Machinist*, Winona Lake: Eisenbrauns, 2013.

Michalowski, P., "Sumerian Royal Women in Motown", in P. Corò (ed.),

Libiamo ne'lieticalici: Ancient Near Eastern Studies Presented to Lucio Milano on the Occasion of his 65th Birthday by Pupils, Colleagues and Friends, Münster: Ugarit-Verlag, 2016.

Molina, M., "New Ur III Court Records Concerning Slavery", in P. Michalowski (ed.), *On the Third Dynasty of Ur: Studies in Honor of Marcel Sigrist*, Boston: American Schools of Oriental Research, 2008.

Molina, M., "The corpus of Neo-Sumerian tablets: an overview", in S. J. Garfinkle and J. C. Johnson (eds.), *The Growth of an Early State in Mesopotamia: Studies in Ur III Administration. Proceedings of the First and Second Ur III Workshops at the 49th and 51st Rencontre Assyriologique Internationale, London July 10, 2003 and Chicago July 19, 2005*, BPOA 5, Madrid: Consejo Superior de Investigaciones Científicas, 2008.

Molina, M., "Archives and Bookkeeping in Southern Mesopotamia during the Ur III period", *Revue d'Histoire des Comptabilités*, Vol. 8 (2016).

Molina, M., "Cases on Malpractice by Provincial Officers at Umma", in P. Corò, et al (eds.), *Libiamo ne'lieticalici: Ancient Near Eastern Studies Presented to Lucio Milano on the Occasion of his 65th Birthday by Pupils, Colleagues and Friends*, AOAT 436, Münster: Ugarit-Verlag, 2016.

Molina, M., "The Looting of Ur III Tablets after the Gulf Wars", in W. Sommerfeld (ed.), *Dealing with Antiquity: Past, Present & Future RAI Marburg*, AOAT 460, Münster: Ugarit-Verlag, 2020.

Molina, M., "Who watches the watchers? New evidence on the role of foremen in the Ur III administration", in A. Jördens and U. Yiftach (ed.), *Legal Documents in Ancient Societies: Accounts and Bookkeeping in the Ancient World*, Wiesbaden: Harrassowitz Verlag, 2020.

Nadali, D., Polcaro, A., "The Early Stages of the Sumerian City at Tell Zurghul: New Results from Recent Excavations", *Origini: Prehistory and Protohistory of Ancient Civilizations*, Vol. 39 (2016).

Nadali, D., Polcaro, A., "Archaeological Discoveries in the Ancient State of Lagash: Results from the Italian Excavations at Tell Zurghul/Nigin in Southern Iraq", *Ash-Sharq*, Vol. 2, No. 1 (2018).

Nadali, D., Polcaro, A., Verderame, L., "New Inscriptions of Gudea from Tell Surghul/Niĝin, Iraq", *Zeitschrift für Assyriologie und Vorderasiatische Archäologie*, Vol. 106, No. 1 (2016).

Neumann, H., "Handel und Händler in der Zeit der III. Dynastie von Ur", *Altorientalische Forschungen*, Vol. 6 (1979).

Neumann, H., "Beer as a Means of Compensation for Work in Mesopotamia During the Ur III Period", in L. Milano (ed.), *Drinking in Ancient Societies: History and Culture of Drinks in the Ancient Near East: Papers of a Symposium held in Rome, May 17 – 19, 1990*, History of the Ancient Near East Studies 6, Padua: Sargon, 1994.

Neumann, H., "Grundpfandbestellung und Feldabgabeunter rechts- und sozialvergleichendem Aspekt (mit Bemerkungen zur Lesung und Interpretation von CST 60, 11 und MVN III 336, 11)", in H. Klengel and J. Renger (eds.), *Landwirtschaft im alten Orient: Ausgewählte Vorträge der XLI. Rencontre Assyriologique Internationale Berlin, 4.-8. 7. 1994*, Berliner Beiträge zum Vorderen Orient 18, Berlin: Dietrich Reimer Verlag, 1999.

Neumann, H., "Staatliche Verwaltung und privates Handwerk in der Ur III-Zeit", in A. Bongenaar (ed.), *Interdependency of Institutions and Private Entrepreneurs*, Leiden: NHAII, 2000.

Notizia, P., "Hulibar, Duhduh(u) NI e la frontieraorientale", in M. G. Biga and M. Liverani (eds.), *ana turrigimilli: studidedicati al Padre Werner R. Mayer, S. J. da amici e allievi*, Vicino Oriente-Quaderno 5, Rome: Università degli Studi di Roma "La Sapienza", 2010.

Notizia, P., Pomponio, F., "A New Annual Account of Wool from the Neo-Sumerian Province of Umma", *Revue d'Assyriologie et d'Archéologie Orientale*, Vol. 113, No. 1 (2019).

Notizia, Palmiro. "How to 'Institutionalize' a Household in Ur III Ĝirsu/Lagaš: The Case of the House of Ur-DUN", *Journal of Cuneiform Studies*, Vol. 71 (2019).

Oh'e, S., "On the Meaning of Sag-rig$_7$", *Al-Rafidan*, Vol. 9 (1988).

Ouyang, X., "Administration of the Irrigation Fee in Umma during the Ur III

Period (ca. 2112 – 2004 BCE)", in L. Kogan, et al (eds.), *City Administration in the Ancient Near East: Proceedings of the 53e Rencontre Assyriologique Internationale Vol.* 2, Babel und Bibel 5, Winona Lake: Eisenbrauns, 2010.

Ouyang, Xiaoli. "Managing the Treasuries of the Gods-Administration of the KÙ. AN in Ur III Umma", *Journal of Ancient Civilizations*, Vol. 35 (2020).

Owen, D. I., "Tax Payments from Some City Elders in the Northeast", *Acta Sumerologica*, Vol. 3 (1981).

Owen, D. I., "Random Notes on a Recent Ur III Volume", *Journal of the American Oriental Society*, Vol. 108, No. 1 (1988).

Owen, D. I., "Syrians in Sumerian Sources from the Ur III Period", *Bibliotheca Mesopotamica*, Vol. 25 (1992).

Owen, D. I., "The Ensis of Gudua", *Acta Sumerologica*, Vol. 15 (1993).

Owen, D. I., "Ur III Geographical and Prosopographical Notes", in G. D. Young, M. W. Chavalas and R. E. Averbeck (eds.), *Crossing Boundaries and Linking Horizons: Studies in Honor of Michael C. Astour on His 80th Birthday*, Bethesda: CDL Press, 1997.

Owen, D. I., "The Royal Gift Seal of Silluš-Dagan, Governor of Simurrum", in S. Graziani (ed.), *Studi sul Vicino Oriente antico dedicati alla memoria di Luigi Cagni*, Napoli: Istituto Universitario Orientale di Napoli, 2000.

Owen, D. I., "On the Patronymy of Šu-Suen", *Nouvelles Assyriologiques Brèves et Utilitaires* 2001/17.

Owen, D. I., "New Additions to the Iri-Saĝrig/Al-Šarrākī Archives", in P. Corò, E. Devecchi, N. De Zorzi, M. Maiocchi (eds.), *Libiamo ne' lieticalici: Ancient Near Eastern Studies Presented to Lucio Milano on the occasion of his 65th Birthday by Pupils, Colleagues and Friends*, Alter Orient und Altes Testament 346, Münster: Ugarit-Verlag, 2016.

Owen, D. I., "The Cosmopolitan Society of Iri-Saĝrig", in I. Arkhipov, L. Kogan and N. Koslova (eds.), *The Third Millennium. Studies in Early Mesopotamia and Syria in Honor of Walter Sommerfeld and Manfred Krebernik*, CM 50, Leiden and Boston: Brill, 2020.

Ozaki, T., "On the Calendar of Urusaĝrig", *Zeitschrift für Assyriologie und Vorderasiatische Archäologie*, Vol. 106 (2016).

Paoletti, P., "Elusive Silver? Evidence for the Circulation of Silver in the Ur III State", *KASKAL. Rivista di storia, ambienti e culture del Vicino Oriente Antico*, Vol. 5 (2008).

Pomponio, F., "The Reichskalender of Ur III in the Umma Texts", *Zeitschrift für Assyriologie und Vorderasiatische Archäologie*, Vol. 79 (1989).

Pomponio, F., "Lukalla of Umma", *Zeitschrift für Assyriologie und Vorderasiatische Archäologie*, Vol. 82 (1992).

Pomponio, F., "The Hexapolis of Šuruppak", in F. Pomponio and G. Visicato (eds.), *Early Dynastic Administrative Tablets of Šuruppak*, Napoli: Istituto Universitario Orientale di Napoli, 1994.

Pomponio, F., Verderame, L., "The Neo-Sumerian Economy", *Rivista di storia economica*, Vol. 1 (2015).

Potts, D., "Adamšah, Kimaš and the miners of Lagaš", in H. D. Baker, E-. Robson and G. Zolyomi (eds.), *Your Praise is Sweet: A Memorial Volume for Jeremy Black from Students, Colleagues and Friends*, London: British Institute for the Study of Iraq, 2010.

Powell, M. A., "Sumerian cereal crops", *Bulletin on Sumerian Agriculture*, Vol. 1 (1984).

Powell, M. A., "Metron Ariston: Measure as a Tool for Studying Beer in Ancient Mesopotamia", in L. Milano (ed.), *Drinking in Ancient Societies: History and Culture of Drinks in the Ancient Near East*, HANES 6, Padova: Sargon srl, 1994.

Prang, E., "Das Archiv des Imgûa", *Zeitschrift für Assyriologie und Vorderasiatische Archäologie*, Vol. 66 (1976).

Reid, J. N., "Runaways and Fugitive Catchers during the Third Dynasty of Ur", *Journal of the Economic and Social History of the Orient*, Vol. 58 (2015).

Reiner, E., "The Location of Anšan", *Revue d'Assyriologie et d'Arché Ologieorientale*, Vol. 67 (1973).

Renfrew, J. M., "Cereals cultivated in Ancient Iraq", *Bulletin on Sumerian*

Agriculture, Vol. 1 (1984).

Renger, J., "Oikos-Wirtschaft und tributäre Wirtschaftsformen-Die dominanten-Strukturen der Wirtschaft in Mesopotamien im 3. und 2. Jt. v. Chr. ", in J.-W. Meyer and W. Sommerfeld (eds.), *2000 v. Chr.: Politische, Wirtschaftliche und Kulturelle Entwicklung im Zeicheneiner Jahrtausendwende*, CDOG 3, Saarbrücker: Saarbrücker Druckerei und Verlag, 2004.

Richardson, S., "Goodbye, Princess: Iltani and the DUMU. MUNUS LUGAL", *Journal of Cuneiform Studies*, Vol. 69 (2017).

Roehmer, R. W., "Uruk-Warka", in E. M. Meyers (ed.), *The Oxford Encyclopedia of Archaeology in the Near East*, Volume 5, New York and Oxford: Oxford University Press, 1997.

Röllig, W., "Politische Heiraten im Alten Orient", *Saeculum*, Vol. 25 (1974).

Rowton, M. B., "Dimorphic Structure and Topology", *Oriens Antiquus*, Vol. 15 (1976).

Rubio, G., "Sumerian Literature", in C. S. Ehrlich (ed.), *From an Antique Land: An Introduction To Ancient Near Eastern Literature*, Lanham: Rowman&Littlefield Publishers, 2009.

Rubio, G., "Sumerian Temples and Arabian Horses: On Sumerian e_2-*gal*", in L. Feliu, F. Karahashi and G. Rubio (eds.), *The First Ninety Years: A Sumerian Celebration in Honor of Miguel Civil*, SANER 12, Berlin: De Gruyter, 2017.

Sallaberger, W., "Textformular und Syntax in sumerischen Verwaltungstexten", *Acta Sumerologica*, Vol. 22 (2000).

Sallaberger, W., "Schlachtvieh aus Puzriš-Dagān. Zur Bedeutung dieses königlichen Archivs", *Jaarbericht van het Vooraziatisch-egyptisch Genootschap Ex Oriente Lux*, Vol. 38 (2003–2004).

Sallaberger, W., "From Urban Culture to Nomadism: A History of Upper Mesopotamia in the Late Third Millennium", in C. Kuzucuoglu, C. Marro (eds.), *Sociétés humaines et changement climatique à la fin du troisieème millénaire: une crise a-t-elle eu lieu en Haute Mésopotamie? Actes du Colloque de Lyon (5–8 décembre 2005)*, Varia Anatolica 19, Istanbul: Institut

Francsais d'Études Anatoliennes-Georges Dumézil, 2007.

Sallaberger, W., "Festival provisions in Early Bronze Age Mesopotamia", *Kaskal*, Vol. 15 (2018).

Sasson, J., "About 'Mari and the Bible'", *Revue d'Assyriologie et d'Archéologie Orientale*, Vol. 92 (1998).

Scharaschenidze, D. M., "Die sukkal-mah des alten Zweistromlandes in der Zeit der III. Dynastie von Ur", in J. Harmatta and G. Komoróczy (eds.), *Wirtschaft und Gesellschaft im Alten Vorderasien*, Budapest: Akadémiai Kiadó, 1976.

Scheil, V., "Notes d'épigraphie et d'archéologie assyrienne. XI-XVII", *Recueil de Travaux Relatifs à la Philologie et à l'Archéologie Égyptienne et Assyriennes*, Vol. 17 (1895).

Schmidt, C., "Überregionale Austauschsysteme und Fernhandelswaren in der Ur III-Zeit", *Baghdader Mitteilungen*, Vol. 36 (2005).

Schneider, N., "Die höchsten Staats und Kultusbehörden", *Orientalia Series Prior*, Vol. 45–46 (1930).

Schneider, N., "Die Königskinder des Herrscherhauses von Ur III", *Orientalia, Nova Series*, Vol. 12 (1943).

Schrakamp, I., Paoletti, P., "Steuer", *Reallexikonder Assyriologie und Vorderasiatischen Archäologie*, Vol. 13 (2011–2013).

Selz, G. J., "Maš-da-ri-a und Verwandtes. Ein Versuch über da-ri ' an der Seite führen': einzusammengesetztes Verbum und einigenominale Ableitungen", *Acta Sumerologica*, Vol. 17 (1995).

Selz, G. J., "Schrifterfindung als Ausformung eines reflexiven Ziechensystems", *Wiener Zeitschrift für die Kunde des Morgenlandes*, Vol. 90 (2000).

Sharlach, T. M., "Beyond chronology: The *šakkanakkus* of Mari and the kings of Ur", in W. W. Hallo and I. Winter (eds.), *Proceedings of the XLVᵉ Rencontre Assyriologique Internationale. Part II: Seals and Seal Impressions*, Bethesda: CDL Press, 2001.

Sharlach, T. M., "Diplomacy and the rituals of politics at the Ur III court", *Journal of Cuneiform Studies*, Vol. 57 (2005).

Sharlach, T. M. , "Priestesses, Concubines, and the Daughters of Men: Disentangling the Meaning of the Word lukur in Ur III Times", in P. Michalowski (ed.), *On the Third Dynasty of Ur: Studies in Honor of Marcel Sigrist*, Journal of Cuneiform Studies Supplemental Series 1, Boston: American Schools of Oriental Research, 2008.

Sigrist, M. , "Erín-un-íl", *Revue d'Assyriologie et d'Archéologie Orientale*, Vol. 73 (1979).

Sigrist, M. , "Le deuil pour Šu-Sin", in H. Behrens, D. Loding, T. M. Roth (eds.), *DUMU-E₂-DUB-BA-A: Studies in Honor of Åke W. Sjöberg*, Occasional Publications of the Samuel Noah Kramer Fund 11, Philadelphia: The University Museum, 1989.

Silver, M. , "Climate Change, the Mardu Wall, and the Fall of Ur", in O. Drewnowska and M. Sandowicz (eds.), *Fortune and Misfortune in the Ancient Near East: Proceedings of the 60th Recontre Assyriologique Internationale Warsaw, 21 – 25 July 2014*, Winona Lake: Eisenbrauns, 2017.

Snell, D. C. , "The Ur III Tablets in the Emory University Museum", *Acta Sumerologica*, Vol. 9 (1987).

Sollberger, E. , "Sur la chronologie des rois d'Ur et quelques problèmes connexes", *Archiv für Orientforschung*, Vol. 17 (1954 – 1956).

Sollberger, E. , "Ibbī-Suen", *Reallexikon der Assyriologie und Vorderasiatischen Archäologie*, Vol. 5 (1976 – 1980).

Sommerfeld, W. , "The transition from the Old Akkadian period to UrIII in Lagash", in W. Sallaberger and I. Schrakamp (eds.), *ARCANE III. History and Philology*, Turnhout: Brepols, 2015.

Steinkeller, P. , "On the Reading and Location of the Toponyms ÚRxÚ. KI and A. HA. KI", *Journal of Cuneiform Studies*, Vol. 32 (1980).

Steinkeller, P. , "More on the Ur III Royal Wives", *Acta Sumerologica*, Vol. 3 (1981).

Steinkeller, P. , "The Renting of Fields in Early Mesopotamia and the Development of the Concept of 'Interest' in Sumerian", *Journal of the Economic and Social History of the Orient*, Vol. 24 (1981).

Steinkeller, P., "The Question of Marhaši: A Contribution to the Historical Geography of Iran in the Third Millennium B. C. ", *Zeitschrift für Assyriologie und Vorderasiatische Archäologie*, Vol. 72 (1982).

Steinkeller, P., "The Administrative and Economic Organization of the Ur III State: the Core and the Periphery", in McG. Gibson, R. Biggs (eds.), *The Organization of Power Aspects of Bureaucracy in the Ancient Near East*, Chicago: The Oriental Institute of the University of Chicago, 1987.

Steinkeller, P., "The Foresters of Umma: Toward a Definition of Ur III Labor", in M. A. Power (ed.), *Labor in the Ancient Near East*, AOS 68, New Haven: American Oriental Society, 1987.

Steinkeller, P., "The Date of Gudea and His Dynasty", *Journal of Cuneiform Studies*, Vol. 40 (1988).

Steinkeller, P., "On the Identity of the Toponym LÚ. SU (. A)", *Journal of the American Oriental Society*, Vol. 108 (1988).

Steinkeller, P., "Sheep and goat terminology in Ur III sources from Drehem", *Bulletin on Sumerian Agriculture*, Vol. 8 (1995).

Steinkeller, P., "The Historical Background of Urkesh and the Hurrian Beginnings in Northern Mesopotamia", in G. Buccellati and M. Kelly-Buccellati (eds.), *Urkesh / Mozan Studies 3: Urkesh and the Hurrians Studies in Honor of Lloyd Cotsen*, Bibliotheca Mesopotamica 26, Malibu: Undena Publications, 1998.

Steinkeller, P., "On Rulers, Priest and Sacred Marriage: Tracing the Evolution of Early Sumerian Kingship", in K. Watanabe (ed.), *Priests and Officials in the Ancient Near East*, Heidelberg: Winter, 1999.

Steinkeller, P., "AB-tum = èš-tum/*iltu*", *Nouvelles Assyriologiques Brèves et Utilitaires*, 2001/35.

Steinkeller, P., "Archaic City Seals and the Question of Early Babylonian Unity", in Tzvi Abusch (ed.), *Riches Hidden in Secret Places: Ancient Near Eastern Studies in Memory of Thorkild Jacobsen*, Winona Lake: Eisenbrauns, 2002.

Steinkeller, P., "Archival Practices at Babylonia in the Third Millennium", in

M. Brosius (ed.), *Ancient Archives and Archival Traditions: Concepts of Record-Keeping in the Ancient World*, Oxford: Oxford University Press, 2003.

Steinkeller, P., "An Ur III Manuscript of the Sumerian King List", in W. Sallaberger, K. Volk and A. Zgoll (eds.), *Literatur, Politik und Recht in Mesopotamien: Festschrift für Claus Wilcke*, Orientalia Biblica et Christiana 14, Wiesbaden: Harrassowitz Verlag, 2003.

Steinkeller, P., "The Priestess égi-zi and Related Matters", in Y. Sefati, et al (eds.), *"An Experienced Scribe Who Neglects Nothing": Ancient Near Eastern Studies in Honor of Jacob Klein*, Bethesda: CDL Press, 2005.

Steinkeller, P., "New Light on Marhaši and Its Contacts with Makkan and Babylonia", *Journal of Magan Studies*, Vol. 1 (2006).

Steinkeller, P., "New Light on Šimaški and Its Rulers", *Zeitschrift für Assyriologie und Vorderasiatische Archäologie*, Vol. 97 (2007).

Steinkeller, P., "Joys of Cooking in Ur III Babylonia", in P. Michalowski (eds.), *On the Third Dynasty of Ur: Studies in Honor of Marcel Sigrist*, Journal of Cuneiform Studies Supplemental Series 1, Boston: American Schools of Oriental Research, 2008.

Steinkeller, P., "Archival Practices at Babylonia in the Third Millennium", in M. Brosius (ed.), *Ancient Archives and Archival Traditions: Concepts of Record-Keeping in the Ancient World*, Oxford: Oxford University Press, 2011.

Steinkeller, P., "On the Location of the Town of GARšana and Related Matters", in D. I. Owen (ed.), *Garšana Studies*, Cornell University Studies in Assyriology and Sumerology 6, Bethesda: CDL Press, 2011.

Steinkeller, P., "How Did Šulgi and Išbi-Erra Ascend to Heaven?" in D. S. Vanderhooft and A. Winitzer (eds.), *Literature as Politics, Politics as Literature: Essays on the Ancient Near East in Honor of Peter Machinist*, Winona Lake: Eisenbrauns, 2013.

Steinkeller, P., "Puzur-Inšušinak at Susa: A Pivotal Episode of Early Elamite History Revonsidered", in K. De Graef, J. Tavernier (eds.), *Susa and Elam. Archaeological, Philological, Historical and Geographical Perspectives: Proceedings of the International Congress Held at Ghent University, December 14 –*

17, 2009, Leiden and Boston: Brill, 2013.

Steinkeller, P., "On the Dynasty of Šimaški: Twenty Years (or so) After", in M. Kozuh, et al (eds.), *Extraction & Control: Studies in Honor of Matthew W. Stolper*, Studies in Ancient Oriental Civilization 68, Chicago: The Oriental Institute of the University of Chicago, 2014.

Steinkeller, P., "An Estimate of the Population of the City of Umma in Ur III Times", in Y. Heffron, et al (eds.), *At the Dawn of History: Ancient Near Eastern Studies in Honor of J. N. Postgate*, Winona Lake: Eisenbrauns, 2017.

Steinkeller, P., "Babylonian Priesthood during the Third Millennium BCE: Between Sacred and Profane", *Journal of Ancient Near Eastern Religions*, Vol. 19 (2019).

Stepien, M., "The Economic Status of Governors in Ur III Times: An Example of the Governor of Umma", *Journal of Cuneiform Studies*, Vol. 64 (2012).

Sterba, R. L., "The Organization and Management of the Temple Corporations in Ancient Mesopotamia", *Academy of Management Review*, Vol. 1 (1976).

Stol, M., "Old Babylonian Corvée (*tupšikkum*)", in T. van den Hout, J. DeRoos (ed.), *Studio Historiae Ardens: Ancient Near Eastern Studies Presented to Philo H. J. Houwink ten Cafe on the Occasion of his 65th Birthday*, Leiden: Nederlands Instituut voor het Habije Oosten, 1995.

Stol, M., "Old Babylonian cattle", *Bulletin on Sumerian Agriculture*, Vol. 8 (1995).

Stolper, M. W., "On the Dynasty ofShimashki and the Early Sukkalmahs", *Zeitschrift für Assyriologie und Vorderasiatische Archäologie*, Vol. 72 (1982).

Stolper, M. W., "Registration and Taxation of Slave Sales in Achaemenid Babylonia", *Zeitschrift für Assyriologie und Vorderasiatische Archäologie*, Vol. 79 (1989).

Streck, M. P., "Tafel (tablet)", *Reallexikon der Assyriologie und Vorderasiatischen Archäologie*, Vol. 13 (2011 – 2013).

Such-Gutiérrez, M., "Der Kalendar von Adab im 3. Jahrtausend", in L. Feliu, et al (eds.), *Time and History in the Ancient Near East: Proceedings of the 56th Recontre Assyriologique Internationale at Barcelona 26 – 30 July 2010*,

Winona Lake: Eisenbrauns, 2013.

Such-Gutiérrez, M., "Man and Animals in the Administrative Texts of the End of the 3rd Millennium BC", in R. Mattila, S. Ito and S. Fink (eds.), *Animals and their Relations to Gods, Humans and Things in the Ancient World*, Wiesbaden: Springer, 2019.

Such-Gutiérrez, M., "Der Beruf su-si- (ig) im 3. Jahrtausend", *Journal of Cuneiform Studies*, Vol. 72 (2020).

Thureau-Dangin, F., "La comptabilité agricole en Chaldée", *Revue d'Assyriologie et d'Archéologie Orientale*, Vol. 3 (1895).

Thureau-Dangin, F., "Notes assyriologiques", *Revue d'Assyriologie et d'Archéologie Orientale*, Vol. 7 (1910).

Tsouparoupoulo, C., "A Reconstruction of the Puzriš-Dagan Central Livestock Agency", *Cuneiform Digital Library Journal*, 2013/2.

Tsouparopoulou, C., "'Counter-Archaeology': Putting the Ur III Drehem Archives Back in the Ground." In Y. Heffron, A. Stone and M. Worthington (eds.), *At the Dawn of History: Ancient Near Eastern Studies in Honour of J. N. Postgate*, Winona Lake: Eisenbrauns, 2017.

Uchitel, A., "Daily Work at Sagdana Millhouse", *Acta Sumerologica*, Vol. 6 (1984).

Ur, J., "Umma. B. Archäologisch", *Reallexikon der Assyriologie und Vorderasiatischen Archäologie*, Vol. 14 (2014–2016).

VanDijk, J. J., "Une insurrection générale au pays de Larša avant l'avènement de Nūradad", *Journal of Cuneiform Studies*, Vol. 19 (1965).

Verderame, L., Spada, G., "Ikalla, Scribe of (Wool) Textiles and Linen", in S. Garfinkle and M. Molina (eds.), *From the 21st Century B.C. to the 21st Century A.D.: Proceedings of the International Conference on Sumerian Studies Held in Madrid 22–24 July 2010*, Winona Lake: Eisenbrauns, 2013.

Verkinderen, P., "Les toponymes bàd^{ki} et bàd.an^{ki}", *Akkadica*, Vol. 127 (2006).

Waetzoldt, H., "Das Amt des Utullu", in G. Van Driel, et al (eds.), *Zikir Šumim: Assyriological Studies Presented to F. R. Kraus on the Occasion of his*

Seventieth Birthday, Leiden: E. J. Brill, 1982.

Waetzoldt, H., "Review of The Organization of Power: Aspects of Bureaucracy in the Ancient Near East by McGuire Gibson, Robert D. Biggs", *Journal of the American Oriental Society*, Vol. 111 (1991).

Waetzoldt, H., " 'Rohr' und dessen Verwendungsweisenanhand der neusumerischen Texte aus Umma", *Bulletin on Sumerian Agriculture*, Vol. 6 (1992).

Waetzoldt, H., "Zu den Siegeln der Vorsteher der Opferschauer Nannazišagal und Enlilzišagal", *Zeitschrift für Assyriologie und Vorderasiatische Archäologie*, Vol. 96 (2006).

Waetzoldt, H., "The Colours and Variety of Fabrics from Mesopotamia during the Ur III Period (2050 BC)", in C. Michel and M. -L. Nosch (eds.), *Textile Terminologies in the Ancient Near East and the Mediterranean from the Third to the First Millennium BC*, Ancient Textiles Series 8, Oxford: Oxbow Books, 2010.

Waetzoldt, H., "Umma. A. Philologisch", *Reallexikon der Assyriologie und Vorderasiatischen Archäologie*, Vol. 14 (2014–2016).

Wang, J., Wu, Y., "A Research on the Incoming (mu-túm) Archive of Queen Šulgi-simti's Animal Institution", *Journal of Ancient Civilizations*, Vol. 26 (2011).

Westenholz, A., "Was Kish the Center of a Territorial State in the Third Millennium? —and Other Thorny Questions", in I. Arkhipov, L. Kogan and N. Koslova (eds.), *The Third Millennium. Studies in Early Mesopotamia and Syria in Honor of Walter Sommerfeld and Manfred Krebernik*, CM 50, Leiden and Boston: Brill, 2020.

Westenholz, J. G., "Intimations of Mortality", in S. Graziani (ed.), *Studisul Vicino Oriente Antico dedicati alla memoria di Luigi Cagni*, Napoli: Istituto Universitario Orientale, 2000.

Whiting, R. M., "Tiš-atal of Nineveh and Babati, Uncle of Šu-Sin", *Journal of Cuneiform Studies*, Vol. 28, No. 3 (1976).

Whiting, R. M., "Some Observations on the Drehem Calendar", *Zeitschrift für Assyriologie und Vorderasiatische Archäologie*, Vol. 69 (1979).

Wiggerman, F. A. M., "An Unrecognized Synonym of Sumerian *sukkal*, 'Vizier'", *Zeitschrift für Assyriologie und Vorderasiatische Archäologie*, Vol. 78 (1988).

Wilcke, C., "Zur Geschichte der Amurriter in der Ur-III-Zeit", *Die Welt des Orients*, Vol. 5 (1969 – 1970).

Wilcke, C., "Drei Phasen des Niedergangens des Reiches von Ur III", *Zeitschrift für Assyriologie und Vorderasiatische Archäologie*, Vol. 60 (1970).

Wilcke, C., "Eine Schicksalsentscheidung für den toten Urnammu", in A. Finet (ed.), *Actes de la XVIIe Recontre Assyriologique Internationale, Université Libre de Bruxelles, 30 juin-4 juillet 1969*, Ham-sur-Heure: Comité belge de recherches en Mésopotamie, 1970.

Wilcke, C., "Zum Königtum in der Ur III-Zeit", in P. Garelli (ed.), *Le palais et la royauté (Archéologie et Civilisation): XIXe Rencontre Assyriologique Internationale organisée par le groupe François Thureau-Dangin, Paris, 29 juin-2 juillet 1971*, Paris: Librairie Orientaliste Paul Geuthner S. A., 1974.

Wilcke, C., "Die Inschriftenfunde der 7. und 8. Kampagnen (1983 und 1984)", in B. Hrouda (ed.), *Isin-Išān Bahrīyāt III. Die Ergebnisse der Ausgrabungen 1983 – 1984*, München: Verlag der Bayerischen Akademie der Wissenschaften, 1988.

Wilcke, C., "Genealogical and Geographical Thought in the Sumerian King List", in H. Behrens, D. Loding, T. M. Roth (eds.), *DUMU-E$_2$-DUB-BA-A: Studies in Honor of Åke W. Sjöberg*, Occasional Publications of the Samuel Noah Kramer Fund 11, Philadelphia: The University Museum, 1989.

Wilcke, C., "É-saĝ-da-na Nibru^{ki}: An Early Administrative Center of the Ur III Empire", in M. Ellis (ed.), *Nippur at the Centennial: Papers Read at the 35e Rencontre Assyriologique Internationale, Philadelphia, 1988*, Occasional Publications of the Samuel Noah Kramer Fund 14, Philadelphia: The University Museum, 1992.

Wilcke, C., "Der Kodex Urnamma (CU): Versuch einer Rekonstruktion", in T. Abusch (ed.), *Riches Hidden in Secret Places: Ancient Near Eastern Studies in Memory of Thorkild Jacobsen*, Winona Lake: Eisenbrauns, 2002.

Winters, R., "The Royal Herdsmen of Ur: Compensation and Centralization in the Reign of Shulgi", *Journal of Cuneiform Studies*, Vol. 72 (2020).

Wu, Y., "Naram-ili, Šu-Kabta and Nawir-ilum in the Archives of Garšana, Puzriš-Dagan and Umma", *Journal of Ancient Civilizations*, Vol. 23 (2008).

Wu, Y., "The Anonymous Nasa and Nasa of the Animal Center during Šulgi 44 – 48 and the Wild Camel (gú-gur5), Hunchbacked Ox (gur8-gur8), ubi, habum and the Confusion of the Deer (lulim) with Donkey (anše) or šeg9", *Journal of Ancient Civilizations*, Vol. 25 (2010).

Wu, Y., "19 Years' Finance of the Household of Geme-Lamma, the High Priestess of Baba in Girsu of Ur III (Š 31-AS 1 = 2065 – 2046 B. C.)", *Journal of Ancient Civilizations*, Vol. 26 (2011).

Wu, Y., Wang, J., "The Identifications of Šulgi-simti, Wife of Šulgi, with Abi-simti, Mother of Amar-Sin and Šu-Sin, and of Ur-Sin, the Crown Prince, with Amar-Sin", *Journal of Ancient Civilizations*, Vol. 27 (2012).

Yoshikawa, M., "Looking for Tummal", *Acta Sumerologica*, Vol. 11 (1989).

Zadok, R., "Elamites and Other Peoples from Iran and the Persian Gulf Region in Early Mesopotamian Sources", *Iran*, Vol. 32 (1994).

Zarins, J., "The Domesticated Equidae of Third Millennium B. C. Mesopotamia", *Journal of Cuneiform Studies*, Vol. 30 (1978).

Zettler, R. L., "The Geneaology of the House of Ur-Me-me: a Second Look", *Archiv für Orientforschung*, Vol. 31 (1984).

Zettler, R. L., "Tišatal and Nineveh at the End of the 3rd Millennium BCE", in A. K. Guinan, et al (eds.), *If a Man Builds a Joyful House: Assyriological Studies in Honor of Erle Verdun Leichty*, Cuneiform Monographs 31, Leiden and Boston: Brill, 2006.

Zólyomi, G., "CUNES 39 – 01 – 026, a legal record about the repayment of a loan", *Nouvelles Assyriologiques Brèves et Utilitaires*, 2020/48.

三 中文参考书目

《马克思恩格斯选集》第 1 卷，人民出版社 1972 年版。

《马克思恩格斯选集》第 1 卷，人民出版社 2012 年版。

《马克思恩格斯选集》第 3 卷，人民出版社 2012 年版。
《马克思恩格斯选集》第 4 卷，人民出版社 1972 年版。
《马克思恩格斯全集》第 4 卷，人民出版社 1958 年版。
《马克思恩格斯全集》第 8 卷，人民出版社 1961 年版。
《马克思恩格斯全集》第 11 卷，人民出版社 1995 年版。
《列宁全集》第 32 卷，人民出版社 1958 年版。
东北师范大学世界古典文明史研究所编：《世界诸古代文明年代学研究的历史与现状》，世界图书出版公司 1999 年版。
[英] M. I. 芬利：《古代经济》，黄洋译，商务印书馆 2020 年版。
拱玉书：《日出东方：苏美尔文明探秘》，云南人民出版社 2001 年版。
拱玉书：《西亚考古史（1842—1939）》，文物出版社 2002 年版。
拱玉书译注：《吉尔伽美什史诗》，商务印书馆 2021 年版。
拱玉书等：《世界文明起源研究：历史与现状》，昆仑出版社 2015 年版。
顾诚：《隐匿的疆土：卫所制度与明帝国》，光明日报出版社 2012 年版。
顾銮斋：《中西中古税制比较研究》，社会科学文献出版社 2016 年版。
郭丹彤、黄薇编：《古代近东文明文献读本》，中西书局 2019 年版。
国洪更：《亚述赋役制度考略》，中国社会科学出版社 2015 年版。
何盛明主编：《财经大辞典》下卷，中国财政经济出版社 1990 年版。
[美] 亨利·富兰克弗特：《古代东方的艺术与建筑》，郝海迪、袁指挥译，上海三联书店 2012 年版。
黄天华：《中国税收制度史》，华东师范大学出版社 2007 年版。
黄艳红：《法国旧制度末期的税收、特权和政治》，社会科学文献出版社 2016 年版。
黄洋：《古代希腊土地制度研究》，复旦大学出版社 1995 年版。
胡铁球：《明清歇家研究》，上海古籍出版社 2015 年版。
蒋家瑜：《不可不知的古代地中海文明史》，华中科技大学出版社 2019 年版。
[英] 莱昂纳德·W. 金：《古代巴比伦》，史孝文译，北京理工大学出版社 2020 年版。
李海峰：《古巴比伦时期不动产经济活动研究》，社会科学文献出版社 2011 年版。

李海峰：《古代近东文明》，科学出版社 2014 年版。

李海峰：《古巴比伦时期动产交易活动研究》，上海三联书店 2018 年版。

李政：《赫梯条约研究》，昆仑出版社 2006 年版。

李治安：《元代行省制度》，中华书局 2011 年版。

刘昌玉《从"上海"到下海：早期两河流域商路初探》，中国社会科学出版社 2019 年版。

刘家和：《古代中国与世界》，北京师范大学出版社 2010 年版。

刘家和、廖学盛主编：《世界古代文明史研究导论》，高等教育出版社 2010 年版。

刘文鹏主编：《古代西亚北非文明》，中国社会科学出版社 1999 年版。

［美］马克·范·德·米罗普：《希腊前的哲学：古代巴比伦对真理的追求》，刘昌玉译，商务印书馆 2020 年版。

毛亦可：《清代卫所归并州县研究》，社会科学文献出版社 2018 年版。

亓佩成：《古代西亚文明》，山东大学出版社 2016 年版。

［英］塞顿·劳埃德：《美索不达米亚考古》，杨建华译，文物出版社 1990 年版。

施治生、徐建新：《古代国家的等级制度》，中国社会科学出版社 2015 年版。

王俊娜：《乌尔第三王朝王后贡牲机构档案重建与研究》，中国社会科学出版社 2017 年版。

吴宇虹等：《泥板上不朽的苏美尔文明》，北京大学出版社 2013 年版。

吴宇虹等：《古代两河流域楔形文字经典举要》，黑龙江人民出版社 2006 年版。

［日］小川乡太郎：《租税总论》，萨孟武译，商务印书馆 1935 年版。

［英］亚当·斯密：《国民财富性质和原因的研究》（下册），郭大力、王亚南译，商务印书馆 1974 年版。

［美］T. 雅各布森编：《苏美尔王表》，郑殿华译，生活·读书·新知三联书店 1989 年版。

晏绍祥：《荷马社会研究》，上海三联书店 2006 年版。

杨建华：《两河流域：从农业村落走向城邦国家》，科学出版社 2014 年版。

于殿利：《巴比伦与亚述文明》，北京师范大学出版社 2013 年版。

于殿利：《古代美索不达米亚文明》，北京师范大学出版社 2018 年版。
张金铣：《元代地方行政制度研究》，安徽大学出版社 2001 年版。
张守军：《中国古代的赋税与劳役》，商务印书馆 1998 年版。
张雨：《赋税制度、租佃关系与中国中古经济研究》，上海古籍出版社 2015 年版。
赵德馨主编：《中国经济史辞典》，湖北辞书出版社 1990 年版。
郑学檬主编：《中国赋役制度史》，厦门大学出版社 1994 年版。
中国注册会计师协会：《税法》，经济科学出版社 2012 年版。

四　中文参考论文

晁雪婷、董晓博：《乌尔第三王朝贡物中心的档案管理研析》，《古代文明》2019 年第 4 期。
陈艳丽、吴宇虹：《古代两河流域苏美尔人的地下世界观》，《史学月刊》2015 年第 8 期。
崔国强：《罗马帝国税收钱币化探析》，《外国问题研究》2018 年第 3 期。
杜峻峰：《税收返还制度》，《学习与研究》1994 年第 10 期。
顾銮斋：《英国中古前期的税收习惯》，《世界历史》2014 年第 6 期。
顾銮斋：《赋税制度与欧洲政治制度的演进》，《史学理论研究》2014 年第 2 期。
顾銮斋：《赋税变迁与欧洲文明》，《光明日报》2018 年 8 月 13 日。
郭丹彤：《论古代埃及的赋税体系》，《东北师大学报》（哲学社会科学版）2016 年第 3 期。
国洪更、吴宇虹：《古代两河流域和巴林的海上国际贸易——楔形文字文献和考古发现中的狄勒蒙》，《东北师大学报》2004 年第 5 期。
黄洋：《摩西·芬利与古代经济史研究》，《世界历史》2013 年第 5 期。
李海峰：《古巴比伦时期土地租赁活动研究》《世界历史》2009 年第 1 期。
李海峰：《论古巴比伦时期的"雇佣劳动"现象》，《求索》2017 年第 7 期。
蒋家瑜、吴宇虹：《乌尔帝国阿马尔辛前期的饲养场第二系牛羊吏舒勒吉阿亚牟研究》，《古代文明》2013 年第 4 期。
李海峰：《古巴比伦时期动产借贷活动中各方身份探析》，《东北师大报》（哲学社会科学版）2018 年第 4 期。

李万慧：《"后营改增"时代中国税收返还制度改革方向探索——为税收返还制度正名》，《现代经济探讨》2017 年第 2 期。

李学彦、吴宇虹：《从一件大礼品单看乌尔第三王朝国王和王后的豪华生活》，《历史教学》（下半月刊）2011 年第 4 期。

刘昌玉：《麦鲁哈与上古印度洋—波斯湾海上贸易》，《浙江师范大学学报》（社会科学版）2016 年第 5 期。

刘昌玉：《〈乌尔那穆地籍〉译注》，《古代文明》2017 年第 1 期。

刘昌玉：《乌尔第三王朝行省制度探析》，《社会科学》2017 年第 1 期。

刘昌玉：《古代两河流域的乳母与保姆》，《妇女与性别史研究》2017 年第 2 辑。

刘昌玉：《两河流域乌尔第三王朝灭亡原因初探》，《浙江师范大学学报》（社会科学版）2018 年第 5 期。

刘昌玉：《政治婚姻与两河流域乌尔第三王朝的治理》，《社会科学》2018 年第 8 期。

刘昌玉：《丝绸之路开辟前以两河流域为中心的跨区域贸易探析》，《中南大学学报》（社会科学版）2019 年第 3 期。

刘昌玉：《税制与乌尔第三王朝的国家治理》，《古代文明》2021 年第 1 期。

刘昌玉、吴宇虹：《乌尔第三王朝温马地区法庭判案文件译注与简析》，《古代文明》2011 年第 2 期。

刘昌玉、应俊：《欧洲什一税源于古代两河流域》，《中国社会科学报》2018 年 10 月 29 日。

刘健：《苏美尔王权观念的演进及特征》，《东方论坛》2013 年第 5 期。

刘健：《苏美尔文明基本特征探析》，《外国问题研究》2016 年第 2 期。

欧阳晓莉：《两河流域乌尔第三王朝白银的货币功能探析》，《世界历史》2016 年第 5 期。

欧阳晓莉：《两河流域乌尔第三王朝温马省神庙宝库记录初探》，《古代文明》2018 年第 1 期。

欧阳晓莉：《波兰尼的经济模式与两河流域经济史研究》，《史学理论研究》2018 年第 1 期。

欧阳晓莉：《何谓"中央集权"——两河流域乌尔第三王朝国王舒勒吉改革辨析》，《江海学刊》2019年第4期。

亓佩成：《上古时期西亚与中国的经济文化互动》，《史学月刊》2020年第9期。

王光胜、吴宇虹：《乌尔第三王朝贡牲中心档案中的"酒宴用牲"研究》，《古代文明》2013年第1期。

王光胜、吴宇虹：《乌尔帝国阿马尔辛王的贡牲中心结构和总管研究》，《历史教学》2013年第18期。

王俊娜：《乌尔第三王朝昝尔沙那的职能探析》，《古代文明》2020年第3期。

王俊娜、吴宇虹：《阿比新提太后和舒勒吉新提身份同一研究》，《东北师大学报》（哲学社会科学版）2011年第2期。

王三义：《古罗马"赋税名目"考略》，《史学月刊》2002年第6期。

王三义：《罗马税制的积弊与戴克里先税制改革》，《世界历史》2007年第1期。

王献华：《两河流域早王朝时期作为地理概念的"苏美尔"》，《四川大学学报》（哲学社会科学版）2015年第4期。

王献华：《皇族"恩图"女祭司与阿卡德帝国的治理》，《中山大学学报》（社会科学版）2016年第5期。

王献华：《"神庙经济"论与早期两河流域研究》，《社会科学研究》2019年第4期。

吴宇虹：《古代两河流域文明史年代学研究的历史与现状》，《历史研究》2002年第4期。

吴宇虹、董晓博：《乌尔第三王朝历史文献中É.TUM词义辨析》，《史学史研究》2016年第2期。

熊芳芳：《从"领地国家"到"税收国家"：中世纪晚期法国君主征收权的确立》，《世界历史》2015年第4期。

徐国栋：《罗马人的税赋——从起源到戴克里先登基》，《现代法学》2010年第5期。

袁指挥：《阿马尔那时代近东大国的礼物交换》，《东北师大学报》（哲学社会科学版）2019年第2期。

杨巨平：《娜娜女神的传播与演变》，《世界历史》2010 年第 5 期。

于殿利：《古代美索不达米亚的国家治理结构》，《学术研究》2014 年第 1 期。

于殿利：《试论文明初期美索不达米亚国家意识形态管理实践》，《学术研究》2015 年第 9 期。

袁指挥：《阿马尔那时代近东大国的礼物交换》，《东北师大学报》（哲学社会科学版）2019 年第 2 期。

张文安：《古代两河流域神名表与神庙名表的编写传统》，《外国问题研究》2019 年第 2 期。

朱承思、董为奋：《〈乌尔纳姆法典〉和乌尔第三王朝早期社会》，《历史研究》1984 年第 5 期。

五　网络资源

美国加利福尼亚大学洛杉矶分校、英国牛津大学和德国马克斯·普朗克历史科学研究所的"楔形文字数字图书馆计划"（Cuneiform Digital Library Initiative，简称 CDLI），https：//cdli. ucla. edu/。

西班牙马德里高等科学研究院的"新苏美尔语文献数据库"（西班牙语：Base de Datos de Textos Neo-Sumerios，简称 BDTNS，英语：Database of Neo-Sumerian Texts），http：//bdtns. filol. csic. es/。

英国牛津大学的"苏美尔文学电子文学大全"（The Electronic Text Corpus of Sumerian Literature，简称 ETCSL），http：//etcsl. orinst. ox. ac. uk/。

美国宾夕法尼亚大学的"电子版宾夕法尼亚苏美尔语词典"（electronic Pennsylvania Sumerian Dictionary，简称 ePSD），http：//oracc. museum. upenn. edu/epsd2/。

德国图宾根大学的"楔形文字文学目录项目"（Die Keilschrift-Bibliographie，简称 KeiBi），http：//vergil. uni-tuebingen. de/keibi/。

美国安德鲁·W. 梅隆基金会和美国国家科学基金会的"电子工具与古代近东档案"（Electronic Tools and Ancient Near East Archives，简称 ETANA），http：//www. etana. org/。

德国巴伐利亚科学院的"亚述学与西亚考古学专业词典"（Reallexikon der Assyriologie und Vorderasiatischen Archäologie，简称 RlA），https：//

rla. badw. de/das-projekt. html。

美国芝加哥大学的"东方研究所出版物"（Oriental Institute Publications，简称 OIP），https：//oi. uchicago. edu/research/oriental-institute-publications-office。

美国加利福尼亚大学伯克利分校的"楔形文字辞典文献数字库"（Digital Corpus of Cuneiform Lexical Texts，简称 DCCLT），http：//oracc. museum. upenn. edu/dcclt/。

匈牙利科学研究基金会的"苏美尔王室铭文电子文献大全"（The Electronic Text Corpus of Sumerian Royal Inscriptions），http：//oracc. museum. upenn. edu/etcsri/introduction/index. html。

欧美学术界的"分享研究"网，https：//www. academia. edu/。

中国世界古代史研究网，http：//www. cawhi. com。

中国社会科学网，http：//www. cssn. cn/。

中外文专有名词对照表
(按照专有名词首字母顺序)

一　神名

安 An
巴巴 Baba
巴加拉 Bagara
达干 Dagan
杜牧孜 Dumuzi
恩基 Enki
恩利尔 Enlil
加图姆杜格 Gatumdug
美吉伽尔 Mekigal
里希 Lisi
南那 Nanna
南塞 Nanshe
尼努尔塔 Ninurta
宁阿祖 Ninazu
宁达尔 Nindar
宁古布拉加 Nin-gublaga
宁胡尔萨格 Ninhursag
宁吉尔苏 Ningirsu
宁吉什孜达 Ningishzida
宁伽尔 Ningal
宁利尔 Ninlil
宁玛尔 Ninmar
宁姆格 Ninmug

宁舒布尔 Ninshubur
宁荪 Ninsun
宁图 Nintu
宁乌拉 Ninurra
努姆什 Numush
帕乌埃 Paue
沙拉 Shara
舒巴努纳 Shubanuna
乌图 Utu
辛 Suen
伊格阿里姆 Igalim
伊南娜 Inana
伊什库尔 Ishkur
伊什塔兰 Ishtaran

二　人名

阿巴 Abba
阿巴恩利尔金 Aba-Enlil-gin
阿巴古拉 Abbagula
阿巴卡拉 Abba-kala
阿巴纳卡 Abba-naka
阿巴萨加 Abba-saga
阿比拉图姆 Abilatum

中外文专有名词对照表

阿比里亚 Abilia
阿比西姆提 Abisimti
阿布亚姆提 Abyamuti
阿达 Ada
阿杜 Addu
阿尔曼 Arman
阿尔西阿赫 Arshiah
阿古 Agu
阿古阿尼 Aguani
阿胡杜 Ahudu
阿胡玛 Ahuma
阿胡姆巴尼 Ahum-bani
阿胡尼 Ahuni
阿胡瓦卡尔 Ahu-waqar
阿胡亚 Ahua
阿哈尼舒 Ahanishu
阿吉 Agi
阿卡拉 Akala
阿拉德 Arad
阿拉德姆 Aradmu
阿拉德南那 Arad-Nanna
阿拉姆 Allamu
阿马尔达姆 Amar-Damu
阿马尔玛玛 Amar-Mama
阿马尔辛 Amar-Suen
阿玛卡拉 Ama-kala
阿玛特辛 Amat-Suen
阿米尔舒尔吉 Amir-Shulgi
阿穆尔辛 Amur-Suen
阿皮尔金 Apilkin
阿图 Atu
阿亚卡拉 Aakala
阿伊里 Aili
安库 Anku

安纳希里比 Annahilibi
巴巴姆 Babamu
巴巴尼 Babani
巴巴提 Babati
巴尔拉 Barra
巴哈尔 Bahar
巴卡尔图姆 Baqartum
巴姆 Bamu
巴萨 Basa
巴乌什美 Baushme
巴亚加 Baaga
巴亚姆 Baamu
巴亚亚 Baa'a
巴扎姆 Bazamu
巴兹 Bazi
贝里阿祖 Beli-azu
贝利杜 Belidu
比达 Bida
彼杜加 Biduga
布杜尔 Budur
布乌杜 Bu'udu
达达 Dada
达达古 Dadagu
达达加 Dadaga
达达尼 Dadani
达干杜尼 Dagan-Duni
达古尼尔 Dagunir
达米克图姆 Damiqtum
达姆库姆 Damqum
达塞 Dashe
达亚亚提 Daa'ati
丹舒尔吉 Dan-Shulgi
迪库伊里 Diku-ili
丁吉尔苏卡尔 Dingir-sukkal

373

杜杜 Dudu

杜加 Duga

杜伊里 Du-ili

埃阿尼莎 Ea-nisha

埃基 Eki

埃拉巴尼 Erra-bani

埃鲁 Elu

埃什塔尔伊尔舒 Eshtar-ilshu

埃泰尔普达干 Etelpu-Dagan

埃祖恩达干 Ezun-Dagan

恩阿姆伽尔安娜 En-amgal-ana

恩丁吉尔姆 En-dingirmu

恩埃吉阿格 Enekiag

恩卡什 En-kash

恩利尔孜沙伽尔 Enlil-zishagal

恩利拉 Enlila

恩马赫伽尔安娜 En-mahgal-ana

恩纳姆提伊比辛卡塞 En-namti-Ibbi-Suen-kashe

恩南那阿马尔辛拉吉阿格 En-Nanna-Amar-Suen-rakiag

恩尼尔伽尔安娜 En-nirgal-ana

恩尼尔希安娜 En-nirsi-ana

恩尼尔孜安娜 En-nirzi-ana

恩努奈阿马尔辛拉吉阿格 En-nune-Amar-Suenra-kiag

恩乌布尔孜安娜 En-uburzi-ana

恩乌努伽尔安娜 En-unugal-ana

古布乌图 Gub-Utu

古地亚 Gudea

古加努姆 Guganum

哈巴卢吉 Habaluge

哈里鲁姆 Halilum

哈纳姆 Hanam

哈西帕塔尔 Haship-atal

汉谟拉比 Hammurabi

胡巴亚 Huba'a

胡里巴尔 Hulibar

胡姆祖姆 Humzum

吉布拉塔古 Giblatagu

基德达吉 Giddaki

吉尔伽美什 Gilgamesh

吉美埃安娜 Geme-Eanna

吉美恩利拉 Geme-Enlila

吉美南娜 Geme-Nanna

吉美宁利拉 Geme-Ninlila

吉美辛 Geme-Suen

卡拉姆 Kallamu

卡什 Kash

卡亚姆 Ka'amu

库巴图姆 Kubatum

库蒂姆 Kudim

库尔比拉克 Kurbilak

库尔基里尼塞 Kurgirinishe

库鲁布阿达德 Kurub-Ishkur

库鲁布埃拉 Kurub-Erra

库南那 Ku-Nanna

库宁伽尔 Ku-Ningal

拉阿沙 La'asa

拉玛伊里纳 Lamma-irina

拉尼 Lani

拉齐普 Laqip

里布尔－辛 Libur-Suen

里沙努姆 Lishanum

利维尔米塔舒 Liwwir-mittashu

卢巴巴 Lu-Baba

卢巴拉萨加 Lu-balasaga

卢班达 Lu-banda

374

卢丁吉尔拉 Lu-dingira
卢杜加 Lu-duga
卢恩利尔 Lu-Enlila
卢古拉 Lu-gula
卢吉里扎尔 Lu-kirizal
卢吉什巴莱达 Lu-geshbareda
卢基纳 Lu-gina
卢基努尼尔 Lu-Kinunir
卢伽 Luga
卢伽尔阿马尔库 Lugal-amarku
卢伽尔阿马鲁 Lugal-amaru
卢伽尔阿尼萨 Lugal-anisa
卢伽尔阿孜达 Lugal-azida
卢伽尔埃利都 Lugal-Eridu
卢伽尔埃孜姆 Lugal-ezem
卢伽尔古伽尔 Lugal-gugal
卢伽尔库加尼 Lugal-kugani
卢伽尔库祖 Lugal-kuzu
卢伽尔马古莱 Lugal-magure
卢伽尔美兰 Lugal-melam
卢伽尔麦麦 Lugal-meme
卢伽尔内萨格 Lugal-nesag
卢伽尔帕埃 Lugal-pae
卢伽尔沙拉 Lugal-shala
卢伽尔乌舒姆伽尔 Lugal-ushumgal
卢伽尔伊宁基纳 Lugal-inimgina
卢伽尔伊提达 Lugal-itida
卢伽尔扎格西 Lugal-zagesi
卢卡尔卡尔 Lu-kalkal
卢卡拉 Lu-kala
卢玛 Lumma
卢马尔萨 Lu-marsa
卢米尔扎 Lu-mirza
卢南那 Lu-Nanna

卢宁吉尔苏 Lu-Ningirsu
卢宁吉什孜达 Lu-Ningeshzida
卢宁舒布尔 Lu-Ninshubur
卢萨加 Lu-saga
卢沙拉 Lu-Shara
卢舒尔吉 Lu-Shulgi
卢苏卡尔 Lu-sukkal
卢荪孜达 Lu-Sunzida
卢乌鲁基 Lu-uruki
卢乌什基纳 Lu-ushgina
卢乌图 Lu-Utu
玛巴内亚 Mabanea
玛玛尼莎 Mamma-nisha
玛美图姆 Mammetum
曼舒姆 Manshum
美埃阿 ME-Ea
美伊什塔兰 ME-Ishtaran
米特哈尔 Mithar
穆尔特里 Murteli
曼舒姆 Manshum
穆尼 Muni
穆沙尔姆纳古巴 Musharmu-naguba
穆祖 Muzu
纳比恩利尔 Nabi-Enlil
纳比舒尔吉 Nabi-Shulgi
纳比乌姆 Nabium
纳比辛 Nabi-Suen
纳迪 Nadi
纳拉姆伊里 Naram-ili
纳鲁 Nalu
纳姆 Namu
纳姆哈尼 Namhani
纳姆马赫 Nammah
纳姆孜塔拉 Namzitara

纳纳 Nana
纳尼 Nani
纳萨 Nasa
纳西达图姆 Nahidatum
南那卡姆 Nanna-kam
南那玛巴 Nanna-maba
南那伊吉杜 Nanna-igidu
南那孜沙伽尔 Nanna-zishagal
奈奈 NE-NE
尼古鲁姆 Nigurum
尼里达伽尔 Niridagal
宁埃加莱西 Ninegalesi
宁海杜 Ninhedu
宁吉尔苏阿孜达南塞 Ningirsu-azida-Nanshe
宁吉尔苏卡伊萨 Ningirsu-kaisa
宁卡拉 Ninkalla
宁利尔－阿玛古 Ninlil-amagu
宁利尔图库尔提 Ninlil-tukulti
宁利莱马娜格 Ninlile-manag
宁舒巴 Nin-shuba
宁图尔图尔姆 Nin-TUR-TUR-mu
宁希莉娅 Nin-hilia
努尔阿达德 Nur-Adad
努尔达干 Nur-Dagan
努尔埃什塔尔 Nur-Eshtar
努尔辛 Nur-Suen
帕吉娜娜 Pakinana
佩斯图尔图尔 Pesh-TUR-TUR
皮沙希鲁姆 Pishah-ilum
普舒伊奈 Pushu-ine
普祖尔阿比赫 Puzur-abih
普祖尔埃什塔尔 Puzur-Eshtar
普祖尔恩利尔 Puzur-Enlil

普祖尔哈亚 Puzur-haia
普祖尔舒尔吉 Puzur-Shulgi
普祖尔图图 Puzur-tutu
普祖尔乌沙 Puzur-usha
普朱尔因舒西纳克 Puzur-Inshushinak
萨尔贡 Sargon
塞莱普图姆 Shelepputum
塞卢什达干 Sellush-Dagan
塞卢什舒尔吉 Sellush-Shulgi
塞什卡拉 Shesh-kala
沙达孜 Shadazi
沙库吉 Shakuge
沙拉卡姆 Sharakam
沙拉亚 Sharra'a
沙拉伊祖 Shara-izu
沙拉扎美 Shara-zame
沙里玛胡姆 Shalim-ahum
沙鲁姆巴尼 Sharrum-bani
沙特埃拉 Shat-Erra
沙特玛米 Shat-Mami
沙特舒尔吉 Shat-Shulgi
沙特辛 Shat-Suen
舒达姆基纳 Shudam-kina
舒埃拉 Shu-Erra
舒埃什塔尔 Shu-Eshtar
舒恩利尔 Shu-Enlil
舒尔吉 Shulgi
舒尔吉巴尼 Shulgi-bani
舒尔吉基德姆 Shulgi-giadmu
舒尔吉拉玛 Shulgi-rama
舒尔吉尼 Shulgi-ni
舒尔吉萨图尼 Shulgi-satuni
舒尔吉西姆提 Shulgi-simti
舒尔吉伊里 Shulgi-ili

舒尔吉伊里穆 Shulgi-irimu
舒尔吉孜卡兰马 Shulgi-zikalama
舒尔吉孜姆 Shulgi-zimu
舒卡布塔 Shu-Kabta
舒库布姆 Shukubum
舒库尔图姆 Shuqurtum
舒玛玛 Shu-Mama
舒纳亚 Shuna'a
舒－舒尔吉 Shu-Shulgi
舒提鲁姆 Shu-Tirum
舒乌图 Shu-Utu
舒辛 Shu-Suen
舒辛安杜尔 Shu-Suen-andul
舒辛－瓦利德－舒尔吉 Shu-Suen-walid-Shulgi
舒伊丁 Shu-Idim
舒伊里 Shu-ili
苏胡什金 Suhush-kin
塔班达拉赫 Tabba-andarah
塔布尔哈图姆 Tabur-Hattum
塔丁埃什塔尔 Taddin-Eshtar
塔昆马图姆 Takun-matum
塔兰乌兰 Taram-Uram
塔希塞恩 Tahi-shen
塔希沙塔尔 Tahish-atal
泰舒普塞拉赫 Teshup-shelah
泰辛玛玛 Tesin-Mamma
提里干 Tirigan
提亚马特巴什提 Tiamat-bashti
图尔塔 Tulta
图金哈提米格丽莎 Tukin-PA-migrisha
图兰达干 Turam-Dagan
图兰舒尔吉 Taram-Shulgi
图兰伊里 Turam-ili

瓦塔尔图姆 Watartum
瓦塔鲁姆 Watarum
瓦祖姆舒尔吉 Wazum-Shulgi
乌巴亚 Uba'a
乌达 Uda
乌达德孜纳特 Udad-zenat
乌尔阿巴 Ur-abba
乌尔阿什吉 Ur-Ashgi
乌尔巴巴 Ur-Baba
乌尔巴德提比拉 Ur-Badtibira
乌尔达姆 Ur-Damu
乌尔丁吉尔拉 Ur-dingira
乌尔杜牧孜达 Ur-Dumuzida
乌尔顿 Ur-dun
乌尔埃埃 Ur-e'e
乌尔埃伽尔 Ur-egal
乌尔埃宁努 Ur-eninu
乌尔恩利拉 Ur-Enlila
乌尔古地亚 Ur-Gudea
乌尔古恩纳 Ur-guenna
乌尔吉吉尔 Ur-gigir
乌尔库努纳 Ur-kununa
乌尔兰马 Ur-Lamma
乌尔里希 Ur-Lisi
乌尔卢伽尔埃丁卡 Ur-Lugal-edinka
乌尔麦麦 Ur-meme
乌尔美兰 Ur-melam
乌尔美斯 Ur-mes
乌尔纳姆 Ur-Nammu
乌尔纳尼卜伽尔 Ur-Nanibgal
乌尔南那 Ur-Nanna
乌尔南塞 Ur-Nanshe
乌尔尼格 Ur-nig
乌尔尼伽尔 Ur-nigar

乌尔宁埃布伽尔 Ur-Ninebgal	西哈卢姆 Shihalum
乌尔宁库拉 Ur-Ninkura	西马特埃阿 Simat-Ea
乌尔宁荪 Ur-Ninsun	西马特埃什塔尔 Simat-Eshtar
乌尔努恩伽尔 Ur-Nungal	西马特恩利尔 Simat-Enlil
乌尔努斯卡 Ur-Nuska	西马特伊什塔兰 Simat-Ishtaran
乌尔萨加 Ur-saga	辛阿布舒 Suen-abushu
乌尔沙拉 Ur-Shara	伊比辛 Ibbi-Suen
乌尔舒尔吉拉 Ur-Shulgira	伊比伊什塔兰 Ibbi-Ishtaran
乌尔舒尔帕埃 Ur-Shulpae	伊布尼舒尔吉 Ibni-Shulgi
乌尔舒姆吉 Ur-shumugi	伊布尼伊什库尔 Ibni-Ishkur
乌尔舒什巴巴 Ur-Shush-Baba	伊达拉基里 Idarakili
乌尔泰什 Ur-tesh	伊迪迪 Ididi
乌尔塔尔卢赫 Ur-TAR-LUH	伊吉安纳凯祖 Igi-anna-kezu
乌尔图尔 Ur-tur	伊吉哈鲁姆 Igihalum
乌尔辛 Ur-Suen	伊吉恩利尔塞 Igi-Enlilshe
乌尔乌图 Ur-Utu	伊卡拉 Ikala
乌尔伊格阿里姆 Ur-Igalim	伊库米沙尔 Ikumishar
乌尔伊吉孜巴拉 Ur-Igizibara	伊拉鲁姆 Ilallum
乌尔伊什塔兰 Ur-Ishtaran	伊里布姆 Iribum
乌古拉 Ugula	伊里舍里 Ili-seli
乌鲁卡基那 Urukagina	伊里达干 Ili-Dagan
乌马尼 Ummani	伊里姆 Ilimu
乌纳帕塔尔 Unapatal	伊里塔巴 Ili-taba
乌努戴内 Unudene	伊鲁姆巴尼 Ilum-bani
乌什姆 Ushmu	伊姆里克埃阿 Imlik-Ea
乌塔米沙兰 Utamisharam	伊尼姆巴巴伊达布 Inim-Baba-idab
乌图巴拉 Utu-barra	伊宁马伊鲁姆 Inima-ilum
乌图尔玛玛 Utul-Mama	伊宁马亚 Inima-Ia
乌图赫伽尔 Utu-hegal	伊宁南纳 Inim-Nanna
乌图吉 Utu-ge	伊宁南那祖 Inim-Nanna-zu
乌图姆 Utumu	伊宁沙拉 Inim-Shara
乌乌姆 U'umu	伊宁伊南娜 Inim-Inanna
乌孜 Uzi	伊沙尔库尔巴舒姆 Ishar-kurbashum
西阿雅 SI. A-a	伊沙尔里比 Ishar-libi

伊沙尔帕丹 Ishar-padan
伊沙尔舒尔吉 Ishar-Shulgi
伊什比埃拉 Ishbi-Erra
伊什美埃拉 Ishme-Erra
伊什美伊鲁姆 Ishme-ilum
伊图尔伊鲁姆 Itur-ilum
伊图鲁姆 Iturum
伊孜因达干 Izin-Dagan
伊扎里克 Izariq
因塔埃阿 Intaea
因提丹 Imtidam
扎甘比 Zaga-AN-bi
扎里克 Zariq
扎里亚 Zalia
扎亚努姆 Za'anum
孜库尔伊里 Ziqur-ili
孜孜姆 Zizimu
祖巴加 Zubaga
祖比亚 Zubia
祖里姆 Zurium

三 地名

阿巴尔尼乌姆 Abarnium
阿比巴纳 Abibana
阿达布 Adab
阿丹顿 Adamdun
阿尔曼 Arman
阿尔舒辛 Al-Shu-Suen
阿哈 A. HA
阿加孜 Agaz
阿卡德 Akkad
阿拉美 Arame
阿拉普胡姆 Arraphum
阿姆利马 Amrina

阿皮沙尔 Apisal
阿皮亚克 Apiak
阿萨如姆达基 Asarum-dagi
阿什舒 Ashshu
阿淑尔 Ashur
阿瓦尔 Awal
阿万 Awan
阿扎曼 Azaman
安珊 Anshan
巴比 Babi
巴比伦 Babylon
巴比伦尼亚 Babylonia
巴德提比拉 Badtibira
巴尔曼 Barman
巴鲁埃 Balue
巴西姆埃 Bashime
比达顿 Bidadun
布乌达 Bu'uda
布赫兹伽尔 Buhzigar
布伊尔 Bu'ir
达尔图姆 Daltum
达卜鲁姆 Dabrum
达里巴 Dariba
达什提 Dashti
达温马 Da-Umma
达西比韦 Dashibiwe
德尔 Der
德尔—吉孜 Der-KI. ZI
迪克迪卡赫 Diqdiqqah
丁提尔 Dintir
杜杜里 Duduli
杜尔埃布拉 Dur-Ebla
杜尔马什 Durmash
杜恩利拉 Du-Enlila

杜鲁姆 Durum			基努尼尔 Kinunir
埃巴尔 Ebal			吉沙 Kissa
埃布拉 Ebla			吉斯马尔 Kismar
埃杜鲁舒尔吉 Eduru-Shulgi			基什 Kish
埃古拉 Egula			基什加提 Kishgati
埃金卡斯卡尔 EZENxKASKAL			加埃什 Gaesh
埃莱什 Eresh			伽尔库如达 Garkuruda
埃兰 Elam			加布拉什 Gablash
埃利都 Eridu			伽尔奈奈 Garnene
埃鲁特 Erut			伽尔沙纳 Garshana
埃萨格达纳 Esagdana			卡尔达 Karda
埃什努那 Eshnuna			卡尔达希 Kardahi
埃什舒 Eshshu			卡尔卡尔 Karkar
古阿巴 Guabba			卡尔孜达 Karzida
古布拉 Gubla			卡拉哈尔 Karahar
古埃丁纳 Guedena			卡库拉图姆 Kakkulatum
吉吉比努姆 Gigibinum			卡马里 Kamari
古铁布姆 Gutebum			卡扎鲁 Kazallu
哈布拉 Habura			凯什 Kesh
哈尔西 Harshi			库阿尔 Ku'ar
哈马孜 Hamazi			库阿拉 Kuara
胡比乌姆 Hubium			库布拉 Kubla
胡布姆 Hubum			库米 Kumu
胡布尼 Hubni			库特哈 Gudua
胡尔提 Hurti			库提 Guti
胡赫努里 Huhnuri			拉比 Rabi
胡普姆 Hupum			拉尔萨 Larsa
吉安 KI.AN			拉伽什 Lagash
吉尔苏 Girsu			利布里 Libri
吉尔塔卜 Girtab			里姆什 Rimush
吉吉比努姆 Gigibinium			卢卢布 Lullubu
吉里卡尔 Girikal			马尔达马尼 Mardamani
基里塔卜 Kiritab			马尔达曼 Mardaman
基马什 Kimash			马尔哈西 Marhashi

380

中外文专有名词对照表

马尔曼 Marman
马干 Magan
马哈祖姆 Mahazum
马腊德 Marad
马里 Mari
马什坎 Mashkan
马什堪阿比 Mashkan-abi
马什堪加埃什 Mashkan-gaesh
马什堪卡拉图姆 Mashkan-kallatum
马什堪沙鲁姆 Mashkan-sharrum
马什堪乌舒里 Mashkan-ushuri
美索不达米亚 Mesopotamia
穆里克-提德尼姆 Muriq-tidnim
穆什比亚纳 Mushbiana
纳格苏 Nagsu
奈贝尔阿马尔辛 Neber-Amar-Suen
奈贝鲁姆 Neberum
尼达拉什韦 Nidarashwe
尼明 Nigin
尼姆孜乌姆 Nimzium
尼那 Nina
尼尼微 Ninua（Nineveh）
尼普尔 Nippur
尼希 NI. HI
努伽尔 Nugar
努图尔 Nutur
帕西美 Pashime
皮伊尔 PI'il
普赫孜伽尔 Puhzigar
普什 Push
普特沙达尔 Putshadar
普图里乌姆 Puttulium
普兹瑞什达干 Puzrish-Dagan
萨布姆 Sabum

萨拉奈韦 Salla-NE-we
塞希尔 Sheshil
塞提尔沙 Shetirsha
沙尔巴特 Sarbat
沙胡安 Shahuan
沙里安 Shari-A-AN
沙米 Shami
沙尼达特 Shanidat
沙什卢姆 Shashru
舒达埃 Shudae
舒尔布 Shurbu
舒尔吉南那 Shulgi-Nanna
舒尔吉乌图 Shulgi-Utu
舒恩提 Shunti
舒鲁帕克 Shuruppak
舒姆提乌姆 Shumtium
舒辛伊杜格 Shu-Suen-idug
舒伊尔胡姆 Shu'irhum
苏美尔 Sumer
苏萨 Susa
塔布拉 Tabra
塔布拉拉 Tablala
泰尔加 Terga
提兰 Tiran
提马特恩利尔 Timat-Enlil
提威 Tiwe
吐玛尔 Tummal
图姆巴尔 Tumbal
图图布 Tutub
图图尔 Tutul
瓦努姆 Wanum
温马 Umma
乌查尔伽尔沙纳 Usar-Garshana
乌查鲁姆 Usarum

381

乌尔 Ur	亚布图姆 Iabtium
乌尔比隆 Urbilum	亚述 Assyria
乌尔古哈拉姆 Urguhalam	伊巴尔 Ibbal
乌尔凯什 Urkesh	伊杜拉 Id-dula
乌加里特 Ugarit	伊利萨格里格 Irisagrig
乌拉姆 Uraum	伊山米孜雅德 Ishan Mizyad
乌勒 U'ul	伊舒 Ishu
乌鲁阿 Urua	伊舒尔 Ishur
乌鲁克 Uruk	伊舒姆 Ishum
乌鲁姆 Urum	伊西姆舒尔吉 Ishim-Shulgi
乌鲁乌德 URUxUD	伊西姆舒辛 Ishim-Shu-Suen
希比拉特 Hebilat	伊新 Isin
西格里什 Shigrish	因布 Inbu
西马努姆 Simanum	因纳巴 Innaba
西马什基 Shimashki	扎巴巴 Zababa
希拉拉 Sirara	扎巴兰 Zabala
西穆卢姆 Simurum	扎布沙里 Zabshali
西帕尔 Sippar	扎克图姆 Zaqtum
希特 Hit	扎图姆 Zatum
希乌米 Si'ummi	孜比莱 Zibire
亚阿米什 Ya'amish	孜达尼乌姆 Zidanium
亚布拉特 Iabrat	孜姆达尔 Zimu
亚布鲁 Iabru

后　　记

乌尔第三王朝（公元前2112—前2004年）在三千年的古代两河流域文明中虽然只占了了一百多年，却留下了数以十万计的楔形文字泥板文献，是古代两河流域出土文献最为丰富的一个时期。乌尔第三王朝研究是亚述学的一个重要方向，在国际亚述学领域有专门的乌尔第三王朝研究学者，他们贡献了大量的学术成果，从基础的释读楔形文字文献，建立文献数据库，到对乌尔第三王朝各个领域的专题研究，自20世纪初开始，关于乌尔第三王朝的研究已经走过了一百多年的历程。

乌尔第三王朝的社会经济史研究一直以来都是亚述学研究的重点问题之一，诸如美国的沙拉赫对bala税、日本的前田彻对gun_2 ma-da税、芬兰的萨洛宁对zag-u税等进行过个案研究。本书建立在前人研究基础上，对赋税制度进行的综合性研究，是乌尔第三王朝经济史研究诸多成果中的普通一员。赋税制度是国家财政经济制度的重要内容，研究乌尔第三王朝的赋税制度有利于进一步全面了解其经济制度，对于我们正确了解古代西亚文明的社会经济形态有着重要的意义。

本书是国家社会科学基金青年项目"两河流域乌尔第三王朝赋税制度研究"的结项成果（鉴定等级：优秀）。非常感谢项目评审老师的指导与意见，感谢全国哲学社会科学规划办对本项目的资助。同时，本书的写作得到了诸多学界前辈、同行们的大力支持与帮助，在此表示由衷感谢。不仅要感谢亚述学的各位前辈和同仁们的关心与指导，也要感谢埃及学、古典学、中世纪史等专家学者们的无私帮助。在我对乌尔第三王朝的探索中，离不开恩师们的淳淳教诲，感谢我的硕士生导师东北师范大学的吴宇虹先生和尾崎亨先生，感谢我的博士生导师德国海德堡大学的Markus Hilgert教授和Stefan M. Maul教授。此外，我要感谢中国社会科学出版社的编辑们专业、严谨、细致的校对工作。本书也得到了浙江师范大学人文学院和浙江大学人文高等研究院的大力支持，一并表示感谢。最后，我还要感谢我的家人们无微不至的关怀与始终如一的支持。

由于笔者的学术水平有限，书中难免有这样那样的纰漏，诚挚地期待专家和读者批评指正。

刘昌玉

2021 年 2 月 14 日

浙江师范大学历史系办公室